Planned Behavior Change

Behavior Modification in Social Work

Joel Fischer

Harvey L. Gochros

THE FREE PRESS
A Division of Macmillan Publishing Co., Inc.
NEW YORK

Collier Macmillan Publishers
LONDON

For Ursula and Jean,
who have shown
that positive reinforcement
can also mean love

The Free Press
A Division of Macmillan Publishing Co., Inc.
866 Third Avenue, New York, N.Y. 10022

Collier Macmillan Canada, Ltd.

Library of Congress Catalog Card Number: 74-34554

Printed in the United States of America

printing number

1 2 3 4 5 6 7 8 9 10

Library of Congress Cataloging in Publication Data
Fischer, Joel.
  Planned behavior change.

  Bibliography: p.
  Includes index.
  1. Social service. 2. Behavior modification.
3. Professional ethics. I. Gochros, Harvey L., joint
author. II. Title.
HV41.F47   361'.06   74-34554
ISBN 0-02-910250-2

Copyright Acknowledgments

Table 6.1 (see p. 91) reprinted from E.P. Reese, *Analysis of Human Operant
Behavior* (Dubuque, Iowa: William C. Brown, 1966), p. 16

Table 16.1 (see p. 282) reprinted from P.A. Wisocki, "The Successful
Treatment of a Heroin Addict by Covert Conditioning Techniques,"
Journal of Behavior Therapy and Experimental Psychiatry, Vol. 4 (London:
Pergamon Press, 1973), p. 60

Contents

Preface

One of the most enjoyable tasks in producing a book is writing the preface. It is written when a book is just about completed, and it is generally the most informal part of the book. In it, authors can let loose and say pretty much what they want to say without worrying about giving a reference. We have therefore made this preface our "M & M" for completing the manuscript.

In considering what to write in our preface, we have chosen to sit back, review what we wanted to accomplish when we set out to write this book, and reflect on how we went about doing it.

For several years, both of us have included considerable material on behavior modification in our social work practice courses. We have also taught numerous courses and workshops specifically on behavior modification. We therefore decided to use these courses as a model for the form and content of the book. Indeed, the book essentially follows the format of a course, beginning with basic concepts and principles, and going on to aspects of their application in practice, followed by illustrations of strategies of intervention into a variety of problems commonly encountered in social work practice. The book concludes with an extended discussion of ethical considerations in the application of behavior modification in social work practice, which, by being placed last, is not intended to depreciate these issues but to highlight them. The contents of the book were continuously being revised and updated on the basis of our review of new literature, feedback from our students, who were applying behavior modification in their practicum, and our own use of behavior modification with our clients.

This preface is being written at a time when the use of behavior modification is being widely questioned, not only by professionals, but also by governmental agencies and the press. Articles and letters to the editor challenging the ethics of behavior modification have appeared in such diverse places as *Time* and the *New York Review*. A federal agency has even announced that it is withdrawing financial support from any program that uses behavior modification approaches.

We know, not only from the literature, but also from our own practice and that of our students, of the good that the use of behavior modification can achieve, and we believe that its procedures can be used humanely and honestly in dealing with many areas of human suffering. We are therefore distressed at signs of emotional and often irrational rejection of behavior modification. But we are equally concerned about any incidents of inappropriate or unethical use. Behavior modification is a potentially powerful technology, and any possible misuse is to be watched for and condemned. Thus, throughout this book we have tried to discuss how behavior modification can be used ethically and in a way consistent with social work values.

While writing the book, we were frequently concerned that our enthusiasm for the approach (fueled, perhaps, in part by our awareness of the "bad press" behavior modification often receives) could obscure the objective presentation of its application in social work practice. Indeed, one of the authors—who shall remain nameless—would have liked to include extensive, critical comparisons of behavioral approaches with some of the traditional approaches used in social work. It was thought that an exposition of the deficiencies of traditional approaches would buttress the case for the use of behavior modification. However, cooler heads (including that of the other author) prevailed. We decided to present behavior modification as much as possible strictly on its own merits, and to let the strengths of behavior modification speak for themselves. We have tried not to be overly polemical, and to make the major objective of the book, as much as possible, be to educate about behavior modification rather than to proselytize. Nevertheless, we recognize (as the reader doubtlessly will) that our enthusiasm over the potential of behavior modification for social work occasionally exceeded our self-restraint. For that, we apologize.

However, we hope that our readers will not simply accept what we say (no matter how convincing our writing style) without subjecting it to careful, critical evaluation. Our profession (like any other profession) needs to use rigorous criteria to evaluate new ideas, and not just accept them on faith. We hope that this book will help generate interest in trying out these principles in a wide range of social work practice settings with diverse clients and problems. Only then will this book have achieved its purpose.

It occurs to us that writing a book involves the same learning principles as any other set of behaviors. Just about everything we've put into this book, we've learned—from other authors, teachers, our families, friends, students, clients, and each other. Thus, it is probably inevitable that there are places in the book where credit was not given when credit was due. Incorporating the ideas of hundreds of people as we have done, there were times when we may not have adequately distinguished between their ideas and our own. Although we have tried to document carefully the sources of our material, we may inadvertently have neglected some references. We therefore would like to acknowledge by this statement our debt to these unnamed, but appreciated, sources. In the case of figures and tables we have adapted from other sources, we hereby express our appreciation for use of this material, and also indicate beneath each item the place of publication of the original. Figures and tables without source lines are our work entirely.

Several people whose names and affiliations are quite well known to us have made significant contributions to this book, and we do want to thank them for their considerable help:

Dr. Herbert Aptekar, who was our Dean at the School of Social Work, University of Hawaii when this book was being developed, and whose recent death was a great loss both to us personally and to social work as a whole, created an academic atmosphere that reinforced the time and effort we put into the book.

Dr. William R. Morrow, one of the pioneers in organizing behavior modification research for application with human problems, introduced one of the authors to the potential of behavior modification for social work, and stimulated that interest over the years.

Dr. Larry Lister, our colleague and friend at the School of Social Work, University of Hawaii, read the first draft and made numerous invaluable suggestions that were incorporated in subsequent drafts.

Jean S. Gochros reviewed and helped revise major segments of the manuscript at various stages of its development.

Jolene Takita, still in high school at the time, typed almost the entire first draft of the manuscript in a highly professional manner.

Our wives, Ursula and Jean, and our children, Susan, David, Lisa, and Nicole by their support, suggestions, and enthusiasm (kids are great at alphabetizing bibliographies) contributed more than they will ever know to the completion of this book. In fact, after spending so many weekends enjoying Hawaii's beautiful beaches without us, our families have become so used to it, and have grown so much to enjoy each other's company without our interference, that we are constantly being asked by them to quickly get involved in *another* book.

To all these people goes our deepest appreciation for their help and support. Which brings us to us. Our own friendship—despite almost daily confrontations over the progress, form, style, and content of the book—has remained miraculously intact, if not stronger for the experience. For this we are reciprocally relieved and grateful.

Introduction

The field of social work is changing at an unprecedented rate. Today's social workers, charged with the same concern, energy, and social commitment as their predecessors, are both responding to, and creating demands on, the field to adjust to a rapidly changing world with new perceptions of the problems of the people the profession serves. They are seeking orientations for their practice which will lead to effective, efficient, and rational interventions reflecting the rights, competence, and intelligence of the consumers of their services.

Nowhere is this change more evident than in social work education. After decades of educational conformity, students are now exposed to programs presenting different content, focus, orientation, and even time required for completion. The profession seems on the verge of moving from rigid uniformity to questioning of much of the fabric of social work practice and philosophy.

There is indeed a pressing demand for a realistic examination of the theoretical underpinnings and methodology of social work services. Critics of social work practice point to several problems in the field, particularly involving practice with individuals and families experiencing problems in their social functioning (see, e.g., Briar, 1967; Fischer, 1973; Fischer, 1975 a & b). These problems involve not only the conceptual and technological deficiencies of many traditional theories of practice, but also include serious questions regarding the efficiency and effectiveness of practitioners who adhere to such approaches.

In view of these concerns, it is not surprising that many social workers have shown interest in the principles and methodology of behavior modification. This approach has much to offer for social work practice in the areas where most traditional approaches have been deficient: (1) It respects the integrity of the client by focusing on observed behavior and limiting itself to helping diminish maladaptive functioning and increase adaptive functioning. (2) There is accumulating research evidence of the effectiveness of behavior modification procedures with a variety of problem situations. Furthermore, the fact that each case in which behavior modification is used allows for—indeed demands —specifying the problematic behaviors and systematically recording the changes in these behaviors, leads to testing the effectiveness of the procedure with each situation. Thus, the practitioner along with the client knows clearly whether goals have been achieved, and does not have to rely on the vagaries of intuition.

(3) There is a clear, logical connection between the assessment of the case (i.e., what specific current conditions maintain dysfunctional behavior of the client or impede the development of functional behavior), and the resulting intervention plan for modifying the behavior by changing these conditions (what factors in the environment may be used differentially to affect the behavior of the client in a helpful direction). (4) The basic principles of behavior modification are clear and easily communicated. They may be taught to nonprofessional personnel and individuals within the natural environment of the client, thereby giving such personnel an effective, easily comprehensible method of assisting in the process of altering dysfunctional behavior. (5) The behavior modification approach has generated numerous specific procedures which the social worker can differentially apply depending on the nature of the problem, situation, and client. (6) The behavior modification approach is efficient. Many cases and situations can be handled more quickly and with less professional time, either directly or by utilizing people in the client's natural environment, than is possible with other approaches. This is an especially useful consideration in view of the increasing concern about the economic use of the limited manpower available in social work programs. (7) The behavior modification approach encourages "self therapy" by the client himself by teaching him how to arrange the conditions which affect his behavior outside the interview situation. In this process, the client becomes better equipped to handle future problems without the need of professional help. (8) Behavior modification is oriented toward prevention. As noted above, parents, teachers, and others within the natural environment of the client may be taught change procedures, supervised in their administration by social work personnel, in order to more directly affect the behavior in the individual. Beyond this, these same persons may also be taught a perspective for observing and changing behavior—explicit principles and procedures which can be applied beyond the immediate problem situation—either to avoid future problems or to deal with them as they occur, so they need not seek professional help for future difficulties. (9) There is a wide range of applicability of behavior modification both in terms of problems and clients. The procedures of behavior modification have been effectively applied with individuals from upper and lower income groups, including clients without skills at verbal communication. Behavior modification has been effectively used with clients typically seen in family service agencies, outpatient clinics, and with a range of people and problems that traditionally have been considered "hopeless," "retarded," "autistic," back ward residents in psychiatric hospitals, delinquents, and so on. (10) Behavior modification provides principles and procedures for socioenvironmental change, to be applied directly with people, or in altering their natural ecology, the systems of which they are a part. Further, these basic principles are the same at all levels of intervention—individual, family, group, social system. Thus, social workers are provided with a technology with major implications for enhancing a range of practice endeavors, including the development of more desirable large-scale designs for living through social planning and social engineering. (11) Behavior modification is compatible with major ideas of other current conceptual frameworks utilized in social work practice which attempt to understand and modify human behavior in terms of its environmental context, such as role theory, system theory and group dynamics. Thus, these approaches—and a range of others with empirical evidence of success—can supplement behavior modification and its base in learning theory to give a more comprehensive view both of interpersonal behavior and, more importantly for social work, intervention into human problems.

Basic Definitions

Before proceeding any further, it is important to develop a few basic definitions of terms that will be used regularly in this book (see, also, the Glossary). The social worker unfamiliar with the terminology of a new approach would almost naturally tend to be more reluctant to explore the applicability of that approach. This often seems to be the case with behavior modification which, for some, appears to present many of the hazards that exist in learning a new language. But most of the basic terms of behavior modification are actually uncomplicated and concise.

"Behavior," e.g., is simply "what people do." Behavior includes such activities as studying, running, crying, kissing, touching, and, so far as the behavioral approach goes, actually includes any observable or measurable movement, task or activity of a human being, whether this be internal (within the individual) or external (Reese, 1966). As can be seen, this is a far-reaching definition of behavior. But as long as the behavior is somehow measurable (even "anxiety" is measurable by verbal reports, the use of equipment to measure pulse rate, perspiration, etc.), then it is appropriate to the task of behavior modification. Of course, such behaviors as eyeblinks are indeed behaviors. But the emphasis in behavior modification is on *significant* behaviors—those that have some implication for the individual's personal or social functioning. It may be a major behavior, of great value to an individual—e.g., sexual behaviors of husband or wife—or a relatively minor behavior—e.g., a twinge of anxiety before an exam for a student—but if its effect is to produce dysfunctional consequences for that individual, it would be an appropriate target for intervention using behavior modification procedures.

Behavior modification recognizes that much of human behavior is learned. Genetic predispositions and biological differences are of course recognized, but the focus of behavior modification is on those behaviors that are learned. A learned behavior is one that has developed as a result of interaction with the environment. In fact, the environment serves a dual role of not only teaching new behaviors, but evoking behaviors that were previously learned. Thus, the concept of functional relationship with the environment—wherein changes in one part of a relationship produce or lead to changes in the other part—is crucial for both assessment and intervention in the behavioral approach. Changes in an individual's behavior can produce changes in his environment, while changes in the environment can produce changes in an individual's behavior. Of course, one of the most important environments for people is other people, and it is easy to think of countless examples where our behavior is changed—e.g., we become more happy or sad, active or passive—in relationship to the behaviors of those around us.

In the literature generally, the terms "behavior modification" and "behavior therapy" often are used synonymously, although some writers prefer to consider behavior therapy as denoting one "branch" of the field (utilizing respondent principles) and behavior modification to refer to another branch (utilizing operant principles). However, given the general focus on measurable behavior and learning as discussed above, behavior modification will generally be defined, for purposes of this book, as the planned, systematic application of experimentally established principles of learning to the modification of maladaptive behavior.

There are several important concepts embedded in this definition. "Maladaptive behavior" can be viewed as behavior that has dysfunctional or harmful consequences for the individual or his environment. The social worker using behavior modification would attempt to either decrease the occurrence of maladaptive behavior, or increase the occurrence of (or help people learn when to engage in) adaptive behavior. The worker would do this in a planned and purposeful way; choice of procedures would not be haphazard or arbitrary but would be specifically derived from the worker's assessment of the problem, situation and the individuals and environments involved. In fact, behavior modification is not really a single, uniform entity, but a combination of procedures based on systematic application to the resolution of human problems of experimentally validated principles of human behavior. The social worker using behavior modification could call upon a wide variety of procedures that have been demonstrated in both laboratory and practice research to have the capability of bringing about predictable changes in human behavior. Thus, chances for failure in work with clients are considerably diminished. And, because the focus of this approach is on measurable behavior and systematic application of learning principles, the social worker using behavior modification would be careful to collect data on his progress—to be certain as to whether or not his program is succeeding. If anything, this systematic, empirical (or research) standard is the trademark of behavior modification. Although this book is specifically about behavior modification, the real commitment of the authors, and hopefully many other social workers, is to the use of the empirical model on which behavior modification is based—research, systematic application of demonstrated principles, development of techniques to implement principles, methods for studying results, and, above all, commitment to the quest for effective practice.

Finally, several other terms are used frequently in this book. The first is the term "client." Consistent with conventional social work terminology the client is the person (or group or system) who either is the expected beneficiary of social work intervention; or who engages, or contracts for, the services of the social worker; or the person(s) whose behavior the social worker attempts to change. Of course, the person who engages the services of the social worker may or may not be the same person as the one whose behavior is actually the target for change (Pincus & Minahan, 1970; 1973). For example, a mother might come to an agency seeking help in child management. The social worker could directly attempt to change the child's behavior, and/or provide direct services to the mother. If the social worker developed a plan for changing the behavior of the child that was to be implemented by the mother, the mother would then be the "mediator" (Tharp & Wetzel, 1969). The mediator is the person who actually carries out the behavior modification plan in direct contact with the individual(s) whose behaviors are targeted for change (e.g., dispensing reinforcers). This person could be the social worker, another professional or non-professional staff member in a given institution (e.g., a teacher or ward attendant), or someone else from the natural environment of the client (e.g., a parent).

Finally, the behavioral plan generally focuses on "target behavior," the last term to be defined here. Target behavior is behavior that specificially is pinpointed or "targeted" for change, either because it is undesired and needs to be decreased, or because it is desired and needs to be increased.

These are a few of the basic dimensions of the behavior modification approach. The characteristics of this approach will be amplified and discussed throughout this book, in chapters dealing with both the basic concepts and principles of behavior modification, and illustrating their application to a variety of practice problems of importance to social work.

Applicability to Social Work Practice

Behavior modification literature is growing rapidly with reports of successful applications of its basic procedures. These procedures have been applied to a constantly broadening range of problems experienced by people of all ages, ethnic and economic groups, educational and intellectual levels, and who are served in various settings, both open (such as family agencies and psychiatric clinics) and closed (such as mental institutions). As the field of behavior modification is further refined, an infinite number of additional applications likely will be developed, since research on the basic processes of human behavior and its relation to the environment has been inherent in the behavioral model since its inception. It is likely, however, that most new developments in the field will build on the basic knowledge that is presented in this text, since, in recent years, research and practice continue to reflect elaborations on what now appears to be this core set of concepts and principles.

Although the focus of this book is on dysfunctional behaviors of individuals and families, it should not be assumed that behavior modification is therefore applicable only to such situations. Basically, behavior modification is concerned with the impact of the environment on the behavior of human beings. Since one person's behavior is the environment of others, and people are constantly affecting each other's behavior, behavior modification can be equally applicable, and in some instances has already been extended, to understanding and affecting interactive behaviors of not only individuals and families, but of committees, peer groups, formal and informal structures of social agencies, and other collectivities (Burgess & Bushell, 1969). Social workers have long been concerned with the concept of the interplay of man and his environment. People in interaction with their community, their jobs, their family, their friends is the focus which provides the keystone of the behavior modificaton approach.

Further, as the definition of behavior used in this book is intended to indicate, behavior modification does not deal simply with isolated, discrete behaviors, but with a whole complex of observable, measurable tasks and activities. In fact, the socio-environmental emphasis of behavior modification, with a focus on the whole person and change goals involving social functioning, is highly congruent with the type of knowledge that has been described as central for the development of a common base for social work practice (Bartlett, 1970). The point is that, as this book should illustrate, the clients, problems, and settings for the practice of behavior modification are entirely consistent with similar focal points in the practice of social work. In fact, social workers are in the front line of practice in many of the areas where behavior modification has been utilized with demonstrable success.

Current State of Development

The basic theoretical work on which much of behavior modification is based is less than 50 years old. It stems largely from the work on human learning of Skinner (1953), Watson (1930), Hull (1943) and Pavlov (1928); (see Yates, 1970, Chapters 1 & 2 and Ullmann & Krasner, 1969, 1973, for an historical review of the development of behavior modification). The direct application of these theories to human problems is much newer. Much of the "early works" in this area date from the late 1950's (see, e.g., Ullmann & Krasner, 1966, for a collection of some of the earlier case studies).

Yet professionals have long observed the phenomenon of interpersonal influence. Most of us engage in it constantly as we try to influence the behavior or thoughts of our own children, agency staff, students, clients and even people holding political power. In recent years there has been a growing effort to try to find the principles of this influence and test out hypotheses regarding those principles. This has been done largely by psychologists working first in the laboratory and increasingly in the clinics and community. The newness of their discoveries adds to the excitement of the field: most of the founders and leaders in this area are still alive and professionally active. New applications are reported monthly, to the point where literally thousands of illustrations have appeared in a variety of professional journals, several of which have been established to deal solely with reports of progress in behavior modification.* And between the years of 1950 and 1973, hundreds of books have been published on behavior modification, most of which are listed in the bibliography for the convenience of the reader. Yet this excitement and newness creates some problems, especially in the area of interpretation and communication. New vocabularies have had to be developed and used for communication among people doing this work. Agreement on some concepts is still not universal. However, most of the disagreement is on an academic level with strong consensus on the basic principles and ideas of behavioral assessment and change.

Finally, behavior modification is essentially borrowed knowledge developed largely by other disciplines. There are problems inherent in the process of adoption of borrowed knowledge. There are hazards of borrowing out-of-date knowledge with greater certainty because it is borrowed, and of borrowing oversimplified versions of knowledge. All too often, the borrowed knowledge remains an "undigested lump" in the body of the profession, rather than being incorporated specifically into practice (see Kadushin, 1959). Although these dangers do exist, one hopes these pitfalls can be avoided by presenting current thinking regarding the application of behavior modification in a manner appropriate to social work in practice.

Purpose and Organization of the Book

Despite the apparent appropriateness of behavior modification knowledge for social work, and the huge outpouring of articles and books on this subject in other fields, relatively little has been taught in graduate schools of social work in the past regarding behavior modification, and indeed only a few schools now seem to offer more than a cursory review of the approach. Most of the knowledge of social workers who are testing out the behavioral approaches in practice comes from the very few references which have appeared in the social work literature (e.g., Thomas, 1968; Gambrill et al., 1971; Carter & Stuart, 1970; Thomas, 1967; Jehu et al., 1972; Nagoshi 1969), from often misunderstood literature written for the field of psychology by psychologists, and from colleagues in other disciplines. This book was written with the intention of presenting the basic concepts and approaches of behavior modification within the context of socal work values and with awareness of the special problems involved in applying this approach in social work settings.

* See, e.g., *Behavior Research & Therapy, Journal of Applied Behavior Analysis, Behavior Therapy & Experimental Psychiatry, Behavior Therapy, Behavior Modification Monographs, Journal of Behavioral Education, School Applications of Learning Technology.*

It is the intention of the authors to make available in a concise manner the conceptual framework of behavior modification, assessment procedures, and the interventive processes for utilization in social work practice. A variety of behavior modification techniques will be offered with the hope that they will be tried in various social work settings with diverse client problems. Special emphasis is placed on a creative use of social work manpower to involve those in the client's environment in the change process.

To accomplish the above goals the book has been organized into four parts:

Part 1. Basic Concepts and Principles

Covers both respondent and operant behavior modification with special emphasis on the latter, including antecedents, consequences, reinforcers and schedules of reinforcement. Also includes a chapter on modeling.

Part 2. Process and Practice

Overviews of the assessment and intervention process, the techniques of behavior modification, behavioral recording and work in the natural environment.

Part 3. Applications and Illustrations

Selected examples of the use of behavior modification in ten major problem areas.

Part 4. Problems and Issues

A review and discussion of some of the problems involved in using behavior modification, plus several of the major issues in the use of behavior modification.

Of the two major branches of the field of behavior modification—operant and respondent (these terms will be discussed in depth in subsequent chapters) —this book focuses largely on the former, that involving operant principles and procedures. This is because it appears that this area has somewhat broader applicability for social work, because source works on operant behavior modification are more scattered and diffuse than those dealing with respondent procedures (e.g., Wolpe, 1969, 1973) , and because the range of techniques for dealing with common social work problems—and for teaching others to deal with them— appears to be greater using the operant framework. On the other hand, a balanced perspective requires specification of principles and procedures from the gamut of behavioral approaches, especially those with evidence of effectiveness. Since the operant and respondent approaches have much in common, both perspectives will be dealt with, along with the modeling perspective, and, where possible, integrated for purposes of social work intervention.

It is not proposed that behavior modification be the sole approach to social work intervention. Many of the goals and activities of social work practice are either outside the boundaries of behavior modification as an intervention strategy, or are in early stages of development in behavior modification. For instance, mobilizing, modifying, and providing material services and resources is a major area of social work activity. Assisting individuals to make decisions— within the context of a nurturing interpersonal relationship—is perhaps one of the unique and best developed areas of social work practice and is a major component of most social work helping. A whole range of common social work interventive practices involving community and societal change remain virtually untapped in the behavior modification literature.

Furthermore, we do not suggest that behavior modification and its core in learning theory should necessarily be presented as a complete explanation of the development of human behavior. Human behavior is a complex phenomenon resulting from equally complex forces. We do take the position, however, that a technology that is effective in modifying behavior should be examined in its own right. The issue of its theoretical or practical relationship to theory regarding the development of that behavior, while important, must remain secondary. This is particularly true for a profession such as social work, with its mandate to intervene into the processes of, and bring about positive changes in, human problems.

It is hoped that the behavior modification approach will be equally interesting and provocative to undergraduate and to graduate social work students, as well as to experienced social workers. Perhaps this book can provide some of the beginning encouragement to attempt those first difficult steps of implementing a new approach in practice, an approach that offers substantial potential benefits for improving our practice methodologies, and ultimately, benefitting our clients.

PART 1

BASIC CONCEPTS
AND PRINCIPLES

CHAPTER 1.   The Behavioral Model

Behavior modification is a system of intervention, that is, a set of principles and procedures detailing how peoples' behavior can be changed. Behavior modification is not a system for explaining how and why people develop as they do (causal/developmental system). But like almost all intervention approaches, behavior modification has its roots in certain assumptions about, and conceptions of, the nature and development of human behavior. Because those perceptions are at considerable variance with many of the traditional and commonly accepted assumptions about human behavior, and because those ideas generally are crucial in determining the nature and type of interventive efforts derived from them, this chapter will present a brief overview of the behavioral model, which, in its view of human behavior, offers a major alternative to more traditional conceptions of human behavior, particularly those which, because of similarities to medical views of *physical* illness, have come to be called the "disease model."

BASIC ASSUMPTIONS OF THE DISEASE MODEL

The key features of the disease model, from which most of the traditional systems of intervention are derived, are a focus on internal ("intrapsychic") events (represented by such terms as "ego," "self," and "superego"), and the regard of overt maladaptive behavior basically as a sign or symptom of those more important internal factors. This would take the form of viewing a problem manifested in an overt behavior (a "symptom") as an indication that there are more basic problems in underlying dispositions.

A basic assumption of the disease model is that "abnormal" behavior is substantially different from "normal" behavior, with different principles explaining the development of "normal" and "abnormal" behavior. Just as physical ill health—caused, e.g., by a virus—often can be distinguished clearly from physical health, an individual suffering from social or emotional problems is viewed as "sick" within the context of the disease model. Thus, "mental illness" becomes similar to any other illness. This "sickness" is seen as a product of some underlying cause, so that when abnormal behavior is displayed, it is seen as an indication that "something" is wrong underneath ("deep down"). Symptoms, then, are viewed mainly as indicators of an underlying problem; symptoms, or observable, maladaptive behaviors, may not be viewed at all as problems in themselves. Hence, a positive change in behavior—e.g., removal of a symptom, such as a phobia about dogs—may be viewed as unimportant unless the "basic cause" of that problem is known and adequately dealt with.

Following from this set of assumptions comes the hypothesis regarding symptom substitution. Simply stated, it is assumed that if only overt behaviors are treated, and the underlying causes are not removed, another symptom will take its place. So, in the example of the fear of dogs, if this fear were to be eliminated, but the underlying cause for this fear were left untouched, it would be assumed that another symptom —perhaps fear of cats?—would pop up to take its place. Symptoms in this model are important largely in terms of the idea that they represent something related to the inner core problems.*

Basic Assumptions of the Behavioral Model

The most important distinction between the behavioral model and other models of human behavior is that the behavioral model places more emphasis on understanding the functional relationship between the environment and behavior. Specifically, it is assumed—and there is abundant research evidence supporting this assumption—that most behaviors are learned; i.e., they develop out of the interaction between an individual and his environment (see, e.g., Rotter *et al.*, 1972; Mischel, 1968; Ullmann & Krasner, 1969). "Environment" is defined to include not only situations, places, and events, but people as well—parents, peers, teachers, and so on.

The focus of the behavioral model is on *observable behavior*. All behaviors, both covert ("inner") and overt ("outer"), are of concern, especially when the behaviors are subject to measurement or observation. This does not mean that behaviors that are not observable are unimportant or worthless. However, the behavioral model does emphasize that it is hazardous to use such unobservable behaviors—independent of any

* More extensive reviews of the characteristics of the disease model, particularly its implications for intervention, such as focus on verbal communication and insight regarding the underlying causes of problems, are available elsewhere (e.g., Mischel, 1968; London, 1964; Ullmann & Krasner, 1969; Tharp & Wetzel, 1969).

objective validation—to explain those observable behaviors from which the internal behaviors are inferred (Skinner, 1953; Kanfer & Phillips, 1970).

The behavioral—or learning—model assumes that the same principles of human behavior explain both maladaptive ("abnormal") and adaptive ("normal") behavior. This is in contradistinction to the major thrust of the "disease" model which assumes that different principles explain the acquisition of normal and abnormal behavior (Ullmann and Krasner, 1969; Mischel, 1968). Thus, using the disease paradigm, an "abnormal" behavior might be viewed as developing in an analogous manner to a physical illness; hence, a diagnosis is made on the presumption of some underlying "disease." But for the vast majority of social and psychological problems, no "disease," or organic disorder, has been discovered. The behavioral model, emphasizing the universality of the development of behavior—that is, that most forms of behavior develop according to the same principles—is concerned with developing laws regarding behavior—general statements about the empirical relationship between the occurrence of behavior and its causes.

This relates to another major focus of the behavioral model, namely, the use of scientific methods to explore and analyze the complexities of human behavior. Observation, recording, use of data and experimentation are all key aspects of the behavioral model. In fact, it is assumed—and most behavioral research bears it out—that the methods of inquiry appropriate to other sciences are also appropriate to inquiry into human behavior. The point is not that the behavioral model deemphasizes humanity, or human uniqueness, by emphasizing the scientific method. Rather, it is that the behavioral model attempts to use both laboratory and field data to establish causal relationships between variables, and insists that when causal variables are identified, they actually *be* causal variables, and not merely inferred causal variables.

"ABNORMAL" BEHAVIOR IN THE BEHAVIORAL MODEL

Since much of human behavior is assumed to be learned according to common principles (of course, situations, events and individuals differ, thereby accounting for the tremendous richness and variety of individual behavior), differences in human behavior need not be described as "normal" or "abnormal." In fact, from the perspective of the behavioral model, such judgments are seen as functions of the *perceptions* of the behavior, rather than factual statements about the presence of some disease accounting for an "abnormality." This is a crucial concept for the behavioral model. It means that behaviors are either adaptive or maladaptive for the individuals who perform them, not "normal" or "abnormal." Thus, a maladaptive behavior might be one or more of the following (Ullmann & Krasner, 1969): a behavior, the performance of which produces aversive consequences for the individual or people in his environment; the behavior of an individual who might not be fulfilling his regular role expectations; the behavior of someone who does not respond to the stimuli or events in his environment, or have the skills to make an appropriate response; behavior whereby an individual might respond to a given stimulus or event, but do it at the wrong time or wrong place (for example, Connie might have sufficient assertive skills, which she uses well in relation to her peers, receiving encouragement and positive feedback from them, but she might also use these same skills with her teachers, thus bringing aversive consequences).

Indeed, the whole notion of abnormality—at the heart of the disease model—is especially problematic. By whose definition is someone or someone's behavior normal? Is it in terms of a normal curve? In terms of society or of a given culture? Is normality a function of individual or family perceptions? Or is normality a matter of functioning adequately in a variety of roles? The point is that when considering the question of normality and abnormality, so many complex dimensions are involved (see, e.g., Offer and Sabshin, 1966) that the whole concept, just on the face of it, begins to lose meaning. Clearly, the distinction between "normal" and "abnormal" is an arbitrary one; it bears little or no relationship to even overt behaviors, let alone the presumed underlying dispositional and personality differences between people labeled "normal" and those labeled "abnormal."

Therefore, it can be seen that even a term such as "symptom," which implies an abnormality, may be misleading. Not only might there be no underlying pathology to which the symptom is related, but, even more important, behaviors traditionally defined as "symptoms" have different meanings for different people, depending on their own learning histories and their situations. For some, the presence of a given "symptom" may be totally disabling; for others, the same behavior may be ignored, or even cherished by himself or others. For example, the hallucinator may be termed a schizophrenic in one culture and a messianic leader or healer in another.

This fact suggests another major implication of the behavioral model. Perceptions about behavior vary widely—from culture to culture, from society to society, even from individual to individual. An enormous amount of data has been gathered showing how similar behaviors are perceived differently depending on the nature of the observer, and the class, culture, status, and role of the individual performing the behavior (Hollingshead & Redlich, 1958; Ullmann & Krasner, 1969). Thus, any label attached to any given behavior is, from the behavioral point of view, irrelevant.

There are basic reasons to avoid diagnostic labels in general. Labels bias practitioners in terms of attitudes and treatments (Fischer & Miller, 1973). Labels limit the social opportunities of those to whom they are affixed. How many employers wish to hire a "schizophrenic" or even an "ex-schizophrenic"? Labels regarding abnormal behavior tend to lead others to overlook the strengths of people; few individuals are "neurotic" or "schizophrenic" all the time. The behavior of people changes depending on a host of variables; behavior rarely, if ever, remains constant. Finally, not only does a label bias the professional so that he tends to see little beyond the "pathology," but labeling has an even more unfortunate effect on the client, in that labels can severely and negatively affect one's image of oneself. Consider, as an example, the experiment conducted by Rosenhan (1973) wherein several professionals gained admission to a number of psychiatric hospitals around the country. These professionals arranged to have themselves labeled as schizophrenics, i.e., as mentally ill. In no case were any of the professionals found to be sane by hospital professionals. Furthermore, all took extensive notes while in the hospital, behavior which, in several instances, was seen as an aspect of their "pathology." Despite their best efforts to convince the hospital staffs of their sanity, the researchers were finally released as "schizophrenics in remission." Interestingly enough, only the real psychiatric patients were able to identify the pseudopatients as such. Clearly, labels and diagnoses such as "mental illness" are more than mythical (Szasz, 1961); they are dangerous—both to the individuals so labeled and to society at large.

Assessment and Intervention Based on the Behavioral Model

These assumptions and conceptions about human behavior are crucial in determining the direction of behavior modification. The Introduction briefly discussed some of the characteristics of behavior modification. This chapter will illustrate how these characteristics were derived from the underlying behavioral model.

The goal of behavior modification intervention is not to alter inner states, but to alter overt behavior. Not only has the efficacy of this perspective in practice been established in extensive research (Franks, 1969), but such efforts are also congruent with substantial research from the field of social psychology (see, e.g., Goldstein *et al.*, 1966), which demonstrates that behavior can be changed without attempting to change inferred, underlying dispositions. In fact, considerable evidence exists showing that, frequently, insight is achieved and one's attitudes toward oneself and others tend to change *after* changes in overt behavior rather than *before* such changes (see Chapter 8 for elaboration of this point). And, in extensive research, the hypothesis of symptom substitution simply has not materialized as a factor affecting the outcome of behavior modification. In fact, contrary to assumptions that a new symptom related to some core problem will appear following removal of a dysfunctional behavior, extensive research on symptom substitution reveals that such a phenomenon may not even exist at all (Franks, 1969; Mahoney, Kazdin, and Lesswing, 1974).

Using the behavioral model, assessment, intervention, and research are all integrated, with one flowing from the other. The focus is on explicitness—both in defining specific problematic behaviors as targets for change, and in designing techniques to modify those behaviors. This not only aids in goal formulation, but in the process of measuring whether those goals have been attained, and what procedures affected the attainment.

Since the same learning principles are used to explain the development of most behavior, they can be used also to derive procedures for changing behavior. Only a few basic principles of behavior pertain, based on their experimental validation in laboratory and field research (these will be explicated in following chapters). This model, while parsimonious and efficient, nevertheless allows for the development of a variety of procedures or ways of implementing the basic learning principles that can be used to change behavior predictably. In a sense, the behavioral model and behavior modification can be seen as an attempt to systematize and bring under the practitioner's control those principles and laws of everyday behavior that constantly occur but, all too often, are neglected in practice.

Instead of remaining preoccupied with social judgments about the normality or abnormality of a given behavior, labels and diagnoses are largely eschewed by social workers using this model. Instead, there is heavy reliance on the discovery of the environmental conditions that either elicit or maintain a given pattern of behavior, and on the description of what actually occurs. This description, stated in terms of behaviors that may need to be increased or decreased, then leads to the use of precise interventive procedures designed to bring about such changes. Again, most areas of human functioning have been involved as target behaviors for behavior modification procedures, including those related to the subjective self-reports of a client, such as feelings of distress, concern, worry, hopelessness, fear, anxiety, and so forth (see Part 3). But what is important is that when the intervention program is designed, it focuses on those behaviors whose occurrence or nonoccurrence bring about an undesired situation (the "pain") for the individuals involved. The focus is not on hypothesized or inferred events assumed to "cause" the dysfunctional behaviors. The aim of behavior modification is not to exclude or deem insignificant any aspect of human behavior such as feelings about oneself or subjective self-reports, but to help clients and practitioners more objectively identify problems and work toward their solution.

A whole new role for the environment is opened up using the behavioral model. This ranges from clearer perceptions of some of the causes of behavior to clearer and more precise utilization of the crucial aspects of the environment that our everyday experience tells us are particularly influential in affecting behavior. The environment thus becomes the laboratory. Problems often can be treated where they occur, namely, in the natural environment. And, with minimal training, a whole range of people in the natural environment—parents, teachers, spouses, and so on—can be taught to help effectively the people with whom they come in contact. For social work, particularly, this is of extreme importance since the development of principles of socioenvironmental change has always been of primary concern to the profession. Particularly heavy emphasis is placed upon the functional analysis of behavior—the way changes in environmental factors effect changes in behavior, and vice versa—and the direct use of such functional analyses in both assessment and intervention.

There is, finally, a more basic and important point. This book is not an attempt to prove or even argue the validity of the behavioral model. It may be more or less accurate, depending on a complicated set of contextual and situational variables. And it may not be. But what *is* crucial is that the behavioral model has led to the derivation of interventive procedures that constitute the technology—or applied body of knowledge—of behavior modification. Moreover, what *can* be asserted is that the principles and procedures of behavior modification hold great promise for social work, precisely because extensive clinical research has demonstrated their efficiency and efficacy in many settings and with a wide range of problems of importance in social work (Franks and Wilson, 1974; Bandura, 1969; Franks, 1969; Bergin & Garfield, 1971). Thus, the major and most significant effect of the behavioral model can be seen in its application, i.e., what educators, researchers and practitioners have been able to learn about the modification—although not necessarily the development—of human behavior. And for social work and the helping professions, the modification of behavior—intervention—is the core issue.

Clearly, the behavioral model engenders a sense of optimism, perhaps because one can reasonably conclude that if a behavior can be learned, it can be unlearned or modified. No longer is it unrealistic to think of man as infinitely adaptable, with tremendous potential for change, and, thus, for control of his own destiny.

Research in Behavior Modification

One pronounced emphasis of the behavioral model and behavior modification is on research, i.e., the application of systematic procedures to develop, modify, and expand knowledge that can be communicated and verified by other investigators working independently (Tripodi *et al.*, 1969, p. 2). This emphasis can be seen in several areas:

1. the use of experimentally validated principles of learning as the basis for the development of behavior modification procedures;
2. the use of rigorous criteria for evaluating research from areas other than behavior modification that are not primarily concerned with intervention (e.g., social psychological research, dealing with cognitive dissonance as in Goldstein *et al.*, 1966) in the event such material can be used to supplement behavioral procedures;
3. comparisons between behavioral procedures and procedures derived from other therapeutic orientations (e.g., Paul, 1966; DiLoreto, 1971; Franks, 1969; Yates, 1970);
4. the research on behavior modification procedures themselves, and their relative effectiveness with different clients and problems (Franks, 1969; Bandura, 1969);
5. the ongoing objective evaluation of intervention with each client;
6. the overall evaluations of effectiveness using rigorous and sophisticated research designs.

There is a comprehensive literature dealing with what constitutes good research design, such as the use of control groups, random assignment, the use of multiple criterion measures including subjective and objective reports, and so on (see Paul, 1969; Stuart, 1971; Campbell & Stanley, 1963; Tripodi *et al.*, 1969; Goldstein *et al.*, 1966; Fischer, 1975). Therefore, these general topics need not be reviewed here. However, one kind of research is very relevant to the development and verification of behavior modification procedures and to the behavioral model itself, namely, the experimental investigation of single cases. As such, and because of its uniqueness with respect to more traditional designs, the central characteristics of this design will be discussed here.

EXPERIMENTAL INVESTIGATION OF SINGLE CASES

This is the basic design used in the development of the procedures of behavior modification, particularly in operant conditioning. There is considerable bias against this design among many researchers who tend to be more familiar with group experimental designs. However, as noted by McNemar (1940, p. 361) over thirty years ago:

> The statistician who fails to see that important generalizations from research on a single case can never be acceptable is on a par with the experimentalist who fails to appreciate the fact that some problems can never be solved without resort to numbers.

This design is typically used to demonstrate that, first, the procedures used are (or are not) actually affecting the target behavior, and, second, that the target behaviors are (or are not) changing. This design can be a powerful method for the evaluation of behavior change procedures, and, properly used, not only forms an important part of the basis for the evolution of behavior modification, but can give each practitioner the means for assessing his own work. In fact, it is the use of the experimental investigation of the single case that some authors (e.g., Yates, 1970) consider the outstanding distinguishing feature of behavior modification.

The features of the single case design and some of the methodological problems associated with it have been spelled out in considerable detail elsewhere (Yates, 1970; Leitenberg, 1973; Howe, 1974; Baer *et al.*, 1966; Browning & Stover, 1971; Bushell & Burgess, 1969; Stuart, 1970; Chassan, 1967; Skinner, 1966; Honig, 1966), so only the basic dimensions need be described here. In essence, the single case study design attempts to determine whether the changes in a target behavior are lawfully related to the experimental operations that were intended to produce them (Yates, 1970, p. 381). This is a long way from the traditional clinical case study because a number of control features are built in. First, a target behavior is identified and either frequency of occurrence or the length of time it occurs (or both) is measured over a period of time long enough to provide base rate information (see Chapter 10 for a detailed explanation of this procedure). This base rate information is used as a *baseline,* and is collected in a rigorous, planned manner (not retrospectively), and before any intervention begins (Gelfand & Hartman, 1968). This baseline information is then charted, with the frequency or length of occurrence going on the vertical axis, and the period of time during which it was collected going on the horizontal axis. Thus, the baseline chart for a child who rarely smiles or laughs, collected during the same one hour period every day for one week, might look like the chart presented in Figure 1.1.

The collection of the baseline (A) is the first step in the evaluation process and actually forms the basis for all succeeding steps. (Of course the behavior, in this case smiling behavior, must be clearly and specifically defined; see Chapter 10 on Recording.) The next step is to identify the specific techniques to be used either to increase or decrease the

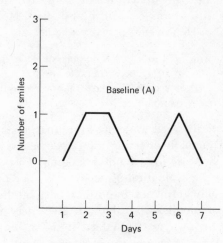

FIGURE 1.1. Number of smiles per one-hour session per day during baseline period.

occurrence of the behavior and to implement those techniques. This is the first intervention period (B), and data continue to be recorded in the same manner as before. In the situation described above, assume that the intervention consisted of positive reinforcement supplied every time the child smiled, the goal being to increase smiling behavior. The chart might look like the one in Figure 1.2.

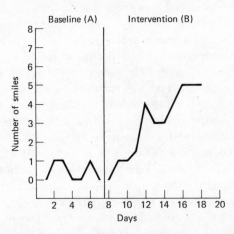

FIGURE 1.2. Number of smiles per one-hour session per day during baseline (A) and first intervention (B) periods.

From a mean of approximately ½ smile per 1 hour period per day during the baseline, the child began to smile roughly five times per 1 hour period per day at the end of the first intervention. This would clearly demonstrate that smiling behavior increased after the intervention started. To find out if this increase was related to the technique used, a third period called baseline 2 or *reversal* (A) could be implemented. During this period, the intervention (positive reinforcement) would be stopped and the individual conducting the intervention would be instructed to behave in the same way he or she had behaved prior to the intervention (at baseline 1). The chart might look like Figure 1.3.

This would demonstrate, at the very least, that the behavior (smiling) decreased, although not to its original level, and strongly suggests that the decrease is related to the cessation of the intervention. Finally, the intervention program would be reinstituted (we can't leave this child a nonsmiler, can we?), and the positive reinforcement for smiling provided again. This is intervention period 2 (B). The chart might look like Figure 1.4.

We once again have a smiling child! And, clearly, the frequency of smiling can be related all along the line to the behavioral techniques and whether they were being applied or withdrawn.

Of course, this example is merely hypothetical and has been oversimplified for purposes of illustration. But the basic evaluation process *is* carried out as described here, and can be of great value both to the individual practitioner and to the field as a whole. It provides the raw, objective data for the continuing development or modification (or both) of intervention procedures, not only for the practitioner involved in a

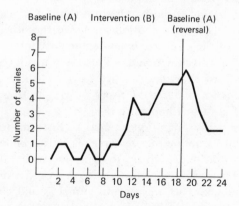
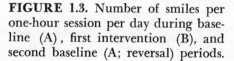

FIGURE 1.3. Number of smiles per one-hour session per day during baseline (A), first intervention (B), and second baseline (A; reversal) periods.

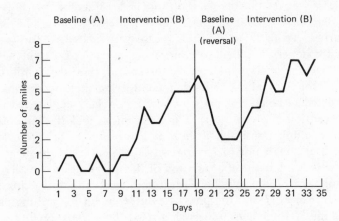

FIGURE 1.4. Number of smiles per one-hour session per day during baseline (A), first intervention (B), second baseline (A; reversal), and second intervention periods.

behavioral program tailored specifically for a given individual, but also for those who use behavior modification techniques so as to be kept informed of ongoing developments. Now it is not necessary for every practitioner to carry out exactly this kind of assessment procedure for every case. On the one hand, this would not only be impractical, but, for ethical and humanitarian reasons, once the desired behavior has been attained, in actual practice it could be highly undesirable to use a reversal stage (baseline 2) and withdraw the intervention to see if the behavior reverts to roughly its preintervention level. On the other hand, the two basic features of this design (the baseline and first intervention periods), which is called the A–B design and is illustrated in Figure 1.2, can easily be incorporated into everyday practice as a continuing tool of assessment. (Suggestions for making the process as interesting and painless as possible can be found in Chapter 10.)

Needless to say, the practitioner's goal is, first and foremost, to help his or her client. Conducting research is of secondary importance, although the use of single-subject designs, especially the A–B design, combines scientific and therapeutic goals: the validation of the success of each technique with each client, thus ensuring that clients are indeed helped. The full design, with all four periods—called the A–B–A–B design—is available for more scientific purposes in the development and verification of procedures to expand knowledge for the helping professions.

Actually, the intention is not to separate scientific and therapeutic purposes, since, in behavior modification research, the two are inextricably intertwined. In fact, the use of the A–B–A–B design should not be completely ruled out for everyday practice. In the first place, much of this research shows that the behavior in the reversal period (second A) rarely returns completely to the rate of the preintervention period (the baseline or first A period). Secondly, the reversal itself can have extremely beneficial effects on behavioral programs because it dramatically demonstrates to the people involved in the program (e.g., teachers, parents, spouses, unrses, ward attendants, other professionals, etc.) that they are indeed influencing the behavior of their clients; hence, the research can act as reinforcement to bolster continuing therapeutic efforts (Krasner, 1971).

Where use of the A–B–A–B design is not feasible or desirable, and more rigor is desired than can be achieved through use of the A–B design, another alternative is available, namely, the multiple baseline design. Not only can this design be used to increase the evidence that observed changes are due to the techniques used, but it does so in a different way than the A–B–A–B design, in that it does not have a reversal condition. With the multiple baseline design, baseline data are collected on more than one target behavior, or are collected on the same target behavior but in more than one setting. Intervention procedures are then applied either on one behavior in more than one setting, or on several behaviors in only one setting. At the same time, data are recorded on all the behaviors and in all the settings. Once the initial target behavior changes, intervention is then applied systematically either to the next target behavior or in the next setting. A multiple baseline design focused on different behaviors (in one setting) is illustrated in Figure 1.5.

In sum, the experimental investigation of the single case, which has been used extensively—well over 110 published reports utilizing the reversal design were published in the late fifties and the sixties alone (Morrow, 1971)—can serve as the foundation for continuing behavioral research. It has proven of inestimable value for knowledge building and for practice, proceeding as it does by progressive modification of hypotheses in the light of discoveries about the relationship between predictions that are based on the principles of learning and behavior that are used and actual empirical results. Replication after replication, which vary such conditions as the type of client, the type of change agent, the type of techniques used and the type of target behavior, provide the basis for the continuing development of behavior modification. In fact, it has been argued that abandonment of this unique feature, i.e., the experimental investigation of the single case, would lead behavior modification to approximate rapidly the traditional disease model approach "with catastrophic effects" (Yates, 1970, p. 381).

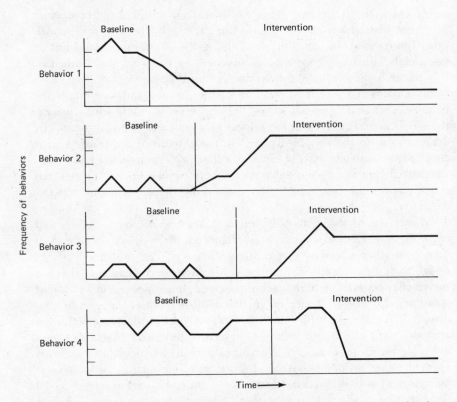

FIGURE 1.5. Multiple baseline design using four different behaviors.

WHAT ABOUT GROUP EXPERIMENTAL DESIGNS?

All the above should not be taken as a plea to abandon more traditional methods of evaluating the effects, and the effectiveness, of behavior modification procedures. Although the single case study design can be used as the primary source of data for the formulation of hypotheses for group experimental studies that test the effectiveness of behavioral procedures against either no-treatment controls or procedures derived from other approaches, single case study designs, even the A–B–A–B, cannot by themselves be used to validate intervention techniques; furthermore, their results cannot properly be generalized to other workers, clients or problems, although they *can* provide evidence that a given technique used by a given worker with a given problem was effective. Rigorously controlled group experimental designs alone can provide conclusive evidence about the effectiveness of any particular technique or set of techniques. In most cases, however, such research can best proceed by being informed *in advance* by the results of numerous single case experimental designs—by testing hypotheses built on solid facts rather than on mere speculation and guesswork. The latter may enhance a research program, or be important to the theorist, but research can proceed geometrically faster and more efficiently (and our clients be helped more effectively when we use such research findings) when the factual basis of hypotheses can be established in advance.

Does this mean that the field of behavior modification has ignored rigorous experimental group designs? Not at all. Not only have most of the underlying principles of behavior modification been the product of extensive research using such designs, but many of the actual *procedures* of behavior modification (systematic desensitization for anxieties and fears, Paul, 1969; conditioning treatment of enuresis, Yates, 1970, chapter 5; modeling, Rachman, 1972, and other techniques) have been so extensively validated in experimental research that they loom as the undisputed interventions of choice for a variety of behavior problems. But such research only adds to what is perhaps the more basic or initial verification of the validity of various intervention techniques that the experimental investigation of single cases provides. In answer, however, to the persistent criticism that behavior modification relies *only* on the single case study design and ignores the more traditional group experimental designs with their usually greater potential for representativeness, control and generalizability, certain facts should be made clear. In the first two decades of the development of behavior modification (1950–1969, but primarily in the sixties), over 170 studies using group experimental designs that showed the positive effects of behavior modification procedures were reported (Morrow, 1971). Such efforts at scientific validation of the actual intervention procedures continue to provide a rigorous and vigorous base for the expanding use of behavior modification. Most important for our clients, such efforts increase their chance of receiving effective help based on the knowledgeable and discriminating use of the results of research on intervention procedures.

Summary

This chapter has reviewed the attributes of the behavioral model, including its basic assumptions, conceptions of "abnormal" behavior, and the manner in which assessment and intervention approaches—behavior modification, per se—are derived. Because of the importance of empiricism—doing whatever possible to evaluate rigorously the effectiveness of practice—a brief review of the unique feature of behavior modification research, namely, the experimental investigation of single cases, was presented. The chapter concluded with a discussion of the notion that such designs work hand-in-hand with traditional methods of research evaluation to provide a firm empirical foundation for the development of behavior modification.

CHAPTER 2.   Basic Principles
of Respondent Behavior

The preceding chapter attempted to set the framework from which the principles and procedures of behavior modification are derived. In this and the following chapters, those basic principles will be described. Although it might be possible to learn and use the techniques of behavior modification without understanding the basic underlying principles of learning, behavior modification is not merely a grab bag of techniques to be applied in some arbitrary or unsystematic manner. Instead, the procedures of behavior modification can be used most effectively when a social worker understands why the procedures were developed and how they relate to the laws of learning. This stance is a liberating one in that the social worker need not merely apply a "cookbook" or mechanistic approach. Instead he can master a variety of procedures, and creatively modify or adapt these procedures—or even develop new procedures, if need be—as the client, problem and situation requires, because he knows the underlying principles. This may seem like a tall order for the novice; it is hoped, however, that these introductory chapters will set the stage for such a practice and for the imaginative use of the intervention procedures that will be described in Part 2 of this book.

Considering the wide range of procedures for changing behavior that is available in behavior modification, it sometimes comes as a surprise that all the procedures essentially have been derived from only three major paradigms of learning. The three paradigms are: (1) respondent conditioning; (2) operant conditioning; and (3) modeling. Since the major focus of this book is on the application of operant principles, succeeding chapters will deal intensively with that topic, followed by a chapter on modeling. This chapter presents an overview of the principles of respondent conditioning.

Respondent Conditioning: Some Basic Definitions

This chapter will lay the groundwork for an understanding of the procedures of behavior modification that are based on the paradigm of learning called respondent conditioning. While respondent procedures are not the major focus of this book, they are of real significance in clinical, or therapeutic, practice, and overviews of several respondent techniques will be presented in later chapters.

Three of the basic terms to be used in this and subsequent chapters are the old stand-bys of learning theory literature: "stimulus" (S), "response" (R), and "conditioning." A *stimulus* is any situation, person, event, or thing (especially environmental but also within an individual) that either does, or can be made to, influence behavior. There are different types of stimuli and it is hoped that these will be made clear in the specific contexts in which each is discussed. *Response* is a term that can be used synonymously with the term *behavior*. Thus, stimuli affect responses (behavior), and responses in turn can become stimuli (e.g., one person's behavior can act as a stimulus affecting another person's behavior, the response). Finally, *conditioning* refers to the process by which a response is learned (or connected with a stimulus). The two basic paradigms of learning that are focused on in this book are operant and respondent conditioning. When a response is learned, i.e., when there has been some modification in an individual's activities as a result of his or her interaction with the environment, and the response has come about through the laws of respondent or operant conditioning, then that response is said to be a *conditioned response*. Conversely, if there is some behavior in an individual's behavioral repertoire which has not come about through interaction with the environment, i.e., was not learned, or is innate, it would be called an *unconditioned response*.

You are very hungry and see a restaurant and your mouth begins to water. A young woman who is afraid of small, enclosed spaces has to ride in an elevator to the top floor of a high-rise and becomes panic-stricken. A cinder flies into one of your eyes while you are driving on a Sunday afternoon, and your eye begins to tear. A tiny infant hears a loud noise and is startled. A student has to make a speech for a class, and breaks out in perspiration when he begins to mount the podium. A bright light is shined into your eyes and your pupils contract. What do all these responses have in common? They are all examples of *respondent behavior*.

Respondent behavior is perhaps best described as behavior that is *preceded* and *elicited* by a stimulus. In a situation where the occurrence of a response bears a one-to-one reciprocal relationship with a preceding stimulus (that is, has been elicited by that stimulus), that response is a manifestation of *respondent behavior*. Respondent behavior is similar to reflexive behavior. It is involuntary, and it is behavior that, most important, is mediated by the autonomic nervous system (the nerves connecting the spinal cord and brain to the glands, blood vessels, heart, and smooth muscles such as the muscles of the intestines, bladder, and so on). A number of common, everyday behaviors are respondent behaviors: perspiring, salivating, tearing (e.g., when a foreign object enters the eye), and becoming pale (the blood vessels contract). Most important for the purposes of social work and behavior modification, our emotions—fear, anxiety, anger (and their physiological correlates such as pulse rate, perspiration, and so on)—can be defined as respondents, i.e., as learned largely through respondent conditioning. Thus, knowledge about the learning and, more important, the modification of dysfunctional respondent behaviors is crucial in developing a well-rounded approach to social work practice.

All the above examples consisted of stimuli eliciting involuntary responses. The sight of the elevator (S) elicited fear (R). The very loud noise (S) elicited a startle reaction (R). The sight of the podium (S) elicited anxiety (R). The cinder in the eye (S) elicited tearing (R), and so on. But there are differences between some of these responses. A closer look reveals that there are two categories of responses: learned or conditioned responses (CR), and unlearned or innate or unconditioned responses (UCR).

An *unconditioned response* is an innate reaction to a particular stimulus. The response has nothing to do with an individual's life history. Thus, the startling of the infant or the tearing of the eye in the above examples were not learned; they were innate reactions or unconditioned responses (UCR). Accordingly, any stimulus which in and of itself elicits a UCR (e.g., the loud noise or the cinder) is called an *unconditioned stimulus* (UCS). We can tell whether a given situation or event is a UCS only by the fact that it elicits the unlearned (innate) response, the UCR.

Pairing

The key concept in respondent conditioning is *pairing* (or association). Extensive research has demonstrated that when a neutral stimulus—i.e., one that elicits little or no response—is consistently and over time paired with an unconditioned stimulus (a stimulus that elicits an unconditioned response), the new or previously neutral stimulus can also come to elicit a response similar to the one that was elicited by the unconditioned stimulus. Thus, the new S becomes a learned or *conditioned stimulus*

(CS), and the response it elicits becomes a learned or *conditioned response* (CR). In the example above, the conditioned stimulus of the image of the restaurant had probably been paired in the past with the unconditioned stimulus, the taste of the food. The taste elicited salivation, which was first a UCR for the taste of food, but then because of pairing with the restaurant, became a CR to the image of the restaurant. This is the basic paradigm of respondent or classical conditioning. It is based largely on the work of Pavlov, whose name probably rings a bell with most social workers. In fact, another term for the same process is "Pavlovian conditioning."

Another example using conventional learning symbols might aid in clarifying the paradigm.

$$S \longrightarrow R$$

Read this as: a stimulus elicits a response.

$$\text{UCS (e.g., a sharp blow)} \longrightarrow \text{elicits} \longrightarrow \text{UCR (fear)}$$

In this example, a sharp blow such as a slap (the UCS) elicits a fright response (the UCR)—composed of numerous physiological reactions and summarized by the term "fear"—fear in the individual who has been slapped (the classic example of fear as a UCS is in Watson & Rayner's, 1920, work with Albert).

Suppose, however, a new stimulus is added, one which has never elicited fear, and the new stimulus is consistently paired with the UCS (the slap). Assume that the new stimulus is a person, say, a female teacher, who is the person slapping a recalcitrant pupil.

(1) UCS(slap) ⟶ UCR (fear)
(2) neutral stimulus (teacher) ⟋
(3) CS (teacher) ⟶ CR (fear)

In this example, the slap serves as an unconditioned stimulus that elicits an unconditioned response of fear. The person doing the slapping, a teacher, is unavoidably associated with the spanking. Eventually, the teacher alone—even when she is not doing any slapping—comes to elicit the fear response in the child. Respondent conditioning has taken place: the fear has become a conditioned response to the mere presence of the teacher.

There are certain aspects of the respondent conditioning process that deserve mention. The order of pairing is critical. For optimal conditioning, the neutral stimulus should be presented before the unconditioned, stimulus. The presentation of the UCS should follow the neutral stimulus within one-half second, and probably no longer than one second (Millenson, 1967, pp. 48, 49). Actually, both of these criteria vary somewhat with the particular $S \rightarrow R$ combination under study. As a rule of thumb, the more times the CS is paired with the UCS, the better the learning. Finally, the new stimulus has been referred to here as originally neutral, in that it presumably elicited no response on its own. Actually, very few stimuli are really neutral—i.e., elicit no response whatsoever from a person. Sometimes, however, the response elicited by the new stimulus is either unknown or somehow undetermined. But more important, to the extent the new stimulus does elicit a response, the question is: which response is stronger or more dominant? In the example above, it is unlikely that the teacher elicited no response from her pupil, either prior to, or independent of, the slapping. However, the slapping and the response of fear was stronger than any other response elicited by the teacher. Hence, the teacher comes to elicit fear in the student as the dominant response to her presence. Obviously, one of the tasks for the social worker who uses respondent conditioning is to insure that the responses he or she wants to condition (e.g., relaxation) are dominant to the undesired responses (e.g., anxiety).

There is an important point about the process of respondent conditioning that may explain why conditioned emotional reactions such as anxiety or fear (which are the respondent behaviors of primary concern to professionals) may sometimes seem so pervasive. In the example of the teacher striking the pupil, other figures similar to the teacher—other teachers at school with characteristics reminiscent of the first teacher, for example—may come to elicit similar reactions. This phenomenon is called *stimulus generalization:* stimuli (other teachers) resembling the CS (the first teacher), can, over time, also come to elicit the CR (fear). The strength of the response elicited by the new stimuli is a function of the degree of similarity between the CS and the new stimuli: the more closely they resemble each other, the stronger will be the response to the new stimuli. Incidentally, this concept of stimulus generalization suggests the crucial importance of establishing a range of positive conditions for children as they develop (respondent conditioning works in exactly the same fashion in the establishment of warm, affectionate, desirable responses; in the example, the teacher, behaving differently, might elicit affectionate feelings in the child that may generalize to other teachers). Not only did one teacher have a negative effect in her own relationship with the child, but it is easy to see how, if that effect were particularly strong, a child could come to perceive many aspects of his school environment as aversive through the principle of stimulus generalization. Clearly, the development of a warm and caring relationship between two individuals—teacher and student, parent and child, and so on—can have major beneficial effects beyond the immediate situation.

This is the essence of respondent conditioning: the pairing—intentionally or accidentally—of any number of situations, events, or even words with stimuli that elicit a range of emotional responses can cause the new, previously neutral stimuli to elicit such emotional responses also. Of course, the process is far more complex than the brief overview presented here may suggest. For example, although it is a more difficult process to establish experimentally, the pairing of entirely new and different stimuli with a conditioned stimulus can lead to the elicitation of responses similar to those of the conditioned stimulus. Thus, instead of a new stimulus being paired with a UCS, a new stimulus can be paired with a CS, and thus elicit a similar response. This is called *higher order conditioning*. Many of the elaborations of respondent conditioning such as this, however, can be found in any basic text on learning (e.g., Hall, 1966; Hilgard & Bower, 1966).

Significance of Respondent Conditioning

This explanation of some of the basic concepts of respondent conditioning was presented for two primary reasons. In the first place, respondent conditioning is a major way of learning maladaptive emotional behaviors; hence, it provides social workers with a clearer understanding of how such disorders develop. This occurs primarily through the pairing of neutral stimuli that elicit little or no response with stimuli that elicit strong aversive or unpleasant reactions such as fear, anxiety, and so on. Thus, many of the disorders traditionally termed "neurotic," including both relatively simple and complex behaviors—fears, anxieties, and phobias, for example—may be more adequately understood in terms of respondent conditioning. A number of disorders such as sexual fetishes, traditionally defined as related to obscure core personality conditions, may be more readily understandable as instances of this process. For example, an individual may at some point experience sexual excitement in response to one stimulus (say, masturbation) while in the presence of an inanimate object such as an article of clothing. Paired consistently and over a period of time, the new stimulus, the article of clothing, could eventually elicit sexual excitement too. In fact, the response of sexual excitement to inanimate objects could eventually generalize to other objects, some only remotely similar to the original object.

Not only is it important to understand respondent conditioning because it enables us to understand better how maladaptive emotional behavior develops, it is also important to gain such understanding because the processes of respondent conditioning underlie two basic sets of principles for behavior *modification,* for changing in a positive direction maladaptive emotional behavior. It is these principles that hold a major payoff for social work intervention. The two sets of principles are called *respondent extinction* and *counterconditioning.* Both sets have associated procedures for changing respondent behavior (i.e., conditioned responses). This is an important point: for the social worker faced with a client whose problems involve emotional behaviors such as fears, anxieties, anger, and so on (conditioned responses), the logic of the assessment process points to the selection of respondent-based procedures to change those behaviors. In other words, for respondent behaviors, consider respondent techniques.

RESPONDENT EXTINCTION

Obviously, it is not always possible for the original unconditioned stimulus (in the example of the teacher, the slap) to be constantly present, forever paired with the new or conditioned stimulus (in this case, the teacher). But the conditioned response, fear of the teacher, will probably persist for some time. However, if the CS (the teacher) is presented over and over again without being paired with the UCS (the slap), the CR (the fear) will dissipate and eventually fade away. The decline in the conditioned response due to repeated presentation of the CS without pairing with the UCS is called *respondent extinction.*

If, after the first days of class, the teacher who had slapped her pupil had stopped the slapping (which elicited the UCR of fear), it is possible that the CR of fear of the teacher would have diminished considerably over time. The teacher (the CS) would have been consistently presented without the UCS (spanking); extinction would thus have occurred. It might also be predicted that the fear which had generalized to other teachers would also have decreased. This phenomenon is called *generalization of extinction.*

As another example of extinction, consider a young woman named Ginger who had a morbid fear of dogs. As a child, she had been badly bitten (UCS) by a dog, naturally eliciting the UCR of fear. The association of the pain with the dog led to the CR of fear, which generalized to all dogs. Intervention consisted of gradual and consistent exposure to one very sweet dog named Cheryl in a very pleasant situation. In a short while, the CR of fear to that specific dog diminished; extinction had taken place. Generalization of extinction also occurred with some easing of the fear of other dogs. With repeated exposure to a number of different well-disciplined, sweet-tempered dogs, culminating in Ginger's attendance at a dog show, the extinction process was complete. Ginger no longer had a morbid fear of dogs.

Incidentally, an issue in behavior modification using respondent techniques involves the failure of "neurotic" behaviors to diminish and fade away in the natural environment. In other words, wouldn't it seem that since the UCS is rarely present, the extinction process would occur automatically? Actually, apart from such obvious reasons as the secondary gains of certain neurotic behaviors (the attention, or reinforcement, created by such behaviors), a pure form of respondent extinction is probably fairly rare. This is because many maladaptive conditioned emotional responses such as anxiety or fear lead to avoidance responses; the individual, because of his fears, avoids the conditioned stimulus (say, dogs, in a dog phobia). Thus, the basic requirement for extinction to occur—repeated presentation of the CS *without* the UCS—never has a chance to take place.

The principle of extinction underlies the behavior modification technique called *implosion* or *implosive therapy* (Stampfl & Levis, 1967). While this technique will be described in more detail in Chapter 14, the essence of implosion is to have the social worker present to the client the CS (whatever the individual is anxious about or afraid of), frequently and persistently, and often merely in imagination, *without the presence of the original UCS*. An intense emotional reaction is elicited initially, but, eventually, with repeated presentation of these anxiety-eliciting stimuli, the emotional reaction diminishes and disappears.

COUNTERCONDITIONING

Some emotional responses cannot occur at the same time as other responses; they are incompatible. Thus, it is difficult for a person to be tense or anxious when he is completely relaxed. It is difficult to feel sexually attracted to someone or something at the same time that one feels pain. *Counterconditioning* simply utilizes this principle: it essentially consists of the conditioning of a new response to the conditioned stimulus. Thus, the new response, which is incompatible with the old response, is elicited when the same CS is presented. If counterconditioning is successful, every time the CS is presented, the new, adaptive response—which is first a UCR such as relaxation, but becomes a CR as it comes to be elicited by the CS—will be elicited rather than the old maladaptive CR. The focus, in other words, is on developing a new response to an old stimulus.

Seth had an intense fear of hats. Whenever someone wearing a hat came close to him, Seth, age 3, would scream at the top of his lungs. Apparently, some very early negative encounters with a hat-wearing babysitter had triggered this response. Seth loved to eat. So, as in the famous early experiment by Jones (1924), the pleasure associated with eating (UCR) was used as the response incompatible with Seth's fear of hats. As Seth ate, an adult wearing a hat quietly entered the room and sat as far away as possible from Seth. Seth noticed but continued to eat. The fact that he was continuing to eat while the feared object was in the room indicated the beginning of counterconditioning. Gradually, and always during mealtimes, the adult wearing the hat moved closer and closer to Seth. Within a week, Seth was playing with the hat as he happily ate his dinner (he had a strong preference for pasta). The pleasure associated with eating (originally a UCR) had overcome the fear of the hat, and was now a CR. This situation might be illustrated as follows:

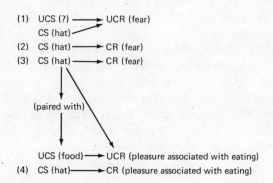

There are three key aspects of counterconditioning that are illustrated above, and serve as general guidelines in the use of counterconditioning processes (Mikulas, 1972):

1. isolate the stimuli that elicit the undesirable response (hats);
2. find other stimuli (food) that elicit desirable responses that are easily elicited, incompatible, and most important, *dominant to* the undesirable responses;
3. systematically pair the two sets of stimuli.

This pairing proceeds carefully, in a planned way, eliciting only small amounts of anxiety. If the hat in the example had been moved too close too quickly, the anxiety elicited would have been dominant to the pleasure associated with the eating. Seth would have been overwhelmed. On the other hand, the anxiety-eliciting stimulus (the hat) could not have been placed so far away that it elicited no anxiety, since counterconditioning would not have occurred. The concept of graduated *hierarchies* of anxiety-eliciting stimuli will be discussed further in Part 2, which will deal in greater depth with respondent techniques of behavior change.

A wide variety of behavior modification procedures has been derived from the principle of counterconditioning. These procedures fall into two major categories, which are described below.

The first category is counterconditioning to overcome maladaptive *avoidance* conditioned responses such as anxieties, fears, and phobias. Much of the work in this area was pioneered by Wolpe (1958, 1966, 1969, 1973). Wolpe hypothesized that a principle called "reciprocal inhibition" underlies the counterconditioning process. Briefly, the principle of reciprocal inhibition can be stated as follows:

> If a response inhibitory of anxiety an be made to occur in the presence of anxiety-evoking stimuli it will weaken the bond between these stimuli and the anxiety (Wolpe, 1969, p. 15).

In other words, anxiety cannot exist in the presence of an incompatible and more dominant response. The development of this principle made the counterconditioning process more suitable for clinical use, since it made clear that the task of the clinician was to find a response which was incompatible with, and dominant to, anxiety, and, applying the rules of counterconditioning, begin the gradual process of reconditioning. Great theoretical, clinical, and empirical strides have been made in this area. At least three procedures have been developed using this principle: *systematic desensitization,* a technique used to overcome a wide range of anxiety and fear responses, and which has the broadest research and empirical support of any single psychotherapeutic or behavior modification procedure; *assertive training,* a procedure used when individuals have anxiety responses in interpersonal contexts that prevent them from saying or doing what is reasonable or right (i.e., what they want to do); *substitution of sexual responses* for anxiety responses in the treatment of sexual problems (Wolpe, 1969). All of these procedures are amplified in later chapters.

The second set or major category of respondent-based techniques is *aversive* counterconditioning to overcome maladaptive *approach* conditioned responses. These procedures have been less widely used than the above procedures because they are often unpleasant to both client and practitioner. However, as evidence accumulates that, in some cases, they may be the only alternative for effective intervention, and when their advantages clearly outweigh their disadvantages, and when clients, with complete awareness of the details of the procedure, voluntarily undertake such treatment, the place of these techniques in the social work armamentarium becomes increasingly important.

The essence of aversive counterconditioning is simply to condition an aversive unconditioned response (UCR) to a stimulus that previously elicited an approach response (CR). The basic paradigm is to pair stimuli (CS) which elicit maladaptive approach responses with stimuli

(UCS) that elicit a stronger aversive response. Among the noxious stimuli that have been used to elicit aversive responses have been chemical substances, electric shock, and pictorial and imagined scenes. Some of the problems that aversive counterconditioning has been used with include alcoholism, sexual fetishes, unwanted homosexuality, and smoking. For example, in working with an individual who wants to stop engaging in homosexual practices, electric shock may be paired with pictures or situations (actual or imagined) relating to homosexual practices. In treating a drinking problem, a chemical inducing nausea or vomiting might be paired with the taste of alcohol, as illustrated in the diagram below.

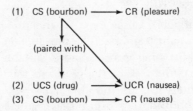

In this case, pairing the conditioned stimulus (the bourbon) with the unconditioned stimulus (the drug) caused the taste of the bourbon eventually to elicit nausea. Bourbon has become a CS eliciting the CR of nausea.

Summary

This chapter has presented an overview of the basic principles of respondent conditioning. Respondent behavior is behavior that is preceded and elicited by a stimulus. The major paradigm of the acquisition of respondent behavior involves the pairing of two stimuli, one of which is an unconditioned stimulus; if this occurs consistently and over time, the new stimulus eventually comes to elicit the same response that previously was elicited by the unconditioned stimulus. This new response is called a conditioned response. The concept of stimulus generalization, where other stimuli similar to the conditioned stimulus also over time can come to elicit the new conditioned response, was briefly discussed. The significance of respondent conditioning for social work practice was discussed in terms of the principles of respondent extinction and counterconditioning. Out of these two sets of principles, several specific techniques of behavior modification have been developed to deal largely with such respondent behaviors as anxiety, fear, guilt, and maladaptive approach responses such as smoking, alcoholism, and sexual fetishes.

The respondent techniques described here have been used mostly by professionals operating in more or less traditional office and clinic settings (although their use is certainly not confined to such places). Hence, their utilization may not have quite the degree of potential for social work practice of some of the other procedures that will be detailed in much of the rest of this book. However, the problems for which these techniques are suitable do constitute a fairly high percentage of the cases of many social workers. As the typology relating behavioral procedures to a wide range of human problems illustrates (see Part 2), knowledge of respondent techniques for effective intervention in a variety of emotional problems is crucial for the social worker interested in a comprehensive base for practice. Respondent techniques logically cannot, and should not, be omitted from the overall behavioral perspective, as they clearly complement the operant procedures to be described later. Thus, overviews of the procedural guidelines for each of these respondent techniques will be presented in Part 2.

It is hoped that, at this point, the reader has begun to develop some familiarity with the basics of respondent conditioning and the ways in which respondent techniques of behavior modification have developed logically from the core principles of respondent conditioning.

It should be clear by now that respondent behaviors are, for all intents and purposes, totally elicited by preceding stimuli. Respondent behaviors do not actually influence the stimuli that precede them; i.e., they do not operate on the environment (the fear of elevators does not really affect the elevators). In addition, the use of the respondent conditioning paradigm is limited to the behaviors that are respondent: reflexive, automatic, and emotional responses. Clearly, a wide range of human behaviors do not fit the respondent paradigm, which involves the pairing of stimuli, involuntary responses, and so on. It seems that a broader and perhaps more comprehensive framework is necessary to explain the wide range of everyday, voluntary behaviors that people engage in, and—more important for the professional social worker—out of which can be developed the range of helping procedures necessary to undergird a sizable portion of social work practice. Such a framework might be at least partially obtainable through a careful examination of the basic principles and procedures of operant conditioning.

CHAPTER 3.   Operant Consequences

Little Bunky runs over to her mother and gets a kiss for picking up her toys. A husband begins to nag his wife for not keeping a neat house, and she breaks down in tears; the husband stops nagging. A group of auto mechanics are told they must complete three tune-ups a day in order to get their weekly bonus. The teacher yells at Dan when he gets out of his seat without permission. All these are examples of the operant process.

Operant behavior, in addition to respondent behavior, is the second major class of learned behavior. Operant behavior involves voluntary or purposeful behavior, i.e., all those movements of a human being that may at some time have an effect on the outside world. In essence, operant behavior "operates" on the environment. In fact, contrary to some criticisms (e.g., Bruck, 1968), the operant framework suggests a conception of man as an actively manipulative organism influencing his surroundings. This framework provides the basis for understanding the complex interrelationships between people and their environment. Man is seen both as "actor" and "acted upon."

Operant behavior involves the gross muscles, i.e., all the muscles used in voluntary activity (hands, arms, mouth, etc.), and the central nervous system (the brain and spinal cord). Actually, the key operant term might be "doing": walking, talking, fighting, singing. Operant behaviors include a wide range of behaviors, ranging from the very simple to the incredibly complex—much of what people actually do and say as they act to promote change in the many aspects of their environment (Wenrich, 1970). This is in contrast to the narrow range of responses called respondent—the automatic, reflexive behaviors. While innumerable behaviors can be described as operant, the major concern of social workers and the primary focus of this book are those operant behaviors that are maladaptive, i.e., those that lead the individual or people in his environment to feel distress or discomfort, and perhaps even to seek professional help. In addition to helping one understand the ways in which maladaptive operant behaviors develop, the application of the basic principles of operant conditioning has led to the development of a wide range of interventive procedures that are designed to deal effectively with maladaptive behaviors.

As was pointed out previously, the focus of operant behavior modification is on the functional relationship between people and their environment. Individuals operate on their environment to get effects (Bunky being kissed by her mother); the environment operates to modify the behavior of the individual (the wife's crying stopped her husband's nagging). Reciprocity between individuals and their environment is the essence of operant conditioning ("what you give is what you get").

The operant conditioning paradigm is characterized by the stress it places on the importance of the *consequences* of behavior. This is generally the key to operant behavior modification: alteration and management of the contingent relationship between the occurrence of a behavior and its consequences (the student gets out of his seat—behavior —and the teacher yells—contingent consequence). In fact, operant behavior modification is often defined as *contingency management*, or the rearrangement of environmental consequences such as rewards and punishments in such a way as to strengthen or weaken specified behaviors (Tharp and Wetzel, 1969).

But operant conditioning (also called instrumental conditioning), and particularly operant behavior modification, involves more than the mere manipulation of consequences. Antecedent conditions—the events or occurrences that precede the behavior—are important also. Thus, the complete operant paradigm can be described as follows:

A (antecedent)—B (behavior)—C (consequences)

These are the ABC's of operant conditioning. Sometimes, in the literature of operant behavior modification, the "A's" are left out of the picture. For example, without considering a particular classroom situation (A), the disruptive behavior (B) of a child and the scolding by the teacher (C) might be improperly understood by the social work consultant. But the analysis of, and intervention in, antecedent events has an important place in the operant framework, and a review of the nature of antecedent conditions from the operant perspective, their relation to respondent antecedent conditions (eliciting stimuli), and their use in behavior modification will be presented in Chapter 5. This chapter will discuss the core of operant behavior modification, the nature of consequences and their varied effects on behavior.

The Nature of Consequences

The body of knowledge underlying operant behavior modification is sometimes referred to as "reinforcement theory" (Keller, 1969). This is because the concept of reinforcement plays a key role in the operant framework. To reinforce literally means to strengthen. Thus, if the consequence of a behavior—its environmental effect—is the application of reinforcement, that behavior will tend to be strengthened or increased. Conversely, if the emission of some behavior results in the removal or withdrawal of reinforcement, that behavior will weaken or decrease. This is where the concept of contingency plays a part. *Contingency* refers to the conditional relationship between the occurrence of behavior and the application or withdrawal of reinforcement. The occurrence of the consequence is conditional upon—i.e., depends on—the occurrence of the behavior. Perhaps a diagram might help clarify this process. Instead of the respondent model of $S \rightarrow R$, the operant paradigm is:

$$R \text{ (response or behavior)} \longrightarrow \text{leads to} \longrightarrow S \text{ (stimulus)}$$

As was mentioned previously, Chapter 5 will discuss possible antecedents to that behavior. The above model merely indicates that the occurrence of a behavior (R) is followed by a specific stimulus (S).

If the stimulus is a reinforcing stimulus, that is, maintains, strengthens, or increases the probability that the behavior (R) will occur again, the notation would be S^+ (a positively reinforcing stimulus or positive reinforcement). This, then, is the formal definition of *positive reinforcement*—any stimulus, situation or event which, when presented as a consequence of a behavior, increases the strength (or frequency of occurrence) of that behavior. Hence,

$$R \text{ (completion of extra work assignment)} \longrightarrow S^+ \text{ (bonus pay)}$$

or

$$R \text{ (a kind word to wife)} \longrightarrow S^+ \text{ (a kiss)}$$

In both situations, the behavior (completing a job or saying a nice word) was followed by the contingent application of reinforcement (a bonus or a kiss).

Not only desired, or positive (prosocial), behaviors are reinforced in real life, though.

$$R \text{ (temper tantrum)} \longrightarrow S^+ \text{ (attention)}$$

If little Angie throws a temper tantrum (R) and its occurrence has been increased or strengthened by her mother's attention (S+), that tantrum has been positively reinforced.

It is probably obvious that the application of positive reinforcement following a behavior is not the only possible consequence. There are several others. It is probably also easy to see the basic importance of these conditions in the development and explanation of human behavior. It is likely that a great deal of presumably complex human behavior can be understood as the effort to maximize the desirable consequences of behavior (rewarding events) and to minimize the undesirable consequences (painful or aversive events). This holds true across innumerable social and developmental dimensions, ranging from the formation of adaptive behaviors to the formation of maladaptive ones. There is increasing consensus in the field of human development that the major determinants of human behavior lie in the complex but specifiable interaction of individuals with their environment (e.g., Hoffman & Hoffman, 1964, 1966; Rotter, Chance, Phares, 1972). However, the task of this book is not to argue the importance of operant conditioning, and learning in general, in the development of human behavior. That has been done elsewhere (e.g., Patterson, 1971; Millenson, 1967; Lundin, 1969; Ferster & Perrott, 1968; Skinner, 1953). Instead, the major importance of the operant perspective for social work lies in those operant procedures that are already available for *changing* behavior. It is largely in these terms—i.e., the implications for intervention —that the remainder of this book will be presented.

Methods for Changing the Rate of Behavior

As mentioned above, there are available to the social worker several possible operations to apply as consequences to behavior "consequating operations"). These operations can either be *applied* or *withdrawn* following, and contingent upon, the occurrence of a behavior; their basic effects are to either *increase* or *decrease* the rate of occurrence of that behavior. This last is a crucial concept for both assessment and intervention in behavior modification. The idea is that there are basically only two directions in which behavior—any behavior—can move. Take the examples of a secretary's typing, a husband's nagging or a student's studying, which are all fairly complex behaviors. In all three cases, the behaviors can only increase (or perhaps be maintained so that they don't decrease), or they can decrease (the rates of typing and nagging and the time spent studying can diminish). The ways to affect these behaviors through behavior modification, including the application or withdrawal of certain consequences, are the subject of this and subsequent chapters.

Given the fact that behavior can be changed only in the direction of an increase or decrease in the occurrence of that behavior (of course, individuals can also be helped to perform behaviors at different times or

T A B L E 3.1.   Contingent Consequences Resulting in Specific
Changes in Behavior

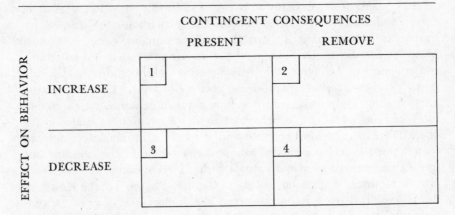

in different places), and that this can be brought about through the application (presentation) or withdrawal (removal) of specific consequences contingent on the performance of that behavior, a four-way table could be developed to illustrate the various possibilities (Mikulas, 1972).

The next task, then, is to fill in the cells in the table with the appropriate concepts, to present the terms for the four operations that, through presentation or removal, result in an increase or decrease in behavior.

POSITIVE REINFORCEMENT

Positive reinforcement refers to the *presentation* of a stimulus (situation, event, item or word) following a behavior which strengthens or *increases* the rate of occurrence of that behavior. This means that the social worker would construct a situation to insure that when a desired (prosocial) behavior occurs, it will be immediately followed by some consequence that will strengthen, or increase the rate of occurrence of, that behavior. While this consequence can generally be thought of as having a pleasurable effect on the individual performing the behavior —that is, it usually is perceived by him as desirable—any of a number of consequences, which will be discussed in the following chapter, might have that effect. The important idea, though, is that the consequence is *presented* (or given or applied, as opposed to being withdrawn), following the behavior and its effect on the behavior is to strengthen or increase the behavior.

EXAMPLE 3.1: Cherie and Larry had been married for five years. How-ever, their marriage was on the brink of divorce. They had a host of com-plaints about each other, which were worked on in a variety of ways by the social worker. One of Cherie's complaints was that her husband never commented positively about her efforts to keep the house clean. Larry's complaint was that the house was always a mess: "What's to comment about?" The social worker helped the couple devise a plan whereby Larry was to comment positively about every effort Cherie made to tidy up the house. Every little thing counted. If he noticed that the carpet had been vacuumed, the dishes washed immediately after dinner, the ashtrays emptied, or any of a number of other possibilities, he was to say so to his wife and show her some affection, perhaps with a kiss or a hug. Within a few weeks following the implementation of this program, not only did the house take on a new and obviously tidy appearance, but Cherie and Larry both commented on their surprisingly improved "communication."

EXAMPLE 3.2: Mrs. Rosemont complained to her social worker that she was having a devil of a time toilet-training her child Jenny, age 3. A physician had determined there was no physical incapacity on Jenny's part. Since Jenny did use the potty once in a while, although she usually simply eliminated in her diapers, a plan was developed to make going on the potty more desirable to Jenny than going in her diapers. Her mother was to watch her carefully for any signs of wanting to eliminate; when she saw such indications, she was to place her immediately on the potty. As soon as she eliminated on the potty, Mrs. Rosemont was to give Jenny a piece of her favorite candy and accompany this with a great deal of attention—praise, clapping, hugging, and so on. Mrs. Rosemont was asked not to make a big fuss out of "mistakes"; after all, this was attention too. She was also in-structed to make the praise and candy absolutely consistent. Mrs. Rose-mont did just that, and Jenny loved it. Within three days, Jenny was going on the potty several times a day just to get all the goodies. Mrs. Rosemont reported complete success within the first week.

In both of these illustrations, the two crucial aspects of the use of positive reinforcement were apparent. In the first example, there was (1) a *contingent relationship* between the occurrence of a behavior (house cleaning) and the *application* of an event (a kind word, a hug); (2) the result was an *increase* in the target behaviors (house cleaning and positive comments). Positive reinforcement was indicated in the second example by the fact that (1) a consequence (candy and praise) was *applied* contingent on a behavior; (2) the occurrence of the target be-havior (eliminating on the potty) *increased.*

Incidentally, if the behaviors had not increased or been strengthened, these would not have been examples of positive reinforcement. If the target behavior had neither strengthened nor increased, the results would have been considered simply to be no effect or a neutral effect, and, therefore, would not have been classified on our four-way table. This will be discussed in greater detail in subsequent chapters, although at this point, it should be obvious enough that, had this plan not succeeded, an alternative involving, say, in the first example, either Cherie's behavior (the target for change), or Larry's behavior (the consequence), or both, would have been utilized.

NEGATIVE REINFORCEMENT

Negative reinforcement, like positive reinforcement, also *increases* behavior. (This often comes as a surprise to many who equate negative reinforcement with punishment.) The only difference between negative and positive reinforcement is that, with negative reinforcement, the consequence is *withdrawn* or *removed* following the behavior (not *applied* as with positive reinforcement). Thus, negative reinforcement can be defined as the *withdrawal* or *removal* of a consequence following a behavior which strengthens or *increases* the rate of occurrence of that behavior.

The notation for negative reinforcement can be written as follows:

$$R \longrightarrow S^{/-}$$

The difference between this and the positive reinforcement paradigm is the change from a plus to a minus sign for the stimulus indicating a negative rather than positive reinforcer (types of reinforcers are the subject of Chapter 4), and the slash through the consequence, indicating its removal rather than presentation. Many everyday behaviors are maintained by negative reinforcement: e.g., when we close a window (increase our behavior) to avoid a draft (remove the consequence); when we take off our shoes to remove a stone—these are examples of negative reinforcement. Each involves some increase in behavior in relation to the removal or withdrawal of some stimulus. In fact, negative reinforcement plays a major role in the learning of many everyday behaviors where people learn to do one thing in order to avoid something else.

Two children are fighting in the family room. Their mother yells and screams at them to be quiet. For the moment, they tone down. The mother has learned, through negative reinforcement, to increase her yelling behavior because it resulted in the removal or withdrawal of some event (the fighting). In other words, the fighting stopped (an aversive stimulus removed) when she yelled at the children; this increases the likelihood that she will use yelling again to quiet her children.

There is a particularly important point about negative reinforcement that might be obvious: all the consequences that were removed or withdrawn in the above examples were unpleasant or *aversive* to the individuals involved. In contrast, most of the consequences in a situation of positive reinforcement are pleasant or rewarding to the individuals involved. This use of *aversive stimuli,* or negative reinforcers, and the corresponding difficulty in establishing situations where aversive events can be removed contingent on the performance of some behavior, makes the use of negative reinforcement not only difficult, but fairly rare in behavior modification. However, knowledge of this basic principle certainly contributes to overall understanding of behavior modification, and there may indeed be some situations in which the use of negative reinforcement is indicated. Generally, these are situations in which increasing some desired behavior through positive reinforcement either is not possible or has not been successful, and when appropriate ethical safeguards have been assured.

EXAMPLE 3.3: David was an 8-year-old boy admitted to a psychiatric institution with a diagnosis of "childhood autism." He never spoke and barely responded at all in a positive way to his environment. In fact, the major reactions that he did demonstrate appeared to be in response to aversive situations. The situation that seemed most aversive to David was playing with other children. When placed in a play situation, he would stand for one or two minutes staring blankly, then run from the scene and hide behind any object that was convenient. One of the first tasks, then, appeared to be to get David to relate in any positive way with other people. It had been demonstrated that he did understand verbal communication, although he would never sit in one place long enough for any staff member to talk with him. The first goal was to help David sit quietly with a staff member. This was done simply by placing David in what appeared to be his most disliked situation, namely, playing with peers—and making it clear to him that the only way he could leave would be to sit down with a staff member in order to avoid the aversive situation of playing with the other children. This step was accomplished fairly rapidly. (Of course, later steps involved helping David actually participate in conversation, and, eventually, play with other children without becoming overwhelmed.)

EXAMPLE 3.4: A withdrawn long-term resident in a psychiatric hospital refused to feed herself (see Ayllon & Michael, 1959). She did like to keep her clothes very neat and clean, however, and it was decided to use this in a program to increase her self-feeding behavior. The nurse, who had been spoon-feeding this resident for some time, casually began to spill little drops of soup and pieces of food on the resident's dress. This was very aversive to the resident who reached for the spoon to prevent further spilling on her dress. Reaching for the spoon immediately terminated, at least for the time being, the aversive event (spilling). Thus, as the program developed, the resident could escape from the spilling by feeding herself. The self-feeding soon began and the aversive situation completely terminated.

The basic aspects of negative reinforcement that were present in the first example were: (1) a behavior *increased* (approaching and sitting with a staff member), and (2) an event, an aversive event at that (play with peers), was terminated or *removed,* or in this example, escaped from or avoided. The second example also illustrates the two basic aspects of *negative* reinforcement: (1) *removal* or termination of a consequence (the spilling of food), (2) *contingent* upon an *increase* in the occurrence of a behavior (self-feeding). Again, this example also illustrates that the behavior was increased to *avoid* or *escape from* the aversive event. Thus, in practice, negative reinforcement is often called *escape* or *avoidance* learning. This latter characteristic, that behavior in negative reinforcement is generally increased in order to avoid or escape from aversive events, is another reason why negative reinforcement is rarely used in behavior modification, at least in comparison with other procedures such as positive reinforcement. Most social workers would far prefer to have their clients learn new behaviors in order to receive desired consequences (as in positive reinforcement), than to have them learn new behaviors merely to avoid aversive consequences. There are several other related reasons why negative reinforcement is infrequently used, and these, too, will be discussed later. Thus, the first two cells in the table have been filled in—the two relating to an *increase* in the occurrence of behavior (see Table 3.2).

Now, how about principles for *decreasing* behavior by contingent use of consequences? In most texts on behavior modification, the two contingent consequences for decreasing behavior are lumped under the term "punishment." However, like the two forms of reinforcement (positive

T A B L E 3.2.   Contingent Consequences Resulting in an Increase in Behavior

		CONTINGENT CONSEQUENCES	
		PRESENT	REMOVE
EFFECT ON BEHAVIOR	INCREASE	1 POSITIVE REINFORCEMENT	2 NEGATIVE REINFORCEMENT
	DECREASE	3	4

and negative) , there are really *two* types of punishment. For the sake of consistency and clarity, these forms of punishment shall be called "positive punishment" and "negative punishment" (Mikulas, 1972). The term "punishment," of course, has very negative implications for many social workers, and some of this is as it should be. This section, however, will explore the meaning of these concepts simply for the sake of clarification. Later sections of this chapter will discuss both pros and cons of their use.

POSITIVE PUNISHMENT

Positive punishment (note the similarities to positive reinforcement) refers to the *presentation* of a stimulus following a behavior which weakens or *decreases* the rate of occurrence of that behavior. This has some similarities to the lay conception of punishment (e.g., the mother spanking her child) with these exceptions: (1) the presentation of the event must be *contingent* on (immediately following and related to) the occurrence of a preceding behavior; (2) the behavior must be *decreased* or *weakened*. If the behavior is not decreased (the mother slaps her child for swearing but he continues to swear), then the situation in behavior modification terms is not punishment. Again, the event following the behavior is usually aversive or unpleasant to the individual being punished, although it is clearly not necessarily painful, as the lay conception of punishment implies. Thus, the task of the social worker using positive punishment is to arrange for some aversive event to follow contingent upon some undesirable behavior in order to decrease the probability that the behavior will occur (i.e., weaken the behavior) .

The notation for positive punishment can be written as follows:

$$R \longrightarrow S^-$$

EXAMPLE 3.5: Bill was a stutterer. He had tried everything he could possibly think of in his 33 years to stop stuttering. His final attempt was to see a social worker who used behavioral techniques. Bill was given a pair of headphones to wear (see Goldiamond, 1965). He was instructed to begin reading a speech. Every time he started stuttering, the social worker administered delayed auditory feedback (i.e., he played back what Bill had been reading just previously) . This was presented contingent on Bill's stuttering. In order to avoid this feedback, which—after brief instructions were provided—was administered by Bill himself, Bill had to slow down his rate of speaking until the stuttering disappeared. Then Bill would increase the rate of speaking to the desired speed without stuttering while the feedback was faded out. Bill's stuttering gradually was eliminated.

EXAMPLE 3.6: Marty was a resident in a small group home for delinquent and "predelinquent" boys. Marty used obscene language quite a lot at the dinner table, and this was a behavior that the staff thought would bring Marty many undesirable consequences after he left the group home. They decided it should be eliminated. While all of the children had certain chores in the group home, one of the most disliked was washing the windows. Normally, this was handled by paid housekeeping staff. In this situation, however, it was decided to use windowwashing as the aversive stimulus to decrease Marty's swearing behavior. Every time Marty swore at dinner, he was immediately assigned the task of washing windows in one of the cottages in the group home (there were several cottages and plenty of windows). Within one week, and after several washed windows, Marty decided the swearing wasn't worth it.

In both of these examples, the essential conditions for positive punishment were present: (1) *presentation* of some aversive event (delayed auditory feedback and window-washing assignment) following and contingent upon the occurrence of an undesired behavior; (2) *decrease* in the occurrence of the behavior (stuttering and swearing). Again, if the behaviors had not decreased, these would not have been examples of positive punishment from a behavior modification point of view.

NEGATIVE PUNISHMENT

If positive punishment results in a decrease in the rate of behavior following the *presentation* of a stimulus, then, to follow the four-fold table, the last remaining characteristic of contingent consequences would be *removal* or *withdrawal* of a stimulus following a behavior which weakens or *decreases* the rate of occurrence of that behavior. That is *negative punishment* (Mikulas, 1972). The social worker using negative punishment would identify undesired behaviors to be decreased, and then, contingent on the occurrence of those behaviors, remove some stimulus in an effort to decrease the probability of the future occurrence of that behavior. Why should the behavior decrease just because some environmental event is removed? Because, generally, the stimulus that is removed is prized or wanted by the individual. He is left with the choice of either decreasing some undesirable behavior or having some desired stimulus taken away. (Contrast this with *negative* reinforcement where the event removed is generally *aversive* and results in an *increase* in behavior.)

The notation for negative punishment can be written as follows:

$$R \longrightarrow \not S$$

EXAMPLE 3.7: Fred just couldn't stop smoking. He was not a particularly heavy smoker, a little less than a pack a day, but he really enjoyed his habit although he realized it was dysfunctional for him. Fred's girlfriend Grace, a nonsmoker, found the habit particularly annoying. So with Fred's cooperation, they worked out a plan. It was determined that Fred was a "social smoker," i.e., he only smoked in the presence of others, and rarely smoked alone, so, rather than requiring Fred to give up his smoking completely, it was agreed that he would smoke only when he was by himself and only in certain places (not in his own apartment or at work). If he did smoke in the presence of others, he would not be able to see Grace for one day (they usually saw each other about 5 evenings a week). In other words, for each violation of the contract, Fred would lose one date with his girlfriend. Fred lost three dates the first week, one the second and none the third. His smoking dropped from an average of 15 cigarettes per day to 2.5 per day.

EXAMPLE 3.8: Laurie loved to watch T.V. But Laurie also would talk back and yell at her mother whenever she was asked to help around the house. Laurie would much prefer to sit and watch the tube. The plan: every time Laurie talked back—defined, essentially, as refusing in a very loud voice to help in response to her mother's request—she would lose one hour of T.V. privileges. Laurie didn't watch T.V. at all the first week of the plan. She just sat around the house and moped. But she soon decided that life was a lot better with a little helping around the house, less fighting, and more T.V. Within three weeks, Laurie not only had her full T.V. privileges reinstated, but she and her mother also reported a happy new mother–daughter relationship.

When negative punishment is used, the basic features are: (1) *withdrawal* or removal of some usually prized event (dates, T.V.) contingent upon and following the occurrence of some undesired behavior; (2) a *decrease* in the occurrence of the behavior (smoking and talking back). Both of these examples illustrate these two dimensions. Negative punishment, when used as a technique of behavior modification, is also called *response cost* (Weiner, 1962) because the performance of some undesired behavior results in a "cost" to the individual (a desired event is removed). Thus, in later chapters, the terms "response cost" should be understood as synonymous with negative punishment while punishment as such will be used to indicate positive punishment only.

The four-fold table is now complete.

Behavior can be *increased* or strengthened by *positive reinforcement* (contingent *presentation* of a consequence), or *negative reinforcement* (contingent *removal* of a consequence). Behavior can be *decreased* or weakened by *positive punishment* (contingent *presentation* of a consequence) or *negative punishment* (contingent *removal* of a consequence).

There is one more potential consequence that can change the rate of occurrence of behavior. As can be seen from Table 3.3, all of the consequences described so far have been applied or withdrawn contingently, i.e., contingent upon a response. The fifth possible consequence

T A B L E 3.3. Contingent Consequences Resulting in an Increase or Decrease in Behavior

	CONTINGENT CONSEQUENCES	
	PRESENT	REMOVE
INCREASE	1 POSITIVE REINFORCEMENT	2 NEGATIVE REINFORCEMENT
DECREASE	3 POSITIVE PUNISHMENT	4 NEGATIVE PUNISHMENT (RESPONSE COST)

EFFECT ON BEHAVIOR

is called extinction (or, technically, and to distinguish it from respondent extinction, operant extinction). *Extinction* involves the termination of a contingent relationship between the occurrence of a behavior and a consequence. Extinction is a procedure for decreasing the rate of occurrence of a behavior, and is based upon the clinical and experimental finding that when a behavior is being maintained by positive reinforcement, complete removal of that reinforcement results in a decrease and eventual extinction of the behavior. Extinction essentially means that the social worker terminates the relationship between a behavior and the specific reinforcing stimulus that is maintaining the behavior. Thus, there no longer is a contingency—the positive reinforcement that is maintaining the behavior is completely withdrawn.

Note the difference between extinction and negative punishment. In negative punishment, some consequence is removed every time a behavior occurs, contingent upon the occurrence of that behavior. Further, the event that is removed (e.g., the T.V. privileges) is *not* the event that is maintaining the behavior (e.g., talking back). Extinction, on the other hand, refers to a complete termination of the relationship between the behavior and the specific consequences that are actually maintaining that behavior. Thus, although it strains the limits of the table somewhat, extinction might be added to our table in the following manner:

EXAMPLE 3.9: The Golds were having trouble getting their three year old son Josh to sleep at night. They'd put him to bed, he'd get out of bed asking for a glass of water, he'd get his water and then be placed in bed

T A B L E 3.4. Consequences Affecting the Rate of Occurrence of Behavior

		CONTINGENT CONSEQUENCES		NON-CONTINGENT CONSEQUENCES
		PRESENT	REMOVE	TERMINATE CONTINGENCY
EFFECT ON BEHAVIOR	INCREASE	1 POSITIVE REINFORCEMENT	2 NEGATIVE REINFORCEMENT	——
	DECREASE	3 POSITIVE PUNISHMENT	4 NEGATIVE PUNISHMENT (RESPONSE COST)	5 EXTINCTION

and this scene would be repeated time and time again. When Josh first began climbing out of bed, his parents thought it was cute. But after nightly recurrences, the situation became almost desperate with the Golds screaming and yelling at Josh to stay in bed and Josh becoming terribly upset, crying and refusing to go. The social worker observed that all of this attention was positively reinforcing to Josh, i.e., it was maintaining the behavior of not going to sleep. The plan was to break the bond between the attention maintaining the behavior, and the getting-out-of-bed behavior. The parents were simply to place Josh in bed at night, tell him he would not be allowed to come out, kiss him goodnight and close the door. If he came out of his room, they were to place him back in bed immediately and close the door—no drinks and no fussing and no yelling. The first night of the plan came as a complete surprise to Josh. He jumped out of bed as usual and was gently but firmly returned. This happened several times to the accompaniment of loud protests by Josh. When he finally did stay in the room, he screamed and cried for almost an hour. The parents had been prepared by their social worker for this eventuality and had been requested to ignore it, which they did, although at several points they could barely restrain themselves from getting up to see if Josh was all right. The second night was a repeat of the first, as was the third night, except for one difference—the third night Josh only cried for one half-hour. The fourth night, Josh stayed in bed and cried for a little less than 15 minutes. The fifth night, Josh stayed in bed whimpering a little, and by the sixth night, Josh fell asleep 10 minutes after being placed in bed. From that point on, Josh willingly went to bed on time, and without a fight.

EXAMPLE 3.10: Boris threw tantrums. That was about the only thing that his mother could think about when she described her son. Whenever he didn't get his way, Boris would throw himself on the floor, twisting and kicking and screaming at the top of his lungs. Of course, his mother reported, she always had to run over and pick him up and hold him so that "he wouldn't hurt himself." The social worker instructed her to ignore the tantrums completely, no matter how tempting it was to comfort little Boris when he was obviously feeling "so upset." For two weeks the mother completely ignored all tantrum behavior. At first, the tantrums seemed to get worse. But by the time the two weeks were up, the tantrum behavior had been completely extinguished.

Both examples illustrate the use of extinction: (1) an environmental consequence (parental attention) maintaining undesired behavior was identified; (2) the *contingency* between the consequence and the behavior (crying and getting out of bed; tantrum) was *terminated;* (3) subsequently the behavior *decreased.* In fact, in both cases, the undesired behavior disappeared completely.

The most frequent use of extinction is on behaviors that are maintained by attention. This is, in part, because it is a fairly simple matter to change the situation by ignoring the behavior instead of attending to it. And, of course, people are among the most powerful reinforcing stimuli for other people. Thus, in these cases, the attention applied to the undesired behaviors was acting as positive reinforcement. Remember, positive reinforcement was noted as follows:

$$R \longrightarrow S^+$$

Extinction simply means the termination of this process, i.e., termination of the contingency between the behavior (R) and the reinforcing stimulus (S+). Hence, the extinction process is written as:

$$R \longrightarrow\!\!\!\!\!/\ \ S^+$$

The paradigm is almost the same, except for the line drawn through the arrow.

These, essentially, are the five basic operations involving the alteration of consequences (contingency management) through operant behavior modification. Other chapters in this book will elaborate the ways in which these principles have been adapted for use with numerous problems into the techniques of behavior modification. But these principles form the core of operant behavior modification for both assessment and intervention. If a client and problem are assessed as having inadequate or missing social and personal skills (e.g., reduced or minimal social skills such as speaking)—a *behavioral deficit*—the appropriate goal would be to increase the quantity and quality of the skills that are lacking. Hence, for increasing or strengthening behavior, the social worker using behavior modification would think first of using positive or negative reinforcement. If the assessment leads to a conclusion that the client engages in maladaptive behaviors that are too frequent or too intense or too long-lasting (e.g., compulsive hand-washing; fighting in class)—a *behavioral excess*—the social worker would consider some form of positive or negative punishment or extinction for reducing the frequency of occurrence (weakening) of those behaviors.

Actually, in behavior modification and in everyday life in general, there is often considerable overlap in the operation of these principles. A nice and neat scheme such as the one presented here is not always possible. In fact, an overwhelming majority of behavior modification programs in practice use more than one of the several principles discussed above, often several in coordinated fashion.

Remember Mrs. Rosemont who was having trouble potty-training Jenny? One part of the plan was not to make a big fuss out of mistakes and to ignore them, because paying attention to the mistakes might have been reinforcing to Jenny and might actually have increased the amount of mistakes. This was an example of an attempt to apply extinction, i.e., ignore the mistakes in an effort to decrease their frequency. At the same time, Mrs. Rosemont was attempting to positively reinforce the times when Jenny actually eliminated on the potty. This use of positive reinforcement and extinction is actually one of the most important techniques of behavior modification. It is called *differential* or *selective reinforcement* (and sometimes called *differentiation;* Lundin, 1969). A social worker using this procedure specifies in advance the behaviors to be increased and the behaviors to be decreased. Then, the behaviors to be increased are reinforced while the behaviors to be decreased are ignored, i.e., simply not reinforced. In other words, a decision is made in advance about which behaviors are to be strengthened, and then these are reinforced while other behaviors are not reinforced. When a specific behavior has been developed or refined through use of differential reinforcement, it can be said that the behavior has become differentiated; i.e., *response differentiation* has occurred. This is a key procedure (or more accurately, combination of procedures) of behavior modification, and its utilization will be illustrated in a number of places throughout the book.

Remember also Bill the stutterer. While this example was intended as an illustration of the use of positive punishment (delayed auditory feedback was *presented* as a contingent consequence to *decrease* stuttering behavior), there was also another side of the coin. By speaking without stuttering, i.e., by increasing his fluent speech, Bill was able to *avoid* the aversive auditory feedback. In other words, negative reinforcement was also in operation (with an *increase* in fluent speech the aversive feedback was *withdrawn* or escaped from). Frequently, both positive punishment and negative reinforcement may be operating in the same approach. The selection of which to emphasize is, of course, determined by whether the goal is to increase (negative reinforcement) or decrease (positive punishment) behavior.

In some of the illustrations, it was noted parenthetically that, if the behavior had not increased or decreased as planned, i.e., the effect of the consequence was not noticeable, none of the principles described in this chapter would have been in operation (their effect would have been neutral). This may be a difficult idea to grasp. When you reward someone following the performance of behavior, isn't that positive reinforcement? When you punish or apply aversive events to someone after performance of a behavior isn't that punishment? When you stop reinforcing behavior that was previously reinforced, isn't that extinction? The answer is yes . . . and no.

The answer is yes *if,* and this is a big if, there is an effect on behavior. If a behavior is rewarded and it tends to increase, then positive reinforcement has occurred. If a behavior is punished and it weakens, then positive punishment is in effect. If a contingency between behavior and reinforcement of that behavior is terminated and the behavior decreases, then extinction has occurred. But if some alteration of consequences takes place, and there is no effect on behavior, then none of the above operations technically can be said to have taken place. They may have been attempted, but they were not successful. In other words, changes brought about through behavior modification are empirically defined; they do not occur in the abstract.

This is a kind of safety precaution in analyzing behavioral procedures. It means, for example, that positive reinforcement has not taken place unless a stimulus is *presented* following the occurrence of a behavior *and* the behavior is strengthened. In this way an observable definition of terms—where an operation cannot be said to have occurred unless it has some real effect on behavior—is clearest, safest, most logical, and most easily communicated to others.

The Pros and Cons of Certain Consequences

All of the consequences discussed here may have been created equally, but some, in practice, may be a little more equal than others. This chapter has already hinted at the idea that there are advantages and disadvantages to the use of some of the consequences. In essence, the rule might be stated as follows: *when possible, use positive reinforcement.* Positive reinforcement is not a panacea for all of the problems with which a social worker using behavior modification is faced. But positive reinforcement, quite simply, is subject to fewer liabilities than some of the other procedures just described. Clearly, each procedure has its place, depending on the assessment and the desired goal. But social workers should also be aware of potential drawbacks.

PROBLEMS WITH USE OF EXTINCTION

When an undesired behavior is being maintained by positive reinforcement, a very efficient procedure for weakening that undesired behavior is to break the contingency between the behavior and the reinforcement by applying extinction. But there may be some problems with this procedure. The behavior of all people can be analyzed in terms of *hierarchies of behavior;* a certain situation may cue one of a number of potential behaviors in the repertoire of a given person. The behavior that actually is emitted is simply the most probable, the second behavior would be the next most probable, and so on. The position of each behavior in the hierarchy is a function of how many times that behavior has been reinforced (or, how well it has been learned). If the topmost or most probable behavior is extinguished, the next most probable behavior may occur and have to be extinguished too, if it is undesirable. Thus, with the use of extinction, the social worker *may* (sometimes, not always) have to spend a great deal of time moving down the hierarchy of behaviors until a prosocial or desirable behavior is reached (Mikulas, 1972). For this reason, extinction is most efficiently used when the hierarchy of behavior is presumably small, such as with the behavior of children. In such situations, the individual simply has not had the time to develop a large hierarchy of behaviors in his repertoire.

There are other problems connected with the use of extinction (Stuart, 1970; Kanfer & Phillips, 1970). Once the undesired behavior is extinguished, the social worker has essentially no control over other behaviors that might replace it (either from the hierarchy or newly learned). Furthermore, extinction may be difficult to apply in certain social situations. For example, a teacher might try to ignore a child's disruptive behaviors in a classroom while the rest of the children reinforce that child with their attention. Extinction requires the elimination of *all* reinforcement for an undesired behavior. Sometimes, all the sources are not known or are not very obvious and cannot be identified; thus, the behavior persists despite ostensible efforts to apply extinction. Extinction is also difficult to apply in potentially dangerous situations (even if a behavior—say, self-inflicted injury—is maintained by positive reinforcement, it is difficult to ignore the individual while he is injuring or harming himself). Also, there often is an emotional response of distress and anguish in the client accompanying the extinction procedure. It is easy to see why an individual, accustomed to receiving positive reinforcement for engaging in certain behaviors, would become distressed when this reinforcement is withdrawn. Moreover, and related to this distress, the behavior targeted for a decrease usually tends to temporarily *increase* when extinction is applied. Thus, the mother instructed to ignore tantrum behavior has to be warned that the tantrums will probably increase before they diminish. This, in fact, is a crucial point for the social worker using behavior modification. Not only the worker, but whomever he may be working with in the natural environment (e.g., a parent or a teacher), must be prepared for this eventuality.

PROBLEMS WITH THE USE OF PUNISHMENT

Both positive and negative punishment are used to decrease undesired behavior. There are, however, certain problems associated with their use (Mikulas, 1972), some of which have already been discussed in the section on negative reinforcement in this chapter. The use of punishment tends to elicit a negative emotional response (fear or anxiety) in the person being punished, which may be respondently conditioned to the situation or punishing agent. In fact, the client may learn just to avoid the situation or person who punished him. For example, if a teacher or parent uses punishment as a way of controlling behavior, the fear elicited by the punishment may become associated with the person doing the punishment, who, in time, can come to elicit the fear reaction even if he or she is no longer using punishment. Of course, for the parent, spouse, or professional attempting to help someone else, this is hardly a desirable situation. The use of punishment might also produce negative modeling in that the individual being punished learns this as the "appropriate" way to behave (the parent who frequently spanks his child may be teaching his child, through modeling, that hitting others is the best way to resolve problems). A person being punished might show less adaptability in the future to changing situations and contingencies. Operating mainly out of fear, he will have learned only what *not* to do and how to avoid unpleasant situations, and not *what* to do and how to deal with such situations.

It is not always clear whether the use of punishment actually extinguishes behavior or simply temporarily suppresses it. One individual may learn to control (reduce) his behavior in the presence of a punishing agent, but not elsewhere. An individual may learn to tolerate the initial level of punishment; if the level of punishment is not increased, the problem behavior may return. (Of course, this is an empirical question, answerable by the collection of data. If undesired behavior never appears again, the results can most likely be judged as satisfactory.) In fact, attempted punishment may even turn out to be positively reinforcing, e.g., as when a spanking, aversive to an outside observer, really functions as attention and positive reinforcement to a child and thereby increases his undesired behavior. (See Galimore *et al.*, 1969, for an example of the positive reinforcing effect of "negative attention.") Again, the collection of data about the effects of intervention should give a clear picture of whether a behavior increases or decreases. While punishment may effectively reduce a behavior, there is no built-in guarantee that a desired behavior will take its place. However, since it is likely that *some* behavior may replace the diminished, undesired behavior, the use of punishment alone provides for no control over what that behavior will be.

The use of punishment may also interrupt an otherwise productive learning situation so that the punished individual may be unwilling to continue in that situation. And, to be effective, punishment should be *consistent,* i.e., delivered every time the undesired behavior is displayed. If it is not, and some of the behaviors to be decreased are positively reinforced, those behaviors may become even more difficult to diminish. Indeed, if punishment is used and then withdrawn altogether, this could lead to an increase in the previously punished behavior. And finally, and on a much broader level, the use of punishment introduces several ethical questions. Is it ethical to use punishment? Is its use consistent with the values of the profession and the people involved? Do the advantages outweigh the disadvantages in a given situation? Are provisions made to see that there is no real danger to the individual involved? As with any intervention procedure adapted from any theoretical orientation, but perhaps even more so with the use of punishment, these issues must be of primary concern.

This is not to say that punishment, especially positive punishment, is *never* the technique of choice. It may very well be, in such situations as the following (Krumboltz & Krumboltz, 1972; Becker, 1971) : (1) When a problem behavior occurs so frequently that there is no desirable behavior available for reinforcement; (2) when the nature or intensity of the problem behaviors leads to serious questions about the safety of the individuals involved; (3) when the use of reinforcement is not effective because other, more powerful, reinforcers are maintaining the problem behavior; (4) when a mild punishment can be used to halt a well-entrenched routine and give an individual the opportunity to try an alternative behavior that can be reinforced.

ADVANTAGES OF POSITIVE REINFORCEMENT

The focus of this book, and behavior modification in general, is primarily on the use of positive reinforcement—teaching human beings to operate on, and actively influence, their environment in order to receive those consequences that they personally have decided are desirable and rewarding. Not only is this consistent with a social work philosophical frame of reference, but the fact that the use of positive reinforcement is not hampered by the drawbacks associated with the use of the other procedures makes this technically justified as well. Furthermore, by the same processes of respondent conditioning described earlier in which an individual becomes associated with the use of punishment and comes to evoke fear, so can a helping person become associated with the positive feelings evoked by the receipt of desired stimuli in positive reinforcement. Thus, the helping person can come to be a more attractive and desirable person himself, evoking a positive response from his clients, and thus become all the more facilitative himself (see also Chapter 8 for a discusison of the personal qualities of the social worker).

Thus, a basic strategy of behavior modification is to use positive reinforcement in three ways:

1. singly, as a way to build or strengthen (*increase*) prosocial or desired behavior;
2. in combination with extinction or punishment to develop or strengthen prosocial behaviors, thereby insuring that the new behaviors that replace the extinguished behaviors will be both predictable and desirable, as with differential reinforcement;
3. to actually *decrease* undesired behaviors by increasing prosocial behaviors which are incompatible with, or take the place of, undesired behaviors (e.g., positively reinforce periods of time when Harry *does not fight* during recess, as when he plays in a non-disruptive way with his peers, rather than punishing Harry when he does fight). All of these possibilities will be discussed in detail in subsequent chapters.

Summary

This chapter has reviewed the basic concepts of operant behavior modification. Essentially, these concepts involve the several operations that can take place following a behavior to increase or decrease the occurrence of that behavior. Four of these operations are contingent on the occurrence of that behavior. Positive reinforcement increases a behavior by applying a stimulus and negative reinforcement increases a behavior by removing a stimulus following the occurrence of that behavior. Positive punishment decreases a behavior by applying a stimulus while negative punishment (response cost) decreases a behavior by removing a stimulus following the occurrence of that behavior. The fifth operation, extinction, refers to a breaking of the relationship between some behavior and the reinforcing stimulus that is maintaining that behavior so that the behavior will decrease. All of these consequating operations have a place in the change agent's armamentarium. However, whenever possible, for several reasons discussed in the chapter, positive reinforcement should be used.

Now, how can a social worker be reasonably sure that what he does present or remove following the occurrence of a behavior will have the desired results? In fact, what are these stimuli—situations, events, materials, words, "things"—that can be used to have such effects on behavior? Together, these stimuli are called *reinforcers,* and they are the subject of the next chapter.

CHAPTER 4.   Reinforcers and Their Uses

In all of the situations discussed in the previous chapter, something had to be supplied or withdrawn in order to result in an increase or decrease in the rate of behavior. That "something" goes under the generic name *reinforcer,* so-called because its presentation or removal results in an increase or decrease in the rate, or frequency of occurrence, of a behavior. There are two types of reinforcers (remember, reinforcer is a "class name" for any number of stimuli): *positive* and *negative.* Positive and negative *reinforcers* are not synonymous with positive and negative *reinforcement.* They are, however, *used* in positive and negative reinforcement as the consequences that when supplied or withdrawn, lead to an increase in behavior. In fact, positive and negative reinforcers are also used as the consequences in punishment (both positive and negative) and in extinction to decrease behavior. Here is how it all works.

Positive Reinforcers

Positive reinforcers are associated with three of the five basic operations of behavior modification: (1) positive reinforcement; (2) negative punishment; (3) extinction.

1. *Positive Reinforcement.* In positive reinforcement, the provision of a positive reinforcer following the occurrence of a behavior will tend to strengthen or increase that behavior. If the behavior does not increase, one may say that the stimulus is not a positive reinforcer (or, at least, that positive reinforcement has not occurred).

> *EXAMPLE 4.1:* Following every smile, Linda was given a piece of candy. Soon, Linda began to smile far more frequently.

> *EXAMPLE 4.2:* Following every smile, Herald was given a piece of candy. After three weeks, there was no observable change in the number of times per day that Herald smiled.

EXAMPLE 4.3: When Kathy threw a tantrum, her mother yelled at her and slapped her. Kathy threw more and more tantrums.

In Example 4.1, positive reinforcement occurred. The candy was administered following each smile and the smiling increased. The candy was a positive reinforcer. In Example 4.2, positive reinforcement did not occur. Assuming all other things were equal (i.e., the program was administered correctly), since the candy did not lead to an increase in behavior, it was, by definition, *not* a positive reinforcer. In Example 4.3, screaming and slapping were "supplied" following the tantrum behavior (although certainly without the intention of increasing it). In this example, screaming and slapping (or possibly the attention) increased the rate of the tantrum behavior. Hence, these stimuli, at least in this example, were positive reinforcers. What do all three examples illustrate about reinforcers in general and their use in behavior modification?

In the first place, the decision about whether a stimulus is a positive reinforcer is based upon its *effects* on a behavior. This means that the social worker should have some idea in advance about the probable effects of the reinforcers he selects. (The basis for selection will be discussed in Chapter 11.) In the second place, some stimuli may be positive reinforcers for some people, and not for others, or may be reinforcing at one time and not at another. In the third place, positive reinforcers may not always be what they appear to be to the outside observer. The screaming at and slapping of Kathy would hardly appear to be positive reinforcers to an outsider. But they *did* increase Kathy's tantrum behavior. Hence, the rule that the only way to tell whether a stimulus is a reinforcer is by determining its effect on behavior.

All of this adds up to one of the most basic principles of behavior modification: *individualization* for the client of the procedures and programs that are selected. This applies throughout the implementation of all the principles of behavior modification: work with every individual must be person-, problem-, and situation-specific. Remember that what has worked with some people may not work with others.

Another point is illustrated by Example 4.2. Reinforcers are not synonymous with "rewards." This may be a fine distinction, but it *is* an important one, since many people tend to think of behavior modification as the simple application of "rewards and punishments." A reinforcer has already been defined as a consequence that has an effect on behavior. A reward may not. A reward may produce a pleasant subjective reaction in an individual; a reward may appear to an outside observer (and perhaps rightly so) capable of increasing behavior. But, as can be seen from Herald's reaction in Example 4.2, the reward of candy (which, incidentally, Herald enjoyed very much) was not a reinforcer because it did not affect the rate of Herald's behavior. Perhaps the candy was not a powerful enough reward to overcome Herald's reluctance to smile. Perhaps, after a while, Herald had just had enough. For whatever reason, this ostensible reward was not a reinforcer.

2. *Negative Punishment* (response cost). Positive reinforcers are also used in the procedure of response cost: the cost for the response is generally something that has been a positive reinforcer. That is, some reward or privilege (a positive reinforcer) is taken away from the individual contingent upon the performance of an undesired behavior. Remember, in response cost, the withdrawal of a consequence results in a *decrease* in behavior.

> *EXAMPLE 4.4:* Every time Robert used a curse word, he lost one hour of socialization privileges in the recreation room out on the ward. Soon, Robert stopped swearing completely.

> *EXAMPLE 4.5:* Every time Matthew used a curse word, he lost one hour of socialization privileges in the recreation room out on the ward. After several days and practically no ward privileges, Matthew's swearing had not decreased at all.

For Robert the withdrawal of privileges had a clear effect on behavior; it decreased dramatically. For Matthew, the procedure had little or no effect. Hence, before using response cost, it must, again, be clear to the worker that the positive reinforcer he intends to remove is indeed a positive reinforcer, and that its removal will have the effect of decreasing behavior. When selecting a reinforcer to withdraw, it is best not to select one that the client has already earned as positive reinforcement (e.g., if a person has earned two hours of T.V., but misbehaves, it would be desirable to withdraw another privilege rather than the two hours of T.V. watching he has already earned).

3. *Extinction.* In extinction, the bond or contingency between the behavior and the specific positive reinforcer that is maintaining it is broken so that no positive reinforcement whatsoever is provided for that behavior (as distinct from negative punishment wherein reinforcers not actually maintaining the behavior are withdrawn on a regular, contingent basis). Hence, the behavior decreases.

> *EXAMPLE 4.6:* Lois would continually jump up out of her seat in class, drawing the teacher's attention and an immediate rebuff. The social worker instructed the teacher to ignore this behavior. Soon Lois was sitting in her seat for longer and longer periods of time.

> *EXAMPLE 4.7:* Judy would continually jump up out of her seat in class, drawing the teacher's attention and an immediate rebuff. The social worker instructed the teacher to ignore this behavior. The teacher consistently

ignored Judy when she jumped up without permission, but there was no decrease in the number of times Judy jumped out of her seat.

For Lois, the teacher's attention was the positive reinforcer that apparently was maintaining the behavior. Withdrawing it decreased the rate of Lois' behavior. Extinction had occurred. For Judy, the teacher's attention apparently was *not* the positive reinforcer that was the primary force maintaining that behavior (perhaps the attention of her peers was maintaining that behavior). When attention was withdrawn, there was still no decrease in behavior.

Negative Reinforcers

Negative reinforcers are sometimes referred to as *aversive stimuli*. This is because there generally is an unpleasant aura associated with negative reinforcers. The person to whom they are applied, in other words, tends to respond with unpleasant subjective reactions; while, because of the typically unpleasant characteristics of aversive stimuli, the individual from whom they are withdrawn tends to respond with pleasant subjective reactions. Negative reinforcers are central to the use of the remaining two of the five basic operant procedures: (4) negative reinforcement; (5) positive punishment.

4. *Negative Reinforcement.* To increase behavior through negative reinforcement, an aversive stimulus (or *negative reinforcer*) is *removed* or *terminated*. Thus, an individual *escapes* from or *avoids* the negative reinforcer.

> *EXAMPLE 4.8:* Jane was warned by her teacher that if she did not finish her assignment, she would have to stay in the classroom during recess. Jane finished 10 minutes before the recess bell rang.

> *EXAMPLE 4.9:* Lucy was warned by her teacher that if she did not finish her assignment, she would have to stay in the classroom during recess. When recess time rolled around, Lucy was sitting idly at her desk playing with her pencil. Her assignment lay untouched.

Jane worked diligently to finish her assignment so that the teacher would not apply the negative reinforcer of having her stay in the classroom during recess. To Jane, this was indeed a negative reinforcer, since she increased her work behavior in order to *avoid* or escape from the aversive stimulus of staying in the classroom during recess. Lucy, on the other hand, didn't care that much about missing recess. To her, this was not a negative reinforcer (or an insufficiently strong negative reinforcer), or, at least, negative reinforcement was not in operation, since she did not *increase* her work behavior in an attempt to avoid or have the aversive stimulus withdrawn by the teacher.

5. *Positive Punishment.* When a stimulus following, and contingent upon, a behavior is *applied* and there is a *decrease* in the probability that the behavior will occur, that stimulus is a negative reinforcer, and the operation is called positive punishment.

> *EXAMPLE 4.9:* The social worker had been working very hard to help Marge, a four-year-old "autistic" child, learn how to talk. Every once in a while, Marge's attention would begin to drift and her eyes would wander about the room. In desperation, the social worker yelled, "No!" Marge stopped gazing around the room and paid attention.

> *EXAMPLE 4.10:* The social worker had been working very hard to help Millie, a four-year-old "autistic" child, learn how to talk. Every once in a while, Millie's attention would begin to drift and her eyes would wander about the room. In desperation, the social worker yelled, "No!" He did this several times, but to no avail. Millie's attention still wandered.

> *EXAMPLE 4.11:* Mrs. Trixon was so happy about her new-found "enhanced communication" with her husband. Her social worker had been right in what he had suggested; try to reinforce Mr. Trixon when he spoke in order to get him to increase his talking with her. They had been having a nice, flowing conversation at dinner one night and Mrs. Trixon wanted to keep it that way. She cut a second piece of apple pie—her husband's favorite—and put it on his plate just as he finished a sentence. Instead of continuing to talk, he said, "No, thank you," and left the table.

If a consequence is applied following the performance of the behavior and the behavior tends to *decrease,* that consequence is a *negative reinforcer* (no matter what the specific nature of the consequence is), and the entire operation is positive punishment. (Punishment should not be used to increase behavior. If a parent wants his daughter to study more, he should not promote it by punishing her and forcing her to study extra hours; instead, he should reinforce positively her study behavior.) For Marge, in the above example, the loud yell was obviously a negative reinforcer. Its application led to an immediate decrease in "gazing-around" behavior. For Millie it was a different story. The yelling may very well have been unpleasant, but, by definition, it was not a negative reinforcer because its application did not result (perhaps it was not strong or aversive enough) in a decrease or weakening of "gazing-around" behavior. Finally, Mrs. Trixon, who was overjoyed with the success of her reinforcement program, apparently overdid it. Her husband had already had a piece of pie and was full. So when Mrs. Trixon attempted to use the pie as a positive reinforcer to increase talking, she failed. The pie, at least at that moment, acted as a negative reinforcer because it led to a decrease in her husband's talking behavior.

The basic characteristics of reinforcers can be summarized as follows:

Positive Reinforcers are those stimuli that:

1. when *presented* contingent upon and following a behavior *strengthen* that behavior (positive reinforcement);
2. when *withdrawn* contingent upon and following a behavior *weaken* that behavior (negative punishment or response cost);
3. when *removed completely* from a contingent relationship with a behavior *weaken* that behavior (extinction).

Negative Reinforcers are those stimuli that:

1. when *withdrawn* contingent upon and following a behavior *strengthen* that behavior (negative reinforcement);
2. when *presented* contingent upon and following a behavior *weaken* that behavior (positive punishment).

To be consistent with the previous chapter, the uses of positive and negative reinforcers can be summarized in a similar table. (The consequating operations involved with each type of reinforcer are included within parentheses):

T A B L E 4.1.   Positive and Negative Reinforcers and their Effect on Behavior

	CONTINGENT USE OF REINFORCERS		NON-CONTINGENT USE OF REINFORCERS
	PRESENT	REMOVE	TERMINATE CONTINGENCY
INCREASE	1 POSITIVE REINFORCERS (Positive Reinforcement)	2 NEGATIVE REINFORCERS (Negative Reinforcement)	——
DECREASE	3 NEGATIVE REINFORCERS (Positive Punishment)	4 POSITIVE REINFORCERS (Negative Punishment)	5 POSITIVE REINFORCERS (Extinction)

EFFECT ON BEHAVIOR

Extrinsic and Intrinsic Reinforcers

Almost any stimulus could be used, in a given time and place, as a reinforcer. The major limitation is the situation itself—the client and what he or she finds reinforcing, the problem, and the available resources. For both conceptual and practical purposes, though, there are ways to classify reinforcers, so that selection from among them may be made more judiciously.

At the broadest level, all reinforcers may be classified as either *extrinsic* or *intrinsic*. *Extrinsic reinforcers* originate externally to the individual, i.e., from his environment. Almost anything in an individual's surroundings might be an extrinsic reinforcer. For example, candy or a demonstration of affection might be extrinsic *positive* reinforcers, while nagging or electric shock might be extrinsic *negative* reinforcers. Remember, whether a stimulus actually *is* a reinforcer is determined only by its effect on behavior. Therefore, whatever examples are discussed here are used only as examples of *potential* reinforcers, ones that have been used frequently in research and practice to attain the desired effects. But with any given individual, these examples may not be reinforcers at all. They have merely, in extensive research, been found to be somewhat more likely than other events to be successful as reinforcers.

Intrinsic reinforcers are *internal* reinforcers, unobservable to anyone but the individual experiencing them. Intrinsic reinforcers are generally pleasant feelings associated with certain behaviors, e.g., a feeling of accomplishment or pride in achieving some desired goal. Intrinsic reinforcers are assumed to be learned by the pairing process discussed in the chapter on respondent conditioning. Briefly, once some behavior has been achieved (e.g., completing homework assignments), the behavior may bring some reward that functions as an extrinsic reinforcer (e.g., good grades). Thus, the *intrinsic reinforcer* (or positive feelings of accomplishment) develops out of association with the extrinsic reinforcer (the grades) that such desirable behavior had produced. Hence, intrinsic reinforcement (positive feelings of accomplishment), which, by definition, leads to a strengthening of behavior, may come to take the place of extrinsic reinforcement once such reinforcement is found to be no longer necessary, or is discontinued, or both. Replacing extrinsic with intrinsic reinforcers would, of course, be a highly desirable outcome of a behavior modification program. However, because intrinsic reinforcement is far less accessible to the change agent than extrinsic reinforcement, most professionals using behavior modification rely on the use of extrinsic (external) reinforcers to help their clients alter maladaptive behaviors.

SUBDIVISIONS OF EXTRINSIC REINFORCERS

Extrinsic reinforcers may be subdivided into two categories: *primary* and *secondary* reinforcers. *Primary reinforcers* are unlearned (innate or unconditioned) reinforcers that deal with (or satisfy) physiological necessities. As with all other forms of reinforcers, primary reinforcers can be positive (e.g., food, liquid, candy), or negative (e.g., a sharp blow). The essence of primary reinforcers is that people tend to respond to this class of reinforcers automatically, without any previous learning experience.

Secondary reinforcers are learned. Presumably, they have become reinforcing because, at some point in an individual's history, they have been paired with either primary reinforcers or other stimuli that have acquired reinforcing value. Secondary reinforcers could be almost anything, and it is easy to see how they might acquire reinforcing value for an individual. Clearly, people are not born with much, if any, ability to discriminate the meaning of others' smiles and frowns. But if the smile is paired consistently, say, for an infant, with mother's milk and the satisfaction accompanying the feeling of drinking the milk, and the frown paired with a slap or another painful stimulus, the smile could begin to take on the properties of a secondary positive reinforcer and the frown those of a secondary negative reinforcer. Either, on its own, may be sufficient, when applied, to alter the frequency of occurrence of behavior.

Of course, what will be a reinforcer for any given individual depends on his or her own learning history—few stimuli can be assumed in advance to be positive or negative reinforcers for a particular individual. On the other hand, some reinforcers, by virtue of the fact that they have been paired with a variety of other reinforcers, become reinforcing for many responses beyond those which were involved during their original establishment. These are called *generalized reinforcers,* and while they are not applicable to all people at all times, they are an important factor for consideration in behavioral programs because they can be used in so many situations and because they are powerful reinforcers. Some examples of generalized reinforcers are praise, money, and attention.

There are several classes of secondary reinforcers available for use by social workers (Bijou and Sturges, 1959). In addition to "consumables"— food, drink, candy, etc.—which would be considered primary reinforcers since they deal with physiological conditions, there are five other major categories of reinforcers (all of which are secondary or learned): (1) *material;* (2) *social;* (3) *activity;* (4) *token;* (5) *"Premack."*

1. *Material reinforcers* include any specific item—e.g., toys, trinkets, jewelry—which has come to have reinforcing value for an individual, and which, if applied consistently and contingent upon the occurrence of some behavior, will tend to strengthen that behavior. Witness the reinforcing value of stamps for the individual—whether child or adult—who is a stamp collector. As another example, the use of toys as reinforcers for small children has a long history of effective usage rooted in the "common sense" art of child-rearing.

2. *Social reinforcers*—essentially, the behavior of other people— probably constitute the single most important category of reinforcers. There are several basic reasons for this. In the first place, people may be the most powerful reinforcers of all for other people. We all, to some extent, care very much about, and often act on the basis of, the reactions of others. An approving smile, a kind word or phrase, a kiss, praise, a frown—all, in the short *and* long run, have tremendous potential for affecting the behavior of others. In fact, a large part of the traditional knowledge base of the helping professions is built on the assumption that the interaction of people with other people ("the helping relationship") can have significant effects on behavior. Secondly, there is ample experimental and clinical evidence that social reinforcers can be successfully used to change maladaptive human behavior. Social reinforcement can be *effective* reinforcement. In fact, social reinforcers are perhaps the most widely used in behavioral programs of all those reinforcers available to the helping professions (Morrow, 1971). Third and finally, social reinforcers are the most widely available of all the reinforcers. They are, perhaps, what might be called the "natural reinforcers"—uncontrived, involving no special expense, usable by anyone (professionals, parents, spouses, peers) involved in a particular situation. A smile, a kind word— almost all of us have this kind of equipment. Indeed, no matter what kind of reinforcer is used in a given program, it is important to use social reinforcers as well. Pairing other reinforcers with social reinforcers is intended to allow whatever behavior has been learned with those other reinforcers to be maintained by social reinforcement. And once a particular behavior modification program is ended, social reinforcement from the natural environment, given in response to the newly adaptive forms of behavior, will be more likely to maintain that behavior. Of course, social reinforcers can be both positive (e.g., smiling, clapping) or negative (yelling, frowning). Again, this is determined by the actual effect the use of such reinforcers has on an individual's behavior.

The use of social reinforcers has great potential for all of us as practitioners and as human beings, in our various roles as parents, professionals, spouses, and so on. As practitioners, understanding the potential efficacy of the use of social reinforcers—attention, praise, the human response—allows us to work with the client's strengths. We can focus on accomplishments in our practice—attend to them, support them, praise them, encourage them—and perhaps even strengthen them. Being aware of the power of one person's behavior to affect another's, we can assess situations and plan programs to maximize the effects of social reinforcers in strengthening prosocial behavior. We can analyze a family system and see how members of a family reinforce undesired behavior in some members of the family, and intentionally or unintentionally ignore or punish desired behavior. We can make alterations in such dysfunctional family systems by planning with the family to rearrange systematically the consequences of behavior so that all members of the family receive social reinforcement for desired behaviors.

In addition, the use of social reinforcers is likely to have powerful effects on our own everyday lives. Most of us think of ourselves as positive reinforcers, i.e., we like to think of ourselves as people who attend to others' strengths, who always have a kind word, encourage the positive behavior of our own family, and so on. The reader might want to try the following exercise. Keep a list for only a few days of all the times you give a kind word to someone in your family or someone at work: a little attention, a kiss, a hug, a "thanks for the great meal," a "that was terrific, Johnny," or some other positive recognition of a family member's activity. And at the same time, keep track of all the times you act as, or give, a negative reinforcer: a yell, spanking, insult, disparaging remark, and so on. Possibly, there will be few of the latter and many of the former. But it is even more likely that just keeping this list will make you even more aware of all the times you could have used social reinforcement, but, for some reason (no time, no energy, whatever) did not. Not only will the planned and generous use of social reinforcers greatly benefit those in your environment, but the more you use social reinforcers, the more you will get in return. People tend to respond to social reinforcement with more of the same.

3. *Activity reinforcers* are the privileges, events, and activities that many of us hold so dear. Such reinforcers are extremely important for most adults and most children. These reinforcers include activities like going out to dinner, to movies, watching T.V., playing games, going on picnics or to the beach, going to the circus, or even taking a brief walk with the family after dinner. Of course, the range of events that can be used as activity reinforcers is infinite, depending on what the individuals involved really enjoy. A behavioral plan might, by contract, make such reinforcing activities contingent upon the performance of desired behaviors; e.g., the performance of some desired behavior such as jogging five times per week will lead to the selection of some desired activity like going out to dinner (Kau and Fischer, 1975).

4. *Token reinforcers* are objects that symbolize various units of value desirable to an individual that can be *exchanged* for something that

person wants. The desired units for which the tokens can be exchanged are called *backup reinforcers* and can consist of anything that is both available to, and prized by, an individual (e.g., specific items like toys, consumables such as candy, special privileges, trips, and so on). The tokens themselves can be points on a chart, poker chips, gold stars, notes to parents (e.g., if Robbie brings home from school five notes stating that he was on time each day, he gets to spend a whole day on the weekend playing with his dad with Robbie choosing the activity), and so on. In other words, any convenient item can be used as the token or symbol; the important idea is that the token has meaning only in terms of what it can be exchanged for. (Incidentally, in everyday life, money functions essentially as a token reinforcer.) The backup reinforcers can also include almost anything that is available and that may be desired by a given individual. In fact, if the resources are available, it is best to have a variety of reinforcers—a sort of "reinforcement menu" (Addison and Homme, 1966)—from which an individual can make selections. Items (or privileges, activities, etc.) on the menu can then be weighted in terms of the accomplishments of the client. For example, for minor, but specific, accomplishments, the client, say a third-grader, might be able to select from three or four types of candy; for moderate accomplishments, from among three or four inexpensive toys; and for major accomplishments, from among three or four prized activities. Thus, the value of the reinforcers to the individual predetermines the type or amount he receives in relation to what he accomplishes. Of course, it is assumed that the value to the individual of all these reinforcers has been established beforehand, and that their use will indeed be reinforcing (i.e., will strengthen behavior). It is also assumed that the operation of the token system will be spelled out in advance to the individual, perhaps in the form of a contract (see Chapter 11 on assessment). In this way, the individual will know just what behaviors he will have to perform, and what he will be able to "buy" with the tokens he receives for their performance.

> *EXAMPLE 4.12:* June and Rich drew up a contract with the help of their social worker. Rich would get one point (token) for every 10 minutes of conversation he engaged in with June. If, at the end of the week, he had 10 points, he would get to select the T.V. programs for the following week (backup reinforcers). If he had 15 points, he would get to select the Sunday activity that they both enjoyed. If he had 20 points, Rich could pick whatever he wanted for dinner for the following week. (Rich loved his food; for him, selection of what to eat was very reinforcing.)

It should be obvious that tokens have a number of advantages (Ayllon & Azrin, 1968). They are portable and can be carried around with minimal difficulty. They can be administered without disrupting others (the difference between a teacher's merely putting down a check mark on a sheet of paper, observed only by the child, versus his giving a child some candy while the entire class looks on). Tokens can be used in situations where other forms of reinforcers are either not available or are impractical to administer. Tokens can be supplied immediately (a basic principle of effective reinforcement—see the following section), and without restrictions as to time or place. Finally, the use of tokens and the concomitant choice from among different backup reinforcers gives an individual far greater freedom of choice among the items and privileges which are reinforcing to him and his changing moods and wishes as an individual.

5. *"Premack."* The fifth category of reinforcers is related to what has been called the *Premack Principle* (Premack, 1959). Briefly, this principle holds that high-probability behavior can be used as a reinforcer for low-probability behavior. Simply put, this means that if one behavior in a "free choice" situation can be observed to occur with a high frequency, that behavior can be used as a reinforcer for a low-frequency behavior (i.e., a behavior that does not occur often and which one wants to increase).

EXAMPLE 4.13: Miss Welch, the teacher, observed that Hilda loved to read, and often used free periods and recess to read one of her favorite books. Hilda also frequently was late turning in math assignments. Miss Welch simply made free time for reading contingent on Hilda's completing her assigned work in math for the day. Hilda soon began turning her math in on time.

Given the idea that people tend to have hierarchies of behavior, behaviors occurring with high frequency on the hierarchy can be used to reinforce those with low frequency. This is especially useful when the behaviors low on the hierarchy (i.e., low-frequency behavior) are behaviors that an individual should perform by virtue of his social role (i.e., studying for school), and behaviors high on the hierarchy are especially pleasing or relaxing to the individual (e.g., sports, games, watching T.V., and so on). Again, use of the Premack Principle assumes that the high-probability behaviors are obtained through observation in a situation where the individual has choices. (This implies the desirability of actual observation when possible rather than simply relying on a client's saying what it is he likes, since this may reflect what he thinks others expect.) Second, as with all situations using behavior modification, this also assumes that the individual is capable of performing the low-probability behaviors (i.e., that the social worker would not be expecting too much), and that their performance would be ethical and productive both for the individual and his environment.

Any or all of these major types of reinforcers—(1) consumables; (2) material; (3) social; (4) activity; (5) token; (6) Premack—can be used together. It has already been strongly recommended that social reinforcement be an integral part of most reinforcement programs. That is, whenever any of the other reinforcers are used, they should be paired with praise, smiles, a pat or hug, and so on. This not only eventually puts the behavior under the influence of real human and personal qualities such as found in everyday social interchanges, but also aids in establishing and maintaining the behavior in the natural environment, where there is no formal behavior modification program and the spontaneous behavior of other people is a major influence on our own behavior.

The notion of the combined use of reinforcers could also be illustrated by the use in a primary school setting of social reinforcers, token reinforcers, and the Premack Principle. The teacher gave each student a point on a chart (token) for completing an assignment. She would, at the same time, smile and verbally praise the youngster. When a student had completed the agreed-upon assignments, he could choose as backup reinforcers from among those activities and privileges that the teacher had observed the students engaging in during recess (Premack Principle).

There is one final note about reinforcers. Try to think of something —anything—that, supplied contingent upon and following a behavior, would strengthen that behavior, for everyone, *all* the time. Actually, there is nothing. Praise, love, food, money—all of these could, and frequently do, affect most of our behavior much of the time. But, for all intents and purposes, *there are no universal reinforcers.* There is nothing that would always and for everyone be a successful reinforcer. This is a crucial point for behavior modification, part of the principle of individualization discussed previously. It means that the specific reinforcers for each individual must be determined on the basis of the uniqueness of that individual at a particular point in time. Certainly, reviewing the literature and other examples and studies of behavior modification with similar problems, plus good old common sense, might give some excellent suggestions to *start* with. But it cannot be assumed that any individual will respond to a specific reinforcer just because many others did or because the *social worker* would under similar circumstances or because "it seems like he should." The task of determining just what is reinforcing for a specific client need not be a lengthy one (see Chapter 11 on assessment), but it is an important one since the use of "non-reinforcing reinforcers" has been responsible for the failure of many presumed cases of "behavior modification."

Effective Use of Reinforcers

Reinforcers cannot be used in a haphazard way. Eight principles, aimed at enhancing the effectiveness of use of reinforcers, have been developed (Michael, 1970; Meacham & Wiesen, 1969), and are proposed here as checkpoints to follow. If all of these principles are implemented, the chances for successfully helping one's client are greatly increased.

1. *Reinforcers (both positive and negative) can be defined only in terms of how they affect the individual.* This is the principle of individualization again. It means that selection of reinforcers must be totally geared to the individual of concern in every project. An initial review of potential reinforcers would probably include examination of the literature for similar problems and clients, and consideration of the social worker's own possible reaction to a similar event, or even the reaction of someone who resembles the client. But, the only *sure* way of knowing whether a reinforcer is indeed reinforcing is to observe it in action, either in the natural environment or in a pilot attempt to affect some other aspect of the client's behavior. Remember, many behavior modification projects run into difficulty because they have failed to identify correctly what is really reinforcing for the client.

2. *Consequences can affect behavior automatically.* This means that it is not necessary for the client to be able to verbalize about the relationship between his or her behavior and the consequence. Ignoring this principle can lead to two types of errors. The first type of error would be failure to attempt to change an individual's behavior "because he won't understand why he's being reinforced." The assumption, presumably, is that because the individual won't understand, he cannot be affected by reinforcers. A conception such as this could stand in the way of delivery of effective services to large numbers of clients. Extensive clinical research has demonstrated the effective use of behavior modification with clients who "didn't understand" the process—e.g., "mentally retarded" or severely disturbed clients (Levis, 1970).

The second type of error that might be committed in ignoring this principle involves failure to work with an individual who verbalizes strong motivation toward achieving some goal, but is not working effectively toward such achievement (Michael, 1970). There is no reason to believe that the addition of some desired reinforcer contingent on performance will not substantially aid in the achievement of that individual's goal.

Now, because behavior *can* be affected automatically by consequences does not mean that the process *has* to be an automatic one. Not only might the awareness and cooperation of the client considerably enhance the effectiveness of the program (in fact, there is research evidence to suggest that this is so; Bandura, 1969), but such cooperation is essential when the social worker and client work out a contract in advance. Thus, when there are rules which must be fulfilled, it seems not only ethical, but also technically more effective, to first inform and discuss with the client the relation between his behavior and the consequences. (There might be one or two exceptions to this rule, namely: (1) when it is necessary first to demonstrate to the client the effectiveness of some reinforcer and the desirability of working toward some prized consequence rather than toward the aversive consequences so many people are subject to; (2) when informing the client in advance will lead to negativism, non-cooperation, and an attempt to sabotage the program.)

3. *Consequences should be very closely related to the desired behavior.* This principle means that the social worker using behavior modification should be very clear about what behavior he is trying to reinforce, and then be absolutely certain that the reinforcement is contingent only on that behavior. It is too easy, for example, to confuse spending time at a task with actually working on the task. Thus, a client might be reinforced for time spent but never achieve the desired goal because the time was spent unproductively. This calls for the social worker to specify *in advance* the desired behaviors—both short- and long-term—and then be quite certain that reinforcers are applied contingent upon performance of those behaviors only.

4. *Reinforcers, to be most effective, should be applied consistently, at all times and in all situations.* Imagine the chaos that would result if, at times, an individual's behavior was reinforced, and at other times, the same behavior was punished. Too often, the person dispensing the reinforcers claims he or she was tired, angry or otherwise preoccupied and "just couldn't manage to supply the reinforcers." There are, of course, limits to human endurance, and the realities of a situation might occasionally preclude reinforcement. But one should be perfectly clear about this—not only will inconsistency hamper a behavior modification program, it might actually render the program ineffective in either affecting overall behavior or accomplishing specific goals. The idea behind this principle, apart from the technical consideration that consistent application of reinforcers is more efficient and effective in developing new behavior, is that reinforcers should not be dispensed at the whims of the reinforcing agent, but according to a pre set plan. This, in essence, requires the social worker to select as the dispenser of reinforcers someone—either himself or a mediator in the natural environment—who will be able and willing to participate on this basis and follow the plan.

5. *Consequences should follow immediately the behavior on which they are contingent.* There should be as little delay as possible between

the individual's behavior and the consequences. If there is too much delay, not only might the reinforcer lose its effectiveness in strengthening the specific behavior for which it was intended, but some other peripheral behavior might be reinforced.

EXAMPLE 4.14: Mrs. Strump's social worker instructed her to praise Scott after every 10 minutes that he played with his brother without fighting. Mrs. Strump watched Scott play for the 10 minutes and started to praise him, but was sidetracked for a moment. When she returned, Scott had just completed punching his brother, although Mrs. Strump didn't notice. "Good boy, Scott," she said enthusiastically.

The principle of immediacy is best applied with all types of clients and behaviors. However, with older and more verbal (or "aware") clients, that is, those who are clearly able to understand and handle a delay, the effect of such a delay may not be as deleterious.

6. *Do not underestimate the optimal amount or frequency of reinforcement.* As a general rule of thumb, if there is any question about how often or how strong the reinforcer should be, it is desirable to reinforce more frequently and with stronger or more potent reinforcers rather than less frequently or with weaker reinforcers. This is especially true if the task is to develop new behavior or behavior that is occurring at very low frequencies. This principle is intended to warn against the error of underestimation. In actual practice, it would be desirable to use the smallest amount of reinforcer necessary to get the job done, since obviously, there rarely is an inexhaustible supply of reinforcers available. While this might seem contradictory to this principle, the rule is that the more effective the reinforcer and the more frequently it is given, the more effectively the behavior being reinforcd will develop. The task in practice, then, is to determine the *optimal* level of reinforcement necessary (not too much since the individual may become satiated, and not too little or the reinforcer will not have an effect), by observation of the effects of specific reinforcers on the client's behavior. This principle is mainly concerned with situations involving *new* learning. For the *maintenance* of desired behavior, it is possible to alter this principle regarding frequency by using different schedules for dispensing reinforcers. These will be discussed in Chapter 6.

Just as there is for every individual a hierarchy of probable behaviors which could be performed in response to a given situation, there is also a *reinforcement hierarchy* for every person. Different stimuli—events, items, situations—have different reinforcing value. Thus, not only does this suggest that a variety of reinforcers will be available to everyone, but that more desired reinforcers may be used as rewards for increasingly desirable performance; that is, lower level (or less desired or less potent) reinforcers can be used for smaller accomplishments, and more desired reinforcers for higher level accomplishments. In other words, the reinforcer should suit the behavior. This is particularly important when using a token system since the most desired reinforcers can be made redeemable for the most points (i.e., highest level of accomplishments). Of course, in view of the above discussion, the obvious problem is to be sure that the lower level reinforcers will in fact be strong enough to be actually reinforcing.

7. *Use small steps.* If the optimal or final goal is too large or too complex to achieve all in one step, it should be broken down into smaller units, with each step spelled out along the way. Again, this capitalizes on the commonsense notion that one has to learn to walk before one can run. In fact, many of the problems with which behavior modification deals involve terminal goals that are far too complex to achieve all at once. Thus, the way to achieve this complex terminal behavior is to design a program which includes many steps to be reinforced such that the client can readily move from one step to the next. This principle is at the core of one of the most important of all the behavior modification procedures—namely, *shaping.*

> *EXAMPLE 4.15:* Mrs. Wong thought her 4-year-old son, Timmie, was old
> enough to help set the table. But Mrs. Wong knew that since Timmie had
> never done it before, he couldn't just set all the plates, glasses, and silver-
> ware the first time. So Mrs. Wong put out the plates, knives, and forks her-
> self, but let Timmie set out the spoons. She gave him enthusiastic praise for
> doing so. The next night, Timmie not only put out the spoons but was
> allowed to put out all the silverware, which he did with a little help from
> his mother. "What a big boy," she said, praising him and giving him a big
> hug. Within a few nights, Timmie was asking to set out the dishes also, and
> by the end of the week, he was setting the entire table.

Shaping is the behavior modification procedure that systematizes the common sense principle "You must walk before you can run." Shaping refers to the delineation of *successive approximations* of the terminal behavior—small steps that gradually come closer and closer to the eventual goal—and the reinforcement of each step along the way to that terminal behavior. In Example 4.15 (above), the terminal behavior was "setting the table," and this was reached by teaching the child each of the steps along the path to that goal. As another example of shaping, a social worker attempting to teach an "autistic" child to speak would not expect such a child to break into the Gettysburg Address the second day of instruction. Instead, each step in speaking must be learned, including proper physical placement of the mouth for making sounds, then actually making the basic sounds, then saying words using those sounds, and, eventually, speaking phrases and sentences.

Shaping requires both careful analysis of the behaviors that are already in an individual's repertoire, to determine a starting point, and the making of a decision in advance about the steps he or she would need to take along the way toward achieving the desired terminal behavior. Then each step or approximation of the behavior is reinforced immediately and consistently (according to the principles of reinforcement discussed in this chapter).

The social worker using shaping must be careful to reinforce appropriately. Too much reinforcement at an early step could result in the client's inability to move beyond those steps. Too little reinforcement or proceeding too rapidly could result either in the extinction of the client's earlier shaped behavior, or in the failure to include in the client's repertoire some of the necessary steps and the consequent inability to perform the more complex behaviors. Several illustrations of the use of shaping will be presented in later chapters.

8. *Insure the effectiveness of the reinforcers.* In using behavior modification, the social worker should avoid taking unnecessary chances and should make sure that the reinforcers eventually selected actually will do their job. This can be accomplished by following these guidelines:

a. *Individualize.* Choose reinforcers on the basis of the uniqueness of each individual.

b. *Wide range.* Offer a wide range of reinforcers for selection if possible. This means that consumables (e.g., candy), material reinforcers (e.g., jewelry), and activities might all be on a "reinforcement menu."

c. *Several types.* Within one category of reinforcers, try to vary what you do select. The purpose of this is to avoid *satiation,* i.e., producing a reinforcer in such abundance that its reinforcing properties are lost, or its presentation becomes aversive (e.g., too much pie for dessert). If you are using candy as a reinforcer, vary the types of candy (chocolate, caramels, gum, peanuts, etc.). After all, how many M&M's can a child eat?

d. *Previous experience.* See that the client has some previous experience with the reinforcer. One cannot expect an individual with no familiarity with a reinforcer to be reinforced by it. A client might, for example, have to be taken on a trip or activity that he never experienced in order to heighten his appreciation for that activity and increase its desirability for him. It is a good idea to require tryout of the reinforcer in the situation in which it is to be used before attempting to use it as a reinforcer (Ayllon & Azrin, 1968).

e. *Modeling.* If necessary, let the client watch—either in real life or on film (or with children, perhaps using dolls)—a similar individual receiving the reinforcer and being very pleased with it. This observation might also add to the desirability of the reinforcer.

f. *Deprive.* While the term seems harsh, in this context it simply means that reinforcers will be more desirable if the individual who prizes the reinforcer is deprived of it for a short while. This simply capitalizes on the commonsense notion that what we want tends to mean more if we cannot have it for a while. Think of how good food tastes when we are especially hungry, or how extra-important that weekly paycheck becomes when it is delayed by only a few days.

Now, it is probably obvious that these principles of reinforcement can rarely, if ever, be strictly adhered to for most people, especially when the program is being conducted in the natural environment. These principles are suggested as guidelines that, if implemented, will optimize the chances for success of any program. That is, when each is followed to the greatest extent possible, there is simply a better chance of attaining one's objectives.

But a program *can* be successful without complete implementation of every principle, depending on the client, the problem, and the extent to which application of these principles varies. A general rule of thumb is that the more basic or elementary the behavior, the greater the need for strict adherence to the guidelines. For example, with a more verbal client, capable of fully understanding the behavior modification program and the contingencies, reinforcement could be delayed considerably. On the other hand, with, say, a "retarded" child, it would be more desirable to make reinforcement as immediate and consistent as possible.

Summary

This chapter has discussed the types of reinforcers available to the social worker using behavior modification. Positive and negative reinforcers were discussed and their use in the various consequating operations was presented. Most reinforcers are extrinsic (originating in the environment) rather than intrinsic. Some reinforcers are considered primary reinforcers, i.e., they are unlearned and satisfy basic physiological conditions (e.g., food). Most reinforcers used in behavior modification are learned, or secondary, reinforcers. These include social reinforcers (the behavior of other people), material reinforcers, activity reinforcers, token reinforcers, (which are exchanged for backup reinforcers) and Premack reinforcers. Examples of the use of most of these reinforcers were presented. Finally, eight principles for effective reinforcement were presented. Adherence to these principles should greatly facilitate a program of behavior modification.

So far, the discussion has centered largely on uses of *consequences*. In an earlier chapter, the place of *antecedents* in the operant framework was alluded to. In fact, the brief discussion above regarding deprivation essentially refers to the alteration of an antecedent condition in order to insure the effectiveness of a consequence. This might serve to highlight the importance of antecedents in the use of operant behavior modification, which is the subject of the following chapter.

CHAPTER 5.   Operant Antecedents

Despite the major focus of operant behavior modification on the effects of consequences on behavior, the analysis of *antecedent* conditions plays an important part both in the assessment and the modification of maladaptive behavior. The social worker using behavior modification will be constantly reminded of this by using the A–B–C paradigm—Antecedent– Behavior–Consequence—as a guide for comprehensive practice.

Before proceeding further, it might be helpful to clarify some of the important differences between the operant and respondent conceptions of antecedent conditions. In the respondent paradigm, the antecedent condition, i.e., the stimulus (S), *elicits* the behavior; there are no other major factors to take into consideration. Hence the respondent stimulus can be described as an *eliciting stimulus—*

$$S^E \longrightarrow R$$

—i.e., the stimulus *elicits* the response.

But the operant conception of an antecedent condition is that it is *not* sufficient, in and of itself, to elicit behavior. In the operant paradigm, an antecedent condition merely *sets the occasion,* i.e., acts like a cue, as, e.g., in setting the time or place for a behavior. Thus a bed, in operant terminology, would not cause or elicit sleeping behavior. The bed would merely signify the place for sleeping.

There can, however, be both respondent and operant dimensions to one behavior. Stuart was playing in the yard when he cut his foot and began to cry. The crying was a respondent behavior since the cut and resulting pain elicited it. However, when he was almost through crying (because the pain had diminished), Stuart's mother came out, and her outpouring of sympathy and attention actually increased Stuart's crying. The crying behavior, at that point, increasingly became an operant; it was being maintained by its consequences (the mother's attention), i.e., the effects it was having on the environment.

One can see a typology relating problems to interventive procedures beginning to take shape:

1. respondent behaviors—anxieties, phobias, etc.—to be treated with respondent techniques;
2. operant behaviors—most behaviors other than respondent behaviors—to be treated by operant techniques;
3. combinations—where both respondent and operant behaviors are problems—to be treated with both respondent and operant procedures, especially when the use of one procedure will enhance the effects of another (e.g., systematic desensitization combined with praise and attention, contingent consequences used to enhance the effects of desensitization).

Antecedent Conditions

Lil was the only girl Tony had ever dated for a sustained period of time. They had a unique relationship characterized by a large number of arguments, a great deal of verbal aggressiveness, and what Tony later described as "some stimulating intellectual discussions." After almost three years, though, Lil went into the Peace Corps. Tony went out with a young woman named Annette who was much less aggressive than Lil. But every time she ventured an opinion, Tony would cut her off with an argument, expecting a renewal of the "stimulating discussions" he had enjoyed with Lil. Tony had a great time, but Annette eventually told her roommate that if Tony were to call, she was to say that Annette had left town.

During the three years that Tony was dating Lil, he was reinforced for his aggressive verbal behavior by the responses of Lil, who also loved a good fight. But Annette was different. In responding to Annette as he had responded to Lil, Tony had failed to *discriminate* the differences between them, and he suffered the penalty. The situation had changed (Lil to Annette), but Tony did not get the message. Had a social worker employing behavior modification been working with Tony, he might have been able, given his assessment based on the A–B–C model, to prepare Tony for possible differences between the two situations.

There are four ways in which antecedents and other factors that influence operant behavior other than consequences can be altered (Stuart, 1970; Goldiamond, 1968). In essence, all function to enhance the effectiveness of the overall behavioral program and, frequently, that of the reinforcer. Thus, antecedents and consequences work hand-in-hand.

DISCRIMINATIVE STIMULI AND DISCRIMINATION

When we perform a behavior in one situation but not another, we exhibit *discrimination*. We drive 65 miles per hour on the highway, but only 20 miles per hour on a residential street. We go to a picnic dressed in old and sloppy clothes, but get all spruced up for a job interview. We talk baby talk to a three-month-old infant ("goo-goo"), but (try to) present a more lucid picture when lecturing to a class of 300 university students. The social worker has two or three alcoholic drinks while attending a party, but drinks a cup of coffee while seeing a client. All of these are operant behaviors differentially performed under different circumstances. Why were these discriminations made? Because we have learned that different consequences follow our behavior in different settings. The settings themselves are called *discriminative stimuli,* situational cues that let us know what type of behavior we could expect to be reinforced.

A discriminative stimulus (S^D; pronounced "ess dee") sets the occasion for reinforced responding. The S^D then becomes the stimulus with which the reinforcement is associated. This occurs when a behavior (e.g., a parent's baby talk) is reinforced (the infant smiles or giggles) in the presence of a specific stimulus (baby in the crib) and not otherwise. As a result of this, the stimulus (situation, time, or place) gains control over the probability that the behavior will be performed. This is called *stimulus control,* referring to the fact that an antecedent condition cues us that if we perform the behavior at a certain time, in a particular place, or with certain people, we will be reinforced. Thus, an individual becomes more likely to respond in one situation rather than in another. Again, it should be clearly noted that the antecedent does not "cause" the behavior to occur, it only *cues* its occurrence. (When no antecedent stimulus can be identified, the behavior is called *free operant* behavior, e.g., the first time an infant, lying by himself in a crib, says "da-da.") The relationships between the discriminative stimulus, the behavior, and the reinforcement can be diagrammed as follows:

Antecedent–Behavior–Consequence

$$S^D \longrightarrow R \longrightarrow S^+$$

(baby in crib)   ("goo-goo")   (baby smiles)

The baby in the crib (S^D) set the occasion for the adult's behavior (R; "goo-goo") which was reinforced (S^+) by the baby's smile.

Since one obviously is not going to be reinforced for the same behavior in all situations, there must be cues (antecedents) that there will be no reinforcement if a particular behavior occurs. These cues are called

S△ ("ess delta"). As a discriminative stimulus (S^D) tells us we *will* be reinforced if we perform a behavior, an S△ tells us we will *not* be reinforced if we perform a behavior. The relationship between the S△, the behavior, and the non-reinforcement can be diagrammed as follows:

$$S^\triangle \longrightarrow R \not\longrightarrow S^+$$

EXAMPLE 5.1: Mark went up to his Dad while his Dad was in the shower and asked for a cookie. He was ignored. Later, when his Dad was in the kitchen, Mark asked again and his father immediately gave him one.

Dad in the shower became an S△ for asking for cookies, while Dad in the kitchen became an S^D for the same behavior. Mark quickly learned to discriminate between the two situations.

Since people are social beings, and our relations with others largely hinge on the ability to perform differential behaviors appropriate to a variety of situations, it can be seen that the ability to discriminate is a pervasive and central concern for everyday living. Eventually almost all operant behavior comes under the influence of antecedent stimuli. Otherwise, a person would never know which behaviors to perform in which situations (imagine a university professor lecturing in baby talk to his students).

But what has all this to do with behavior modification? There are two major implications. The first lies in the behavioral procedure called *discrimination training.* Essentially, this refers to the process of training the client to perform certain behaviors in situations where the behaviors will be reinforced (S^D), and not in situations where no reinforcement will be forthcoming (S△)—in other words, to identify those situations where performance of a behavior will lead to desirable consequences. Such training can proceed in either of two ways. The first way is by actually using reinforcement and extinction to develop prosocial behavior in appropriate circumstances by reinforcing a response in the presence of one stimulus and extinguishing it (say, by ignoring it) in the presence of another (Whaley & Malott, 1971). The second way is to teach a person with some behavior already in his repertoire to discriminate where he can and where he cannot perform it by teaching him to identify the cues as to when his behavior is likely to be reinforced. This can proceed, in addition to reinforcing the behavior when it is performed at the right time and place, by making already present discriminative stimuli more perceptually clear, prominent, and compelling (Morrow, 1971).

EXAMPLE 5.2: The social worker was conducting group therapy with several long-term residents in a mental hospital. Whenever one of the residents spoke lucidly in the group, he was reinforced with a token and verbal praise. If a group member spoke irrationally, he was ignored. This attaching of differential consequences was an attempt to develop discrimination training by reinforcing lucid speech during group therapy so that, eventually, the group meeting itself would become a discriminative stimulus (S^D) controlling or evoking such speech. As is usually the case with discrimination training, the procedure was coupled with positive reinforcement, providing the additional advantage of strengthening desired behavior, in this instance, lucid speech. Of course, continued work with these group members would involve the effort to have the lucid speech generalize to other situations.

EXAMPLE 5.3: When he was in third grade, Craig's teacher was very strict and never permitted the children to ask questions or speak out in class. Craig was a sensitive youngster and quickly learned to keep his mouth shut in class, although when he was out of class with his friends, he was outgoing and boisterous. When he went into the fourth grade, Craig remained quiet and suspicious and never volunteered anything in class although the new teacher attempted to encourage this. With the help of the social worker, who discussed and clarified the differences between the two classes with Craig and encouraged the new teacher to praise Craig for any verbal behavior. Craig soon learned that this class was different, and that he could speak and not be punished but, rather, be reinforced.

The second major implication of discriminative stimuli lies in the utilization of suitable environments for behavioral intervention programs (Schaefer and Martin, 1969). A suitable environment consists of physical surroundings suitable for learning and behavior change, as free as possible from offensive and noxious conditions—noises, odors, and so on—so that the surroundings themselves can function as S^D's for prosocial behavior. A soothing physical environment can become an S^D for the reinforcement derived from relaxation and pleasurable activities. In addition, a suitable environment includes the presence of people to implement programs who can themselves act as positive discriminative stimuli for bringing about prosocial behaviors, and who understand the way people can function effectively as discriminative stimuli for other people.

Schaefer and Martin (1969) note the large incidence of headbanging in one particular hospital for the retarded. It seems that every time a resident banged his head against the wall, the nurses would rush up and comfort him and offer him candy to calm him down. It was not long before the nurses, who were reinforcing the headbanging, became discriminative stimuli—as soon as a nurse entered the ward, the whole group of residents would begin banging their heads. Thus, TLC (tender loving care) was not enough; in fact, the inappropriate use of the TLC was a deciding factor in producing the problems.

POTENTIATING VARIABLES

This second major class of antecedent conditions consists of specific variables that insure the effectiveness of the reinforcer. There are actually two conditions involved—*satiation* and *deprivation*—which may be viewed as two ends of a continuum. The overall goal of alteration of these conditions is to control the effectiveness of the reinforcer. *Satiation* simply describes the phenomenon of decreasing effectiveness of a reinforcer after repeated presentation (Whaley & Malott, 1971). If an individual is full after a large dinner, the use of food as a reinforcer will probably be ineffective. Satiation, of course, is not a permanent condition, since, after a while, it is likely that the reinforcer will once again assume its reinforcing properties. The goal in behavior modification is to avoid satiation by offering a wide variety of reinforcers, and by being careful not to offer too much reinforcement at any one time in order to avoid having it lose its value. Satiation has a fairly specific effect, so that a small variation in the type of reinforcer (say, changing from one type of candy to another) may overcome the ineffectiveness of the previous reinforcer due to satiation.

The opposite of satiation is deprivation. Again, the term conjures up images of clients locked up in dark rooms, deprived of all human contact and treated as animals. But this is a misconception of the use of this term in behavior modification. *Deprivation* simply refers to a procedure that consists of withholding a reinforcer for a period of time. Up to a point, the greater the deprivation (i.e., the longer the reinforcer is withheld), the more effective the reinforcer will become when used (Whaley & Malott, 1971). In everyday life, both satiation and deprivation might best be demonstrated by the dinner hostess who, when she is concerned that she does not have enough of the main course, prepares huge amounts of appetizers in the hope that her guests will become satiated before the entree, or the hostess who holds a very late dinner with no appetizers at all knowing this deprivation will make her guests ravenous and even more appreciative of her cooking.

In behavior modification, deprivation can be used in a number of ways to increase the effectiveness of a reinforcer. The withdrawal of desired privileges, activities, sweets and other goodies for a period of time before the implementation of a program will enhance the effectiveness of these consequences as reinforcers. The client will be just that much more willing to work toward obtaining these reinforcers; thus, increases in desired behaviors would be more probable.

INSTRUCTIONAL STIMULI

These are rules or guidelines provided for the client by the social worker. Not only is this a basic technical necessity, but common sense and ethical practice should guide the social worker in being certain to clarify how the client is expected to behave, the stimuli to which he should respond, and so on. The behavioral technique of *prompting* (or coaching) is one that, in part, relates to instructional stimuli. A social worker would *prompt* a client by first clarifying what behaviors should be performed and under what conditions, and, second and more specifically, by verbally encouraging or assisting the client to perform the behavior that will bring the reinforcement. For the performance of specific behaviors, such prompts or cues should be provided just before the behavior that is to be reinforced. On all occasions, the social worker should be certain that the cue is both crystal-clear and nonpunitive.

> *EXAMPLE 5.4:* In teaching Willie, a mute, "autistic" child to speak, the worker first tried to explain that when Willie made any noise, he would receive some candy. Then the worker said, "O.K., now try to say 'mm'." Willie approximated the "mm" and was immediately given a piece of chocolate candy.

FACILITATING VARIABLES

The final class of antecedent events is composed of the tools, materials, or equipment required to perform the desired behaviors. The social worker using behavior modification should insure that all necessary materials are available. A person could not realistically be expected to learn to brush his teeth regularly if the toothbrush were not available. Nor could an individual be trained to discriminate between different cues or situations if those cues or situations were not provided. While providing facilitating variables seems like an obvious course of action, a small oversight in seeing that appropriate materials are indeed available could considerably damage a behavior change effort, and the social worker would do well to be sure those materials and situations are available *before,* rather than after, the program has begun.

IMPLICATIONS OF ANTECEDENTS

Too often in the process of behavior modification these antecedent conditions are ignored. One novice behaviorist instructed a mother who had been having difficulty handling her child to ignore all his crying because the child just wanted attention. The novice thought that merely by ignoring the crying, extinction would occur. The next day, the child began really screaming in a back room of the house. The mother tried to follow the instructions faithfully and ignored the crying. After several minutes of nonstop crying, however, she finally decided to investigate. She found her child had fallen and cut his arm, and was in real pain. The novice worker had been so sure of his assessment that his recommendations had overlooked not only common sense, but also the development of a more comprehensive plan based on the A–B–C model, including specifically paying attention to antecedent events. In this case, the crying had not been operant crying (i.e., for "attention's" sake) which could have been affected by altering the consequences. The use of the A–B–C model, in essence, then, insures a far more comprehensive and sensitive approach to assessment, including attention to antecedent *and* consequent events.

It also seems to be inefficient to develop a program involving major alteration of consequences when it would be simpler and sometimes more effective to examine and alter antecedents. Some behaviors might be far more adequately performed by providing discrimination training or prompting, or simply seeing that the appropriate facilitating variables are provided. In fact, oftentimes, when it appears as though a behavioral program is failing ("the reinforcer isn't working"), the real problem probably could lie also in the lack of attention to one of the antecedent conditions; the reinforcer itself might be adequate, but overall planning insufficient. In other words, behavior modification is not a half-baked or fuzzy-headed simple "reward and punishment" operation ("just give the monkey a reward and he will perform"). Instead, used appropriately in both assessment and intervention, the behavior modification perspective offers a comprehensive approach to behavior change, not only by altering consequences, but also by altering antecedent conditions and seeing that the behavior is carried out at the right time, in the right place, and with the desired intensity.

Generalization

Another important concept related to antecedent events is *generalization* (or *stimulus generalization*). The chapter on respondent conditioning noted that stimuli similar to the conditioned stimuli also tend to elicit the conditioned response, although to a lesser degree. Such a process also occurs with operant behavior and (unfortunately, because of the potential confusion caused by the terminology) it too is called stimulus generalization or simply generalization. *Generalization* refers to the process that takes place when a discriminative stimulus (S^D) similar to the original S^D begins to gain some control over a particular behavior. Thus, generalization is said to have taken place when behavior learned in one situation occurs in another situation. Of course, the greater the similarity between the two situations (the two S^D's), the greater the probability that the behavior will occur in both (will generalize).

The process of generalization is basic to the performance of adaptive human behavior. If the behavior we learned in one place (e.g., talking to our parents) did not generalize (talking to other people), our behavioral repertoire would be limited to the point where we would have to learn entirely new sets of behaviors every time we found ourselves in a somewhat different situation.

The process of generalization is crucial for behavior modification. In the first place, it means that new behaviors learned in one situation do not have to be entirely relearned in other situations. Second, and even more important, knowledge about principles of generalization can be built into behavior modification programs to insure that the positive effects will be carried over from the intervention situation to the natural environment. Ordinarily, the first choice for conducting a behavioral program would be in the natural environment, thus eliminating the middle step. But if this is not possible, or if the social worker wants to have the new behavior generalize from one part of the natural environment to another, there are certain processes specifically related to antecedents that will facilitate this.

One of these procedures is simply to develop the new behavior in a situation that resembles as closely as possible the real-life situation. The physical setting might be adapted in some way. Some psychiatric hospitals have attempted to eliminate as much as possible the "hospital aura" by keeping the rooms nicely decorated, comfortable, and "homey."

Another procedure is to help the client perform the new behaviors by first practicing them through a technique called *behavior rehearsal* (which is discussed in more detail in later chapters), and then by encouraging the client to perform the behaviors *in vivo* (in real life), with appropriate verbal reinforcement from the social worker for any attempts to perform them.

Finally, the procedure called *fading* introduces an important ingredient to the generalization process. *Fading* refers to the procedure of gradually changing a situation controlling an individual's behavior to another situation. The social worker would decrease the differences between the situations gradually so that the first S^D comes to resemble the second S^D. In one psychiatric hospital, the staff attempted to implement fading for residents preparing for discharge by wearing "civilian clothes," spending less time with the residents, encouraging more trips to the community, beginning home visits on weekends, and transferring residents to halfway houses that were run primarily by the residents. Gradually, residents were able to perform the behaviors in the newer situations, gradually approximating life in the community. As another illustration, a social worker who had been working with a "school-phobic" child attempted to generalize his hard-won gains from his office to the school by introducing in the office dolls and playhouses that "resembled" the school and the teachers; he then reinforced the boy for playing with these toys without fear. The social worker also brought in the boy's teacher and had her praise the boy's efforts, so that an *in vivo* fading process gradually occurred—the stimulus control exerted by the social worker and his office were replaced by the stimulus control of the school and the teacher.

A related procedure is the use of *stimulus change,* in which the client is helped to remove himself from, or change, the stimulus field (i.e., the constellation of situations and events) that has been associated with the problem behavior. For example, some couples find that they can more easily work toward an improved relationship on a vacation than at home ("motel therapy"). Another example would be the social worker who deals with a particularly nonverbal individual who is able to speak more comfortably or freely when he and the worker leave the office and go for a walk or a cup of coffee.

Summary

The process of behavior modification involves consideration of the three-term paradigm: A (antecedents)–B (behavior)–C (consequences). This chapter concentrated on the A (antecedents). In operant terms, antecedents set the occasion for behavior to occur; they let the individual know whether or not he will be reinforced, insure that the reinforcer will be effective, and insure that the appropriate materials for the program will be available. The four major classes of antecedent variables were described as discriminative stimuli, potentiating variables, instructional stimuli and facilitating variables. Techniques for altering antecedent conditions were also briefly presented, e.g., discrimination training, deprivation, prompting, and fading. The process of generalization, whereby behavior learned under the control of one stimulus occurs under the control of other stimuli, was also reviewed. The basic points of this chapter were, first, it is sometimes far more efficient and effective to alter antecedents rather than consequences; second, the full process of behavior modification should involve consideration of both antecedent and consequent conditions in any intervention program.

Obviously, the use of behavior modification procedures requires a social worker who is willing and able to make creative use of a variety of ideas and procedures that are available. If one simple procedure can be used ethically, effectively, and efficiently, it should be used. But human beings and their problems are so complex that one can hardly expect resolution of those problems by the simple alteration of one or two variables. The whole process of behavior modification involves careful consideration of a variety of factors that are potential contributors to behavior problems, and judicious selection from among the many procedures available those that would be most effective with the particular individual and problem. This chapter has suggested ways in which the traditional operant emphasis on consequences can be expanded into a more specific and detailed, yet, at the same time, broader, conception of both human behavior and intervention into human problems.

CHAPTER 6.　Schedules of Reinforcement

The last three chapters have discussed the basic principles of operant behavior modification, including the role of the antecedents and consequences of behavior, and the nature of reinforcers. But one important question has not yet been dealt with directly: how often and when do we reinforce? Reinforcement must be used in a planned way, and in order to carry out such a plan, the social worker should choose in advance a schedule for the use of reinforcers. *Schedules of reinforcement* specifically refers to the patterns by which reinforcers are related to behavior: the numerical and temporal relationships between reinforcers and responses. This chapter will cover the basic principles involved in establishing schedules of reinforcement.

Continuous Reinforcement and "New" Behavior

The fastest way to establish a new behavior, or strengthen a behavior already in a client's repertoire, is to reinforce every occurrence of that behavior. Reinforcement of *every* occurrence of a desired behavior is called *continuous reinforcement,* and the reinforcement is said to be supplied on a *continuous* (or regular) *schedule* (abbreviated, CRF). Reinforcement applied on a continuous schedule is applied according to all the principles of reinforcement discussed in Chapter 4. When differential reinforcement, involving both reinforcement and extinction, is used, the schedule is called the DRO schedule (differential reinforcement of other behaviors).

But what if the desired behavior is not in an individual's repertoire at all; what if the client never performs it? How does the social worker get the behavior to occur in the first place so that it can be reinforced? Obviously, behaviors do not occur magically. Actually, most of the procedures for establishing a new behavior have already been discussed in slightly different contexts in previous chapters. To summarize, there are five ways to bring about the occurrence of entirely new behavior (Mikulas, 1972). These procedures are: (1) shaping; (2) fading; (3) modeling; (4) prompting; (5) physical guidance.

1. *Shaping*. This is the basic technique used to develop new behaviors. It consists of the reinforcement of small steps that are successive approximations of some terminal behavior. Shaping utilizes any response in a person's repertoire that is related to the final behavior, even though the relationship is only tangential. With the terminal behavior in mind, the social worker begins "where the client is," i.e., with whatever responses the client has that can be gradually shaped into more complex behavior. Thus, teaching a child to talk might mean reinforcing first a movement of the lips, then perhaps a single sound, and each successive approximation of normal speech until the desired terminal point, speaking, is reached. (Incidentally, the process just described is typically carried out in real life, as when an infant first begins to make sounds and is reinforced by attention, praise, and so on. The eventual result of the reinforcement of basic sounds is the development of speech.) The point of shaping is to start with a minimal (but related) response, and then gradually reinforce small steps as the individual progresses.

2. *Fading*. Although used far less often than shaping, one can use fading to get "new" behavior to occur or, more specifically, to get behavior to occur in new situations. The use of fading to develop new behavior involves getting behavior that occurs in one situation to take place in another by gradually changing the first situation into the second. Thus, an individual comfortable in one setting could be made comfortable in another by introducing him to situations that gradually approximate the second setting. The gradual decrease in the differences between one stimulus situation and the other means that the second situation will also become a discriminative stimulus that eventually evokes the behavior that previously occurred only in the first setting. In a sense, fading involves approximation on the stimulus side, whereas shaping involves approximation on the response side (Mikulas, 1972).

3. *Modeling*. Behavior totally absent from a person's repertoire can be introduced into that repertoire by having a model perform the behavior and having the client imitate him. In everyday life, modeling, too, has a great deal to do with the learning of new behaviors, and it can be a valuable asset to the social worker who wants to aid his client in the development of new behavior.

4. *Prompting*. Prompting (also called coaching) consists of having the social worker advise the client what behavior he should perform in order to implement the program.

5. *Physical Guidance*. If the new behavior is some motor behavior that involves the voluntary muscles, the social worker could demonstrate by simply guiding the part of the client's body that is involved (e.g.,

facial muscles for talking, positioning the feet for a non-ambulatory client to aid in developing walking, and so on).

Of course, for many situations in which social workers are involved, such procedures are not necessary. But in case a potential client does have a serious behavioral deficit, i.e., when the adaptive behaviors simply are not in his repertoire at all, these procedures are available.

This section has discussed not only the establishment of behaviors that are not at all in the client's repertoire, but also the development—or strengthening—of behaviors that are already in his behavioral repertoire. All may be reinforced on a continuous schedule. Behavior learned under a continuous schedule is generally learned fairly rapidly. However, one problem the use of a continuous schedule entails is that if the reinforcement is ever withdrawn or stopped, there is likely to be a brief increase in the rate of occurrence of the behavior, followed by a rapid decrease (extinction), which may be accompanied by emotional distress. In other words, behavior learned only under a continuous schedule extinguishes rapidly. Still another problem with a continuous schedule is that it is not really the most economical way of reinforcing behavior, since it obviously requires both that the dispenser of reinforcers be available continuously and that every correct response be reinforced. This can become impractical, since one of life's realities is that we only have so much time in a day to spend with one client.

A continuous schedule is the method to use in establishing and strengthening a new behavior. But once the behavior has reached the desired frequency and strength, and the client is performing it at the optimal rate, the social worker should "thin out" the schedule—i.e., deliver fewer reinforcements. This is done by changing from a continuous to an *intermittent schedule,* which involves the reinforcement not of every occurrence of the behavior but rather that of *selected* occurrences. Not only does an intermittent schedule provide the social worker with a more economical system, but, as will be discussed in detail below, behavior learned under such a schedule is more resistant to extinction than behavior learned under a continuous one. Hence, the social worker who has helped his client strengthen a desired, prosocial behavior may increase its resistance to extinction by using an intermittent schedule.

Intermittent Schedules

There are two major categories of intermittent schedules: ratio schedules and interval schedules. A *ratio schedule* is a schedule in which reinforcement is dispensed after a *predetermined number of responses* are made, as when a child is reinforced after going to school five times, for example. An *interval schedule,* on the other hand, refers to reinforcement dispensed after the *passage of a predetermined length of time,* as when a child is reinforced after staying in school for five hours.

Both ratio and interval schedules may be either *fixed* or *variable.* A schedule (whether ratio or interval) is said to be *fixed* when the reinforcement is completely predictable and regular. The reinforcement of a child after every five words spoken (fixed-ratio) or after every five minutes of speech (fixed-interval) are examples of fixed schedules. A *variable schedule* is one in which either the number of responses (variable ratio) or length of time (variable interval) *varies* around some mean, such that to the individual receiving the reinforcement, the reinforcement is neither predictable nor regular.

Intermittent schedules of reinforcement may seem confusing at first, but understanding the nature of schedules of reinforcement is important to the social worker as he or she attempts both to make new behavior more resistant to extinction, and to generalize new behavior from a behavior modification program into the natural environment. By way of clarification, each type of intermittent schedule will be discussed in greater detail below.

Ratio Schedules

When the goal of the intervention program is to reinforce the client for making a certain *number* of responses, a ratio schedule is used.

FIXED RATIO SCHEDULES

A *fixed ratio* schedule of reinforcement means that a behavior is reinforced regularly after a certain set number of occurrences. For example, a fixed ratio schedule of 4 might be established to help a child who is learning to do arithmetic. This means that after every four problems are completed, the child would receive the reinforcer (whether it be direct reinforcement, a token, or both). If the child were required to solve two problems before receiving the reinforcer, it would be a fixed ratio schedule of 2. (Note that regardless of which reinforcement schedule is used, the basic principle of *immediacy* applies: reinforce immediately following the targeted, scheduled, correct response). A fixed ratio schedule of 4 is written as FR: 4.

To reiterate, in a fixed ratio schedule, the individual receives reinforcement only after a fixed number of responses have been made. The basic rule for determining the ratio is to start low (begin where the client is) and *gradually* increase the ratio. In fact, both the change from the continuous to the fixed ratio schedules and the increase in the ratio (of required behaviors to reinforcements) should be gradual to avoid extinguishing the desired behavior. One common example of a fixed ratio schedule in everyday life is piece work, where the worker is paid a fixed sum of money for completing a fixed amount of work, say, for repairing three instruments, or packing six boxes of pineapples.

CHARACTERISTICS OF FR SCHEDULES

Since reinforcement under the FR schedule depends on the rate of behavior, an FR schedule tends to reinforce speed because the faster an individual responds, the more rapidly he is reinforced. Thus, work output would be high under an FR schedule. One caution is in order here: high output does not necessarily mean accurate or high-quality output. A student might quickly finish five problems but do them all incorrectly. Thus, the reinforcement should be given only if five problems are completed *accurately*.

The FR schedule typically leads to high (and stable) rates of responding (Bandura, 1969). Higher rates of responding (i.e., more frequent occurrences per unit of time of the target behavior) can be reached by starting with a low ratio of reinforcement to responses required, and gradually raising the number of responses required before reinforcement is dispensed (e.g., from FR: 3 to FR: 20). Sometimes, however, there is a tendency for individuals to withdraw from schedules requiring high rates of performance to get minimal rewards. Thus, the FR schedule is used when the ratio is not too high so that the effort required to receive the reinforcement, which must be strong enough, is within reasonable limits (Lundin, 1969). If too large a number of responses is needed, the frequency of occurrence of the behavior may decrease (*pause*) following the reinforcement, presumably because the individual knows the reinforcement will not come until after he has performed a certain number of responses (e.g., having difficulty getting back to the job after completing a piece-work assignment and collecting your pay.)

If a fixed ratio schedule is withdrawn, i.e., the reinforcement is stopped, extinction (or the diminishing of the response) occurs much in the same way that it does with a continuous schedule. There is a brief spurt in the rate of response, followed by a fairly rapid drop in the frequency of occurrence of the behavior.

VARIABLE RATIO SCHEDULES

Reinforcement with a variable ratio schedule (VR), as with the FR schedule, is supplied after a predetermined number of correct responses, but with the VR schedule, the number of responses required before reinforcement is given is systematically varied around some average number of responses. For the individual being reinforced on a VR schedule, the number of responses required to get the reinforcement is not predictable. Thus, to increase the number of words correctly read, reinforcement might be given after 3 correct words, then 5, then 7, then 5 again; the overall mean would be 5, written VR: 5. One instance of behavior in everyday life maintained by VR schedules is gambling, which is maintained by the anticipation of a "killing" and the infrequent, unpredictable wins (reinforcement).

CHARACTERISTICS OF VR SCHEDULES

Reinforcement under a VR schedule leads to a high and relatively stable state of responding. With a VR schedule, there are not many pauses after reinforcement and the behavior is maintained at a high rate of occurrence. The rate of responding is even higher than under a fixed ratio schedule because with a VR schedule, the individual cannot predict when the reinforcement will come; therefore the behavior is performed regularly in anticipation of the reinforcer. The VR schedule is perhaps the most powerful schedule in maintaining behavior (Bandura, 1969). However, as with FR schedules, the VR schedule requires that the number of responses be counted, since reinforcement is delivered only after a certain number of responses. This, at times, may be impractical for the social worker or whoever is administering the reinforcement.

The VR schedule produces behavior that is very resistant to extinction. During extinction (i.e., when reinforcement is withdrawn), the rate of behavior is fairly well maintained, although there are some pauses. Eventually, the pauses tend to increase and the overall rate of behavior decreases.

Interval Schedules

When an individual is reinforced after a certain period of time has passed (as opposed to a certain number of responses occurring), he is being reinforced on an interval schedule. In general, interval schedules produce lower rates of responding than ratio schedules (i.e., fewer occurrences of a behavior take place). This is so because reinforcement depends on how much time passes, not on how many responses are made.

FIXED INTERVAL SCHEDULES

When a fixed interval (FI) schedule is used, a certain length of time is set in advance and reinforcement is regularly supplied following that period of time. (This assumes that the desired behavior has occurred at least once.) Thus, if Margaret is told that she will be reinforced after every ten minutes during which she is sitting quietly at her desk, she would be on a fixed interval schedule of 10 (FI: 10). If the time were increased to 30 minutes, it would be FI: 30. The weekly or monthly payment of salary is one example of the FI schedule in everyday life.

CHARACTERISTICS OF FI SCHEDULES

With the FI schedule, there is usually a pause after reinforcement, followed by a gradually increasing rate of response as the time for reinforcement approaches. This pause occurs because, after reinforcement, no matter what type of behavior is performed, the individual knows (either because he is told or because he soon figures it out) that he will not be reinforced until a given period of time has elapsed. As the end of that period approaches, people tend to increase their rates of behavior in anticipation of the coming reinforcement. The FI schedule usually produces only a minimal amount of behavior in any given situation (i.e., there is a fairly low rate of responding). The rate of behavior tends to vary with the length of the interval—the longer the interval between reinforcements, the lower (usually) rate of responding. This occurs because the pause (or decrease in the rate of responding) after reinforcement tends to increase as the length of the interval increases.

In general, behavior under an FI schedule is fairly resistant to extinction (Reese, 1966); when reinforcement is withdrawn, it tends to maintain a more regular response rate than behavior learned under a continuous schedule.

VARIABLE INTERVAL SCHEDULES

With a variable interval schedule (VI), the length of time between reinforcements varies around some mean (contrast VI with VR schedules, where the *number of responses* varies around some mean). Thus, reinforcement might be given after the first 10 minutes, then 6, then 20, then 8 again, with an overall mean of 11, written VI: 11. These intervals should be set in advance, starting with shorter intervals (which will produce somewhat higher rates of responding), then gradually increasing the length of the interval. Of course, using such interval schedules—both fixed and variable—requires keeping track of the time, which may be an inconvenience. The "strange" behavior of the devoted fisherman, who is up at the crack of dawn, might be explained in part by the VI schedule of reinforcement for catching fish.

CHARACTERISTICS OF VI SCHEDULES

Variable interval schedules produce a higher rate of responding, and more stable and consistent performance, than fixed interval schedules. As with FI schedules, the longer the interval, the lower the rate of responding. The steadier, more nearly constant rate of responding under the VI schedule may be attributed to the fact that the individual cannot gauge the interval between reinforcements, which appear to occur at random. Thus, the rate of responding remains stable because the reinforcement is expected to occur at any time (e.g., the fisherman expecting to catch his fish).

Behavior learned on a VI schedule is very resistant to extinction. When reinforcement is withdrawn, behavior is characterized by a low, steady rate of responding before a gradual decrease in the frequency of occurrence of the behavior. In fact, responses maintained by the two interval schedules (FI and VI) are more resistant to extinction than those maintained by other schedules; FI and VI schedules are the ones to use if the primary goal is to maintain the behavior for a long time after the termination of the behavior modification program (Reese, 1966). It can also probably be seen why intermittent schedules in general entail less emotional distress during extinction than continuous schedules. Under a continuous schedule, the change to nonreinforcement (extinction) is a drastic change. But when the individual is accustomed to not being reinforced, particularly for long periods of time (as under intermittent schedules), the change to nonreinforcement is far less dramatic. Thus, the rate of behavior tends to persist longer, and the decrease in behavior (particularly with both interval schedules and the variable ratio schedule) occurs more gradually than with a continuous schedule.

For illustrative purposes, Figure 6.1, redrawn from Reese (1966, p. 160), presents an overview of the differences in performance under the four basic types of intermittent schedules.

Use of Schedules

In everyday life, most schedules of reinforcement are unplanned rather than planned. Unfortunately, this frequently holds true in behavior modification programs as well. One reason for this is that administrators

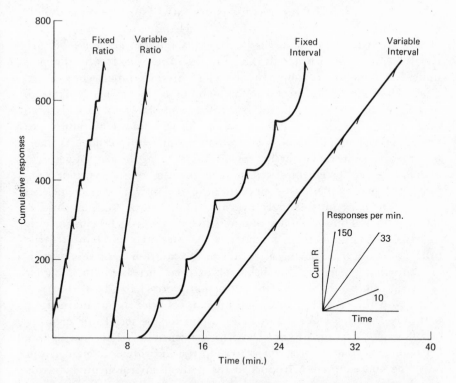

FIGURE 6.1. Stylized records of responding under basic schedules of reinforcement. Diagonal marks indicate reinforcement; the slope of various response rates is indicated at lower right. Fixed Ratio: high rate, with brief pause following reinforcement and abrupt change to terminal rate. Variable Ratio: high sustained rate; no pausing after reinforcement. Fixed Interval: low overall response rate due to pause following reinforcement; length of pause increases with length of interval; gradual increase to high terminal rate as interval ends. Variable Interval: low sustained rate; no pausing after reinforcement.

Source: E. P. Reese, *Analysis of Human Operant Behavior,* Dubuque, Iowa: William C. Brown, 1966.

of reinforcement cannot constantly attend to the behaviors of others— either by counting or by keeping time. This, to some extent, may prove beneficial, since reinforcement supplied under such a system (or non-system) is, by definition, intermittent reinforcement; as such, it may help to maintain some desired behavior. But this also has undesirable side effects, since undesired behaviors (say, a child's tantrum behavior) may be reinforced intermittently as well, making them equally difficult to extinguish.

In everyday life in the natural environment, much of human behavior is maintained by a variety of schedules, called *concurrent* or *complex schedules* when several are in effect at the same time, or *multiple schedules* when two or more operate sequentially. Thus, there are usually all types of schedules—ratio and interval, fixed and variable—operating at any given time for all of us. Knowing about the existence of such schedules can be a distinct advantage to the social worker who wants to understand and modify human behavior. An individual who has received continuous reinforcement for many of his behaviors is likely to become easily discouraged and frustrated, and likely to actually stop responding, when faced with failure or the withdrawal of reinforcers. On the other hand, a person used to intermittent reinforcement is likely to persevere in his behavior for some time, even in the face of setbacks and loss of reinforcement. In fact, such patterns of intermittent reinforcement may explain why deviant or maladaptive behavior persists even in the face of seemingly aversive consequences (such as institutionalization). Thus, when one attempts to extinguish such behavior only to have it persist, there is a tendency to "give in" and reinforce the behavior again (e.g., paying attention to the tantrum "just this once"), and this may strengthen the behavior or even increase it to a higher rate than prior to the start of the extinction process (Bandura, 1969).

Despite the fact that much of human behavior is maintained by naturally-occurring schedules, it is important for the social worker using behavior modification to know how to *use* schedules. The goal of any behavior modification program is to help the individual client perform satisfying and adaptive behaviors in the natural environment. Behavior modification programs do not last forever; once the individual starts behaving in ways acceptable to himself and his environment, the goal of the social worker is to see that the desired behavior will still occur in the natural environment after the formal program is terminated. One very important way to insure this is to change the schedule from a continuous schedule to intermittent reinforcement (ultimately, a variable schedule). The behavior will then become more resistant to extinction and will be more likely to "transfer" from the consistent and friendly confines of the formal intervention program to the more haphazard reinforcements of the everyday world. Once the behavior is satisfactorily maintained through intermittent reinforcement in the program, the client will be better prepared to face the reduction in reinforcement he is likely to find in the natural environment. Of course, the transfer should not be a dramatic one, so that the natural reinforcers in the environment—the behavior of other people, salaries, and so on—will take over and continue to provide some intermittent reinforcement to maintain the desirable new, or reinstated, behavior of the client. The goal is for the adaptive behavior of the client to *stimulate* such reinforcement, on the grounds that others in his environment will be responding positively in reciprocity to the positive behaviors of the client. "You give what you get."

Overall Guidelines for the Selection of Schedules

Following are some of the key points to consider in selecting schedules for use in behavior modification.

1. For the development of new behavior, and to achieve the highest frequency of occurrence, use a *continuous schedule.*
2. For the highest resistance to extinction (i.e., the most enduring behavior), use a *variable* schedule, preferably a variable interval schedule.
3. If you cannot keep a count of the number of responses (which is required for the use of a ratio schedule), use an *interval* schedule.
4. If you cannot keep track of the passage of time (required for the use of an interval schedule), use a *ratio* schedule.
5. Generally, interval schedules are easier to administer than ratio schedules because timekeeping is easier than counting specific behaviors.
6. For increasing or maintaining a certain number of responses a client is to perform (the rate of responding), use a ratio schedule.
7. For strengthening certain behaviors performed over a *period of time,* use an interval schedule.
8. Use a *variable ratio* schedule if the goal is to develop a high, sustained rate of behavior (i.e., when performing a certain number of responses is the crucial criterion).
9. Use a *variable interval* schedule for a low sustained rate of behavior (i.e., when the number of responses, per se, is not the crucial criterion).
10. For all intermittent schedules, start with low performance requirements for behavior to be reinforced, and *gradually* increase the perfomance required in order to receive reinforcement (e.g., from VR: 3 to VR: 30).

Summary

Schedules refer to the patterns in which reinforcement is dispensed. Continuous schedules—the reinforcement of every desired, correct response—are used to develop new behavior. Intermittent schedules are used to maintain and strengthen desired behavior. The four basic types of intermittent schedules are fixed and variable ratio schedules (supplied after a certain number of responses are made), and fixed and variable interval schedules (supplied after a certain period of time has elapsed) .

Intermittent schedules are important because: (1) they result in different rates of behavior; (2) they (particularly the variable schedules) increase the resistance of behavior to extinction; (3) they can be used to facilitate the transfer of desired behaviors from a formal intervention program into the natural environment.

CHAPTER 7. Modeling

A good deal of human behavior is learned by watching others. The process of changing one's behavior by observing and copying that of others is called modeling. After respondent and operant behavior, modeling is the third major category of learning from which all the basic principles and procedures of behavior modification have been derived. This chapter on modeling is placed after the three chapters on operant behavior because, as shall be illustrated below, one of the major issues regarding modeling is the extent to which reinforcement plays a part in the learning of behavior through observation.

Basic Principles of Modeling

Extensive research (Bandura, 1965; Bandura & Walters, 1963; Rotter, Chance, & Phares, 1972) has demonstrated that nearly all behavior that is learned as a result of direct experiences can also be learned on a vicarious basis through observation of the behavior of others. This has obvious significance in considering the development of both adaptive and maladaptive behavior in that a good deal of "everyday learning" takes place through modeling, as when young children, for example, watch and imitate their parents. But beyond this, and of central concern for this book, is the importance of using modeling to obtain therapeutic effects. Much of this work has been stimulated and conducted by Bandura and his colleagues, and extensive reviews of the processes and issues involved in modeling are available in Bandura's work (Bandura, 1969; 1971).

DEFINITIONS

In a recent review of the clinical applications of modeling, Rachman (1972) has suggested distinguishing between several terms related to modeling. "Observational learning" is viewed as any change in behavior which is acquired as a result of observing the behavior of another person, by definition, a social phenomenon. "Imitation" is viewed as a change in behavior acquired as a result of observing the behavior of a person or an animal or of an inanimate occurrence (e.g., a sound); imitative behavior would be noted by its similarity to the observed event or experience and is often a deliberate attempt to approximate that event or experience and is not necessarily a "social phenomenon." Finally, "modeling," per se, is viewed as *social imitation*—a subclass of both imitation and of observational learning, but not synonymous with either.

On the other hand, Bandura (1969, pp. 118–119), in reviewing the variety of terms under which vicarious phenomena are grouped, rejects the premature use of differential terminology on the grounds that there is no clear evidence that the vicarious learning of different classes of behavior is governed by separate variables. Thus, in the absence of evidence that different antecedent, mediating, or behavioral variables are involved in different processes of vicarious learning, and since similar processes appear to apply in most forms of vicarious learning, imitation, observational learning, social learning, vicarious learning, and identification will all be considered synonymous with *modeling*, which is defined as a change in behavior as a result of the observation of another's behavior. Tacit support for this is also provided by Rachman (1972), who, after makinig the distinctions described above, proceeds virtually to ignore them in the remainder of his paper, acknowledging that the key issue is their application in clinical practice.

PROCESSES INVOLVED IN OBTAINING A MODELING EFFECT

There are a variety of possible explanations for an individual's change in behavior after observation of another's activities. Bandura (1969) reviews several of these:

1. classical and associative conditioning theories (i.e., a conditioned response is developed through observation of someone else);
2. reinforcement theories (which assume that observational learning is contingent upon reinforcement of imitative behavior);
3. affective feedback theory (which emphasizes the classical conditioning of positive and negative emotions accompanying reinforcement to stimuli arising from matching responses, e.g., Mowrer, 1960);
4. contiguity–mediational theories (e.g., where the observer acquires a new behavior but does not actually perform it, suggesting the importance of cognitive or representational mediators assumed to be learned on the basis of a temporal contiguity learning process).

Drawing from these theories and the large amount of empirical research on modeling, Bandura (1969; 1971) suggests that modeling involves at least four interrelated subprocesses: attention, retention, motoric reproduction, and reinforcement.

Attentional processes refers to the importance in modeling of being sure that the observer attends to, recognizes, and differentiates the distinctive features of the model's behavior. Several attention-controlling variables may be involved in this process, including characteristics of the model, characteristics of the observer, and incentive conditions. One of the keys to effective modeling may involve manipulation of these conditions, many of which are within the control of the social worker. The model should be someone who can attract the observer's attention and who will be important to the observer. This might mean an "expert," a celebrity, an especially attractive person, a high-status or especially competent person, or just someone who will attract the observer's attention (e.g., a cartoon character for a child). Similarly, there should be a clear relationship between the activities of the model and the activities of the observer. For example, a six-year-old child may be more willing to approach a feared dog if he sees another six-year-old child, rather than an adult model, approach the dog.

Changing incentive conditions is another way of increasing the effectiveness of the observer's attending behavior. For example, it is particularly helpful to inform observers in advance that they will be asked to reproduce a model's behavior, and that they will be rewarded for the number of elements of the behavior performed correctly. In addition to the use of incentives to direct attention, the modeled behavior should be simple enough and performed at a rate that is within the observer's capacity to perform. Moreover, the modeled behavior should be highly discernible to the observer, since such behaviors will be more readily performed than more subtle ones.

The second subprocess involved in modeling is the *retentive* or *memory capacities* of the observer. Obviously, it is necessary for the observer to be able to retain the new learning. Both overt and, when overt is impossible, covert rehearsal operations—i.e., practice of the modeled behavior—facilitate retention. However, symbolic coding operations may be even more helpful in facilitating long-term retention of modeled behavior (Bandura, 1969). This is because the observer must retain the original input in some symbolic form in order to perform modeled behavior without the continued presence of external modeling cues (e.g., the model continuously being present). Such symbolic coding may include representing stimulus events in vivid imagery (i.e., images of modeled sequences of behavior) and translating action sequences into abbreviated verbal systems. Of these two symbolic coding systems, imaginal and verbal, Bandura (1971) suggests that verbal coding of observed events to serve as guides for subsequent reproduction of matching responses is probably more efficacious.

The third subprocess involves *motoric reproduction,* the use of symbolic representations (imaginal or verbal) of modeled behavior to guide overt performances. Actual practice of the modeled behavior (whether guided by external cues such as the model's behavior, or by symbolic cues in delayed modeling) is especially necessary when complex behaviors that require many motor components are involved. Modeled responses are often acquired and retained in symbolic forms, but are not reproduced because of physical limitations, social constraints, or other limiting factors.

The final subprocess in modeling involves *reinforcement* and *motivation.* Research has documented the fact that a person may acquire or learn new behaviors through observation of models, but, for a variety of reasons (e.g., negative sanctions), may not perform such behaviors (i.e., translate new learning into action). This suggests that the presence of reinforcement is not always essential to learning through modeling. Indeed, research has verified the acquisition of learning through modeling without the presence of reinforcement for the observer, a phenomenon Bandura has labeled "no trial learning." On the other hand, research shows equally clearly that reinforcement for the observer is particularly facilitative for actually performing observed behavior (Bandura, 1969). In fact, the performance of modeled behavior by the observer is greatly facilitated by rewarding such behavior in either the observer or the model (or both). Indeed, the social worker who repeatedly demonstrates desired responses, instructs the client to reproduce them, manually prompts the behavior when it fails to occur, and administers potent reinforcers to the client, will, in the vast majority of cases, eventually elicit matching responses (Bandura, 1971).

Effects of Modeling

There are three major effects of modeling when used in a therapeutic or behavior modification context. The first is to develop new behaviors or new patterns of behavior, the second to eliminate anxieties and fears, and the third to facilitate the performance of already established behavior.

DEVELOPMENT OF NEW BEHAVIORS

Modeling has been found to be the procedure of choice when considering the development of new behavior. Obviously, shaping and differential reinforcement can also be used to develop new patterns of behavior, but in order to use reinforcement, some aspect of the behavior must already be in the client's repertoire so that it can be reinforced. This is not a requirement when modeling is used.

Among the most prominent of the behavior modification research regarding the development of new behavior through the use of modeling is the material on language development and elimination of deficit conditions (Lovaas, 1966; Lovaas, *et al.*, 1967). These clinicians/researchers have taught language, self-care skills, play patterns, intellectual skills, and a variety of interpersonal skills to children labeled as "autistic." The basic program involves the following steps: establishing control over the child's attending behavior; using modeling activities in small steps of increasing difficulty starting with simple behaviors and moving to gradually elaborate complex behaviors; physically guiding the child if he does not respond; gradual withdrawal of the physical prompts; reinforcement for performance of the modeled behavior; a gradual shifting of stimulus cues from modeling the behavior to verbal stimuli and appropriate environmental events.

This graduated, guided, reinforced modeling program appears to have important implications for overcoming behavioral deficits. Variations of these procedures have also been used to help "juvenile delinquents" develop appropriate social skills (Sarason & Ganzer, 1969) and to overcome social withdrawal among preschool children (O'Connor, 1969). Furthermore, research has documented that the effects of such modeling go beyond "mere mimicry," and can generalize to innovative behavior, to different settings, and to different stimulus conditions (Bandura, 1969).

ELIMINATION OF ANXIETIES AND FEARS

The elimination of anxieties and fears and associated avoidance behaviors through modeling is achieved by exposing fearful observers to modeled events in which the model performs the feared activity without experiencing any adverse effects (and, preferably, enjoying the activities). There is considerable evidence bearing on the effectiveness of modeling as a procedure for reducing anxiety. A review of research on this topic (Rachman, 1972) reported on fourteen studies using a no-treatment control or systematized own-control for comparison purposes, in which modeling was superior to no treatment and achieved significant amounts of fear reduction. This fear reduction tended to be enduring and tended also to generalize to similar situations and stimuli.

The positive effects of modeling in achieving elimination or reduction of fears and anxieties may be facilitated by using graduated modeling, i.e., gradually increasing the fear-arousing value of the modeled situation after starting with clients observing the model interacting in a positive manner with situations that have low fear-arousing value. Use of multiple models also appears to have a more beneficial effect than use of only one model. While there appear to be no major differences between the efficacy of live and symbolic (e.g., films) modeling, there does appear to be a slightly more powerful effect on particularly difficult avoidance behaviors when the modeled performance is live. Finally, the use of participant modeling, whereby the client is encouraged to actually participate in performing the feared behavior after exposure to a model, is superior to the effects obtained by merely observing (without participating) a fearless model.

Most of the research on the fear-reducing properties of modeling used (in addition to actual behavioral measures) a variety of psychometric and attitude-change assessments that demonstrated positive effects similar to those obtained by using other behavior modification procedures (e.g., actually handling the feared object). On the other hand, most of these studies used "nonpsychiatric," volunteer samples, were focused on relatively simple fears (e.g., fear of dogs or snakes), and most used children or students as subjects. Thus, while there is little reason to believe that the results reported here cannot be replicated with a variety of actual client samples, such studies have yet to be conducted.

FACILITATION OF ESTABLISHED BEHAVIOR

The third and final type of effect of modeling is to facilitate the expression of behavior that an observer has already learned, but has not performed due to a lack of social support. Extensive research evidence attests to the fact that a wide range of behaviors already in an individual's repertoire can be substantially increased by having him observe a model performing such behavior. In such situations, the behavior of the model functions as a discriminative cue to facilitate expression of the desired behaviors.

Bandura (1969) has listed a wide range of behaviors that both laboratory and field research has shown can be facilitated through modeling. Such behaviors include the following: volunteering one's services; performing altruistic acts; assisting persons in distress; seeking relevant information (e.g., regarding employment); selecting certain types of foods, activities or articles. Susceptibility to the social facilitation effects of modeling appears to be related to three sets of variables (Bandura, 1971):

1. reinforcement control of the matching behavior (if either the model or the observer—or both—is rewarded, matching behavior is more likely to be performed);

2. characteristics of the model (models who possess high status in terms of prestige, power, and competence are emulated to higher degrees than those of lower status;

3. observer characteristics (persons who have been frequently rewarded for imitative behavior, who tend to lack self-esteem or to feel incompetent or highly dependent, as well as those who are similar to the model on such dimensions as sex, age, race, and socioeconomic status are most likely to pattern their behavior after successful models).

Optimal Conditions for Effective Modeling

Modeling is a particularly valuable behavior modification procedure because of its inherent flexibility. Modeling can be conducted live or symbolically, and can be used with individuals or with groups. Modeling has been shown to be effective when used alone in developing new behaviors and decreasing anxieties and fears, but also has great value when used in conjunction with other procedures—for example, in facilitating a shaping process, aiding in behavior rehearsal (having the client first watch the worker perform the behavior, then perform it himself)—and when combined with guided participation and in vivo desensitization in the technique called "contact desensitization" (Ritter, 1968; see also Chapter 13).

In order to make modeling optimally effective, a number of conditions should be implemented. While all of these conditions have not been proved unequivocally to be necessary, most have some degree of empirical evidence supporting their utilization. Until further research can identify the specific conditions contributing to the effectiveness of modeling, the following list (compiled from Bandura, 1969, 1971; Rachman, 1972) would appear to offer the most effective package when using modeling:

1. Use models who are important to the observer and who will attract and maintain the observer's attention (e.g., high-status, prestigious models).

2. Show the model being reinforced for prosocial behavior.

3. Reinforce the observer for imitating the model's behavior.

4. Use clear pretherapy instructions; supplement with relaxation training when possible.

5. Use multiple models.

6. Demonstrate clearly the relationship between the events affecting the model and those affecting the client, in terms both of similarity of problem and of age, sex, and race.

7. Provide preliminary incentives for the observer to attend to, and imitate, the model.
8. Progressively increase the difficulty or the fear-arousing value of the modeled behavior.
9. Have the model describe his progress, and provide verbalized guidance or reinforcement (or both).
10. Use repeated modeling experiences.
11. Use repeated practice for the observer.
12. Provide guidance and encouragement during observer practice.
13. Graduate practice exercises (from less to more difficult).
14. Provide feedback for practice.
15. Provide favorable conditions for practice.
16. Arrange for regular reinforcement of newly acquired behavior to insure that it endures.
17. Arrange for reinforcement from the natural environment as soon as possible.
18. Use guided participation in practicing the real-life behaviors whenever feasible, preferably at each step in the sequence of activities.
19. When using symbolic modeling such as movies, use a combination of audio and visual presentations.
20. Use as many successful exposures—and as much time of exposure —of the observer to the model as possible.
21. Make the modeled behavior clear and highly discernible to the observer.

Summary

Modeling is an effective procedure for developing new behaviors and decreasing anxieties and fears. Modeling can also be used to supplement a variety of other behavior modification procedures. In this chapter, various definitions of modeling were reviewed, followed by a review of the basic subprocesses assumed to underlie modeling. These processes are attention, retention, motoric reproduction, and reinforcement. The three basic effects of modeling were presented as developing new behavior, decreasing anxieties and fears, and facilitating the performance of already established behavior. The chapter concluded with a listing of the optimal conditions for achieving effective modeling.

PART 2
PROCESS AND PRACTICE

CHAPTER 8.   Introduction to the Practice of Behavior Modification

The first part of this book presented the basic concepts and principles of behavior modification. The task of the second part is to weave those principles into the practice of behavior modification in social work. This practice consists of the application of basic learning principles to a diverse range of behaviors frequently encountered in social work settings. This chapter is a brief introduction to the process of behavior modification that highlights some of the issues and varying contexts of its application.

Goals of Behavior Modification

The social worker who uses behavior modification will generally shift from asking *why* questions to *what* questions (Ullmann & Krasner, 1969). Hence, the worker might ask: What is the person doing? Under what conditions are particular behaviors being performed? What are the effects of those behaviors, i.e., what changes occur after they are emitted? What situations are being avoided? What environmental circumstances are maintaining the behavior? What environmental circumstances can be altered to diminish maladaptive behavior and increase adaptive behavior? What reinforcers can be supplied (by the social worker or significant others)? Most important, the social worker asks, what does the client want and what are the most efficient and effective means at my disposal to help him get it? Presenting problems, the initial complaint, are considered of major importance, although intervention need not stop there. On the other hand, intervention is not considered successful or complete unless the presenting problem is modified. This means that a man who initially complains of loneliness would probably not be considered successfully helped until the loneliness has been diminished or eliminated, no matter how much he comes to understand himself and his problem.

Thus, the goals of behavior modification are, specifically, to decrease maladaptive, undesired behavior and increase adaptive, desired behavior.

Such adaptive behavior has certain characteristics (Ullmann & Krasner, 1969, p. 92): (1) people must be able to attend to, and receive, social stimuli; (2) they must have the skill to perform the appropriate response; (3) they must perform the response; (4) they must perform the response at the right time and place.

If these terms sound too "behavioral," too much like the jargon of laboratory psychology, perhaps the following might be more acceptable: the goal of behavior modification is self-actualization for every individual! A self-actualized person is someone who functions more fully and lives a more enriching life than does the average person. He or she is someone who utilizes and develops all of his or her unique capabilities and potentialities, free of the emotional turmoil and inhibitions of the less actualized (Shostrom, 1968; Maslow, 1954). Does such a paragon of virtue exist? Perhaps not. But such qualities are not inconsistent with the definition of the general objectives of behavior modification. For behavior modification, all of the above can be summarized as the following goals: (1) to maximize the control an individual has over himself or herself and over the environment; (2) to maximize the development and use of one's own abilities as well as environmental opportunities.

The difference between behavior modification and other approaches is that, given agreement that "self-actualization" is a noble and desired goal, behavior modification proceeds to a more detailed definition of self-actualization." The social worker who uses behavior modification would define for each individual client what self-actualization actually means: when a person is (or becomes) "self-actualized," what behaviors will he or she be performing and under what conditions can the behaviors be expected to occur? Without such specific definition, self-actualization may be a worthless concept. For the struggling writer, self-actualization may include the ability to sit at his desk and write for several hours. For the young mother, self-actualization may mean the ability to rear her children without excessive emotional turmoil. For the newlywed, self-actualization may mean the ability to perform sexually in a manner satisfying to both partners. Thus, attempting to bring every client to the point of the completely self-actualized individual as described above would be inappropriate, if not downright impossible. Self-actualization must begin with what the client wants or needs to be, and can no more be applied as an indiscriminate and global goal for every client than can, say, the same behavioral techniques be used with every problem.

The use of specific goals for each individual also has important practical advantages. For example, how many social workers, working with children in a school would consider their assignment to be to help decrease a shy child's "shyness," or to work with a child who is "immature?" From a behavioral perspective, terms such as "shyness" and "immaturity" are merely labels, providing little basis for making rational decisions about intervention. It would be far more appropriate to find out what it is that an individual does that leads others to attach a particular label to him. For example, the "shy" child may be so labeled because he does not initiate conversations with adults or peers. The "immature" child may be so labeled because he frequently leaves his seat in class or because he fails to follow instructions. Such specificity in setting goals—e.g., decreasing the frequency with which Dale leaves his seat without permission, or increasing the number of times that Rita initiates conversations with others—allows choice of specific interventive procedures for specific behaviors. It is surprising how often global impressions of others (like "immaturity") with their negative labeling effects and inferential qualities are based on impressions about a series of specific behaviors. When these behaviors are changed, the basis for such global diagnostic impressions no longer exists.

Finally, one of the myths about behavior modification is it ignores feelings, and considers changes in feeling trivial. In fact, several techniques of behavior modification deal directly with and have important, salutary effects on feelings (e.g., systematic desensitization of anxiety and behavior rehearsal to overcome lack of assertiveness). But beyond this, both from a behavioral and a social work perspective, any changes in any type of problem configuration must be translated into changes in social functioning. Enhancement of social functioning is the central concern of social work, and should always be the primary goal in any intervention program.

THE ROLE OF COGNITION

One of the more obvious aspects of behavior modification is the emphasis placed on environmental or external control of human behavior. This is so mainly for one reason: there is strong and persuasive evidence that the alteration of environmental factors along the lines suggested here can have clear positive effects on human behavior. But does this mean, *ipso facto,* that *only* environmental events are of concern to social workers using behavior modification, or that internal factors, especially cognitive ones, are ignored? The answer is no. The suggested basis for the use of behavior modification is that *the social worker who uses behavior modification should use any ethical approach where empirical evidence suggests its application will be effective in resolving clients' problems.* One hopes that the goal of the practitioner who uses behavior modification is not to demonstrate the superiority of his or her techniques over other techniques, or to conduct a clinical case study using the real problems of another human being just for the sake of research, but to effectively help people with problems. So where does the role of cognitive factors fit into all this?

It is hoped that this section of the book, and later chapters that discuss the techniques of behavior modification, will clearly illustrate how behavioral procedures attempt to utilize all aspects of human existence to promote positive behavior change. The technique of systematic desensitization might serve as an example: utilizing cognition (the client's imagination and memory) in addition to affective (feeling) and motor responses, the social worker weaves together a package involving all three of the major modes of human functioning (cognitive, affective, overt behavioral). In fact, several of the techniques of behavior modification are specifically designed to employ cognitive processes (covert reinforcement, thought stopping, etc.). An entire branch of the field is concerned with helping people achieve some degree of self-modification, and this obviously includes cognitive processes (see, e.g., Mahoney & Thoresen, 1974; Goldfried & Merbaum, 1973). It might be argued that such self-control is the ultimate goal of each and every behavior modification program.

A secondary concern might be, do cognitive processes play a part in all behavioral techniques? Considerable research suggests that cognition clearly cannot be assigned a predominant role in the explanation of the changes brought about by behavior modification procedures (Mikulas, 1972; Lang, 1969; Bandura, 1969). On the other hand, there is ample room for further research on this topic; the role of cognition in facilitating behavioral techniques need in no way be ruled out at this juncture. But for the *practitioner,* the question of *why* behavioral procedures work must play a subordinate position to the more important one of determining when and with whom they do work, and of being able to apply the procedures flexibly. Helping people comes first; knowing exactly why they are helped, though of obvious importance in understanding and extending change processes, must await future research.

THE ROLE OF INSIGHT

Does behavior modification mean that the social worker using it should ignore helping his client achieve some insight into the nature of his problems?

Why should it? If insight can facilitate positive change, then insight should be part of the behavioral package. This may be partly a question of emphasis. How important is the achievement of "insight"—or emotional and cognitive understanding and awareness of the internal and external relationships between events and the "experiencing" of such awareness—to behavior change?

There is, in the first place, no clear, substantial evidence that achieving insight is a necessary or sufficient condition for changing behavior. People may clearly understand their problems—e.g., internal motives and their effects on relationships and behaviors with others—but still not be able to *act* to solve their problems. For insight to be helpful, there must be present a variety of other social and behavioral skills to implement the behaviors that are to be changed once it is understood what those behaviors are.

In the second place, it is not at all clear that insight must *precede* behavior change. In fact, there is increasing evidence—from behavior modification research (Bandura, 1969), from social psychological research (Festinger, 1962; Goldstein *et al.*, 1966), and even from the work of psychoanalytically oriented practitioners (Spregel & Linn, 1969)—that insight can *follow* behavior change. The very act of bringing about the successful change of dysfunctional behaviors has been followed in several cases by a change in attitudes and clients' reports that they more clearly perceive and understand themselves in a way that links both feelings and thoughts, including those of which they previously were not aware (Ullmann & Krasner, 1969; Bem, 1967).

Finally, there is clear evidence that awareness or understanding of the factors that govern the occurrence of one's own behavior in relation to the behavior of others can facilitate both the learning and the performance of adaptive behaviors (Bandura, 1969; Locke *et al.*, 1968). In other words, when an individual understands what he is doing, in terms both of his behavior in the natural environment and of the program worked out with the change agent, there is a greater probability of achieving success in changing his or her behavior. This is not intended to imply that extensive time and energy must be expended in helping an individual achieve insight into his problems before an active program of behavior change can begin. It does mean, however, that, given the available time and capabilities of the client, an optimal intervention program will foster and encourage both the client's understanding of, at the very least, the conditions of that program, in addition to understanding the arrangement of the environmental conditions necessary to bring about a decrease in maladaptive behavior and an increase in adaptive behavior.

The Helping Relationship: The Context of Behavior Modification

Behavior modification usually proceeds in the context of a direct relationship between the social worker (or other professional) and the mediator or client. Thus, anything that facilitates the positive aspects of that relationship is likely to enhance the positive effects of the program. This touches on one of the more unfortunate criticisms of behavior modification: that the behavioral approach is cold and mechanistic, and pays little or no attention to feelings, or to "affect."

Nowhere in the behavioral literature are there admonitions to be "cold" or "distant" or "removed" from the client. In fact, just the opposite pertains, and practitioners who utilize a behavioral approach, just as their counterparts who use more traditional approaches, are urged to be warm, empathic, concerned, kind, and humane (Thomas, 1970; Wolpe, 1969; Lazarus, 1972).

Recent evidence indicates that this is actually true in practice. An experimental study involving practitioners professing one of three theoretical orientations—behavioristic, Freudian or ego psychology, and humanistic—showed that there were no significant differences in actual practice in the qualities of the relationship, as measured on the dimensions of empathy, warmth and genuineness, between the practitioners of any of the three groups (Fischer *et al.*, 1975). This is an important finding, since it offers tentative evidence to suggest that the notion that behaviorists are any different in their interpersonal skills than practitioners from any other theoretical orientation may be just a myth.

But such a finding only illustrates that there are no differences. Based on the principle that the social worker who uses behavior modification will use whatever effective resources are available, the issue must be: Can social workers actually improve their interpersonal skills to the extent that such skills clearly facilitate client changes? This seems to be the case. An increasing body of research has established the core conditions of empathy, warmth, and genuineness (core because these conditions may be thought of as basic to all human processes of interaction) as basic to the training of practitioners in the field of interpersonal helping— *regardless* of theoretical orientation. This research has been conducted with institutionalized and clinic clients, with several diagnostic categories, using individual and group therapeutic methods, practitioners of diverse theoretical orientations, and a variety of subjective and objective outcome measures. The results are clear and uniform: practitioners who possess high levels of these qualities—as measured on scales designed specifically for that purpose—are significantly more successful in helping their clients than practitioners with lower levels of empathy, warmth, and genuineness.

This research, and the methods for training practitioners to communicate higher levels of the three core conditions, has been reviewed extensively elsewhere (Carkhuff, 1969; Fischer, 1975, 1973; Truax & Mitchell, 1971; Truax & Carkhuff, 1967), so there is no need to elaborate here. But the point must be made clear—such interpersonal dimensions cannot be ignored, whether one is using behavioral approaches or not. Moreover, because training for these interpersonal skills has been demonstrated empirically to be effective, and is significantly different from the traditional approaches to training practitioners in qualities of relationship (see Fischer, 1975, for both training procedures and the outcome of research evaluating such training), such components should be part of every training program in the area of interpersonal helping. The authors, for example, always attempt to combine training in behavior modification procedures with concurrent training in the core conditions of empathy, warmth, and genuineness.

There are several reasons for this. The first and most obvious is that this is a direction clearly indicated by the research literature. Second, the application of behavior modification procedures requires the utmost in clinical sensitivity in understanding the client and in deciding on procedures. Third, such training is judicious for ethical reasons. High levels of communication of empathy, warmth, and genuineness help to insure a practitioner who will be nonpunitive and nonmanipulative, sensitive to, and understanding of, the client's feelings, and able to proceed at the client's pace. Fourth, there is both case study (Bergin, 1969) and experimental evidence (Vitalo, 1970; Mickelson & Stevic, 1971) that practitioners who communicate high levels of empathy, warmth and genuineness are more effective in their use of behavior modification procedures.

The success of practitioners with high levels of these interpersonal skills may, at least in part, be explained by referring to some of the basic principles of learning described in the first part of this book. In the presence of a practitioner communicating high levels of the core conditions, respondent extinction might take place. The client feels comfortable and able to talk, and repeated evocation of the distressing emotions in the presence of high levels of empathy, warmth, and genuineness, and *in the absence* of the original unconditioned stimulus, would lead to a gradual extinguishing of the dysfunctional emotional responses. It is also likely that these interpersonal skills function as reinforcers in that practitioners high on the three dimensions are more effective social reinforcers for the client. Using the process of differential reinforcement, such practitioners, by their attention, praise, and concern, reinforce the positive aspects of the client's perception of himself or herself, and reinforce efforts at adaptive functioning, at the same time paying little attention (operant extinction) to negative or self-defeating aspects of the client's functioning (Truax & Mitchell, 1971). This is truly "working with the client's strengths"—the positive aspects of human functioning. This also illustrates the way knowledge of reinforcement principles can greatly facilitate the core conditions and vice-versa.

Finally, it has also been postulated that the success of practitioners who possess high levels of empathy, warmth, and genuineness may be due to the "principle of reciprocal affect" (Truax & Mitchell, 1971; Truax & Carkhuff, 1967). Briefly, this principle states that in any interpersonal situation, the affect elicited in one person is in kind and proportion to the affect communicated by the other. Thus, the practitioner who communicates high levels of warmth tends to elicit high levels of warmth in response from the client. As stated in Part 1: "You give what you get."

Empathy, warmth, and genuineness can be utilized in numerous ways, particularly when one is aware of their value as social reinforcers. In the first place, the effectiveness of social reinforcement in changing behavior has already been noted. Hence, the greater or more accurate the communication of the core conditions, the more potent the social reinforcement, and the greater the degree of effectiveness in practice. Thus, understanding the nature and appropriate use of social reinforcement allows an even more facilitative use of empathy, warmth, and genuineness and, reciprocally, allows the social worker who uses behavioral procedures to make more truly human and personal use of himself. Because of their reinforcing qualities, they would increase (in social psychological terms) the "attractiveness" of the practitioner, and consequently the desire and motivation of the client to work with the practitioner.

The core conditions (at the expense of making these complex dimensions sound oversimplified and too concrete) also can be employed in any interviewing situation to reinforce clients' strengths and their positive perceptions of themselves and their efforts at success. The core conditions can be used (and have been demonstrated to do so) to facilitate the use of other behavioral techniques (systematic desensitization, positive reinforcement, and so on). The core conditions can be used in working with mediators—to move at their pace, enhance their involvement, and socially reinforce their efforts. The core conditions can, in sum, be used throughout the entire process of behavior modification, from assessment to intervention, directly with clients, indirectly with mediators and significant others; finally, they can be used in the development and implementation of behavior modification programs to overcome prejudices that the behavioral approach is, somehow, necessarily inhumane.

Applications in Interviewing

As noted previously, the primary focus of behavior modification intervention is not the interview itself. Instead, the interview between social worker and client is usually just the context in which a behavioral program, involving the use of specific techniques with specific problems, is implemented. On the other hand, since interviews between social worker and client (or mediator) do occur, one should provide optimal conditions for the enhancement of future interactions between the parties involved. To that end, behavioral principles can be used to facilitate the social worker's role; at least they can provide part of the foundation knowledge to increase the worker's effectiveness during the interview.

A good deal of the underpinning for the application of behavioral principles in the interview process comes from research on verbal conditioning. (For summaries of this work, see Kanfer & Phillips, 1970; Kanfer, 1968; Krasner, 1968.) To summarize this material briefly, there is clear evidence that interviewers, first, *can* influence the verbal (and other) behavior of interviewees during interviews; and second, that interviewers, even of the presumed most "non-directive" sort *do* influence the verbal behavior of interviewees during interviews (Truax, 1966). This influence appears to occur in large measure through the employment of positive and differential reinforcement, operant and respondent extinction, modeling, and punishment, all of which are communicated both verbally and nonverbally (gestures, grimaces, etc.) by the interviewer.

The point of all this is that, if such processes are indeed occurring in interviews anyhow, would not the most logical and helpful (to the client) conclusion be that they should be used intentionally to achieve optimal positive effects? Some of this material has been covered in a slightly different context in the preceding section on the conditions of empathy, warmth, and genuineness. The following discussion is intended only to highlight and make more explicit the behavioral principles involved.

The first and perhaps most obvious use of behavior modification in interviewing is the use of positive reinforcement to increase desired behaviors. In this instance, the positive reinforcement is largely social reinforcement, i.e., the social worker's praise, attention, interest, and encouragement. Such social reinforcement can be used to help the client speak and to increase his verbalizations if need be; to strengthen positive self-references, thereby increasing the client's favorable beliefs about himself; to encourage and reinforce change efforts by the client, including both verbalizations about efforts ("I think I might try that next week.") and the efforts themselves; and so on. Social reinforcement can be used in a variety of ways—from simple nods of the head to "mm hmm" to smiles and enthusiastic, genuine praise. And both in-interview and outside-of-interview behavior can be changed by the consistent and intentional use by the social worker of positive reinforcement for desired behaviors.

Another use of behavioral knowledge in interviewing is in the application of operant extinction, i.e., the withdrawal of positive reinforcement that is (or may be) maintaining certain behaviors. The potency of the social worker's attention in maintaining the client's verbalizations is well-established (Kanfer, 1968; Krasner, 1967). But there are several instances where the worker might want to decrease undesired behavior that his attention may have been maintaining. When the client is expressing excessive and inappropriate discouragement, depressive thoughts and feelings, inappropriate or potentially harmful aggressive thoughts, irrational thoughts (e.g., delusions, rambling, "word salad," etc.) the social worker, by withdrawing his attention, might attempt to decrease these. Of course, the key, and this may involve a rather fine line, deals with the "appropriateness" of the behavior—a difficult judgment at best. The point is not that the worker just sits and ignores the client whenever a given class of behaviors appears. Rather, the worker has to discriminate between those occasions when increased attention (e.g., to the constant reiteration by the client of depressed feelings) can prove dysfunctional to the client, increasing rather than decreasing the severity of the problem.

Actually, extinction is best used in combination with positive reinforcement in the form of differential reinforcement. Thus, the worker would selectively pay attention to adaptive, positive behaviors, and selectively ignore (when it appears as though continued attention will be harmful) undesired behaviors.

Another example of the application of behavior modification in interviews is in the use of modeling procedures. The social worker endeavors, through his own personal conduct, to provide a model for desired behaviors for the client. This might be done through the social worker's expression of empathy and warmth for the problems of others, or in his acceptance of hostility when under attack. For example, working with parents, a social worker might demonstrate how to deal with a variety of situations by his own behavior in dealing with the children. Furthermore, by his own example, he might function as a problem-solving model, demonstrating how he approaches a problem, considers alternatives, and moves toward a solution. Again, all of this is done with the knowledge that the clients are carefully observing, and with the explicit intention that they engage in similar behavior.

The social worker might function in a way that promotes a decrease in anxiety through respondent extinction. When the client discusses behavior that has previously brought undesirable consequences and hence promoted anxiety, the social worker very specifically acts as a nonpunitive audience. The worker does not make judgments about, criticize, or disapprove of, the client's behavior, but, instead, encourages the client to talk about it in an atmosphere of warmth, acceptance, and understanding. This, of course, is probably in contrast to many of the responses the client has received (or perceives himself to have received) from other listeners.

As the client gradually feels freer to speak, and does indeed speak of the anxiety-producing behavior or situation, the anxiety decreases through a process of respondent extinction. This is because, in the first place, the client is no longer avoiding the subject or the behavior (avoidance which may have maintained it previously); and second, because the behavior (the conditioned response) is permitted (even encouraged) to occur in a warm, accepting atmosphere, away from, and without any further pairing with, the unconditioned stimulus (see Chapter 2). Hence, with repeated discussion, the behavior might gradually begin to diminish and eventually cease to occur.

A final example of the way behavioral principles might be used in interviewing is in discrimination training. The client might begin to learn to perceive the environment differently. For example, the client can be taught to discriminate between responses realistically related to his present situation (e.g., relations with adults and peers) and those related to the past (e.g., relations with parents). He might also learn through discussions with his social worker to discriminate real from artificial dangers. The client might learn to discriminate among a variety of stimulus conditions leading to a problematic response, perhaps with the social worker supplementing from his own experiences those probable contingencies between stimulus dimensions and responses that are appropriate for the situation (Kanfer & Phillips, 1970). And finally, through prompting and reinforcement from the social worker, the client might learn to view his milieu differently, once the behaviors that are already in his repertoire are connected to realistic discriminations.

In sum, the purpose of this section has been only to highlight a few of the many potential uses of behavioral principles in the interview situation. The intent is not to make the interview the only focus for behavioral intervention or an end in itself. But the intent is to clarify and optimize the way behavioral principles and procedures can be used to facilitate one form of communicative process that, in turn, can facilitate the implementation of a range of other specific behavioral techniques.

Applications in Groups

Behavior modification principles most often have been applied with individual clients or families, one at a time. Only recently has the potential of using groups and group processes to bring about behavioral change begun to be fully explored. Already, however, behavioral approaches are being used in a wide variety of situations. For example, Paul and Shannon (1968) have used systematic desensitization in groups to treat anxiety; Miller and Miller (1970) reinforced self-help group activities of welfare recipients; Hedquist and Weinhold (1970) used group approaches to increase the assertiveness of chronically anxious college students; Rose (1974) helped parents of disturbed children to modify their own and their children's behavior through a group experience; Lawrence and Sundel (1974) used short-term, small-group approaches for such adult problems as child management, anxiety, marital discord, depression and interpersonal difficulties with friends, family and co-workers.

Group procedures which have been effective with children have been reported by a number of authors. Barrish, Sanders and Wolf (1969), for example, developed a "good behavior game" for children exhibiting disruptive behavior in the classroom, and Sulzbacker and Houser (1968) and Packard (1970) used group contingencies to reduce disruptive and inattentive classroom behaviors (other examples of the use of group approaches to various problems are presented in Part 3 of this book).

The application of behavior modification in groups is built upon substantial research regarding the impact of behavior modification on individuals in group settings (Fo & Robinson, 1972). Shapiro and Beck (1967) showed that the behavior of group members who monopolized group attention, avoided expressions of anger or distanced themselves from group interaction could be modified through programmed use of the group leader's attention and approval. Heckel, Wiggins and Salzberg (1962) were able to eliminate nonproductive silences in groups through negative reinforcement. Several studies have demonstrated that the group leader's use of operant conditioning methods can increase group members' verbalizations leading to desirable group outcomes. Liberman (1969, 1970 a & b) found that the group leaders can have considerable deliberate impact in shaping, modifying and eliciting verbal behavior from group members leading to greater group cohesiveness. Further, the group leader can successfully reinforce desirable group independence from the leader.

Such procedures can be of use to leaders of any therapeutic group. Indeed, many behavior modification-oriented groups share a number of concepts with other treatment groups, such as an emphasis on group cohesion and reinforcement of individuals within the group. However, despite the diversity of groups utilizing behavior modification, there is much that is characteristic of the roles of the group leader and group member in groups with a behavior modification orientation as described by such authors as Frankel and Glasser (1974), Fo and Robinson (1972),

Rose (1972, 1974), Lawrence and Sundel (1974), and Liberman (1972). A few of the basic similarities are described below.

THE GROUP LEADER

Behaviorally oriented groups tend to be highly structured. "Spontaneous and free-flowing group process and interaction are discouraged and the therapist takes a more task-oriented educational role with his group" (Liberman, 1972, p. 149). The group leader, therefore, takes the major role in planning and implementing the group process and deciding on the general content of group activity. The group leader assumes the responsibility of a teacher with his group, explaining the behavioral approach, and seeing the group through the stages of pinpointing problem behaviors and modifying them.

THE GROUP MEMBERS

Unlike other treatment groups, the members of the group do not generally take responsibility for the direction the group takes—at least until they have gained some mastery of behavioral approaches. As in individual treatment using behavior modification, each member of the group generally focuses on a specific problem behavior which will hopefully be changed as a result of the group process. The problem is clearly identified and pinpointed either before the members enter the group or as a result of group discussions. The desired outcome of group participation for each member is specified in behavioral terms rather than in terms of general personality change or enhanced self-awareness.

GROUP CONTINGENCIES

Group contingencies can significantly affect the behaviors of individuals in groups. The procedure, in general, involves withholding specific reinforcements from all group members until one or more group members complete certain identified tasks. Since the reinforcement of all group members is contingent upon the behavior of individual members, they can generally be expected to reinforce positively the desired behavior through praise, affection, and greater inclusion in the group and reinforce it negatively through verbal and perhaps physical hostility and possible rejection from the group.

There are several hazards, however, in using group contingencies. For example, in an open setting, if the pressure to perform the assigned task becomes too great, a group member may simply elect to leave the group. If the group member finds the task impossible to complete, or the pressure too great, he may find it more reinforcing to undermine the plan and thus punish the group. Frankel and Glasser (1974) suggest three alternative methods of overcoming these problems: 1) set individual contingencies for each group member appropriate to his ability to perform the assigned task; 2) provide group contingencies that will allow for reinforcements to be given out even if not all group members complete their assigned tasks. "Bonus" reinforcements can be provided when additional members complete their tasks; or 3) start at a level of task assignments which all members should be able to complete with little difficulty and build up expectations as tasks are successfully completed.

THE SETTING

The group setting provides the social worker with powerful tools in implementing a behavioral change strategy with his clients. It offers group members the opportunity to model after other members who are successfully engaging in changing behaviors similar to theirs. For example, in a group of fathers of retarded adolescents, one father might model another father's disciplinary procedures. In fact, it is likely that the group leader would structure role playing exercises to facilitate that modeling.

Once a group achieves cohesion, or ". . . intermember behaviors which reflect mutual interest, concern, empathy, affection, support, assistance and acceptance . . ." (Fo & Robinson, 1972, p. 4), it takes on powerful social reinforcement potential for group members. This potential can be used to reinforce reported or observed steps taken by group members to change their problem behaviors. While such reinforcement usually occurs as a regular part of group sessions, group reinforcement can also occur between sessions. Rose (1969), for example, reported that he encouraged group members to remind each other outside of group sessions to carry out behavioral assignments, and Packard (1970) described a buddy-system extension of a group in which a more assertive group member accompanied a less assertive group member to coach and reinforce him in carrying out a group assignment.

In most respects, behavioral principles of assessment and intervention in groups are similar to those that will be described for interventions with individuals in the succeeding chapters. Those procedures which are unique in the application of behavior modification in groups, particularly in the areas of selection of members for groups, group assessment, group problem solving, group norms, and group process have been described in detail by Lawrence and Sundel (1972), Frankel and Glasser (1974), and Rose (1972).

As in making any other clinical choice, the decision to modify a particular problem through a group or individual approach will depend on the nature of the problem, as well as available resources. It can be expected, however, that a greater variety of problems will be treated in the future through the potent combination of behavior modification and group influence.

Applications in Consultation

Since behavior modification provides a body of knowledge which is easily understood and readily translated into intervention, it is well suited to consultation, an increasingly important function of a wide range of social work agencies. Further, the principles of behavior modification provide direction for, and understanding of, the consultation process itself.

Depending on the needs and requests presented by the consultee, the social worker familiar with behavior modification can be helpful in four ways:

1. by providing basic information about how behavior is learned, and how it can be changed;
2. by helping the consultee consider how these basic concepts can be applied to understanding common learning experiences which tend to affect the behavior of those client groups with which the consultee works, such as particular age and cultural groups, sub-cultures and institutional populations (e.g., oppressed minorities, adoptive parents, the aged, institutional offenders, etc.);
3. by considering how this knowledge can be related to developing assessment procedures and options for interventive strategies and programs in a particular setting (e.g., prison, home for the aged, school for the retarded) in which the consultee is working;
4. by applying behavior modification assessment and interventive strategies and techniques to specific problems or cases that consultees are confronting in their practice.

An increasing body of knowledge on the consultation process is being developed and is available for use by social workers (e.g., Caplan, 1970). Obviously, prior to the beginning of consultation, the consultant should thoroughly familiarize himself with the specific agency's organization, formal and informal structure, and problems. In terms of the specific use of behavior modification, the consultant should try to create a relationship with the consultee(s) which will positively reinforce the consultee's efforts to learn, evaluate, and subsequently utilize the ideas emanating from the consultations. Such a relationship will enable the consultee to objectively evaluate the extent to which the practices and/or personnel in the consultee's organization, and perhaps the consultee himself, may, in some measure, be sustaining and even reinforcing the very behaviors the consultee wishes to alter. The social worker may facilitate such explorations by helping the consultee develop objective observation and reporting procedures which will systematically record not only the pinpointed target behaviors, but antecedent and consequent events as well. Using such objective procedures introduced by the consultee reduces the aura of subjective blame or guilt associated with the problems.

Based on these procedures, the social worker/consultant can explore with the consultee alternative interventive strategies that might be applicable given the nature of the problem, the setting in which the problems occur, the capacities of those available to plan and mediate interventions and the presence of other resources which may be required for various interventive strategies. The social worker may then inform the consultee of procedures used successfully in situations similar to that encountered by the consultee, or may help the consultee think through innovative uses of the available resources for particular interventions where there is no known precedent. The social worker/consultant may help the consultee evaluate whether referral is preferable, and if so, explore the options available for referral.

If the consultee is to proceed with intervention, the social work consultant may offer assistance, by role playing or modeling some of the suggested interventive procedures, and, perhaps, do some of the direct intervention with the consultee or other potential mediators observing. The consultant then follows through as any subsequent problems emerge during intervention.

Throughout the process of consultation, the social worker must evaluate the effect of the consultation process on the behavior of the consultee. Certainly the consultations themselves should not be allowed to become aversive to consultees by overwhelming them, or making them feel incompetent. The consultee should be helped to approach the consultation with neither unrealistic expectations nor fear of embarrassment.

Going along with consultees or agencies step by step without expecting them to take on more than they can handle at any point can avoid failure and consequent discouragement (along with a wholesale rejection of the behavior modification approach), and increases the chances of success and the positive reinforcement of change efforts.

The consultee's attempts to carry out plans derived from consultation are further reinforced by the awareness that the social work consultant understands and appreciates the consultee's goals, problems and limitations, and offers help in overcoming realistic obstacles which may impede an interventive plan. Another source of reinforcement is the consultant's enthusiasm and praise as positive results of intervention begin to appear. On the other hand, the consultant can help consultees anticipate and respond constructively to failures, recognizing the resulting frustrations, anger, and, occasionally, guilt as well as evaluating the possible sources of failure and planning a revised approach. And, of course, the consultant should always be available for follow-up, to provide additional consultation or simply positive reinforcement for obtained results.

Behavior modification, in essence, offers a variety of important factors that can be helpful in consultation:

1. by facilitating functioning in the role of consultant;
2. by providing a specific body of knowledge as the topic of consultation;
3. by enhancing the consultation process, per se.

Thus, professional social workers may find not only that they, as consultees, may benefit from such consultation, but that, functioning as *consultants,* they can greatly increase their own efficiency in providing services to others by consulting both with other social workers, and with a wide range of nonprofessionals and people in the natural environment.

Summary

This chapter consists of an introduction to the practice of behavior modification. The goals of behavior modification were explained both in terms of self-actualization and in terms of specifying for each person what behaviors he will be engaging in when he is self-actualized. The role of cognition and insight in behavior modification was explored with the conclusion that insight may be a helpful, but usually not a necessary or sufficient, condition for achieving change in overt behavior. The context of behavior modification—the helping relationship—was described as the core conditions of empathy, warmth and genuineness. It was pointed out that these personal qualities of the social worker should be inextricably interwoven with his or her techniques. Finally, some of the ways behavior modification principles can be used in the interview situation, in groups and in consultation were described.

CHAPTER 9. Working with Mediators

Behavior modification operates primarily though the alteration of contingencies in the client's environment so as to increase desirable behavior and decrease undesirable behavior. Such contingencies must generally be closely associated in time with the target behavior. In applying the basic concepts of behavior modification, the social worker chooses the most effective reinforcers available that might override competing reinforcers in the client's environment. Often, the client himself is able to manipulate the contingencies of his behavior so that, with the help of the social worker (and sometimes without), he can modify his own behavior.

There are situations in which the social worker himself has access to powerful enough reinforcers so that he can directly modify the client's behavior either in his office or in the client's natural environment. Generally, however, the most powerful reinforcers are possessed and manipulated by other people in the client's world. Such reinforcers are often preferable to any that the social worker might have to offer in his office for several reasons:

1. They may be administered immediately after the desired behavior occurs in the natural setting of the behavior.
2. They may be administered by people who are significant to the client and who can pair the provision of tangible reinforcements with their own social reinforcements.
3. With few exceptions, there is little that the social worker can offer his client that exceeds the potential power of reinforcements that exist in the client's natural environment.
4. Using a significant person in the client's natural environment may counteract faulty reinforcements (or lack of reinforcements) provided by others in the environment; it may even improve the significant other's own behavior toward the client. For example, Mrs. Loo would nag her daughter to clean her room, but usually ignored her when she followed through on her chores. After intervention, Mrs. Loo discontinued nagging, but played canasta with

her daughter each night, an activity much-enjoyed by both of them, contingent on the daughter's cleaning up her room.

5. Behavior which is modified in the natural environment tends to be "naturalized" more easily than behavior altered in an artificial environment such as an agency office. For instance, a child who is reinforced for focusing on, and solving, arithmetic problems in the classroom, with the attendant distractions and other stimuli typical of such a setting, will have an easier time continuing this new behavior in the classroom than a child who learns such behavior in an isolated, quiet office.

Given the value, then, of the modification of the behavior of clients in their own home, work, or social environment, it becomes clear that the social worker must have an agent working on his behalf in that environment. Such an agent is called a mediator.

Working with mediators allows the social worker to spread his or her services geometrically to a far larger number of people who have problems than would otherwise be possible. Apart from being able to work with several individuals simultaneously, each mediator can, through his training and experiences with the social worker, learn to apply behavior modification with subsequent clients (or himself) with decreasing social work supervision. The social worker can teach potential mediators not only the principles and procedures to deal with specific problems, but also an entirely new perspective on changing behavior.

It becomes the mediator's task, working in cooperation with the social worker, to carry out an intervention plan in the client's natural environment. This generally entails, first, the observation of the client's behavior and the events which seem to affect it; second, the modification of antecedent events which might lead to the undesired behavior; and third, the provision or withdrawal of certain reinforcers to the client contingent on the performance of the specified desired behavior. It may also be the mediator's task to keep records of the client's behavior before and after the intervention. The social worker's function in relation to the mediator is to:

1. select an appropriate mediator;
2. develop assessment and treatment strategies with the mediator;
3. motivate the mediator to carry out his tasks;
4. educate the mediator about the basic concepts and processes of behavior modification and how they apply to the specific target behaviors;
5. anticipate and work with the stress that may be associated with being a mediator;
6. reinforce the mediator for performing his role;
7. help the mediator in the process of naturalizing the new behavior.

Each of these functions will be described in the following sections.

Selecting the Mediator

It is likely that the client comes into daily contact with a number of significant people who may have influence over the client's behavior. These potential mediators may include parents, spouses, employers, friends, co-workers, teachers, classmates, nurses, ward technicians, siblings, fellow group members, fellow patients, volunteers, and so on.

To select more than one or two of these people to act as mediators would be organizationally cumbersome and likely to cause confusion. Therefore, how does the social worker go about selecting a particular mediator?

Such a decision is based on the evaluation of the possible candidates on a number of criteria:

1. *Is the candidate nearby when the target behavior is most likely to occur?* If the specific behavior to be increased is affectionate behavior by a wife, for example, the most likely candidate for mediator is obviously the husband. If the specific behavior to be reduced is disruptive behavior in a classroom, the most likely candidate may be the teacher.

2. *Does the candidate have access to significant reinforcers?* The mediator should have at his disposal, or have easy access to, effective reinforcers. In the case of social reinforcement, the candidate, by the very nature of his relationship with the client, may be a powerful reinforcer. In children's institutions, for example, cooks are often perceived with affection and, thus, endowed with considerable potential reinforcing power. Sometimes a cookie and a big hug given for a specified desired behavior may go a long way in an intervention plan.

4. *If aversive stimuli are to be presented to the client, it must be determined that the mediator can bring himself to participate in such a plan.* Conversely, if the mediator is generally angry at the client, it should be determined whether the mediator can participate in the plan without displaying anger or vengeance.

5. *Will the candidate find the client's new behavior reinforcing?* Mutual reinforcement for a client and mediator as a result of the changed behavior of the client enhances the probability of a successful outcome. Mediators whose only reinforcement would come from feeling they are doing a worthwhile job, or from being praised by the social worker, are less preferable than mediators who would obtain genuine intrinsic and extrinsic reinforcements from the client's new behavior.

6. *Is the candidate willing to work with the plan jointly agreed upon with the social worker?* This can be determined by going over the general concepts of behavior modification and the various roles of the partici-

pants in the program, and eliciting the candidate's reaction to working with the social worker on the intervention. The social worker should be sensitive to the reaction of the candidate to both the clients and the intervention plan. Is he willing, and does his situation permit him, to establish reinforcements on contingency? It may be essential to elicit and discuss any hesitation and provide the information and support necessary to evaluate the candidate's potential level of cooperation and motivation.

There are situations in which no one in the client's environment clearly satisfies all these criteria. It then becomes necessary for the social worker to choose the candidate who comes closest and, using behavior modification concepts, attempt to enhance his potential to be an effective change agent.

Developing Assessment and Treatment Strategies with the Mediator

The mediator's role is usually broader than simply providing contingencies for target behaviors. In early interviews with the mediators, the social worker can gather information for an assessment of the problem behaviors, and develop strategies for changing them. Generally, such comprehensive explorations with the mediator occur before any planned intervention with the client is begun.

Effective interventions depend on the social worker's acquisition of sufficient accurate information about the target behavior and the environmental circumstances that affect it. The individuals the social worker has selected as mediators (by reason of their proximity and familiarity with the client and his environment) should be in a position to provide a substantial amount of this information. The client's, mediator's, and even social worker's impatience to get on with the intervention should not push the social worker into premature, and perhaps misdirected, interventions before all the relevant and necessary observations have been made, reported, and integrated into an intervention plan.

In acquiring this information, the social worker may want to follow a series of steps that not only lead to an understanding of the problem, but also contribute to effective decision-making about the procedures to be used in modifying problem behaviors. The following nine-point outline is based on a guide for interviews with parents whose children were experiencing a variety of problems (Holland, 1970); it is equally applicable to work with other mediators such as school teachers, spouses, nurses, and ward attendants when the mediator is also the person identifying the target behavior. Like most outlines used in connection with therapeutic interventions, this one should be used as flexibly as particular situations demand.

1. *Have the mediators indicate their general goals and complaints about the client's behavior.* This initial step may be the easiest, since mediators are usually quickly able to say what they see as the problem and what they would like to see changed. The social worker's function in this step may be largely one of clarifying the mediator's specific expectations about the client. Often the mediator has only a vague idea of what he does not like about the client's behavior. A common problem in such situations is that the mediator has never been clear himself, or made clear to the client, exactly which behavior he would like changed. Clarification of the problem behaviors with the mediator may well facilitate subsequent clarification with the client. This, in turn, may lead to significant improvements in behavior before any other interventions are initiated.

2. *Help the mediators list the specific behaviors which they would like to see either increased or decreased in frequency.* In this step, the mediators move from their general complaints and wishes about the client's behavior to listing and ranking a number (five to ten) of specific behaviors they wished would increase, and a similar number of specific behaviors they wished would decrease. This information provides a basis for setting priorities in interventions.

3. *Have the mediators select a particular target behavior from the list to which they wish to give major attention.* Generally the behavior chosen is the one that is most aversive to the mediators, or the most dangerous for the clients, or both. Focusing on a particular problem tends to eliminate the diffusion of attention and the feelings of futility that often plague parents, ward personnel, and teachers. By focusing on a particular problem rather than on a multitude of problems, the mediator is able to focus his or her efforts and feel somewhat more comfortable about giving up the responsibility of trying to cope with the other problems. Such a process of concentration increases the chances that the mediators will meet with some success, giving them more confidence in both their social workers' and their own abilities.

4. *Help the mediators present a clear behavioral description of the specific behavior they want to change.* This step may lead to the presentation of baseline data on a chart for the behavior (see Chapter 10). Focusing on the observable manifestations may lead the mediators to alter their perceptions of the problem; it may even change the incidence of the undesired behavior.

5. *Help the mediators present a clear behavioral description of the terminal behavior they are hoping for.* The mediators should be helped not only to describe clearly and specifically what they feel is the "wrong" behavior, but they should also be helped to explicate what they think

would be right. Once the social worker, client, and mediators are clear about what the "A" of the situation is (what the behavior is now), and the "Z" of what they would like it to be (the terminal behavior), then it becomes easier to determine the intervening steps.

6. *Plan with the mediators the intervening steps between the present behavior and the terminal goal.* When the mediators and social worker are clear where the current behavior is ("A") and what behavior they are working toward ("Z") the task becomes one of determining the intervening steps, with special emphasis on the first step ("B"). The social worker recognizes the desire of the mediator and perhaps the client to move immediately to "Z." This might prove disastrous: whereas success can reinforce, failure can extinguish. The terminal behavior may be beyond the behavioral skills of the client, or might even be initially aversive to him. Careful selection of the initial steps in the intervention increases the chances of success and may also reveal skills of the client which had been previously overlooked by those in his environment.

7. *Help the mediators list stimuli which they believe would act as reinforcers for target behaviors.* Preparing such a list could help the social worker considerably in developing a treatment plan. However, except for obvious items (such as sweets, movies, staying up late for children), it may be difficult for mediators to identify accurately what is potentially reinforcing for the client. They may overestimate the reinforcing power of such socially acceptable items as praise and material objects, and overlook more potent reinforcers such as privacy, or the freedom to be different. While the choice of actual reinforcers may depend on more objective procedures (such as observing the client's behavior), the process of exploring the mediator's perceptions of potential reinforcements may be useful in assessing the environmental resources available to the mediators, and in helping the mediators understand the client's behavior.

8. *Explore what possible deprivations of the client are possible.* The potency of any reinforcer depends, in part, on the client's either being deprived of, or satiated with, the reinforcer. The noncontingent presentation of any reinforcer will, in time, reduce its effectiveness. It may be necessary to deprive the client of a particular reinforcer except as a reinforcement for the target behavior. This might even include expressions of praise or admiration not contingent on goal-directed behavior. Mediators, particularly parents, may take exception to the use of deprivation, especially of such basics as affection and praise, even when the indiscriminate use of such reinforcements may be doing more harm than good.

The mediators may accept the use of deprivation more readily if they understand that it can ultimately bring the client more positive reinforcement—not only from the mediators, but from others as well—as a result of his changed behavior. Also, the mediators might consider that the target is already deprived of many things which he may want, not only as a result of any dysfunctional behavior but as one of the realities of his circumstances. Few of us have everything we want. But behavior modification involves attempting to help the client get what he wants as a result of changing his behavior.

9. *Clarify what the mediators are willing to do in order to modify the target behavior.* Mediators, particularly parents, are often primarily concerned with decreasing behaviors they consider aversive. The social worker may help the mediators change their goal to the more effective strategy of *increasing* behaviors which are opposite to, and incompatible with, the undesirable behaviors. The social worker then explores with the mediators their willingness to start providing the particular positive reinforcement required to change the client's behavior in the desired direction.

Motivating the Mediator

The social worker must apply many of the same principles to the mediator that he expects the mediator to apply with the client. That is, the mediator's work in cooperation with the social worker must be maximally reinforcing, and minimally aversive. The social worker lays the groundwork for a satisfying working relationship with the mediator.

In institutional settings, this groundwork may have been laid a considerable time before a particular intervention begins. All too often there is a split in such settings between those on the "firing line"—that is, house parents, teachers, and guards—and those who "sit in their offices" and have "nothing but book learning"—administrators, social workers, and consultants. Often the direct contact personnel (who may be excellent candidates for being mediators) see working with the social worker or other professionals as aversive. They may see social workers consistently "putting them down," showing them little respect, indicating little concern for, or interest in, their problems in carrying out *their* jobs or even their perceptions of the problems around them. Indeed, they may view the entire counseling staff as disruptive to the work of the school, prison, or institution. In this environment of mutual lack of respect, of distrust and disharmony, it is unlikely that the social worker would find many willing candidates for his behavior modification "schemes." Also, if such an environment prevails, any plan may be sabotaged.

Conversely, if there has been a history of cooperation, mutual consideration, respect, trust, and even reinforcing social contact, there is a much greater chance that the social worker will gain the cooperation and commitment of the direct service staff. Once there is a history of such interventions proving successful, cooperation will be perceived as more reinforcing by potential mediators—especially if there is a reduction in the dysfunctional and disruptive behavior of the clients, who are part of the daily environment of the direct contact personnel.

Whenever possible, the social worker should involve the mediator in assessment and the development of the intervention plan. Such a procedure enables the social worker to make full use of the mediator's first-hand knowledge and observations. Furthermore, being a full participant in intervention planning tends to increase motivation in following through with the intervention.

It is possible to enhance cooperation by giving priority to those problem behaviors which have most immediate consequences for the mediator. For example, if the mediator is a teacher, decreasing disruptive classroom behavior may be an early goal; if the mediator is an overworked mother, completion of house-cleaning chores by a child might be the first goal. If the mediator is a friend, keeping appointments on time may be a logical choice.

In addition, it is important for the mediator, as it is for the client, to choose relatively tractable—but annoying—behaviors that are likely to be successfully changed as the first steps in intervention. While these initial changes may not be of major consequence in themselves, the effects of success reinforces and motivates both client and mediator to attempt additional, perhaps more difficult, goals and strategies.

Certainly the core conditions of basic warmth, empathy, and genuineness should be displayed by the social worker to the mediator. His awareness of the difficulty of the mediator's tasks must be conveyed along with suggestions and procedures for reducing the stress. Finally the social worker must communicate his appreciation and praise for the mediator's efforts, and, if possible, provide reinforcements for the mediator for his help. Such simple courtesies as having coffee with the mediator, patting him on the back and praising him on the success of his intervention, and carefully going over charts he may have filled out further reinforce the mediator's participation in the intervention plan. In giving this support, the social worker must avoid seeming patronizing.

The social worker must also be aware that the mediator (who is attempting to modify the target behavior) is in turn under the influence of others in his environment, who may be either supporting or punishing the mediator's efforts. For example, Mr. Orren and his five-year-old daughter, Laurie, resented the amount of time Mrs. Orren was spending carrying out an intervention plan to reinforce the socially appropriate behavior of her seven-year-old daughter, Robin, who had been attacking her sister and had been generally destructive in their home. The social worker empathized with the pressure Mrs. Orren felt to give "equal attention to all the members of her family." The husband was subsequently instructed by his wife in record-keeping activities, and given the task of reinforcing certain behaviors of the younger child and organizing a weekly Saturday morning excursion for the whole family. It was also agreed that each evening, after both children were in bed, Mr. and Mrs. Orren would spend half an hour relaxing with each other over a much-enjoyed glass of beer. The social worker thus attempted to have the sum total of the reinforcements for the mediator's efforts on behalf of the client exceed any possible aversive elements.

Teaching the Mediator

Not only must the mediators be motivated to work cooperatively with the social worker, but they must also be familiar with the basic underlying concepts and principles of behavior modification. Such knowledge facilitates their active participation in the intervention program. The mediator is in a position, once he understands the intervention strategy, to gather information about the availability of reinforcers, the nature of the client's response patterns, and the client's typical activities, all of which aid in developing the intervention plan. Also, it is likely that the mediator will feel much more inclined to work with the social worker if he feels he is part of a team, and not merely a convenient extension of the social worker.

The education of the mediator can be provided either individually or in small groups of mediators working on similar problems (for example, a group of fathers of adolescent delinquents, or ward technicians in a state hospital). Groups offer the advantages of efficient use of the social worker's time, the mutual sharing of the experiences and ideas of the group members, the mutual social reinforcements once intervention strategies begin to succeed, and encouragement when some fail.

Programs can be developed to train individuals not usually viewed as potentially effective mediators. For example, Weinrott (1974) has described a program based in a behaviorally-oriented educational camp for retarded children in which eighteen siblings of retarded children were trained as mediators of their own siblings' behavior. The children were taught basic learning theory, and given the opportunity to observe the application of operant procedures. They were also supervised in applying some of the procedures themselves. For example, they learned how to "employ tokens, checkmarks, timers, and other devices as means of building attention, task completion, and more appropriate social behaviors" (p. 369). The siblings were videotaped while they were interacting with their brothers and sisters. The videotapes were then reviewed with them to illustrate learning concepts and offer constructive criticism.

The training program enabled many of the siblings to learn how to ignore some undesired behaviors of their brothers and sisters. Since ignoring (thus helping to extinguish) such behavior is an "unnatural" response, learning the procedure was found very worthwhile and productive. When parents were contacted two months after the training program, they reported that the sibling training had been quite useful. "With only one exception, siblings were noted to have moderately or vastly improved the 'quality' of their interaction with the retardate" (p. 372).

The social worker's educational activities have several major goals: to introduce the mediator to behavior-specific observation and understanding, to help the mediator reinforce, punish, or extinguish behavior contingently, and to teach the mediator to record behavior when indicated.

The mediator is taught how to provide punishment or reinforcement. The social worker should emphasize certain cardinal principles which might even be written and given to the mediator. Such principles might provide the framework for a contract between the mediator and social worker that explicates mutual expectations. The directions must be succinct: the social worker should choose carefully what concepts to convey in order not to overwhelm the mediator by their cumbersomeness. They should be limited in number and be given in clear, simple language. The reasoning behind each step in the process should be clearly understood. For instance, a parent may be helped to modify his child's behavior more effectively if he is given the following instructions and rationale by the social worker:

1. Check Ben's chart *immediately* after he does each of the specific chores assigned to him: taking out the garbage, making his bed, and clearing the table. Immediacy is important: not only does it avoid forgetting, but it connects the ultimate reward with the activity, and makes doing appropriate things immediately rewarding.
2. Praise him at the same time you are checking his chart (*eventually* we will stop using the chart, and your praise will be enough to reinforce the behavior).
3. Do not record other activities on the chart besides the three mentioned, or fail to check the chart because he has displeased you in some other way. (It confuses what we are trying to do, and might sabotage the overall plan.)
4. If Ben refuses to carry out these activities, or at any point shouts, kicks his sister, or is destructive, instruct him quietly to go to his room for a period of exactly five minutes. Do this calmly, without expressing anger or depreciation. If he does not go voluntarily, you can physically carry him to his room.

5. Remember, these are only first steps, but even the longest trip starts out with a single step!

Since the mediator is often the person who originally asked for a program that would help with some problem, he can often become an active participant in defining the problem as well as in setting up the situations in which intervention will occur. Significant decisions about intervention strategies can result from discussions between the social worker and mediator on several of the following eleven aspects of the management of the target behaviors, as suggested by Holland (1970):

1. *In which situations should the desired behavior occur?* The mediators can identify the discriminative stimuli that might lead to desired behavior, and then attempt to present these stimuli in the expectation that the desired behavior will occur, and subsequently be reinforced. In a psychiatric ward, for instance, ward meetings or certain games may serve as discriminative stimuli for desirable social interaction. A light bedtime snack may be a pleasant discriminative stimulus for a child going to bed.

2. *In which situations are the undesired behaviors apt to occur?* The mediator explores the nature of the discriminative stimuli that provide cues for the client to exhibit undesired behavior. On the basis of this information, the mediator can attempt to either remove the stimuli or have the client avoid them. For example, a couple observes that they almost always have a fight after visiting a particular relative's home; an ex-prisoner notes that he always ends up drunk and frequently in trouble when he visits friends at a particular bar; a woman notes she always eats too much at restaurants but rarely at home. The reduction of exposure to such stimuli can reduce the probability of occurrence of the undesirable behavior.

3. *Choose a situation that would increase the likelihood that some part or aspect of the desired behavior will occur.* Almost every person displays at least some part of the desired behavior somewhere, sometime. The mediator may be aware of the circumstances under which the client already exhibits such behavior. The truant child may sometimes go to some classes; the unresponsive husband may sometimes respond; an apathetic young adult may sometimes seek work; fighting siblings will sometimes play together. The social worker and mediators should actively respond to those opportunities for providing reinforcement, so that the likelihood of recurrence of the desired behavior is strengthened. Careful observation by the mediators may reveal attributes of situations that may have contributed to positive behavior so that, if possible, they can be repeated.

4. *Explore with mediators the use of immediate positive reinforcement contingent on desired behavior to increase such behavior.* The me-

diators' effectiveness in using this core behavior modification procedure depends on several variables: their willingness and ability to apply reinforcement immediately after each occurrence of the target behavior; their access to effective primary reinforcers; their creativity in using secondary reinforcers. Often the mediators must learn how to pair the presentation of tangible reinforcements with verbal and nonverbal social reinforcers such as genuine praise and smiles. Ultimately, the mediators are helped to fade out tangible reinforcers and focus on the more natural social reinforcers that exist in the client's real world.

5. *Explore with mediators how they might increase desired behavior by removing negative reinforcers immediately after the occurrence of such behavior.* While positive reinforcement is usually more widely applicable, negative reinforcement might be preferred by the mediators in some situations. For instance, the client can be relieved of some unwanted chore or responsibility contingent on his performance of some other, more useful, task, such as a husband taking over some of the housekeeping chores to encourage his wife to spend more time playing with the children.

6. *Explore with mediators the procedures that might be used to decrease unwanted behaviors.* While increasing desired behavior is usually more effective with the majority of problems than decreasing undesired behavior, the social worker may want to review with the mediators procedures for decreasing behaviors. Both should keep in mind the tendency of mediators to focus on behaviors they want to stop, rather than on the behaviors they may want to increase, and the hazards involved in such tendencies.

7. *Help the mediators determine the timing of reinforcement schedules.* Explain the necessity of continuous reinforcement until the new behavior becomes established and the desirability, then, of moving to an intermittent schedule. The social worker may be able to provide specific rules to guide this transition, or may simply be able to guide its timing. Mediators should be urged to prepare their targets for the eventual shift from continuous to intermittent reinforcement.

8. *Encourage creativity and spontaneity on the part of the mediators in administering their program.* The mediators generally know their own and the client's situation better than the social worker. If they can combine this familiarity with the skills and guidance provided by the social worker, they can be most effective. Latitude may be provided in terms of the choices of reinforcements used (to avoid satiation), and the nature of the social reinforcement to be provided concurrently.

9. *Explore how the mediators may modify two or more behaviors simultaneously.* Often, mediators will be working on more than one target behavior of one or more individuals at any particular time. Typically, if the mediator is trying to reduce an undesirable behavior, he will, at the same time, be trying to increase one or more desirable behaviors.

Juggling several procedures at once, and perhaps charting each, may be complicated, but in the long run may be necessary in successful intervention into any given problem cluster.

10. *Make sure the mediators understand the principles and procedures of the intervention.* The social worker should avoid the risk of assuming the mediator understands the procedures simply because he has stated them. It is safer to have the mediator go over each step of the agreed-upon procedures in detail before he attempts to modify the target behavior. Role-playing and behavior rehearsal may be useful.

11. *Explore ways of enhancing the quality of the mediator–client relationship.* There is considerable potential for stress between the mediator and the person whose behavior he will be changing during the intervention program. This stress can even lead to the withdrawal of the mediator from the intervention. Conversely, good rapport between the mediator and client not only enhances the effectiveness of social reinforcement, but also increases both the mediator's and the client's willingness to bring about change. The social worker can explore with the mediator procedures for improving the quality of his relationship with the client, and be available to discuss ways of decreasing tension.

The Mediator as Record Keeper

The mediator often has the responsibility for maintaining records of the changes in the target behavior. The purposes of such recording should be clearly understood by the mediator, and again, he should be fully involved in the development of the recording plan, including such matters as where the chart is to be placed, how it should be used, and so on. It is essential that recording and charting systems be simple, uncomplicated, and clear. The social worker should avoid making excessive demands on the mediator.

Whenever possible, the social worker should work out the specific procedures for collecting data on the target behavior to avoid vagueness or confusion for the mediator. If a chart is to be kept, the social worker might set up the chart rather than expect the mediator to do it. Many people have learned to be intimidated by charts and the collection of data. "Research" has an aura of mysticism that the social worker may have to cut through if he wants the mediator to collect the necessary data. A little time spent in preparing the necessary material and going over it with the mediator can avoid confusion and mistakes later.

It can sometimes be helpful to review data collected in similar situations and problems to provide a model for the mediator. Hypothetical situations can be set up and the mediator asked how he would go about recording in such situations.

Anticipating Stresses on the Mediator

The social worker can help the mediator best if he anticipates some of the problems which may inevitably result from the intervention plan. First, he must recognize a common, reasonable reaction of some people, mediator as well as others, to behavior modification: "Changing people can't be that easy." Often, intervention plans seem deceptively simple, especially when they begin—as they so often do—with collecting baseline data on the behavior before intervention begins, and, even then, starting with limited goals. If the mediator has been a victim of the client's dysfunctional behavior, it is understandable that he may well be impatient to see some significant results of his intervention immediately rather than go through the often tedious process of first collecting baseline data and then following through step by step. Here the social worker can show understanding of the impatience, empathize with the problems the mediator is experiencing, and, through his confidence in the potential effectiveness of the intervention plan give the mediator hope that his investment will pay off.

Sometimes mediators have objections to participation in behaviorally-oriented programs based on genuine philosophical concerns (Tharp & Wetzel, 1969, pp. 127–130). Objections may be expressed over whether these procedures violate democratic concepts of self-determination or equal rights, and whether there is an element of "bribery" involved ("People should do what is right and not have to be paid for it"). Although most of these issues are discussed in Chapter 26, it may be noted here that the issue of bribery is often raised by individuals who are comfortable in using aversive control over behavior, but object to the positive reinforcement of desired behavior. This is not surprising when the anger many potential mediators feel toward "offending" target individuals is considered. It is much easier to punish someone who has hurt you over an extended period of time than to reward him. In such situations, it is possible that the mediator may hedge on his reinforcements, or provide them grudgingly, along with aversive comments or expressions. The social worker should anticipate such problems: he should work with the mediator's hopes to alter the target behaviors, recognize his anger, and reinforce him for cooperating with the intervention plan. If the target behaviors begin to change, the mediator will be reinforced for his efforts.

When the interventions begin, the social worker can help the mediator anticipate setbacks. For instance, if an extinction strategy is initiated (e.g., for dealing with a child exhibiting temper tantrums, or for a nagging spouse), the social worker must point out that there is likely to be an increase in the unwanted behavior upon the withdrawal of reinforcement before there is any improvement. Furthermore, the mediator can be warned that any weakening, giving in and reinforcing ("just this once") on his part is tantamount to the provision of intermittent reinforcement for the undesired behavior, thus making extinction even more difficult to achieve.

Regardless of the good intentions of both the mediator and the social worker, other difficulties may be encountered. People and their environments are not computerized; therefore, there can be few perfect intervention strategies. The social worker should carefully point out the possibility of failures and setbacks along the way and establish a willingness to try again.

The social worker should also recognize, with the mediator, that the client constantly operates under the influence of many individuals in his environment who are not members of the intervention team. The social worker and the mediator can therefore anticipate who in the client's natural environment might be adversely affected by his changed behavior. They should consider the extent to which these others might bring pressure upon the client to maintain his dysfunctional behavior, and try to avert it. Similarly, the mediators themselves are under the influence not only of the client and the social worker but others in their environment. Again it would be useful to anticipate these pressures and help the mediators devise ways of minimizing their impact.

Often, the mediator may find that his work with the target is quite time consuming. While the social worker can point out that the intervention in the long run may well save the mediator time, it is also desirable to explore with the mediator the most efficient methods of carrying out his tasks, and help in implementing them. Sometimes it may be necessary to reduce the expectations of the mediator. For example, if the mediator is intimidated by recording, it might be delayed until some preliminary interventions have taken place.

Finally, the social worker should consider the problems inherent in the social worker–mediator relationship. The mediator may feel himself under the scrutiny of the social worker, especially in relation to the adequacy of the mediator's recording procedures. The mediator may feel he is being evaluated (in the case of other professionals or paraprofessionals such as nurses, teachers, houseparents) and resent the "smart-aleck" social worker's attempt to "supervise" him. The mediator may even feel patronized by the social worker. Often, the best way to handle this (assuming, of course, he is *not* patronizing) is for the social worker to bring up for discussion any perceived problems in their relationship in as nondefensive a manner as possible, and indicate an understanding of the mediator's competence and commitment. Paying lip service to such attitudes is, of course, meaningless unless the social worker shows respect and concern to the mediator—which, in itself, can be reinforcing.

In initial discussions with the mediator, the social worker can set up hypothetical situations that the mediator might encounter and ask how the mediator would go about handling them, giving genuine praise (social reinforcement) in response to reasonable replies:

What if David only half-cleans the table?
What if he deliberately spills the garbage on the way out?
What if your wife volunteers to make his bed for him?
What do you do if you're working late some night and aren't around to chart David's behavior?

Articles and books aimed at lay audiences about the use of behavior modification with problems common to children (e.g., Patterson & Gullion, 1968; Patterson, 1971; Krumboltz & Krumboltz, 1971) and with marital problems (Knox, 1971) are available and may be provided to the mediator (and often to the targets as well) to facilitate their understanding and cooperation in the intervention plan. In fact, there are a variety of programmed texts available (e.g., Becker, 1971) that provide the basics about behavioral principles; they also present for professionals clear guidelines for training mediators.

Problems which might be anticipated in carrying out the intervention plan can be role-played, with the social worker initially playing the role of mediator and later with the mediator attempting to role-play himself. It can also be useful in difficult situations to have the social worker function as the dispenser of reinforcers in the natural environment, with the mediator observing. At an appropriate time, the mediator could take over the dispensing of reinforcers, with the social worker observing.

Reinforcing the Mediator

As noted previously, the mediator's behavior is obviously under the influence of other reinforcers besides the social worker's. The client himself may well be continuing to behave in a manner aversive to the mediator. Others in the mediator's environment may be jealous of the time involved in the intervention, envious of the reinforcements the mediator is providing the client, threatened by the client's changed behavior, or deprecating of the whole process. The social worker can help to counterbalance such aversive stimuli by the nature of his own relationship with the mediator.

The relationship with the mediator has essentially the same three components as any other helping relationship:

1. The social worker shows positive regard and respect for the mediator by his interest in him as a total human being (i.e., not just as a

mediator). He reveals a real concern for the mediator's well being, including the hopes and frustrations associated with the client's problems. He treats the mediator in an egalitarian manner, shows respect for the mediator's competence, and makes clear that the mediator's own concerns, and problems associated with the intervention, are worthy of the social worker's attention. The social worker shows that he cares about the mediator, and not only about the client. Simple procedures such as seeing to the mediator's comfort, providing him with the materials necessary for intervention, and taking the time to engage him in informal chats contribute to rapport and reinforce the mediator's participation in the program.

2. The social worker shows empathy for the mediator by communicating his understanding of the mediator's experiences in connection with the intervention. He attempts to perceive, and reports to the mediator if he senses, that the mediator is ambivalent, overwhelmed or confused by the plan, despondent over the lack of success in carrying out the intervention, or, on the other hand, is pleased with his appropriate efforts and the resultant changes. Such a relationship encourages openness on the part of the mediator, which might avoid problems in carrying out the intervention, and facilitates expeditious modifications when necessary as the intervention progresses.

3. The social worker is genuine, not "phony," in his relations with the mediator. He avoids an artificial, defensive, professional veneer that would tend to set him apart from the mediator. The social worker also acts in a nondefensive manner. For example, the social worker should avoid arguing with the mediator, attempting to prove him wrong on the basis of the weight of the social worker's credentials.

In choosing target behavior, the social worker might give priority, at least initially, to goals that have a high priority for the mediator as well. Also, in choosing reinforcements, the social worker should choose reinforcements that are not aversive to the mediator (e.g., too expensive, or in violation of the mediator's reasonable values). Generally, the intervention plan should not require so much time or effort that it becomes an unpleasant, unwelcome task.

To further reinforce the mediator for his cooperation, the social worker might try to determine what reinforcers he has available for the particular mediator for his efforts. For example, the social worker might offer a teacher who is a mediator with a disturbed adolescent consultation on the teacher's own problems with colleagues or administration.

Finally, the social worker can further reinforce the mediator's participation by being available, taking the time to go over the mediator's charting in detail, giving him time to complain about the plan and mention problems he may be having in carrying it out, and recognizing and praising the mediator's efforts.

Helping the Mediator Naturalize the New Behavior

It may be quite reassuring to point out to the mediator that the structured reinforcing and charting expectations should ultimately be replaced by "chartless," spontaneous, intermittent reinforcement coming from the environment. In other words, the new behavior will become naturalized.

The mediator can enhance this naturalization of behavior in various ways:

1. by seeing to it that praise and other social reinforcers from the mediator and others accompany desired behavior, and that natural reinforcers eventually replace artificial reinforcers as they are phased out;
2. by changing from a continuous reinforcement schedule to a steadily decreasing intermittent reinforcement schedule as the rate or duration of the desired behavior increases;
3. by training others in the client's environment to attend selectively to, and reinforce, the client's desired behavior.

Summary

In many situations in behavior modification, neither the social worker nor the client is in the best position to alter the contingencies that affect the target behavior. In such cases a third party, or mediator, can be selected to work with the social worker to modify the target behavior.

Almost anyone in the client's environment can be considered for the role of mediator: parents, spouses, other family members, employers, friends, co-workers, teachers, classmates, nurses, ward technicians, and others. The selection of a mediator from among these candidates is based on:

1. who is present when the target behavior is exhibited;
2. who has access to effective reinforcers;
3. who is able and motivated to provide them contingently;
4. who besides the client is likely to profit from improved behavior;
5. who is motivated (or specifically charged) to work with the social worker on the client's behavior.

Once a mediator is selected, the social worker works with the mediator in assessing the target behavior and developing an intervention plan, and seeks to motivate the mediator to participate actively in the plan. The social worker then proceeds to teach the mediator the basic concepts and procedures of behavior modification and how they apply to the specific target behaviors.

The stresses, disappointments, and tension that the mediator may experience in connection with the intervention are anticipated and worked with. As intervention progresses, the social worker attempts to reinforce the mediator for his efforts and successes. Finally, the social worker works with the mediator in planning the naturalization of the reinforcements for the desired behaviors in the client's natural environment.

CHAPTER 10. Behavioral Recording

While behavior can, of course, be changed without keeping any records, maintaining objective data on the target behavior before, during, and after intervention usually makes success in bringing about change more likely. Since the goal of behavior change is generally either to increase or decrease behaviors, recording is directed toward giving clear evidence that the direction and duration of such changes are compatible with the interventive goals.

But why must there be written records? Aren't they a dehumanizing carry-over from the laboratory origins of behavior modification? Isn't record-keeping needlessly cumbersome and really unnecessary busy work that intrudes upon the client–social worker interaction?

Quite simply, recording is used because it has been found to be the most effective, accurate way of determining the efficiency and effectiveness of behaviorally-oriented interventions. The ethics of our profession require that we be accountable for our interventions. Therefore it is crucial for social workers to document the success of their interventions and to record the evidence of any damage that may result from their efforts. Data such as those obtained by behavioral recording serve this need for documentation.

There are alternatives to the objective record keeping described above. The methods most often relied upon by social workers include their impressions of changes in the target behaviors or attitudes, or the client's own impressions of general improvement in his condition. In interventions that focus only on increasing self-awareness, or improving decision-making, there may be few alternatives to impressionistic data. However, in planned behavior modification, such data have limitations. First, they are imprecise: they often fail to measure the slow but steady changes that occur in some cases. Second, the accuracy of such observations is questionable. The need to succeed, or frustration in case management, may bias the social worker to see progress when none exists, or conceal failures (even retrogression) because he chooses not to see them. Clients' verbal reports can be equally inaccurate. They may distort or slant their reports to the social worker in order to please him either because they like and respect him, or because they fear him, or to avoid any aversive quality of continued contact with a social worker or agency. Of course, such distortion is possible even in recorded reports (i.e., faked data), particularly if the client keeps the record himself. But the maintenance of recorded data makes such distortion more difficult and more unlikely, especially if the social worker verifies the recorded data, and helps the client or mediator in a positive, constructive way to see the advantages of accurate recording.

ADVANTAGES OF RECORDING BEHAVIOR

Although the principal purpose of recording is to assess more accurately the target behavior and the effects of intervention, record keeping has other significant advantages:

1. Recording enhances assessment and intervention planning by forcing one to choose specific *behaviors* as targets. It is difficult, if not impossible, to chart generalizations such as "ego strength," "effective discipline," or "affection." It is possible—and much more effective—to chart specific behaviors (e.g., applying for a new job, leaving one's classroom seat without permission, and hugging or kissing).

2. Recording enables the social worker to determine case progress at any time, to perceive plateaus, regressions, or the establishment of a behavior at a desired level. It alerts the social worker to alter interventive strategies without undue delay when they seem ineffective.

3. Recording of progress in behavioral change serves as an immediate, tangible reinforcer for the intervention activities of the client, the mediator, and even the social worker. Such reinforcement encourages continued efforts on the part of all involved in the case, and provides hope and enthusiasm to replace the hopelessness and lethargy which may have existed prior to the intervention. Conversely, recorded data that clearly show that goals are not being achieved can jar the social worker and mediator out of any complacency about everything going well when, in fact, it is not.

4. Recording provides the social worker with a tool that can be used to correlate behavioral change with concurrent environmental events, including those that seem to interfere with the goals of the intervention (such as a child's tantrum behavior concurrent with visits from certain relatives).

5. Small but continuous changes that would otherwise be overlooked can often only be perceived through recording.

6. Recording of a wide range of cases can provide data that can later be analyzed to determine the nature of a class of problems as well as the characteristics of effective interventions.

7. In some cases, recording in and of itself leads to positive changes in behavior, particularly when the client is reminded of each occurrence of the target behavior by the written record. In cases where undesired behaviors are being extinguished, such changes might not last long unless reinforcement for desired behaviors is supplied.

WHO SHOULD DO THE RECORDING?

Record keeping can be done either by the person exhibiting the behavior (the client) or by a separate observer (the mediator). There are both advantages and disadvantages to each.

The clients are, of course, always present at the time their behaviors are exhibited. They may well be more motivated than mediators to change their behavior and thus do the requisite recording. They may or may not be more sensitive as to *when* the actual behavior occurs. On the other hand, clients may not notice the occurrence of target behaviors, perhaps out of habit, or perhaps because they are not necessarily willing to alter their behavior.

Since behavior modification involves the alteration of environmental contingencies that are often controlled by people other than the client, it is often preferable to have those people, rather than the client, record the behavior. Another person can often determine more objectively whether a behavior has indeed occurred than can the person engaging in the behavior. For example, behavior that the client perceives as a gesture toward social interaction—say, a smile to a new acquaintance—may not be perceived as such by a mediator who is probably in a position to evaluate or describe more accurately the behavior of the client. Sometimes an observer can note dysfunctional behavior that the client is not even aware he is exhibiting. Recording done by a mediator also tends to be less disruptive to the ongoing behavior of the client and tends to interfere less with spontaneity.

In determining who is the best person to record behavior, the social worker should use the criteria presented in Chapter 9, dealing with the selection of mediators. However, there are additional questions the social worker may want to consider in choosing a recorder:

1. Does the recorder understand and accept the value of recording?
2. Will the recorder in the natural course of events be present when the target behavior occurs?
3. Is the recorder sensitive to the exact nature of the target behavior (i.e., will he know *when* it occurs)?

4. Is the recorder motivated to follow through with the recording procedure? If not, can the social worker create a situation in which the record keeper is reinforced for maintaining the records?

Given satisfactory answers to the above, the social worker may still have a wide choice of candidates for record keeping. In addition to the client himself, observation and recording may be done at home by the parents, spouse, children, or siblings of the client. In school, recording can be done by teachers, aides, parents, volunteers, school social workers, or classmates. In institutions and hospitals, houseparents, social workers, psychiatrists, psychologists, nurses, aides, volunteers, and fellow residents can be called upon to record behavior.

How Is Behavior Recorded?

Essentially, recording is simply a process in which problem behavior is specifically defined or "pinpointed" as a particular behavior unit and then counted.

The first step in recording, then, is the definition of the target behavior, partially and sequentially. (Chapters 11 and 12 discuss the process in which dysfunctional behavior is partialized and target behavior placed into a sequence of interventions.) Such definition must be done before the intervention planning can proceed. Each target behavior (whether it is to be increased or decreased) must be focused or "pinpointed" into units of behavior that can be observed and counted by an objective record keeper.

Even if the goal of intervention is not perceived initially as specific behavioral change, it is still the component behaviors that are counted. For instance, the *goal* of intervention may be weight loss, acquisition of new friends, or improvement of school grades. While it is possible to record the progress toward such goals (through weight charts, a count of friends, or a report card), such recording would not focus attention on the specific behaviors that lead to the goal. For example, "losing weight" is not a behavior *per se;* it is a condition that is a consequence of a set of behaviors such as eating less or exercising more. Similarly, "making friends" is not a behavior, but the result of engaging in behaviors that lead to making friends. And "making good grades" is not a behavior but, it is hoped, an end product of doing those assignments that meet instructors' expectations or lead to better test performance.

Of course, there are many situations in which there is no simple behavior–goal attainment connection. Establishing a good marriage, being an effective parent, and reversing delinquent patterns all usually involve a complex of behaviors that often involves more than one person. Such complexes of behavior may require a series of records of the component target behavioral units that in turn lead to the ultimate goal.

Each behavioral unit is usually defined as a cycle in order to have a clear unit of occurrence (that is, a beginning and an end) and facilitate an accurate count. For example, a behavioral unit could consist of job seeking on the telephone, calling a potential employer found through searching the newspaper ads, calling to determine if the job is open, exploring the possibility of filling the job description, asking if there is indeed a possibility of employment, and setting up a job interview if indicated.

Specificity in defining behavioral units is especially important in helping mediators who work with a large number of individuals experiencing similar dysfunctional behavior. For example, Werry and Quay (1969, p. 468) reported defining "student-out-of-seat" behavioral units for teacher-mediators as " . . . any situation in which the normal seating surface of neither buttock is applied to the child's seat or in which there is movement of his desk or chair so that its ultimate stationary position is altered (thus swinging a seat on its axis or tilting a chair on its leg is excluded)." Such specificity may seem extreme, but it avoids vagueness in one's expectations about the target behavior and anticipates any questions about which behavior is to be reinforced.

Occasionally, behavioral units do not have a clear beginning or end, such as "husband getting home in time for dinner," or are the product of a combination of behaviors, such as "child keeps his room clean." But even such concepts as these have their hazards, and social workers should work toward defining target behaviors in as succinct, observable, and specific behavioral terms as the situation and their creativity permits. This orientation obviously eliminates vague, global behavioral units such as "Cheryl is helpful in class," "Joe communicates badly with his wife," or "Jody makes more boyfriends." Such global behaviors may be reasonable, if vague, ultimate goals of intervention, but they are difficult to operationalize in terms of recording (as well as altering contingencies), and are subject to considerable variability in interpretation by observers, thus leading to inconsistent and unreliable data. To avoid such problems, the characteristics of recorded behaviors must be clearly understood by the recorder and the client, must be precisely defined, and must be countable.

Each occurrence of the specific behavior which is being counted is called a "behavior unit." Behavioral units may be recorded as either of the following:

1. frequency of occurrence of behavior unit, that is, how often the behavior occurs;

2. duration of the behavioral units, that is, how long each occurrence of the target behavior lasts.

Both of these methods of reporting have their uses. Since combining these two methods could make the record confusing, the social worker should determine which method to use. The choice is made by deciding which approach is more logical and which approach will more parsimoniously record data specifically related to the intervention goal. Generally, the decision is based on the following two considerations:

First, if the problem is that a target behavior occurs too often or not often enough, so that the goal is to increase or decrease the frequency of occurrence of that behavior, then a record should be maintained on the *frequency* of the behavior units. Frequency recording is usually quite simple since it requires only that the behavior unit be carefully described, and the number of times it occurs during a specified period of time be counted. Examples of the situations which lend themselves to frequency recording include the frequency of children's completion of assigned chores (each chore is a unit), the number of times a student speaks out of turn in class (each occurrence is a unit), the number of times a wife comments on her husband's good qualities (each comment is a unit), the number of cigarettes smoked (each cigarette lit is a unit), the number of letters written to family and friends (each letter written is a unit).

Second, if the problem is that the target behavior lasts too long, or not long enough, then records should be maintained on the *duration* of the behavior units. Duration recording is somewhat more complicated than frequency recording, since it requires the equipment (e.g., a stopwatch) necessary to measure how long each occurrence of the target behavior lasts. It also requires careful determination of whether the target behavior is actually occurring during the period studied. For example, a student may be at his desk, but not doing his homework; a father may be in a room with his child, but not playing or talking with him. Here again, the specificity of the target behavior is essential. Examples of situations that lend themselves to duration recording include the length of time spent studying, exercising, or in family recreational activities.

In some situations, the initial assessment may seem to call for either frequency or duration recording, but subsequent events lead to the conclusion that the other might have been more appropriate.

EXAMPLE 10.1: Rita was a generally well-functioning college student who was disturbed only by the fact that she spent too much time repeatedly washing her hands at night before going to bed. She was aware that this could be a dysfunctional carry-over of an old interaction with a beloved nurse who instructed Rita when she was a child to wash her hands carefully before saying her bedtime prayers, but she still could not stop. She asked her social worker (one of the authors) to help her get rid of this "annoying habit."

The social worker instructed Rita to put a piece of paper next to her sink and gather baseline data for a week on how often she washed her hands before going to sleep (frequently recording). The first week she reported an average frequency of four hand-washings per night. The social worker instructed Rita that, after each hand-washing, she should pat her hands dry, apply an expensive hand lotion, and dry her hands for 15 minutes under a lamp bulb.

In this case, the strategy was to attach several cumbersome contingencies to the hand-washing, which, in effect, would make Rita decrease the frequency of hand-washing in order to avoid its consequences. After another week, Rita reported she was down to one hand-washing a night, but that it now lasted from 15 to 20 minutes! The undaunted social worker switched to duration recording and instructed Rita to record her cumulative hand-washing time each night. She was asked to allow herself three minutes per hand-washing and follow each three minutes of hand-washing with the same drying process described above. Rita dropped to one three-minute hand-washing per night and in a three-month follow-up had no further related problem.

BASELINING

One of the most common reasons for the failure of intervention plans that use behavior modification is the absence or inadequacy of baselining, a process in which data on the frequency or duration of the target behavior and, perhaps, its controlling events, are collected and recorded *prior to* any planned intervention. People who exhibit dysfunctional behavior are understandably impatient to initiate intervention and go about the important business of changing their behavior. Sometimes this impatience is shared by the mediator or social worker. Baselining is often seen as needless, "scientific" trivia.

However, premature intervention should be avoided. Without the foundation of baseline data, it is difficult to assess the effectiveness of the subsequent intervention and the impact of environmental factors (such as time of day, location of behavior, day of week) on behavior. The existence of a baseline enables the social worker to discriminate slow and subtle changes in behavior from no change at all. It also facilitates the solution of problems in the process of data gathering before actual interventions are initiated.

There are probably only two kinds of situations in which baselining can be bypassed (Watson & Tharp, 1969): (1) when, prior to intervention, the desired behavior never occurs; (2) when the occurrence of a dysfunctional target behavior is dangerous to the client or to others in the environment.

A final factor to consider in favor of the use of baselining is the research that indicates that baselining often has the additional advantage of being sufficient in and of itself to affect behavior. There are numerous reports of the decrease of dysfunctional behavior (Rutner & Bugle, 1969), and the increase of functional behavior (Tharp & Wetzel, 1969; McFall, 1970) following the process of baselining alone. It would seem that merely perceiving and reporting information about a behavior accurately can positively affect it.

Baseline data should be accumulated until the social worker thinks he or she has a fair idea of the usual rate or patterns of the target behavior and of the nature of the variables that seem to control its occurrence. The more stable the occurrence of the behavior, the more quickly baselining can be accomplished. Generally, if the target behavior is occurring with any regularity, a week or so of baselining will be adequate. If there seems to be considerable variation in the occurrence of the behavior from day to day, then perhaps two weeks or more might be necessary.

Methods of Recording

Recording should not become a fetish or an end in itself. In fact, the social worker should be aware that many potential mediators (and clients themselves) may be put off from cooperating in an intervention program by the imagined or actual complexity and cumbersomeness of a recording procedure. This could, of course, sabotage the intervention plan and make the entire procedure aversive. Recording should be no more complicated or difficult than is absolutely necessary for adequate case management. Recording can and should be a simple procedure that enhances the intervention by reinforcing collecting and reporting data, rather than punishing it. The degree of complexity of the recording procedures depends very much on the complexity of the problem, the capabilities and motivation of the record keeper, and the nature of the problem itself.

Essentially, there are two basic related tools used in recording: (1) data gathering instruments; (2) presentations of accumulated data on charts.

DATA GATHERING INSTRUMENTS

Data may be gathered in an infinite variety of ways. The criteria for determining the manner in which the data are gathered include:

1. Is the method portable enough to be easily used where the behavior occurs? In many situations, for instance, a clipboard or large chart would be most inconvenient, while a small notecard may serve well.

2. Is the method unobtrusive enough not to be distracting to the client or others in the natural environment, or embarrassing to use?

3. Is the method *likely* to be used? No recording method is of any value if it is not used. Can a method be found that would be interesting or even enjoyable to use? Frequently, the client and mediator can provide imaginative suggestions on ways to gather data.

Many simple but effective data gathering instruments have been reported. Some examples of these instruments and the situations in which they can be used are:

1. Cards kept by residents at an institution for adolescents can be initialed or punched by a houseparent for each occurrence of a desired behavior.

2. Coins can be moved from one pocket to another (or from one compartment to another in a purse) contingent on the occurrence of specified behavior, such as making friendly overtures to others at social gatherings.

3. Poker chips are frequently used because they can be easily redeemed for desired items at specified intervals, and simplify the counting of completed behaviors.

4. Small cards kept in a pocket or purse are portable and easy to use for collecting data on a wide range of behaviors. For example, they can be tucked in the back of a pack of cigarettes to record the number smoked each day.

5. Inexpensive golf-score counters worn on the wrist provide a versatile instrument for collecting data by inconspicuously "clicking off" behaviors on the knob. Knitting stitch counters can be used similarly, e.g., by a parent to record the number of times one child teases another.

6. Small pieces of masking tape, taped to the wrist, on which checks can be made each time a target behavior occurs are an even less expensive device which can be used in places where other instruments might be impractical (at a beach, for example).

7. In many situations a small portable cassette tape recorder can be used to record incidents of behavior as they occur, for later review with the social worker. For example, a social worker can narrate a running commentary as he watches a family interact through a one-way mirror.

8. Data also may be accumulated in brief written reports. For example, in reviewing spouse interactions (Knox, 1971), each partner in a couple experiencing marital problems can maintain records of interaction with the other, using three columns: (1) spouse's desirable behavior ("what your spouse does that you like"); (2)

spouse's undesirable behavior ("what your spouse does that you don't like"); (3) own reaction (to both). Each entry is presented in a concise manner. Such an instrument has the advantage not only of recording target behavior, both functional and dysfunctional, but of allowing for an analysis of both antecedent and consequent events.

9. Some behavioral procedures are actually self-recording. For example, Lindsley (1968) reports on a "Sunday Box" approach to modifying family members' patterns of leaving personal possessions in inappropriate places around the house. In this procedure, any items found out of place at the end of the day are placed in a box from which they cannot be removed until the following Sunday. The success of such an intervention can be measured by the amount of items in the box each Sunday.

Each of these procedures can be made more useful if the mediator informs the client after the intervention program begins, in situations where it is practical, that he or she is marking down any occurrence of the target behavior. If the behavior being recorded is one that is to be increased, the mediator might accompany the statement "I am recording another one" with social reinforcement, or any other planned contingency. If the behavior is one that is to be decreased, the mediator announces "there is another one" or makes some other nonhostile comment to the effect that another undesired behavior has occurred. The mediator should avoid getting into an argument about the behavior, and simply record it.

HOW MANY BEHAVIORS SHOULD BE COUNTED AT ONE TIME?

The basic rule for recording behavior is: keep the procedure simple. This is especially necessary for the clients' or mediators' initial attempts at behavioral change. Focusing on too many behaviors simultaneously may lead to confusion and frustration. Generally, a mediator should not be expected to record more than two or three target behaviors of a particular individual at any one time.

It is possible, however, to record several *aspects* of a specific target behavior. For example, a man may record not only how many times he loses his temper, but also who is the target of his anger (e.g., boss, wife, child), and what time of day it occurs (morning, during dinner, at bedtime). A teacher may note not only how often each day a particular student leaves his seat without permission, but also how often during each particular class this behavior occurs (to determine whether there is a possible relationship between the frequency of disruptive behavior and the subject being studied). Such specific data are particularly useful in the baseline stage of intervention and may be useful in focusing on a particular interaction, a particular time or day, or a particular setting as being the time or location of intervention.

WHEN SHOULD RECORDING OCCUR?

Obviously it would be impractical, to say the least, to develop a recording plan that requires continuous recording of a client's behavior. Attempting to record all instances of an individual's display of the target behavior would be impractical and awkward. A *sampling* of target behavior is therefore the most useful method of recording. In order to sample effectively, a specific period of time each day is chosen in which there is a high probability that the target behavior will occur (e.g., one hour, 15 minutes, the duration of dinner, a particular class period). Of course, if this will not secure a *representative* picture of the target behavior, more than one period of observation per day may be necessary.

It is preferable that the period of time and the circumstances in which the behavior is observed be similar in subsequent observations so as to guarantee that there will be consistent opportunities for the event to occur. For example, comparing a child's behavior in the half-hour before breakfast on one day, for two hours at school the next day, and one hour watching television the third day might not permit a reliable evaluation of any changes in behavior brought about by any new consequences.

Sometimes the logical period of time for observing a target behavior varies from day to day. For instance, the observation of the insults exchanged between children in a family from the end of dinner to bedtime may vary by an hour or so each night. In such cases, the data collected can be a *rate* of behavior over a given time, determined for each day by dividing the frequency of the observed behavior by the number of minutes in the observation period. For example, in the illustration below, the parents recorded the number of times each of their two children insulted ("put down") the other from dinner until bedtime, and divided that figure by the number of minutes in the interval (e.g., $\frac{14}{180} = .08$).
The results are shown in Table 10.1.

In reviewing such data it is the rate of behavior that is emphasized, rather than the number of times the behavior occurs.

T A B L E 1 0. 1. Rate of Put-Downs per Hour Made by Alan and Laurie

CHILD	Number of PD's		Period Covered	Number of Minutes	Rate per Minute
LAURIE					
Monday	~~HHT~~ ~~HHT~~ ~~HHT~~	(14)	6:30–9:30	180	.08
Tuesday	~~HHT~~ ~~HHT~~ 11	(12)	7:00–8:45	105	.11
Wednesday	~~HHT~~ 111	(8)	7:00–9:00	120	.07
Thursday	11	(2)	6:45–8:30	105	.02
Friday	~~HHT~~	(4)	7:00–9:30	150	.03
ALAN					
Monday	11	(2)	6:30–9:30	180	.01
Tuesday	~~HHT~~	(5)	7:00–8:45	105	.05
Wednesday	11	(2)	7:00–9:00	120	.01
Thursday		(0)	6:45–8:30	105	0
Friday		(0)	7:00–9:30	150	0

Charting

It is often useful to convert the data gathered by methods such as those presented above into a stationary chart. Such a chart presents a comprehensive overview of the history of the effect of intervention on the target behavior, and can be a major tool for intervention planning and review. Moreover, the observability of the recorded data to others may serve as an additional reinforcer, or aversive stimulus, for the behaviors being charted. While there are many ways such a chart can be made, the simplest way is to use standard graph paper, which is available in most stores selling school supplies. Alternatively, a chart may be drawn on a plain sheet of paper.

In some situations where the target behavior usually occurs at one particular place, data on the frequency or duration of the target behavior may be placed directly on the chart rather than on some portable data gathering instrument. For example, snacking behavior may be directly recorded on a chart taped to the refrigerator, toothbrushing behavior on a chart pinned to the bathroom wall, sexual behavior on a chart next to the bed, classroom behaviors on a class bulletin board, and so on.

The chart offers a visual representation of changes in the frequency or duration of the target behavior over the interval from the initial baselining of the target behaviors, through the initiation of one or more interventions by the social worker, to the termination of the interventions. A chart's primary function is to help the social worker, mediator, and client evaluate the effect of the interventions on the frequency or duration of the target behaviors, and consider the other factors that may be having an effect on the target behavior. (The use of such charting in behavioral research is also briefly discussed in Chapter 1.)

HOW ARE DATA PRESENTED ON THE CHART?

It is generally preferable for the social worker, in consultation with the record keeper, to prepare the material for keeping a cumulative chart prior to the collection of data. The record keeper then need only fill in the indicated data on the spaces on the chart.

There is no "right way" to present accumulated data. For example, sometimes the accumulated data is merely a set of check marks on a calendar. However, some conventions are emerging which facilitate understanding of more formal charts and communication among those familiar with formal charting.

Below is an illustration of a typical behavioral chart, Figure 10.1. In this case intervention was directed at the poor school attendance of a 16-year-old boy.

A chart as illustrated in Figure 10.1 generally includes the following information:

Behavior units: The vertical axis is a record of the occurrence of behavioral units, described in terms of frequency (the number of times a behavior occurs during a consistently observed period of time), rate (frequency divided by varying periods of time), or duration (the length of time the behavior is exhibited per period of observation). In Figure 10.1, John's behavior units are measured by the number of days of school attendance per week. (The duration of behavior is assumed to be all day, although separate recording of duration would be necessary to illustrate

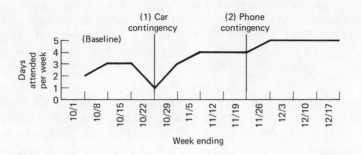

FIGURE 10.1. Number of days per week John attended school.

this.) The chart reflects the possible range of the rate of such behavior: 0 to 5 days attendance per week. One of the reasons for baselining is to determine the range of frequency of occurrence of a behavior during a specific period of time. We can see before intervention that John's rate of school attendance ranged from 1 to 3 times a week.

Time Units: The units of time during which observations are reported are arranged along the horizontal axis. The time units in the illustration are simply weeks for which the behavior was recorded.

Sequence: The sequence of time, i.e., number of hours or days over which the behavior is recorded, reads from left to right.

Baseline: The frequency or duration of the target behavior is observed and recorded for a period of time *prior to* the intervention. In the illustration, school records revealed that John had attended school twice the fourth week before intervention, three times each the third and second week before intervention, and only once a week immediately before intervention.

Intervention: The introduction of the intervention is indicated by a solid vertical line drawn at the point of time (as indicated on the horizontal axis) that intervention is initiated. In the illustration, car use on weekends was made contingent on school attendance of at least four days a week (intervention number 1). School attendance improved to approximately four days a week. A second intervention (intervention number 2) made phone use contingent on daily attendance at school. This stabilized attendance at five days a week for the remainder of the charted period.

Charts can also be used to record changes in the duration of target behavior:

EXAMPLE *10.2:* Babs was a "retarded" adolescent in a special education class. Her attention span had been rather short, and thus, she spent little time working at her programmed-learning machine. In reviewing her case, the social worker learned that Babs loved hair ribbons. The social worker, the teacher, and Babs agreed that she would be given a point each day her time at the machine equalled or surpassed her quota. Five points (represented by tokens) would earn her a hair ribbon. Quotas were raised each week, after the teacher reviewed the previous week's chart, and were kept within her capacity at each step. In Figure 10.2, below, minutes spent at the machine each day are indicated on the vertical axis, days of the week on the horizontal axis, and quotas are in heavy vertical lines.

A common form of chart frequently used in both intervention and research is known as an "ABAB" (see Chapter 1). In such a chart, baseline data on the frequency or duration of a particular behavior are acquired (A^1). An intervention designed to change either the antecedents or the consequences of the behavior is introduced (B^1) and the subsequent frequency recorded. The intervention is then withdrawn to see the

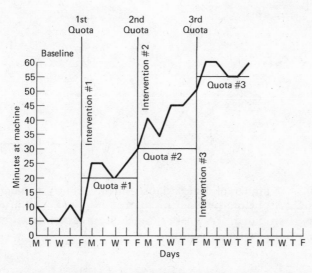

FIGURE 10.2.   Length of time Babs spent each day working at the learning machine

effect of its removal on the behavior (A²). Finally, the intervention is reintroduced (B²), and its effect noted. Such a procedure can be useful in double-checking the effects of an intervention's introduction and removal on a target behavior.

EXAMPLE 10.3: Time-Out for Dale: The Wolks were houseparents in a state institution for delinquent adolescents. They were curious, but certainly not convinced, about the possible effectiveness of behavioral techniques on the boys in their cottage. In reviewing with the cottage social worker the behavioral problems they were encountering in their cottage, both Mr. and Mrs. Wolk agreed that a major discipline problem was the fights which occurred while the boys were watching television at night. They had tried various approaches to eliminate the fights, including ignoring them, shouting at the boys, and taking away privileges. Nothing worked. The social worker suggested discussions of nonviolent ways of settling disputes along with the initiation of a time-out procedure: putting both boys involved in a fight into their rooms for a ten-minute "cooling-off period" as soon as they began to fight. Dale, a boy with a "violent temper" and one of the more "incorrigible" fighters in the group, was selected as a trial target.

The Wolks were dubious about how successful such a procedure would be, and whether it would be worth their effort. The worker therefore suggested a test of the procedure. The Wolks, with their social worker's help, agreed to maintain an ABAB charting procedure that would clearly show the effect of the procedure on Dale's behavior.

When the procedure was completed, a month later, the chart (see Figure 10.3) showed the following:

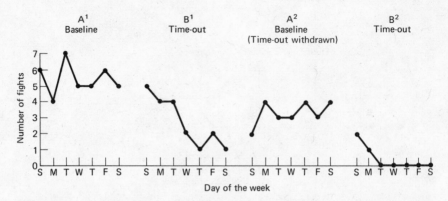

FIGURE 10.3. Number of Dale's fights during nightly two-hour television sessions: (A¹) before time-out program is initiated; (B¹) after time-out program is initiated; (A²) after time-out program is withdrawn; (B²) after time-out program is reinitiated.

A¹ *(first baseline period)*. During this baseline period the Wolks were to react to Dale as they would normally. The number of times Dale got into fights each night during the two hours he watched television was recorded. The chart shows that Dale averaged about five fights each night.

B¹ *(first intervention period)*. At the beginning of the second week of the program, the Wolks were to introduce the time-out procedure and use it every time Dale began to fight. By mid-week, he was starting fights only one or two times a night.

A² *(the second baseline period)*. To test whether the reduction in fighting was a result of the time-out procedure, the Wolks were instructed to discontinue the procedure during the third week. They could return to any procedures they had previously used to reduce Dale's fighting. Their chart revealed that Dale's fighting increased to about three fights a night, higher than the first intervention period, but not quite as high as during the first baseline period.

B² *(second intervention period)*. In the final week of the test, the time-out procedure was reinstituted. There was an almost immediate cessation of Dale's fighting.

The Wolks were pleased with the results of their research, which showed an elimination of Dale's fighting as a result of their intervention program as verified by their own chart.

RECORDING MEDIATOR BEHAVIOR

Sometimes the behavior recorded is that of someone other than the principal target. It might be desirable, for instance, to have parents who punish their children frequently but tend to overlook functional behaviors maintain records of the number of contingent social reinforcements given out to their children for good behavior. The social worker might also use a similar method by reviewing taped interviews with mediators and counting the number of empathic statements the social worker makes during each contact.

INSURING RELIABILITY

There are several procedures the social worker can use to minimize the chances that inaccurate data will be collected and reported:

1. Clearly define the target behavior so that there is little chance of confusion as to whether or not the target behavior has indeed occurred.
2. Role-play the target behavior or in some other way set up a situation in which the recorder can test his ability to determine whether the target behavior has occurred.
3. If the client himself is recording the behavior, and he has a tendency to fail to notice the very behavior he wants to modify (Watson & Tharp, 1972), instruct him to engage in the target behavior (whether functional or dysfunctional) while actively paying attention to what he is doing (e.g., acting hostile, being friendly, making undesired sounds, scratching, taking out and lighting a cigarette). In recording behaviors they themselves are to modify, clients could ask those in their environment to tell them when they are engaging in the target behavior.
4. Do not set up a recording situation in which the recording becomes aversive to the recorder. Conversely, whenever possible arrange for the recording procedure to be enjoyable.
5. Try to develop record keeping into a habitual routine. This can be facilitated by insuring that the recording instrument is available at the time the observations are to be made. When the social worker is teaching the client self-modification, the Premack Principle can be utilized. That is, the social worker can help the client make certain that he engages in a particular high-probability behavior only after charting is completed.
6. See that the recording of behavior takes place immediately after the occurrence of the behavior. Delays often lead to distorted or incomplete data.
7. If necessary, verify data by having a second independent observer and recorder. This is especially useful and practical when collecting group data.
8. Make use of the data. It is pointless to accumulate data that are not reviewed by client, mediator, or social worker; people who

collect data that are not used will probably lose interest in recording.

Group Recording

It is often useful to record simultaneously the behaviors of groups of individuals, such as students in a class, residents of a ward, or members of a social group. As with individual behavior, data can be recorded in terms of either frequencies or duration of behavior. If a houseparent wants to change the duration of such behaviors as cleaning up after dinner (i.e., reducing the time it takes), talking within the group before the start of discussion sessions, doing homework, or other behaviors where the time element is important, then data on the duration of these behaviors would be collected. A stopwatch, regular watch, or even kitchen timer may be used to collect such data. Timing begins at the point the group understands the target behaviors are to begin, and ends when the last group member terminates the target behavior (Rose, 1972).

In other situations, the goal is to increase or decrease the frequency of particular group behaviors; for example, the number of social amenities exchanged in a chronic psychiatric ward, the number of fights during recess at a school, or the number of chores completed by a group of "retarded" children. Generally, all that is needed to record such data is check marks for specific target behaviors placed beside each name on a list of group members. Mediators such as teachers and ward technicians are more likely to keep accurate counts if they have prepared tabulation charts than if they have blank pieces of paper only (Rose, 1972). The lists then will provide cumulative data on the frequency of particular behaviors in the group as a whole (see Figure 10.4), as well as data on the effect of environmental consequences on both individual and group behavior.

Although group recording is usually used to survey total group behavior (such as the number of residents on the ward making their own beds after initiation of a policy that requires they do this before having lunch), it may also be used to determine which particular group members tend to be most—or least—likely to exhibit a particular behavior, or to provide a vehicle for differential reinforcement of various members in a group.

EXAMPLE 10.4: Mrs. Clark's Chore Chart: Mrs. Clark, a widow, was overwhelmed in trying to have her four children consistently follow through with their household chores without considerable nagging from her. Following a family session, a "chore chart" was developed (see Table 10.2) and placed conspicuously above the television set. Each child was to put a check mark on the chart immediately after he or she had completed each assigned task. Check marks were added up at the end of the week. The chart was accompanied by a statement of the individual and group consequences of the recorded activities. Check marks could be exchanged at predetermined rates for special privileges, such as choosing television programs for a particular night, or selecting a dessert for a particular dinner. If a minimum of 60 check marks was recorded for all the children during a week, the whole family would go out for a movie on the weekend (thus adding group contingencies as well as individual motivation) .

Useful data can also be collected in certain group situations using the "Freeze Approach" (Blackham & Silberman, 1971). In this procedure, the group leader or data collector asks the group members to stop and stay still when the leader yells "freeze." As an example, in a shop class, the teacher complained to the social worker that students were frequently away from their bench, wandering around the room or hall. The teacher was instructed by the social worker to call "freeze" periodically when she noticed such wandering behavior. Once the students were still, the teacher placed a mark by the name of each student at his bench. At the end of the day, the students with a certain number of check marks were reinforced for staying at their benches.

A checklist of problem behaviors can be developed by the social worker (or group leader) or can be adapted from already existing lists. For example, Rose (1972), offers a checklist that teachers can use to

T A B L E 10.2. *Mrs. Clark's Chore Chart:* **Chores Completed by Mrs. Clark's Four Children, Along with Weekly Totals for Each, and Total for the Four.**

	7/1	7/2	7/3	7/4	7/5	7/6	7/7	Total
BARRY								
Clothes picked up	X	X	X		X	X		
Bed made	X		X		X	X		
Garbage removed	X	X	X	X	X	X	X	16
BETH								
Clothes picked up	X	X	X	X	X	X	X	
Bed made	X	X	X	X				
Table set	X	X	X	X	X	X	X	18
MAGGIE								
Clothes picked up				X				
Bed made				X		X		
Dishes washed	X	X		X	X	X	X	9
OSCAR								
Clothes picked up	X	X	X	X	X	X	X	
Bed made	X	X	X	X	X	X	X	
Carpets swept	X	X	X	X	X	X	X ·	21
	Total	Score						64

estimate the frequencies of problem behaviors for the group or to keep a record of the problem behaviors of particular students. Once the checklist has been maintained for a while, the social worker can help the teacher focus on specific problems. Rose's list (1972, p. 55), which can be altered to fit the age and other characteristics of a particular group, follows:

1. *Gross motor*
   a. Getting out of seat
   b. Standing up
   c. Leaving room
   d. Turning around in seat
   e. Rocking
   f. Squirming
   g. Rocking
   h. Other
2. *Objectionable noise*
   a. Tapping pencil or object
   b. Stamping feet, hands
   c. Desk or chair noises
   d. Other
3. *Disturbance of others' property*
   a. Grabbing objects
   b. Throwing objects
   c. In possession of another's property
   d. Destroying another's property
   e. Other
4. *Contact*
   a. Hitting
   b. Kicking
   c. Shoving
   d. Pinching
   e. Slapping
   f. Striking with object
   g. Other
5. *Verbalization*
   a. Talks without permission
   b. Makes irrelevant comments
   c. Swears
   d. Cries
   e. Talks with self
   f. Screams
   g. Tattles
   h. Tells others what to do

    i. Threatens others
    j. Teases
    k. Name-calls
    l. Lies
    m. Speaks in discussions
    n. Talks back
    o. Other

6. *Task behavior*
    a. Assignments completed
    b. Time on task
    c. Other

7. *Isolate behavior*
    a. Plays by self
    b. Participates in group activities
    c. Other

8. *Expressive behaviors*
    a. Sulks
    b. Has temper tantrums
    c. Has bad moods
    d. Maintains eye contact
    e. Smiles or laughs when reprimanded
    f. Other

9. *Other*
    a. Wets in pants
    b. Soils in pants
    c. Complains of illness
    d. Injures self
    e. Mouths object
    f. Absences
    g. Tardinesses
    h. Smells
    i. Other

Similar checklists can be developed for institutional, family, or social groups to pinpoint specific problem areas in those settings.

CHARTING GROUP BEHAVIOR

Whatever procedure is used to collect data, charting similar to that used with individual behaviors may be used to present summarized group behavior. These charts can point out problems and trends in group behavior, and—like individual behavior charts—can be effective in reinforcing goal-oriented behavior. Figure 10.4 shows the cumulative record of the activities of one cottage in an institution's cleanup campaign.

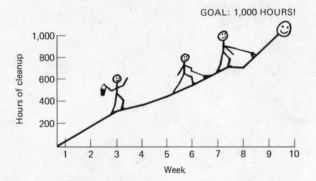

FIGURE 10.4. Cumulative hours of cleanup activities by the Blue cottage during the cleanup campaign.

Reinforcement included praise from the staff and the pride in the chart itself. Cumulative charting (each week's count includes the total from all previous recorded weeks) emphasizes progress when the goal is to increase behavior. However, when the goal is to eliminate a behavior, a noncumulative chart is generally used since it makes decreases more apparent (Rose, 1972).

Charts used as a stimulus for group behavior should be displayed conspicuously. They can be made more effective if presented in a creative, even flamboyant manner. For example, one group worker stretched strips of bright-colored paper up a wall to show group progress. A teacher put a penny in a glass bowl on her desk every time a difficult, task was completed by the students in her class. When the bowl was full, she used the money to pay for a party for the class. Group charting, as in individual charting, can be more effective if it includes elements of creativity and fun.

Summary

This chapter reviewed the value and technology of collecting and recording behavioral data. Recording enables the worker to assess accurately the effects of interventions on the target behaviors. It also forces specificity in defining the target behavior, provides immediate feedback and reinforcement for both mediator and client when there is progress, provides a vehicle for correlating target behavior with environmental events, and allows for research analysis of interventions with classes of similar behavior.

While the social worker often has a choice of record keepers, those selected should:

1. understand and accept the value of recording;
2. be present when the target behavior usually occurs;
3. accurately perceive the target behavior;
4. be motivated—and reinforced—for keeping records.

Prior to intervention, the baseline of the target behavior is determined so that the effects of intervention can be accurately determined. The units of behavior to be recorded should be specifically defined and may be recorded in units of frequency or duration, depending on which is more appropriate in terms of target goals.

Procedures for recording are flexible, and are determined by situational demands and the social worker's resources. They should be as simple and nonaversive as possible. Two related tools are used in behavioral recording: (1) data gathering instruments, and (2) presentations of accumulated data on charts. Data gathering instruments should generally be portable, convenient, and inconspicuous. Whenever possible, the instrument should be pleasant to use. The cumulative record should clearly display the course of behavior over time.

The reliability of the data can be enhanced by clearly specifying the target behavior, preparing the record keeper for receiving and recording the data, making record keeping reinforcing to the record keeper, ensuring the immediacy of recording after the target behavior has occurred, and using a second observer as a check. Data can also be collected and presented for group behaviors using procedures similar to those for individual behaviors.

CHAPTER 11. An Overview of the Assessment Process

Assessment in behavior modification is a process through which answers to the following questions are obtained:

1. What aspects of the problem are due to specific behaviors of the individuals involved?
2. What specific behaviors are to be changed?
3. What factors maintain the dysfunctional behaviors, or prevent the occurrence of functional behaviors?
4. What resources in the client's environment, or elsewhere, are available for use in changing the behaviors?
5. What procedures are most likely to have a positive effect on the target behaviors?

The purpose of the assessment process is to develop the simplest intervention plan that will effectively help the client and those in his environment at the least cost to all those involved.

Assessment procedures do not stop when intervention begins; throughout intervention they are subject to revision as new data emerge. Since behavioral intervention is often carried out in stages, each intervention builds upon previous behavioral changes and the ongoing evaluation of their effect on the target behavior.

The Assessment Process

The process whereby behavioral principles are applied in changing problem behaviors is fairly clear and direct, and is based on procedures developed in practice in various settings with diverse groups of clients and different problems. Although the presentation of the general process may seem simple, the *application* of the principles to specific cases is complicated by virtue of the fact that many variables affect a given client's behavior at any given time. The problem behaviors encountered by social workers typically involve a number of subproblems that are often maintained by a complex of social, cultural, and economic variables. Poverty, racism, sexism, economic displacement—all can play a role in creating and maintaining such difficult problems as child abuse, delinquency, desertion, and so on. It is possible that having a narrow clinical orientation can blind one to the sources of the problems of many individuals. Thus, a child's behavioral problem in school may reflect either an inadequate educational program or his faulty hearing; a man's unwillingness to look for a job may reflect fear of job discrimination; a family's fighting may be a consequence of overcrowded and inadequate housing.

While the *principles* underlying the processes of behavior modification are relatively invariant, the *application* of these principles calls for flexibility, ingenuity, perceptiveness, creativity, and, perhaps most of all, patience and perseverance. Because the application can be very complex, the social worker must carefully assess each case to determine to what extent the client's problems are due to his own or others' behaviors, and to what extent the problems call for the alteration of environmental pressures or deficits. If the latter, the first step of the social worker may be to move to alleviate environmental stresses and facilitate the client's use of community resources. In the role of "social broker" (Briar, 1967), for example, the social worker can help obtain community resources for those who need them but do not have them, either because they are unaware of the existence or source of such resources, or because they are having trouble getting access to them. The social worker can also serve as an advocate, acting as a client's adviser, supporter, or representative in dealing with problems with organizations like hospitals, courts, and schools, and helping the client obtain his rights. Such roles not only meet the needs of the individuals who come to the attention of the social worker, but, if performed by enough social workers, cause social institutions to become more responsive to such individuals (Grosser, 1965; Briar, 1967).

However, if the problem, or some part of it, appears to be due to dysfunctional behaviors (i.e., what the clients, targets, or people within the immediate environment are doing or not doing) that are having undesired effects on the personal or social functioning of one of the parties involved, the social worker proceeds to assess the behaviors in their environmental context in order to develop a strategy to change those behaviors.

EMPHASIS ON PRESENT

Assessment for behavior modification focuses on changing observable behavior. There is no attempt to find historical explanations for behavior; rather, there is an attempt to define empirically what seems to be maintaining undesirable behavior and preventing the occurrence of desirable behavior. The basic principle of behavior modification is that most behavior is controlled by the environment, and can be altered by changing specific elements in the current environment. The key words in this statement are "current environment." Habitual patterns of behavior do exist, and their careful analysis may illuminate current problems, and be helpful in planning intervention programs. Any behavior may have a long history of reinforcement. Genetic predisposition may well have an effect on behavior. Such variables and others may have led to the development of the current environmental-behavioral configuration that *is* the subject of assessment when intervention is undertaken. However, no matter what role these factors may have played in the development of the problems (and hypotheses about such roles are often infinitely complex and untestable), when they are in the irretrievable past, they generally are subject neither to objective assessment nor effective intervention.

It is largely current experiences with the environment that influence and constantly mold behavior. Changing these experiences in a planned, focused way can change behavior. Thus, it is the ways in which the environment can—and does—affect the target behaviors, and the ways in which the client, in turn, affects his environment, that is the subject of this chapter.

DIAGNOSTIC LABELING

The behavioral orientation toward assessment generally precludes the use of traditional diagnostic classifications to pigeonhole people into diagnostic categories. There are many routes to more or less similar problem behaviors, and many routes away from such behaviors. Instead of focusing on historical and psychiatric labeling, behavioral assessment focuses on the selection of individualized, precise descriptions of the problem behaviors and the environmental factors that affect those behaviors. The only purpose of assessment is the collection of enough information about a problem behavior to design a focused intervention plan to change it. For example, the product of an assessment procedure may be a judgment that a child's lack of speaking skills interferes both with his learning in school and his acceptance by his peers and teachers. The intervention plan drawn from such an assessment would be the use of the reinforcements (chosen as a result of data acquired in the assessment) needed to increase appropriate speaking behavior.

In sum, assessment is the essential foundation for all behavioral interventions. It is a highly pragmatic process: its major purpose is to select a strategy for, and techniques of, intervention.

Sources of Information

Various methods are available to the social worker for obtaining data for behavioral assessment. The choice of which methods—or combination of methods—to use depends on the nature of the problems, the situations in which they occur, and the resources available to the social worker. *Interviews, checklists and inventories,* and *direct observation* are the basic assessment tools in behavioral modification.

INTERVIEWS

Assessment begins, in most cases, with interviews with the individuals who are either experiencing problems in their own behavior or complaining about that of others. This process, as noted in Chapter 8, is best conducted when the social worker communicates high levels of warmth, empathy, and genuineness, and works toward establishing a trusting relationship with the client.

Interviews are structured to obtain answers to the following questions:

1. What, specifically, do the individuals involved see as the problem behaviors?
2. Who is complaining or suffering as a result of these behaviors?
3. Who is participating in the problem behavior? Is more than one person involved in reciprocally hurtful behavior (e.g., a couple always fighting in a "Who's Afraid of Virginia Wolfe?" marriage)?
4. At what time and under what circumstances do the problem behaviors seem to occur? What events precede them? What consequences seem to follow them?
5. Can the problem behaviors best be described by their frequency (behavior exhibited too often, or not often enough), duration (too long, or not long enough), or appropriateness (occurring when they should not, or not occurring when they should)?
6. Who, in the environment of the person exhibiting the problem behaviors, has the time, motivation, and resources to help modify the behaviors?
7. How would the person exhibiting the problem behaviors and those in his environment like to see the situation changed? What are their long-range behavior goals?
8. Which stimuli seem to serve as reinforcers for this person? Are they available in his environment?

In addition to eliciting information about the problem behaviors and the resources available for use in modifying these behaviors, the social worker can use the initial interviews to go over the basic concepts of behavior modification and how they might be applied to the problems under discussion. Assessment interviews also allow for the establishment of a relationship with the client and set the stage for future reinforcement by the social worker.

CHECKLISTS AND INVENTORIES

Printed or mimeographed checklists of various kinds can elicit valuable information from the clients or from other people in their environment. Such checklists provide convenient, concise, and comprehensive vehicles for obtaining essential information that might otherwise require extensive, time-consuming, and often incomplete explorations through other means. Often, too, individuals may be more comfortable indicating information of a personal or, perhaps, unusual nature on an impersonal checklist than in early interviews. Sometimes, of course, the opposite is true, emphasizing again the need to establish a good relationship between the social worker and his informants as a solid foundation for an adequate assessment.

Several kinds of inventories are available. Three examples are discussed below.

MARRIAGE INVENTORIES

A marriage inventory was developed by Knox (1971) for couples with marital problems. In addition to general information about the marriage, it asks for clinical information: couples are asked to underline descriptive statements that apply to them (e.g., life is empty; I feel guilty; I feel depressed), and asked about problems in the marriage in the areas of sex, communication, money, in-laws, religion, recreation, friends, alcohol use, and children. They are also asked to rank these problems in the order that they would like to deal with them.

Next the couples are asked to list those of their behaviors that please them. They then indicate the specific behaviors they would like increased and developed in their spouses and themselves. Finally they are asked to provide any other information that they feel may aid in better understanding their problems and how these may be solved.

SEXUAL SURVEY SCHEDULES

A series of schedules for women and men were developed by Annon (1971) to provide an opportunity for people with sex-related problems to check the degree to which they either fear or enjoy a wide range of sexual stimuli (e.g., various parts of the anatomy, specific sexual activities, interpersonal situations). This type of survey allows clients to supply information of a sexual nature more readily than in a face-to-face interview (especially if they consider their behavior bizarre), since all they have to do is choose among printed options.

REINFORCEMENT SCHEDULES

The selection of effective, problem-specific reinforcers for increasing the rate, intensity, or duration of desirable behavior is a critical step in behavioral assessment. Since one man's reinforcement is another man's boredom, the use of reinforcement schedules facilitates the tailoring of reinforcements to individual targets.

The "Reinforcement Survey Schedule" (Cautela & Kastenbaum, 1967) was developed to aid in the selection of reinforcers. The first part provides a checklist for indicating how much pleasure is derived from various objects and events such as particular foods, beverages, people, recreational activities, listening to various kinds of music, watching or participating in various kinds of sports, reading various kinds of literature, gardening, hiking, being praised about various attributes, flirting. It also includes other interpersonal activities as varied as "winning a bet" and "having somebody pray for you."

The second section of the survey presents various situations such as the following: "You have just led your team to victory. An old friend comes over and says, you played a terrific game. Let me treat you to dinner and drinks!" The client is then asked to indicate how much he would enjoy being in each of these situations.

Finally, the client is asked to list things he does or thinks about doing more than 5, 10, 15, or 20 times a day. Such information is useful in applying the Premack Principle (Premack, 1959), i.e., finding high probability-behaviors that can be used to reinforce low probability-behaviors.

A short schedule for identifying potential reinforcers for children with school problems was developed by Blackham and Silberman (1971, pp. 173–174). The questionnaire asks children five questions:

1. What games would they buy, if they could?
2. What three things do they like to do in their classroom?
3. What three jobs do they most like in their classroom?
4. What would they most like to buy with 25 cents?
5. What other things do they enjoy doing at school (in the building or playground)?

It may be useful for social workers to develop their own assessment instruments for special problem clusters or settings such as working with retarded young adults, handicapped individuals, or residents in a home for the aged.

DIRECT OBSERVATION

While some useful observations about a client's general behavior and his behavior toward others can be made in the office, such observations may be of limited value. A client's patterns of interacting with the social worker may be quite different from the way he interacts with employers, family members, teachers, and others. Thus, the most effective observations are those made by the social worker or other trained observers of the client in his natural environment. The best time and place for observation is that in which problem behaviors are most likely to occur.

The initial observations made in the client's environment should focus on the detection of gross patterns of behavior, as well as those events that tend to precede the problem behaviors (antecedent events) and those events that tend to occur immediately after, as a consequence of the behaviors. Such observations may lead to some tentative hypotheses about the events that provide cues to the client that it is time to exhibit particular problem behaviors, and the events that tend to reinforce or prevent them.

For example, direct observations by the social worker may lead to the conclusion that a working mother's return to a home made untidy by her children leads to a series of screaming, nagging behaviors on her part, which negatively reinforces the children for cleaning the house, which, in turn, positively reinforces the mother for screaming at the children.

Bijou *et al.* (1968) suggest that recording a running description of such family episodes is one of the initial steps in understanding the behavioral patterns of dysfunctional families. In such descriptions, the observers record all interactions as they occur, with no inferences made as to why they are occurring. Specific behaviors are recorded ("Mother called son 'lazy' "), rather than labeled ("hostile, punitive"). Bijou *et al.* emphasize the need to understand the *temporal* relationship of events and therefore organize their data in three columns (antecedent events-responses-consequent events). The antecedent events and consequences are generally behaviors of those in the client's environment, the responses are generally the dysfunctional target behaviors.

Considerable work has been reported about the use of professional observers to record dysfunctional behavior in families (Patterson, 1968; 1971). This work has generated several procedures to minimize the obtrusiveness of the observers, which could impair typical spontaneous interactions. One such method of eliminating these distortions is to train the participants in the target behavior to observe their own reciprocal behavior. In his treatment of marital problems, Knox (1971) provides both husband and wife with charts on which each records the other's desirable and undesirable behaviors and his or her own response to them. For example, a husband reports that his wife "emptied my liquor bottle" and that his response to her behavior was to "cut down her rose bush." She also "served a delicious supper of steak, potatoes, salad, fresh green peas, wine, and so on," and his response was, "I kissed her and suggested that we see a movie." The wife observed that her husband "told me he hated my mother" and her response was, "I cried." Later, however, she observed that her husband "told me he thought I was a good wife," and her response was, "I smiled, kissed him, and led him to the bedroom."

Data accumulated from such observational procedures enable the social worker to reconstruct recurrent chains of events in problem behaviors: an antecedent event (usually the behavior of significant others) provides a cue for a response (the target behavior) which is followed by the behaviors of significant others in such a way as to reinforce the response or extinguish it.

Time Needed for Assessment

The length of time necessary to conduct a behavioral assessment varies with the particular situation, problem, and client. If the assessment is to be carried out in an institution, e.g., in a ward of a psychiatric hospital, there may be less pressure to begin intervention, and more time available (and necessary) to obtain information; thus, the assessment, including recording procedures, interviews with clients and ward personnel, and so on, might take several weeks. On the other hand, in a situation in a family service agency where the client is seeking immediate help, the assessment might take only two hours. The fact that assessment can progress rapidly in such a situation, and tangible, concrete intervention begin, may enhance the client's motivation not only to continue in the program, but to cooperate in its implementation. Thus, at least part of the reason for the excessively high drop-out rates in many forms of traditional programs—with up to 50 and 60 percent of clients dropping out after the first interview (Garfield, 1971; Briar, 1967)—might be eliminated; a behavioral program can provide immediate and tangible intervention procedures. The behaviorally-oriented social worker will not explore the client's problems interminably; he will be oriented to action, and to taking responsibility for such action.

All of this assumes, of course, that the social worker is moving at the client's pace, working to establish rapport with the client, and coordinating his efforts with what the client needs and wants. It also assumes that there is no formal end to the assessment process in behavior modification. Throughout the intervention program, recorded data and feedback from the client insure that if new strategies are necessary, or old ones need to be revised, such adaptations can and will be made.

Phases of Assessment

A cardinal principle intrinsic to the nature of the practice of behavior modification is that each target behavior is unique: it is emitted by a unique person, at a unique time, under a unique set of circumstances. As a result, the social worker must be flexible and creative in his application of behavioral concepts to each situation.

Nevertheless, there *is* a series of more or less sequential steps that may be useful in assessing a problem and developing an intervention strategy. Frequently, these steps logically would occur out of sequence, and often several procedures may occur concurrently. There are also situations in which not all the steps are necessary. These steps, then, are only suggested. It should be noted that, while many of these phases are appropriate to any behavioral assessment, they are largely derived from, and intended for use in, interventions with an operant emphasis. When respondent features are present in a given problem configuration, e.g., anxiety, irrational fears, and so on, the social worker should consider some of the assessment procedures designed specifically for respondent behaviors. Specific guidelines for the assessment of respondent behaviors are presented in Chapter 19.

The basic steps in behavioral assessment are to:

1. evaluate the presenting problem;
2. survey the functional and dysfunctional patterns of the client's behaviors in their environmental context;
3. specify the target behaviors;
4. establish priorities;
5. determine who can best mediate;
6. determine the location for the intervention;
7. collect and analyze baseline data on the target behavior;
8. specify the controlling events;
9. establish terminal goals and interim objectives;
10. select the intervention plan and specific modification techniques;
11. evaluate and select potential reinforcers;
12. collect and analyze data on changes in behavior subsequent to intervention.

1. EVALUATING THE PRESENTING PROBLEM

Despite social work's efforts to take the initiative in identifying human problems and to offer help assertively when needed as early as possible, in most situations it is not the social worker who first identifies a problem. More often, the problem has been known for some time to someone else—the client himself, those who have been adversely affected by his behavior, or, possibly, some agent of society who is concerned about his disturbing behaviors. The problem, initially presented to the social worker, may be an inappropriate focus for the ultimate intervention. In family agencies, problems may be described to the social worker by an angry spouse or an anxious mother. Problems may be brought to the school social worker by a harried, overworked teacher, to social workers in hospital or outpatient clinics by a misinformed doctor, in welfare agencies by a frustrated volunteer, and in institutions by rule-oriented attendants. In such situations, some semblance of behavioral change goals have already been established by the complainant, if not by the client. The social worker's first task, therefore, is to evaluate the definition of the problem and its putative source.

It is easy to suggest that the social worker has no right to challenge the goals of those who seek help in changing the behavior of others, if the behavioral goals are, indeed, socially acceptable. But the social worker's responsibilities are broader than running a behavioral-change department store: they include concern for the social context of the behavior and its implications for others in the client's environment.

As was noted in the Introduction, the term "client" is used throughout this book to refer to those individuals who are complaining about, or being hurt by, others' behaviors, and to those individuals whose behavior ("target behavior") is identified by themselves or by others (when the social worker concurs with this evaluation) as requiring change. The target behavior must be changed to ease the discomfort of the "client system," that is, the individual or individuals who are suffering because of the target behavior. It is clear, however, that any problem usually involves more than one individual in any social system, whether it be marital, parent—child, or institution—resident relationships.

Furthermore, the target behaviors of individuals in such social systems are often mutually reinforcing; the problem or target behavior of one (nagging by wife, truancy by child, nontalking of patient) is often partly a product of the behavior of the other (staying out late by the husband, parents belittling the value of education, lack of social stimulation from other residents or staff). Both sets of behavior are subject to the same learning principles. The chain of reinforcements through the series of reciprocal interactions that culminate in the target behavior is a long and complex one, and a major subject of assessment. However, it is generally helpful to focus on a few central problem behaviors that are the sources of greatest irritation to those exhibiting the behavior, or those in the environment, or both. One might expect (although this should be tested) that the network of responses to improvement in these target behaviors will be equally widespread.

The social worker must also consider a number of other factors.

First, are the changes reasonable? Are they consistent with reasonable goals for the client and those in their environment? Sometimes requests for change are attempts to subvert an individual's efforts to attack or remove unfair, oppressive factors in their environment, such as inhumane prison conditions, restrictive welfare laws, racial prejudice, sexual oppression, parental overcontrol, and so on. In such cases, a social worker's values should preclude his participation in efforts to suppress reasonable attempts to change such environmental systems. Rather, the social worker might direct his or her efforts to altering the goals or behavior of those who are pressing to change a person's behavior, helping the client develop more effective ways of dealing with the oppression, and perhaps serving as, or finding others to act as, an advocate for the client's cause.

In effect, the social worker must participate in the process of deciding what (and who) is to be the target of intervention, if any. Should the social worker aid in suppressing dissension among rebelling residents in a poorly run institution, condition compliance in emotionally abused children, or manipulate sexual behavior to coincide with dysfunctional or arbitrary sexual codes?

In many situations, social workers must see their role as broader than an individually-oriented change agent and consider a more basic social-work role in bringing about social change, which, in turn, will serve to increase those factors in society that reinforce functional, satisfying human behavior and relationships, and decrease oppressive forces.

Even in situations in which individuals seek specific behavioral change, the question should be asked: what pressure is being exerted on the individuals to change their behavior? What personal cost is involved in their changing this behavior, and is there an alternative line of action if the behavior is not changed? The social workers should ask themselves whether they must accept all requests presented to them by clients for change, or whether they have the responsibility to use whatever influence they have to urge clients and others in their environment to evaluate change goals.

A second factor to consider is whether changes in clients' behavior will enable them to function more effectively in their general life situation, within the context of the laws and reasonable conventions under which their chosen reference group operates.

Here, the social worker must be aware of the expectations of significant others for the client's behavior and evaluate their reasonableness. The social worker must also consider the *norms* of the particular sociocultural group with which the client identifies. While it is dangerous to evaluate cultural norms through the filter of one's own culture and experience, it is equally hazardous to accept any group of norms as acceptable simply because they exist.

It would be inappropriate here to explore all the issues associated with the development of a point of reference from which to evaluate the norms that guide behavior and the expectations about behavior. This is not to discount, however, the importance of this issue. The social worker must be conversant both with the behavioral expectations of the groups he works with at any point in time, and with the methods through which the social control of particular groups influence behavior. There may be pronounced behavioral differences between people from urban and rural environments, with different religious affiliations, educational levels, and from different ethnic groups. There are also significant variations within each of these groupings.

Despite the awareness about the controlling influences of behavior, social workers should not make the questionable assumption that what is done by most is "good," and what is done by a few is "bad." Furthermore, social workers should not make the assumption that any particular individual shares—or *should* share—all the behavioral expectations of their particular reference group. In the final analysis, it is the choice of the clients, made without unreasonable pressure from others, and aimed at nondestructive, self-fulfilling, and satisfying behavior on their part—however they define satisfying—which should determine behavioral goals.

Another important consideration is whether or not the identified problems lend themselves to behavioral change. Often, problems brought to a social worker can be identified as primarily ones of decision making (e.g., should I get a divorce; should I relinquish my unwanted child or get an abortion; should I move from my rural home to the city?). In such cases, help in evaluating the options and making an intelligent choice becomes the appropriate goal.

Helping clients with decision making can be an integral part of the behavior modification process. The social worker can help the client make a rational choice among the options he or she has open. In order to do so, the social worker helps the client seek answers to such questions as:

1. What are all the specific behavioral options I have open to me at this time?
2. Will these options change in the foreseeable future?
3. What would be the probable short-range and long-range positive

and negative consequences of each possible behavior for myself and for other people in my environment?

4. What additional information do I need to make a decision?
5. To what extent can I try out these behavioral options?
6. To what extent would anxiety interfere with various options?

Premature focus on an apparent specific problem area, without consideration of the decisions implicit in altering a particular behavior, should be avoided. A client's difficulty in focusing on a particular problem or following through on a particular plan may be an indication that focus on that problem is either inappropriate or, at least, premature. Zealots for "getting to the action" of behavior change may overlook the essential foundation work of determining not only who the target of behavior change is to be, but what indeed is the behavior to be changed, and what are the goals of the worker's activities.

> Jill and Randy approached the agency with a request for sex counseling. Neither were enjoying their sexual relationship and Randy had become increasingly sexually uninterested in Jill. The social worker proceeded to have the couple engage in behavioral exercises to enhance their sexual awareness and "pleasuring" of each other. After several weeks of treatment, it was obvious that Randy was using various means to avoid carrying out his social worker's "homework assignments." The social worker noted Randy's avoidance, suspended the "homework" and explored in greater depth Randy's feeling towards the marriage. Randy anxiously revealed that he considered his marriage to Jill a mistake; he never really loved her, but married her only to rid himself of family pressure (Jill's parents were Randy's parents' closest friends). Randy had loved—and still loved—Belle, who came from a family Randy's parents did not like. Subsequent discussions with Randy and Jill led to the dissolution of the marriage (Jill actually preferred to pursue her career in music and wanted "freedom" more than marriage, but had previously felt guilty about this) and Randy's ultimate marriage to Belle.

Finally, the social worker evaluates the extent to which the problem behavior is a product of emotional (or respondent) reactions to life situations that impede behaving in a functional manner. Most often such respondent behavior is found in the form of anxieties, fears, guilt, and anger. Decreasing these dysfunctional emotional reactions through such procedures as systematic desensitization can pave the way to more functional behaviors, which may be increased through the use of operant procedures. For example, an individual who is prevented by his anxiety from approaching potential employers can be freed, through an anxiety-decreasing procedure such as systematic desensitization, to engage in the operant behaviors (brought about through modeling and positive reinforcement) needed to find and keep a job.

2. SURVEYING THE FUNCTIONAL AND DYSFUNCTIONAL PATTERNS OF THE CLIENT'S BEHAVIOR IN THEIR ENVIRONMENTAL CONTEXT

Initially, problems may be perceived as the client's own general discontent about his situation, or a cluster of more or less vague complaints by those in his environment. It is often useful to have the client, or those seeking change in the client's behavior, complete one of the questionnaires or checklists mentioned earlier. These can provide the initial data to objectify the client's patterns of behaviors and the variables in the environment that seem to control his behavior. Kanfer and Saslow (1965) have developed a comprehensive instrument as a guide for the worker in eliciting preliminary information in situations in which behavioral change seems indicated. The five major areas they recommend exploring are discussed below.

CLASSIFY EXCESSES AND DEFICITS

A description of the various complaints and problems is obtained to develop some conception of the total range of problems. Major complaints are then classified in terms of behavioral excesses and deficits. For each excess and deficit, the frequency, intensity, duration, and appropriateness of form or location are described. This would include behaviors that are perceived by the client or significant others either because they occur, or fail to occur, in situations where the prevailing social attitudes are against their occurrence or nonoccurrence.

EVALUATE THE CLIENT'S ASSETS

In addition to assessing dysfunctional behavior, it is equally important to explore assets or strengths, both in terms of the client's functional behavior (i.e., what he does well) and in terms of the human and material resources the client has in his environment. This material will be useful not only in determining what resources the social worker has available in developing an intervention strategy, but also for the necessary task of establishing priorities for intervention and predicting the effectiveness of that intervention. In line with this, the social worker explores what attempts the client and those in his environment have made to modify the client's behavior in the past. To what extent have these attempts been successful; what ideas does the client currently have for modifying the target behavior; what changes in behavior or situation does the client hope for; finally, what are the client's expectations and preconceptions about the help the social worker will provide?

ANTICIPATE THE IMPACT OF CHANGE

No problem exists in a social vacuum. Assessment includes the collection of information about the reciprocal interaction between the problem behaviors and their environmental determinants. Preliminary explorations lead to the determination of who is suffering as a result of the problem behavior, as well as who is profiting from it. While all those involved with the client may protest—and perhaps believe—that they are upset by the problem behavior, there are often social systems (families, teacher–student relationships, patient–staff relationships) in which some individuals profit from the dysfunctional behavior of others, and, as a result, reinforce the very behavior they object to.

Typical examples of this sort of situation would be the lonely mother who keeps her child dependent on her, or the husband of an alcoholic who maintains her as a dependent, undemanding child. Such situations pose serious problems for intervention, since the improvement of the client's behavior may well remove reinforcements from those in the client's environment. Such reinforcements (or punishments) may be difficult to counter with reinforcements for functional behavior. The first step toward removing them—and offering the purveyor of the dysfunctional reinforcements new, less destructive behaviors—is their detection. Observation of the client's interaction with key people in his environment, especially at points when dysfunctional behavior is exhibited or at points when absent functional behavior should be exhibited, can facilitate such an assessment.

As noted previously, one individual's behavior is often another's environment. Changes in the client's behavior will generally affect the behavior of those in his environment, just as the behavior of those in the environment affect the client's behavior. Therefore, in considering any intervention, the social worker must try to anticipate how these changes will, in turn, affect those in the client's environment, and how this effect will ultimately affect the client's total situation. Teaching a client to subvert a dysfunctional social system from which he cannot extricate himself may ultimately boomerang on the client. Similarly, there is little question about the undesirability of helping people develop behaviors that are ultimately destructive to other members of our society.

Another implication of the reciprocal nature of behavior change is the need to consider and often involve people in the client's role network who both affect the client's pattern of behavior and will be affected by any changes in that pattern. Liberman (1970) suggests that in the application of a behavioral change model to family therapy, each member of the family should be asked two questions:

1. What behavior would you like to see changed in the other members of the family?

2. In what ways would you like to be different from the way you are now?

The answers to these questions provide some direction in choosing target behaviors, as well as some clues about how each family member's behavior influences that of the others.

The client may well be getting reinforcement for dysfunctional behavior, or fear loss of reinforcements or even punishment if he relinquishes the dysfunctional behavior. The social worker should attempt to anticipate what the long-range results of changing the target behavior in the client's environment will be. If these are anticipated and shared with the client and others working with him, their negative impact may be minimized.

PHYSIOLOGICAL AND BIOLOGICAL CONSIDERATIONS

Behavior is obviously not determined or maintained exclusively by the environment, but by physiological and organic factors as well. The social worker is obviously limited in what he or she can evaluate in the area of physiological functioning. Indeed, there is much that is not yet known about the physiological basis for human behavior. Referral to a physician in many cases can be expensive, time-consuming, and perhaps unnecessary. However, if there is some suspicion of physical illness or other organic basis for the problems at hand, the social worker should arrange for the client to see a physician.

The social worker should also consider to what extent the client's physical makeup has a clear influence on his behavior. The client's general health, energy, physical attractiveness, handicaps, and intellectual capacities, and the client's own perceptions of these variables, may all have a profound effect on his behavior. If there is a physical problem that impedes behavioral change, the social worker, in consultation with the appropriate medical personnel, should consider whether or not it is reversible, and, if so, what the history of attempts to remedy the situation has been. The social worker might also think about the behavioral consequences of any unusual physical problems or handicaps and the extent to which they will influence behavioral change. If these problems are amenable to medical treatment, early assessment may be directed toward helping the client obtain the resources that will remove, to the extent possible, such physical obstacles to behavior change.

A recent case in which one of the authors served as consultant illustrates the necessity of checking possible physiological causes to be sure the intervention is adequately planned. A young mother sought help in stopping her four-year-old daughter's whining and crying which could be traced to no antecedent events. A behavioral program was begun emphasizing time-out (negative punishment) and positive reinforcement. After two weeks with no apparent success, the program was being re-evaluated. At the same time, and coincidentally, the mother brought her daughter to a physician for her annual check-up, during which the physician discovered, deep in the ear of the child, a seed that she had apparently stuck in there several months before. (At the previous physical exam, the physician had not noticed the seed.) The discomfort from the seed, about which the child had been afraid or embarrassed to tell her mother, had produced the intermittent whining. Once the seed was flushed out, the child's "irrational" whining and crying stopped immediately.

ASSESS THE PEOPLE IN THE IMMEDIATE SOCIAL ENVIRONMENT

Assessment often focuses on the individuals within the client's family and other significant persons (such as employees, co-workers, teachers, nurses, etc.). Observation of the relationships between these individuals and the client focuses on the ways in which they mutually affect each other's behaviors—for example, does a husband tend to control his wife through guilt, ridicule, fear, or statements of love? An analysis of this kind becomes even more important in assessing mutually destructive relationships. The task, then, is to determine what maintains such relationships. Such data lead to procedures to strengthen the relationship, or perhaps to procedures that will hasten its dissolution in a way as satisfactory as possible for all concerned.

A survey of the people who have potential or actual influence on the client's behavior will aid later in the selection of a mediator. It will also suggest possible contingencies to be used in the intervention plan. An assessment of the mutual expectations of the client and those in his environment can also help in selecting people who can be helpful in interventions.

3. SPECIFYING THE TARGET BEHAVIORS

The purpose of this part of the assessment is to determine what specific behaviors should be changed, in terms of frequency, duration, form, or location. The importance of specifying the exact behavior to be modified cannot be overstated. This, of course, does not mean ignoring complex behaviors, but being as clear and concise as possible in specifying what those behaviors are, including breaking them down into their component parts when possible. Without this important step, subsequent efforts may prove worthless. If such specification is lacking, it is quite possible for the social worker to have difficulty in "knowing where to start." When looking at what appears to be a global and complex problem, he may feel frustrated, if not overwhelmed, by the futility of trying to cope with such vast, global problems. Furthermore, the selection of specific interventive procedures to be used without knowing the specific problems would be extremely difficult. But given such specification, one can go on to a more systematic, step-by-step selection of interventive procedures appropriate to the specific target behaviors, and one has both the basis for gradually changing complex problems as well as a criterion for the ongoing evaluation of effectiveness. As each component behavior of the problem is changed, the entire complex of problem behaviors is modified.

It is important to note that these descriptions should be of specific behaviors and not generalizations or descriptions of their products or effects. Thus, the problem should be stated, "The child doesn't do his homework"—*not* "The child isn't working up to his potential." And the complaints of the husband should be that, "The wife doesn't wash the dishes after supper," *not* "She is a poor housekeeper." While the wife's complaints should be that, "The husband doesn't take showers," *not* that, "He smells bad."

One reaction to such specification often is that "the problem is broader than that" or "these are only part of the problem." This may well be true. But the totality of human experience is a composite of such small behaviors. Small changes in behavior are frequently cumulative; they lead to larger changes, both through the principle of generalization and through a reciprocating effect. The easing of tensions in one area sometimes leads to a similar easing in other areas, and to an increase in reciprocal reinforcement. Once an individual in a relationship modifies even a small behavior in a way that is reinforcing to his or her partner, the environment is changed—albeit in a small way. However, as the goodwill of significant others increases, the rate and duration of the individual's desirable behavior is likely to increase, and his undesirable behavior will tend to extinguish. Finally, only when behaviors are specifically defined can any changes brought about in their rate, duration, or intensity be accurately detected, and progress evaluated. Thus, such specification is an important aid in the determination of effectiveness.

Disagreement over the choice of target behaviors can be a major hurdle to behavioral change. The social worker must often negotiate with a number of influential individuals, each of whom may have different notions about what the behavioral goals should be. These may not coincide with the social worker's—or the client's—choice. For example, parents may wish their children to comply with every demand, reasonable or not; teachers may wish to have every child sit still with his hands folded through interminable classes; wardens may expect religious conversions and monastic behavior from their prisoners; wives may expect unconditional affection without sexual demands from their husbands. All of them may expect the social worker to intervene to achieve their goals. The social worker in these situations has the task of demonstrating empathy for these wishes, yet rephrasing the problems in such a way as to achieve some sort of equilibrium between the rights and expectations of all those involved in the problem.

Such an equilibrium may often test the social worker's values, since the behavior the social worker helps the client achieve will not be occurring in the context of the best of all worlds. Contemporary marriage may be a flawed institution; imprisonment may be an inhumane, socially discriminative, destructive process; racial and economic prejudices may affect societal expectations about individual behavior (the poor must behave more morally than the rich); school curricula may be archaic, and irrelevant to contemporary needs. Yet social workers often find themselves in the position of changing behaviors to conform to these imperfect institutions. While social workers have the responsibility of attempting to modify and improve these social institutions, they must also accept their limitations in doing so. At best, such institutional changes are slow to come, and the clients social workers see live in the present, and need help now. Thus, social workers may reluctantly, but necessarily, find themselves in the position of teaching the child how to function optimally in the school system, the couple how to optimize their own fulfillment through their marriage, and the oppressed minority group member how to get optimal benefits from an oppressive society. The alternative—refusing to get involved with the individuals until the system changes—seems a cruel and futile alternative that victimizes the wrong people. Social workers operate in systems neither completely of their own making nor of their choice; they must help people get the most out of life in an imperfect world.

4. ESTABLISHING PRIORITIES

This part of the assessment deals with the establishment of the order in which the target behaviors are to be modified. In most situations encountered by social workers, there is more than one specific target behavior. In such cases, some system of priorities or sequencing must be established.

There are, of course, situations in which there is a clear-cut priority dictated by the danger posed by a particular behavior to the client or to those around him. The prevention of genuine efforts at suicide might precede the improvement of social relationships. The prevention of fire-setting should take priority over the improvement of school attendance. However, it could be that such problems are interrelated, and that when the client achieves success and satisfaction in socially acceptable behaviors (e.g., social activities, employment, schoolwork), the potentially harmful behaviors that have obvious aversive qualities (such as suicidal gestures, fire-setting, and fighting) will tend to diminish. Certainly the client's wishes—based on his own discomfort and his own goals —are important. The client's motivation for change is in itself a major reinforcer of change in those behaviors he finds unpleasant. If the people in the client's environment who have significant influence on him are suffering as a result of his behavior, and if they are also capable of dispensing powerful reinforcers to the client, then their major concerns are given consideration in the setting of priorities.

Often, however, neither the client nor others in his environment will have a clear choice for the initial target behavior, or the one with the highest priority. More likely they will present an unordered, vague complex of problem behaviors. Several criteria can be useful in setting priorities:

1. *Choose target behaviors that are annoying but have a high probability of being successfully changed.* All other things being equal, it is wise to select as a first target behavior that which appears most amenable, at that time, to intervention. Generally, the earlier in the intervention program, the higher the probability of success should be, particularly if the task is small. The feeling of accomplishment, along with the praise (social reinforcement) that comes with the successful completion of a task, tends to reinforce not only that task, but can generalize to subsequent attempts to modify one's behavior. Success in changing behavior is highly motivating to the client and the mediator (not to mention the social worker), and increases their confidence in attempting to deal with more difficult problems. Conversely, failure can impede progress toward terminal goals by making attempts at behavioral change aversive not only to the clients but to the frustrated mediators and other individuals in their environment.

Mrs. Palama had been treated by a succession of welfare workers who had made valiant efforts to attack her wide range of problems, which included desertion by her husband, truancy and "predelinquent" behaviors by her children, a grossly run-down house, and general apathy and hopelessness on the part of Mrs. Palama and her four children. The previous social workers had tried with little success to find her a job, encourage her to seek medical care, and engage her in efforts to work on her children's behavior. She would manage to be out or to have company whenever they came, and the workers considered her "untreatable".

Her new social worker thought that Mrs. Palama had been overwhelmed with comprehensive programs for her family's rehabilitation and discouraged by false hopes generated by the previous social workers, as well as by her own excessive expectations for improvement in her situation.

The new social worker took Mrs. Palama out to lunch (a "bonus" reinforcement for the relationship), and attempted to demonstrate empathy for her past frustration and anger at the welfare workers. She also began to explore those factors in Mrs. Palama's life that were bothering her the most. Mrs. Palama spoke of her major frustration—the thing that really got her "down in the dumps"—the "mess" all over the house.

The social worker showed understanding of the fact that keeping the whole house clean was a "big hassle," and wondered if there was something in particular that annoyed her most. Mrs. Palama nodded, and said it was "the mess all over the floor." Focusing even more, the social worker wondered if there was a particular room in which the mess on the floor was most bothersome. Mrs. Palama answered that the kitchen was the worst—and that was where she spent most of her time. The social worker wondered if they could establish the goal of working on the kitchen floor. Mrs. Palama said she did not really know how to proceed, she did not even have a waste basket! The worker got together with Mrs. Palama and her children at their house, and suggested that the children get a cardboard box from the supermarket and decorate it as a family project. Then everyone in the family could place trash in the box. The preparation of the box, and, indeed, the cleaning of the kitchen floor, became a reinforcing family project.

A few days later Mrs. Palama displayed the clean kitchen floor to the social worker, who reinforced her with considerable praise. Mrs. Palama's small but clearly observable success paved the way for further efforts at cleaning the house, and gave her and the children hope and incentive for other changes.

2. In addition to illustrating the value of careful selection of initial and intermediate goals with a high probability of success, the above case also illustrates a second guiding principle in problem selection: *think small.* Too often, goals are stated in global terms, and attempts to achieve such long-range goals are taken in steps that are too large. The social worker can explain to the client and other interested parties that their long-range goals are valid, but trying to reach them in too few steps can be futile and destructive.

It may be useful to diagram this concept for clients as well as those in their environment by indicating that the client is currently at "A" and hopes to get to point "Z." It would be nice if it were possible to get there in one step. But, unfortunately, this is not often realistic.

Indeed, if clients keep reaching for "Z," they may never get there. Rather, it becomes important to identify the steps (intermediate behavioral goals) along the way to "Z," and work toward each in sequence. As noted above, each individual step should have a high probability of success. However each step should not be so simple that there is no challenge or feeling of success.

Often, the behavior required in a particular step is not exhibited at all by the client, or seems beyond his or her current abilities. Sometimes the goal behavior is actually a complex of behaviors. In such situations, the behavior is divided into sequential component parts, and each behavioral segment then becomes an interim target behavior.

This process of shaping requires careful selection of the intermediate goals. Again, each should be manageable and have a high probability of success, yet not be so simple as to be boring or unchallenging for the client. Each subsequent behavior builds on both the behavioral skills and the self-confidence generated by the previous step.

3. The third guideline is to *choose a behavior that, although perhaps limited and specific, will tend to help the client improve some important aspect of his social functioning.* Such behavior will tend to continue, and be maintained by the client's natural environment, even after the social worker leaves the situation. This "relevance of behavior rule" (Ayllon, 1968) suggests that only those behaviors that will be useful in the future should be the goal of intervention. Such behaviors themselves tend to generalize. That is, a functional behavior learned in one situation can be readily applied by the client to cope with other situations.

Parents follow the "relevance of behavior rule" in teaching their children to speak. Functional words like "water," "yes," "no," or "cookie" are taught early, before less functional words like "stone" and "atom." Similarly, the social worker may choose to focus first on developing basic social skills, assertiveness, and work habits in clients who have related problems.

In preparing a client to engage in more functional job behaviors, for example, specific behaviors such as promptness, courtesy, and cooperation may be learned. Discrimination training may be offered in such matters as when to ask questions of supervisors and when to try to figure things out oneself.

In social situations, the client can learn such building blocks as how to start a conversation with a stranger, or discrimination in the matter of what clothing to wear in which circumstances. Such behaviors will be functional not only in the present problem situation, but will help the client adapt and find reinforcement in unforeseen situations in the future.

4. A fourth guideline is that *it is generally preferable to think through the problem and establish intervention goals in the direction of increasing the incidence, duration, or intensity of behaviors rather than decreasing behaviors.* In situations of clear and present danger to clients or those in their environment, such an orientation may not be possible, since the dangerous behavior (such as physical attacks or illegal acts) must be confronted directly. However, it is difficult and sometimes impossible to remove the various reinforcements that maintain some dysfunctional behaviors. Extinction is a difficult process; many behaviors

are maintained by intermittent reinforcement, and they are likely to continue unless *all* reinforcements are eliminated.

In addition to extinction, positive or negative punishment may be employed to decrease the incidence of the undesired behavior. But these procedures have some hazards, as detailed in the first part of this book, and their use is best limited to situations in which there are no other options, or where they are at least used in combination with positive reinforcement.

Positive reinforcement has fewer side effects, and tends to be more effective; it is generally far easier to develop new behaviors than to remove old ones. Furthermore, the process builds on success, does not necessarily compete with other reinforcers in the natural environment, and generalizes to positive feelings toward the entire intervention process by encouraging the client's participation in further change efforts.

When problems are conceptualized in terms of increasing functional behaviors, and these socially desirable behaviors are indeed reinforced, then the undesirable behaviors often tend to disappear. When an individual is able to get what he wants in socially approved ways, he tends to use socially disapproved ways less often.

In summary, then, the selection of priorities for target behaviors includes consideration of what is urgent, and what clients and others around them want. The behaviors selected (especially initially) should: (1) have a high probability of success; (2) preferably be ones to be increased (rather than decreased); (3) be divided into a logical sequence of steps that build toward the long-range goal; (4) involve behaviors that will tend to be useful in a wide range of situations.

5. DETERMINING WHO CAN BEST MEDIATE

The implementation of a behavioral change strategy requires that: (1) someone create new consequences for the target behaviors; (2) someone undertake the collection of any data about the behavior deemed necessary by the social worker. The choice of that "someone" is another product of the assessment procedure.

Changing the consequences of behaviors and recording them can be done either by the social worker, a mediator (that is, someone who is concerned about the problem and spends time with the client in his natural environment) or the client himself. If the client is motivated to change, capable of recognizing his target behavior when it occurs—a skill that can be taught—and capable of supplying new contingencies for the behavior, then it is better that the client serve these functions himself, with or without the assistance and guidance of the social worker. (A useful guide to such self-modification is available; Watson & Tharp, 1972.)

However, the client may neither be in a position to control the contingencies of his behavior, nor be motivated, nor be able to alter or record them. In such a case, a third party should be selected to work with the social worker in developing an intervention plan, providing the new consequences of the target behavior and recording the results. For example, in marital and other familial situations, various family members may serve as mediators in planned, voluntary attempts to modify each other's behavior. (The process through which mediators are chosen, along with the procedures for working with them are discussed in Chapter 9). Generally, the choice of a mediator is based on who is motivated, has access to reinforcements, and is frequently present when the target behavior occurs.

Sometimes, it is possible for the social worker himself to provide contingencies for the target behaviors. In most cases, however, the social worker is rarely at the place where the problem behavior occurs at the time it occurs. Furthermore, the social worker is rarely part of the client's natural environment, and his mere presence may interfere with the occurrence of the client's typical behavior patterns. Any new contingencies initiated by the social worker may be difficult to generalize.

Exceptions to this, of course, are institutional settings where the worker has frequent contact with residents, such as working with "autistic" children, whose behavior is uncontrollable or intolerable to those in their natural environment, or in those situations where initial behavioral changes are so subtle or critical (such as in developing speech patterns) that time-consuming, exacting work is demanded in creating new contingencies for the target behavior (Lovaas, 1965). Even in those situations, however, the social worker can help in training technicians, aides, and relatives to carry out the requisite day-to-day activities. In fact, in many situations the social worker might initially carry out the intervention while potential mediators such as teachers, nurses, or parents observe the process and later take on the responsibilities for provision of contingencies themselves.

6. DETERMINING THE LOCATION FOR THE INTERVENTION

This phase of assessment examines the potential locations for the primary intervention process, e.g., home, school, worker's office, ward, and so on.

Generally, the location in the client's natural environment at which the target behavior usually occurs—or should occur—is the most desirable site for intervention. In cases where one wants to decrease behavior, it is obviously most desirable to have intervention take place at the times and in the places where the dysfunctional behavior usually occurs. In cases where what is desired is to increase behavior, reinforcement should be provided at the time and the place in which it would be appropriate for the desired behavior to occur. The social worker's office might be used to help the client acquire the appropriate behavior through modeling or behavioral rehearsal, or to train the client in the particular behavioral skills necessary for effective behavior in his natural environment.

The availability of motivated and competent mediators may also determine the locus of intervention. If a child has problems in both his history and English classes, but has a motivated, concerned, and relatively less burdened English teacher, and a punitive, overworked history teacher, the social worker might initiate behavioral change in the English class, hoping that any new behaviors will generalize to the history class.

Finally, determining which location will provide the highest probability of success should be a prime factor in making this decision. This includes considerations of such factors as which setting will be most hospitable (or be least inhospitable) to the intervention, which has the greatest resources available, and in which can the target behavior be dealt with directly and specifically.

7. COLLECTING AND ANALYZING BASELINE DATA ON THE TARGET BEHAVIOR

In order to understand the target behavior more fully, and to set the stage for evaluating the results of intervention, baseline data on the incidence of behavior prior to intervention is collected by the social worker, mediator, or self-modifying client. Baseline data are nothing more than a count of the frequency, or the measurement of the duration, of target behaviors prior to intervention. These data aid in assessment and are essential in accurately describing the current level of the behavior in its natural state. Only when such material is collected can the social worker best determine what seems to be the actual frequency or duration of the target behavior. The social worker may well find that the client or those in his environment have exaggerated the frequency or duration of occurrence of the target behavior. Baselining also enables one to develop hypotheses as to when, and under what conditions the target behavior occurs, thus facilitating intervention planning. For example, such data can provide answers to questions such as: in which classes does a child tend to engage in disruptive activity; in what situations does the young adult think about suicide; when and where are arguments most likely to occur in a family; how often and under what circumstances does grandfather come home drunk?

Baseline data enable the social worker to assess the effectiveness of intervention plans through later comparison of the baseline occurrence of behavior with post-intervention occurrences. The length of time involved in collecting such data varies, but, in general, baselining goes on until the social worker is reasonably certain that a more or less stable rate of behavior can be discerned, so that the change in rate caused by the planned behavioral change can be evaluated.

Baseline data are accumulated in various ways. Generally, data are collected for a consistent period of time (e.g., the first five minutes of each hour), and at a fixed time (e.g., dinner hour, English class). However, it is important to be aware that these periods may not accurately represent the full range of target behaviors so that more flexible data collection may be necessary. Further, the greater the probability that a behavior will occur, the shorter the period of observation required. Methods of collecting baseline behavior are discussed in Chapter 10.

The acquisition of baseline data is more complicated—but equally necessary—in complex family interactions. Patterson and Reid (1970) developed a reliable method of collecting data on the rate of a wide range of reciprocal social behaviors in family units by defining and coding both specific target behaviors and their consequences for four days a week, over two week periods, for approximately one hour per day. All observations occurred in the family's kitchen, in which a major portion of the significant family interactions occurred.

Clients and others in their environment often resent baselining procedures, and are eager to get on with the intervention. The degree to which data collection is considered aversive by teachers and parents can be a more important factor in determining mediator cooperation than the concern over the problem behavior (Tharp & Wetzel, 1969). Since data acquired through baselining is often essential in a well-formulated intervention plan, the social worker should provide reinforcement for data collection, and attempt to diminish its aversive consequences. Procedures for doing this are presented in Chapter 9 and Chapter 10.

8. SPECIFYING THE CONTROLLING EVENTS

The goal of this phase of assessment is twofold: (1) identification of the conditions or events that precede the target behavior—discriminative stimuli (S^D) for operant behavior and eliciting stimuli (S^E) for respondent behavior; (2) identification of the counterproductive consequences of behavior—the events or conditions that reinforce undesirable behavior or do not reinforce desirable behavior. Such identification may provide the information necessary to decide on a specific intervention. For example, with respect to antecedents, it may be possible in the situations cited earlier, to determine in which classes a child tends to engage in disruptive activity; in which situations the young adult thinks about suicide; when and where family arguments tend to occur; and the circumstances under which grandfather comes home drunk. The social worker may be able to take his cue directly from this information to design his intervention program to build in more effective discriminative stimuli, provide discrimination training, supply the necessary tools or materials for a particular program, and so on.

Similarly, with respect to consequences, the social worker might be able to determine that a given undesirable behavior is being reinforced and suggest withdrawal of the reinforcement to decrease the behavior; or he might determine that positive reinforcement is lacking in some situation, and such reinforcement can be built in to increase desired behavior.

The identification of controlling events usually proceeds in conjunction with baselining. Forms that are used for baselining can also include spaces for jotting down specific antecedent and consequent events. In fact, one of the advantages associated with baselining and determination of pertinent antecedent and consequent conditions is that maladaptive behavior is often observed to decrease purely as a result of such recording and the resulting recognition by the client or mediator of dysfunctional patterns of behavior.

9. ESTABLISHING TERMINAL GOALS AND INTERIM OBJECTIVES

Using all of the previous information—ranging from presenting complaints to baseline data—ultimate or terminal goals are established. These goals may well be tentative, but they should be identified as specifically as possible in terms of the relevant behaviors to be performed; that is, given a particular desired goal, the social worker and the client should determine which specific behaviors will accomplish the desired ends, how the client will behave when the aims are achieved, and the conditions under which the behaviors can be expected to occur. The establishment of terminal goals also means clear specification of the kinds of changes that are desired—e.g., an increase or decrease in the frequency of occurrence or duration of a behavior, a change in the location in which the behavior typically occurs, and so on. This specification insures not only that the goal will be precise and its achievement (or nonachievement) evident enough for evaluative purposes, but also that it will be clear enough for the client to obtain feedback on the progress of his own program (Bandura, 1969).

Specific criteria for termination are also established. These, of course, are directly related to goal specification. When the goal involves changing the frequency of occurrence of some behavior (either upward or downward), the criterion for termination would be the achievement of a pre-set rate of that behavior, maintained over a pre-set period of time to insure its stability. Thus, if the goal is to eliminate Andy's tantrum behavior, the criterion for termination could be no tantrums (as specifically defined) over a period of three weeks. If the goal is to increase Kay's conversation with her husband, the termination criterion (in addition to satisfaction of both spouses) might be that Kay initiates at least two conversations per evening for two weeks.

If the goal involves changing the duration of a given behavior or set of behaviors, the termination criteria should be set in terms of intervals. Thus, if the goal is to increase the amount of time Chris spends studying for his doctoral examinations, termination of at least the formal part of the intervention program might come when the data indicates that Chris has been studying nine hours per day, six days a week (even doctoral students deserve a day off) for one month.

As noted previously, most terminal goals can only be reached by setting specific behavioral objectives as interim steps in the process of attempting to reach the ultimate goal. The social worker and client establish *sequential, manageable* steps, each one being mastered before a new one is attempted. Each step must be highly specific in its description and must be described in terms of the requisite behavior, rather than the ultimate goal. Thus, an ultimate goal for a young woman might be acquiring boyfriends. An intermediate goal might be "looking better," defined at least partly as weight loss. However, while the intermediate goal may be defined as weight loss, the steps for achieving this loss are defined as specific behaviors necessary to achieve the weight loss, such as not eating between meals, or increasing the hours per week spent in exercising.

Now the interim steps should not be seen as ends in themselves. Embracing one's spouse, dressing oneself, gaining confidence in talking to others, having conversations with one's children during dinner, teaching a child not to jump out of his seat or yell in class, all of these must be evaluated in terms of their contribution to the achievement of broader goals for each individual. Each may comprise an important component that contributes to the overall success of a behavioral program.

10. SELECTING THE INTERVENTION PLAN AND SPECIFIC MODIFICATION TECHNIQUES

The social worker reviews all of the preceding material with the client, or mediator, or both and attempts to match the assessment with a specific intervention strategy and the appropriate behavior modification techniques. Thus, analysis of what the problem is, where it occurs, how serious it is, who is involved, the type of behavioral change sought, the physical material and social resources available, and so on, all play a part in determining the type of intervention. This is the heart of the assessment process—its *raison d'etre*. Strangely enough, however, this is probably the easiest part of the process, because the entire assessment has been carried out in terms directly relevant to intervention. Thus, at the most basic level, when the problem involves the goal of decreasing undesired behaviors, the intervention program involves the selection of procedures to decrease or weaken behavior. Similarly, when the problem involves the necessity for increasing desired behaviors, the social worker selects a program to increase or strengthen behaviors (see Chapter 15 for overviews of such programs). The social worker familiar with the specific situation of his particular client also should be either familiar with the literature or have access to it (or have a pretty good consultant or supervisor), so that he might determine the kinds of strategies and procedures that have been used successfully with similar problems in the past. He can then select and adapt those procedures to the existing situation (see Part III of this book, which provides illustrations of behavior modification applied to problem areas frequently encountered in social work practice).

Since the topic of Chapter 15 is an overview of the various intervention strategies available, no more need be said at this point about how to select them. Similarly, Chapter 12 presents specific criteria for technique selection, so further discussion of specific techniques is deferred until then.

11. EVALUATING AND SELECTING POTENTIAL REINFORCERS

Most behavioral intervention strategies include positive reinforcement, not only because positive reinforcement is one of the most effective, adaptable, and universally available forms of behavior modification, but also because its use tends to involve fewer potential complications and dangers than other behavior modification procedures, namely, extinction, negative reinforcement, and punishment.

The use of positive reinforcement, however, requires the careful selection of reinforcers. There is no way to guarantee the effectiveness of a reinforcer chosen *a priori*. By definition, a stimulus can be considered a reinforcer only if its presentation indeed affects the subsequent frequency, duration, or intensity of the target behavior. There are no universal reinforcers. What is reinforcing for one person's particular behavior may not be for another's. Futhermore, what is reinforcing to an individual today may have no effect on him several weeks later. The differences may be due to the nature of the behavior that is being reinforced. Also, if a client has been deprived of a reinforcer which he normally likes (food, candy, praise), then he will be more likely to be reinforced by its presentation. Conversely, if he has had too much of the reinforcer, he becomes satiated, and it ceases to reinforce.

An error commonly made by social workers is to assume that what is reinforcing for them will also be reinforcing for their clients. What might be reinforcing for a social worker in a given situation may be quite insignificant to someone else. Such differences may be attributable to differences in cultural background, personal style, social class, and so on. In general, social reinforcers such as praise and smiles ultimately tend to be more functional than primary reinforcers, but they may be less effective in early stages of intervention. Reinforcers vary greatly from individual to individual and from situation to situation. In view of this, as wide a choice of reinforcers as possible should be available.

How does the social worker evaluate possible reinforcers? There is no perfect system. Each attempt at reinforcement is a trial to be confirmed or rejected on the basis of subsequent observed change—or lack of change—in the target behavior. There are several methods, however, that often prove useful in selecting effective reinforcers. Since most of these have been discussed before, only a brief summary of the methods for selecting reinforcers is necessary here.

In considering different reinforcers, the social worker keeps in mind three basic criteria (Reese, 1966):

1. Can they be presented immediately following a desired behavior?
2. Can they be used without inducing satiation?
3. Are they in reasonable supply (i.e., are they available at reasonable expense)?

Following are several methods for selecting reinforcers:

OPEN-ENDED SELECTION BY THE CLIENT

The client can be asked to list those things he most likes to do, or the items he most enjoys. To make the task easier, a reinforcement checklist such as the Reinforcement Survey Schedule (Cautela & Kastenbaum, 1967) may be used. However, open-ended selection by the client can lead to choices that are often too expensive or otherwise unsuitable to use as reinforcers.

REINFORCEMENT MENU

The client can make selections from a reinforcement menu (Addison, 1966), that is, a list that includes only those reinforcers that the social worker has determined are available and practical to use. For example, Clements and McKee (1968) have developed a reinforcement menu for prisoners—including such items as use of the radio, access to magazines, and use of the typewriter—that was effectively used in modifying prisoner behavior. This menu is an example of the use of the range of reinforcements already available within an institution, and involving no additional cost.

PREMACK PRINCIPLE

A more complicated but often more effective way than the reinforcement menu to select reinforcers is the Premack Principle (Premack, 1959). It suggests that to increase the occurrence of a low-probability behavior (that is, something that a person does not do very often), make a high-probability behavior (something that the person *does* very often) contingent on his performance of the low-probability behavior. In other words, the behavior that tends to occur more often in the person's ordinary life experiences will serve as a reinforcer for the desired low-occurrence behaviors. In order to select high-probability behaviors, the social worker or mediator observes what the client tends to do most often at the time and place in which the desired behavior is to occur.

PREVIOUS EXPERIENCE

Another method of selecting reinforcers is to determine what has been reinforcing to the client previously, and to consider those reinforcers for possible use. For example, one of the authors found his daughter to be highly reinforced during potty training by little, gift-wrapped, inexpensive toys. These reinforcers were used again successfully roughly one year later in other circumstances. Of course, what is reinforcing at one point in time may not be reinforcing at a later point in time; this is a matter to be determined both logically (does it seem likely that a given reinforcer will continue to work?) and empirically (does it, in fact, work?).

REVIEW OF THE LITERATURE

Reviewing the literature to see what reinforcers have been used in other programs with similar clients and problems might yield several suggestions. Again, though, whether a given reinforcer will work for a given client at a given time is a matter to be tested empirically.

SOCIAL REINFORCEMENT

While there may be no really universal reinforcer, genuine praise and attention (social reinforcement), if not selected as the major reinforcer, should always be built into programs to accompany other forms of reinforcement. Social reinforcement is the least expensive, yet one of the most effective and easily generalized forms of reinforcement. Thus, a concrete reinforcer can eventually be phased out so that the social reinforcement may become sufficient in and of itself to maintain the desired behavior.

12. COLLECTING AND ANALYZING DATA ON CHANGES IN BEHAVIOR SUBSEQUENT TO INTERVENTION

The assessment procedures described so far in this chapter are intended to guide the development of intervention strategies. Assessment does not stop, however, with the implementation of an intervention program.

The success or failure of the intervention cannot be adequately evaluated through the subjective impressions of either the social worker or the client. Even the most objective social workers tend to filter their impressions of client progress through their own and their client's hopes, expectations, and mood swings. In addition, frequently, the social worker and the client may not be in a position to describe accurately changes in the target behaviors. Whenever possible, evaluation of an intervention strategy should be made through the use of objective records (see Chapter 10).

Records of the frequency or duration of occurrence of target behaviors can, when compared to baseline data, provide information on the rate of progress, the extent to which progress has been stabilized (which can lead to such decisions as changing from a fixed to a variable reinforcement schedule), and evidence of any retrogression. Such ongoing analysis allows the social worker to mold the intervention program as it proceeds, move on to new target behaviors, or steps in shaping, and, as the intervention progresses, move back a step if there is retrogression, or decide that termination of the intervention is indicated. If termination is indicated, the worker should generally plan follow-up contacts (as described in Chapter 15) with the client, or those concerned with the client's behavior, or both, to evaluate whether the changed behavior has been sustained.

Summary

Effective behavior modification requires careful, comprehensive assessment and definition of the client's problems in the context of his natural environment and the specific target behaviors to be changed.

Assessment includes consideration of the factors that may be maintaining the problems in the client's environment. When these include either obstructed access to legitimate social and economic opportunities, or oppression from those who have control over the client, social workers must assess to what extent and through what channels they might successfully intervene. Social workers practice in an imperfect world with imperfect social institutions, however, and they must balance their efforts at social change with their efforts to help clients derive optimum satisfaction from a flawed environment.

When it appears that some change *must* occur in the behavior of an individual, the social worker can draw on several sources of information to determine what behaviors should be changed, and what resources are available to effect those changes. These sources of information include interviews, checklists and inventories, and direct observation of the problem behaviors.

The major steps in assessment for behavior modification include:

1. Evaluation of the presenting problem;
2. Survey of the functional and dysfunctional patterns of the client's behaviors in their environmental context;
3. Specification of the target behaviors;
4. Establishment of priorities;
5. Determination of who can best mediate;
6. Determination of the location for the intervention;
7. Collection and analysis of baseline data on the target behavior;
8. Specification of the controlling events;
9. Establishment of terminal goals and interim objectives;
10. Selection of the intervention plan and specific modification techniques;
11. Evaluation and selection of positive reinforcers;
12. Collection and analysis of data on changes in behavior subsequent to intervention.

CHAPTER 12.   The Tools: Increasing Behavior

For the social worker engaged in the day to day realities of attempting to deal with a wide variety of complex problems, the core of practice, no matter what the theoretical orientation, lies in the techniques or procedures used. One of the early points made in this book is that the development of specific techniques to deal with specific problems is at the heart of the behavioral approach. It is in clear definition for both worker and client of the procedures to follow that behavior modification has so much to offer. A good deal of this book focuses on the basic principles out of which the techniques were developed, as well as on the strategies of assessment, recording, and working with mediators. But the actual implementation of behavior modification calls for a deliberate specification of the techniques available and the ways in which they are used. This chapter and the next two chapters will review the major techniques of behavior modification; subsequent chapters will present illustrations of their application.

What Are Techniques?

For many social workers, the term "techniques" seems to imply a mechanistic, dehumanizing, and oversimplified approach to complex human problems. Perhaps this stems, in part, from some confusion over just what the word means. In the context of the helping relationship, "something" has to be done by the helper. Unless the worker is doing "something," he would be sitting passively, unengaged in therapeutic interactions. The questions then, are, what does a worker do, and how does he decide what to do?

In the first place, of course, the worker doesn't "do" theory. A theory, or a complex set of ideas, in itself cannot be applied to a person. There must be some way of translating the theory, or a principle of the theory, into action. The translation, the application with people, is the "technique." The techniques of helping are merely the ways the worker attempts to use the theory, or make the theory come alive in practice. Without the techniques, social workers could never accomplish their goals, or even offer any services. The techniques are the expression in action, in a precise form, of what the helper does in a given situation with a given client with a given problem.

Social workers have always known this. Many of the traditional approaches to social work practice at least acknowledge the necessity for the use of techniques as a way of implementing the various approaches (see, e.g., Hollis, 1970; Perlman, 1970). However, although the necessity of techniques has always been recognized, the *development* of such techniques has lagged considerably, to the point where there are few definitive guidelines available in traditional approaches as to what techniques to apply, to what kinds of problems, with what kinds of clients, in what kinds of situations.

Even such complex interactions as verbal communication and "relationship" are expressed through the means of techniques. Increasingly, innovative systems intended to provide specific training for helping professionals in what heretofore have been considered the subtle and complex skills of "relationship" are being developed and tested (Truax & Carkhuff, 1967; Carkhuff & Berenson, 1967; Fischer, 1975a). Thus, the notions of "relationship" and "techniques" are in no way antithetical. Techniques are the warp and woof of practice, what the social worker actually does. To be sure, the techniques should not be the master of the social worker. Rather, the worker must be able to select his techniques flexibly and appropriately; he must not be confined to the application of only one technique to all his clients' problems because it is the only one he knows. Developing a wide repertoire of interventive procedures is the essence of professional skill and preparation for practice.

The social worker who uses behavior modification has the distinct advantage of having at his command a wide range of techniques to deal with a wide range of behaviors. If the techniques are applied in a rigid fashion, however, they will probably be less effective; furthermore the social worker will be losing one of the important ingredients of good practice, namely, creativity and sensitivity in using available knowledge to meet the unique needs of his clients.

Selection of Techniques

There are several criteria which the social worker might use in selecting a technique for intervention (Thomas, 1970; Jehu, 1972):

1. Obviously, the wishes and values of the client and significant others are a primary consideration.
2. The social worker should decide whether he should attempt to modify the client's responses to some aspect of the environment, or the environment itself. Frequently, both tactics are used, but it is generally preferable to reduce external stress first, if possible, rather than to modify the client's responses to external stresses.
3. The social worker must determine whether he is dealing with an excess or deficit in behavior. If there is a behavioral excess, the social worker would choose a technique designed to decrease the magnitude, frequency, or duration of that behavior. If there is a behavioral deficit, of course, the choice would be a technique designed to increase that behavior.
4. The class of problem behavior involved—whether predominantly operant or respondent—would offer another guideline for selection. In general, operant techniques are appropriate for operant behavior problems, and respondent techniques for respondent problems.
5. Based on the assessment, the social worker will have to decide whether to focus on modifying antecedent conditions or to concentrate on altering consequent conditions.
6. The relative effectiveness of different techniques is another important consideration. For example, in cases involving maladaptive anxiety, the worker would be able to choose between, say, systematic desensitization and implosion. Because of the considerably larger body of evidence attesting to the effectiveness of desensitization, this procedure would generally be favored.
7. The efficiency of the procedure would be another consideration in that, usually, only a limited amount of time is available, and, for both ethical and practical reasons, the easiest and most efficient procedure would be the procedure of choice.
8. The availability of resources is still another factor to take into account. Financial considerations, the availability of mediators, and the presence of time and materials for implementation of the intervention are all contributing factors in the selection of one technique over another.

COMBINATIONS OF TECHNIQUES

The techniques presented in this and the next two chapters will be discussed separately for purposes of clarity and ease of identification. But in actual practice, most problems are complex enough to require the use of more than one technique, depending upon the nature of the client and the problem. This point is illustrated in the bibliography compiled by Morrow (1971); it lists hundreds of intervention programs, the vast majority of which utilized more than one technique. The use of a single technique is the exception rather than the rule; the typical client problem demands the use of more than one technique. Thus, the reduction of anxiety through desensitization may be only the first step in a behavioral program that would also include the use of positive reinforcement, modeling, and behavior rehearsal to increase some other desired behavior and develop new skills. It is this multiplicity in options for the practitioner that is one of the hallmarks of behavior modification. An individualized, comprehensive package of techniques for each client, rather than just the routine and single-minded application of one technique, is generally the optimal outcome of the behavioral approach to intervention.

Of course, once a technique has been chosen, there is no guarantee it will be successful. A faulty assessment, a change in the situation, or depletion of the resources required for use of the technique may result in failure; hence, the strong suggestion throughout this book that systematic data be kept, and that ongoing feedback from the client and others be reported to the social worker. Given the records and the feedback, the social worker will have the information to evaluate the effectiveness of the procedure, to reassess the situation, and to decide (with the client and the mediators) whether or not the procedure should be modified or replaced.

In gauging the effectiveness of the procedure, one of the considerations must be the current frequency of the target behavior. For example, the techniques of time out and extinction could generally be expected to have an effect on tantrum behavior within three to six days. However, if the tantrum behavior occurs only once a day, its extinction would be expected to take somewhat longer. If the tantrums occur several times a day, obviously less time would be needed to demonstrate the effects of the program (since the program would then be implemented several times per day).

At some point in a behavioral program, a social worker may even think of a more appropriate or effective procedure, and introduce its application. The decision to make such changes, though, should proceed as much as possible from what the data actually show and the extent to which the client, the social worker, and relevant others are satisfied with progress. The goal should always be effective help for the client; at times, workers must be cautioned against unswerving loyalty to a technique in the face of evidence either that it is not working or that more suitable alternatives are available.

Organization of Techniques

The techniques of behavior modification presented here are grouped according to the type of behavioral change they are intended to produce. Thus, there are three categories of techniques—those designed to increase the magnitude, frequency, or duration of a behavior; those designed to decrease a behavior; and "complex" techniques, those procedures that may increase and decrease behaviors at the same time. This classification is at times arbitrary because many of the techniques described here have been used both to strengthen and to weaken behavior (e.g., positive reinforcement to increase a desired behavior that is incompatible with, and will therefore decrease, some undesired behavior). Thus, the techniques have been categorized on the bases of what they have been either primarily *designed* to do, or primarily *used* to do. Other ways organizing this material—e.g., by whether the technique is operant or respondent, or focused on antecedents or consequences—would have been possible, but they would probably be less useful than a goal-oriented schema.

Each technique will be discussed in terms of its roots—operant, respondent, or "complex"—its primary focus (whether on antecedent or consequent events) and the kinds of behaviors with which it has been used successfully. A technique is referred to (Thomas, 1970) as "complex":

1. when two or more techniques are combined;
2. when both operant and respondent features are involved;
3. when its use involves a focus on both antecedent or consequent events;
4. when it can be used both to increase and decrease behavior; and/or
5. when there is some lack of clarity as to some of its essential features.

Most of the techniques described here are not confined to work at only one level of intervention—only with individuals, say, or only with families. Most have been used in a variety of very complex situations. But whether they be used on hospital wards, in one-to-one counseling in an office, or in groups, they are all derived from the basic techniques presented here. The adaptation of any procedure used predominantly with individuals for use with groups, say, (Paul & Shannon, 1967; Rose, 1972), or couples and families (Erickson & Hogan, 1972), or even larger assemblages such as hospital wards, organizations, or institutions (Ayllon & Azrin, 1968; Burgess & Bushell, 1969; Thomas, 1967) depends largely on the social worker's ingenuity and flexibility. Since a substantial portion of other parts of this book are devoted to explicating basic operant principles and procedures, only a brief review of eight basic operant techniques—such as positive reinforcement, shaping, punishment, and so on —will be presented.

Techniques Used to Increase Behavior

1. POSITIVE REINFORCEMENT

Positive reinforcement refers to the presentation of a stimulus contingent on the occurrence of a behavior so as to strengthen that behavior. Positive reinforcement has been used as the primary technique in developing new behavior or strengthening existing behavior in almost every type of social welfare setting and with almost every kind of problem. Positive reinforcement has been used with children in the school, in the home (Patterson, 1971), and in hospitals and clinics (Ashem & Poser, 1973; Graziano, 1971). Positive reinforcement also has been used with adults in institutions, clinics, offices, and natural or home settings (Krasner, 1971; Franks, 1969). With both children and adults, positive reinforcement has been applied to a broad range of problems including those involving "retardation," chronic and acute psychiatric disorders, and problems of everyday life (e.g., in the schools).

Positive reinforcement can be provided in two general forms, either directly or through the use of tokens. In the direct use of positive reinforcement, the social worker would, upon the performance of some prespecified behavior, immediately present the actual rewarding stimulus. In a token system, he would present a symbolic object such as a chip or star on a chart, which could be exchanged at a later time for a desired reward. Well over a hundred token programs with adults, youths, the aged, and various units of society have been established (Krasner, 1970). The stimuli actually used as reinforcers include such diverse ones as food and candy, praise and attention (social reinforcers), activities and privileges, and a variety of forms of personal companionship, including sexual relations between spouses (Stuart, 1969).

Because of the great versatility of positive reinforcement, it has been used not only in formal behavioral intervention programs, but also as a way of systematically increasing desired behavior in counseling interviews as well as in training couples and parents to reinforce each other (Knox, 1971; Stuart, 1969; Paterson, 1971). Almost every form of operant behavior has been the target of change through positive reinforcement: the verbal interaction of spouses; delinquent behaviors such as stealing and fighting; dysfunctional sexual behaviors; maladaptive work habits and inadequate work skills; self-care behaviors such as feeding and toilet training; speech disorders; school-related problems such as learning disabilities and classroom disruption; parent–child problems such as sibling arguments and defiance of parents; severely disturbed behaviors such as hallucinations and delusions (Morrow, 1971). Positive reinforcement is the major foundation of the behavioral approach, and it often plays a direct or indirect part in the use of several other techniques.

2. SHAPING

Shaping refers to the development of a desired behavior—either completely missing from the client's repertoire or in rudimentary form—through the sequential reinforcement of successively closer approximations to that behavior.

The positive reinforcement used in shaping, of course, can be provided either directly or through tokens. The nature of shaping is such that it is generally (although not always) used on more basic behaviors such as feeding oneself, toilet training, grooming, dressing; developing basic social skills including appropriate play behavior and relevant social greetings; developing basic motor skills including walking; and building appropriate academic behaviors including paying attention in class and studying (Morrow, 1971; Franks, 1969; Krasner, 1971). Most shaping programs operate using direct rather than token reinforcement although either is possible depending on the capabilities of the clients involved.

3. COVERT REINFORCEMENT

Covert reinforcement is a relatively new technique (Cautela, 1970) that uses reinforcing thoughts to bring about changes in behavior. The social worker helps the client identify scenes or thoughts that are pleasurable and can be imagined quickly and clearly. The client is taught that when he is in a distressing situation, he may cue himself by using a particular word, say, "love" or "reinforcement," that evokes pleasant thoughts and increases the desired behavior in that situation. Clients learn the technique by practicing (with the social worker) thinking about disturbing situations, having the social worker (and later the client himself) state the one word ("reinforcement"), then imagining the pleasant scenes. Cautela (1970) has illustrated the use of covert reinforcement in helping a young man make heterosexual approaches (e.g., phoning for dates), and Knox (1971) has used this technique with a variety of marital problems. Covert reinforcement is promising less as a unitary technique than as an adjunct to other procedures and as a way to help the client generalize positive results into the environment. It may, however, be useful in teaching clients self-control and methods of conducting their own therapy (see the section on self-control in Chapter 14).

4. NEGATIVE REINFORCEMENT

Negative reinforcement consists of the removal of an aversive stimulus contingent on the occurrence of a behavior so as to increase that behavior. Essentially, negative reinforcement increases behavior by inducing the individual to escape or avoid the aversive stimulus. Hence, it has also been called escape or avoidance conditioning (Morrow, 1971; Rachman & Teasdale, 1969). It has been defined as "a training procedure in which the learned movement circumvents or prevents the appearance of a noxious stimulus" (Kimble, 1964, p. 477). The aversive stimuli (or negative reinforcers) to be avoided or escaped have included both delayed auditory feedback and loud noises to increase nonstuttering speech (Flannagen, et al., 1958; Goldiamond, 1965a); mild electric shock to increase heterosexual behavior (Feldman & MacCullough, 1971; Birk, 1969, cited in Liberman, 1972); spilled food to increase self-feeding behavior (Ayllon & Michael, 1959).

It should be noted that negative reinforcement or avoidance training is one of three procedures subsumed under the broader term aversive conditioning or aversive therapy, which, unfortunately, leads to some confusion. The other techniques are operant punishment and respondent aversive counterconditioning. Obviously, all three are similar in that they use aversive stimuli. However, since the procedures are otherwise generally distinct, and in order to avoid confusion, the three techniques will be discussed separately.

On the whole, negative reinforcement or avoidance learning maintains many everyday behaviors that involve avoidance or escape from aversive consequences (e.g., safe driving to avoid tickets and accidents; law-abiding behavior to avoid imprisonment; wearing sunglasses to avoid glare). Except for Feldman and MacCullough's (1971) work with individuals who wished to terminate their homosexual responses, clinical examples of these techniques are relatively scarce (compared, say, to the use of positive reinforcement; see Sherman & Barr, 1969, for a brief review of negative reinforcement applications). But Feldman and Mac-Cullough (1971) argue that, for certain difficult problems, such as undesired homosexual behaviors, avoidance learning may be the best procedure since it eliminates old, unwanted responses by generating new responses, incompatible with the old, that also are quite resistant to extinction. Their procedure, in essence, consists of presenting an aversive electric shock, coincident with pictures of men (the clients were men), that could be terminated or avoided by the client by pressing a switch.

Contiguous with this termination, pictures of attractive females were presented. The authors report that undesired homosexual behavior in the natural environment declined, and heterosexual interests increased.

5. PROMPTING

Prompting, or coaching, consists of the verbal or nonverbal (e.g., pictorial) presentation of a cue that a behavior should occur. The prompt could range from simply providing an individual with the information about what he is to do, to a very specific cue to bring about an immediate specific response (e.g., "OK, Willy, now try to make this sound . . . "). As such, prompting is not actually a technique to be used alone, but is mainly a method for preparing an individual to emit a behavior that will be reinforced; it has largely been used in a formal sense in educational settings with a variety of academic behaviors (Meacham & Wiesen, 1966), and in teaching people basic self-care and speaking and social skills (as in work with retarded youngsters; Gardner, 1971).

6. FADING

Fading refers to the gradual merging of stimuli from one situation where desired behavior occurs into the stimuli in another situation so that the desired behavior will occur in the second situation. Fading can also refer to the gradual elimination of stimuli that control a specific behavior (e.g., a prompt) such that the behavior becomes autonomous. The key in both situations—where the controlling stimulus is eliminated, or where it is merged with other stimuli that come to control the behavior—is *gradualism*. The necessity for such fading is occasioned either by the fact that a given stimulus is no longer necessary for a behavior to occur, or that one wants to get a prosocial behavior that already occurs in one situation (e.g., reading a book at home) to occur in another (e.g., reading a book in school). The task of the social worker is to merge the two stimulus conditions gradually by one of two basic methods. The first involves increasing the similarities between the two stimulus conditions, evoking the behavior in one situation and maintaining it in more and more dissimilar situations. The second involves decreasing the duration, frequency, or intensity of the first set of controlling stimuli so that it gradually loses its control over the behavior; at the same time, new stimuli are presented, which gradually gain control over the behavior. Fading is frequently used in academic and institutional settings (Meacham & Wiesen, 1966; Gardner, 1971; Whaley & Malott, 1971) to increase a variety of academic (e.g., reading and studying), self-care, and social behaviors.

7. CHAINING

Chaining is a technique used for increasing the complexity and temporal length of a given response sequence (Tharp & Wetzel, 1969). The key word here is sequence, because in chaining, the reinforcement of one response is used as the cue for the next response. Thus, the reinforcement and cue become virtually identical resulting in a continuous chain of behaviors in which one runs into the next. The procedure involves having the worker make the (antecedent) discriminative stimulus for a response already in the client's repertoire contingent upon a new response. This produces the "chain" of behaviors, in that the reinforcement for the response follows the completion of the last behavioral link. In this way, the client comes to engage in behavior of increasing complexity, reinforced both by the same reinforcer for which he produced the original behavior, as well as by the several stimuli associated with the behaviors in the chain which have also become reinforcing (Tharp & Wetzel, 1969). When using chaining, the continuous reinforcement schedule may be thinned so that reinforcement is presented on a less frequent basis. In this way, the client would learn to engage in an increased number of behaviors for less frequent, and perhaps fewer, reinforcers.

Five essential conditions for utilizing chaining have been described by Gagné (1970): (1) the separate stimulus response (S-R) links must be learned before they can be chained; (2) each link must be executed by the learner or client in the correct sequence; (3) the S-R units should be performed in close time succession, thus ensuring that the links are chained together; (4) the sequence should be repeated until the desired learning has been accomplished; and (5) positive reinforcement should be present in the learning of chains.

A wide range of behaviors in the natural environment can be viewed as chains, such as, dressing in the morning, playing a musical instrument, playing games, going to bed at night. Each of these requires a variety of behaviors performed in a chained of linked fashion. Chaining has been used in behavior modification primarily to develop a range of complex behaviors such as involved in language development, self care, playing games and studying.

8. BEHAVIOR REHEARSAL

Behavior rehearsal is a complex technique that consists of helping the client role-play with the social worker the very behaviors that he will be called upon to perform in the natural environment. Just as modeling by the social worker and positive reinforcement for the client's performance play a part in behavioral rehearsal, so does behavior rehearsal play a part in other techniques, such as assertive training (described in Chapter 15). The main purpose of behavior rehearsal is to enable the client to learn how to behave in a variety of situations by acting out those situations. The social worker demonstrates to the client how to play the role he will be engaged in, and then helps the client role-play the situation with him to the point where the client is comfortable in engaging in the desired behaviors. The client is then encouraged to attempt the behaviors in real life. Although the major goal of behavior rehearsal is to strengthen the performance of prosocial behaviors, it often results in a great reduction in anxiety about the performance of those behaviors since excessive anxiety is frequently associated with their performance. Behavior rehearsal is often used to help people develop such appropriate assertive behaviors as dealing with significant people in their environment (family, employers, friends, and so on). Behavior rehearsal has also been used to help people learn job-application skills, social and interpersonal skills, conversational skills, and in practicing for oral examinations (Lazarus, 1966, 1971; Wolpe, 1969).

Such procedures as behavior rehearsal, modeling, and others where the client is encouraged to practice the performance of behaviors, have several advantages (Sturm, 1965):

1. they generate vivid, lifelike behavior and cues, thereby maximizing the possibility that there will be generalization to the natural environment;
2. they condition a *total* behavioral response—verbal, motor, physiological, and ideational—rather than just a verbal one;
3. they use as dispensers of powerful reinforcers enacted models and other characters who in real life dispense such reinforcers.

Summary

This chapter has discussed the meaning of techniques, and their use in behavior modification. The criteria for selection of techniques were presented, and emphasis was placed on the notion that most techniques are used in combination, based on the nature and complexity of problems, rather than singly. The format for organizing the current presentation of the techniques of behavior modification was presented in terms of the types of behavior changes they are intended to produce—increasing behavior, decreasing behavior, or both (complex). This chapter also discussed eight techniques for increasing behavior: (1) positive reinforcement; (2) shaping; (3) covert reinforcement; (4) negative reinforcement; (5) prompting; (6) fading; (7) chaining; (8) behavior rehearsal.

CHAPTER 13.   The Tools: Decreasing Behavior

The preceding chapter described eight behavioral techniques designed primarily to produce an increase (or strengthening) in the target behavior. This chapter describes fourteen techniques designed primarily to be used when there is an excess of behavior and the goal is to decrease (or weaken) that behavior.

Techniques Used to Decrease Behavior

1. SATIATION

When used as a behavioral change technique (rather than as a means of increasing the reinforcing effect of a reinforcer) satiation refers either to the provision of such an abundance of a stimulus that its reinforcing properties are lost, or to the continuous reinforcement of a response until it no longer is performed (Blackham & Silberman, 1971). In both cases, the goal of satiation is to eliminate a problem behavior emitted by an individual constantly seeking a particular reinforcer by providing so much of it that he no longer desires it. Using satiation, Resnick (1968) eliminated smoking behavior by having his clients smoke so much they no longer desired to, and Ayllon and Michael (1959) and Ayllon (1963) eliminated two types of hoarding behavior (magazines and "junk" in the first instance and towels in the second) by providing so much of the desired objects that the objects became so aversive to the individuals involved that the hoarding gradually decreased.

2. NEGATIVE PRACTICE

Using negative practice, the social worker attempts to have an individual with a problem behavior such as a tic, twitch, or stammer repeat the behavior over and over again, in prolonged repetition in massed trials. The resulting fatigue results in the maladaptive habit's becoming aversive or painful and perhaps more under voluntary control, and therefore, far less likely to be performed. Negative (or massed) practice has been used with such behaviors as stuttering, tics, nailbiting and teethgrinding (Case, 1960; Yates, 1970; Blackham & Silberman, 1971).

3. POSITIVE PUNISHMENT

Positive (operant) punishment refers to the reduction of the probability that a behavior will occur by presenting an aversive stimulus (negative reinforcer) contingent on its occurrence. As a result of this punishment not only should the behavior in question be reduced *during* the punishment process, but its probability of occurrence in the *future* should be reduced as well in order to have an effective, empirical definition of whether punishment has actually occurred. The success of punishment depends on a host of variables (Azrin & Holz, 1966; Yates, 1970). Among these are: the manner of introduction of the punishing stimulus (the more sudden, the better); its immediacy and intensity (the more immediate and intense, the better); the schedule of punishment (it should be continuous, but not extended over too long a time); whether or not the punished response is also being reinforced (it should not be); whether or not alternative desired responses are available (if not, they should be developed). For the reasons discussed in Chapter 3, punishment is used mainly when there are no other suitable behavior change alternatives, and when the effects of behavior to be decreased are more dysfunctional than the potential negative effects of the punishment procedure. The point is, of course, that the social worker who contemplates the use of punishment must be aware of the ethical and behavioral implications of its use, communicate his awareness to the client, and then decide *with* the client when possible whether or not to use it.

A wide variety of stimuli have been used as punishing agents, including verbal remarks ("No"; "that's incorrect"), undesired activities (e.g., washing windows), chemical agents (such as apomorphine for inducing nausea to overcome addiction; Raymond, 1964), and, most commonly, electric shock. Operant punishment has been applied to a wide range of behaviors typically considered by social workers to be among the most difficult to diminish, namely, unwanted homosexual behaviors, addictive behaviors, self-injurious behaviors, smoking, drinking alcohol, tics, inappropriate verbal behaviors, fetishes, and so on (Yates, 1970; Azrin & Holz, 1966; Rachman & Teasdale, 1969). The punishment procedure typically consists of the presentation of an aversive stimulus (e.g., an electric shock) immediately after the occurrence of the undesired behavior (e.g., sexual arousal in response to a picture) until the behavior diminishes.

Such a procedure generally requires repeated sessions—as many sessions as are necessary to get to the point where the behavior not only does not occur either during the punishment process or in the natural environment. Also typically, almost all instances of the use of punishment (and related aversive techniques such as negative reinforcement and aversive counterconditioning) have been conducted with the voluntary consent of the client. The only instances where this may not have been the case is where the behaviors (say, self-injurious behavior) were performed by individuals without the capacity to evaluate the proposed interventions, and such behaviors were deemed dangerous to the health and welfare of the clients (say, severely disturbed children).

4. NEGATIVE PUNISHMENT (RESPONSE COST)

Since positive punishment is seldom used as a technique for decreasing maladaptive behavior in settings other than clinics or institutions, social workers should consider negative punishment or response cost as an alternative that may be used in many more situations and settings, including clinics and institutions. Response cost refers to the removal of a positive reinforcer contingent on the occurrence of an undesired behavior. In other words, when an undesired behavior is performed, the social worker or mediator immediately removes or withholds some customary reward or privilege such as watching T.V., use of automobiles, allowances, and so on. These reinforcers are removed temporarily, of course, and their removal is contingent upon the performance of the behavior. Furthermore, the reinforcers that are removed are not the ones that are presumably maintaining the behavior, although their removal is intended to affect the behavior. (These latter two points—[a] contingent removal of [b] reinforcers not maintaining the behavior—distinguish response cost from operant extinction.) The amount of the decrease in behavior due to the use of response cost is a function of the relative magnitude of the opposing consequences (Bandura, 1969). Obviously, removing T.V. privileges for 15 minutes would not be sufficient to overcome complex, long-held, or highly rewarding behaviors (e.g., stealing or fighting). But when the "punishment fits the crime," when the privileges removed are indeed powerfully reinforcing to the individual involved, response cost can be a highly effective procedure.

Response cost can be used either directly—removing a privilege at the time the undesired behavior occurs—or through the use of tokens—e.g., loss of a certain amount of points leading to the loss of certain rewards or privileges. Either way, the most judicious use of response cost would be to develop a contract beforehand so that all parties to the interaction know where they stand. Response cost has been used primarily with children and adolescents to decrease a variety of undesired behaviors such as fighting, swearing, thumbsucking, tantrums, self-destructive behaviors, and so on (Sherman & Baer, 1969; Blackham & Silberman, 1971; Bandura, 1969).

5. TIME-OUT

Time-out is a variant of response cost in which, contingent upon the performance of an undesired behavior, the individual client is withdrawn from the situation in which the undesired behavior is occurring and where the reinforcement is operating. The basic operation—which has been used predominantly with children—is to place the child immediately in a room where the child will obtain little or no reinforcement. This means that the child's own room, equipped with toys, books, and so on, would be a poor choice, as would rooms with other people continuously passing through, or rooms where there may be a T.V. set or radio. On the other hand, great care should be taken to insure that the room will not be frightening to the child, e.g., a closet or a room that is too dark or confining. (The point is to withdraw reinforcement, not to frighten the child!) No one should speak to the child while he or she is in the room; the child should be placed in the room with no emotional recriminations, and as calmly as possible. Firmly but gently, the mediator or social worker should place the child in the room after a brief statement that the form of behavior he just engaged in will not be tolerated. There should be a definite time limit. Since this is a particularly effective technique, one way to gauge the time limit is to see empirically how much time is necessary to decrease the behavior. (Temporary suppression, though, is not the only goal; rather, one should strive for long-term extinction of undesired behaviors.) As a general rule of thumb, start with a minimal amount of time—two to three minutes; frequently, three to seven minutes is sufficient. There should, however, always be a definite time limit, set in advance by the mediator and not the child. A period of up to 15 or 20 minutes may be considered a maximum, although periods of 30 minutes and more have been used with adolescents who engage in behaviors that are extremely difficult to extinguish.

As with other procedures, time-out is most effective (technically and ethically) when used consistently and fairly, and not at the whim of the mediator or in some other arbitrary fashion. Surprisingly, few children react adversely to time-out after the experience is over. In the initial stages, however, the social worker and the mediator should be prepared for the possibility of the child's crying or yelling while in the time-out room. The target child should be informed that the confinement interval *begins* when he is quiet, so that five minutes in time-out may actually be 15 minutes if the child complains or cries during the first ten minutes. Time-out is an extremely useful, nonpunitive technique to teach parents and teachers; it has been used with a variety of problems such as inappropriate yelling and screaming, fighting, swearing, disobedience and defiance, dangerous climbing, self-destructive behavior, tantrums, and so on (Ashem & Poser, 1973; Patterson, 1971; Blackham & Silberman, 1971; Kanfer & Phillips, 1970).

6. OPERANT EXTINCTION

Extinction refers to the discontinuance of the presentation of any and all reinforcement for a specific behavior contingent upon the occurrence of that behavior such that its probability of occurrence is reduced. In other words, the social worker or mediator arranges a situation so that undesired behavior is not rewarded (reinforced). Assuming the behaviors have been maintained by that reinforcement, repeated nonreinforcement should produce a decline in the occurrence of the behavior. The intervening agent must, first, insure that all sources of reinforcement are removed, and, second, be prepared to deal with the probability that the nonreinforced behavior may actually increase at the start of extinction and that there may be some emotional distress associated with the removal of reinforcement. Extinction has been used primarily for behaviors maintained by the attention of others. Thus, extinction most commonly consists of not replying, not watching, or in no other way interacting with the client while the undesired behavior is being performed. Whatever way the behavior is ignored, a decline in its frequency and intensity will indicate whether or not extinction is being used effectively.

Extinction has been used successfully in decreasing many different child and adult behaviors, including vomiting, crying, tantrums, "psychotic talk," refusal to eat unassisted, excessive drinking of alcohol (the target drinker's companions were requested to ignore or leave the client when he began imbibing), and compulsive scratching (Kanfer & Phillips, 1970; Bandura, 1969). Because there is no guarantee, using extinction, that desired behaviors will replace the extinguished behaviors, and in order to help develop suitable alternative ways of behaving, extinction is often used in conjunction with the positive reinforcement of desired behavior. This technique is called differential reinforcement, and will be discussed in the following chapter on "complex" techniques.

7. POSITIVE REINFORCEMENT OF ALTERNATIVE OR INCOMPATIBLE RESPONSES

One of the best ways to decrease undesired behaviors is to find some desired behavior that is either an alternative to, or incompatible with, the undesired behavior. Using positive reinforcement, the desired behavior is strengthened or increased; the undesired behavior tends to decrease as it becomes replaced by the new, prosocial behavior. Here, positive reinforcement is actually used to *decrease* behavior. Assuming the newly reinforced behavior is strong enough to overcome the undesired behavior, or is simply more rewarding to the client, the undesired behavior will not occur. Again, used in this fashion, positive reinforcement is most frequently combined with extinction in the technique of differential reinforcement. But, used alone, when the goal is to reinforce an alternative response, the social worker or mediator attempts to reinforce a different, prosocial way of responding in a particular situation so that the client will find the prosocial way of responding more desirable, e.g., reinforcing an isolated child every time he makes a move to play with other children as a method of decreasing social isolation (rather than reinforcing the isolation by paying attention to him while he is sitting alone).

When the goal is to reinforce an *incompatible* response, i.e., one that prevents the occurrence of some other behavior, the social worker attempts to strengthen a prosocial or desired behavior that cannot occur at the same time as the undesired behavior. There are any number of examples of incompatible behaviors: one cannot smile and frown at the same time, or sit and walk, or be quiet and scream, or bang one's head on the wall while one is clapping one's hands and rocking in time to music (Lovaas *et al.*, 1965; Watson & Tharp, 1972). The social worker who uses this technique should ask: what directly opposed behavior could be increased while decreasing the undesired behavior; are there any behaviors that would make it impossible to perform the undesired behaviors (Watson & Tharp, 1972)? The task for the change agent then is to provide reinforcement for the desired behavior so that it will take the place of the undesired behavior.

There are relatively few well-documented cases where positive reinforcement to decrease behavior (as opposed to "differential reinforcement," which formally incorporates extinction procedures as well) has been isolated as a specific technique. The few instances have included target behaviors such as hyperactive classroom behavior, social isolation, fighting, screaming and yelling, and self-destructive behavior (Lovaas *et al.*, 1965; Reese, 1966; Bradfield, 1970). Nevertheless, the use of positive reinforcement to strengthen a desired behavior as a means of decreasing or weakening undesired behavior may in many instances be a very efficient and effective alternative to the use of extinction or punishment procedures alone; moreover, it may have far fewer potential side effects.

8. SYSTEMATIC DESENSITIZATION

This respondent technique is perhaps the most thoroughly researched and widely used clinical technique of behavior modification. Extensive controlled research, plus numerous less well-controlled individual and group case studies validate its effectiveness over a wide range of maladaptive emotional behaviors. This technique is of particular significance and value to social workers working with any of the traditionally defined "neurotic" disorders one might typically expect to encounter in outpatient clinics and counseling agencies. Because the basic procedure of systematic desensitization has been covered elsewhere so extensively and in such detail, and in terms appropriate for a social work audience (Wolpe, 1969; Marquis *et al.*, 1971; Fischer, 1973a and b), only a brief overview of the technique will be presented here. It is hoped that the reader will want to gain a fuller understanding of the use of desensitization, and review one or more of the references cited.

In essence, systematic desensitization utilizes counterconditioning processes (as presented in Chapter 2) to overcome maladaptive emotional avoidance responses such as anxiety and fear. The purpose of using this technique is to develop a new, adaptive response (say, relaxation) that will be incompatible with the old response (anxiety) but elicited by the same stimulus (the frightening situation or event). There are five basic steps—or more properly, phases—in the desensitization process:

a. ASSESSMENT

This stage of the process, as with other behavioral procedures, involves development of case history information, exploration of current relationships, and use of specific instruments (which are nontechnical and easily administered—see Chapter 19 and Wolpe, 1969), all designed to pinpoint areas of dysfunctioning and to determine the appropriateness of the use of desensitization. The goal is to develop a clear understanding of stimulus–response relationships, i.e., what kinds of situations elicit what kinds of maladaptive reactions (anxiety, fear, etc.).

b. CONSTRUCTION OF ANXIETY HIERARCHIES

If the decision is made to proceed with desensitization, the areas of difficulties discussed during the assessment are classified into common themes based on the nature of the stimulus condition. Then, the client and worker together develop these themes into hierarchies that can range from 5 to 25 items (generally about 1 to 14 is the norm). The hierarchies (and there may be more than one depending on the nature of the problem) begin with the situation arousing the lowest level of anxiety up to the item eliciting the greatest amount of anxiety; they are arranged to constitute a reasonably spaced progression of anxiety from item to item (there should not be too great a jump in the amount of anxiety elicited by one item over the preceding item). The decision about which item elicits the greatest anxiety is made by the client, so that two individuals with similar problems and similar hierarchies may have the items on the hierarchy arranged quite differently. Following is an example of a hierarchy dealing with one person's anxiety at being in situations where she is the center of attention, with the most feared item as number 1 and the least feared as number 14 (Marquis *et al.,* 1971):

1. You have fainted at church just before mass and are lying there conscious but unable to get up, your dress is up to your waist, you are by yourself, people are staring and giggling.
2. You are giving a speech to the Parent-Teacher Association on child rearing and your voice cracks and you sound nervous.
3. You have fainted down the street from your home before a small crowd and are lying there conscious but unable to move, your dress is up to your waist, you are by yourself, people are staring and giggling.
4. You ask the speaker a question at the Parent-Teacher Association.
5. You are shaking hands with a candidate for the House of Representatives at a tea.
6. You are at a jewelry party.
7. Next door neighbor having a cup of coffee, watching intently while you get dinner.
8. You are going into a strange hardware store, not too many people.
9. Entertaining two couples, someone asks you a question, all eyes are on you, you answer easily.
10. You drop a bag of groceries at the store, you laugh and pick them up and kid with the man who helps you pick them up.
11. You are at your sister's house and someone says, "What a lovely dress"; all turn to look.
12. Neighbor: "You're not as tense as you used to be."
13. Therapist actually stares at the patient for two seconds, interval gradually increased to one minute.
14. Your family is watching you cook dinner.

c. TRAINING IN RELAXATION

The most common response used to overcome the anxiety reaction (i.e., the response incompatible with or antagonistic to anxiety) is relaxation. Based on the work of Jacobsen (1938), the procedure involves selecting one muscle group at a time (e.g., lower arm) and illustrating the contrast between tension and relaxation. The client is instructed to tense up that muscle group for 15 to 20 seconds, then to relax it and attend to the contrast between the pleasant, tingling sensation and eventual relaxation and the previous feelings of tenseness. This process is repeated with the same muscle group, and eventually all of the muscle groups of the body, until the client can completely relax his entire body for brief periods of time, preferably when cued with some words such as "relax," or whenever the client wishes to do so. This training period can last from one to six sessions, depending upon how fast the client learns to relax, and includes 15 to 30 minutes of practice per day at home.

d. IMAGERY TRAINING

Since the basic process of desensitization is implemented by having the client imagine items on the hierarchy while relaxing, the next step is to train the client to be able to "image" (or imagine) scenes. The client is requested to imagine a scene evoking neutral, or, preferably, pleasant emotions (e.g., relaxing on a sunny beach in beautiful Hawaii). The client is helped to attend to all of the senses potentially involved, tactile, visual, auditory, olfactory, until the scene is at least as clear as a vivid memory, and to the point where the client sees himself as a participant in the scene rather than as a passive viewer. A variety of scenes can be used to help establish the basics of imagery.

It may, at first glance, appear as though simply imagining an anxiety-provoking scene while in the social worker's office would be insufficient to desensitize the anxiety that occurs in real situations. However, a substantial body of research, almost all of which has been conducted using this imaginal process, consistently demonstrates the generalization into everyday life of successful desensitization using imagery (Franks, 1969).

There is, however, an alternative to the use of imagery, and that is conducting the desensitization process *in vivo*—in real life. Thus, instead of imagining the feared items on the hierarchy, the client and worker develop a hierarchy of anxiety-eliciting situations in real life, and proceed up the hierarchy by using the actual feared objects or situations themselves. This *in vivo* process may be called for in the 10 to 15 percent of the cases where the client has difficulty in visualizing (Wolpe, 1969), particularly when the client is a child (Garvey & Hegrenes, 1966). *In vivo* desensitization also has the advantage of utilizing far more of the behavioral repertoire of the client (not only the cognitive and affective components); thus, when the hierarchy is completed, it means that the client actually has been able to face the most feared situation without anxiety.

e. IMPLEMENTATION

Once all of the above is completed, actual implementation begins. Each session begins with the client imaging a control scene, i.e., one evoking pleasant emotions. Then, the lowest item of the hierarchy is presented. The client imagines the scene for 5 to 7 (and later, up to 12) seconds, then terminates it on instruction from the worker. If the client feels any anxiety while imagining the scene, he raises a finger as a signal, whereupon he is immediately instructed to terminate the scene, and go back to the control scene. The difficult scene is either tried again, or the client goes back to the previous item which could be imagined without anxiety, or a new item is added to the hierarchy midway between the preceding item and the scene causing the difficulty. In this manner, the client is led all the way up the hierarchy, repeating each scene two or three times after it no longer elicits anxiety. The purpose of the hierarchy, of course, is to extinguish the fear response and to re-condition the relaxation responses to the stimuli which previously elicited anxiety. Obviously, the point of the gradual, step by step progress up the hierarchy is that moving at too fast a pace would elicit too much anxiety; the relaxation response must always be strong enough to overcome the anxiety response, and this is generally insured by seeing that the anxiety is appropriately extinguished at each step of the hierarchy.

Systematic desensitization, although only one out of several techniques available for use in a behavioral program, has achieved an almost remarkable—and clearly documented—success with a wide range of emotional problems. These problems have included a variety of fears and phobias such as fear of heights, closed spaces, small animals, and examinations, as well as far more complex and generalized difficulties including fear of criticism and devaluation, general and "existential" anxiety, feelings of guilt and jealousy, anxiety-related sexual problems, depression, and problems with authority figures (Wolpe, 1969; Paul, 1969; Marquis *et al.*, 1970).

9. SUBSTITUTION OF SEXUAL RESPONSES

Applying the principle of reciprocal inhibition, Wolpe (1969) has substituted sexual responses (rather than relaxation) with certain sexual problems. When the problem is one in which anxiety is a prime factor, e.g., either inadequate erections or premature ejaculation in the male, and desensitization is either not possible or is unsuccessful, and a cooperative sexual partner is available, this technique may be used. The essence of the technique is slowly to introduce the client into the feared sexual situation and gradually proceed step by step from the point of preparing to enter the specific situation all the way to the desired terminal goal (e.g., successful intercourse). At each step, the partner soothes and encourages the client, and when the actual sexual performance begins, only proceeds to a point agreed upon in advance, say, stopping with heavy necking until such necking can be completed without any anxiety. The complete disappearance of anxiety is the criterion for moving to the next stage. As in shaping, each success should be heavily praised, but there should be no effort to move the client too quickly, say to the point of orgasm in intercourse, until the previous steps leading up to the attempt at intercourse have been successfully negotiated. The technique has been used primarily with males with such problems as impotence and premature ejaculation, but has also been used with females who complain of orgasmic dysfunction (Wolpe, 1969).

10. AVERSIVE COUNTERCONDITIONING

Aversive counterconditioning is based on the same set of conditioning principles as systematic desensitization, but it works in an opposite way. Instead of conditioning a positive response (relaxation) to a stimulus that previously elicited an avoidance response (anxiety), aversive counterconditioning conditions a *negative* or aversive response to a stimulus that previously elicited a positive, or approach, response. This is done by pairing the stimuli to which the maladaptive or undesired approach response have been learned with stimuli (UCS) that elicit a stronger aversive response in such a way that the undesired response will begin to extinguish (Mikulas, 1972). Since aversive counterconditioning subsumes a variety of specific procedures, most of which have been discussed thoroughly elsewhere (Rachman & Teasdale, 1969a and b; Eysenck & Beech, 1971; Bandura, 1969), this section will present only a brief outline of its basic elements.

Almost any strong, unpleasant stimulus may be used in aversive counterconditioning. Among the stimuli that have been used are chemicals that induce nausea, electric shock, excessive stale smoke from cigarettes, ugly or unpleasant pictures, and so on. In all situations where aversive counterconditioning is used, however, the basic steps remain the same. First, a maladaptive approach response is identified. This may be such behaviors as smoking, alcoholism, sexual fetishes, or undesired homosexual responses. Next, assuming voluntary participation on the part of the client, an aversive stimulus is selected. Recently, practitioners have tended to prefer the use of electrical stimulation since it allows for easy control of such important aspects as onset, duration, and intensity; it produces fewer potential side effects than, say, drugs; it can be used by the client in his everyday life by carrying a portable shock unit; it generally seems less unpleasant to use for both practitioners and clients than other aversive stimuli. Once the aversive stimulus, say, electric shock, is selected, and some level of its administration determined—i.e., one that will be unpleasant to the client though, of course, not dangerous—some system of presenting the stimuli that previously elicited the approach behavior is found. Assume that the behavior undesired by the client is his homosexual behavior, and that the eliciting stimuli will be presented in the form of a variety of pictures of men of varying degrees of attractiveness to him. The final task, then, is to pair the previously attractive pictures of men with the unpleasant electric shock (Feldman & MacCulloch, 1965). When the client states that prior attraction has turned to indifference or dislike, the next picture is presented and the process repeated until the client reports—and his behavior in real life bears out—that he is no longer sexually aroused by other men.

The counterconditioning process, in essence, is that the new, unpleasant response has been counterconditioned (i.e., has been learned in place of the old maladaptive response to the same stimulus). The process may be facilitated by an *aversion relief* procedure whereby the termination of the aversive stimulus, which is pleasant and thereby rewarding in contrast to the aversion process, is paired with positive stimuli or those to which one wants to condition an approach response. In the above example, this might be done by pairing the pictures of attractive females with the termination of the shock. It is also helpful to have the client return for booster sessions—regularly scheduled additional sessions—even though the client is not reporting any recurrence of the old maladaptive approach responses (Vogler *et al.*, 1970).

Aversive counterconditioning has been used with some of the most difficult and persistent behaviors, including some that have proved almost impossible to change by any other methods, such as alcoholism, undesired homosexuality, sexual fetishes, and smoking. The results have been extremely encouraging, particularly in comparison with other forms of intervention, although, perhaps because of the very difficult nature of the behaviors with which they have been used, success rates have been somewhat more variable than with other behavioral procedures. As will be noted in Chapter 14, for most behaviors, it is likely that the greatest amount of success will result not from the use of one isolated technique, but from behavioral *programs,* i.e., combinations of techniques used to deal with the variety of specific problem behaviors that comprise such global problems as alcoholism and homosexuality.

11. COVERT SENSITIZATION

Another of the self-control procedures of behavior modification, covert sensitization is actually a variant of aversive counterconditioning, using an *imagined* scene as the aversive event rather than an external aversive stimulus (Cautela, 1967; 1969). Since the aversive stimulus is imaginal, covert sensitization provides the worker and client with a far wider range of aversive stimuli. At the same time, the use of this procedure allows one to avoid many of the unpleasant aspects involved in the use of an external aversive stimulus such as the cumbersomeness of apparatus or the dangers of drugs. The process involves asking the client to visualize the pleasurable (but undesired) object (e.g., liquor). When he is able to clearly visualize the glass of liquor about to touch his lips, he is told in graphic detail that he is becoming sick, that (in imagination) he is vomiting, and that the vomit goes all over himself, his friend, the drink, and so on. Alternate scenes are also presented in which the client abstains from the drink and experiences relief, say, the feel of cold, fresh air or an invigorating shower. After several practice trials, the client is requested to continue on his own by means of homework assignments, and to imagine the aversive scene every time he is tempted to indulge in the maladaptive behavior. The goal is for the clients to monitor effectively their own behaviors in their own particular problem area (Cautela, 1966). The process of covert sensitization, then, actually involves both aversive counterconditioning, where the (imagined) aversive stimulus is paired with the response to be reduced, and, to a certain extent perhaps, avoidance training or aversion relief in that the client learns to associate pleasant responses with the avoidance of the maladaptive behavior. Covert sensitization has been used with many of the same behaviors as aversive counterconditioning, including smoking, overeating, alcoholism, and sexual fetishes.

12. IMPLOSION

Implosion or implosive therapy is the name of the approach developed by Stampfl (1970; Stampfl & Levis, 1967) to reduce maladaptive emotional behavior such as fear and anxiety. Implosion uses the principles of respondent extinction: the conditioned fear- or anxiety-eliciting stimulus is continuously presented without any further pairing with the unconditioned stimulus (with which it was originally paired in learning the fear or anxiety response), resulting in the reduction and eventual disappearance of the conditioned response (the maladaptive anxiety or fear). Implosive therapy works by first getting the client used to the method and illustrating that, in the safety of the office (and without the presence of the UCS) even great anxiety is not unbearable. The practitioner then develops with the client a hierarchy of cues related to the client's fears, such as objects or situations with "high anxiety-eliciting value." These cues are then presented to the client with a great deal of imagery. For example, as one item, a client with a fear of spiders might be told to imagine spiders crawling all over his body, up his arms, into his mouth and eyes, and so on. These cues are all selected to elicit a great deal of anxiety, with higher items on the hierarchy chosen to elicit progressively more anxiety.

Each item is presented until it fails to elicit any anxiety, and the hierarchy is worked through until the anxiety or fear related to all areas of the problem is extinguished. Following are two out of a total of nine cues used to extinguish the anxiety in a severe school phobia of a 13-year-old (Smith & Sharpe, 1970):

> Item 4: After walking through the halls of the school, which are deserted and strangely silent, Billy finds himself at the stage door of the auditorium. The door opens and Billy is confronted by the leering school principal, who says, in a sadistic tone of voice, "We want Billy." Billy looks at his mother for assistance, but she coldly says, "I'm through taking care of you. You're on your own from now on." She turns and leaves.
>
> Item 7: Billy is ordered to his literature classroom by the principal. The room is dark and strange, and the chairs have been pushed to the sides of the room. Students begin silently filing into the room. It is too dark to identify them. Tension grows as Billy wonders what will happen. The students encircle him, pressing very close, and begin to murmur, "Crazy Billy," and "Stupid, stupid, stupid." They then begin to jostle and strike him.

Implosion has been used with a variety of phobias and fears such as snake and rat phobias, school phobias, and neurotic and psychotic affective disorders (Hogan & Kirchner, 1967; Smith & Sharpe, 1970; Hogan, 1968; Levis & Carrera, 1967). When it is successful, implosive therapy achieves its results in a relatively short time, between 5 and 10 sessions. However, some studies (Fazio, 1970; Hodgson & Rachman, 1970; Mealiea, 1967) have reported either that implosion was not effective, or that anxiety actually *increased* during intervention. Hence, if implosion is to be used at all, it should be used with extreme caution and only in highly controlled situations. In fact, pending clearer evidence, implosion is probably not an intervention of choice, and counterconditioning procedures such as systematic desensitization remain the preferred techniques for reducing maladaptive anxiety.

13. CONTACT DESENSITIZATION

Contact desensitization is a technique developed by Ritter (1968, 1969a, 1969b) that basically combines modeling and *in vivo* desensitization procedures. During the process, the worker acts as a live social model in the presence of the client, plus uses actual physical contact with the client while shaping his performance. There are three major steps in the process:

1. modeling or demonstrating behaviors by the worker which the worker and client have mutually decided are relevant to the problem;
2. assisting the client in repeating the behavior which has been modeled by the worker using behavioral prompts such as placing the client's hand on the worker's while the worker touches a feared object or holding the client's arm while walking in a crowded area;
3. gradual fading out of counselor prompts while fading in of independent behavioral rehearsals by the client; i.e., the client gradually begins to approach the feared object on his own (Ritter, 1969b).

The entire process works from least difficult behavior at the early stages to gradual introduction of more difficult behaviors as proficiency in the less demanding behaviors develops.

Contact desensitization, as an entire package, has been found to be effective with adults and children, individually and in groups, with a variety of fears including snake phobia, fear of dissecting animals, fear of heights, and environmental fears such as fear of crossing the street. Of course, contact desensitization can only be used when the feared situation can readily be modeled and approached in real life.

14. THOUGHT STOPPING

Thought stopping is a complex self-control technique designed to decrease obsessive thinking, hallucinations and delusions, and compulsive behavior (Cautela, 1969; Wolpe, 1969). The procedure consists basically of instructions and demonstrations by the social worker, who begins by asking the client to think of a typical disturbing thought pattern (e.g., "I want to kill my wife"). The client raises his index finger to signal when he is thinking such thoughts and the social worker suddenly shouts "Stop!" Then the worker points out to the client that the thoughts actually do stop. This process is repeated several times, each time with the social worker clearly illustrating the way the thoughts actually do disappear. Then the social worker asks the client to try the process himself, and imagine that he is yelling "Stop!" to himself when he thinks the distressing thoughts. This is repeated several times; the client is warned that the thoughts will probably recur, but that every time they do, he must interrupt them again. The client is helped to develop this technique so that it is entirely under his own control and hence always available. The goal is to help the client stifle any distressing thoughts as soon as they appear, and to have such thoughts return with less and less frequency until they eventually disappear. It is particularly helpful to design some alternatives for the clients to think about or do as soon as the distressing thoughts disappear. The technique of covert reinforcement (which was discussed in Chapter 12), where the client is taught to think of pleasant, rewarding ideas and fantasies, is, for this purpose, a good addition to thought stopping.

Summary

This chapter has presented fourteen of the basic techniques available in behavior modification to decrease or weaken an undesired behavior. The techniques are: (1) satiation; (2) negative practice; (3) positive punishment; (4) negative punishment (response cost); (5) time-out; (6) operant extinction; (7) positive reinforcement of alternative or incompatible responses; (8) systematic desensitization; (9) substitution of sexual responses; (10) aversive counterconditioning; (11) covert sensitization; (12) implosion; (13) contact desensitization; (14) thought stopping.

CHAPTER 14. The Tools:
Complex Techniques

A few techniques of behavior modification can be used both to increase and to decrease target behaviors at the same time. These procedures, six of which follow, are called "complex techniques."

Techniques Used to Increase and Decrease Behavior

1. DIFFERENTIAL REINFORCEMENT

This is perhaps the core technique of operant behavior modification. Differential reinforcement consists of the reinforcement of certain prespecified behaviors and the concurrent nonreinforcement of certain other prespecified behaviors. The first step in differential reinforcement is the selection both of behaviors that are desired and to be increased, and those behaviors that are undesired or maladaptive. To the former, the desired behaviors, positive reinforcement is applied, following all the guidelines developed in Chapter 4. To the latter, the undesired behaviors, extinction is applied; they are carefully examined as to their source of reinforcement, and the contingent relationship between the reinforcement and the undesired behaviors is terminated. If the sources of reinforcement cannot be identified, or if the extinction process does not result in a satisfactory reduction in the undesired behaviors, some form of punishment may be used, e.g., time-out for the objectionable behavior of a child. In this way, using differential reinforcement, adaptive desired behaviors will be strengthened and will take the place of the maladaptive undesired behavior.

Differential reinforcement provides the basis for a comprehensive behavioral approach to many human problems. This procedure, which is a combination of more basic procedures, has been at the heart of behavioral programs in the home, in schools, in hospitals, in clinic offices—in essence, both in and out of the natural environment. Differential reinforcement forms the core of sophisticated forms of social engineering such as token economies. Differential reinforcement also has clear value in more traditional forms of therapeutic interviewing, in reinforcing clients' positive comments about themselves and their efforts, and in ignoring, or applying extinction to, self-defeating comments. Differential reinforcement is used by professionals in such fields as social work, psychology, and psychiatry in direct practice with clients; it forms the basis for instructing other people such as teachers, parents, nurses, attendants, and so on in the procedures of behavior modification.

Differential reinforcement has been applied to many forms of human behavior, including most of those listed under the separate techniques of positive reinforcement, punishment, and extinction. A brief listing of some of those behaviors can only hint at the scope of the utilization of differential reinforcement: making vocational decisions; problem-solving; a range of academic and educational behaviors; self-care behaviors; maladaptive or undesired sexual behaviors; delinquent behaviors; addictive behaviors; work and employment problems; speech disorders. And, of course, within each of the above categories there are several specific behaviors that have been the focus of differential reinforcement procedures (e.g., with respect to school and academic behaviors: disruptive classroom behaviors; study habits; truancy; poor performance in a variety of courses; see Morrow, 1971). Note that differential reinforcement—whether used with the most basic form of behavior such as developing new speech patterns, or with the most complex of cognitive and problem-solving behaviors—is nothing more than the systematic reinforcement of desired behavior and the nonreinforcement of undesired behavior. The application of this procedure will be illustrated in subsequent chapters.

2. DISCRIMINATION TRAINING

This operant procedure focuses on helping the client distinguish between situations where discriminative stimuli are present (S^D: tell the client he will be reinforced for performing certain behaviors) and where stimuli delta are present ($S\Delta$: tell the client that if certain behaviors are performed, they will not be reinforced).

The purpose of discrimination training is to place behaviors under stimulus control so that a behavior will produce predictable and specifiable consequences in the presence of another stimulus (say, a classroom). In other words, clients are helped to identify the right time and place for performing certain behaviors. The most common form of discrimination training is to see that a behavior is reinforced when one stimulus is present (e.g., reward a child who is reluctant to play with peers when he makes some move to play in the presence of his peers, but not reward him for playing alone or only when the teacher is present). Thus, this is primarily a technique not for decreasing undesirable behavior or for increasing desirable behavior but for helping the client perform the appropriate behaviors under the appropriate circumstances. Discrimination training may also take the form of verbal instructions to clarify or emphasize already existing discriminative stimuli, although the subsequent appropriate responses should then be reinforced to maintain them.

Discrimination training has been used in a variety of cases including those involving reading difficulties, lack of self-care behaviors, aggressive behavior, training parents to deal with their children, speech disorders, sexual problems between spouses, maladaptive school behaviors, undesired homosexual behavior, delinquent behavior, and overeating (Morrow, 1971; Whaley & Malott, 1971; Goldiamond, 1965).

3. ASSERTIVE TRAINING

The goal of assertive training is twofold: to reduce the anxiety that inhibits people from asserting themselves, and, at the same time, to increase their assertive behaviors. Assertive training actually consists of various combinations of other techniques such as modeling, behavior rehearsal, structured assignments ("homework"), and positive reinforcement. Wolpe (1969) conceptualizes assertive training as an essentially respondent procedure in that the actual expression of assertive feelings (and behaviors) is antagonistic to, and therefore reciprocally inhibits, anxiety. However, it is considered here as a complex technique.

The most commonly used combination of procedures in assertive training consists of: (a) practicing assertive responses in the social worker's office; (b) carrying out a series of graded assignments in the natural environment. Once the areas of maladaptive interpersonal functioning are pinpointed (i.e., the situations in which the anxiety or lack of assertiveness take place), and the decision to utilize assertive training made (see Wolpe, 1969, chapter 5, for some aids in assessment), the social worker begins by modeling a variety of assertive behaviors that the client might perform in the distressing situations. Then, through behavior rehearsal, the social worker and client role-play those situations, first with the social worker playing the part of the client, then with the client performing the assertive responses himself. The social worker should attempt to reinforce the client for his efforts, and initially be nonpunitive in his own responses, thereby providing the client with successful experiences in being assertive. As the client becomes more capable of performing assertive responses, the social worker should provide a wider range of feedback, including, when the client can tolerate it, some potentially negative feedback to give the client some experience in dealing with it.

Once the client has mastered the performance of the responses in the social worker's office, i.e., not in the actual interpersonal situations, the social worker and client together develop a hierarchy of anxiety, similar to that used in systematic desensitization, which is related to the client's specific problem. This hierarchy is then used for structured assignments ("homework"). The client is instructed to perform in real life the lowest items on the hierarchy, that is, those that tend to elicit the least anxiety. Thus, for a male college student who has difficulty in asking women out for dates and in handling personal encounters with women in general, the first item on the hierarchy might merely be, "saying hello to a female friend while passing her on campus," the next item might be, "stopping a woman on campus to ask her the direction of a building," and so on up the hierarchy until the client has mastered all the behaviors that form the steps of the hierarchy and can perform all of them without any anxiety. Of course, for each success, the client is reinforced not only by the social worker, but also by the success itself—having accomplished behaviors that were previously impossible. Thus, in a way similar to the process of shaping, the terminal desired behavior is reached on a step-by-step basis.

Assertive training should not be used if the act of assertion leads to aversive effects from the environment. At the barest minimum, the worker and client should explore fully all the possible implications and consequences of increasing assertive behaviors, including the probable reactions of others to such behaviors.

Assertive training has been used with a number of problems involving overdependence or lack of assertive behaviors, including shyness, inability to apply for jobs, marital problems (e.g., nagging, minimal verbal communications), frigidity and impotence, a range of interpersonal phobias, general anxiety, and depression (Wolpe, 1969; Morrow, 1971; Lazarus, 1971). One important possibility to consider is the use of assertive training in combination with systematic desensitization, using the latter first to overcome anxiety reactions, and assertive training to develop the adaptive behaviors or assertive skills that were previously missing.

4. MODELING

Modeling consists of the presentation of some example of adaptive behavior for observation by the client. Through observing this model, the client may learn and perform the behaviors he has observed. This complex technique may be used in and of itself to develop new behavior or to decrease fears and anxieties. Further, modeling has great value as an adjunct to other techniques such as shaping (e.g., having a child who is learning a new skill first watch another child perform that skill and then be reinforced himself as he approximates the modeled behavior), behavior rehearsal, and *in vivo* desensitization ("contact desensitization").

One of the special values of modeling is the flexibility of this technique in that it can be presented live or symbolically (such as in movies or pictures), and can be used with individuals or groups. Modeling will be more effective when: (1) the model is important to the observer and will attract and maintain the observer's attention; (2) the model is reinforced for performing the appropriate behavior; (3) the observer is reinforced for initiating the modeled behavior; (4) the observer is led through guided participation to practice the actual modeled behaviors (see Chapter 7 for a complete list of the optimal conditions for effective modeling). Modeling has been used to develop social and vocational skills; self-care skills; prosocial play patterns; appropriate sex role behaviors; intellectual skills; linguistic skills; assertive responses; problem-solving skills; efficient study habits; parental child-rearing skills; and a variety of social skills and to decrease such anxieties and fears as snake and dog phobia and fear of heights (Bandura, 1969; 1971).

5. ADVICE AND INSTRUCTIONS

The provision of advice and instructions is rarely used as a procedure sufficient in and of itself to produce positive behavior change. There is, however, increasing evidence that in many situations, clients want advice (Reid & Shapiro, 1969; Mayer & Timms, 1969). There is also evidence that advice and instructions, provided as components of a planned behavior change program, can facilitate its results. Typically, advice refers to practical recommendations for action, while instructions refers to the act of furnishing information in a systematic way. However, when used in behavior modification, advice and instructions may be divided into three categories: The *first* category is actually giving suggestions to the client as to a recommended course of action in dealing with problems. This might take the form of suggesting that the client bring in a family member for counseling, providing alternatives for meeting stressful situations, making referrals, giving information as to where certain desirable consequences might be obtained ("Our local Y.M.C.A. has a club for unmarried parents. This might be something you'd like to consider as a way of meeting other people."), and so on. The *second* category—although traditionally not considered as advice in approaches emphasizing such verbal techniques as interpretation, reflection, and clarification—deals with pointing out relationships between client problems and controlling events, whether residing in the client (e.g., dysfunctional attitudes) or in the environment (e.g., transactions with others). The purpose of advice in this context is to help the client recognize these interrelationships, to make him aware of the control certain events exert over his problems, and to develop out of this awareness the possibility of moving more efficiently and effectively toward the solution of his problems. The point is, of course, that such recognition is not the end in itself, but simply one way of facilitating an intervention program. These procedures have been used fairly widely by Wolpe (1969) and Lazarus (1971) in such situations as helping to clarify the way an inaccurate attitude or opinion about, say, certain sexual practices, has promoted maladaptive functioning, and in easing problems stemming from the client's overgeneralization and stereotyping ("all women are like mother"), dichotomous thinking ("You're either with me or against me"), "oversocialization" (total acceptance of dysfunctional cultural myths), or just plain faulty information ("masturbation causes mental illness"). The *third* category is perhaps the most frequently used, and consists of supplying the necessary information to carry out behavioral procedures adequately. This might consist of instructions on self-control procedures (see section below), prompting, discrimination training, behavioral contracts, use of reinforcement, and so on.

Again, advice and instruction are rarely used alone, but are frequently integral components of a behavioral program. Four general guidelines for the use of advice and instructions are:

1. They should only be provided when the problem is thoroughly understood. To advise prematurely is to court disaster.
2. They should be provided only when there is a good chance that they will actually be followed. Most clients have been told what to do by everybody—friends, relatives, even the hairdresser. Professional advice should not just be an expensive version of lay advice ("Stand up to your mother-in-law!"). If clients have not been able to follow advice previously, the reasons should be thoroughly explored.
3. Advice should be given only when there is a substantial chance that following the advice will lead to successful results for the client. All of the possible consequences, positive and negative, as well as alternative ways of reaching the goal, should be spelled out.
4. The advice and instructions should be crystal clear, presented in terms understandable by the client. Feedback from the client as to his understanding of the instructions should always be solicited.

6. MODIFICATION OF STRESSFUL ENVIRONMENT CONDITIONS

Strictly speaking this is not a technique of behavior modification, but it should be a part of every assessment, and should be implemented, when necessary, as a precondition to, part of, or alternative to, a behavioral program. It is, in other words, one of the first avenues the social worker should consider in making his behavioral assessment (see Chapter 11). The question to be answered is: are there any environmental conditions that need to be altered that are either preventing or suppressing desired behavior, or that tend to lead to an increase in undesired behavior (Reese, 1966)?

This could include any number of different types of intervention and should be a familiar part of interventive strategy to most social workers. On the broadest level, environmental modification could mean increasing the client's opportunities, or at least his access to such opportunities (e.g., job counseling for the unemployed), or remedying his social or material deprivation (e.g., inadequate housing) as a way of decreasing his anxiety and hostility (stemming from overcrowding or lack of privacy). Environmental interventions, arising, say, out of a referral of a presumably "disturbed" child, might include making modifications in a school system (speaking with a principal, rearranging classes, having a student transferred to a different class). Given that the system is the disturbing factor, changes within the system, almost independent of the child, may lead to a complete extinction of the child's undesired behavior. To give a similar example, one might reduce a parent's punitive behavior toward a child in order to lessen the child's fear. A third example might be work with the employers of discharged residents of psychiatric institutions to educate them about the potentialities of such people, reduce their tendency toward overprotection, and so on.

All of this, of course, implies that making a comprehensive assessment will preclude accepting individuals for direct behavioral practice until it is clear that the most efficient, effective, and ethical intervention will lie in direct work with the client, and not the system in which he or she is functioning.

Finally, on a more technical level, environmental intervention may facilitate the use of behavioral techniques by bringing about changes in secondary sources of reinforcement. For example, working with a teacher or parents to diminish a child's aggressive behavior might have a far better chance of success if the child's peers can be convinced to stop encouraging (or attending to) the child when he fights or yells. In all of these situations, any of the behavioral techniques described in this and the preceding two chapters may be used to facilitate such environmental changes. But the basic point is that it is often far more ethical as well as effective to modify the conditions controlling the client's behavior than to modify the client's *reactions* to the conditions.

Behavioral Programs

A basic feature of behavior modification is its evolutionary nature: behavioral procedures are continuously developed and revised as new information becomes available. As was emphasized earlier, these procedures are not described here in an effort to encourage their indiscriminate use —use without adequate assessment, planning, and individualization. In fact, one would hope that the social worker who uses behavioral procedures will be familiar with several techniques to be used *if*, and only if, the situation calls for their application. This means, of course, that a social worker will not apply only one technique to every case, but will know how to combine several procedures, if necessary, to deal with the various components of the complex human problems he typically encounters. The very complexity of human problems, in fact, precludes a narrow or mechanistic utilization of techniques, and instead calls for the use of behavioral *programs*.

A behavioral program consists of a combination of techniques selected on the basis of an individualized assessment—the nature of the problem, the client, and the situation. A behavioral program should be designed for each client: the social worker should not simply apply "Program X" to this type of client and "Program Y" to that type. For example, in dealing with problems involving severe and pervasive anxiety (Cautela, 1966), the social worker might consider:

1. relationship formation, encouragement, reinforcement of positive comments by the client about himself, and reassurance that the social worker will be available to help;
2. systematic desensitization for aspects of the anxiety amenable to it;
3. assertive training using modeling and behavior rehearsal;
4. a variety of self-control measures such as thought-stopping for obsessive thoughts.

Similarly, in dealing with problems involving excessive alcohol intake (e.g., McBrearty *et al.*, 1968), the social worker might consider:

1. aversive counterconditioning, in which onset of the electric shock is paired with the taste and smell of alcohol and words describing alcoholic beverages;

2. aversion relief, in which onset of the shock is paired with drinking juice or soda;

3. covert sensitization to the intake of alcoholic beverages;

4. systematic desensitization for the anxiety related to (or perhaps causing) drinking;

5. behavior rehearsal to train the client in areas of behavioral deficits such as conversation at parties, refusing alcoholic beverages, dealing with former drinking companions, and so on.

Perhaps the most sophisticated of the behavioral programs is the token economy. The goal of a token economy is to develop behaviors that will lead to social reinforcement from others, and to use behavioral techniques to train the individual client to control his own environment in such a way that he will both elicit positive responses from others and assume a responsible social role (Krasner, 1970). Token economies are established by:

1. defining certain behaviors as desirable;

2. developing mediums of exchange, i.e., the tokens (the term "economy" refers to the supply and demand and exchange characteristics of the programs that determine the value of the token);

3. developing a way to utilize the tokens, namely, the exchange for direct reinforcers ("the good things in life").

Token economies, or other sophisticated programs that are based on similar operant principles but without the tokens (because the clients have difficulty in using them, e.g., some "autistic" children), combine a wide variety of techniques:

1. positive reinforcement;

2. shaping for basic behaviors;

3. differential reinforcement to develop desired behaviors and extinguish unwanted behaviors;

4. extinction;

5. discrimination training and prompting;

6. modeling;

7. mild punishment for destructive behaviors (e.g., time-out for tantrums).

All kinds of skills are taught in such programs, from such basic ones as speaking, good personal hygiene, reading and writing, to what are often considered more complex skills, such as displaying affection, playing or interacting with peers, working regular hours, speaking in groups, developing good study habits, and living in the community. Similarly, a variety of undesired behaviors—including tantrums, delusions, hallucinations, fighting, stealing, isolation, noncooperative play, swearing, apathy, self-mutilation, absence of response to social situations, and so on—are extinguished.

The range of settings and types of clients and problems with which such sophisticated programs have been used is particularly impressive. They have been used with children, young and middle-aged adults, the aged, "mentally retarded" individuals, and delinquents, in such diverse settings as psychiatric institutions, schools, day care centers, halfway houses, and correctional facilities (Sherman & Baer, 1969; Davison, 1969; Krasner, 1970 and 1971). These sophisticated, carefully planned programs are being used with increasingly diverse populations and problems, and with increasing skill and care as new developments become available.

Self-Control: Helping Clients to Help Themselves

"Helping clients to help themselves" is perhaps one of the most misused phrases in traditional social work. Based perhaps on noble philosophical principles, this phrase has, in practice, frequently amounted to an abdication of responsibility on the part of the social worker, and often has served as an excuse for passivity and for an inability to make specific plans with the client to deal with present and future problems. Yet, regardless of whether or not one uses behavioral procedures, the ultimate goal in professional intervention indeed is to provide the client with the skills and resources necessary to lead his own life as adequately and independently as possible. The area of self-control has gained increasing momentum in behavior modification, as research and practice have contributed to the development of a number of procedures to aid clients in establishing autonomy.

Self-control refers to the ability of an individual to decrease those of his own behaviors that are perceived as harmful to himself or to others, and to increase the behaviors that are perceived as functional. An individual is said to have good self-control if he is able to inhibit undesirable responses that are likely to occur under certain conditions, and increase or perform other behaviors that are desirable under certain other conditions. It is the individual himself who determines the goals to be achieved, and who deliberately selects, arranges, and implements the strategies he will undertake to bring about behavior change (Cautela, 1969; Goldfried & Merbaum, 1973; Mahoney & Thoresen, 1974). The goal of the social worker who uses behavior modification would be to help his client develop the knowledge about how, when, and where to use such strategies. Success, however, would be defined in terms of the client's actually being able to use those strategies on his own at the appropriate time and place.

As with any other behavioral program, the social worker would carefully base the planning of such interventive strategies upon the specific characteristics of the client. Obviously, people will differ in their ability to use self-control procedures; some people will be able to learn a sufficient amount to prepare them to deal with a variety of problems for an indefinite period of time. Other people may be able to learn a self-control procedure to deal only with their current problem, and may need additional sessions in the future to learn to cope with new or different problems.

As with all other behavior modification programs, two points pertain: First, the social worker, in helping the client learn self-control procedures, not only takes an active hand in teaching and demonstrating, but applies behavioral procedures in teaching (e.g., positive reinforcement for success); Second, specificity in the procedures is the essence of the behavior modification approach to self-control. A client is taught specific methods for dealing with specific problems, and the ways he can implement specific techniques. The basic principles of behavioral assessment and technique selection are followed, e.g., whether the goal is to increase or decrease behavior (or to change the time or place of its occurrence), whether the behavior to be changed is respondent or operant (or complex), and so on.

Several of the techniques described in this and the last two chapters were actually designed for use in self-control programs. These techniques include covert reinforcement, thought stopping, and covert sensitization (see Cautela, 1971; 1972). Other procedures, although not generally used in self-control programs, have some promise, e.g., systematic desensitization and assertive training. In fact, the relaxation procedures that are usually part of the desensitization package may have some promise as therapeutic tools in their own right (i.e., teaching clients how to relax in certain situations, e.g., before going to sleep; Cautela, 1969). Operant procedures have been used more frequently in self-control programs dealing with such problems as smoking, overeating, marital friction, lack of good study habits, and lack of exercise (Goldfried & Merbaum, 1973; Kau & Fischer, 1974). Such procedures have included behavioral contracts, self-reinforcement, response cost (withdrawing privileges if agreed-upon tasks are not completed), and discrimination training (Goldiamond, 1965). Since the use of most of these procedures as self-control techniques have been clearly described in some recent publications (Goldfried & Merbaum, 1973; Watson & Tharp, 1972; Cautela, 1969, 1971, 1972; Mahoney & Thoresen, 1974), there is no need to review them all here. But it is essential to realize a basic point: whichever self-control procedure is used, the social worker approaches the client and problem in the same way as he would any other situation in behavior modification—with careful assessment and careful technique-selection. The basic process is the same. The only real difference is that, instead of applying the procedures himself, or training a mediator, the social worker trains the client to apply them to himself.

One relatively early conception of self-control was Homme's (1965) description of use of *"coverants."* Homme suggested that internal responses such as thoughts and imagination are merely covert operants ("coverant" merely being a contraction of the two terms), and that they are therefore subject to the same laws as any operant. Hence, self-control from this perspective simply consists of teaching the individual to manage his own contingencies through self-administered verbal contracts. Thus, the client who wants to improve his study behavior might tell himself: "When I finish my math problems, I can treat (reinforce) myself with a chocolate sundae." A recent case study (Johnson, 1971) reported successful application of this coverant technique.

In summarizing the basic steps of self-modification, Watson and Tharp (1972) have developed a multi-step guide that the social worker and client can use together:

1. List current dissatisfactions.
2. Select one particular problem and state the problem in terms of the *behavior* that occurs *in particular situations*.
3. Describe the problem using the appropriate behavioral terms (e.g., "I withdraw from social conversation to *escape aversive consequences.* Hence, my withdrawal is maintained by *negative reinforcement*.").
4. Be as precise as possible in stating the behaviors that occur and the situations in which they occur. Describe some behavior-in-a-situation that you wish to increase or decrease.
5. Gather your own baseline data. Count every instance of target behavior and keep a record of your count (include time and place).
6. Catalog your reinforcers. Answer three questions for each potential reinforcer: (a) Is it a reinforcer specifically for me? (b) Is it a strong reinforcer? (c) Is it accessible (can I find some way to use it)?
7. Draw up a contract with yourself. State what the target behavior is and what reinforcement you will gain for performing it. Specify the ways in which you will obtain reinforcement, e.g., the shaping schedule. (At times, it might be helpful to designate a significant other, spouse or friend, as the dispenser and withholder of reinforcers to insure there will not be any "cheating;" Fischer and Kau, 1974).
8. List, and attempt to verify through self-observation, possible antecedents to problem behaviors. Devise a plan for intervention,

for altering antecedent (or stimulus) control. Do not implement the plan.

9. Identify the emotional components of a problem (e.g., anxiety response) and devise an *in vivo* or self-desensitization plan. Develop hierarchies and practice relaxation.

10. Select one of the plans you have developed (item 7, control of consequences; item 8, control of antecedents; item 9, desensitization) and begin that plan.

11. Continue to collect data on the problem behavior. Make a graph of the data to determine if the intervention plan is working. If not, reanalyze or change the plan or choose an alternative plan.

12. Consider termination if the plan is successful:
    a. list the opportunities in the natural environment for practicing new behavior;
    b. rate these in terms of their likelihood for receiving "natural" reinforcement;
    c. test for generalization (perform the new behavior in a variety of situations);
    d. institute intermittent reinforcement to maximize resistance to extinction;
    e. continue counting target behaviors during all of the above;
    f. implement the next plan (e.g. numbers 7, 8, or 9) if additional maladaptive behaviors are present.

PROBLEM SOLVING

One aspect of self-control that has received considerable attention in traditional social work practice is problem solving, defined here as a behavioral process that makes available a variety of response alternatives for dealing with a problem situation, and increases the probability of selecting the most effective responses from among those alternatives. A behavioral approach to training in problem solving may be conceptualized as a form of self-control training in that the client learns how to solve problems, thereby discovering for himself the best way of responding and deciding upon the most effective course of action when confronted with a problem situation (D'Zurilla & Goldfried, 1971).

The behavioral problem-solving process is not a single technique but rather a combination of techniques to provide the client with the ability to use the following five steps in coping with problems (Goldfried & Merbaum, 1973, p. 27):

1. being able to recognize problem situations when they occur and making an attempt to resist the temptation to act impulsively or avoid, or do nothing to deal with, the situation;

2. defining the situation in concrete or operational terms, and then identifying the major aspects with which he or she must cope;
3. generating a number of alternative behaviors that might be pursued in this situation;
4. deciding on the course of action most likely to result in positive consequences;
5. implementing the decision in real life and verifying the effectiveness of the behavior in resolving the problem situation.

The social worker decides to use this approach to problem solving on the basis of his assessment, and could use any number of procedures to implement this approach. The provision of advice and instructions would probably characterize some of the interaction as the social worker explains the various parts of the program. The client could be trained to observe and record his own behavior in problem situations. When such situations occur, desensitization might be used to decrease anxiety responses. Assertive training through behavior rehearsal and modeling could help provide the client with the skills necessary to confront problem situations actively. Positive and differential reinforcement would be used to reinforce the client for success during the interview, for example, for moving through the various stages of the process and for effectively coping with problems in real life, outside of the social worker's office.

Summary Table of Techniques

This and the preceding two chapters have described a number of the major techniques of behavior modification. These techniques will probably be continually revised, and new ones developed, as research and practice in behavior modification continues. But one hopes that the selection and application of techniques will continue to occur in the same systematic way as these techniques are currently selected and applied: based on careful assessment, evaluation of the kind of behavior involved (say, respondent or operant), whether the behavior is to be increased or decreased, and after reference to previous efforts (as reported in the literature) where specific techniques were effectively used with specific behaviors. Most of these features can be ascertained by reviewing Table 14.1, which summarizes the salient characteristics of the major techniques of behavior modification.

TABLE 14.1. The Techniques of Behavior Modification.

A. Techniques Primarily Used for Strengthening (Increasing) Behavior

Technique	Class of Behavior	Focal Events	Sample Behaviors
1. Positive Reinforcement	Operant	Consequences	Delinquent behaviors (fighting and stealing); marital verbal communication; work and employment problems (work habits and skills); self-care behaviors; sexual problems; speech disorders; academic problems (e.g., studying); hallucinations and delusions; parent–child problems.
2. Shaping	Operant	Consequences	Self-care behaviors (feeding, toilet training, dressing, eating); basic social skills (smiling, appropriate greetings, playing); developing speech; academic behaviors (attention in class).
3. Covert Reinforcement	Operant	Consequences	Marital problems; approaching members of opposite sex.
4. Negative Reinforcement	Operant	Consequences	Talking in group therapy; stuttering; homosexual and heterosexual behavior; self-feeding.
5. Prompting	Operant	Antecedents	Academic behaviors; self-care; basic speaking skills.
6. Fading	Operant	Antecedents	Academic behaviors; self-care behaviors; basic social skills
7. Chaining	Operant	Complex	Language development; social play; self-care behaviors; studying.
8. Behavior Rehearsal	Complex	Complex	Assertive behaviors; job and interview skills; social and interpersonal skills (conversation); examination-taking.

B. Techniques Primarily Used for Weakening (Decreasing) Behavior

Technique	Class of Behavior	Focal Events	Sample Behaviors
1. Satiation	Operant	Complex	Smoking; hoarding.
2. Negative Practice	Operant	Complex	Tics, nail-biting, stuttering, teeth-grinding.

3. Positive Punishment	Operant	Consequences	Inappropriate verbal behavior; smoking; homosexual behaviors; self-injurious behaviors; fetishes; tics; tremors; stuttering.
4. Negative Punishment (Response Cost)	Operant	Consequences	Fighting; stealing; swearing; defiance and disobedience; tantrums; thumbsucking; self-destructive behaviors.
5. Time Out	Operant	Consequences	Yelling and screaming; fighting; swearing; dangerous climbing; self-destructive behaviors; tantrums; disobedience and defiance.
6. Extinction	Operant	Consequences	Vomiting; crying; tantrums; excessive alcohol-drinking; "psychotic" talk; refusal to eat unassisted; compulsive scratching.
7. Positive Reinforcement of Alternative Response	Operant	Consequences	Hyperactive classroom behavior; fighting; self-destructive behavior; screaming and yelling.
8. Systematic Desensitization	Respondent	Antecedents	Fear of criticism and devaluation; sexual problems (e.g. impotence); "existential anxiety;" feelings of guilt and jealousy; fears and phobias (e.g., of closed spaces, heights, examinations, small animals); general anxiety; depression.
9. Substitution of Sexual Responses	Respondent	Antecedents	Impotence; frigidity; premature ejaculation.
10. Aversive Counter-conditioning	Respondent	Antecedents	Alcoholism; homosexual behavior; smoking; sexual fetishes.
11. Covert Sensitization	Respondent	Antecedents	Smoking; sexual fetishes; alcoholism; overeating.
12. Implosion	Respondent	Antecedents	Snake phobia; rat phobia; school phobia; "psychotic" affective reactions.
13. Contact Desensitization	Complex	Complex	Snake phobia; fear of heights; fear of crossing the street.

TABLE 14.1. The Techniques of Behavior Modification. (continued)

14. Thought Stopping	Complex	Complex	Obsessive thoughts; hallucinations and delusions; compulsive behaviors.

C. COMPLEX TECHNIQUES—INCREASE AND DECREASE BEHAVIOR

TECHNIQUE	CLASS OF BEHAVIOR	FOCAL EVENTS	SAMPLE BEHAVIORS
1. Differential Reinforcement	Operant	Consequences	Making vocational decisions; problem solving; academic and educational behaviors (e.g., school performance); delinquent behaviors; self-care behaviors (e.g., eating, dressing); maladaptive sexual behaviors (e.g., impotence); hallucinations and delusions; addictive behaviors (e.g., alcoholism); speech disorders (e.g., stuttering, lack of speech).
2. Discrimination Training	Operant	Complex	Reading problems; self-care behaviors (e.g., feeding); aggressive behavior and fighting; training parents; speech disorders; homosexual behavior; academic behavior (e.g., studying); overeating.
3. Assertive Training	Complex	Complex	Shyness; making job applications; marital problems (e.g., nagging, lack of verbal communication); frigidity and impotence; interpersonal phobias; general anxiety; depression.
4. Modeling	Complex	Complex	Problem-solving skills; self-care skills; prosocial play patterns; appropriate sex-role behaviors; intellectual and linguistic skills; assertive responses; child rearing; dog phobia; fear of heights.
5. Advice and Instructions	Complex	Complex	Any of the above.
6. Modification of Stressful Environmental Conditions	Complex	Complex	Any of the above.

Summary

This chapter described six complex techniques that can be used both to increase and decrease behavior. The techniques are: (1) differential reinforcement; (2) discrimination training; (3) assertive training; (4) modeling; (5) advice and instructions; (6) modification of stressful environmental conditions. Behavioral programs such as the token economy were also described. In such programs a variety of techniques are used in combination depending on the nature of the client, the problem, and the situation. The behavioral perspective on self-control—a remedial and preventive function—was presented. Using behavior modification, people can be helped to help themselves, thus, it is hoped, minimizing the need for future professional services. Problem-solving was also briefly described as one aspect of self-control. Finally, the major procedures of behavior modification that were described in this and the preceding two chapters were presented in a single table, both for summary purposes, and as a guide to aid the reader in the selection of techniques by providing an overview of the type of technique, its goal, the class of behavior with which it is primarily concerned, its focal events (antecedents, consequences, or both), and some examples of the behaviors with which each technique has been successfully used.

As mentioned several times in this and the previous chapters, behavioral procedures are rarely applied singly or in a vacuum. Instead, they are the product of an individualized assessment, and are also applied in the context of an on-going interventive process. The following chapter describes the way the procedures of behavior modification are integrated and differentially applied as part of an overall interventive process, again, one hopes, the logical outgrowth of the assessment process.

CHAPTER 15. An Overview of the Intervention Process

Although behavior modification often involves a sequence of steps—from initial assessment, through contracting, to intervention and evaluation—it should not be interpreted as requiring a rigid lockstep process from which the social worker never deviates. Behavioral approaches require an awareness of differences in environmental and behavioral patterns as well as changes over time in an individual's responses. The application of behavior modification techniques to the complexity and infinite variety of human problems requires flexibility and creativity in dealing with each new problem.

Steps in the Interventive Process

As described in Chapter 11, the core of behavior modification is the assessment of the behavior to be changed and the variables that affect—or could affect—such behavior. Assessment not only precedes the application of behavior modification procedures but should also be carried out during and after the application of the procedures.

This Chapter presents a series of interventive steps that integrate the use of techniques described in Chapters 12–14 and that can serve as a guideline in planning and carrying out interventions based on behavioral assessment. This assumes that, conditions permitting, the 12 phases of assessment presented in Chapter 11 have been carried out. As with assessment, the major thrust of this chapter is concerned with operant behavior and intervention. When the problem behavior includes respondent features, the guidelines in Chapter 19 may also be applied. The general model of the interventive process includes the following steps:

1. developing contracts between the participating individuals;
2. preparing mediators;
3. altering significant elements in the client's environment to increase the probability that desired behavior will occur;

4. making the new behavior acceptable to the client;
5. establishing the effectiveness of the reinforcers;
6. applying all the principles of effective reinforcement;
7. strengthening or increasing desired behaviors in frequency, intensity, or duration;
8. weakening or decreasing undesired behaviors in frequency, intensity, or duration;
9. arranging for generalization to the natural environment;
10. keeping objective records of the target behavior;
11. terminating the formal intervention program and planning follow-up contacts.

1. DEVELOPING CONTRACTS BETWEEN THE PARTICIPATING INDIVIDUALS

Once the social worker is prepared to proceed with an interventive program based on the assessment of the behavioral problem, he works with the client or mediator in structuring and carrying out the intervention plan. Of course, much of the interaction between the social worker, mediator, and client will be spontaneous and revolve around unanticipated events that will inevitably develop as the interventions take place. Indeed, many of the reinforcements for goal-related behaviors may be a function of serendipitous events, such as when the social worker notices and comments on the attractiveness of a brightly colored new dress worn by a generally withdrawn, apathetic client.

However, most of the interventions in behavior modification are planned—albeit subject to revision. As little as possible should be left to chance. Interventions are often more effective if they are carried out on the basis of more or less formal oral or, if possible, written contracts between the social worker, the client, and, if there is one, the mediator.

Intervention contracts may state: (1) what the mutual goals are of those who are participating in the intervention; (2) that each of the parties involved (i.e., the social worker—by himself and as an agent of his agency—the client, and the mediator) agree to engage in specified activities in exchange for the other participants' engaging in other specified activities; (3) what, specifically, the client is expected to do in order to obtain reinforcements from the social worker or the mediator. The contract may specify how long a period of time the agreement will be in force, or the circumstances under which the agreement will be terminated, or both. However, it should be clear that the contract is subject to renegotiation whenever any party to it considers it unworkable or unfair (Krumboltz & Thorensen, 1969). A comprehensive written contract is presented in the case illustration at the end of Chapter 21.

Implicit in the concept of contracts is an openness between the client and the social worker about behavior programs. Just as there is no need for secret labeling in assessment, there is no need for secret plans in intervention. Assuming that the social worker and the client (or the social worker and the mediator) are aware that a behavioral change is being planned, then a logical step to take is to develop an explicit intervention contract. An intervention contract can facilitate the subsequent interventions in three ways (Rose, 1972). First, if a client knows about a treatment procedure and expresses a willingness to participate in it (especially if the client commits himself to it in writing), then the intervention is more likely to be successful. Second, knowing specifically what one is supposed to learn has been found to lead to successful learning. The more one knows about a situation, the less likely (generally) one will be to feel anxiety about the learning process. It is possible that the high drop-out rate of many therapies is a function of the failure of the social worker (or other therapist) to communicate clearly to the client what he expects the client to do, and what procedures are to be used. The explicit contracts often used in behavior modification may be a factor in the relatively low drop-out rate of this approach. Third, all concerned in behavioral change efforts may be on firmer ethical ground when social workers and mediators are open about what they plan to do with respect to the client's problems.

Contracts may cover any or all phases of intervention. For example, the following oral contract might have been proposed in an early session focusing on the assessment of a parent who requested help with her "uncontrollable rages," which had often culminated in her physically attacking her six-year-old daughter, Brenda:

> I will work with you toward finding ways of reducing your unwanted behavior toward your daughter, and try to help you improve your relations with her, if, for the next week, you will do the following things:
>
> 1. Every time you feel you are beginning to react to your daughter in a way that could lead to your rage, inform your husband, and leave the room you are in immediately, and stay away for a period of 10 minutes *after* you feel you have cooled off.
>
> 2. While you are out of the room, you will jot down on a piece of paper the date, the time of day, and all the events and thoughts that you noticed were associated with your getting angry at Brenda at that time.

The social worker may also negotiate a contract for the intervention itself, specifying the behaviors expected of the client.

> Mary Schaar, caseworker, agrees to arrange for Colin Omori, resident of Cottage 7, to have home visits (including bus fare) for each of the next four weekends provided that Colin meets the following requirements for each of the four weeks:

a. No fights participated in by Colin at mealtimes (fights in gym, under supervision, permitted)—to be certified at week's end by cottage supervisor.

b. All math assignments to be turned in on time—to be certified at week's end by math teacher.

[Signed] _____   _____
       Colin Omori   Mary Schaar
                                    [dated] November 14, 1975

A more informal oral contract may be made by a social worker and his or her clients in an early marital counseling interview: "I will meet with you to explore how I can help you with your marriage for the next six weeks, without fee, provided *both* of you develop and keep up the reciprocal behavior checklists we discussed this evening."

The social worker can also help a mediator develop a contract with an individual or group for which he or she dispenses reinforcers:

CONTRACT

Gwen Angell (mother) and Ben Angell (father) agree to give their son, Charley, points on our "Behavior Chart" (to be posted at all times on the kitchen cabinet door next to a copy of this contract) according to rates specified below for the things we'd like him to do. Each Friday he can exchange these points for things he'd like us to do, or "deposit" them for bigger things as described in this contract.

We, the parents, agree to enter the "points" with smiles on our faces, and promise not to withhold them because of other things Charley does, even if we don't like some of the other things he does.

To show our good faith, we, the parents, have deposited $50 with the Boone County Family Service to be held by a social worker until February 12th of next year to be returned only if we follow through with this plan, subject only to revisions sanctioned by our social worker. (If we renege, the money is to revert to the agency's emergency fund.)

This plan goes into effect immediately and will be revised or terminated on February 12, 1976.

Charley Gives (Parents Get)

Activity	*Points*
Attends school all day (per day)	5
Works 2 hours a day at farm chores	5
Baby sits for younger sisters (per evening)	5
Goes to church on Sunday morning with family	5
Watches and discusses evening news with father	5

Parents Give (Charley Gets)

Item	
Use of family car on Saturday (day)	25
Use of family car on Saturday (night)	30
Use of family car on week night (7 to 10 p.m.)	20
Choice of menu for Sunday dinner	20
Calf of his own (to raise for fair)	500

New trumpet (approximately $300)   500
    Car of his own (VW—circa 67–69)   1,000
[signed]

_____

Gwen Angell

_____

Ben Angell

_____

Charley Angell

_____

Helen Silloh   (Social Worker—Witness)

[dated] September 24, 1975

In preparing oral or written contracts, as little as possible should be left to chance. For example, contracts should always be clear as to what consequences will follow what behaviors. To minimize misunderstandings, it may be desirable to spell out in writing the terms of the agreement, and to have all parties to the agreement (e.g., social worker, mediator, and client) sign the contract, as in the illustrations above. This avoids misunderstandings, misapprehensions, and subsequent recriminations.

Some social workers consider the use of contracts to be a separate technique of behavior change. Indeed, merely participating in such an agreement can produce some degree of behavioral change, even before formal implementation of other techniques. However, the extent of such changes would probably be limited in most cases.

2. PREPARING MEDIATORS

If, as a result of the assessment, a mediator is to be used, the social worker and the mediator should explore their mutual expectations and responsibilities. The mediator and the social worker should discuss the means of data collection, the frequency and nature of contacts with the client, arrangements for periodic reviews and emergency conferences with the social worker. The mediator should be actively involved in the choice of reinforcements and in the development of the intervention strategy. Goals of their cooperation should be explicated, and potential problems discussed. For example, if a token economy is to be established on a psychiatric ward, the negative reactions of staff and residents on other wards may be anticipated, along with complications in the mechanics of setting up the program. The social worker could help minimize these problems and devise ways of making the efforts of the staff worthwhile.

Consider the case of parents who are reluctant to act as mediators for their child. They may feel that there is no use in trying, that the intervention plan sounds "silly," and that they have already tried several approaches to modify their child's behavior. The social worker empathizes with the parents' fatigue, offers them support, models appropriate behavior for them, and suggests a trial period of a specified length of time to try the new approach.

The social worker might also help the mediator develop his relationship with the client. Whenever possible, the mediator (or the social worker) should discuss with the client the intervention plan, methods of behavior modification, and the contingencies of reinforcement. The details of whatever oral or written contract is developed between the mediator and client (see previous section) can then be worked out.

In some situations involving such involuntary clients as young children or severely "retarded" or disturbed people, it may not be possible to establish a reciprocal contract. But even in such situations, the mediator should make every attempt to define clearly the contingencies of reinforcement.

3. ALTERING SIGNIFICANT ELEMENTS IN THE CLIENT'S ENVIRONMENT TO INCREASE THE PROBABILITY THAT DESIRED BEHAVIOR WILL OCCUR

This component of intervention calls for the participation of the client or mediator (or both) whenever possible; it involves structuring the client's environment in such a way as to make it more likely that cues that lead to desired behaviors will occur or be more prominent, or that cues that lead to undesired behaviors will be less pronounced, thus encouraging the occurrence of desired behaviors.

The client should learn the cues which signal it is appropriate for the desired target behavior to occur; a mute child should learn when it is "good" to speak, an "unresponsive" husband should learn when it is appropriate to give affection, and a student should learn when it is appropriate to persevere in an argument with a teacher and when to keep quiet. Often these cues exist, but the client does not perceive them. In such situations the social worker or mediator may help the client be more *sensitive to* these cues. The procedure of discrimination training may be called for: the social worker teaches the client to attend to the differences between those cues (discriminative stimuli—S^D) that suggest that succeeding behavior will be reinforced and those (stimulus delta—S^Δ) that suggest that succeeding behavior will not be reinforced.

The rules or instructional stimuli for the program or for exhibiting specific behavior should be clear. The client needs to understand those characteristics of situations that call for certain behaviors, or preclude certain other behaviors. Furthermore, the client must be provided with the skills and materials necessary to engage in the goal behaviors. The client may find himself without these skills or resources. He may not have a car, access to a telephone, or adequate vocabulary or social skills. The social worker uses his creativity here to see to it that the client acquires the necessary tangible resources or skills to carry out desirable behaviors when they are called for. To acquire tangible resources, the social worker can engage in such traditional social work activities as advocacy, brokerage, and resource development. If the goal is to change the individual's interactions with other people, the social worker can use such procedures as the following:

PROMPTING

In prompting, the social worker gives clear directions on how the client may best react to typical environmental cues. He can do such coaching most effectively at the place and time at which the target behavior is to occur—at home after dinner, for example, when parents are attempting to react appropriately to their children's temper tantrums. Or the social worker might whisper suggestions while a client is making phone calls to find employment. Some clinicians have experimented with such procedures as remote coaching through an ear phone for family interactions observed through one-way mirrors, and the use of signal lights operated by a mediator to provide cues for prearranged behaviors.

MODELING

In modeling, the social worker acts in ways that the client can observe and replicate in his own behavior. People will more likely model behaviors in individuals they perceive as "successful" and who have reacted to them in a warm, empathic, and genuine manner. The social worker may model how to engage in constructive arguments and how to express recognition for a job well done. Indeed, the social worker may model in his relationship with the client (or perhaps, another social worker) how the client might relate more effectively with others in his environment. In group settings the client can model the behavior of those in the group who have successfully completed a task similar to that confronting the client.

BEHAVIOR REHEARSAL

In behavior rehearsal, the social worker reproduces typical problem situations by portraying the client or another key person associated with the target behavior (e.g., teachers, spouses, parents, supervisors, boyfriends, etc.). The social worker sets up a situation with particular cues to which the client responds, and reinforces or otherwise reacts to the client's behavior in the same way that significant others might. The social worker then uses modeling and coaching to show how the client's behavior might be altered to bring about more desirable consequences. Changes resulting from such experiences may generalize to the natural environment of the client, and bring about effective reinforcement from those in the client's environment.

NEGATIVE PRACTICE

Sometimes people are unaware of their dysfunctional behavior until someone in their environment points it out to them. For instance, a father may not be aware he is shouting when he criticizes his children; a child may not be aware of a tic or atypical speech pattern; a "retarded" adult may not be aware of his tendency to button his shirt improperly. In negative practice the client is taught to be more aware of such dysfunctional behaviors, and to bring them under purposeful control by deliberately repeating the dysfunctional behavior and attending to how it looks or feels. For example, the shouting father may role-play a situation in which he criticizes his child—all the while shouting at his typical level; the child is asked to exhibit his tic over and over again in front of a mirror; the retarded adult is instructed to deliberately button his shirt askew. Once the client becomes more aware of the sensations associated with the dysfunctional behavior, he becomes more able to control it.

It may be necessary to *remove cues* for behavior that are incompatible with goal behaviors or that will lead to undesirable behaviors. The social worker can help the client learn what events or cues lead him to engage in undesirable behaviors. He then helps the client avoid being in situations that would provoke undesirable behaviors by either staying away from such situations, or, if possible, by removing the cues for undesirable behaviors from the client's environment.

For example, the person with an alcohol problem giving up the use of alcohol will stay away from cocktail parties and bars; the overeater will avoid buffets; the drug user will avoid going to places frequented by pushers; the young woman concerned with her "promiscuity" will avoid being alone on dates in isolated places; the habitual smoker will avoid situations, such as lingering at the dinner table, that are associated with smoking.

Whenever possible, the client is helped to be more aware of when he is entering a situation that would probably lead him to engage in problem behaviors. The worker might review with the client the characteristics of such situations. The goal is to provide the client with cues that previously reinforced behavior will no longer be reinforced.

4. MAKING THE NEW BEHAVIOR ACCEPTABLE TO THE CLIENT

Behavior modification (or, for that matter, almost any type of professional intervention) usually begins as an artificial intrusion into the natural life patterns of the client and those in his environment. The very existence of the intervention may provoke anxiety or anger in the individuals whose behavior is to be changed. They may feel—perhaps correctly—that they are being asked to give up behaviors that have previously been reinforced and, even worse, to relinquish the reinforcements themselves. These negative emotional reactions to intervention could obviously impair the effectiveness of any intervention program.

Such anxiety or anger may be kept to a minimum by emphasizing behavioral goals that involve increasing new behaviors through positive reinforcement, and avoiding as much as possible goals that involve decreasing old behaviors via punishment or extinction. For example, it would be preferable to reinforce a child for school attendance rather than punish him for truancy, or reinforce couples for behaving affectionately to each other rather than withdraw reinforcements for ignoring each other.

Negative emotional reactions to the social worker or the mediator can be further reduced by using procedures (see Chapter 8) that enhance the worker's communication of warmth, empathy, and genuineness to the client. If it is at all possible, similar skills may be taught to mediators such as ward staff, teachers, and parents. Associating the social worker or mediator with positive reinforcement further minimizes negative emotional reactions. It is an old technique, but a valid one, for a social worker to have discussions with clients over a cup of coffee or a soft drink. Recognition of the client's and mediator's efforts to alter the problem behaviors prior to the present intervention may dispel their feelings of guilt and prevent their feeling threatened by the social worker. When punishment or extinction must be used, the social worker should attempt to create situations in which desirable behavior is reinforced.

In essence, the social worker and mediator should try to associate themselves with positive consequences to the client, so that they will come to be discriminative stimuli for the client (i.e., cues that positive reinforcement is forthcoming). They should also attempt to avoid any associations with criticism, punitiveness, or other behaviors that might lead the client to perceive himself as sick, immoral, incompetent, or inferior. Conversely, the behavioral modification program should become a cue to the client for hope and the promise of future increased life satisfactions. Once the intervention program has begun, "bonus reinforcements" outside of the reinforcement schedule may be provided to the client from time to time to reinforce his participation.

5. ESTABLISHING THE EFFECTIVENESS OF REINFORCERS

Once the program has begun, and after selection of the reinforcers, the worker determines whether the reinforcers are indeed reinforcing. Since this topic has already been discussed in Chapter 4, only a brief summary of the procedures for insuring the effectiveness of reinforcers will be presented here.

1. Make certain the reinforcers are highly individualized, i.e., client-specific.
2. Offer a wide range of reinforcers if possible.
3. If only one type of reinforcer is used, e.g., candy, use different varieties.
4. Avoid satiation.
5. Give the client an experience with the reinforcing effects of the reinforcer.
6. Model another individual receiving a similar reinforcer. For children, it may even be possible to show a doll receiving a similar reinforcer and being "highly pleased" with it.
7. Manipulate antecedent conditions; if necessary, deprive the client of the reinforcers to enhance their effectiveness when reapplied.

6. APPLYING THE PRINCIPLES OF EFFECTIVE REINFORCEMENT

The basic principles of effective reinforcement were presented in Chapter 4. To the extent possible, these should be followed in implementing an interventive program involving positive reinforcement.

7. STRENGTHENING DESIRED BEHAVIORS IN FREQUENCY, INTENSITY, OR DURATION

A number of procedures can be effective in strengthening desired behaviors:

PROMPTING, MODELING AND BEHAVIOR REHEARSAL

If the desired target behavior is not in the client's repertoire, that is, the client *never* exhibits the target behavior, the social worker can help the client develop the requisite basic behavioral skills through prompting, modeling, and behavior rehearsal, described in Chapters 12–14.

DISCRIMINATION TRAINING

If the client exhibits a desired or acceptable behavior at an inappropriate time or place, or fails to exhibit it at an appropriate time or place, the social worker can provide the client with discrimination training, that is, training to discern antecedent events that would indicate whether a particular behavior is likely to be reinforced in a particular set of circumstances. This may be achieved by role playing in the social worker's office or it may be done in the client's natural environment. In either case, specific behaviors are reinforced *only* when certain cues are present, and not when they are absent. Thus, a mother may be taught to attend to her child when he is behaving in a desirable manner, e.g., seeking help with homework or iodine for a cut, and to ignore him when he is having a tantrum or making demands for affection that are impossible to meet. In such discrimination training, however, the worker must emphasize that the point is not to decrease the sum total of attention for the child, but to reorient that attention toward increasing desired behavior.

Discrimination training may also include learning that "there is a time and place for everything." For example, students can be taught to study more effectively by emphasizing a clear division of time and place for studying and recreation. Goldiamond (1965) reported a case in which he helped a disorganized college student study more effectively by specifying: "If she wished to write a letter, she should do so, but in the kitchen; if she wished to day dream, she should do so, but was to go to another room; at her desk she was to engage in her school work and her school work only. Within a few weeks, the student was studying at least three hours a day—at her desk. The new discriminating behavior became naturalized by her improved test performance" (p. 854).

SHAPING

If the terminal goal behavior is not currently a behavior in the client's repertoire, but some approximation of the terminal behavior is, the social worker should use shaping, that is, the reinforcement of *successive approximations* of the goal behavior.

Often terminal goal behaviors are beyond the present competence of the client, despite the presence of adequate motivation or the availability of powerful reinforcers. In such cases, a shaping program is developed.

Rod and Babe used shaping in toilet training their thirty-month-old son. Both parents knew the grunting sound their child made while defecating in his diapers. In the first week of training they gave him a candy if the sound occurred within 20 feet of the bathroom, the second week, the child had to be within 10 feet of the bathroom to be reinforced, the third week *in* the bathroom, and, finally, in the fourth week, defecation had to occur on the potty. Praise accompanied all candy-giving (a small jar of candies was kept nearby, and the child could subsequently help himself to a candy whenever he performed on target). Toilet training was completed pleasantly, quickly, and with relatively little fuss.

The following case is an example of shaping applied to a more complex situation.

Kurt was a shy high school junior raised in an all male institution for dependent children who confided to his welfare worker that he was embarrassed around girls, did not know how to approach them to ask for a date, and certainly would not know how to behave on a date. His goal was to have a warm, intimate relationship with a girl his age. The social worker learned that Kurt had virtually no contact with girls either at his institution or at school. For the first week of shaping the social worker used modeling and behavior rehearsal to teach Kurt to smile and say "Hi" to three different girls whom he wanted to know better. Based on the social worker's knowledge of Kurt, it was possible for Kurt to do this with minimal anxiety. When Kurt reported that he had successfully completed his "homework" the following week, the social worker (who did have a good relationship with Kurt) praised his efforts and assigned him his next task: to say at least one sentence to each of the same three girls immediately after classes during the week. The kinds of sentences that he might use and the situations in which he might use them were role-played with Kurt.

In the following weeks, increased expectations were communicated to Kurt: from carrying on a conversation with six interchanges, to offering to take one of the girls out for a coke, to double-dating to a movie and, later, to a dance. In addition to the social skill training and secondary reinforcements coming from the social worker's praise, Kurt's growing pride in, and enjoyment of, his new relationships reinforced his increased competence in relating to young women.

In the process of shaping new behavior, the social worker should be careful to minimize the impact of any unsuccessful steps along the way to new behavior. In the event the client is unsuccessful in completing any "homework" assignments, the social worker tries to discount the failure, and suggests that the client repeat the prior step. Feelings of failure and any possible resistance toward trying again may be minimized by discussing possible setbacks with the client when the shaping process is initiated.

Shaping, and the strengthening of behavior through positive reinforcement in general, proceed most effectively when the following guidelines are observed.

1. Divide the process of reaching a desired terminal goal into an orderly series of sequential approximations to the goal based on the assessment of the client's skills, capacities, and motivation.

2. Start with an initial behavior that is already in the client's repertoire, is relatively easy for the client to perform, and is accompanied by relatively little anxiety.

3. If the first step seems unclear to the client or is too difficult for the client to perform, break the behavior down into its component parts.

4. Using the procedures for selecting reinforcers discussed in Chapters 4 and 11, reinforce the successful completion of each approximation on a continuous schedule (see Chapter 6).

5. Pair nonsocial reinforcers with social reinforcers from the mediator or social worker whenever possible in order to facilitate the naturalization of the desired behavior and the withdrawal of extrinsic nonsocial reinforcements.

6. Set the shaping in the environment in which the terminal goal behavior is to occur, or move it to that environment as goal behavior is approached—for example, from the social worker's office to the home, or from an institution to a halfway house to the community.

7. Create situations in which significant individuals in the natural environment provide social reinforcers for the approximations to the terminal goal behavior.

8. Gradually raise the criteria for reinforcement. As shaping proceeds, reinforce successively more difficult or more complex steps. Indeed, as time passes, even praise should be reserved for more and more goal-approximating behavior. Generally this will lead clients to expect more of themselves. Their successes on earlier steps tend to give them hope and motivation for taking increasingly greater steps toward the terminal goal. However, the client, social worker, and mediator should not get carried away with their enthusiasm. Whereas success reinforces behavioral change efforts, failure tends to make such efforts aversive. The client should not be pressured into moving too quickly into having behavioral expectations that he cannot meet. Conversely, the client should not be kept at a step that he has already mastered. Boredom is also aversive. In most cases, clients will give cues about their ability to move on to a new step or need to repeat an old one.

9. If the behavior required in any step is unclear to the client, use procedures such as prompting, modeling, or role playing (see 3 above) to facilitate his understanding.

10. If the client fails to achieve the goal behavior for any step, return to an earlier step, being careful to discount his failure. The client should be prepared for such a possibility when the intervention begins.

11. To make reinforcers more potent, limit their availability in situations other than immediately following the occurrence of desired behavior. If a client readily obtains the reinforcer, its reinforcing potential for the target behaviors is reduced. Furthermore, the overuse of any specific reinforcer can lead to satiation. That is, the overused stimulus ceases to possess reinforcing potential, and may even acquire aversive qualities; it becomes "too much of a good thing."

12. When any desired intermediate behavior is of sufficient strength —that is, it seems to be occurring at a fairly stable level—change over to intermittent reinforcement (see Chapter 6).

a. If the goal is to increase the *frequency* or *rate* of response, change from a continuous ratio to a *variable ratio* schedule of reinforcement. For example, instead of continuing to reinforce a child every time he turns in his math homework, switch to reinforcing him after he has turned in his fourth, seventh, and eleventh (and so on) assignments. Once a psychiatric hospital resident begins to engage in better self-care, the ward nurse no longer gives her a token every day she combs her hair, but every "once in a while," the variable ratio being determined in advance to avoid reinforcement by chance or through favoritism.

b. If the goal is to increase the *duration* of the desired behavior, change from a continuous reinforcement schedule to a *variable interval* schedule —that is, reinforce the individual after he has been exhibiting the desired behavior a certain length of time, say, 3 minutes, then 4 minutes, and so on. Reinforcing practice on musical instruments, doing homework, and carrying out chores can be best maintained in this way. Most operant behavior in real life is reinforced on intermittent schedules. Thus, switching to such schedules helps to naturalize the behavior.

13. Gradually increase performance criteria on an intermittent schedule. That is, the client must exhibit increasingly more desired behavior to bring about reinforcement from the mediator (for instance, moving from a ratio of one reinforcement for each six target behaviors to one reinforcement for each ten target behaviors). Again, such an increase in performance expectations parallels the demands of the natural environment, in which each occurrence of target behavior does not necessarily evoke reinforcement from the environment. Increasingly, the reinforcement comes from feelings of success and from the positive consequences of the new behavior in the person's life.

14. Provide bonus reinforcers for progress. When it appears that the client is performing the target behavior at an increasing rate and seems to be "catching on" to the program, reinforcement over and above that specified by the initial contract or plan may be given intermittently. The purpose is to reinforce the client's overall response to the behavior

change program. Bonuses may be simply an extra unit of the regular reinforcement (an extra token, for example) or something special or informal such as treating the client to a drink. Certainly extra praise that occasionally accompanies comments on the client's progress can reinforce the client's efforts at changing his or her behavior.

TOKEN ECONOMIES

If a program is developed to strengthen a variety of target behaviors among a number of people in such settings as schools for "retarded" children, psychiatric and penal institutions, group homes or hospitals, then a token economy system may be employed. Tokens are given contingent on the client's exhibiting specified target behaviors (or intermediate steps if a shaping procedure is being attempted). These tokens may be exchanged for reinforcing objects or privileges at a predetermined rate of exchange at specified intervals. Often a reinforcement menu is employed. The reinforcement menu in a hospital might provide such items as special meals, a private room, an extra hour with a therapist, extra trips to town, or weekend passes. Children may choose from menus offering such items as toys, candy, or tickets to movies.

Token economies tend to be more effective when the following conditions are met:

1. Mediators (such as nurses, house parents, guards, etc.) understand the purposes of the program, and participate in its planning, development and evaluation. The client's participation in the program is reinforced by receiving praise, interest, time, and any appropriate material reinforcement the social worker can provide.

2. The clients understand the rules and procedures of the token economy, and are given some practice in the economy, starting with the use of noncontingent introductory bonus tokens.

3. The system is applied consistently and fairly to those involved (reinforcing favorites and ignoring the desirable target behavior of unpopular individuals must be guarded against).

4. The reinforcement menu is as broad as possible, increasing the probability that there are items on the menu that will be optimally reinforcing for most of the clients most of the time. To avoid conflicts with budget officers and administrators of schools and other institutions with limited funds, the social worker (along with other consultants), mediators, and clients can use their imagination and creativity to develop inexpensive reinforcement menus. Often, community organizations may be approached about providing items for such menus. Clients themselves may participate in the selection of items for the menu and may supply reinforcement items to the menu. For example, a person institutionalized in

a psychiatric hospital with a background in hairdressing might provide special hair styling sessions for a certain number of tokens.

5. Social reinforcement (i.e., praise) accompanies the presentation of tokens.

6. Tokens themselves are made more effective reinforcers by pairing them initially with a rapid exchange (not more than a few hours or a day) for items on the reinforcement menu. The tokens should be given to the client as quickly as possible after the occurrence of the target behavior.

7. Tokens, although at least initially presented each time a target behavior is exhibited, are allowed to be redeemed only after increasingly longer intervals. However, the delay in redemption should not be so great as to decrease the probability of occurrence of the behavior. This can be checked out on any records or charts maintained on the target behaviors. As long as the tokens seem to have reinforcing power, a delay in redemption will serve to increase the tokens' intrinsic reinforcing power, as well as the relative influence of the social reinforcers accompanying the tokens, and ultimately the environmental reinforcers that are products of the new behavior.

8. WEAKENING OR DECREASING UNDESIRED BEHAVIORS IN FREQUENCY, INTENSITY, OR DURATION

If the terminal goal includes decreasing or weakening certain behaviors, proceed as follows.

See to it that all reinforcers for the undesired behaviors are withdrawn from all sources. The process of eliminating a behavior by systematically withdrawing its reinforcers (extinction) is described in Chapter 3. The necessity of completely terminating all reinforcement from all sources for the dysfunctional behavior makes it a difficult process. Since most behaviors in the natural environment are maintained by intermittent reinforcement, occasional reinforcements occurring in the client's natural environment may serve to maintain undesired behaviors. It may be difficult to help those in the environment of the client be absolutely consistent about withdrawing reinforcement. Individuals in the client's environment may be negatively reinforced for "giving in" once in a while to provide the reinforcement that will at least temporarily terminate the client's undesired behavior. The parent might say: "Oh, we let our son stay up for just another 10 minutes, just to get him quiet—he gets so agitated we get scared!"; or, "I told my husband after he got drunk that I'd go to work in the store for him just once more—I just can't stand to see a grown man cry;" or, "How could I as a nurse ignore Louise when she babbles so? She's obviously miserable, and I just have to comfort her." Such incidents of "giving in," however occasionally, tend to sustain the behavior while giving only temporary relief to those in the client's environment. The rationale for withdrawing reinforcement completely in order to extinguish unwanted behavior must be clearly explained to the mediators.

Do not unintentionally reinforce the behavior. The mediators, through role playing, prompting, and so on, can be made more sensitive to the characteristics of the target behavior and their usual patterns of responding to it. Then, new procedures for responding to it can be taught, particularly, ignoring the behavior and trying at the same time not to criticize the client. It is possible that criticism—or any other form of negative attention—may unintentionally reinforce the undesired behavior.

Help the mediators anticipate that behaviors undergoing extinction typically increase in frequency, intensity, or duration before they subside. In effect, the client may be searching even harder for the reinforcers he had received previously. Such temporary strengthening in behavior may be easily seen in the mediator's recording. The temporary increase can be quite unpleasant, even frightening, to the mediators, especially if they had considered the target behavior already aversive at its "natural" level. They may feel that the increase in the dysfunctional behavior is evidence that the intervention plan is worthless. Anticipating such a pattern and preparing them for dealing with it will help to sustain the mediators, and help them avoid the temptation of "giving in" to the client and giving up on the intervention.

Try to modify the client's environment to decrease the possibility that the undesirable behavior will be elicited. The social worker, mediator, and client might anticipate which situations are likely to provoke the undesired behaviors, and then plan strategies to help the client avoid getting into these situations. For instance, an overly aggressive child might be kept from competitive situations, a person with an alcohol problem from bars, a suicidal ruminator from being alone.

Consider the use of negative punishment (response cost). Unlike extinction, in which the reinforcers for undesirable behaviors are eliminated, response cost involves the withdrawal of *other* currently reinforcing stimuli contingent on the occurrence of the undesirable behavior. Withdrawal of a positive reinforcer is done as soon as possible after the target behavior is exhibited. The withdrawal of a reinforcer should be made without punitiveness or recrimination, but with the clear understanding that the removal of the reinforcer is a direct consequence of the client's having engaged in previously defined undesirable behavior. Most important, the withdrawal of positive reinforcers should be made after *every* occurrence of the target behavior witnessed by the mediator or social worker. Whenever possible, response cost should be established on a contractual basis, so that all parties to the transaction are clear about the consequences of undesired behavior. The contract, ideally, will also establish positive consequences for desired behavior.

Withdrawal of reinforcement from oneself contingent on the occurrence of undesired behavior is also possible. For example, a social work educator was concerned about what she considered to be her overuse of profanity in her classes. She decided to consequate every use of profanity by immediately becoming silent for 10 seconds. She quickly was able to reduce her use of profanity.

Consider the use of time-out from reinforcement (see Chapter 13). Destructive behavior can be reduced by removing the client from a reinforcing environment (family room with television on, gymnasium during a recreational period, and so on) contingent on his exhibition of dysfunctional behavior (e.g., fighting, shouting, whining). Time-out is most effective if the room or other area to which the client will be sent is selected in advance. This place should have minimal reinforcing potential. Time-out would be less effective, for instance, if the child were sent to a room full of recreational equipment. Again—as with all other intervention strategies—time-out should be used as soon after the occurrence of the target behavior as possible. It should be used without punitiveness or recrimination, but only as a direct consequence of the target behavior. The mediator should establish the duration of the time-out at the time of, or prior to, the occurrence of the target behavior. The time-out should start as soon as the exhibition of the target behavior ceases (e.g., immediately after floor pounding and other loud noises stop). Generally, time-out should not exceed 15 to 20 minutes and should last at least 2 or 3 minutes. However, if the target behavior recurs soon after a time-out, the subsequent time-out period can be lengthened. The mediator—not the client—decides on the duration. Finally, time-out should be applied consistently to similar classes of behavior.

While attempting to decrease undesired behavior, reinforce opposite, desired behavior. Often "good" behavior competes with the "bad." The extinction of undesired behavior, by itself, is difficult and sometimes impossible to achieve unless the social worker can create situations in which the client can be reinforced for functional behavior that either competes with or achieves somewhat the same goals as the behavior which is being eliminated. (See the steps outlined above regarding the strengthening of behavior plus Chapter 12 for procedures to strengthen behavior.)

If the desired behavior is not in the client's repertoire (i.e., the client does not exhibit reinforceable behavior) the social worker can help him develop that behavior through shaping, making sure that the reinforcers are indeed reinforcing. The social worker should couple nonsocial reinforcement with praise to insure that new behavior is generalized to the client's natural environment.

9. ARRANGING FOR GENERALIZATION TO THE NATURAL ENVIRONMENT

The terminal goal behavior, whenever possible, should be structured so that the behavior will generalize to the appropriate situations. A new behavior will add little to the social functioning of a client if it occurs only under limited circumstances. A client who learns to relate only to his caseworker, a resident in a psychiatric hospital who learns to accommodate only to a token economy, a student who learns to complete homework only for a particularly warm teacher, a parent who can deal only with certain specific behaviors of a particular child—all may well run into difficulty if they cannot make the transition from such limited applications to the more general situations. The following procedures facilitate the generalization (or naturalization) of behavioral change to the natural environment of the client:

1. Before a program to generalize prosocial behavior to the natural environment is begun, that behavior should be established in the controlled environment at the desired level, i.e., the level at which it is likely to be supported by the natural environment. For example, the self-care behavior of a psychiatric patient should reach a fairly consistent level of performance before one can expect the individuals in the patient's natural environment will comfortably reinforce such self-care behaviors rather than continue their earlier pattern of simply caring for the patient on his return home.

2. Whenever possible, reinforce behaviors in situations in which the desired behavior will eventually have to occur. For instance, for child-parent problems, one might choose to reinforce appropriate interactions in the family home rather than simulations of such interactions at a clinic. When this is not possible, use fading, that is, gradually change the situation in which reinforcement is being supplied so it resembles the situation where reinforcement will be supplied in the natural environment. An example of fading would be the transfer of a back ward resident of a psychiatric institution, contingent on her behaving appropriately, to an open ward, then to a group home, a halfway house, foster home, and finally her own home. Similarly an imprisoned offender might move from his block to a more open block, and then to a conditional release center which gives him successively longer home leaves.

3. Modeling and behavior rehearsal procedures can be used to optimize generalization. In these procedures, the social worker demonstrates, and then encourages, the client to role-play the very behaviors the client will be called upon to perform in the natural environment. As the client gains skill and confidence in engaging in those behaviors, the probability is increased that he also will be able to engage in them in the natural environment.

4. Establish people in the client's natural environment (for example, parents, teachers, ward staff, house parents) as reinforcement dispensers by initially reinforcing target behavior in their presence. Gradually have these individuals in the natural environment take over reinforcement after ascertaining their clear understanding of the plan for behavior change and how to apply reinforcement. The social worker might role-play reinforcement procedures with the client and might also have the mediators initially reinforce the emerging behavior—usually using social reinforcement—in the presence of the social worker. To further facilitate naturalization of the goal behavior, the social worker can arrange or provide reinforcement (his own praise as a minimum) for the cooperation of those in the client's environment. An example of such a procedure would be a child who exhibits considerable withdrawal in school. He might first be reinforced for verbal and other classroom-related behavior in the social worker's office, later with one of his more responsive teachers present in the office, still later by just the teacher, then with the teacher alone in her classroom, and, finally, with the teacher along with the other students in the class.

5. If there is no one in the client's natural environment who seems able or motivated to serve the function of reinforcing the client's behaviors, the client may be introduced to, and coached in, self-modification procedures (see Chapter 14 and Watson & Tharp, 1972). Indeed, clients may even be taught to reinforce themselves. Such self-reinforcement—whether covert or overt—can be integrated into any behavioral program (see Cautela, 1969; Goldfried & Merbaum, 1973). Furthermore, as a program progresses, the behavior initially controlled by extrinsic reinforcement may eventually be maintained by intrinsic reinforcement, i.e., the feelings of satisfaction and self-worth that accompanied the extrinsic reinforcement used.

6. Finally, and perhaps most importantly, the social worker should always be completely sure the desired behavior is firmly established and resistant to extinction before he terminates the program. This is done by utilizing intermittent schedules of reinforcement, as described above, perhaps initially fixed, eventually variable. Too often, social workers who use behavior modification are content to show through a reversal design (A—B—A—B) using continuous schedules of reinforcement that the behavior is related to environmental contingencies, and neglect to change those schedules from continuous to intermittent ones. In such cases, one would expect the behavior to extinguish once the continuous schedule is removed and the program terminated. This is perhaps the most important way to insure generalization, because it is almost totally under the control of the worker, and less susceptible than any of the other ways to "the slings and arrows of outrageous fortune."

Behavior modification, of course, focuses primarily on actual behavior (not verbal or symbolic representations of such behavior), regardless of the locus of the program. If intervention is carried out in the client's natural environment, one would ordinarily expect the behavioral change to persist, since no differences exist betwewen the behaviors learned in the behavioral program and those to be performed in the natural environment.

This focus on real-life behaviors—reducing maladaptive, undesired behaviors and increasing adaptive, desired behaviors—should help the client become the recipient of already existing sources of reinforcement in his or her environment ("you get what you give"—the principle of reciprocal affect). With positive changes in behavior and new, more desirable ways of relating to others, people in the natural environment would tend to respond more positively, and their social reinforcement would help maintain the new, desired behavior.

However, people in the natural environment can and should be trained to provide reinforcement for the prosocial behaviors. The above should not be left to chance. Spouses, parents, teachers, and friends can all be given brief but careful instructions as to how to reinforce adaptive behavior and ignore maladaptive behavior. Such structured training of people in the natural environment should be part of every behavioral program. Indeed, training people in the natural environment to handle problems can have a prophylactic effect in that the skills and techniques learned to resolve current difficulties can be applied in other new situations.

10. KEEPING OBJECTIVE RECORDS OF THE TARGET BEHAVIOR

The rationale and procedures for collecting data and maintaining records are discussed in Chapter 10. These records are used to evaluate the progress of behavioral change. If change in the desired direction does not seem to be occurring, several questions may help in determining the source of the problem:

1. What competing reinforcers are operating in the client's environment? To what extent, and how, can they be modified?
2. Are the reinforcers well-chosen? Are they reinforcing? Has satiation occurred?
3. Are there factors impeding the effectiveness of the mediator? Is he being reinforced for his participation? Is he clear about the intervention procedures?
4. Has intervention proceeded too quickly? Are the goal behaviors within the client's repertoire? If not, can they be shaped? Does the client possess the requisite skills for behavioral change?
5. Is it necessary to move back to an earlier stage in the intervention plan, or to an earlier step in shaping?

11. TERMINATING THE FORMAL INTERVENTION
PROGRAM AND PLANNING FOLLOW-UP CONTACTS

When the previously agreed-upon target behaviors are well established in the client's behavioral repertoire and adequately supported in
his altered natural environment, the formal program can be terminated.
If possible, one should create a situation in which there is likely to be at
least social reinforcement of the goal behavior on an intermittent schedule in the natural environment.

The client should understand that no one's situation remains stable
forever and, therefore, the requisite behaviors and skills to adapt to a
person's situation may change over time. One would hope that there has
been specific planning toward that end so that the interventions initiated
by the social worker will equip the client to cope with the environmental
stresses and changes that inevitably occur.

Since the behavioral model by its very nature can remove much of
the stigma from seeking help in dealing with behavioral problems, and
since it does not belittle clients nor make them less able to operate
autonomously, any necessary return for additional help in achieving behavioral change can be sought out with minimal trauma or loss of self-
esteem.

In any event, before the formal intervention program is terminated,
at least one follow-up contact, and perhaps more than one on a progressively diminishing basis (e.g., after one month, three months, six months,
and a year), might be scheduled. The length of the interval before follow-
up depends on the severity of the problem and the apparent stability of
the goal behavior at the point of termination. The follow-up is used not
only to assess results, but also to assure the client and others involved
about the social worker's continued interest and availability. Furthermore, follow-ups can also be used to help the client cope with any new
problems.

Frequently, clients will choose to maintain some records of their own
behaviors even after termination. Such data can make the follow-up contact a simpler matter. If the problem has recurred or if new problems
have emerged, the worker would follow through with a new assessment
(see Chapter 11). If goal behavior has been sustained by the client and
others involved, or if any efforts in that direction have been made, the
worker can reinforce him with praise.

Having gone through the experience of planned behavior change
may well equip the client and others in his natural environment with
competence in modifying problem behaviors as they occur in the future.
If such is the case, they will probably have no further need for the social
worker. In fact, this whole process can be facilitated when the social

worker assumes the role of teaching clients and significant others not only the specific procedures for dealing with current problems, but also the principles and the process underlying the behavioral approach. This might help clients understand and deal with future problems, either by preventing their occurrence or by dealing effectively with them as they occur.

Why Behavior Modification Fails

Fails? Given all the above (not to mention what follows), is it actually possible that behavior modification can fail to produce successful results? Unfortunately, yes, although this failure is frequently less a failure of the behavioral procedures themselves than a failure to apply them properly. Thus, the probable reasons for failure that will be outlined here might be thought of as guidelines for successful use of behavior modification, or, rather, a checklist of conditions to avoid in order to give the behavioral program an optimal chance of succeeding. Each of the following, then, should be considered in the implementation of a behavioral program.

1. Failure to record data, from baseline through intervention. Such an omission means the change agent will not know what effect the program is having, and, consequently, whether or not a change in the program is necessary (see Chapter 10 on Recording).

2. Failure to individualize reinforcers, or adherence to a reinforcer after it has lost its reinforcing value. All rewards are not reinforcers; the reinforcer selected must be chosen on the basis of its reinforcing value for the particular client involved. Moreover, if the client becomes satiated, new reinforcers must be used. It is a good idea to offer several different reinforcers if possible.

3. Failure to eliminate reinforcement for maladaptive behaviors. Frequently an undesired behavior is maintained by reinforcement from sources unsuspected by, or inaccessible to, the change agent. Thus, the behavior continues.

4. Inconsistency of administration. If reinforcement for new (desired) behaviors (on continuous schedules), or punishment for old (undesired) behaviors is to be successful, it should be administered as consistently and regularly as possible each time the target behaviors are performed.

5. Failure to consider antecedents of specific behaviors. Sometimes, the simplest way to change a behavior is to alter its antecedents, e.g., by changing the discriminative stimuli to change the time and place for the occurrence of the behavior. The examination of antecedents also

enables one to insure that the appropriate tools, resources, and materials for the behavioral program are available. Finally, attention to antecedents insures that operant techniques like extinction (e.g., ignoring a child's crying) are not inappropriately applied to respondent behaviors (e.g., crying elicited by a fall).

6. Premature use of behavior modification procedures. This may result either in the use of the wrong procedure because of an incomplete assessment, or in the use of behavior modification techniques to change the client's behavior when the correct thing to do is to remove some stressful environmental condition that is responsible for the maladaptive behavior.

7. Attempting to develop a behavior too quickly. Be sure that you move at the client's pace. Shaping techniques can be of great value in developing a behavior previously absent from the client's behavioral repertoire.

8. Failure to reinforce (or be available to, or help) the mediator. The success of many behavioral programs depends on the successful use of mediators. It is extremely important for the social worker to insure that the mediator is willing and able to participate, to maintain such willingness, and to demonstrate some success at changing behavior as early as possible—all of which mean, among other things, forestalling intervention until there are enough indications that it will be effective. The social worker should first attempt to develop a trusting relationship with mediators and clients, and foster their willingness and ability to engage in the program. It is also a good idea to start the program, if possible, with some behavior that can easily be changed in order to demonstrate the effectiveness of the approach, and provide social reinforcement for all participants for future efforts.

9. Failure to prepare participants in the program for the reactions of significant others to the changes in behavior. Generally, it is assumed that when undesired behaviors are decreased or desired behaviors increased, there will be a reciprocal increase in positive reinforcement from those in the natural environment. And, whenever possible, planning to insure such reciprocity should be an integral part of the behavioral program. But there are some situations where a change in behavior could have aversive consequences. In comprehensive case planning, the worker should always examine the possible aversive consequences so that: (1) the client can choose whether to continue with the program in the face of such possibly undesirable effects; (2) preventive intervention can avoid such effects; (3) another type of intervention with fewer potential negative side effects can be implemented.

The situations where negative effects are most likely to occur are those where different individuals have different perceptions of what is desirable; for example, from the client's perspective, an increase in his or her assertive behaviors may be highly desirable, but obnoxious from an employer's point of view. More difficult to anticipate are those situations where all parties to the interaction appear to agree to a desired change in behavior, say, decreasing the wife's crying behavior, but find when that behavior has been decreased, that the attention focused on the wife for her crying was an important ingredient in maintaining family unity. The point, of course, in both situations is not that the dysfunctional behavior should be left alone, but that all the possible consequences of changing the behavior should always be made as clear as possible in order to prepare the client and significant others for the occurrence of any of them. The social worker must attempt to avoid situations where the behavior is changed but the program fails ("the operation was a success but the patient died").

10. Failure to follow any of the basic principles for effective use of reinforcement (see Chapter 4).

11. Failure to arrange for generalization to the natural environment. This may be the most common reason of all for the failure of behavior modification programs. One of the great strengths of behavior modification is the availability of a number of ways to increase the generalization of adaptive behavior from the artificial (office or institution) setting to the natural environment. Several of these methods were described in section 9, above. But obviously, availability does not insure implementation, and the social worker must take care to see that methods to enhance generalization are utilized whenever necessary.

Summary

This chapter presented an overview of the steps in the process of behavior modification intervention. These steps, which are based on an ongoing, careful assessment of the target behaviors and the factors that influence, or potentially influence, the behaviors, include:

1. the development of contracts between the participating individuals;
2. the preparation of mediators;
3. the alteration of significant elements in the client's environment to increase the probability that desired behavior will occur;
4. making the new behaviors acceptable to the client;
5. insuring the effectiveness of reinforcers;
6. application of the principles of effective reinforcement;
7. the use of procedures for strengthening or increasing desired behaviors in frequency, intensity, or duration;
8. the use of procedures for weakening or decreasing undesired behaviors in frequency, intensity, or duration;

   9. arranging for generalization to the natural environment;
  10. keeping objective records of the target behavior;
  11. termination of formal intervention and the planning of follow-up contacts.

The chapter concluded with the presentation of a checklist to follow in order to reduce the chances of failure of a behavior modification program.

PART 3:

APPLICATIONS AND
ILLUSTRATIONS

Introduction

Behavior modification is a relatively new approach to human problems. As noted in Chapter 1, the leaders of the field are still very active in developing and refining the applications of behavior modification to an expanding range of problems. Despite its newness, the reports of successful applications in diverse settings and with various problem behaviors are extensive. In *Behavior Therapy Bibliography,* Morrow. (1971) lists over one thousand documented reports, published between 1950 and 1969, of the successful application of behavior modification procedures to human problem behaviors.

In this part of the book, a review of a small sampling of these reports is presented in ten problem areas which social workers often encounter in practice. The problem areas are addictive, antisocial, depressive, emotional, marital, parent–child, school, self-care, severely disturbed, and sexual behavior problems.

There are any number of ways these illustrations could have been organized. The practice of behavior modification could be categorized by the setting for practice (e.g., home, hospital, office, institution; Ulrich *et al.,* 1970), or by the degree of severity of disorder (mild, moderate, severe; Ullmann & Krasner, 1966), or by technique or principle (Wolpe, 1969; Bandura, 1969), or even by diagnostic classification (Ullmann & Krasner, 1969; Yates, 1970). Instead, the illustrations are categorized according to the kind of problem behavior involved. This was done for three major reasons:

1. it avoids many of the biases inherent in the other categorizations (e.g., categorizing principles and techniques by diagnostic categories—diagnostic categories are unreliable and tend to lead to stereotyping and mere labeling; furthermore, a range of behavior problems are not confined to any specific diagnostic categories);
2. social workers can probably best use such illustrations when they are ordered in terms of problem *behaviors*. When working with a particular behavior that is included here, one might simply turn to the chapter dealing with that behavior;

3. this categorization builds on previous work (Morrow 1971), so that further references categorized by problem behavior can be easily found.

It therefore seems logical to organize a presentation of the application of behavior modification around types of dysfunctional behavior, since it is problem behavior, and not such variables as methods of approach, setting, or other constructs, that is the focus of those using behavior modification. Unfortunately, no generally agreed-upon typology of dysfunctional behavior has yet emerged in the behavior modification literature. Certainly, the classifications in these chapters are not presented as a logically consistent listing of mutually exclusive entities (for example, marriage and sexual problem behaviors, as well as parent–child and school problem behaviors often overlap). Some categories include problems found in particular settings (e.g., school problems), some in particular role relationships (e.g., marriage and parent–child), and still others refer to clusters of behaviors commonly considered intrinsically undesirable (e.g., addictive, depressive, emotional, and antisocial behaviors). However, all the categories refer to problem areas frequently encountered by social workers and all are germane to social work practice.

Obviously, the reviews of these problem areas are not represented as including all that is now known on these subjects. They are, however, intended to be illustrative of some conceptual and practical considerations in the application of behavior modification to common problems. They also are intended to serve as a means of integrating much of what has already been presented in this book—basic concepts combined with the process of practice. In each problem area, the types of problems encountered in the area are considered along with the factors that may bring about and maintain the problems. A sampling of successful interventive strategies that have been reported are then reviewed, and, finally, a detailed case illustration, including assessment and interventive procedures, is presented to provide in-depth examples of practice.

Some of the original reports on which these chapters are based were incompletely reported, with significant data omitted. Some reveal methodological weaknesses such as unreliability of observations or the use of inadequate measures of effectiveness. The chapters that follow have, moreover, oversimplified many reports. The reader is therefore referred to the original sources to evaluate more adequately the procedures described.

The reports are largely the work of individuals who consider themselves researchers as well as practitioners. Most of them would agree that they present their work not as ideal approaches or end points of the development of interventive strategies for complex human problems. Rather, they are steps—often tentative—along the way to developing, testing, and constantly refining applications of basic behavior modification concepts to the diverse problems experienced by different people in various sets of circumstances. This tentativeness is consistent with the scientific base of the practice of behavior modification.

> The scientific method and all that is implied in the term remains the best way man has yet devised to order his experience in this world. One major test of a well-constructed theory and good scientific work is that it can be improved. At best, observations and procedures are so defined that they can be verified, extended, refined and replaced. The scientific enterprise not only permits but demands ceaseless progress [Ullmann & Krasner, 1969, p. 599].

It is with this orientation that the following survey of the application of behavior modification is presented.

CHAPTER 16. Addictive Behavior Problems and Substance Abuse

Behaviors that are variously characterized as "substance abuse" or "addiction" provide a particularly difficult challenge to behavior modification practitioners. Although the behaviors can be clearly destructive to an individual—psychologically, physically, and socially—their use is, at the same time, highly reinforcing to that individual. Any reinforcers used to increase behavior incompatible with the addictive behavior would have to be very potent. Conversely, any punishment contingent on addictive behavior would have to be equally potent. Several addictive patterns—particularly the use of "hard" drugs—are extremely difficult to alter, and have been resistant to most conventional interventive strategies. Such problems may require the combined approaches of counseling, medication, and the provision of carefully controlled environments.

Types of Behavior Included

"Addiction" means different things to different people. As Ullmann and Krasner (1969) point out, even the diagnostic and statistical manual of the American Psychiatric Association avoids a definition. They go on to point out (p. 489) the various concepts often subsumed under addiction including ". . . physiological addiction, psychological dependence, abuse, likelihood of becoming addicted, and the social and physiological consequences of prior indulgence." Each of these concepts has a different meaning, even though they may often overlap. The degree to which any individual may be "addicted" to a particular substance may vary, depending on what definition of addiction, abuse, dependency, or indulgence one chooses to use.

For the purpose of this chapter, addiction and substance abuse refers to the habitual use by individuals of substances of any kind to the extent that they adversely affect the individual's physical, emotional, or social well-being. Assessment procedures, of course, will determine to what extent the individual and the people around him are being harmed by his use of the substance, the degree to which he feels dependent on the substance as a major or exclusive source of satisfaction, and his motivation to give up its use.

Addicted individuals may indeed find it aversive to give up or modify the use of the problem substance. Its use may be found to be highly reinforcing for several reasons:

1. the predictable pleasure it brings;
2. a general reduction of anxiety, an increase in relaxation, or a blurring of cognition of other problems;
3. enjoyable or interesting fantasy experiences when using the substance;
4. social approval for its use from peers.

Not all abused substances bring all these "benefits" at all times to all those who use them. But even some of these reinforcements, along with some of the temporary pleasing physiological effects of some substances, can greatly reinforce the associated behavior.

The most common behavioral patterns associated with addiction and substance abuse include:

1. excessive use or dependence on alcohol (e.g., solitary drinking, need to have a drink before facing routine tasks);
2. use and abuse of hard drugs (e.g., heroin, amphetamines, etc.);
3. overeating (i.e., to the point of obesity and endangering one's health);
4. cigarette smoking (i.e., to the point of risking heart disease or cancer).

Interventive Strategies

Self-control of such behaviors as those listed above is often the most practical intervention goal. While organizations such as Alcoholics Anonymous and Weight Watchers provide effective group and individual reinforcement and guidance for the reduction of substance-abuse behaviors, they, too, emphasize the need for self-control procedures. This emphasis recognizes that the target behaviors often occur either when a mediator is not present (e.g., solitary use of drugs, alcohol, midnight raids on the refrigerator) or when the addicted individual is in a social situation in which environmental control is difficult (e.g., smoking at work, overeating in a restaurant).

Many of the strategies for intervention with addictive behavior seem to be equally applicable to several forms of mediation and thus will be discussed together.

One paradigm that may be used as a general approach to the enhancement of self-control has been developed by Homme (1965, 1966). Homme's approach is oriented toward helping people manage their own behavior through contingency management. This is essentially a process in which the individual controls his own behavior through the use of the Premack Principle (1965, p. 132). This procedure may offer a first line of defense against addictive behaviors that an individual wishes to change. In Homme's approach, the individual trying to overcome undesirable behavior carries out the following general procedures:

1. specifically identifies stimuli that tend to precede an unwanted behavior;
2. introduces a thought incompatible with the target stimuli;
3. introduces a thought that reinforces the desirability of an alternative nondestructive behavior;
4. reinforces himself for refraining from the undesired behavior.

For example, overweight individuals wishing to avoid snacking might note that the thought of snacking occurs usually when they feel bored or restless. When they experience the pre-snacking stimuli, they might imagine a grotesque image of their inflated appearance, and then find some other activity to substitute for the usual eating response. They might also think about and imagine the new clothes they will buy and their new attractiveness after they lose weight. Finally, each time they resist the snacking urge they might put a nickle into a jar, with the plan that when the jar is full, the money will be used to buy a new (and, one hopes, smaller) item of clothing.

Another approach that has shown general utility in decreasing addictive behavior is covert sensitization (Cautela, 1967; see also Chapter 13), which pairs imagined aversive stimuli with the imagined use of the addicting substance of behavior. This procedure can be taught to the client by the social worker, and then be self-administered subsequently by the individual with the problem. In Cautela's approach, the individuals are taught to relax (probably reducing any anxiety related to giving up a powerful reinforcer), and to visualize a situation in which they are about to enjoy the use of the addictive substance (e.g., a cigarette, an ice cream cone, a glass of bourbon). As the individuals imagine themselves getting closer and closer to the actual use or enjoyment of the substance, they are asked to imagine vividly their getting more and more nauseous. Just before the point at which they imagine they would actually be using or consuming the substance, they are asked to imagine themselves vomiting. Then, as they remove themselves from the substance, the imagined nausea disappears and they feel better. The social worker helps the clients imagine these events in sharp detail, to the point that they often feel nausea as they experience the images. The clients then practice the procedures in their natural environment, especially when in situations in which there is temptation to engage in the target behavior.

Cautela describes the following instructions a social worker might provide a client with an alcohol problem (1973, p. 227):

> You are walking into a bar. You decide to have a glass of beer. You are now walking toward the bar. As you are approaching the bar you have a funny feeling in the pit of your stomach. Your stomach feels all queasy and nauseous. Some liquid comes up your throat and it is very sour. You try to swallow it back down, but as you do this, food particles start coming up your throat to your mouth. You are now reaching the bar and you order a beer. As the bartender is pouring the beer, puke comes up into your mouth. You try to keep your mouth closed and swallow it down. You reach for the glass of beer to wash it down. As soon as your hand touches the glass, you can't hold it down any longer. You have to open your mouth and you puke. It goes all over your hand, all over the glass and the beer. You can see it floating around in the beer. Snot and mucus come out of your nose. Your shirt and pants are all full of vomit. The bartender has some on his shirt. You notice people looking at you. You get sick again and you vomit some more and more. You turn away from the beer and immediately you start to feel better. As you run out of the bar room, you start to feel better and better. When you get out into fresh clean air you feel wonderful. You go home and clean yourself up.

A similar process of self-administered imagined aversive conditioning has been successfully employed in the treatment of overeating, cigarette-smoking, undesired homosexual behavior, and dysfunctional interactions with parents (see Goldfried & Merbaum, 1973, p. 22; Morrow, 1971; Yates, 1970). The long term efficacy of these approaches is dependent on: (1) repeated use of the self-administered process even after a decrease in "temptation" has occurred; (2) the learning of alternative behaviors that provide satisfaction to the individual without addiction or other deleterious consequences.

The above procedures emphasize use of the imagination to facilitate self-control. Stuart (1970) presents a system for the control of the addictive behavior of overeating that aims at reinforcing the development of self-control skills in the overeater through his own success, the reduction of aversive consequences of the absence of self-control, and specific instructions and social reinforcement by the social worker. Intervention is carried out through a series of specific suggestions presented and discussed in sessions held three times a week over a four to five week period, with subsequent sessions as needed. The rationale for the frequent initial sessions is the learning efficiency of "massed trials," that is, the provision of a large number of learning experiences in rapid succession. This provides greater opportunity to monitor target behavior and make reinforcement of success more likely and immediate. Immediate success is considered essential if the procedures are to work.

In early sessions, procedures and routines are explained and the clients are taught to analyze objectively their own eating habits and the variables that maintain and can also modify these behaviors. Two daily records are kept throughout the program:

1. *Food Data Sheets:* These sheets present comprehensive data regarding the time, nature, quantity, and circumstances of all food and drink intake.

2. *Weight Range Sheets:* These sheets provide an ongoing record of fluctuation in the client's weight, which is recorded four times a day. This serves the purposes of accumulating data on patterns of weight fluctuation, providing regular reminders of the weight loss program, and leading to an immediate awareness of the direct results of eating on weight. This overeating is regularly and almost immediately followed by a mild aversive stimulus: the recording of the client's weight.

In addition to these two records, clients are asked to provide a list of their high-probability behavior patterns (excluding eating) that, according to the Premack Principle, are reinforcing (e.g., caring for African violets, watching television). They are also asked to list their most urgent fears about their being overweight (e.g., disease, death, social ostracism).

Based on these materials, the "Behavior Curriculum" proceeds along the following six steps:

Step 1: The client is to interrupt each meal for a specific period of time (initially, usually two to three minutes, gradually increased to five minutes), during which he is to put down his eating utensils until the specified time is over. This teaches the individual that he *can* control an aspect of eating behavior.

Step 2: The client is instructed to remove food from all rooms in the house other than the kitchen. Also, he is to keep only food that requires preparation (other than salad greens and the like) and to prepare only one portion at a time. This step helps make "absentminded" eating less likely. Eating can only be the result of a deliberate series of activities and snacking occurs less often. Both the trip to the kitchen and the procedures to prepare food may serve as a deterrent to undesirable eating.

Step 3: The client is instructed to make eating a "pure experience." Eating is to be paired with no other activity such as reading, chatting with friends, or watching TV. This proscription avoids pairing excessive eating with other pleasant events and thus creating a conditioned response of eating while engaging in the other behaviors.

Step 4: The client is instructed to put only a small amount of food in his mouth at a time, and put eating utensils on the table until each mouthful is chewed and swallowed. Since it has been noted that obese people tend to eat rapidly, Stuart points out that this process tends to intervene and give the individual some control over this steam shovel approach. Slow eating enhances enjoyment of the quality—rather than the quantity—of the food, so satiation may be achieved with smaller amounts of food.

Step 5: The client is instructed to engage in one of the previously listed high-probability behaviors at a time when he would normally eat. For instance, the client might read a magazine or call a friend (if these are high-probability behaviors) at a time when he would normally be having a superfluous meal. Before doing this, the client repeats the phrase, "I can control my eating by engaging in other activities that I enjoy." This pattern cuts down on the hazards of between-meal snacks, which are usually highly reinforcing to overeaters. Its substitution is highly reinforcing, and, it is hoped, less aversive.

Step 6: The client is instructed to use a variant of covert sensitization to reduce the chance of eating particular foods, or of eating under particular circumstances. In this process, Stuart adapts Cautela's (1973) approach by having the client, in his imagination, vividly pair the eating of the problem food (e.g., milk shakes, French fries) with an imagined aversive stimulus (e.g., the client's spouse engaging in an affair with a more attractive partner).

These steps are serially introduced over the twelve sessions, and are accompanied by ongoing reviews of the food data sheets and weight range sheets, individualized suggestions by the worker and client, and praise for successes.

A simpler procedure, used with a more "disturbed" client, that illustrates the power of social reinforcement was reported by Moore and Crum (1969). The client was an overweight woman (Mrs. S.), diagnosed as having "chronic undifferentiated schizophrenia," who had a long history of excessive eating. Mrs. S. had two very attractive and successful siblings. In contrast, Mrs. S. had always been physically unattractive, and had frequent academic and social failures. The major behavior that brought acceptance by Mrs. S.'s parents was eating. (Her mother reportedly felt this was evidence that she was taking good care of her daughter.) Later, when Mrs. S. was hospitalized for "schizophrenic" behavior, weight loss was chosen as an initial procedure to reverse Mrs. S.'s dysfunctional patterns of responding to her environment. Since Mrs. S. was quite responsive to others' acceptance and approval, it was decided to use these social reinforcers to help her inhibit her excessive eating.

As a first step, a therapist initiated a number of contacts with Mrs. S., giving her attention and verbal reinforcement so that he began to be perceived by Mrs. S. as an agent of social reinforcement. Mrs. S.'s ward chart showed that her weight had been consistently high (165–170 lbs.) the last year. Also, to verify a baseline, Mrs. S. was weighed by an attendant at three-day intervals for a period of two weeks. Following the determination of the baseline, the therapist had Mrs. S. brought to the ward chart room each weekday to have her weight checked and then recorded on a wall chart. If she lost weight from the previous day, praise and acknowledgement were given. If there was no weight loss or if there was an increase in weight, the therapist would only shake his head sadly, record the weight, point out the difference, and return her to her ward. Time spent together averaged five minutes a day. Within two weeks, Mrs. S. came to the chart room on her own initiative, without ward staff prompting. The procedure continued for a period of approximately five months. During this period she lost thirty-five pounds. In the eighth week, Mrs. S. had a one-week home visit during which she gained 8½ pounds. Upon her return to the hospital, she resumed her weight loss. However, when she made a subsequent two-week home visit eight weeks later, she was able to maintain her weight level, suggesting some degree of self-control without any apparent reliance on social reinforcement. Following the initial five month program, Mrs. S. was weighed in the therapist's presence only intermittently for one month, with no increase or decrease in weight. Mrs. S.'s weight loss was subsequently maintained for a five-month "unreinforced" period.

While other approaches to overeating—such as Stuart's (1970), described earlier—emphasize influencing eating behaviors directly, this approach, apparently used with success in the reported case, provided reinforcement for the *outcome* of behavioral changes brought about by the improved self-control of the client—a fact made more impressive by Mrs. S.'s otherwise generally dysfunctional behavior over a long period of time.

Numerous other studies of behavior modification approaches to overeating have been reported. Abramson (1973) has reviewed forty such experimental studies and case reports. Treatment approaches reported in these articles included aversive conditioning, covert sensitization, therapist-controlled reinforcement, and client self-control of eating. Abramson reported that although two of the cited studies of self-control of eating had discouraging results, "the preponderance of favorable outcomes suggested that this approach may hold the most promise" (pp. 552–553). Further, he found that self-control was especially successful when supplemented by therapist-controlled reinforcement.

Although many of the procedures reported for eliminating addictive behaviors rely largely on teaching self-control, some have made good and creative use of environmental supports. For example, a community-based behavioral approach to alcoholism has been reported by Hunt and Azrin (1973). They developed a program for eight men with a history of hospital admissions for alcoholism. The program rearranged ". . . the vocational, family and social reinforcers of the alcoholic such that time out from these reinforcers would occur if he began to drink" (p. 93). The men also received counseling to improve their job performance, marital relationships, sexual behavior, and social relationships. For example, it was found that most of the close friends of the men also had serious drinking problems. As a result, drinking had become a behavior that was at least in part reinforced by their friendships. The men were therefore encouraged to improve their social relationships, and discouraged from contacts with their "drinking buddies." They were particularly urged ". . . to schedule social interactions with friends, relatives and community groups with whom alcoholic drinking was not tolerated" (p. 95).

To facilitate this, a former tavern was converted to house a self-supporting social club for the men. The club provided a band, jukebox, card games, dances, picnics, fish fries, bingo games, movies, and other social activities. Wives and friends were frequently invited to join in the club's activities. It was hoped that this package of reinforcers would compete, and be incompatible, with the "social" drinking of the past. A follow-up after a six-month period showed that the "mean percent of time spent drinking, unemployed, away from the home and institutionalized was more than twice as high for the control group as for the community reinforcement group" (p. 97).

DRUG ADDICTION

This section, thus far, has focused on the application of behavior modification procedures to such addictive problems as overeating and alcoholism. It has barely touched on drug abuse for two reasons: (1) there are few reports of the successful use of behavior modification procedures to treat drug addiction; (2) many of the behavioral approaches that have been used emphasize the employment either of medications or of shock, and few social workers, to date, have been willing to use such methods, or are trained in their application. Most of the procedures have been applied in institutional settings, using aversive conditioning, covert sensitization, and other procedures to eliminate addiction to analgesics (Wolpe, 1964), methadone (Raymond, 1964), morphine (Leser, 1967), tranquilizers (Anant, 1968), heroin (Liberman, 1968; O'Brien, Raynes, & Patch, 1972; Steinfield, 1970), and amphetamines (Gotesman et al., 1972). In several articles Kraft (1969a, 1969b, 1970) reports on the elimination of addiction through the use of systematic desensitization for the social anxieties that he believes often maintain drug usage.

Miller (1973) has reviewed a number of published research reports on behavior modification of drug addiction. Many of these studies reported some success in treating various drug addictions using such techniques as aversive conditioning, relaxation training, systematic desensitization, assertive training, and token economics. However, Miller notes that, despite these reported successes, "to date, no well-controlled experimental studies on the effects of behavioral approaches on drug abuse have been reported" (p. 517).

Wisocki (1973) provides one of the few detailed case reports of an outpatient behavioral program for addiction using procedures easily adaptable to many social work settings. She presents the case of a 26-year-old man who had been dependent on heroin for several years. His habit required at least twenty "bags" a day. He had previously frequently used barbiturates, amphetamines, and mescaline. He was pushing drugs and involved in various other criminal activities to support his habit. Wisocki used such procedures as covert sensitization, covert reinforcement, and thought stopping to accomplish three major concurrent goals: (1) elimination of his addiction; (2) improved self-concept; (3) more positive attitudes toward society. The last involved getting a job, attending social functions, and overcoming his loneliness and fear of rejection.

After only four months of therapy (twelve sessions) the man was no longer dependent on drugs; he was ". . . determined that he would never return to drugs, and felt happy and confident that he could handle his problems" (p. 59). At his eighteen-month follow-up session the man reported that he was still off drugs, and had no desire to return to his old ways. Further, "he had taken a job as a counselor for emotionally disturbed children and delighted in it. He had married, despite opposition from the girl's family, and was experiencing an active social life" (p. 54).

Table 16.1 summarizes the treatment approaches used to accomplish these goals.

Before leaving this case, it should be noted that the author herself comments that the case may be atypical of most addiction problems since the client was ". . . educated, highly motivated, presented himself for therapy voluntarily . . . and on a paying basis" (p. 60).

It is hoped that research in the application of behavior modification approaches will lead to effective and flexible procedures to eliminate drug addiction in the foreseeable future. Meanwhile, such "nonprofessional" approaches to drug addiction as the Synanon program (as well as Weight Watchers for those with problems of overeating and Alcoholics Anonymous for those with alcohol-related problems) seem to be effective in altering addictive behavior.

TABLE 16.1.   Summary of Course of Therapy and Behavioral
Methods Used in the Treatment of a Heroin Addict.

TREATMENT GOALS	*Number of therapy sessions required* 1 2 3 4 5 6 7 8 9 10 11 12	TECHNIQUES USED
I. Elimination of heroin addiction	. . . .	Covert reinforcement Covert sensitization Thought stopping
II. Improvement of self-concept	. . . .	Thought stopping Covert reinforcement
III. Establishment of pro-social behaviors	. . . .	Covert reinforcement Sampling Covert reinforcement Thought stopping

Source: Wisocki, P. A. (1973). "The Successful Treatment of a Heroin Addict by Covert Conditioning Techniques," *Journal of Behavior Therapy and Experimental Psychiatry,* Vol. 4, p. 60.

The Synanon approach focuses on the specific dysfunctional be-havior—the use of drugs—and avoids a disease orientation. It seeks to provide a new set of functional behaviors for the individual and to reinforce the new behaviors via social approval (Ullmann & Krasner, 1969). Following a mandate of "Let's learn from what seems to work," such an approach can provide ideas for social work in altering similar forms of dysfunctional behavior.

Case Illustration

Sometimes the social influence principles derived from programs such as Synanon or Alcoholics Anonymous can be successfully applied to indi-vidual cases. Sulzer (1965) reports a case of a man who was frequently intoxicated and self-labeled as an "alcoholic." Despite frequent vows of abstinence, numerous aversive consequences of his drinking, and a period of intensive traditional psychotherapy, no significant reduction had oc-curred in his drinking.

The intervention goal was the complete elimination of—or major reduction in—drinking liquor. Unlike many individuals with alcohol-related problems, the client rarely ·drank alone, and had a job (which he did not want to quit) that required that he frequently visit taverns and cafes.

The client was particularly concerned over the potential loss of his friendship with two lifelong friends who, while not abstainers themselves, found the client increasingly intolerable in his drunken states. Since the desire to be with his friends was a high-probability event and thus reinforcing, the change agent chose to use the friends as mediators to reinforce nonalcoholic drinking.

The client and his friends agreed to participate in the following program: At least once a week, after work, the three would meet in a particular tavern for "a drink" before going home. Although the friends could drink anything they wished, the client could only have soft drinks. If the client ordered or drank an alcoholic beverage, the friends would leave immediately. The client would also invite the friends to his house on all occasions when alcohol was being served to guests, but they would stay only as long as the client abstained. The client would also be invited to the friends' houses, but no alcohol would be served.

The first day of the plan passed without incident and the plan was, in fact, met with additional reinforcements at the friends' favorite haunt from the bartender, who was pleased at the client's sobriety, and was much friendlier to the client than he had been previously. The next day, at the practitioner's suggestion, the client made his business trips only to eating places that served no alcohol. Except for drinking an excessive amount of coffee, the client reported no problems. During the next several days, the client's work necessitated his visiting taverns and he did drink some liquor, but less than before. At the end of the week, the client again made arrangements to meet his two friends for a drink. When they arrived, the client, who had arrived early, had already had several glasses of liquor. Under the circumstances, the friends were not sure whether to remain, but did stay with the client, who refrained from drinking any more liquor. During the two hours that followed, as the client sobered up he felt at ease, and had little desire to imbibe alcohol. That was the last day the client was known to consume an alcoholic beverage.

He continued in his work, visiting taverns frequently, and enjoying the friendships with the bartenders, who tended to reinforce abstinence. He continued to meet his friends periodically after work, but they soon began to meet in places other than bars.

During this period, the client met with the practitioner twice a week and received considerable social reinforcement. The client and his family also moved into a new neighborhood in which his new neighbors were not exposed to the same objectionable behaviors that had led his old neighbors to disapprove of him and approach him with disgust. Their more positive reactions to him added further reinforcement for his new behaviors.

CHAPTER 17.   Antisocial Behavior Problems

All societies have codes of conduct specifying both acceptable and pro-scribed behaviors for their members. Certain elements of those codes are formalized into laws that are differentially enforced over time—depend-ing on community consensus about their importance—not only to protect the lives, property, and mores of individuals, but to maintain the social systems as well. Social work is one of the professions that has been charged with (and that has accepted) the responsibility for social con-trol—attempting to decrease or modify destructive antisocial behaviors. While behaviorally oriented social workers are concerned about the victims of antisocial behaviors, they are equally concerned about the aversive effects of antisocial behavior on the offenders. There are at least three major factors that make interventions to do this difficult:

First: antisocial behaviors in varying degrees are often consequences of social circumstances such as poverty and racism, and the aversive consequences of illegal behaviors seem differentially (and inequitably) applied according to these same variables.

Second: social workers may not share the same perception as others (e.g., judges, police, large segments of a community) as to what indeed is an antisocial act requiring intervention. There is considerable disagree-ment—as well as variations in community and state laws—about the degree to which certain behaviors should be decreased or prevented, rather than left to the choice of individual citizens. These "crimes" can include such diverse behaviors as viewing pornography, civil disobedi-ence associated with efforts toward social change, abortion, engaging in atypical sexual behaviors, smoking marijuana, evading the draft, and circumventing unjust welfare laws. In such cases, the social worker may choose to help the offender evaluate his options in light of the conse-quences of his behavior, or work toward changing the community stan-dards and attitudes that support unjust laws or unjust enforcement of such laws, or both.

Third: as noted elsewhere, punishment is the most common public response to an individual who engages in undesirable behavior. Nowhere is this more apparent than in the "treatment" of antisocial behavior. Our legal system is oriented toward seeking out, adjudicating, and punishing criminal acts. The ultimate punishment (short of execution) is imprisonment. Despite efforts by many social workers and others at rehabilitation in prison, the primary effect of imprisonment is still punishment. And within prisons—and most other correctional institutions—the major form of behavioral intervention is punishment. Desirable behavior is essentially ignored, while undesirable behavior is punished; and punishment, as noted previously, rarely teaches new, effective behavior, but rather teaches the individual to escape aversive consequences. Imprisonment rarely results in improved social functioning, unless the social reference group is essentially antilegal. Recidivism rates indicate either that imprisonment is highly reinforcing, or that skills that would facilitate functioning well socially and legally outside of prison are not provided by the imprisonment. Many people—adults and adolescents—who leave a punitively oriented correction facility are even more bitter, more hostile, and more likely to engage in antisocial behaviors than when they entered. If they have learned any significant new knowledge, attitudes, or skills, they are those that will make them even more competent in antisocial behaviors and, thus, more dangerous (Ullmann & Krasner, 1969). It is a paradox, then, that social workers in some correctional facilities are working toward decreasing antisocial behaviors in a setting that, in the final analysis, fosters them.

The goal, then, of the social worker concerned with individuals engaging in antisocial behavior is to work toward developing programs that, first of all, reduce social and environmental encouragement and reinforcement for antisocial behavior; second, that reduce economic or ethnic discrimination in the application of social justice; third, that teach and provide opportunities for offenders to obtain reinforcements for prosocial behaviors (e.g., work, satisfying social and sexual relationships) that are incompatible with behaviors that violate the reasonable rights of others. If placement in a correctional institution is unavoidable or necessary, then the social worker does what he can to establish in the institutions those conditions that will teach and reinforce those behaviors that will lead to effective social functioning outside the institution.

Types of Behavior Included

Antisocial behavior can be categorized in two ways: (1) criminal behaviors, i.e., those specific behaviors that society at any point in time considers dangerous enough to legislate against; (2) characteristic behavior patterns of those individuals who repeatedly engage in destructive violations of other people's rights. The first category would include the following five behaviors:

1. assault to persons (including rape and murder);
2. damage to property (ranging from vandalism to arson);
3. stealing property (theft, robbery, fraud, etc.);
4. self-destructive behavior (suicidal behavior and drug usage);
5. offenses to public sensibilities and morality (public nuisance, prostitution).

These specific categories of behavior have had limited attention from behaviorists. For one thing, as noted throughout this book, it is preferable to focus on increasing desirable behaviors incompatible with antisocial behaviors rather than on decreasing undesirable behaviors such as antisocial acts themselves. Furthermore, behavioral approaches are generally concerned with frequency of occurrence, and many of the behaviors in the above list of "criminal" offences occur rarely for any particular individual. The seriousness of an offense does not usually correlate with its frequency: murderers rarely are recidivists, but bad-check passers often are (Davis, Kausch & Gochros, 1968). Also, the fact that a criminal offense has been identified may be a happenstance of detection and the legal process, as much as it is that particular dysfunctional patterns of behavior occur. Antisocial behaviors may be reinforced by peers in a manner that may be beyond the control of the social worker and the mediators. Finally, there is little likelihood that those individuals who repeatedly commit crimes will be engaging in those particular criminal behaviors while in the presence of mediators, in or out of correctional institutions.

The reasons for the inability of many individuals to achieve adequate reinforcements through prosocial, noncriminal behaviors are varied. Some have had no access to reinforcement for socially approved behavior, because of lack of resources, poverty, or discrimination. Criminal activities may have become a major alternative. Often, individuals have not learned the interpersonal and vocational skills necessary to acquire and hold a job. Others lack the knowledge, experience, and, perhaps most important, models for such diverse skills as resolving differences, seeking intimacy and sexual satisfaction, expressing hostility, or obtaining material goods through appropriate behaviors. Still others have found antisocial behaviors reinforced by their peers, and even by their families. Their heroes, after whom they may model, may have shown that crime *does* pay. Behaving in socially approved ways, which may be approved in society at large, may be ridiculed in the individual's own group. Indeed, those individuals whose behaviors are labeled "sociopathic" may have learned well the art of using their charm and facility at deceit to achieve reinforcement through novel, exciting behavior with little aversive consequences.

Finally, as noted previously, our correctional programs themselves may teach antisocial behavior. The emphasis on punishment may result in only more contempt for society rather than more concern and empathy for fellow human beings and a desire to learn those skills required for effective social functioning.

The behavioral approach to serious antisocial behavior is not essentially different from the approach to other dysfunctional behaviors. Rather than being perceived as a disease deeply ingrained in the individual (e.g., sociopathy or a "character disorder"), serious antisocial behavior is seen as having been learned and maintained in the same way as any other type of behavior, and, thus, subject to change by the same learning principles and processes.

Interventive Strategies

Much of the reported efforts of behavior modification with those engaging in serious antisocial behaviors have focused on teaching socially acceptable behaviors (e.g., work habits, interpersonal skills) that are incompatible with antisocial behaviors. Many of these approaches have been used in institutional settings in which efforts have been made to replicate the valid expectations, contingencies, and reward systems of the community. These programs have tended, of necessity (and sometimes by choice), to be group programs, and most have involved the use of token economies. Some examples of these programs are described below. Other programs have focused on the use of modeling to teach effective, socially functional skills. Finally, some examples of innovative outreach programs (involving efforts to identify individuals in their natural environment who are likely to engage in antisocial acts, and to reduce the likelihood of their occurring), are described.

TOKEN ECONOMIES

Token economies offer help on two levels for the successful transition from the institution to the community. On the first level, they offer discrimination training, which facilitates learning the advantages of engaging in socially desirable behavior. On the second level, the individual is reinforced for learning the skills that will enable him to function effectively when he leaves the institution.

An illustration of the effective use of a token economy is the Intensive Training Program at Murdoch Center, a special unit for retarded adolescents who had frequently engaged in antisocial behavior (Burchard, 1967). The objective of this program, which was staffed largely by nonprofessionals (university students, attendants, workshop instructors, etc.), was to shape socially acceptable practical skills (personal, social, educational, and vocational) by way of systematic, response-contingent punishment and reinforcement. Burchard engineered his program to increase the probability of occurrence of desired behavior, and decrease that of undesired behavior. The behaviors selected for reinforcement were those considered essential for the residents' functioning and those that would be more likely to be reinforced when the residents returned to the community. Target behaviors included maintaining a job, staying in school, budgeting money, buying and caring for clothes, buying food and meals, and cooperating with peers and adults.

Since verbal reinforcement had not proven to be an effective reinforcer for those who frequently display antisocial behavior (Cleckey, 1955; Johns & Quay, 1962; Quay & Hunt, 1965), reinforcing objects and tokens were given by staff members immediately after desirable behavior. These tokens were redeemable for money or for such items as special foods, smoking articles, clothing, books, grooming aids, and other commissary items; recreational activities such as riding bicycles and go-carts, hiking, and fishing; and such miscellaneous items as bus tickets for trips to town and visits home.

Punishments were designed to be administered immediately following undesirable responses and to be of short duration, but of sufficient intensity to decrease the frequency of such responses. It was considered preferable to punish less extreme behaviors as often as they were observed rather than delay punishment until the frequency or intensity of the misbehavior built up. This avoided severe or extended punishments. The behaviors selected for punishment were ones that are usually punished in the community, including fighting, lying, stealing, cheating, verbal and physical assaults, temper tantrums, and property damage.

Punishments were accompanied by two verbal responses—"time out" and "seclusion"—that signified both the loss of tokens and a time out procedure. The difference between "time out" and "seclusion" was one of intensity, with "seclusion" signifying a longer separation and a greater loss of tokens. Each, occurring as soon as possible after the unacceptable behavior, was contingent on different behaviors. Generally, time out was for nonviolent behaviors, and resulted both in the loss of four tokens and banishment for 3 to 5 minutes to a time out area of the dayroom. Seclusion was generally related to violent behavior toward property or individuals, and involved both the loss of 15 tokens and staying in an isolation room for 30 minutes after the resident became quiet. If the resident went through the seclusion period in an orderly fashion, he was reinforced with five tokens when the period was over. Staff members were instructed to handle the punishments in a matter-of-fact manner, avoiding arguing with the residents.

The program also used the concept of response cost. Residents were charged one behavior credit each day they did not pay their token debts for that day. Also, if a minimum balance of tokens could not be maintained by a resident, the cost of all reinforcers was raised. On the other hand, if the resident did maintain a minimum balance, he was given free access to the play area outside his unit and the right to purchase a trip to town or recreation time with female residents.

The effect of these token procedures was tested on such activities as the residents' sitting at their desk during school and workshop and completing specified activities. A modified A–B–A–B analysis was used, in which desired responses were reinforced with tokens in the first phase, not contingently reinforced in the second phase, and contingently again in the third phase. Each period lasted five days. A reinforcement of five tokens was given contingent on the performance of specific tasks while the resident was seated at his desk in the first and third periods. In the second (middle) period, five tokens were given contingently. As shown in Figure 17.1, there was a drop in length (in minutes) of school

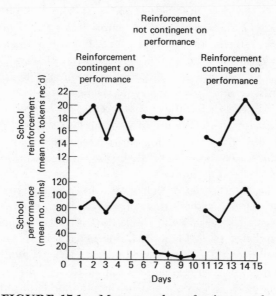

FIGURE 17.1. Mean number of minutes of school performance by nine residents.
Source: J. D. Burchard, "Systematic Socialization: A Programmed Environment for the Rehabilitation of Anti-social Retardates." *Psychological Record*, 1967, vol 17, p. 470.

performance during the noncontingent period, and a recurrence of higher performance in the final period. Similar results were found when the procedures were used in workshop performance.

Burchard noted the importance of developing more natural contingencies for the behaviors to be modified. Frequent and immediate material reinforcements for desired behaviors are not as likely to occur in the natural environment. Neither are punishments as immediate nor structured in the community as they are in Burchard's program. Salary, for example, is given only after a considerable amount of time—and behaviors—has passed. Therefore, an effective institutional behavior modification program must include a provision to move from the basic structured token reinforcement, time out, punishment and response cost programs to more natural reinforcement, such as occasional praise and social approval for behaviors that are part of a chain of behaviors leading to material reinforcement.

Since it is not possible to simulate completely the complex network of a natural community in an institution, residents who make optimum progress under such programs as Burchard's should be moved to the community or to settings (e.g., work-out programs, halfway houses, boarding houses) that more closely approximate living in the community.

One such program, called "Achievement Place," has been described by Phillips (1968). He and his wife were the houseparents, behavioral engineers, program planners, and mediators in a community-based group home for boys referred by the local court. These boys had been to court for a variety of minor offenses, and had histories of school problems and other disruptive behavior. Within the group home, boys often showed behaviors such as inappropriate aggressiveness and poor speech habits that were considered by the houseparents to be incompatible with adaptive behavior in the community. They also singled out cleanliness, punctuality, and completing homework assignments as behaviors that should be increased because of their importance in the boys' future functioning in the community.

After selecting the target behaviors, the houseparents developed a token reinforcement system that involved recording points on 3×5 cards that each boy carried with him. Boys received points for desirable behaviors, and lost them for undesirable behaviors. At the end of each week, the cards could be exchanged for certain privileges. Table 17.1 shows the range of privileges boys could earn.

The "economy" was developed in such a way as to guarantee that a boy who did all the basic tasks expected of him and lost a minimum in fines could expect to obtain all the privileges without being required to perform additional tasks.

In addition to the items on the lists, other "one-of-a-kind opportunities" were auctioned off each week to the highest bidder. Such privileges

T A B L E 1 7. 1. Privileges That Could Be Earned through the Point System.

Privileges (for the week)	Price in Points
Allowance	1,000
Bicycle	1,000
TV	1,000
Games	500
Tools	500
Snacks	1,000
Permission to go downtown	1,000
Permission to stay up past bedtime	1,000
Permission to come home late after school	1,000

Source: E. L. Phillips. "Achievement Place: Token Reinforcement Procedures in a Home-Style Rehabilitation Setting for Predelinquent Boys," *Journal of Applied Behavior Analysis,* Vol. 1, No. 3 (Fall, 1968), p. 215.

included the right to first choice for the week of seats in the group home's car, or to be the manager for the week of certain household chores. (The manager could earn or lose points as a result of the quality of his job as rated by the houseparents.) Boys could also earn or lose points on the basis of their manners in the presence of guests in the house. Table 17.2 shows the kinds of behavior that could earn or lose points for the boys.

Data were accumulated by the houseparents on the effect of their program on certain behaviors, ranging from saying "ain't" to making aggressive threats toward other boys.

"Aggressive statements" were chosen as an area of intervention in recognition that aggressiveness was considered an undesirable characteristic in the school records, court summaries, psychological test reports, and in the general comments of those who knew the boys. On further inquiry, however, it was noted that the aggressiveness was generally limited to comments made by the boys such as, "I'll kill you," or, "I'll smash any car that gets in my way." It was felt that such comments were ultimately self-defeating, and thus the houseparents developed the following program to eliminate them. (The results of the program are summarized in Figure 17.2.)

"Aggressive" comments (defined as statements by the boys that threatened to destroy or damage any object, person, or animal) were recorded for each of three boys (Don, Tom, and Jack) three hours a day while they were doing woodwork in the basement workshop. During the baseline period (see Figure 17.2) no contingencies were placed on the boys' "aggressive" statements by the mediators. During the "correction" phase, the three boys were told the definition of an "aggressive" com-

T A B L E 1 7. 2.   Behaviors and the Number of Points That They Earned or Lost.

BEHAVIORS THAT *Earned* POINTS	POINTS
1. Watching news on TV or reading the newspaper	300 per day
2. Cleaning and maintaining neatness in one's room	500 per day
3. Keeping one's person neat and clean	500 per day
4. Reading books	5 to 10 per page
5. Aiding houseparents in various household tasks	20 to 100 per task
6. Doing dishes	500 to 1,000 per meal
7. Being well-dressed for an evening meal	100 to 500 per meal
8. Performing homework	500 per day
9. Obtaining desirable grades on school report cards	500 to 1,000 per grade
10. Turning out lights when not in use	25 per light

BEHAVIORS THAT *Lost* POINTS	POINTS
1. Failing grades on the report card	500 to 100 per grade
2. Speaking aggressively	20 to 50 per response
3. Forgetting to wash hands before meals	100 to 300 per meal
4. Arguing	300 per response
5. Disobeying	100 to 1,000 per response
6. Being late	10 per minute
7. Displaying poor manners	50 to 100 per response
8. Engaging in poor posture	50 to 100 per response
9. Using poor grammar	20 to 50 per response
10. Stealing, lying, or cheating	10,000 per response

Source: E. L. Phillips. "Achievement Place: Token Reinforcement Procedures in a Home-Style Rehabilitation Setting for Predelinquent Boys," *Journal of Applied Behavior Analysis,* Vol. 1, No. 3 (Fall, 1968), p. 215.

ment, and that such statements were not to be used. Subsequently, a corrective statement by the mediators, such as, "Stop that kind of talk," was made by the mediator contingent on an aggressive statement.

After 15 sessions, a fine of 20 points was made contingent on each aggressive statement. After the 25th session, fines and corrections were dropped as contingencies, but there were threats at several points by the mediators to reinstate the fines if the rate of aggressive comments did not decrease. "Threats" were stated: "If you boys continue to use that aggressive talk, I will have no other choice but to take away points." In the 55th session, an announcement was made that fines were to be reinstated, now at the rate of 50 points a comment, instead of 20.

In reviewing the results of the program as shown in Figure 17.2, Phillips noted that correction alone reduced the aggressive comment rate of only one boy, while fines dramatically reduced the comments of

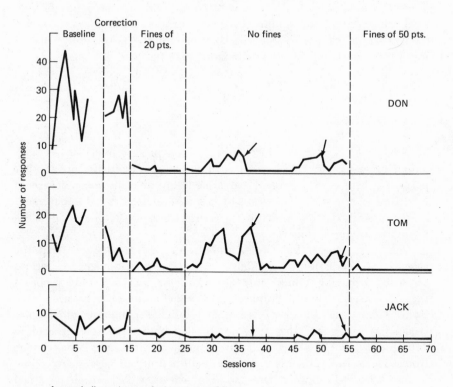

Arrows indicate threats of reinstatment of fines

FIGURE 17.2. Number of aggressive statements per three-hour session for each youth under each condition.
Source: E. L. Phillips, "Achievement Place: Token Reinforcement Procedures in a Home-Style Rehabilitation Setting for 'Pre-Delinquent Boys." *Journal of Applied Behavior Analysis,* vol. 1, no. 3, fall 1968, p. 217.

all the boys. The comments gradually returned after the fines were dropped, but disappeared altogether when the fines were reintroduced. Early threats during the "no-fine" period had some effect, but, perhaps as a result of their not being carried out, subsequent threats had less effect. Although the procedure does seem to show that the use of a response cost program can decrease aggressive comments, the authors do not indicate how well the learning generalized to other settings in and out of the group home, or if the fine was indefinitely levied.

It is noted that in this project the boys maintained most of their own records on their own behavior, and cheating did not appear to be a problem, partly because of the severe penalty for cheating on the token point cards. It is further noted that the reinforcements provided are not consumable, generally cost nothing, and are the kinds of contingencies available in unlimited amounts in most homes or institutions. The program seemed to show that the use of the point system had a significant effect on the boys' behavior.

MODELING

Modeling, as described in Chapter 7, is a process in which an individual observes, and takes on the behavioral characteristics of, another person. Inherent in almost any treatment approach is some degree of modeling. Certainly the success of a program such as "Achievement Place," described above, rests to a certain extent on the modeling of the mediators by the residents.

There is considerable evidence about the major influence that the absence of adequate role models has on the development of serious antisocial behavior. Glueck and Glueck's (1950) classic study reported that 81 percent of the delinquents in Massachusetts reformatories come from homes in which there were other criminals. Ullmann and Krasner (1969) have suggested that it is not broken homes per se that lead to delinquency, but the fact that given many adult figures who change from time to time, there is a greater likelihood of noninterest, rejection, inconsistency of reinforcement contingencies, or lack of a sustained model for socially acceptable behaviors. The impact of the absence of a socially responsible role model was reported by McCord and McCord (1958), who studied the family patterns of a large number of lower-class urban families, and twenty years later studied those in which children became delinquents. The study concluded that the presence of a parent who provided a criminal role model, unless counteracted with consistent discipline and warmth from at least one parent, led to delinquent behavior by the child.

Since modeling is a prerequisite of empathy, and lack of empathy is often an attribute of those who repeatedly carry out serious antisocial acts (Ullmann & Krasner, 1969), it might be expected that the modeling of socially useful behavior would have the additional advantage of developing empathy with others and thus of decreasing the probability of antisocial acts.

Sarason and Ganzer (1969) describe a project in which adolescent delinquent boys were provided opportunities to observe and imitate successful accepting adults role-playing situations involving: (1) vocational planning; (2) motivation and interest; (3) attitudes toward work and education; (4) the utility of socially appropriate behavior. The authors justified their emphasis on modeling vocational and educational skills by pointing out that these are areas that are crucial to the effective social functioning of adolescents. They also emphasized that modeling can be effective only if there is good rapport between the models and the boys. The models must be liked, and be people with whom the boys would want to identify.

At the beginning of the project, the mediators met several times with a group of delinquent boys to discuss their problems, their perceptions of peers and adults in general, their feelings about themselves, and their goals and needs. The mediators then did a content analysis of these sessions and chose the major problems and interest areas described by the boys. Subsequently, groups of boys were asked to role-play some of these situations, such as interacting with an authoritarian teacher, reacting to discipline from a teacher, and one boy encouraging another to experiment with narcotics. Based on a study of these and other role-played vignettes, the authors developed a series of 16 to 20 scripts on such subjects as how to interact appropriately with a police officer, how to act at a job interview, how to respond to peer pressure, and how to make a good impression without "conning" someone.

After the scripts were refined by the four models, they were presented in a series of one-hour sessions that were punctuated by breaks for soft drinks and various other activities to maintain interest. Recognizing the nonverbal, action orientation of many delinquents, the models had the boys move around a great deal during the sessions and emphasized the importance of affect and nonverbal communication in their role playing. The playback of tapes of the role-played vignettes and the use of verbal summaries by the boys of what they observed during the role playing also facilitated active participation in the modeling process.

Modeling sessions were held three times a week for about forty minutes. Each day the models would role-play different situations involving two to four people. The boys were asked to observe the role playing, and then take turns themselves in playing the same roles. Video tapes of the sessions were observed. They then discussed their impressions of the role playing, and the way it related to their own lives. Self-reports and observations by others showed the modeling program had a positive effect on the boys' subsequent adjustment. For example, boys who took part in the program showed more positive behavior change as rated by cottage staff on a behavior rating scale than did a control group. The boys' own subjective evaluation was that the experience was useful in helping them prepare for re-entry into the community. Indeed, in follow-up reports, the boys had put the modeling to good use through practical application of the learned skills, particularly in the area of job seeking and performance.

PREVENTION THROUGH OUTREACH AND OPERANT CONDITIONING

Anna Freud (1958), among others, has noted that adolescents are difficult to get into treatment, as evidenced by their missing appointments, being late, refusal or inability to introspect, and general lack of cooperation. Many social workers will attest that this is even more true of adolescents with a history of delinquent acts.

An unorthodox, but effective, system for motivating adolescents with a history of delinquency to participate in programs having the goal of behavior change has been reported by Schwitzgebel (1964, 1967). Beginning in 1958, he and a group of researchers found that money was an effective reinforcer for encouraging delinquents to be interviewed for research purposes. They went directly into areas with high crime rates to hire adolescents with a history of delinquency, from pool halls and street corners, to come to their "Street Corner Research Center," which they established in an old neighborhood store. They were paid $1 an hour to engage in tape-recorded interviews about their life experiences, and were also provided with other reinforcements such as food and cigarettes. After several sessions, the researchers noted that the "subjects" seemed to enjoy the sessions; consequently, they were gradually shifted to therapeutic sessions, using counselors with a variety of counseling orientations. The adolescents were seen an average of three times a week for about nine months. A follow-up study of the first 20 adolescent employees (Schwitzgebel, 1964) three years after termination of their employment revealed that the employees had about half the rate of arrests and incarcerations as a matched control group. The researchers also noted that the degree of "unorthodoxy," directness, and concrete expression of feelings on the part of the interviewers, regardless of their theoretical orientation, seemed most significantly related to change in the adolescent's behavior.

In a subsequent project, Schwitzgebel (1967) tested a further hypothesis: therapeutic interventions that provide planned differential consequences for interview behavior would result in different treatment outcomes. Once again, contacts with subjects were made on street corners. Subjects were told by the mediators that they were from the university and were doing research on individuals who had court, prison, or police records. Subjects were invited to go with the mediator to a restaurant of their choice to talk about topics that interesed them. They were then offered employment in the research project. The adolescents later took part in several controlled studies to determine the effect of reinforcement on their behavior. Schwitzgebel matched two groups of adolescents whom he treated differently during a series of interviews on four types of behavior: hostile statements, positive statements, prompt arrival at work, and behaviors associated with general employability. In the study group, hostile statements during interviews were followed by a mild aversive consequence (inattention and mild disagreement), while the other behaviors were followed by positive consequences (praise, candy, cigarettes, cash, opportunities to work on and operate electronic equipment at the center, and so on). No such consequences were supplied to the control group. The results showed an increase for the study group in the positive behaviors (measured both in and out of the research center). However, little change was noted in the hostile statements. The participants in Schwitzgebel's programs showed a lower frequency of, and shorter time in, incarceration for milder offenses than the control group, although there was no significant difference in the number who eventually were returned to some form of imprisonment.

Case Illustration

Sometimes a specific antisocial act is of serious enough proportions to require intervention that will quickly eliminate the behavior from an individual's behavioral repertoire. Fire setting is such a behavior. In the case that follows (Welsh, 1968), the principal approach was to deal directly with the fire setting through satiation, which is the repeated presentation of a stimulus that initially has reinforcing properties but upon repeated presentation becomes aversive.

The client was a seven-year-old boy who had, on several occasions, obtained matches and then burned articles around the house, including his own bed. The mother had thus far been successful in preventing any major conflagrations.

The boy had numerous other problems including voracious eating episodes at midnight, a fear of the dark, a fondness for climbing telephone poles, and a tendency to lie to and disobey his parents. It was decided, however, that fire setting was to be the first behavior to be modified, because of its potential danger.

Following brief sessions with the mother in which the intervention approach was explained and her questions answered, intervention took place in several sessions in the consultant's playroom. As soon as the boy entered the playroom, he was presented with a pack of paper matches and was told he could light the matches if he followed four safety rules (actually designed to encourage fatigue).

1. He was to remove one match at a time and close the cover before he struck it.

2. When the match was lit, it was to be held at arm's length over an ashtray.

3. The arm holding the match could not be rested on the table or supported by the other hand.

4. The match must be largely burnt before it is put out.

The boy spent three sessions eagerly burning and blowing out matches with little evidence of boredom. The fourth session was therefore extended to an hour and forty minutes. Ten minutes before the end of that session, the boy asked to stop the match burning and play something else with the consultant.

When the mother returned with the boy for the next session, she reported a dramatic change for the better in the boy's overall behavior. After three additional playroom satiation sessions, the boy said he would rather not light any more matches. The mother subsequently returned for counseling sessions for six months on the boy's other problems, but reported no further incidents of fire setting.

CHAPTER 18. Depressive Behavior Problems

Depression is a ubiquitous condition. Most people feel at least mildly depressed sometimes, and some people feel quite depressed—even to the point of suicide—often. It is one of the most common complaints of a large segment of clients seen by social workers.

Traditional psychotherapeutic approaches have devoted considerable attention to the description and etiology of depression, if not to specific interventive procedures. Psychiatric nosologies are replete with such disease labels as "manic–depressive reactions," "involutional melancholia," "agitated depressions," "post-partum depressions," and "schizo–affective disorders," as well as with such vague labels as "mixed" and "masked" depressions.

Yet, despite its prevalence and frequently disabling characteristics, depression, and the constellation of behaviors associated with it, has received relatively scant attention from behaviorally oriented researchers and practitioners. Morrow (1971), for example, lists only 15 references of effective behavioral interventions with depressive behaviors.

There are several possible reasons for this relative inattention by behaviorists to the problem of depression. First, it is difficult to define depression operationally and to identify behaviors that are specifically derived from or that reflect the problem of depression. Depression may indeed be one of those "inferred inner states" that the behaviorally oriented generally avoid. Further, depressive behaviors involve both operant and respondent processes, and often blur any supposed differences between these two learning processes.

To complicate matters further, such supposed depressive behaviors as crying and reduced motor behavior may actually have nothing to do with depression, (they may, for example, stem from an organic base), yet be falsely mistaken as evidence of it. Finally, the feelings associated with depression are highly subjective and are therefore often difficult to objectify and measure, as behaviorists prefer to do. It is difficult to count despair and dejection, to assess the level of misery or feelings of futility. With such profound emotional experiences, any suggestions to measure the rate of speech or the percentage of accurate memories or to count "the number of tears" may indeed seem insensitive, superficial, and mechanistic.

Despite these difficulties, however, depression *can* be approached from a behavioral framework. With such an orientation, depression can be understood as the behavioral and affective consequences of loss of reinforcement—resulting from such events as the death of a significant relative or friend, the loss of a job, or a move to a remote city—or the sustained absence of positive reinforcement. Such an orientation would suggest behavioral assessment and intervention procedures that have the goal of establishing or re-establishing a network of reinforcement.

Types of Behavior Included

There are a number of specific behaviors observed by the social worker or reported to him that may be associated with depression, such as crying, the loss of an ability to see humor in one's situation, difficulty in concentrating and remembering, insomnia, and loss of appetite. Statements from depressed clients often reflect their hopelessness, feelings of worthlessness, general unhappiness, and, often, thoughts about suicide. At the same time, there is a significant decrease or absence of behaviors that help to cope with environmental demands and to bring about reinforcement from the individual's natural environment. The depressed person often seems apathetic and withdrawn from the potential reinforcers in his environment.

The common denominator of this pattern of behavior is a low production of task-oriented behaviors that are typically positively reinforced by those in a person's environment. However, it may happen that some of these "depressed" behaviors (e.g., crying, protestations of being a "burden" on those around them) may elicit reinforcement in the form of statements of concern, affection, and general attention from those around the depressed person—sometimes including professional helpers— that may serve to *reinforce* and thereby increase the depressed behavior, rather than soothe or comfort the depressed person and decrease the depressed behaviors.

As noted above, depression may have respondent as well as operant components. For example, an antecedent aversive stimulus may serve, solely by its occurrence, to elicit feelings and behaviors that could be called depressive (see Case Illustration). A depressed affect about certain thoughts or events can be respondently conditioned by its repeated association with loss or pain (e.g., memories of a dead, loved relative or friend) so that thoughts of these events or related cues elicit sadness.

A typical set of components involved in a state of depression, then, may be viewed in the following way (Lewinsohn, *et al.,* 1969). The rate of activity and talking of the depressed individual may be a product— or, more accurately, the lack of a product—of the low rate of reinforcement the individual receives. The low rate of reinforcement elicits a depressed affect that, in turn, provides discriminative stimuli for such operant behaviors as crying and self-depreciating comments. The relatively few reinforcements the individual *does* receive from his social environment (e.g., expression of sympathy and willingness of others to readjust their lives to meet the depressed person's moods and take over some of his responsibilities) may come in response to these depressed behaviors or to the individual's low rate of functional behaviors and withdrawal. This might initially reinforce the depressed behavior (e.g., crying, suicidal ruminations, statements of being a failure and a burden) and extinguish much productive task-oriented behavior. Eventually, however, even these reinforcements are withdrawn by those close to the depressed person, since *they* may be decreasingly reinforced for their behaviors toward the depressed person by a reduction in reciprocal reinforcement from the depressed person. This ultimate continuing withdrawal of reinforcement from the depressed person may further accentuate the depression, for example, after the funeral, or mourning period, is over.

Depression may also be the long-term product of an individual's lack of skill in obtaining social reinforcement. "Social skills, defined as the emission of behaviors which are positively reinforced by others, are seen as an area of deficit especially important in the development of depressive behaviors" (Lewinsohn *et al.,* 1969, p. 232).

Another important factor in many cases of depression may be "conditioned helplessness" (Wolpe, 1973), in which individuals have been put (or put themselves) in situations in which repeated efforts to escape an aversive stimulus have proved to be ineffective. Eventually, the individual just stops trying, and sees no hope of a solution for his undesirable situation. Subsequently, when another individual (such as a social worker) attempts to show a way out for the person who has learned to be helpless, the response may be apathy, hopelessness, or "intractable negativity" (Maier *et al.,* 1970). The depressed individual may therefore be the victim of a two-edged reinforcement-pattern sword: The behaviors used to cope with his environment may be decreasing through extinction, while, at the same time, he may be reinforced for the acquisition of depressive behaviors. Thus, the depressed individual may not be responding to an overall loss of reinforcement, after all, but a distribution of reinforcements weighted toward his depressed behavior and deficient for his other, more functional, task-oriented behaviors.

Certainly some degree of depression is to be expected and is part of most people's lives: we all at some point suffer losses, feel helpless, and enjoy the concern and support of others. However, the focus of this chapter is on certain patterns of depressed behavior that are *dysfunctional* and may require social work intervention. For example, in developing a typology of dysfunctional depression for clinical purposes, Wolpe (1973) has suggested three categories of depression, each of which can include several of the respondent and operant characteristics of depression described above.

1. EXAGGERATED AND PROLONGED REACTION TO LOSS

An overwhelming feeling of helplessness is a natural reaction to a major disappointment or to the loss of something or someone emotionally important, either through death or other irreversible separation. However, if such a reaction of grief is sustained for an extended period of time, it may reflect the individual's inability to replace, to some degree, the reinforcements that came from the relationship that has ended. Alternatively, it may mean that a conditioned response of depression has occurred as a result of the individual's suffering a sequence of major losses. A situation of conditioned helplessness (described earlier) may be precluding efforts of the individual to readjust his life to accommodate to the loss.

2. REACTIVE DEPRESSION ASSOCIATED WITH SEVERE ANXIETY

Anxiety and depression are closely related emotional reactions and often found concurrently in the same individual. Generally, depression follows the occurrence of anxiety, and may take its place, again as a result of conditioned helplessness. An individual who is continually subjected to stress and whose repertoire of behaviors to cope with the stress has been exhausted without success may ultimately give up and suffer the stress in a state of depression, with the anxiety more or less fading out.

3. FAILURE TO CONTROL INTERPERSONAL SITUATIONS

Although many interpersonal relations are characterized by one individual's domination over another as a result of role relationships, prestige, or other sources of power, such relationships do not usually result in depression for the dominated person. But depression can result when one individual accepts the domination of the other not as a product of the dominant individual's actual power, but as a result of conditioned submissiveness and anxiety about assertiveness. Rather than attempting to deal with the dominator, the dominated person becomes depressed. If the dominated individual's feelings of powerlessness and lack of assertiveness pervade most of his relationships, he will probably be generally depressed.

Interventive Strategies

The depressed client is generally characterized by a relatively high proportion of undesirable depressive behavior as a response to, and reinforced by, the client's environment and a relatively low amount of desirable task-oriented, or problem-solving, behaviors. Therefore, the goals of intervention are generally a reduction of the former and an increase of the latter.

Since much depressive behavior is a response to a massive loss or absence of reinforcement from the client's natural environment, it is useful to explore the client's social situation to assess the ways the client is reacting to a bleak reinforcement constellation. Such an assessment should include an inventory of the significant potential sources of reinforcement: marriage, family, work, avocations, and friendships. To the extent possible, the social worker then works with the client to re-establish or build in reinforcements in those areas in which they are missing. Such procedures as behavior rehearsal, assertive training, modeling, prompting, social reinforcement for attempts, and systematic desensitization may decrease anxiety about, and facilitate the development of friendships, hobbies, and improved work situations.

Whichever interventive strategies are used, they should not result in the further reinforcement of the client's depression. Indeed, a part of intervention should be the reduction of *any* reinforcements for depressive behaviors. Burgess (1969) lets her clients talk about their "sad state of affairs" only once (during their first interview), and only to acquire the data needed to develop an assessment of the depression. The assessment covers four areas:

1. any desired behaviors formerly exhibited by the client that are not presently in the client's repertoire;
2. those reinforcers for functional behavior, and their accessibility, that might have a significant effect on the client;
3. the manner in which any depressive behaviors are being currently reinforced;
4. the description of the circumstances surrounding the onset of the depression.

REINFORCEMENT REINSTATEMENT AND TASK COMPLETION

Intervention strategies are logical products of such an assessment. For example, if the depression seems to be a reaction to some specific loss (e.g., a friend, relative, job, or status), then intervention may be directed toward finding replacements for the lost reinforcements.

Often the depression is a result of less specific losses of reinforcement, or the loss itself is not so easily replaced. In such cases, "Reinforcement Reinstatement" may be effective (Burgess, 1969). In this procedure, the client is first asked to attempt several task-oriented behaviors that meet two requirements: (1) they involve minimal effort; (2) they have a high probability of being reinforced if successfully completed. Since depressed people often develop a pattern of not completing tasks, the product of their unsuccessful efforts is often not only the absence of the reinforcement that task completion would have provided, but also an increase in anxiety resulting from repeated abortive attempts to achieve reinforcement. Thus, the social worker helps the client select and carry out realistic, manageable goals. After any initial successes, the social worker helps the depressed client choose and carry out increasingly difficult tasks that successively approximate the client's predepression behavior. An outside mediator such as a close relative may be able to provide additional reinforcement for the client's task-oriented behaviors in the natural environment. In any event, the depressed client should be provided with fairly frequent contacts with the mediator or social worker during the initial stages of task completion, perhaps daily. The frequency of such contacts can be decreased as the natural reinforcers for the client's new behaviors begin to take effect.

TIME PROJECTION

Operating on the hypothesis that the saying, "Time heals all wounds," does *not* say that the passage of time *itself* is therapeutic, but rather that the passage of time allows greater opportunity for new adaptive responses to be emitted and reinforced, Lazarus (1968) presents an interventive strategy that dramatically accelerates this process.

In this procedure, depressed clients (who may or may not be put into a state of deep relaxation first) are asked to project themselves vividly in their imagination into the future. They are first asked to think of themselves a day later, then a couple of days, a week and so on until they are eventually imagining themselves six months from the date on which the interview takes place. In each of these projections, they are asked to imagine themselves doing those things that the social worker has previously learned the client enjoyed doing before the onset of the client's depression. Clients are asked to picture themselves in these enjoyable reinforcing situations in the midst of a busy and pleasant life. Finally, when they are imagining themselves six months hence, the clients are asked to look back, in fantasy, on what they had done during this period, and to think "back" to the present when they were (are) so upset. They are then asked how they feel in retrospect. If their situation still bothers them, they are asked to tell the social worker. If they report continued depression, the process continues with longer excursions into the future, up to two years. If, however, the clients indicate that their current episodes no longer upset them, they are asked to recount their experiences.

For example, a young woman artist whose disturbing depression was triggered by her boy friend's telling her he was going to marry another woman reported after the procedure that in retrospect she could explain her feelings in three ways: "First, I feel kind of foolish; second, there are lots of pebbles on the beach; and number three, there's something inside that really wants to find an outlet on canvas." During the following week, the woman reported that she had had a productive week, had regained her appetite, and that she had been sleeping soundly for a change. Progress in the lifting of depression is further reinforced by helping the client actually participate in those activities that will bring about reinforcement. Using these procedures with 11 clients in one-session trials, Lazarus (1968) reported excellent results with six depressed clients, moderate success with two, and no improvement in three cases.

USE OF THE PREMACK PRINCIPLE

A novel application of the Premack principle to depressed clients is suggested by Lewinsohn *et al.* (1969). Since certain behaviors (e.g., statements about feelings of unhappiness, guilt, worthlessness, and being a burden) may be emitted by depressed clients at a fairly high rate, these behaviors could reinforce other low-frequency behaviors (e.g., constructive, assertive task-oriented behaviors) by making the former (depressive) behaviors contingent on the latter (constructive) behaviors. For example, Lewinsohn *et al.* (1969) cite the case of a young man who had been wandering aimlessly from city to city following the break-up of his marriage. In his intake interview, he looked unkempt, talked about considering suicide, and spent his time criticizing himself for mistakes he had made in his marriage, his use of money, and his work. He had changed career goals several times, and his educational and vocational planning had been unrealistic. The therapist and the client made a contract about a series of specific economic and vocational steps the man would have to take in order to get himself on his feet, including the formation of some realistic plans, such as get a loan, contact training programs, find out about possible jobs, and so on. In subsequent interviews the therapist listened to the client talk about his depressions and past failures *only* if he completed some specific goal-directed behaviors since the last appointment. If the client had made no such progress, the therapist would quickly end the appointment, and suggest that the client return in a few days, after he had completed his assigned task. In a matter of a few weeks, the client made and carried out several important work decisions, and reported to the therapist that he felt much better.

AFFECTIVE EXPRESSION

Traditional psychotherapeutic approaches have often advocated that the depressed client should attempt to direct anger at people in his environment as a way of alleviating depression, since depression is viewed as "anger turned inward." There is very little objective evidence to support this view of the etiology of depression. However, the work of Lazarus (1968), based at least in part on a reciprocal inhibition framework, does tend to provide support for the hypothesis that any strong expression of feeling can give relief to individuals in a depressed state.

Lazarus (1968) points out that depressed individuals seem to have developed a lowered response to external stimuli. Therefore, any stimulus that breaks through this apathy will tend to decrease depressive behaviors, at least temporarily. The presence or expression of anger *seems* to be incompatible with depressive behavior. "In general, . . . anger (or the deliberate stimulation of feelings of amusement, affection, sexual excitement, or anxiety) tends to break the depressive cycle" (p. 88) .

The implication of this observation for any intervention is that when appropriate, the social worker, in his discussions with the depressed client, can reinforce appropriate reaction of "righteous indignation" toward the source of the depression, such as national economic policies resulting in job loss, a drunken driver causing an accident, the inability of medical science to prevent death, or the faithlessness of a girl friend who did not return proffered love. The reinforcement of such anger, which reciprocally inhibits the feelings of depression, may reduce depression and even serve as "first aid" in cases of suicidal thoughts. On the other side of the coin, being helped to see and to express the humor, or irony, or senselessness of the situation that confronts a person (without belittling the reaction to it) may further facilitate the reduction of depressive behavior.

DESENSITIZING DEPRESSIVE FEELINGS

As noted earlier, anxiety and depression are often closely related, and both can respond to systematic desensitization. Dengrove (1966) has used systematic desensitization in the treatment of exaggerated or prolonged grief reactions in cases in which grief has been associated with death (or other forms of loss) of a loved person. The process involves vividly recalling the lost person in a variety of happy situations that occurred in the past. Then, when the depressed individual is in a state of deep muscle relaxation, he is asked to recall a series of such vignettes in a sequence slowly leading up to the lost person's death and funeral. In situations in which the mourner experiences guilt over the death or fears death himself, these reactions are interspersed in the desensitization hierarchy.

GROUP APPROACH

Group treatment can be useful for the many depressed individuals who are socially isolated, have few friends, or lack the social skills that would facilitate the development of social reinforcers. Structured group experiences can teach such skills and provide interpersonal situations in which to practice them. Lewinsohn *et al.* (1969) describe a group of nine depressed clients that met 18 times over a three-month period. The focus of the group, which was described to the members as a "self-study" group, was to teach each of the group members about his or her patterns of relating and the social consequences of such patterns. Information was provided directly to the group about the development and maintenance of depressed behavior. Subsequently the group operated in ways similar to many therapy groups, with members discussing their various problems and reacting to each other's as well as the group leader's behavior.

The group leaders, however, did not focus primarily on the specific problems or feelings expressed in the group. Rather, they collected data and reported on the quantity and quality of the interactions among the group members. This material was specifically collected for each member, and presented to them at regular intervals. The data were organized around three aspects of social skills:

1. *The relationship between amount of behavior emitted by the individual and the amount of behavior directed towards him:* These data showed that for each individual there was considerable variation each session in the number of behaviors emitted, and that there was also a strong relationship between the number of behaviors each group member emitted and the number of behaviors other group members directed

at him. Thus, the concept of social reciprocity was taught and reinforced by the data. Those who had a low rate of behaviors were strongly reinforced by the group leaders and fellow group members for increasing the rate of behaviors directed toward other members.

2. *Interpersonal efficiency:* There was also considerable variation in the group members' "interpersonal efficiency," that is, the ratio of the number of behaviors directed towards the individual divided by the number emitted by him. Upon inspection of these data, the most active group member in number of behaviors directed toward other group members was found to be especially "inefficient." Despite *his* activity, there were relatively few behaviors directed toward him. When he aggressively confronted the group with these figures, the group responded (with good documentation), that on the occasions when group members directed behavior toward him, they were met with aversive responses of criticism and general hostility.

3. *Use of positive reaction categories:* According to the group leaders' data, there were several group members who rarely emitted any positive interpersonal behaviors, such as statements of praise, affection, approval, agreement, or positive humor toward other group members. The data on one such member who did have high "interpersonal efficiency" revealed that his pattern of behavior toward other group members was largely critical and challenging (for example, he told one group member that his problem was ". . . trivial and easily soluble"), leading to defensive responses. His response to the presentation of this information was to reveal his concern that this probably reflected his inability to make friends despite his considerable efforts. He was subsequently encouraged to focus on emitting more positive and fewer negative responses to others.

This group approach obviously combines elements of self-awareness groups along with such behavior modification procedures as specifying behavior, collecting related data, and creating consequences such as group reinforcement for the behaviors. Results of an administration of the MMPI and other ratings of group members showed increased social skills and fewer depressive behaviors by the end of the group session.

McLean *et al.* (1973) describe an eight-week treatment program for depression which focused on clients' interactions with their spouses. Based on their conviction that depression is the product of unsuccessful attempts to control one's social environment, they organized a program which included three procedures:

1. *Teaching basic learning theory, including a behavioral explanation of depression:* Couples were given homework assignments utilizing these principles on their relationship at home.

2. *Providing immediate feedback of perceptions of interactions between the client and spouse by way of a small electrical apparatus:* During specific interaction sessions at home in which they were instructed to discuss sensitive interpersonal matters, "couples were instructed to push

a green light whenever they felt their spouse was being supportive, constructive, complimentary or otherwise positive in reaction to their discussion. Conversely, each patient and spouse was instructed to push the red button each time they considered their spouse to be sarcastic, contemptous, indifferent, or, generally speaking, negative towards them" (p. 325).

3. *Training in developing and using reciprocal behavioral contracts:* Couples were asked to specify behaviors each wanted from the other. For the first three weeks, each was asked to comply with the other's requests even if the spouse didn't. For the remaining five weeks, requested behaviors were to be carried out only on contingency. Thus to receive a desired behavior, each spouse had to produce a desired behavior.

When compared to a control group of clients who received a variety of conventional treatments for depression, including medication, and group and individual therapy, those in the experimental group showed significant improvement in their problem behaviors, and in objective measures of depression.

Case Illustration

Stuart (1967) presents a case in which a variety of interventive strategies were used to deal with both the respondent and the operant aspects of depressive behavior.

Miss A. Z., a twenty-five-year-old unmarried secretary, was referred by a psychiatric hospital to a family agency with a diagnosis of "severe depression," following her hospitalization for a second suicide attempt. She reported that she had cut her wrists (as she had done in her first suicide attempt) after she had been alone for several days, was feeling quite unhappy and felt she had few prospects for any activities that were likely to relieve her depression.

Miss A. Z.'s behavioral pattern was conceptualized as follows: the eliciting stimuli for her depression involved being alone and having few prospects for pleasurable activities; her depression triggered off (i.e., was a discriminative stimulus for) the operant behaviors associated with the suicide attempts, which were reinforced by the anticipated or actual attention both from a friend whom she called upon for help and from solicitous hospital attendants. Such attention was not only reinforcing in itself but decreased the aversive stimuli of loneliness. Thus, Stuart diagrammed Miss A. Z.'s problem as follows:

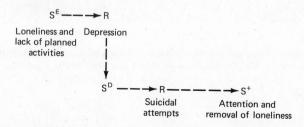

INTERVENTIVE GOALS

Both the referring hospital and Miss A. Z. hoped that intervention would prevent future suicidal attempts. Furthermore, Miss A. Z. wished to avoid her recurrent episodes of depression, to find greater satisfaction from her job, to make some friends of her own age, and to have some hope for the future.

INTERVENTIVE STRATEGIES

Miss A. Z.'s difficulties seemed to revolve around three interrelated problems:

1. DEPRESSION AND SUICIDE

Intervention with this problem was directed toward controlling Miss A. Z.'s suicidal rumination and providing her with life satisfactions that would be incompatible with depression. Based on the information that Miss A. Z. was particularly interested in religion and reading, the social worker gave Miss A. Z. the following instructions to carry out at those times when she was alone and began to feel depressed: (a) she was to "think about the glories of God" and how she could help carry out God's will in her daily life; (b) she was to make an effort to translate parts of the Bible and Apocrypha into contemporary English. It was anticipated that such activities would be satisfying to Miss A. Z. and incompatible with depression and thoughts of loneliness. These behaviors would be reinforced both by the reduction of aversive thoughts and by praise and recognition from the social worker for her avoiding depression and engaging in desirable behaviors.

2. DULL WORK SITUATION

Although Miss A. Z. was bored by her current position as a bookkeeper, she was afraid to look for a new job because of the possibility that her history of job changes would create the impression that she would not be a reliable employee. The social worker did not reinforce Miss A. Z.'s general anxieties about change, but, based on his knowledge of the local job market, he did point out the reality of her being quite employable in view of her particular job skills, and that her work history was not a likely threat to future employment. After reviewing the attributes of positions that would be attractive to Miss A. Z., the social worker set up a program in which Miss A. Z. was to call an employment agency within five days and follow this up with at least two job interviews within ten days. In essence, the worker encouraged Miss A. Z. to assert herself in following through with improving the quality of the reinforcements from an important segment of her life, namely, her job. She was coached in several behaviors associated with her job seeking, and a structure was provided for her to carry out the necessary job-seeking activities to combat her depressive inaction.

3. SOCIAL ISOLATION

Despite Miss A. Z.'s strong desire to make some friends of her own age, she found herself avoiding situations in which she was likely to meet people. The social worker dealt with this pattern of avoidance by helping Miss A. Z. improve her appearance, locating settings in which she could meet compatible young people, and teaching her behaviors that would help her approach and become friends with these people. Miss A. Z. was able to express herself well and was responsive to her worker. However, she appeared unkempt, was overweight, and tended to wear clothes that made her appear less attractive and older than she was. Specific directions were given to her to improve her appearance, including a behaviorally oriented weight reduction program. The program had as its goal Miss A. Z.'s losing approximately one and a half pounds each week for three months. As a concrete reinforcement, her social worker reduced the agency fee by one-third for any week in which she achieved her weight-loss goal. She agreed to put any money she saved this way into a special fund to buy a new dress at the end of the three-month period.

Although Miss A. Z. did have basic social skills, she was unassertive in social situations. Her social worker, therefore, provided her with assertive training, beginning with the assignment of approaching someone she did not know at church and initiating a conversation of at least two sentences. She was also to note the specific aspects of such approach behavior that made her anxious. Specific suggestions to reduce this anxiety and to reinforce emerging friendships were presented. She was socially reinforced by her social worker—and by her natural environment—for her efforts to join groups that reflected her interests in religion, reading, knitting, and swimming. She was also encouraged to pursue her interest in going to college. Her new appearance, her positive assertiveness in social situations, and her participation in a wider range of social activities combined to provide her with a much wider base of social reinforcement. For the first time since high school, she made friends with people who were within ten years of her age.

Her assertive training, combined with social reinforcement from both her social worker and her growing pool of friends, overcame her anxiety and reinforced her for new, more functional, social approach behaviors.

Stuart (1967) points out several attributes of the approach to this situation. Four types of reinforcement brought about change in Miss A. Z.'s behavior and replaced depressive behaviors with functional behaviors. The first was increased success in coping with situations she had previously avoided. Second, the worker encouraged her to engage in specific desired behaviors and then praised her after completion of the behaviors. Third, her new behaviors eventually brought about greater reinforcement from her natural environment. Fourth, the social worker provided Miss A. Z. with concrete reinforcements for the completion of target behaviors such as the "new dress" reinforcement in her weight loss program.

The social worker specifically avoided giving Miss A. Z. any subtle reinforcement for statements about her depression in interviews. Whenever she began to discuss her sadness, she was quickly asked to evaluate critically the behavior associated with such ruminations. The incidence of such comments in the interviews rapidly decreased.

Miss A. Z.'s progress was impressive. She soon found a new job which gave her both more money and more interesting responsibilities. She became successful in making more social contacts through church, and, ultimately, through other social groups. She also began taking night courses in college, which brought her additional educational and social reinforcement.

CHAPTER 19.   Emotional Behavior Problems

A substantial part of social work practice has traditionally been concerned with intervention with, and amelioration of, "emotional problems." In fact, to some extent, traditional social work approaches have considered emotional problems to be part and parcel of almost every client problem—regardless of its nature—with which a social worker is faced (see, e.g., the several approaches described in Roberts & Nee, 1970). The focus on "affect" or on "feelings" and their communication in the social worker–client relationship is perhaps the essence of traditional clinical practice in social work. This focus has sensitized social workers to some of the ways in which human emotions act as barriers to efforts to resolve a range of complex problems, and has also served to sensitize practitioners to the desirability of having warm and caring relationships between social workers and clients.

But this focus on emotions has had some deleterious effects. In the first place, emotions have been poorly defined. Too often, such distinct configurations as anxiety and fear, anger, sadness, depression, and so on have been lumped together under the rubric of "feelings" or "neurosis." Furthermore, they generally have been based more on inferences about behavior than on behavior itself. Indeed, since almost all types of problems have been seen as composed at least in part of emotions, few specific techniques have been devised to deal with specific kinds or classes of emotional problems. It never has been clarified as to which specific types of emotional behavior should be addressed by any given verbal communication by the worker, when or how they are to be addressed, or how these communication skills actually affect emotional problems beyond simply allowing a cathartic or ventilating experience. In other words, the gap between assessment (awareness of the presence of emotional factors) and treatment (intervention into, and modification of, those factors) has never been adequately bridged.

DIFFERENCES IN BEHAVIOR MODIFICATION

One of the very unfortunate stereotypes about behavior modification is that behaviorists ignore feelings and deal only with concrete motor responses or superficial behaviors. Nothing could be farther from the truth. In fact, the area of emotional behavior problems—problems involving human feelings—has probably received more attention from professionals using behavioral techniques in research and in practice than any of the other behavior problems discussed in this book. It is in the area of emotional behavior problems that the procedures of behavior modification have had the greatest amount of validated success, as reported in extensive case study and group experimental research.

Behavior modification with emotional problems has tended to be the more clinically oriented branch of the field. Problems are often worked on in traditional office-therapy arrangements, with the professional in the therapeutic role. Usually, there is a one–to–one relationship between client and professional; sometimes the professional applies his behavioral techniques in small groups. There has been minimal use of mediators and nonprofessionals as the purveyors of behavior modification in this clinically oriented work. Thus, the behavioral approach to emotional behavior problems—direct intervention by the professional—may seem somewhat more familiar, and perhaps more comfortable, to many social workers.

But the basic elements of the behavioral approach nevertheless are present in dealing with emotional behavior problems. As always, the social worker who uses the behavioral perspective should attempt to ascertain the observable dimensions of the problem. In this case, with emotional responses of primary concern, the worker should ascertain not only how the client expresses the emotion, i.e., verbally, physiologically (e.g., perspiration), motorically (e.g., avoiding certain objects or situations), but also what factors or events precede the occurrence of the behavior, what events follow it, and in what situations it occurs. The emotional response would be broken down into component parts and a process of *direct retraining* would be begun. The goal of such retraining is twofold: to diminish or extinguish the maladaptive emotional response (e.g., dysfunctional anxiety), and to help the individual develop new adaptive behaviors in response to situations or events that he might have avoided previously (Ullmann & Krasner, 1969). This, in fact, is the primary contribution of the behavioral approach to work with emotional problems: breaking down emotional responses into specific categories of problem behaviors, and developing specific techniques for dealing with these categories—in other words, bridging the gap between diagnosis and treatment.

Types of Behavior Included

In order to avoid the traditional practice approach of lumping together a number of distinct configurations under the term "emotional problems," and to avoid the resulting confusion for interventive purposes, such behavior will be given a very specific meaning here. Emotional behaviors are taken here to include anxiety, tension, fears and phobias, and the accompanying behaviors (such as avoidance behaviors) that result from such conditions. Such a grouping may be somewhat narrower than the typical conception of emotional behaviors. This grouping, however, provides a more concrete basis for discussing intervention since: (1) there appear to be common denominators in the way these behaviors are generally learned; (2) they include some of the most omnipresent and pervasive of the behavior disorders; (3) there are common techniques for intervention for all of them. This, of course, is not to say that other disorders may not also be considered "emotional." A whole range of problems may have emotional components (see Ullmann & Krasner, 1969, chapters 15, 16, and 21). Some of these disorders, e.g., "depression," are discussed in separate chapters in this book. But the logical consistency of behaviors such as anxieties, fears, and phobias compels their discussion as separate behaviors.

Emotional behaviors, in the first place, are composed of multisystem responses. Indicators of such problems may be noted in verbal terms, in motor activity, and in physiological terms (e.g., perspiration, rapid heart beat). Interestingly, several studies have shown that different measures of the presence or intensity of anxiety or fear do not correlate very well with each other (Yates, 1970), so that one or all of these indicators may be most obvious at any given time. Thus, it appears that what typically has been considered anxiety or fear may simply be a shorthand term for a complex pattern of responses characterized by subjective feelings of apprehension and tension accompanied by, or associated with, physiological excitation (Paul, 1969). Most typically, such behavior is not under the voluntary control of the individual (the fact that elevators will not realistically harm a person does not necessarily diminish a person's fear of elevators).

Emotional behaviors are learned reactions. (It is hardly necessary to point out that this discussion is couched in terms of *maladaptive* emotional behaviors, with results dysfunctional for the individual rather than those forms of anxiety or fear that are realistic or perhaps even motivating to functional behavior.) In Chapter 2, the respondent basis for the learning of emotional behaviors was explored. The respondent process essentially involves the pairing of previously neutral stimuli with stimuli that elicit emotional reactions such that the new stimuli also come to elicit such reactions.

But it is unlikely that such a conception accounts for the development of all dysfunctional emotional behaviors. There also can be operant factors in the development of emotional behavior. There are, in the first place, obvious operant responses performed as a *function* of the emotional responses, e.g., running to avoid a feared object. But, just as clearly, there may be an emotional reaction based on operant conditioning when a previously reinforcing event is removed, as in response cost, or the contingent relationship between positive reinforcement and behavior is broken, as in extinction (as represented by increased agitation or anxiety when previously reinforced behavior is not reinforced). The presentation of an aversive stimulus (positive punishment) also is likely to evoke an emotional reaction such as anxiety. And the termination of an aversive stimulus that reinforces or increases operant behavior by its termination may also elicit emotional responses (Ferster & Perrott, 1968).

Thus, almost all instances of the development of emotional behavior —either from an operant or a respondent perspective—include the presentation or termination of powerful stimuli, either as antecedent or consequent events. In most cases, a prime feature of emotional behavior is the disruption, or disturbance, or change that occurs in an individual's behavior at the point at which an "emotional situation" occurs (Millenson, 1967). Most often, those (changed) behaviors include avoidance of (or escape from) the situations that tend to produce the emotional responses (a student afraid of being criticized may not go to school to avoid potential criticism; a man with a great fear of failure may avoid asking out women for dates because he fears being rejected). These avoidance behaviors tend to reduce the emotional response (e.g., fear) and are therefore reinforcing. Hence, such avoidance behaviors would tend to be maintained. Of course, the behaviors one engages in to reduce fear and anxiety are a function of one's learning history, the type of skills in one's repertoire, available alternatives, the type of situation, and so on. While there may be a number of theoretical distinctions in the way such behaviors are learned, at the present time these distinctions make little difference to the way such dysfunctional emotional behaviors are *changed*.

Interventive Strategies

ASSESSMENT

The goal of the assessment process for emotional behavior problems is to select the appropriate procedure for effectively dealing with the problem. As with all other forms of behavioral assessment, the social worker attempts to be as specific as possible, in terms not only of the specific emotional responses distressing the client, but also of the specific stimuli eliciting or following the emotional response. At times, this is easier said than done, but the extent to which it is accomplished is probably directly related both to the efficiency and the effectiveness of intervention. The point, of course, is not to oversimplify the true complexities of human behavior, but to be as clear as possible about the behaviors of concern in order to facilitate the selection of intervention procedures.

To that end, the assessment of emotional behavior problems attempts to ascertain (Ullmann & Krasner, 1969):

1. what problems or areas the client wishes to work on and what benefits he or she wishes to derive;
2. what the specific problems are (i.e., the nature of the responses);
3. what responses should be diminished or acquired;
4. where and when dysfunctional reactions occur (i.e., the circumstances, the eliciting stimuli);
5. what behaviors the person is actually performing (e.g., avoiding a particular situation);
6. what the consequences of performing such behaviors are (e.g., reduction in anxiety; reinforcement from others in the form of secondary gain);
7. what conditions may be maintaining the dysfunctional behavior.

Again, the goal of this information is to help guide the selection of techniques for dealing with the problem.

It is very important, however, to keep two cautions in mind. The first involves avoiding the selection of techniques without adequate information. Too many professionals, for example—understandably, perhaps, because of the clear, and often dramatic, record of success of desensitization—tend to use desensitization as soon as any sign of anxiety or fear becomes obvious. (Anxiety may be a realistic response to an aversive environmental event. Removal of that event or situation may be the more appropriate and efficient intervention.) But the goal of assessment is not only to establish the similarities between a given client's problems and the problems of other clients so that similar, successful techniques can be applied, but also to *individualize* the case, to learn the unique factors involved in the client's problem configuration so that a range of appropriate procedures can be flexibly and differentially applied to the client's special situation.

The second caution is based on the fact that most of the techniques used to deal with emotional behavior problems are designed to help the client cope more adaptively with his or her problem. But, if the assessment identifies situations or events the removal or presentation of which evoke the emotional response, a far more parsimonious, effective, and perhaps ethical solution would be to intervene in the *situation* rather than with the client. This might mean that instead of helping an anxious student cope with his anxiety about a truly punitive teacher, intervention would be directly with the teacher, or, if this were not possible or successful, it would mean helping the student transfer out of that teacher's class.

In addition to the assessment guidelines discussed in Chapter 11, a number of procedures have been developed specifically for the assessment of emotional behavior problems (see, e.g., Wolpe, 1969, chapter 3; Lazarus, 1971, 1972). Many of these procedures involve the collection of assessment information from at least six sources (Marquis *et al.*, 1971).

1. *The client's presenting complaint:* These are always taken seriously. Often, the basis for an entire course of intervention may be found here. Certainly, there may be a great deal more involved than the initial complaint indicates, but, in the last analysis, intervention cannot be judged effective unless these problems have been successfully handled.

2. *Historical information:* The purpose of obtaining this information is not only to give the worker some perspective on the problem, but also to provide a background for succeeding steps and possible clues to current relationships (Wolpe, 1969, pp. 22–28). A questionnaire developed by Lazarus (1971, pp. 239–251) requesting the client to report a range of background information, as well as information about current problems, may be filled out by the client at home, and can be very helpful in obtaining these data.

3. *Instruments:* The most commonly used instrument is the Fear Survey Schedule (Wolpe, 1969, pp. 283–286), an 87-item instrument asking the client to rate, on a 5-point scale of fear or anxiety, such items as "speaking in public," "entering a room where other people are already seated," "making mistakes," "feeling rejected by others," "prospect of surgical operations," and so on. This is a very useful method of categorizing the client's responses into anxiety-related themes (e.g., fear of failure), and it can be used without extensive technical training. Another instrument recommended for assessment is the Willoughby Personality Schedule (Wolpe, 1966, pp. 279–282), which includes 25 items asking the client more detailed information about his fears and anxieties. Finally, the Bernreuter Self-Sufficiency Scale (Wolpe, 1969, pp. 287–290), is a 60-item questionnaire to be used when problems of overdependency or lack of self-assertion seem to be involved. Extensive technical training in the use of these instruments is not necessary; they are available for rapid and easy implementation in practice by social workers.

4. *Client note-taking:* The client can be asked to take notes about his own behavior, specifically, when and where dysfunctional emotional behaviors occur.

5. *Social worker observation:* An obvious and important source of information consists of the social worker's own observations of the client,

whether this occurs in the office or the client's home. The latter instance may be particularly advantageous as it allows observation of the client's patterns of interaction with others.

6. *Client–social worker interaction:* The client may, in his discussions with the worker, actually begin to demonstrate some of his difficulties with others. "Shyness," difficulties in talking about a particular problem area, "hostility," all may be elicited by either the material being discussed or some dynamic of the social worker–client relationship. When these are noted by the social worker, they can be explored for further clarification of the problem situation, and for their implications for relationships with others.

Of course, such assessment is an ongoing process. New data and new information almost always are constantly emerging as the social worker–client relationship intensifies. In fact, such new information should be encouraged by the social worker, who might specifically explore at each interview whether any new dimensions to the problem have developed. Such information may lead to any number of changes, including changes in procedure, e.g., from assertive training to desensitization on the grounds that debilitating anxiety has to be overcome before the assertive training can proceed further. All of the above information will, one hopes, be collected with the greatest of clinical sensitivity, not only in following subtle leads, but also in helping the client discuss difficult areas the mere discussion of which elicits strong feelings of anger or anxiety. By the time the initial assessment process is completed (anywhere from one to two interviews), the social worker will begin making decisions as to the types of techniques to employ, basing such decisions on the numerous criteria discussed in Chapters 11 through 14.

INTERVENTION

There are generally two potential focal points for intervention with emotional behavior problems. The first is to focus on the anxiety or fear response itself. The second is to focus on the avoidance behaviors produced by the anxiety. In actual practice, both of these areas are usually combined to produce optimal benefits for the client. This is because the ultimate goal in working with a client suffering from dysfunctional emotional responses such as maladaptive anxiety is to have him eventually enter the situation or participate in the event that elicits the anxiety. In some situations, simply removing the anxiety response would be enough. Paul (1966), for example, clearly demonstrated with the technique of systematic desensitization that removing anxiety about public speaking was sufficient for those clients to enable them to make speeches without incapacitating fear. On the other hand, if an individual avoids certain situations because of anxiety, the social worker might best help by concentrating directly on helping the client to perform the previously avoided responses. This was demonstrated by Neuman (1969), who used assertive training and behavior rehearsal to overcome a problem that involved the avoidance of heterosexual contacts and interpersonal contacts with peers and family. A further benefit of using assertive training and behavior rehearsal is that both the previously avoided response *and* anxiety are focused on simultaneously. Performing the previously avoided responses is incompatible with, and therefore decreases, the anxiety.

It should be emphasized again that simply removing anxiety may not be sufficient. For example, if some of Paul's (1966) clients (discussed above) had not had sufficient skills to make the speech even after their anxiety had diminished, the therapeutic task would have been to help develop those skills through such techniques as behavior rehearsal, positive reinforcement, modeling, and shaping. Or, in a similar situation, systematic desensitization could be conducted *in vivo,* thus decreasing the anxiety as the real life response is made at the same time.

Because of the prominence of respondent features in anxiety and fear responses, the bulk of the work on emotional behavior problems has been conducted using respondent techniques. Of these, systematic desensitization is by far the most frequently used. An extremely important factor in the selection of systematic desensitization as a primary technique for dealing with emotional behavior problems is its outstanding success record, validated in extensive experimental research. Assertive training and behavior rehearsal have also been used quite frequently, particularly when the problem involves failure to perform assertive or affirmative interpersonal behaviors. To a lesser but growing extent, implosive therapy (respondent extinction; Stamfl, 1970), modeling (Bandura, 1969), and thought stopping and other forms of self-control (Cautela, 1969, 1971, 1972) have also been used. And, of course, as in all behavior modification intervention, positive reinforcement in the form of praise and attention is used to reinforce adaptive efforts by the client. Indeed, in the typical behavior modification program dealing with emotional behavior problems, it is likely that several of these techniques will be used in combination, according to the specific nature of the client's problems. To recapitulate, using behavior modification, emotional behavior problems are dealt with through direct retraining by removing the dysfunctional emotional or avoidance response, or substituting an adaptive response, or both.

Increasingly, the literature reflects the fact that a large majority of behavioral interventions directed toward reducing emotional problems employ more than one technique. However, for illustrative purposes, three case studies, each of which emphasizes the use of only one technique, will be briefly summarized here, followed by a Case Illustration which features a complete program of several techniques employed in combination. In line with the discussion above, the first of these cases describes the use of systematic desensitization to focus directly on the anxiety response itself; the second describes the use of behavior rehearsal and assertive training focused on the avoidance behaviors elicited by anxiety; the third describes the use of modeling or imitative learning to decrease anxiety.

One of the standard criticisms of systematic desensitization—if not behavioral approaches as a whole—is that only highly specific, encapsulated problems can be handled, while more complex, ill-defined problems remain refractory to behavior modification. The case study reported here, however, is focused on dealing with "existential" anxiety, involving a series of multidimensional, complex, and ill-defined problems (Nawas, 1971). The client was a 20-year-old college student who felt his "world [was] falling apart," and had problems in every area of functioning— college, interpersonal relations, family, dating, and work. He had trouble making decisions, was vague and unsure of himself, and, when asked how he sees himself five years in the future, replied, "All I can say is that I may be dead or alive, but I don't have the slightest idea what would become of me."

Although this was an uncontrolled case study, an interesting strategy for enhancing the demonstration value of the case study was used. Essentially, the client served as his own control and underwent periodic psychological testing, using a variety of tests including the MMPI, TAT, Maslow Security-Insecurity Inventory, and the PIL. These tests were administered in six phases: (1) screening; (2) pretreatment; (3) after a three-week period to assess the effects of a no-treatment time lapse; (4) three weeks after relaxation training (for desensitization) was initiated and to recheck the effects of a no-treatment time lapse; (5) prior to implementation of desensitization (a special instrument developed by the author to specifiy the conglomeration of problems underlying existential complaints); (6) post-treatment. Excluding the post-treatment phase, none of the instruments (except one scale on the MMPI after relaxation training) showed any appreciable changes, thus attesting to the facts that testing and retesting, relaxation, and the overall relationship between client and worker had little therapeutic effect on the client.

Using the instrument developed by the author to classify existential complaints, the problems were categorized into the following areas: (1) relations with authority figures; (2) inability to assert oneself; (3) problems with the opposite sex; (4) interpersonal relations in general and inability to feel a part of a group in particular; (5) fear of self-disclosure; (6) generalized lack of self-confidence. Items for desensitization hierarchies were developed for each of these six problem areas, and ranked by the client as to degree of anxiety each elicited. Actual implementation of desensitization lasted twenty sessions spaced roughly three days apart.

The client began to report improvement in several areas after fifteen sessions, and with continuing reports of improvement, and the end of the college semester in sight, treatment was terminated after five more sessions. The PIL, MMPI, TAT, and Maslow Inventory were then re-administered. On all but the Maslow Inventory, significant positive changes between pre- and post-treatment were found. Scores on all of the tests were now in the "normal/healthy" range. Follow-up at five months revealed continued positive effects, with the client doing well in school, engaged to be married, no longer feeling in need of treatment, and having made, for the first time, a firm commitment to a college "major"—psychology.

The second case study involves the use of assertive training to decrease the social anxiety and increase the range of interpersonal skills of an outpatient group of men and women with a mean age of about forty, all of whom had been diagnosed as "chronic schizophrenics" (Bloomfield, 1973). Prior to this report, there was no report in the literature on the use of assertive training with a similarly diagnosed outpaient group.

The author had decided to try assertive training with this group after observing a more or less typical pattern of excessive compliance, submissiveness, and social inhibition and anxiety among most of the members of the group. The purpose of the use of assertive training was to decrease the social anxiety and increase the interpersonal skills of the group members, all of whom were taking major tranquilizers. The decision to use assertive training was made despite warnings by colleagues regarding the fragility of the "schizophrenic ego."

The group was composed of eight to ten people and met on an open-ended basis one hour per week. The group used assertive training to deal with the full range of assertive behavior including forthright statements of anger and resentment, genuine expressions of love, difficulties with employers, problems in expressing a variety of emotions, and was also used to deal with the "here and now" business of the group, teaching members to express feelings of warmth and approval, as well as irritation, for one another. Group interaction and cohesiveness were utilized to facilitate the use of the assertive training.

The report focused on the use of assertive training with one of the group members, J. C., a 33-year-old woman. J. C., who presented a very fragile, compliant picture of herself, had been having trouble with a light-sleeping downstairs neighbor. The neighbor complained, among other ways, by knocking on the ceiling, that J. C. was making too much noise and commotion, despite the fact that J. C. was making every effort to be reasonably quiet. J. C. had not confronted the neighbor and was becoming increasingly anxious, depressed and suspicious of rumors that the neighbor might be starting about J. C. among other tenants.

The sequence of steps in the intervention process was as follows:

1. Identification of J. C.'s excessive compliance and submissiveness; this was facilitated by members of the group pointing out inappropriate behaviors.
2. Identification of adverse consequences of J. C.'s compliance; emphasizing differences between reasonable assertiveness and aggressiveness; discussion of other group members' successful assertive behavior; group encouragement for J. C. to assert her rights.
3. Specific behavioral rehearsal including role reversal with the therapist acting out, first, the neighbor's part, then J. C.'s; modeling by the therapist of assertive behaviors; role playing by J. C. with several members of the group.
4. Specific feedback during behavior rehearsal regarding J. C.'s verbal content, facial expression, tone of voice, etc.; group support and approval to reinforce new behavior.
5. Practice of specific assertive behavior in which J. C. not only expressed displeasure but provided information to facilitate more acceptable interaction.
6. Provision for positive feedback from the environment; assurance from another group member who knew the neighbor that the neighbor would "respond well" to J. C.'s assertiveness; repeating and refining of behavior rehearsal; preparation for the range of possible reactions from neighbor; support for first "confrontation" with neighbor (which J. C. spontaneously volunteered to undertake).

After this training, J. C. reported a successful series of interchanges with the neighbor over a period of weeks during which they reached a mutual understanding and had begun to establish a more friendly relationship. J. C. reported that she no longer felt suspicious, depressed or anxious, and felt better able to trust her emotions.

Although modeling is most often thought of as the procedure of choice for developing new behavior, it also has proved highly effective in eliminating anxiety (Rachman, 1972). In the first, and now classic, controlled study to demonstrate this effect, Bandura, Grusec, and Menlove (1967) focused on a group of young children who were very frightened of dogs. Four groups of children were used. The first group, in eight brief sessions, observed a fearless peer model exhibit progressively more fear-provoking interactions with a dog. This behavior was presented within the context of a highly positive party (designed to counteract the arousal of anxiety). Once the party had started, a fearless four-year-old boy brought a dog into the room and performed a variety of prearranged interactions with the dog for roughly three minutes per session. The fear-eliciting properties of the modeled performances were gradually increased from session to session by simultaneously varying the physical restraints on the dog, the directness and intimacy of the modeled approach behaviors of the boy, and the duration of interaction between the boy and his dog.

The second group of children observed the same performances between the boy and his dog, but this time outside the party context, in a neutral situation. For controls, a third group of children observed the dog in the context of the party but without the model being present, and a fourth group of children participated in the party with neither the dog nor model present.

All the children were administered tests for avoidance behavior before and after the programs, and at a one-month follow-up. These tests included approaching and petting two dogs, releasing them from a playpen, removing their leashes, feeding them dog biscuits, spending a set amount of time alone in a room with each dog, and, finally, climbing into a playpen with each dog, petting it, and remaining alone with the dog under those confined conditions.

The modeling procedure produced highly stable extinction of the avoidance behaviors. Children in both groups that had observed the model interact with the dog displayed significantly greater approach behavior toward both the experimental dog and an unfamiliar dog than did children in either of the two control groups (which did not differ from each other). The positive context, the party, contributed little to the favorable outcome. Further, 67 percent of the children who had observed the model were able to remain alone in the room confined with the dog in the playpen, while only a few of the children in the control conditions were able to attain this.

Case Illustration

There are no cases or situations that are "typical" examples of behavior modification with emotional behavior problems. In fact, the task of illustrating intervention strategies becomes somewhat complicated by the fact that there are so many illustrations of such intervention, most of which employ a variety of behavioral techniques chosen on the basis of careful analysis to deal with specific components of a problem. Thus, the illustration presented here is only one of many which might have been selected, although this report, by Geisinger (1969), not only involves a change strategy that emphasizes the use of multiple techniques, but also a great deal of flexibility and sensitivity on the part of the practitioner.

The client was a 23-year-old married woman from a lower-middle-class background, which included parents, described as alcoholics, who were punitive in their treatment of the client as a child. The client, whose name was Naomi, got married at age 21 to a man who was a graduate student and with whom she reported getting along very well. At initial contact, Naomi appeared gloomy and cheerless, poorly groomed, over-weight, and generally morose and drab. The first two hours of contact with Naomi were spent in detailed assessment of the circumstances sur-rounding her concerns, including: (1) exaggerated sensitivity to criticism, particularly from her husband and people in the office where she worked as a secretary; (2) a marked lack of assertiveness, shyness, and a tendency to withdraw from interpersonal interactions; (3) numerous and per-sistent feelings of jealousy about her husband, which she knew had no factual basis. Based on the assessment, the following techniques were selected: (1) systematic desensitization; (2) assertive training; (3) behavior rehearsal and modeling; (4) positive reinforcement (praise from the clinician) for accomplishments.

The third session was spent in helping Naomi refine and elaborate the particular situations in which she became anxious. She was instructed in the rationale and process of desensitization, and was asked to think about specific situations involving criticism and jealousy. Behavior re-hearsal and assertive training were started in the fourth and fifth sessions. Naomi was angry and resentful about her employer's giving her an excessive amount of work, which resulted in her frequently having to work overtime without compensation. This made her want to leave her job, particularly because she felt unable to confront the situation di-rectly. The therapeutic task was to help her learn to deal more directly with such situations rather than avoid them, and in a way that would not bring destructive responses from others. The author role-played the part of her employer and Naomi played herself in a typical office inter-action. At first Naomi played her part in a faltering way and seemed quite ill at ease, although this diminished after several attempts and after listening to tape recordings of her efforts. The author and Naomi re-versed roles and the author modeled explicit and more assertive ways of behaving with her employer. After several attempts, Naomi became able to handle the situation comfortably. The therapist suggested that she practice what she had learned whenever the opportunity arose.

Several sessions were spent in teaching relaxation techniques, in de-veloping desensitization hierarchies, and in beginning the desensitization process itself. The "criticism" hierarchies consisted of 24 items. Some of these items were: (1) "at the office building, Cathy, another secretary, says, 'Why don't you wear your hair down?' " (8) "At the office, the boss brings back a letter I've composed and says, 'Next time it might be better not to be so blunt in telling the customer that he's made an error.' " (16) "At the office while taking shorthand, I misunderstood a word and sent the letter out with the wrong word on it. The boss's attention is called to the error and he tells me, 'You should have caught that.' " (24) "At home, Aaron [her husband] said, 'Your thighs used to be so big that I could see no distinction where your butt ended and your thighs began!' "

The "jealousy" hierarchy had 21 items such as: (1) Aaron and I are at Ron and Dora's house. Aaron and Ron are talking to each other and laughing." (6) "In front of the office building I introduce Aaron to Helen (another secretary), and he is very charming and cordial." (14) "Aaron and I are at a roller rink. It is the girls' turn to have the floor to themselves for doing tricks and Aaron watches them intently." (21) "Aaron and I are at a friend's house. We are about to leave and a woman who boards there comes out to the doorway of her bedroom in her panties and bra. She looks at us and says, 'You aren't leaving so early, are you?' "

Naomi reported considerable improvement in her mood by the twelfth session, which coincided with progress on the criticism hierarchy and in assertive training. She reported that she was even able to be more assertive with her boss with no anxiety, and by the fourteenth session reported being able to joke with the office manager for the first time. By the seventeenth session, Naomi reported that: (1) she had played the piano at a friend's house in front of a group of people although she had previously been too self-conscious and afraid of making mistakes to do this; (2) she had phoned a prospective employer who had delayed making a definite commitment to her, and told him diplomatically but assertively that she expected to hear from him one way or the other about a particular job. Naomi stated, "A number of people told me that I'm completely changed, that I'm a new person."

Naomi revealed during the twenty-second session that she was still excessively jealous about her husband. The author began to suspect that this might be related to her feelings about her own physical appearance, which, for all intents and purposes, had not changed. He began to encourage Naomi's efforts at physical change by verbally reinforcing (praising) all such efforts (such as starting a new diet) or even verbal expressions of such efforts. Behavior rehearsal was conducted several times during which she played herself bringing up the matter of buying new clothes to her husband, who seemed to resent this. She gradually decided to make major efforts to change her appearance. By the twenty-fourth session, Naomi appeared wearing a new coat and make-up, saying that she was beginning to feel better about herself, and that she had not felt jealous all week.

After roughly 30 sessions, Naomi and her husband decided to move to another city where Aaron had accepted a job (he had graduated from the university). Naomi was considerably changed, having eliminated several phobias, having become more assertive and more relaxed in her social interactions, and having improved her relationship with her husband and her thoughts and feelings about herself. Ten months after termination, the author happened to see Aaron at a professional meeting and asked him how his wife was. Aaron tapped the shoulder of a young woman who was standing next to him chatting with a group of people and said, "You can ask her yourself." As the author relates this incident (Geisinger, 1969, p. 465), he could hardly believe his eyes. "It was Naomi. Her hair had been cut and set in an attractive new style, her figure was lithe, and she was wearing a bright new dress, tastefully applied make-up, and had even changed her eyeglass frames. She seemed poised, outgoing, and told [me] how well things had been going for her."

CHAPTER 20   Marital Behavior Problems

A generation ago, Margaret Mead said of contemporary American marriage: "It is one of the most difficult marriage forms that the human race has ever attempted" (Mead, 1949, p. 7). There seems little reason to believe that it is any less difficult today.

From a behavioral point of view, a major difficulty in the American "marriage form," especially in middle-class families (perhaps the greatest source of candidates for marital counseling), is the almost exclusive dependence of each partner in the marriage on the other for social reinforcement. In less industrialized, less urban, and less transient societies, the network of individuals who provide social reinforcements (e.g., expression of praise, affection, and concern) for any particular individual is fairly broad. This network may include a large number of friends, neighbors, and members of the extended family. In much of American society, where family transience is increasingly a way of life, these networks are often broken, if they ever existed. Such transience, and the resulting relative isolation of the nuclear family, is becoming more and more a pattern at all economic and educational levels. The loss of these reinforcement networks leads many individuals to hope to find in their spouse a permanent, portable reinforcer. Pressure for reciprocal reinforcement in such areas as companionship and self-evaluation from just one other individual (rather than a range of individuals) often places demands on a marriage that one or both partners find difficult to meet.

Under such stress, what are the behavioral characteristics of a relatively successful marriage as contrasted with an unsuccessful one? Stuart (1969) suggests that most individuals enter marriage with the expectation that their relationship will be mutually reinforcing and that each spouse will give to, and receive from, the other. Indeed, marriage partners are generally attracted to each other to the extent that they feel currently or potentially reinforced. Thus, marriage usually begins with each spouse giving the other considerable noncontingent praise, affection, and tangible positive reinforcers (e.g., flowers, restaurant dinners, favorite homecooked foods, sexual favors). A "successful" marriage, then, is one in which this pattern of mutual reinforcement is essentially sustained, and one in which ". . . both partners work to maximize mutual rewards while minimizing individual costs" (Stuart, 1969, p. 676). In other words, marital partners, like anyone else, feel close to those who make them feel good, and who tend to behave in a manner that is reinforcing to them without requiring excessive reinforcement (or other behavioral influence procedures) on their part. For example, a wife will more likely reinforce her husband if he comes home for dinner on time without being begged, talks about subjects she is interested in without being badgered, and agrees to her independent activities without being ridiculed as a chauvinist (assuming these behaviors are reinforcing to her). A husband will more likely reinforce his wife if she occasionally prepares meals he likes without his threatening to eat out on his own, attempts new sexual experiences without being argued into it, and seems interested in his work concerns without being criticized for her apathy (assuming these behaviors are reinforcing to him).

An unsuccessful marriage, on the other hand, is one in which one partner (or both) has become less successful in receiving reinforcements from the other, or one in which the costs for receiving reinforcements have become excessively high. In such marriages one partner (or both) may reduce his investment in the marriage and expect less and less reinforcement from the other. In essence, they may have found that the giving of reinforcers has not been reinforced. In such marriages the partners generally resort to either of two patterns in relation to their spouse (Stuart, 1969). The first is coercion, in which one partner (or both) uses negative reinforcement (e.g., nagging, ridicule, sarcasm, threats) to obtain the behavior desired of the other. Coercion makes the spouse's grudging compliance to the coercion less reinforcing for subsequent positive behaviors, and, finally, it demeans the response. The second is withdrawal, in which one partner (or both) withdraws from the marriage emotionally or physically and turns from the spouse to other sources of reinforcement. Withdrawal can lead to such behaviors as engaging in a dysfunctional relationship with a child, or in an extramarital sexual relationship. Withdrawal provides little to mutually reinforce the marital relationship even though it may preserve the marriage by avoiding open conflict.

Based on these behavioral perspectives of marital interaction, the task of the social worker is to assess the potential for mutual reinforcement for the couple, their motivation or desire to make the marriage work, the patterns of behavior each wants the other to increase or decrease, and then to reverse the negative patterns and contingencies of behaviors in the couple's relationship so that they each will generate greater amounts of reciprocal reinforcement with minimal recourse to aversive control.

As will be noted in the remainder of this chapter, the reported behavioral expectations of a significant proportion of marriages encountered in marital counseling—as elsewhere—reflects sex role stereotyping. Indeed the case illustrations in most articles and books on marital problems (some of which are referred to below) are replete with wives who wait patiently at home, hoping their husbands can be modified to "communicate" with them when they return from the "real world" of work, and husbands whose major reinforcements from their wives are well-cooked meals and sexual favors.

Many who reject such a model for female-male relationships may well be offended by these expectations of the couples and the marriage therapists alike. While the sexism implicit in the existence of these problems and in social workers' approaches to these problems is an important emerging concern for all professionals, these *are* the types of problems reported in the literature, and they are still typical of many of the husband-wife relationships encountered in daily practice. Hence, these problems still appear to be an appropriate focal point for social work interventions.

Types of Behavior Included

Marital problems are different from most of the problems discussed in the other chapters in this part of the book in that it is always the patterns of dysfunctional or inadequate *reciprocal* reinforcement that constitute the problems. The inventory of stimuli that are reinforcing or aversive to any individual at any point in time is almost infinitely varied. The fact that marriages involve the intermeshing of significant reinforcements of two individuals creates a complex set of behaviors and contingencies for the social worker to study. Furthermore, other significant behavior problems are often superimposed, created, or maintained by the marital problems. (See the case illustration at the end of this chapter.) It is not surprising, therefore, that behaviorists have just recently begun to approach the complexities of intervention in marital behavior problems.

Perhaps because of the complexity of specifying the types of marital dysfunctioning, Morrow (1971) lists only "sexual" and "nonsexual" as target behavior subdivisions for marriage problems (p. 4). The difficulties in conceptualizing and developing effective interventive strategies for marital problems is reflected by the presence of only eight reported successful approaches to marital problems (p. 136) in Morrow's bibliography. This chapter deals primarily with nonsexual problems in marriage. Sexual problems (in and out of marriage) are discussed in Chapter 25.

It is perhaps pointless to attempt to define various types of marital disharmony since their essential characteristic is that whatever behaviors one partner exhibits are either insufficiently reinforcing or excessively aversive (or both) to the other. Thus marital problems can occur in such areas of interaction as the frequency and nature of sexual activity, relations with in-laws and friends, the use of money, the number, spacing, and discipline of children, recreational activities, religion, and communication with each other in general (Knox, 1971). The factors that bring about or maintain unsatisfactory complementarity in such areas or in the marriage in general can include the partners' lack of adequate models for the reinforcement of marital behavior, excessive or exclusive expectations of reinforcements from partners, selection of a partner whose basic characteristics (e.g., age, appearance, intelligence) never did, or have ceased to, reinforce the other partner adequately, changes in either partner's needs for reinforcement, unclear or inconsistent cues for desired behaviors, respondent conditioning in which a partner has been paired with aversive stimuli (e.g., partner has been paired with the feeling of being tied down), or behaviors that are reinforcing to one partner (e.g., having many children) becoming aversive to the other.

Interventive Strategies

ASSESSMENT CONSIDERATIONS

The goal of assessment in behavior modification with marital problems is to determine:

1. the patterns of reciprocal behavioral influence;
2. the behaviors each partner wants changed in the other, in terms of direction, frequency, duration, or intensity;
3. the procedures each has been using to elicit these behaviors, such as nagging, seeking support from other relations, bartering with physical attacks, threats of desertion, etc.;
4. the factors that seem to be maintaining the undesired behaviors and preventing the desired behaviors of each;
5. the resources or potential reinforcers each has that might be used more effectively to alter the other's behavior.

It is, of course, possible that one partner (or both) may not perceive the other as having the potential resources for reinforcement and thus demand radical changes in the other that are antithetical to the other's own goals or wishes in order to preserve the marriage. In such situations, a decision making process is entered into in which each partner evaluates whether the marriage is worth the personal costs of altering his own behaviors, and whether the partner any longer has real potential for reinforcement.

While it is not within the scope of this book to explore comprehensively a behavioral conception of "love," it may be inferred that love certainly will be absent if the reinforcing potential from a spouse becomes minimal. One then turns to the consideration of the potential assets and liabilities of a divorce as compared with that of preserving the marriage.

Assuming, as often happens, that there is sufficient reinforcement available in the marriage to sustain it (or enough perceived aversive consequences to a divorce), then the focus shifts to an assessment of the marital goals of each partner, and of variables within the marriage that may be altered to increase the positive reinforcers in the marriage and decrease the aversive aspects of the marriage.

In doing this, the social worker avoids functioning as a judge whose job is to determine who is at fault or even who is engaging in the worst behavior. Such requests essentially call for the social worker's joining the "offended" partner in applying aversive controls on the putative "erring" partner. In more functional marriages, not only does each partner recognize his own dysfunctional behavior, but each is also willing to accept responsibility for trying to deal with any dysfunctional behavior exhibited by the other (Knox, 1971). An early stage in the behavioral approach to marriage involves not only helping each partner identify mutually dysfunctional behavior, but also changing the consequences of the problem from either punishment or withdrawal to acceptance, concern, and a willingness to help each other with the problem in a positive way. Such a commitment tends to dissolve the punishments that were previously associated with working on marital problems and that have previously prevented cooperative behavioral change (Knox, 1971; Stuart, 1969).

Assessment, of course, must also take into account the impact on the marital relationship of contingencies outside the marriage, such as the partners' employment situation, economic problems, relationships with friends and relatives, cultural expectations of the couple and of significant others around the couple, and even marital expectations and behavioral fads communicated by television, books, and magazines. Finally, the couple's dysfunctional perceptions and expectations of each other must be understood and dealt with before the marital interaction itself can be modified.

On the basis of his assessment, the social worker may proceed to restructure the reciprocal reinforcement patterns of the couple through positive reinforcement rather than coercion, and teach each partner how to provide more of each other's reinforcements at as little "cost" as possible. If the mutual expectations are too high, or of such a nature that one partner (or both) cannot provide sufficient reinforcement, the social worker might explore the possibility of one partner's achieving, with mutual consent, reinforcements outside the marriage. For example, if a wife's only source of companionship is her husband, while he has a wide circle of friends, the wife may be helped to expand her circle of friends. The marriage must be treated in the context of the surrounding pool of potential reinforcers as well as of the external aversive stimuli that infringe on the marriage.

As noted previously, the number of reported successful applications of behavior modification to complex marital problems has thus far been limited. In this section, three interventive strategies will be discussed: (1) stimulus change and self-control procedures; (2) planned reciprocal reinforcement or exchange contracts; (3) prompting or coaching.

STIMULUS CHANGE AND SELF-CONTROL

Seemingly innocuous environmental stimuli may provide many discriminating stimuli for everyday behavior. A rapid way to facilitate change for some specific undesirable behaviors (in and out of marriages) is, therefore, to change the general circumstances—or stimulus field—under which they occur. The creation of new stimuli, or the rearrangement of old stimuli coupled with the establishment of new consequences designed to alter the undesirable behaviors, may produce changes in such behaviors more quickly than they would in the milieu of the old stimuli (Goldiamond, 1965b). A new hairdo or outfit of clothes, or a new job, especially when accompanied by new consequences of old behavioral patterns, can strengthen desired new behaviors. Stimulus change strategies can be especially effective when applied to marital behavior problems in which there is some motivation to change specific behavioral problems. Generally, this strategy is a helpful supplement to more extensive procedures. Often each partner's appearance, along with the various stimuli in and around the various rooms in which the couple lives, can set off subtle chains of events that contribute to their problems. Having the couple rearrange the household furniture can provide a visual cue for a new set of behaviors.

Sometimes, a complete change in surroundings can facilitate the initiation of the modification of reciprocal patterns. One of the authors, in his practice, generally advises couples experiencing marital problems to plan a weekend at a motel or hotel early in the treatment process. (Some couples who can not afford this have been able to trade apartments for a night.) Generally, spending time in new surroundings—especially a motel—adds a hopeful, romantic note and a feeling of a new beginning for the discussions and new patterns of reciprocal behaviors that the couple are asked to carry out.

Goldiamond (1965b) cites several examples of the use of stimulus change in marital cases. In one case, he recommended the rearrangement of furniture and change in the patterns of use of various rooms in the couples' house. He also suggested that since the husband had difficulty having discussions with his wife without shouting at her, he should have their discussions, for a short while only, in semi-public places where shouting was less likely to occur. When shouting was thus brought under control, the husband began to sulk. Goldiamond instructed the husband that he could continue to sulk, but only in the garage on a special "sulking stool." The aversive elements of the procedure, as well as its humor, probably contributed to the effectiveness of this use of stimulus control.

In another case described by Goldiamond (1965b), a successful young business executive took courses at night and never seemed to have time to spend with his wife. Goldiamond suggested that the husband "schedule" his wife two nights a week in his appointment book. This worked for a few weeks. However, since there were clear differential consequences for failing to keep his business appointments, and less clear consequences for not keeping his appointments with his wife, the program failed. The husband himself came up with a suggestion on how to make the system work. Since both he and his wife were extremely well groomed, prized each other's looks, and went regularly to hairdressers, the husband suggested that going to the hairdressers be contingent on his and his wife's keeping their appointments. After one failure, and one week of messy-looking hair, the appointments were kept for some time thereafter, while, presumably, other elements in the marriage were explored and altered to provide natural reinforcements for their interaction.

RECIPROCAL POSITIVE REINFORCEMENT, AND EXCHANGE CONTRACTS

Since the behaviors of partners in a marriage (or other close relationships) are, to a substantial degree, reciprocally contingent, a logical approach to the treatment of dysfunctional marital relationships is the planned alteration of the consequences of each partner's behavior toward the other. Knox (1971) offers procedures for couples to record each other's target behaviors and assess and intervene using a variety of procedures with reciprocal marital behaviors in such areas of disagreement as sex, communication, alcohol, in-laws, friends, religion, money, recreation, and children.

Based on his perceptions of the basis of marital problems in reciprocal expectations, behaviors, and reinforcements, Stuart (1969) offers a structured four-step program that he presents to couples in the form of a game to alter their dysfunctional marital interactions.

STEP 1

The social worker presents the logic of this treatment approach to the couple. Understanding the approach has two advantages: (1) it reduces each partner's biases about the other's behavior; (2) it puts the partners in a better position to participate actively in treatment planning and implementation.

The explanation of the logic of the approach focuses on two basic premises. (1) The impressions each partner has of the other are based to a large extent on the behavior of the other, and, therefore, once a partner changes his or her behavior, the other's impressions and expectations of him or her will also change. This notion parallels Goldiamond's clinical instruction to husbands: "If he wished his wife to behave differently to him, then he should provide other stimuli than the ones which produced the behaviors he did not like" (Goldiamond, 1966, p. 118). (2) To change the relationship in a marriage, each partner must initiate changes in his or her own behavior before he can reasonably expect behavior change in the other. In other words, neither partner can hope for change if he waits for change in the other before he initiates it.

STEP 2

Each spouse is asked to list three behaviors ("wishes") that he or she would like the other to increase in frequency. Stuart notes several difficulties that must be overcome in carrying out this step: In view of their negative interactions at the point at which they seek help, most couples will want to emphasize those behaviors of their spouses that they would like to *decrease* rather than increase. This approach is, of course, contraindicated since decreasing undesired behavior calls for extinction or aversive procedures, which dysfunctional couples probably have already used excessively in their relationship. Second, couples tend to describe behaviors they want changed in broad, vague terms rather than in specific ones. For example, a husband might request that his wife be more "feminine" rather than pinpointing (and evaluating) the discrete behaviors that comprise his concept of femininity. A third problem in choosing specific behaviors to alter is many people's expectations that their spouse should be a mind reader: that the husband or wife should already know what they want, and that if they have to list their wishes, it proves that their partner is inadequate, unfeeling, or uncaring. The fourth problem in carrying out this step is that the specific behaviors chosen are often middle sections of behavioral chains that begin and end with negative behavior by the spouse (i.e., a negative behavior from partner "A," the desired behavior from partner "B," and another negative behavior from partner "A"). Such "sandwiched" desired behaviors must first be considered in the context of the other's negative behaviors. Once any blockages from these four sources are removed, the couple can proceed to Step 3.

STEP 3

Once each partner has selected three wishes, they are each transcribed on a "behavior checklist" that is posted in the couple's home. Each partner then notes on the checklist the frequency with which the partner exhibits the desired behaviors. Recording at this point not only provides a baseline for evaluating subsequent changes, but may (as noted earlier in the chapter on Recording) positively influence the rate of the behavior.

STEP 4

Finally, if there is some reciprocity in the marriage, an exchange contract—that is, an agreement for a more or less equal exchange of desired behaviors—is worked out. Stuart notes that, typically, an increase in communication is high on the list of behavioral goals of couples, which means, in essence, an increase in undefined patterns of mutual reinforcement. In this step, each partner begins to compensate the other for behaviors that are considered reinforcing. For example, one husband chose the following behaviors as those he wanted his wife to increase: (1) greeting him at the door when he came home from work; (2) cleaning up the family room before he came home; (3) serving meals on time. His wife requested that the husband: (1) spend more time with their children; (2) take her to movies; (3) comment on meals when they were well prepared. Each of these behaviors was made the subject of a behavior checklist, and each partner kept note of the frequency with which these behaviors were exhibited. When the couple agreed that the behaviors were occurring at a satisfactory rate, new goals were added.

In those marriages in which reciprocity was at a minimum and the principal interactions consisted of coercion or withdrawal, Stuart introduced a token economy: tokens were given by one spouse to the other contingent on the occurrence of target behaviors. The tokens were redeemable for reciprocal behaviors listed on a reinforcement menu. He noted several advantages of the use of tokens in these marriages:

1. they can be provided immediately after the behavior is exhibited;
2. they can be exchanged for the specific reinforcement the recipient elects at a particular point in time;
3. they are concrete and unambiguous;
4. the exchange of tokens is generally associated with positive relationships;
5. they enable behaviors that do not immediately follow each other to be exchanged.

Stuart (1969) reports on the effectiveness of such a token exchange system in the treatment of four couples, all of whom were on the verge of divorce when they came to treatment. In all four cases, the wives felt "shut out" by their husbands, and chose as their main wish that the husbands converse more with them. Criteria for giving husbands tokens for conversing with their wives were established; conversations were timed by the wives (using a kitchen timer) and reinforced with tokens. If the husband failed to meet certain conversation criteria, the wife was obliged to offer clear suggestions to the husband on how his conversations could be improved.

The tokens given to the husband could be redeemed at the husband's request for reinforcements from a menu stressing physical affection, including sexual activity. (Each of the couples had been engaging in sex infrequently, averaging less than once a week, and as rarely as once a year.) Each couple wanted to have sexual intercourse more often, averaging three times a week. Therefore, husbands were charged three tokens for kissing and "light petting," five tokens for "heavy petting," and fifteen tokens for intercourse. Figure 20.1 shows the results of these procedures with one of the couples whose response to treatment was fairly typical of the others. The rates of the couple's conversations and sexual activities rose sharply after the start of treatment and remained high through a 24-week follow-up period. Marital satisfaction inventories were also completed by the couples at the beginning and end of treatment, and at follow-up. These inventories indicated: (1) their own satisfaction with the marriage; (2) their perceptions of their spouse's satisfaction; (3) their commitment to the marriage. According to the responses on these inventories, the couples' satisfaction with their marriages greatly increased.

PROMPTING (COACHING) THROUGH MECHANICAL CUES

Modification in reciprocal patterns of communication can be critical to the improvement of marital relationships. A group of social work educators at the University of Michigan developed an electromechanical

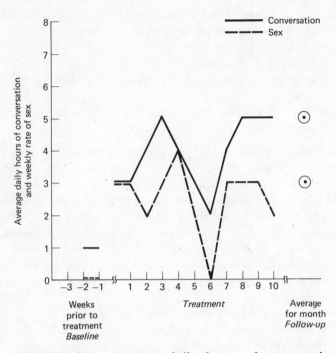

FIGURE 20.1. Average daily hours of conversation and weekly rate of sex of couple before, during, and after operant marital therapy.

Source: R. B. Stuart, "Operant Interpersonal Treatment for Marital Discord," *Journal of Consulting and Clinical Psychology,* vol. 33 (16), December 1969, p. 679.

signalling system, referred to as "SAM" (Signal System for the Assessment and Modification of Behavior), which has been effectively used with problems in marital and parent–child communication patterns (Thomas, Carter, & Gambrill, 1969). Based on assessment procedures they developed to describe patterns of reciprocally reinforcing verbal exchanges, they demonstrated that couples could be taught to communicate in more reinforcing ways (e.g., decreasing a husband's pattern of dominating conversations). Using SAM, the social workers offered feedback to the couples on their interactions, and reinforced effective communications. Following prior instructions, the social worker, or either spouse acting as mediator for the other, would use SAM's light signals as a cue, a conditioned reinforcer, or punishment for a spouse in response to comments during conversations (Thomas, Carter, Gambrill, & Butterfield, 1970). A more complex system has been developed that combines SAM with other behavior modification procedures, involving the feedback of the couple's conversation along with the light signal data (Butterfield, Thomas, & Soberg, 1970).

While these procedures seem to have been useful, they may be excessively expensive and complex for most social work applications. However, simpler feedback systems and visual or auditory cues could be adopted based on the same principles as described with SAM.

Case Illustration

Liberman (1970) reports on the use of differential reinforcement as an approach to marital problems. He notes that spouses often unwittingly reinforce their partner's dysfunctional or undesirable behaviors over the years with their anger, nagging, babying, conciliation, invitation, or sympathy. These behaviors may superficially appear aversive but may, indeed, negatively reinforce the unwanted behaviors. In response to these patterns, Liberman recommends that the therapist and the couple engage in a three-step process: (1) specify the undesirable behavior; (2) determine reasonable alternative desirable behaviors; (3) teach and guide the couple to alter the contingencies of their reinforcement patterns from reinforcing undesirable behaviors to reinforcing desirable behaviors.

Liberman describes the application of this process to the marriage of Mrs. D., a 35-year-old housewife with a 15-year history of severe migraine headaches for which she was hospitalized frequently, despite the fact that no physical cause for the headaches could be found. Although she had received intensive psychodynamically-oriented psychotherapy for a year and a half, she still found that the only relief for her headaches was to use narcotics and stay in bed for periods ranging from a few days to a week at a time.

When Liberman entered the case, he concluded that couple therapy was indicated, on the assumption that Mrs. D.'s headaches had a major role in the couple's marital relationship, and vice versa. Mr. D. was a busy, action-oriented man who rarely talked at length with his wife. When he came home from work he would get involved with watching TV, reading the newspapers, or doing repairs on his car or around the house. He paid attention to his wife only when she developed her headaches, took to bed, and retreated from her housekeeping role. Mr. D. would then respond with considerable attention, give Mrs. D. her medication, and stay home from work to care for his wife and children and arrange for visits from Mrs. D.'s physician.

Believing that Mrs. D.'s headaches and her pattern of retreating to bed may have been reinforced by Mr. D.'s solicitousness, Liberman decided to redirect Mr. D.'s reinforcements from caring for his wife's illness to reinforcing her more desirable behaviors as wife and mother. He shared this analysis with the couple in ten 45-minute sessions, and, having developed a strong positive relationship with the couple, encouraged them to restructure their reciprocal reinforcement patterns.

Subsequently, Mr. D. began to focus his reinforcements on Mrs. D.'s efforts as wife and mother through attention and praise. Upon coming home, instead of disappearing into the newspaper or garage, he would chat with his wife about any problems she may have had with the children. He would occasionally take his wife to the movies or to dinner (which he had rarely done in the past), and, even while watching TV, would sit close to his wife or have her sit in his lap.

In turn, Mrs. D. was taught to reinforce her husband's attentiveness with affection and praise, and to prepare special dishes for dinner. There was also considerably more kissing, which, in technical terms, turned out to be reciprocally contingent.

Mr. D. was instructed that, in order to decrease his wife's headaches in intensity and frequency, he should pay little attention to them when they occurred. He was not to give his wife her medicines, call the doctor, or "cater" to her. At those times, he was to encourage his wife to carry on her routines around the house as much as possible. Liberman emphasized that " . . . he should not, overall, decrease his attentiveness to his wife, but rather change the timing and direction of his attentiveness" (p. 127). In other words, Mr. D. was to transfer his reinforcements from his wife's headaches to her housework, from her sickness to her functioning as a wife, mother, and "whole person."

By the end of ten sessions Mr. and Mrs. D. reported that they were enjoying each other more, that their sex life had improved, and that they had learned how to apply their understanding of behavior to their children, with the result that their children were better behaved. Mrs. D. had also found and taken a job as a salesclerk, which, in turn, further reinforced "non-sick" behavior and gained still more reinforcement from Mr. D. for bringing in extra money.

Although Mrs. D. still had occasional headaches, they were milder and briefer than in the past, and she was well able to take care of them herself without contacting the physician. A follow-up a year after termination showed that the couple had maintained their improved relationship, and while there were still occasional mild headaches, Mrs. D. had not required hospitalization, and no longer felt the need to retreat to bed when they occurred.

CHAPTER 21   Parent–Child Behavior Problems

Those who study child behavior from a behavioral perspective generally conclude that a child's behavior largely reflects the reinforcing contingencies of the child's environment (Skinner, 1953). These researchers do not overlook the fact that children both think and feel, and that these "internal" processes indeed influence their behavior. However, because of the power of the contingencies used by adults in a child's environment (most usually, parents and teachers), these reinforcement contingencies become a major variable in shaping a child's behavior, both functional and dysfunctional. As children grow older, their behavior is influenced by a progressively wider circle of people: teachers, siblings, peers, neighbors, and so on. But at least in their early years, the behavior of children is most clearly influenced by their parents' behavior toward them.

Furthermore, just as parents are very much reinforced by the feelings of pride and joy that result from the functional behavior of their children, they are aversively affected by their children's antisocial or dysfunctional behavior: they feel embarrassment, guilt, anger, and so on because of behaviors of their children that they (and others) consider inappropriate. Thus, the behavior of children and parents can be reciprocally reinforcing or reciprocally aversive.

The research on the reciprocal behavioral patterns of children and the significant adults in their environment suggests that the adults clearly tend to reinforce a wide variety of undesirable behaviors. Reviewing such research, Patterson (1971) states that the findings support the utility of analyzing dysfunctional behavior patterns and altering the contingencies provided by the adults in the child's environment, since ". . . the social environment provides positive social reinforcers contingent upon deviant child behaviors that are sufficient to maintain these behaviors" (Patterson, 1971, p. 752).

For example, Hawkins, Peterson, Schweid, and Bijou (1966) reported on a study that showed that not only do parents reinforce their children's aggressive and negative behaviors, but also that the quantity of the parents' positive reinforcers tended to covary with their children's "unwanted" behaviors. Similarly, when Patterson, Ray, and Shaw (1968) studied the families of children who exhibit disturbed behavior, they found that the family members provided such social reinforcers as attention, interest, approval, or positive physical contact contingent on such apparently undesirable behaviors as teasing, yelling, hitting, and noncompliance. The positive reinforcers for these behaviors were provided on a schedule and with an intensity that were clearly stronger than those of the aversive consequences offered concurrently, and which were generally limited to mild nagging, scolding, or unfulfilled threats.

The reinforcements provided by parents and siblings in such studies can maintain a broad spectrum of dysfunctional behaviors. The careful study of contingencies provided for dysfunctional behaviors also suggests that the reinforcement can be quite subtle and thus easily overlooked, such as fleeting warm or hostile facial expressions, or just paying attention to the child contingent on certain behaviors. However, in the long run, an awareness of these reinforcements could prove essential to eliminating problems in parent-child interactions. "While at first blush we may seem to do little but 'unearth the commonplace,' if these commonplace contingencies are not altered, the effects of intervention programs will likely be short-lived" (Patterson, 1971, p. 752).

Types of Behavior Included

The problem behaviors often subsumed in the category of "parent-child problems" cover a wide area and have no common denominator other than that they are manifested within the parent-child relationship and are considered dysfunctional by either the parents or the child or by both.

The very definition of the problem presents the initial difficulty in approaching these problems. These problems occur in a relationship in which there are two major roles: parent and child. It is almost always the problem behavior of the child (e.g., the child's tantrums, unresponsiveness, or belligerence) that is initially identified and presented to the social worker; it is rarely the problem behaviors of the parents. Thus a social worker bias is possible, at least initially, since the parents present themselves as a client system, and the child is perceived as the target of intervention. The fact that parents report dissatisfaction with their child's behavior and request a social worker to change it may be an insufficient motivation to initiate change strategies. The problem may lie in the inappropriate or excessive behavioral expectations for the child, or the inability of the parents to tolerate such possibly functional behaviors of the child as assertiveness, competitiveness, anger, or sexual expression. To go along with the requests of parents to modify such behaviors simply because they are more articulate and have more power than the child would be a violation of the child's rights and might contribute to the impairment of the child's future development. Furthermore, the social worker and the parents must recognize and adapt to a variety of functional behaviors of children that may change over time, from place to place, and from one reference group to another.

Three criteria would seem useful, then, in deciding whether to initiate a behavioral change program for a child (Blackham & Silberman, 1971):

1. The target behavior must occur fairly often. Occasional fighting or an incident of petty theft may be blown out of proportion by an anxious parent, and the subsequent "treatment" may become more dysfunctional than the episodic behavior.
2. Were the target behavior to continue, it would clearly damage the child or those in his environment. For example, a child who continually responds to anger with violent physical attacks on his siblings, his parents, or even household furniture must learn new ways of dealing with his anger.
3. The target behavior is interfering with the child's adaptation and functional development, for example, when the child persists in infantile or excessively dependent behavior.

A further criterion, of course, would be that functional behaviors occur often enough. If a necessary behavior is absent from a child's repertoire, or if it occurs with insufficient frequency or intensity (such as in the withdrawn or nonspeaking child), it must be developed or shaped.

Guidelines for evaluating functional child behavior are difficult to articulate. Unfortunately, many that have been offered are to some degree culture-bound, or may reflect a college-educated, middle- to upper-class bias (see, for example, Maslow, 1954, and Erikson, 1963).

However, recognizing these limitations, and recognizing that a child's behavior develops over time, it is possible from such sources and others to distill a limited framework for evaluating not only the behavior of a child, but also the learning experiences provided by parents (and others) that are major factors in shaping the child's behavior:

1. Is the child able to assess his environment and make choices that bring about reinforcement?
2. Is the child able to derive pleasure from interaction with people in his environment in a way that is not injurious to himself or to others?
3. Does the child comfortably take pleasure from the genuine expressions of affection from others, and can he display or express affection selectively to those whom he likes or loves?

4. Is the child spontaneous in much of his behavior, and is his behavior congruent with his feelings?

5. Is the child able to accept the responsibility for the outcome of his behavior, whether positive or negative, and alter his subsequent behavior accordingly if necessary?

6. Does the child take satisfaction from accomplishing tasks?

7. Does the child seem willing to take reasonable risks in order to gain satisfactions for himself and for others?

8. Does the child seem to understand the expectations for his behavior of those around him and appropriately respond to those that are reasonable?

9. Can the child express himself effectively when he feels his rights are being violated, and take reasonable actions to defend his rights?

Most children (and probably most adults as well) would fall short of optimum functioning as judged by these criteria. They are ideals, however, that many parents would generally support for their children. What factors, then, within a family bring about problems, and limit the child's ability to achieve an optimum level of social behavior? The possible reasons are legion, but four common sources of problem behavior follow.

First: Much of the subtle behavior of children is learned through modeling. Unfortunately, children often model their parents' dysfunctional behaviors as much as they do their functional behaviors. Thus, learned dysfunctional behavior can be transferred from generation to generation. There may also be a scarcity of positive behaviors modeled by the parents.

Second: As noted earlier in this chapter, parents often reinforce the dysfunctional behavior of their children. As an example, they may well "give in" to tantrum behavior or whining behavior "just to shut them up," and thus reinforce the very behavior they would like to extinguish.

Third: Parents may ignore functional behavior and attend only to undesirable behavior; punishment thus becomes the major vehicle of parent-child communication. If no alternative behavior is taught and reinforced, the child learns how to avoid punishment rather than how to achieve reinforcement. He may well become evasive, his behavior may become incongruous with his feelings, and, as a result of respondent learning, his attitudes and responses to his parents (and, by generalization, to other potential dispensers of punishment) may become colored by fear, anxiety, or hostility.

Fourth: Parents may not know or understand the typical behaviors, needs, and problems of children, as well as effective positive means of socializing their children. They may also respond to conflicting points of view of child management. As a result, they may either withdraw from presenting clear contingencies for their children's behavior, or they may act in an inconsistent manner, thereby confusing their children and failing to provide them with clear, consistent, reinforced directions for their behavior. Sometimes, when these dysfunctional parental patterns occur, problems may be manifested outside the home or in other aspects of the child's behavior (as discussed in other chapters in this section), such as school behavior, antisocial behavior, self-care problems, or severely disturbed behavior. However, they are most often reported to social workers in the reciprocal relationships between parents and children in their own homes. These problems are described by parents in many forms, such as:

"The child won't 'behave,' he won't mind, is disobedient and negative, and he won't go to bed when we tell him or eat his food."

"The child is destructive, he hits me and his siblings, he calls us dirty names, he destroys our furniture."

"The child is sloppy, he doesn't wash, dress properly, or brush his teeth. His room is a mess."

"The child is constantly demanding things from me. He's under my feet all the time, wanting things. He's always whining."

"He's got to have things his own way, or he'll cry or have a temper tantrum."

"He just seems afraid of me."

With relatively few exceptions, such problems reflect difficulties in reciprocal reinforcement patterns between children and their parents. The behavior of each, to a greater or lesser extent, reflects the contingencies provided by the other. The role of the social worker, along with the family, is to discern these patterns of reciprocal control and alter them.

Although the problems listed above are the types of problems most often described by parents seeking help, they are obviously biased in the direction of parents' complaints, or at least, concerns, about the behavior of their children. It is a rare occurrence for young children to seek help about the unacceptable behavior of their parents. Another dimension, then, of parent-child problems, is the dysfunctional behavior patterns of parents, which may be a response to the child's aversive behavior or a product of other influences that reinforce the dysfunctional behavior patterns of parents (e.g., grandparents reinforcing their adult children for stern methods of child "discipline"), or simply lack of knowledge or information about the basics of being a good parent. In some situations, the child's behavior may be appropriate, but the parents' behavior inappropriate. An extreme example of this is child battering. Common patterns of dysfunctional parental behavior include excessive demands for behavior not in the child's repertoire, lack of attention to the child's needs, inconsistent reinforcement, or excessive use of aversive stimuli to control the child's behavior. As in most close interpersonal relationships, the problems are reciprocal, and although either the parent or child may clearly be suffering more, or exhibiting more problem behavior, the social worker's focus will probably be on modifying the behaviors of both.

Interventive Strategies

The trend in the application of behavior modification to parent-child problems is to move from the professionals to the parents as mediators, and from the professional's office to the family's home as the site of intervention. This shift in emphasis tends to diminish the artificiality of office-based attempts by a professional to alter those behaviors that occur much more often in another environment under different contingencies. This avoids difficulties in generalizing any newly learned behavior. Home-based behavior modification can affect behavior over much longer periods of time than office sessions. It also provides a more reliable vehicle for observing the initial problem and its change over time. A comprehensive review of home-based procedures is presented by Berkowitz and Graziano (1972).

The first three interventive strategies described in this chapter have as their goal the facilitation of parental modification of their own behavior and that of their children. The final interventive strategy is presented as an alternative for those situations in which, for one reason or another, contingencies provided outside the family must be called upon to alter the child's behavior. Examples of the following approaches are described:

1. modification of parental contingencies through office and laboratory guidance;
2. group parent training and preventive programs;
3. guidance of parents' mediation in their own homes;
4. direct mediation of the child's behavior by the professional helper.

1. MODIFICATION OF PARENTAL CONTINGENCIES THROUGH OFFICE AND LABORATORY GUIDANCE

The intent of these procedures is to modify parental behaviors in a laboratory or office setting so that parents, in turn, alter the contingencies of their children's dysfunctional behaviors in their homes.

One of the prototypes of such an approach was reported by Williams in 1959. He described training parents, in a series of office visits, how to respond to their children's temper tantrums. They were made aware of how their previous behavior may have served to reinforce these tantrums, and they were taught how to discontinue such social reinforcement. The length and incidence of temper tantrums as recorded by the parents subsequently decreased dramatically.

Straughan (1964) was one of the earliest investigators to report the deliberate use of the investigator interacting with a child in a playroom as a model for the parent. Although instructions to, and modeling for, parents are often sufficient to improve significantly the parents' interaction with their children, more complex procedures may be called for with many problems (Patterson, 1971). Some problems require carefully supervised training of parents in procedures designed to modify their children's behavior.

Studies reported by Martin (1967) and by Kaswan, Love, and Rodnick (1968) focused on training parents in an important aspect of parental effectiveness; that is, carefully attending to their own and their children's behavior. Often parents seem unaware of their children's specific behaviors, both desired and undesired, and also seem insensitive to their own behavior and how it might affect their children. Martin's training programs helped parents attend to their children's and their own significant behavior. This attention resulted in the improved behavior of the children both in the laboratory and in the classroom as subsequently assessed by the children's teachers. Lindsley (1966), also recognizing that parents are often vague both in their descriptions of their children's dysfunctional behaviors as well as in their expectations of such behavior, placed considerable emphasis on teaching parents to observe—or "pinpoint"—the specific behaviors that were to be changed. He also expected parents to keep detailed records of the occurrences of these pinpointed behaviors. He found that the act of pinpointing the behaviors and then counting them probably served as an aversive consequence for the child, which, by itself, significantly changed the frequency of the target behavior in the desired direction in 20 percent of the cases studied. Such an approach, of course, requires that parents be both able and motivated to maintain such records. Patterson (1971) observed that while such procedures are desirable and effective, some parents experience difficulty in following through with them. His clinic assists such families (and reinforces their efforts) through such procedures as having staff members call parents daily to prompt recording and reinforce it when it is done.

Beyond teaching parents to observe, pinpoint, and record their own and their children's behavior, parents may have to be trained to reinforce desired behavior effectively. Bernal, Duryee, Pruett, and Burns (1968), for example, carefully observed the interaction between a mother and her eight-year-old son in a laboratory and used these observations to instruct the mother on more effective reinforcement contingencies than those previously used. The presenting problems were the boy's temper tantrums, aggressiveness, and bizarre verbal behavior. Based on their observations, they taught the mother to give fewer verbal responses to the boy in general and to "selectively ignore" the boy's provocative behavior, which ranged from sulking to physical attacks. The goal was to help the mother make more careful discriminations about which behaviors should be responded to, and which ignored. Furthermore, the mother was taught to pair certain cues (especially frowning, an angry voice, and orders to stop) with physical punishment, thus developing some conditioned negative reinforcers. If her anger and orders to stop were not followed by the boy's terminating the undesired behavior, she was to spank him. The rationale was that these conditioned negative reinforcers alone, if successfully paired with spanking, would ultimately serve to terminate unwanted behavior. Videotapes were made of the mother's pre-intervention sessions with her son, and these were shown to the mother along with videotapes of subsequent sessions. She was helped to observe how her own actions were related to her son's inappropriate behaviors. In sessions with her son, a brief tone, which was audible in the playroom, was sounded whenever the boy was observed to be behaving in an abusive manner. The buzzer served as a cue for the mother to emit one of her conditioned negative reinforcers. After each training session, the mother herself was reinforced by the trainer for making the appropriate responses. After only nine such sessions, there was significant improvement in the child's behavior.

A somewhat similar method was utilized in a study reported by Wahler *et al.* (1965). In this project, the authors observed interactions between mother and child from two observation rooms adjoining a clinic playroom. Prior to these sessions, the mother (apparently without the father and siblings) was instructed to play with her child just as she might if she were home. While the mother attempted to do this, two observers working in separate observation rooms recorded both the child's and the mother's behavior. From these observations, four classes of behavior were listed:

1. the child's dysfunctional behaviors based upon similarities between the observed behavior and the problem behaviors at home previously reported by the child's parents (e.g., commanding behavior);
2. the child's behaviors that were incompatible with the deviant behavior (e.g., cooperative play);
3. the mother's ways of reacting to her child's deviant behavior (e.g., compliance with the child's inappropriate demands);

4. the mother's ways of reacting to those of her child's behaviors that were incompatible with the deviant behavior (e.g., ignoring belligerent demands and playing with the child when the child is not attempting to control).

Interventive strategies become a logical extension of such observations. After the procedure described above, Wahler *et al.* (1965) proceeded to coach the mother, who was again under direct observation in the playroom, to reinforce desired behavior and (generally) ignore undesired behaviors. Following the accumulation of baseline data on both desired and undesired behaviors in the initial sessions, the mother was provided with instructions on how to react to her child's behavior in subsequent sessions. To aid her, signal lights were flashed on to provide cues to her as to when to reinforce her child's behavior and when to ignore it.

As the sessions progressed, the function of the light cues was changed to reinforce the mother's appropriate responses. In these sessions, the mother was asked to observe her child's behavior and respond appropriately without the "coaching" of the cue lights. Now the lights were cued to provide instant feedback to the mother concerning her correct and incorrect responses to her child's behavior, thus reinforcing the mother's own appropriate responses. In general, the goal of the training sessions was to diminish the mother's reinforcement of her child's undesired behavior, and increase her reinforcement of the predetermined incompatible, desired behaviors. Thus, assuming the mother was a powerful source of reinforcement for the child, undesirable behaviors would be weakened as a result of both extinction and the reinforcement of desired behaviors incompatible with the dysfunctional behavior.

To aid the mother in making these discriminations, she was shown the baseline data by the observers, who explained them to her in detail. They also provided numerous examples of both the undesirable behavior and the incompatible behavior. She was told that in subsequent sessions she would reinforce the incompatible behaviors but ignore the undesired behavior. (In one case, because of the resistance of the child's dysfunctional behavior to extinction, time out procedures had to be added.) The signal light was described as an aid in carrying out the instructions. Unless the light was lit, she was to sit in a chair reading a book and so on, but avoid looking at or talking with the child. The observers would only flash the light immediately following an incompatible behavior.

As soon as the data collected by the observers suggested that the mother was responding appropriately to the observers' light cues, she was directed in subsequent sessions to make her own decisions to respond to or ignore her child's behaviors. The light would now be used to indicate when she made a correct decision.

2. GROUP PARENT TRAINING AND PREVENTIVE PROGRAMS

Most of the reports of behavior modification programs reflect work with either a single family or, at most, a few families. More and more investigators are describing group programs involving large numbers of families. The cost benefits of such an approach are obvious.

Walder and his associates (Walder *et al.*, 1966, 1967a, 1967b, 1967c, 1971) have reported extensively on a comprehensive fifteen-week training program for parents that prepares them to understand family behavior better and apply operant reinforcement independently to complex family interactions. Parents of children bearing various psychiatric labels and exhibiting a wide range of problem behaviors were included.

The training program required each family to enter into a contract that stipulated the expectations for their participation in the program. Each family would then attend a series of weekly group meetings with several other families. At these sessions, the families were taught basic concepts of human behavior from a learning theory perspective as well as basic concepts of behavior modification. The instruction included lectures, assigned readings, written homework, films, role playing, modeling, and discussions.

In addition to group sessions, each family was also seen separately by a "therapist-consultant" to discuss the application of the general principles provided in the group sessions to their specific family situations. Parents were held responsible for developing behavior programs for their children at home by identifying, observing, recording, and modifying problem behavior. Furthermore, they were encouraged to apply these procedures independently as any new problems emerged in the future, thus emphasizing the preventive as well as the therapeutic aspects of the program. To demonstrate, as well as reinforce, the family change resulting from the program, Walder carried out a series of "before" and "after" tests with the parents using videotapes of family interactions as well as standard personality tests.

To reinforce parental involvement further, Walder used a variety of contingencies with the families including "debits" for incomplete homework that resulted in the parents' losing money from previously written checks, coffee socials with other families and staff, and home visits by the staff.

Ray (1965), Wahler (1965), and Lindsley (1966) have also reported on group programs to educate parents to act as more or less independent behavior modifiers of their children's (and their own) behaviors. Ray (1965) reported on observing mothers interacting with children exhibiting serious behavior problems in their own homes during twelve 20-

minute baseline sessions. The mothers were then seen together for five group sessions, during which programmed instruction on behavior principles and reinforcement concepts for children were presented. After these sessions were completed, the mothers and their children were again observed in their homes for twelve sessions. The changes in the interactions were significant, especially in the increase in the children's nonaversive approaches to their mothers, the increase in the mothers' positive responses to their approaches, and the general increase in the mothers' use of positive approaches to their children.

Lindsley (1966) reported on a unique program that focused on the role of fathers as behavior modifiers in contrast to the far more common emphasis on mothers. In a preliminary report on a group of 24 fathers of retarded children, nine were able to pinpoint a problem behavior exhibited by their children and initiate contingencies for its modification (or, in Lindsley's words, "consequate" it). Lindsley reported that as a result of the fathers' pinpointing, recording, and "consequating" dysfunctional behaviors, the majority were able to change the undesired behavior successfully. Furthermore, several of these fathers later organized other self-help parents groups to teach and jointly plan behavior change programs for their retarded children.

Patterson (1971) describes a program, which he conducted, that included home and school observations as well as group parent training. Candidates for the program collected two weeks of baseline data based on observations of family interactions. The parents then completed a programmed text on social learning theory (Patterson & Gullion, 1968). Once this assignment had been carried out, a member of Patterson's staff spent an hour with the family to help pinpoint one or two of the children's problem behaviors and establish a schedule for the parents to observe the pinpointed behavior systematically. Staff members then called the parents daily to encourage the observations and reinforce them when they occurred. Once the parents had collected several days' worth of consistently good data, they were reinforced by admission to the parents group.

This group was composed of three to five families, at least one of which had a child exhibiting antisocial behavior. At the group sessions, each parent was allotted 30 minutes (a timing device provided the necessary "stimulus" control) to present to the group his current data on his intervention program, describe the program, and discuss any management problems. In the rare situation in which parents had no data for the session, their behavior was negatively reinforced by having to present their material last. The group examined the data and responded to them and to the problems presented. They also participated in planning interventions, evaluating progress, and suggesting modification of ongoing intervention strategies.

Staff members again carried out home observations after four weeks of group membership, and, again after eight weeks. If, after four weeks, progress was apparent, parents "earned" the right to have staff begin school-based interventions, if such interventions were necessary. Arrangements were made to observe the child at school and collect baseline data on school behavior. Plans for the modification of any school problems were also initiated.

Families were followed up systematically six months after the school, home, and group programs were terminated. Patterson indicates that the data collected thus far suggest that these are "promising procedures."

Programs such as those described above illustrate the potential behavior modification might offer to social workers as an underpinning for large-scale preventive programs. In a sense, most of the parent-child behavior modification programs involve the prevention of future problems in that parents are taught practical and effective principles they might use in their future interactions with their children. Thus, not only can current problems be handled, but future problems can also be avoided. Should problems arise again, the parents are equipped with the basic principles for understanding and modifying undesirable behavior.

It would, of course, be preferable to teach such principles before problems arise. Unfortunately, our society provides no formal training for the vast majority of its citizens to be effective parents. A logical setting for this sort of education (which might include not only familiarity with the principles of being an effective parent, but also an exploration of the reciprocal rights and responsibilities of parents and children) would seem to be the public schools. Public education has already been assigned the responsibility of taking over many of the increasingly complex socialization responsibilities—such as sex education and personal hygiene—that were traditionally in the domain of the family.

Knowledge about how to be an effective parent is not innate. The formal education in social learning principles would supplement that acquired, often haphazardly, from observations of one's own parents, who may or may not provide effective models for successful social behavior.

Obviously, such programs can proceed at many levels, from programs developed in public and private agencies to programs formally included in the curricula of high schools. For example, pupils in the seventh, eighth, and ninth grades could be offered a series of progressively more complex courses on basic principles and issues of human behavior, concluding with specific applications of behavior modification to problems that could develop in families. Field observation, and actual experience in the application of such principles, could be made available in infant nurseries, obstetric clinics, pre-schools, and grammar schools. Children can be taught to anticipate and avoid problems, and how to apply their knowledge in resolving them should they occur.

3. GUIDANCE OF PARENTS' MEDIATION IN THEIR OWN HOMES

The thrust of many recent reports about behavior modification of parent-child problems—especially those focusing on younger children—is to carry out the assessment as well as the intervention in the child's own home:

> It seems likely that some families . . . will find that training in an interview, laboratory or group situation will be ineffective, simply because the procedures are not systematic enough to control their behavior or because the relevant reinforcing contingencies (for parent and child), cannot be properly presented. The necessity for additional precision in training for such families is provided by having the behavior modifier go into the home and carry out the training program in that setting [Patterson, 1971, p. 756].

A number of such programs have been reported. For example, in a case presented by Hawkins *et al.* (1966), home observations of a child described as extremely difficult to manage or control revealed nine specific behaviors that were called, generically, "objectionable." These included the child's:

1. biting his own shirt or arm;
2. sticking out his tongue;
3. kicking or hitting himself, others, or objects;
4. calling someone or something a derogatory name;
5. removing or threatening to remove his clothing;
6. saying "No!" loudly and vigorously;
7. threatening to damage objects or persons;
8. throwing objects;
9. pushing his sister.

The undesirable behavior of a child previously diagnosed by a psychiatrist as an "immature brain damaged child with a superimposed neurosis [and] seriously disturbed" was redefined after a period of observation by O'Leary, O'Leary, and Becker (1967) as kicking, hitting, pushing, and throwing objects at his brother. This behavioral description provided specific targets for change, as well as minimized negative effects of labeling.

Direct observations of the child in his own environment can facilitate the assessment of the stimulus condition that seems to be associated with the undesirable behavior, both of the child and the parents. For example, Hawkins *et al.* (1966) noted on a home visit that the undesirable behavior of the child seemed to be reinforced by his mother's attention. When the child misbehaved, the mother would attempt to explain why his behavior was wrong, and would then try to distract him with toys or food.

Such procedures generally tended to reinforce the related behavior. Occasionally the child would be punished by the mother, who would take away a misused toy or object only to be quickly persuaded by him to give it back.

Similarly, the home observation reported by Zeilberger, Sampen, and Sloane (1968) showed that the reported objectionable behavior (defined as screaming, fighting, disobeying, and bossing other children) of a four-year-old boy was often reinforced by excessive attention from his mother, who was inconsistent in applying aversive consequences to these behaviors. She was also quite unclear to her son about the contingencies between the undesired behavior and her punishments, offering instead long, complex explanations of the punishments to him (both parents were college graduates).

Many of the home-based programs such as those above make use of outside observers to observe, define, and record parent-child interactions. Others, however, emphasize teaching parents to attend to, and accurately observe, their child's target behavior (Walder et al., 1967; Patterson et al., 1968; Thorne et al., 1966). These programs also devote considerable time to teaching the parents, either in their own home or in the office, the basic principles of behavior modification. Formal seminars for parents (Walder et al., 1967) and programmed texts (Patterson et al., 1967, 1968) are also sometimes used to facilitate the parents' subsequent functioning as effective mediators of their children's behaviors in their own homes.

Home-based programs involving a variety of problem behaviors (thus far, however, largely limited to pre-adolescents) and approaches have been reported. Peine (1969) describes a series of six one-hour home sessions with the parents of a three-year-old boy labeled autistic who had had a series of grand mal seizures. Prior to intervention, the child would scream and cry up to fourteen hours a day. Moreover, he was highly aggressive in his interaction with others, often biting them as well as himself. The parents were taught to observe and record the boy's undesired behavior, and to use both time-out procedures and attention as contingencies for his behavior. Improved behavior was maintained through a six-month follow-up.

Hawkins et al. (1966) used a coaching approach with a mother to modify the behavior of her young son. The target behaviors included the boy's tantrums, hitting himself, destroying his clothes, and general belligerence.

After trained observers collected baseline data of the boy's "objectionable behavior," an intervention period was begun in which the mother was taught to respond to three signals which were to be given to her by observers in the home in response to her child's behavior. One signal meant that the mother was to stop an objectionable behavior. A second signal indicated that the child should be put into his room with his playthings removed (time out). The third signal indicated that the mother was to notice her child's desirable behavior, praise him, and embrace him. Outside of these sessions, the mother was instructed to behave in her usual way.

After six of these signaled treatment sessions, a second baseline was recorded: the frequency of undesired behaviors seemed stable, and the contingencies operating during the first baseline period were re-instituted. The mother was instructed to interact with her child as she had before intervention. When the second baseline period was completed, the signaling procedure was re-introduced for six additional sessions, with the exception that the third "reinforcement" signals were dropped. No observations or contacts were then made with the family for 24 days. On follow-up in three 1-hour sessions, observers recorded the child's behavior, and the mother was told to use any procedures she felt appropriate to deal with the child's behavior. Data obtained during the follow-up showed that the improvements in the child's behavior, noted during the second baselining, had continued. Furthermore, the mother reported that her child was now much better behaved and less demanding than previously. From the data summarized below in Figure 21.1, it would appear

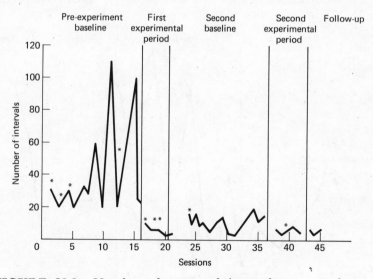

FIGURE 21.1. Number of 10-second intervals, per one-hour session, in which objectionable behaviors occurred. Asterisks indicate sessions in which reliability was tested.
Source: R. P. Hawkins, R. F. Peterson, E. Schweid, and S. W. Bijou, "Behavior Therapy in the Home: Amelioration of Problem Parent-Child Relations with the Parent in a Therapeutic Role," *Journal of Experimental Child Psychology,* 1966, vol. 4, p. 105.

that the mother's changed patterns of responding to her child had been retained and had, indeed, generalized from the "signaled" treatment hours, to the other hours of the day.

Zeilberger, Sampen, and Sloane (1968) worked with both parents (although, as in most home-based programs, the mother appeared to be the principal mediator) of a four-year-old boy whose typical behaviors included bossing of other children, screaming, fighting, and general "negativism." Two observers worked with the parents in their home, focusing on, and reporting, the boy's interaction with his mother. The parents were trained to reinforce the boy differentially by ignoring certain undesired behaviors, instituting time-out procedures for others, and pairing food and toys with social reinforcement of desirable behavior. The results of the application of these contingencies (see Figure 21.2 below) was a significant increase in the percentage of parental instructions the boy followed, from an average of 30 percent in the baseline period to 78 percent in the final sessions of the intervention. The observers initiated a return to baseline conditions to impress on the parents that, to a large extent, their child's behavior was influenced by the contingencies the parents—the mother in particular—provided.

O'Leary, O'Leary, and Becker (1967) demonstrated that using the parents as mediators in the home can effectively modify reciprocal be-

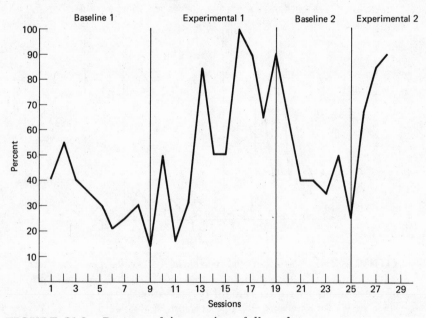

FIGURE 21.2. Percent of instructions followed.
Source: J. Zeilberger, S. E. Sampen, and H. N. Sloane, Jr., "Modification of a Child's Problem Behaviors in the Home with the Mother as Therapist," *Journal of Applied Behavior Analysis,* 1968, vol. 1, p. 49.

havior problems between siblings. In the case described, a six-year-old boy was reported to be destructive, hyperactive, and subject to temper tantrums and running away from home. He was also in constant conflict with his three-year-old brother. Home observations led to the conclusion that parental attention to the children was largely contingent upon loud, destructive fights between the boys. The parents were taught to use time-out procedures to decrease the fights, but were encouraged to emphasize the use of social and tangible reinforcers to increase cooperative play between the boys. Although there was no reported follow-up, at the end of the intervention the observers noted both an increase in positive interaction between the boys and a decrease in their mutually destructive interactions.

Figure 21.3 shows the progress of the intervention as measured by the percentage of cooperative behavior divided by deviant and cooperative behavior. The chart covers four phases:

1. a baseline observation period;
2. an intervention period in which the trained mediator provided food reinforcers (M&M's) and, later, a token system for cooperative responses;
3. a second baseline period, in which the mediator was not present, but observations continued to demonstrate the impact of planned contingencies on the child's behavior;
4. a second intervention period, in which the mother was trained to mediate the token system as well as a time-out system for unacceptable behaviors.

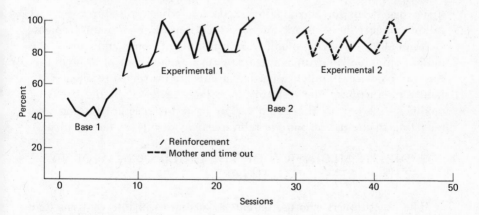

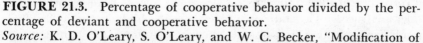

FIGURE 21.3. Percentage of cooperative behavior divided by the percentage of deviant and cooperative behavior.
Source: K. D. O'Leary, S. O'Leary, and W. C. Becker, "Modification of a Deviant Sibling Interaction Pattern in the Home," *Behaviour Research and Therapy,* 1967, vol. 5, p. 115.

While there are differences in the manner in which these and other home-based programs are carried out (such as using parents versus outsiders as observers and recorders of the children's behaviors), there are some marked similarities in the reports, and some common problems. Emphasis is generally placed on both reducing the often unnoticed reinforcement of undesired behaviors, and teaching parents to notice and provide reinforcement for desirable behavior. Several programs utilize token systems or other tangible reinforcements to supplement the parent's social reinforcement, since many children who chronically exhibit unacceptable behavior seem unresponsive to their parents' putative social reinforcers (Patterson *et al.*, 1967; Patterson, 1971; Wahler, 1967). The ineffectiveness of parental efforts at social reinforcement can tend to extinguish their efforts. Therefore, Patterson (1971) recommends the use of more potent reinforcers—such as a strong token system—by the parents early in intervention programs to reinforce the parents' efforts as well as changes in the child's behavior. Furthermore, pairing the behavior of the parent with the provision of nonsocial reinforcers ultimately enhances the parents' effectiveness as social reinforcers.

One of the recurrent problems in the modification of children's behaviors occurs at the very time that their behavior seems to be responding to the interventive procedures. Zeilberger *et al.* (1968) and Patterson (1971) noted that once the child's behavior begins to respond to the contingencies that the parents are deliberately providing, and the parents are directed to fade out these procedures slowly, allowing them to be brought under the natural social contingencies provided in family life, the parents often begin to take the modified behaviors for granted and "forget to reinforce them." To avoid this problem, Patterson (1971) offers some suggestions for encouraging successful fading procedures, such as calling parents daily to ask about the current stage of reinforcement. Occasionally a behavior modifier returns to the home and guides the mother's interaction with her child with a remote-control "bug-in-the-ear" radio device. In other cases, the parents are instructed to tape-record family interactions. The recordings are later reviewed in the behavior modifier's office with the parents as a basis for specific training and modeling in the use of positive reinforcement during its fading phase.

4. DIRECT MEDIATION OF THE CHILD'S BEHAVIOR BY THE PROFESSIONAL HELPER

The practitioners who use parents as mediators in interventions that involve parent-child problems (as described above) have reported considerable success. Generally, improvements in children's behaviors that result from changes in parental behaviors reinforce the parents' new behaviors. Unfortunately, there are many parents who are insufficiently motivated to change their behaviors toward their children. There are parents, for example, who see the social worker, ostensibly to change their children's behavior, only because a school, court, or other agency requires it. They may consider their child's behavior unimportant, or may not perceive their child's behavior as aversive, and thus may have little interest in having their children change. Some parents may, indeed, be very much reinforced by their child's behavior, even when it is considered "deviant" or unacceptable by others, and may consider the *termination* of such behaviors as aversive.

Such parents have long posed a frustrating problem for social workers and others concerned with the welfare of children. Various approaches have been tried with parents who seem inaccessible to the usual behavior modification strategies (Patterson *et al.*, 1968; Patterson & Reid, 1970; Patterson, 1971) such as making money, appointments with hairdressers, and driving lessons available to parents contingent on their carrying out reinforcement programs for their child's problem behaviors. Such strategies may have limited success, however, since long-lasting changes in a child's behavior are probably dependent on more or less enduring changes of the contingencies within the family system. Behavior modifiers must always address themselves to what will sustain any new desirable behaviors once the formal intervention procedure is terminated.

One possibility—and sometimes the only one available—is to attempt to modify the child's behavior through procedures outside the home, using mediators other than the parents, with the goal that the child be taught new behaviors that will be more reinforcing to the parents than their previous behaviors. The child's new behavior, then, will reinforce those parental behaviors that sustain the new behavior.

There are, of course, many mediators outside the family who may be able to bring about changed behavior in a child. Other relatives, teachers, "Big Brothers," or other volunteers can be enlisted, supervised, and reinforced for their efforts by the social worker. Another option, of course, is for the social worker or other professional or paraprofessional to act as mediator.

The case illustration that follows presents a situation in which the professional helper contracts with a family to bring about specific changes in a child's disturbing behavior outside the family. As a result of these efforts, one is hopeful that the child's behavior has been changed sufficiently so that the parents' behavior toward him will also change and continue to reinforce the new behaviors.

Case Illustration

A case reported by Ayllon and Skuban (1973) illustrates the use of a mediator outside a family to bring about significant changes in those behaviors of the child that had been problems in the parent-child relationship. Of perhaps greater interest, it describes a treatment intervention that emphasizes the professional's accountability to the recipient of intervention services. The intervention was built around a contract between the worker and the family requesting help. The goals of treatment were thus made quite explicit, avoiding any misunderstanding about what the parents could expect, and what the social worker did expect, to be the results of the contracted services.

The focus of intervention was the behavior of Mike, an eight-year-old boy living with his mother, stepfather, and 2½-year-old sister in a middle-income apartment complex.

Mike's mother described him as having always been "bad" and "different" from other children. She considered him extremely difficult to manage, especially in public places where she was frequently embarrassed by his behavior. He responded to most of his mother's requests with noncompliance and tantrums. The parents had attempted, unsuccessfully, to control Mike by putting him in the bathroom, withholding privileges, hitting him, and calling him names.

The mother described life with Mike as "hell on earth." He was expelled from kindergarten as a result of his uncontrollable behavior. When tested by a psychologist he showed serious problems in visual perception and motor coordination. His EEG patterns showed little that was unusual, but neurological examinations suggested some brain damage. A psychologist's evaluation stated:

> Within the first hour he changed from a helpless-looking child who seemed unable to speak, to a wild tornado screaming and grabbing all the loose things he could find in the room and throwing them on the floor . . . Because of his uncontrollable behavior in a demanding test situation, all results indicate that Mike is functioning at a severely retarded level. There were several. instances of echolalic speech patterns and almost constant screaming at a temper-tantrum level. The manipulativeness of these outbursts was evident from the first; there were no tears and there was no affect behind the screams [Ayllon and Skuban, 1973, p. 21].

Mike's parents decided to seek help in a program directed by Dr. Ayllon when their application for Mike to enter a special school program was turned down on the basis of the psychologist's report.

As a first step in the treatment process, Mike's behavior in relating to adults was observed in an empty classroom. The observer noted that Mike responded with loud crying whenever the observer did not do exactly what Mike said he wanted. Also, Mike responded to requests with tantrums. It appeared to the observer and the author that these responses were Mike's attempts to control adults.

Mike's behavior problems were therefore pinpointed as a low incidence of following instructions, and a high incidence of engaging in tantrums. Both behaviors were subsequently explicitly defined, and the

baseline frequency of following directions and the frequency and duration of temper tantrums were recorded in observation sessions.

Based on the parent's requests, and these observations of Mike's
behavior, which seemed at that point beyond the control of the parents,
a written treatment contract was negotiated between the parents and
those who agreed to attempt to modify Mike's problem behaviors. The
contract specified the ultimate goal of the interventions, which was to
equip Mike with those social and academic behaviors necessary for admission to school. More explicitly, the contract stated that the interventions agreed to in the contract would, within 35 days, reduce Mike's
tantrum behaviors from the baseline of 46 percent to a posttreatment
level of 5 percent, and increase his rate of following adult requests from
a baseline rate of 59 percent of the time to more than 80 percent. These
would be tested in a session with the parents at the conclusion of the
program. If the contracted gains were fully achieved, the mediator would
receive his full, specified fee. If they were not achieved, the parents would
pay only two-thirds of the fee.

The full contract (Ayllon, 1973, pp. 22–23) is reproduced below by
permission of Teodoro Ayllon.

A CONTINGENCY CONTRACT FOR THERAPY

I. Overview of problem and therapeutic program

The overall objective of this therapeutic program is to develop and
stabilize Mike's behavior patterns so that he may be considered for admission
to school this fall. In general, this will involve strengthening some requisite
behaviors such as following commands from an adult, and eliminating
others, such as the screaming and tantruming that accompany most of his
refusals to follow instructions.

Mike has a discouraging behavior history for most teachers to consider
working with. Because his characteristic reaction to requests is to throw
tantrums, he is considered "untestable" by standard psychological means.
This does not necessarily mean that he cannot do the items on a test, but
rather that he has little or no control over his own behavior. His uncoopera-
tiveness quickly discourages most people from making much of an effort
to work with him. What is clearly needed is an intensive rehabilitation
program designed to enable Mike to build patterns of self-control which
would lead to the elimination or drastic reduction of his disruptive behavior.
This, in turn, would open other possibilities for developing Mike's potential,
that is, the avenues which are blocked by his unmanageable behavior.

The overall goal of this 8-week program will be the development of
self-control with its reciprocal outcome of decreasing or eliminating tantrums and disruptive behaviors. Implementation of this program will

require that the child and his trainer engage in such activities as trips to the zoo, museums, parks, movies, swimming pools, shopping centers, supermarkets and so on, as well as having lunch and snacks together. These settings are included to expose Mike to a maximal number of normal situations where expectations of a standard of conduct are imposed by the setting itself.

As much as possible, the techniques used in the day program will be designed with the ultimate objective of utilization in the home. An attempt will be made to see that procedures used in the program are transferred to home management at the termination of treatment. The therapist will give instructions weekly to the parents by phone to insure that efforts both at home and in rehabilitation do not conflict.

II. Behavioral objectives of therapy

1. The objective of the therapeutic program is to teach Mike to comply with between 80–100 percent of the verbal commands given to him by an adult (s). Compliance will be defined as Mike's beginning to perform the behavior specified by the command within 15 seconds after it has been stated and then completing the specified task.

2. In addition, we intend to eliminate or drastically reduce Mike's excessive screaming and tantruming. The goal is not to tantrum more frequently than once out of 30 commands and for no longer than 1 minute at a time.

3. Evaluation of treatment outcome: The decision as to the attainment of these specific objectives will rest upon Mike's performance during a 30-minute test session to be conducted in a classroom situation. At this session the therapist, the parents and an additional person will make 10 verbal requests each of Mike, for a total of 30 verbal requests. Mike must comply with 80–100 percent of these requests for the program to be considered a success. In addition, he must have tantrumed not more than once, and for not more than 1 minute, during this final evaluation.

III. Time and place of therapeutic intervention

1. The therapeutic program will start on _____ and terminate on _____ . Evaluation of the effectiveness of treatment will be held on or about the termination date of the therapeutic program.

2. Location: The meeting place will be at the _____ . Session activities, however, will involve time spent elsewhere, for example, having lunch, trips to shopping centers, amusements, and other special events. If the facility is not available, some other agreeable place can be designated as meeting and base center.

3. Days of training: Therapy sessions will be scheduled 5 days per week. The specific days may vary from week to week to comply with the objectives of the program. The family will be advised of the therapy schedule 1 week in advance.

4. Hours per day: Therapeutic sessions will be scheduled for 7 hours a

day. Session time may be extended when therapeutically necessary as decided by the therapist.

5. Absences: There will be four notified absences allowed. The mother is expected to notify the therapist at least 1 hour before the scheduled therapy session. Any additional absences will require an additional fee of $10 per absence.

IV. Fees

Achievement of the behavioral objectives is expected to take 7 weeks of training from _____. This training will cost a total of _____. The monies will be disbursed in the following manner.

1. A check for two-thirds of the total amount will be given to the therapist at the beginning of therapy.

2. The balance of one-third will be paid to the therapist upon the achievement of the program objectives as specified above on about the date of termination of the program. In the event that the above objectives are not reached by this date, therapy will be discontinued and the balance will be forfeited by the therapist.

3. All expense incurred during training will be defrayed by the therapist. This will include admission to baseball games, the city zoo, swimming pools, and so on, as well as the cost of field trips, lunch, and snacks.

* * *

By my signature I do hereby attest that I have read the above proposal and agree to the conditions stated therein.

_____

Parent

_____

Supervising Therapist

_____   _____

Date   Cotherapist

Following the agreement on the contract, Mike spent approximately 210 hours over the 35 days—with a single behavioral mediator—a substantial investment of time. In order to increase the generalization of any new behaviors learned, the time was spent almost entirely in public places such as banks, supermarkets, department stores, restaurants, parks, a zoo, gas stations, shopping centers, and homes of acquaintances.

During the first phase of the program, observations and recordings were made (approximately every hour) of the number of requests Mike complied with, the number of requests precipitating tantrums, and the length of tantrums. These measures, using a variety of mechanical counters (a wrist counter, a hand counter, and two stopwatches), were used as an ongoing evaluation of the interventive procedures.

At first, the major procedure used to increase Mike's compliance with adult requests was the presentation of positive reinforcement (money), while tantrums were followed by time out from positive reinforcement. A penny or nickel, coupled with praise, was given to Mike contingent upon his complying with the mediator's request within ten seconds. Mike could use these coins either to operate pinball or vending machines, or as tokens redeemable for such privileges as access to playground equipment for a particular period of time, swimming privileges, pushing the buttons on an elevator, or even being tickled by the mediator. (The total money thus expended averaged about $2 per day, or $75 altogether for the treatment program.)

Tantrums were brought under control by a time-out procedure that involved the use of a stopwatch as a discriminative stimulus. When the stopwatch hanging around the mediator's neck was moved into a certain position, Mike understood that reinforcements were available. The stop watch was then left running until Mike engaged in a tantrum, at which time the stopwatch was conspicuously turned off, and the mediator reprimanded Mike with a firm "No." The mediator would then turn away from Mike and ignore him, unless his behavior was potentially dangerous to his environment, in which case Mike was dispassionately restrained by the mediator with a firm grip of his arm. One minute after the termination of the tantrum, Mike was told that the stopwatch was on again, and that he could once again earn coins through compliance with the mediator's requests.

As soon as a considerable improvement was noted in Mike's social behavior, that is, a decrease in tantrums and an increase in compliance with requests, attention was directed toward increasing his academic skills by reinforcing his correct responses with pennies. Target behaviors included such tasks as writing his name, counting to five, and discriminating between left and right. Mike began to see such "schooltime" tasks as a new cue for reinforcement, and sought them out from the mediator.

To strengthen changes in Mike's behavior, the mediator increased the requirements for reinforcement. For example, he was now given only praise for each of those requests complied with outside of "schooltime." However, when he received five "praises" he earned a nickel, which he could exchange for a "schooltime" session. He was also given his own counter to wear around his neck, thus modeling the mediator, and was instructed to count the "good boys" given to him.

A final phase of intervention was initiated to transfer the contingencies for Mike's behavior to the natural consequences that might be provided by Mike's parents. Praise was now used as the principal reinforcer for Mike's following directions. Contingent on receiving recurrent praise on a day's outing, Mike would intermittently be reinforced with special treats. Tantrums, when they did occasionally occur, were ignored. Mike's counter, along with most of the mediator's equipment, was no longer used. Only the mediator's wrist counter was maintained to record the frequency of praise given to Mike as a guide for the provision of treats that were given at a variable exchange rate to simulate natural contingencies more closely.

By the end of this phase, Mike was following instructions 97 percent of the time, as opposed to 59 percent at the time of assessment. His tantrums were only two percent of the amount seen at assessment. The length of tantrums—which had been as long as 33 minutes at assessment —dropped to about two minutes.

As specified in the treatment contract, a test session was held at the conclusion of the intervention. The test included giving Mike 30 requests by adults—10 from his regular mediator, 10 from an adult Mike had not previously met, and 10 from his father. The only directions given to the adults involved in the test were that they "smile and act naturally" whenever Mike followed through on their requests. The test results were gratifying to all involved. The contract specified that Mike was to follow 80 percent of the instructions presented to him. He successfully completed 97 percent. He was also not to have more than one tantrum during the test session, and that for not more than one minute. Mike did have one tantrum, but it lasted only five seconds.

The parents indicated full satisfaction that the stipulations of the contract were satisfactorily carried out, and they paid the therapist in full. Mike was subsequently admitted to a special class in a regular elementary school.

CHAPTER 22 School Behavior Problems

The experiences children have in school affect not only the knowledge they absorb in the subjects they study, but also their future approach to work and interpersonal relations. Children spend almost a quarter of their lives in school. During this time they are very much under the influence of teachers who have considerable power to shape their behavior (Blackham & Silberman, 1971). Experiences with fellow students in school can also significantly influence students' behavior and self-perceptions. But even the influence of students' peers is to some degree under the control of the teacher.

Although teachers may be very well aware of their influence on students, and although they may be committed to providing a quality education, they are also faced with problems of classroom management. This may mean accomplishing curriculum objectives while trying to maintain order in a crowded classroom. Indeed, some teachers claim they devote almost as much or more of their time to dealing with disruptive behavior, inattention, and emotional difficulties as they do to teaching. Skinner (1968) has observed that teachers tend to rely on aversive methods to deal with such problems, and that these methods have very limited success. As noted in previous chapters, procedures of aversive control often have more undesired than desired consequences. For example, the student may learn to avoid punishment or the punisher rather than modifying the problem behavior to meet the expectations of the teacher. Such common problems as truancy, tardiness, poor study habits, hostility to school and teachers, vandalism, and learning difficulties can often be traced to the preponderance of aversive procedures in teachers' approaches to students or in the school situation in general (Blackham & Silberman, 1971; Krumboltz & Krumboltz, 1972).

In his approach to school difficulties, one of the major contributions of the social worker may be to create more positive consequences for children's school experiences and to reduce the avoidable aversive elements. The social worker can help teachers use positive procedures to influence student behaviors. Such an approach requires an understanding of the pressures and limitations particular teachers may be working under, such as demands from administration and limited opportunities for individualized attention to the students. The social worker who attempts—with little understanding of teachers' working conditions—to offer simple solutions to the difficult problems of teachers is likely to have little positive effect on their behavior. Direct observation of classroom problems, along with observation of the teachers' own behavior and patterns of reinforcement and punishment, can lead both to more accurate assessment and to more acceptance of the social worker's suggestions by the teachers. Assistance in working out some of the teacher's practical classroom problems can also pave the way to a working partnership with the teacher.

Since teachers often feel the pressure of time, any procedures recommended by the social worker that can offer more efficient and effective disciplinary procedures than the teachers are already using are more likely to be used. Once the teacher has found consultation with the social worker reinforcing, the teacher may be more accepting of direction in sensitive areas (for example, having the teacher deliberately use himself as a role model for students, or modifying patterns wherein teachers identify some children as intrinsically bad rather than perceiving some of their *behavior* as bad).

Some teachers may respond to behavioral change programs in the same ways as some parents. For instance, they may be impatient to see change (as in an extinction process), and give up before the procedure has had an opportunity to work. They may also perceive any reinforcement programs, especially those using tangible reinforcers, as bribery, and refuse to take part. They may, perhaps, refuse to reinforce a desired behavior as a form of punishment for earlier behavior that was not desired. In such situations, the social worker must understand the teacher's point of view and, through a mutually reinforcing relationship, encourage the teacher to re-evaluate his approach to behavior change procedures, and persuade him to "try them and see if they're at all useful."

In many situations involving school-related problems such as truancy and school phobias, the mediator would more logically be the parents than the teachers. In such cases, the parents' pattern of behavior in relation to their children's school activities might be the target of intervention. For example, if a lonely mother cried and complained of her loneliness each morning as her child was about to leave for school, the mother's behavior might well be the logical target for intervention in the child's truancy.

Types of Behavior Included

School is, of course, a setting, not a problem per se. There are, however, a number of problems associated with optimizing learning experiences, managing classroom behavior, and intervening with students' interpersonal problems in schools that have been the subject of extensive behavior modification research and practice with both "normal" and "exceptional" children. In fact, there are few settings in which behavior modification approaches have been more often applied and tested than schools.

For example, Morrow (1971) lists the following categories of school behavior problems: "disruptive classroom behaviors (talking out, looking around, getting out of seat, roaming about, throwing things, hitting, sassing, diddling, etc.); performance in 3R subjects (reading, writing or arithmetic); performance in non-3R subjects; study habits and techniques; truancy; miscellaneous school behaviors" (p. 4). The number of reports of successful applications of behavior modification in these areas is substantial. In just one area, disruptive school behaviors, Morrow (1971) lists 74 cases of successful behavior modification procedures reported from 1950–1969.

Many factors can contribute to the educational and behavioral problems displayed by children (Blackham & Silberman, 1971). As noted previously, teachers and fellow classmates are prime reinforcers of a child's behavior in school. A teacher may have learned well the subjects she teaches but may not have learned effective procedures to see that a child learns or that his behavior is appropriate to classroom goals.

> Teachers often say, and rightly so, that they have for the most part been poorly prepared to cope with many of the student difficulties that arise in the classroom. There has been little effort made to provide teachers with useful classroom techniques which would enable them to carry out their professional teaching responsibilities in as effective a manner as possible [Klein, Hapkiewicz, & Roden, 1973, p. viii].

Many attempts to influence behavior in classrooms are aversive in nature, such as threats of punishment (e.g., being sent to the principal, or being given bad grades). Such experiences, as noted previously, can teach the child how to avoid being punished (e.g., how to cheat without being caught) rather than new, desirable skills. If punishment or ridicule are used extensively, the student might learn to pair the anxiety or embarrassment associated with one teacher or learning experience to education in general. For example, a child who has been ridiculed by his classmates or teachers for inaccuracy in doing arithmetic problems at the blackboard may subsequently approach all learning experiences in mathematics with anxiety.

While threatened or applied aversive consequences may be used to excess in trying to influence behavior in some classes, social reinforcement from teachers in their daily interaction with students may be used minimally. Based on their observations of teacher-student interaction in the primary grades, Patterson *et al.* (1969, p. 15) concluded that, "In many respects the classroom is a barren wasteland when one compares it to other, normally reinforcing interactions." Often reinforcements are limited to test results and report card grades.

A possible result of having few social reinforcers for desirable behavior is that children may learn to use various undesirable behaviors to coerce their teachers (and perhaps their peers) to respond to them. Indeed, there is much data to suggest that inappropriate classroom behavior is maintained, and perhaps taught, by teachers and peers. For example, classroom studies have shown that a considerable part of the "hyperactive" behavior of children is reinforced by teachers and peers (Ebner, 1967), and the majority of aggressive behaviors of preschool children seem to be reinforced by peers (Patterson, Littman, & Bricker, 1967).

In many situations, a child who frequently displays undesirable behaviors teaches his teachers (or parents or peers) to reinforce his undesirable behaviors (Patterson & Reid, 1969). For example, if a child lacks the skills to acquire reinforcement for desirable behavior, he might obtain attention through disruptive behavior, which he exhibits until the teacher responds, perhaps chastising, reasoning with, or cajoling the child to "behave." At that point, the child might temporarily decrease his undesirable behavior, thus negatively reinforcing the teacher for provoking the attention. Indeed, the child's and teacher's behavior may become mutually reinforcing. Thus, Ebner (1967) has observed in classroom studies that disruptive children obtain more social reinforcers than other children in their classroom. Indeed, such undesirable behaviors may be further strengthened by the observed tendency of teachers and peers (as well as parents) to *ignore* the socially desirable behaviors of children who more usually engage in undesirable behavior (Hotchkiss, 1966; Warren & Mondy, 1968; Patterson, Shaw & Ebner, 1969).

Often, there is little reinforcement of positive school performance or even school attendance, and the school experience itself may become aversive. For example, the expectations of a teacher may be excessive, or class activities may be uninteresting, irrelevant, or accompanied by competing distractions from peers.

Finally, the source of problems in school may lie outside the classroom. Parents or others may reinforce behaviors incompatible with school attendance. For example, parents may convey to their children that homework, classwork, or even formal education itself is of minimal worth in the "real world," and instead reinforce the child for other activities incompatible with his formal education.

Interventive Strategies

The problems encountered in the school setting can take many forms. Basically, however, the problems can be considered as either behavioral excesses or behavioral deficits. Behavioral excesses would be those behaviors which occur too often (getting out of seat without permission), with too much intensity (yelling), or at the wrong time or place (a child who engages in appropriate, unrestrained exuberance with peers on the playground attempting to interact with his teacher in the same way). Behavioral deficits would be those behaviors that do not occur frequently enough (not responding to teacher's questions), or with too little intensity (speaking too softly; social withdrawal). In essence, the task for the intervening agent is to decrease the undesired behaviors (excesses) and increase the desired, prosocial behaviors (deficits).

Those who have attempted to use behavior modification with school problems have used a wide variety of interventive approaches with each of these subcategories (see Klein, Hapkiewicz, & Roden, 1973; Blackham & Silberman, 1971; Benson, 1969; Sloggett, 1971; Krumboltz & Krumboltz, 1972). This chapter will touch only briefly on some of these problems by offering illustrations of interventive approaches. The school-related problems discussed are: (1) social withdrawal; (2) inadequate learning patterns; (3) talking too much or too little; (4) disruptive behavior; (5) chronic absenteeism.

1. SOCIAL WITHDRAWAL

In a busy classroom, the shy, withdrawn child may be easily overlooked. However, a child's social isolation may reflect a considerable anxiety about interpersonal relations that impedes both his educational and social development.

One common method to draw out the shy child is to use the powerful reinforcers of the shy child's peers (Blackham & Silberman, 1971). To draw the child out, classmates receive reinforcements (candy, etc.) contingent on appropriate social interaction from the shy child who, in turn, is reinforced for appropriate social interaction by the other students.

Bandura (1967) reported on the use of successive approximation by teachers in drawing out shy children. Noting that teachers sometimes actually reinforce withdrawal behavior by paying attention to shy children only when they are conspicuously withdrawn (e.g., sitting alone in a corner), Bandura suggests that the teacher can be more helpful by doing the opposite, that is, attending to the child contingent on the child's interaction with classmates. Initially, even looking at the other children would be reinforced by teacher attention; later the child would be reinforced for moving toward groups of classmates. In such procedures, the teacher may require support and assistance from the social worker.

The use of modeling procedures has also been reported to be useful in drawing out shy children. O'Conner (1969) showed a film to withdrawn children that presented a series of interactions of nursery school children in which the chief character increasingly participates in social interaction with reinforcing consequences. The children who watched the film subsequently increased their social interaction, while a control group, which did not see the film, showed no change in its behavior. In another project (Sulzer, Mayer, & Cody, 1968), classmates who tended to do well in social interactions were used as role models for those children who did not. An unsuccessful child was seated next to a successful child who was consistently praised by the teacher (by plan) for his or her good work. In this approach, "models" should be rotated so as not to create a situation in which any particular child becomes labeled by peers as "teacher's pet," thus losing his effectiveness as a role model.

2. INADEQUATE LEARNING PATTERNS

Teachers may unintentionally reinforce poor academic performance by giving individual attention to children when they are doing poor work, and more or less ignoring them when they do as expected. Zimmerman and Zimmerman (1962) reported on an effective system for teaching spelling accuracy. A child was given a spelling test and then asked to correct his spelling errors at the blackboard. The teacher did not respond to the child's errors, or make statements about being a poor speller, but praised him for words spelled correctly. When all the words on the test were correctly spelled, he was given an "A" and invited to join the teacher in an enjoyable classroom project. A somewhat similar process was used to improve the spelling of an entire class by making listening to the radio in class contingent on perfect performance on spelling tests and excusing individual students from taking spelling quizzes for the rest of the week once they had received a perfect score on a test (Lovitt, Buppy, & Blattner, 1969).

Many learning problems can, of course, be traced to children not paying attention to information given in classrooms. Teachers recognize that attention is essential to learning and exert considerable effort to encourage it. Tokens awarded on completion of classroom tasks, recorded on a card maintained by each child, have proved effective in maintaining students' attention. Wolf, Giles, and Hall (1968), for example, used a rather elaborate system for a group of low-achieving fifth- and sixth-grade children living in a poverty area. The children were given a booklet that had different colored pages marked with small boxes. Each page (and color) represented a particular reward that would be given to the child when all the boxes on that particular page had been checked. Rewards included items that could be obtained relatively quickly—such as small amounts of money, snacks, and a weekly field trip—as well as longer-range goals. As soon as the child completed an assignment, the teacher would assess the assignment and determine the number of points to be indicated in the child's book. Bonus points were given for good grades.

Whereas children with mild attention problems seem to do well with teachers who give praise contingent on the students' paying attention, students with more pronounced attention problems seem to require more tangible reinforcements such as those offered through token economies. Such procedures seem effective with school children of all ages. Younger children seem to respond best to trinkets while older children (junior high and older) seem to prefer activities or special privileges as reinforcements (Blackham & Silberman, 1971; Sloggert, 1971).

3. TALKING TOO MUCH OR TOO LITTLE

One of the socializing products of school experiences is learning how much talking—and under what circumstances—is socially functional. In many segments of Western culture, lack of verbal fluency is considered a handicap to learning, while excessive talking is disruptive to the learning of other students. Social withdrawal (discussed above) and talking too little are, of course, frequently encountered in the same child.

"Culturally deprived" children, who are often perceived as either socially withdrawn or nonverbal in classrooms, may be responding to the alien atmosphere or peculiar interpersonal characteristics of their school experience, and may require more appropriate educational experiences (Riesman, 1963; Blackham & Silberman, 1971). However, children of all economic levels who have difficulty in verbalization have been shown to respond quite well to role-playing situations, combined with reinforcements from the teacher, that encourage children to act out dramatically, rather than only to conceptualize the problems or ideas under discussion (Greenspoon, 1955; Krasner, 1962; Verplanck, 1955).

Detailed procedures for the use of role playing are provided in Shaftel and Shaftel (1967).

The teacher should particularly reinforce, through smiles and praise, those comments made by the relatively nonverbal students that have been elicited in the discussion following role playing. The teachers should planfully reinforce successive approximations of meaningful comments made by the children. Such role-playing activities may be more successful if initially removed from the classroom setting (which may be aversive to many nonverbal children), carried out in the playground, auditorium, gymnasium, and so on, and later transferred to the classroom (Blackham & Silberman, 1971).

Reinforcement by the teacher for children's use of adjectives has also shown to be effective in increasing verbal responses. This approach encourages nonverbal children to amplify and color their otherwise spartan conversations (Hart & Risley, 1968).

In a somewhat related approach, provision of materials to nonverbal children for classroom projects was made contingent on verbal interchanges with the teacher. The double reinforcements of the materials and teacher attention increased the rate of spontaneous comments from the children (Reynolds & Risley, 1968).

There are, of course, children in classrooms who talk too much rather than too little—a major problem for many teachers. Smith and Smith (1966) suggest a group approach to this problem. Each day, for at least two weeks the class members are given a 10-minute assignment that they are to do by themselves, with clear instructions that they are to be silent, and not ask any questions. During this period the teacher does not respond to any behaviors such as raised hands, lack of attention, or getting out of seats. However, if a child talks, the teacher reminds the child of the rule that he is not to talk. The teacher keeps records of the students' inappropriate talking to evaluate the effectiveness of the approach. The teacher can anticipate an increase in limit testing during these sessions. However, these behaviors will extinguish if the teacher remains consistent. Smith and Smith (1966) note that this approach leads to generalization to other situations, and that inappropriate talking can be reduced for increasingly longer periods of time.

Another group approach (Barrish, Saunders, & Wolf, 1969) is to establish teams in a class that can win certain reinforcement (a victory tag, being first in line for lunch, having free time, etc.) contingent on how infrequently team members got out of their seats or talked out of turn.

Hunter (1967) suggests an approach in which the teacher informs a student who tends to talk excessively or inappropriately that these specific behaviors are not acceptable. She also says that she will maintain a record of the frequency of inappropriate talking, which the child (but not the others in the class) will observe. This will generally reduce the inappropriate talking of the child. At the same time the teacher reinforces evidence of the child's *listening* behavior by making positive comments to the child, sending notes commenting on the child's increasing attentiveness home with the child, or otherwise reinforcing him. As the child's listening behavior becomes stronger, his talking behavior is likely to become more appropriate.

4. DISRUPTIVE BEHAVIOR

Occasional disruptive or "atypical" behavior of otherwise well-functioning children is to be expected, and may even be a characteristic of creative, experimenting childhood. Chronic disruptive behavior, however, impedes not only the learning of the disruptor, but that of the other children in the class, and is a major problem for most classroom teachers. Problems involving children who frequently disrupt classes are among the most common presented by teachers to social workers for resolution.

Some disruptive behaviors are encountered in groups of children in a classroom and can best be handled through group contingencies applied by the teacher. Sulzbacher and Houser (1970) reported on an effective procedure to eliminate obscene finger gestures and related comments, laughter, and giggling in a class of 14 educable retarded children. After baseline data were obtained, the teacher put a desk calendar bracket with 10 numbered cards in front of the class and informed the students that there would be a 10-minute recess at the end of each day. However, if the teacher saw a "naughty finger" or heard about it, she would flip down one of the cards in the holder, and the class would have one minute less of recess. A significant reduction of exhibitions of "naughty fingers" resulted.

The Premack Principle can also be used with groups of children. For example, Homme *et al.* (1963) noted that children in a classroom are more likely to engage in the low-probability behavior of sitting quietly while reading material on the blackboard if this is intermittently followed by giving the children an opportunity to engage in higher-probability behavior such as running or jumping.

Often, however, the teacher is concerned about the disruptive behavior of particular children. The use of time-out procedures to decrease undesirable behavior and develop self-control is equally adaptable to home and school (Kubany, Weiss, & Sloggett, 1971; Sulzer, Mayer, & Cody, 1968). Such a procedure terminates whatever environmental reinforcement the child derives from his misbehavior, particularly any reinforcement from classmates. If a child continues to be disruptive, time out continues until appropriate behavior is demonstrated and 5 to 10 minutes thereafter. Time out should commence as soon as the teacher becomes aware of the disruptive behavior.

Most misbehavior that is not too severe can effectively be reduced by the teacher's ignoring it, and consistently using praise to reinforce more appropriate behaviors (Hall, Panyan, Rabon, & Broden, 1968; Ward & Baker, 1968; Hall, Lund, & Jackson, 1968; Thomas, Becker, & Armstrong, 1968; Madsen, Becker, & Thomas, 1968). As noted by Blackham and Silberman (1971), many teachers find this process frustrating and give up after observing that the disruptive behavior may initially increase when such an extinction/reinforcement program is presented. The social worker may be helpful by anticipating such an eventuality and be available in the classroom to observe the results of the process and provide feedback to the teacher that might facilitate the procedure.

For children whose behavior is more disturbed, and perhaps not amenable to regular time out procedures, a more drastic procedure has been developed by Keirsey (1965, 1969). This procedure, called "systematic exclusion," requires the participation of the teacher, the child's parents, and the principal. The teacher notes when the child begins to exhibit his disruptive behavior, and immediately gives him a signal to go home. The child agrees to go home on that signal for the rest of the day. The principal supports and enforces the teacher's order. The parents do not ask about or criticize the particular behavior that led to the exclusion from school. Keirsey (1969) reports excellent results from the procedure if all partners cooperate. Their cooperation may indeed be the subject of the social worker's efforts in such a case. Despite concerns of parents, teachers, and principals to the contrary, most children who are excluded on this basis do not usually welcome the opportunity to go home. In using this approach the child should not be reinforced when he goes home, but should remain in a room with very few reinforcement opportunities until the time he would normally come home from school (Blackham & Silberman, 1971). The fear of loss of learning as a result of the process is countered by the fact that the child will learn little anyway as long as his behavior is unchanged.

5. CHRONIC ABSENTEEISM

Chronic absence from school may be the result of many factors. Children may not go to school because they are ill, resist the authority implicit in school attendance, embarrassed about their appearance or clothing, fear either their classmates or their teacher, kept at home by a parent for practical or emotional reasons, or simply bored. Whatever the factors that prevent a child from going to school, truancy is a serious concern, since it can grossly interfere with the continuity essential to effective learning. The assessment procedures of the social worker in such situations should involve a determination of whether a student's chronic absence reflects either an absence of reinforcers in school sufficient to make school attendance worthwhile, or the presence of a fear of attending school. Such an assessment leads to the determination of which part of a child's problem the social worker's efforts should be focused on. For example, many children from "culturally deprived" backgrounds may be subtly (or, perhaps, not so subtly) discouraged from going to school by their parents, who might consider school a waste of time. In such cases, the social worker's efforts might be directed toward changing the parents' attitudes about school, or, perhaps, making the school experience more useful for the child.

An effective method for increasing the likelihood that a student who is excessively absent will attend school is to use the principle that when children are reinforced for changes in the behavior of another child, that child's behavior is more easily changed. In the case of truancy, Blackham and Silberman (1971) have utilized the "triangle method." Each child who tends to be chronically absent is placed with two other children who are his friends, and who also attend school regularly. The three children are then assigned an ongoing group project, which will enable them to earn toys, candy, and special privileges as long as all three children are working on the project in school on particular days. Thus, the two school attenders cannot achieve their goals without the attendance of the child who is chronically absent. There is considerable motivation on the part of the absentee to maintain his friendships, and since his friends can only obtain the particular reinforcement by his attendance, he is likely to obtain social reinforcement for school attendance. "Of course, the absentee's school attending behavior is further encouraged by the fact that the two other group members tend to use some persuasion in increasing his school attendance" (Blackham & Silberman, 1971, p. 116).

The approach to school phobias (in which the child experiences considerable fear of school) is more complex than for situations in which only the differential reinforcement of school attendance and staying at home is involved. In cases of considerable anxiety, respondent counterconditioning techniques may be called for. In a case reported by Lazarus, Ravison, and Polefka (1965), both operant and respondent procedures were used with a nine-year-old boy with a school phobia. The therapist's approach to the boy's school phobia was to follow a series of steps of systematic desensitization about school attendance in the child's natural environment. The child was brought closer and closer to full-time school attendance while he was helped to relax. For example, the therapist chose a Sunday afternoon to walk to the school with the boy, attempting to keep his anxiety to a minimum by using humor and other distractions. On the next two days the therapist took the boy on walks to the schoolyard and home again while reducing his anxiety by "emotive imagery" (i.e., leading the discussion to pleasant memories of Christmas and a visit to Disneyland). On subsequent days, the therapist brought the boy to his classroom after school was over, and later brought him to stay in the classroom for several days until morning exercises were over. Later the child would stay for the entire day while a therapist stayed in the classroom. Still later, school attendance was maintained by awarding tokens contingent on school attendance that could be used to purchase a baseball glove.

The complex problems encountered in treating another case of school phobia are described in the case illustration that follows.

Case Illustration

As noted earlier, no problem related to school is as potentially destructive to the child as his refusal or inability to attend school. The case example that follows (Ayllon, Smith, & Rogers, 1970) demonstrates an operant-based program for a school phobia involving several attempted interventions in both the child's and her mother's behavior. It also demonstrates the frustrations and difficulties often encountered in carrying out even the most carefully planned intervention programs. It shows an "if at first you don't succeed . . ." approach in which four different procedures had to be initiated before the goal was achieved. The procedures involved a considerable investment of time by the people involved—time that may not be available in other similar cases. The interventions culminated in the mother's use of a successful, but unplanned and perhaps questionable, interventive strategy to bring about the desired goal.

The client was Valerie, an eight-year-old girl living with her three siblings and parents in a low-income neighborhood. Starting in second grade, her school attendance gradually decreased until she stopped going to school altogether. She had attended only a few days of third grade. Her mother reported that whenever she attempted to take Valerie to school, she would have a temper tantrum, scream, cry, become almost impossible to move, and claim she was sick. On the occasions on which Valerie's mother would try to accompany her to school on the bus, Valerie would become stiff, begin shaking, and scream. Her mother alternated between coaxing and punishment to get her to go to school, but she was generally unsuccessful.

The mother had sought help from a school counselor, medical specialist, and social worker, and received conflicting advice ranging from ignoring Valerie to severely punishing her. None of the advice worked, nor did her own attempts at coaxing and punishment.

In addition to her school phobia, Valerie experienced numerous other problems, including insomnia and a lack of friends both at home and at school. When she did attend school, she was quiet and withdrawn. She would not play with the other children.

When Valerie was asked, during an intake evaluation at a pediatric clinic, why she was afraid to go to school, she reported an incident that occurred when a young boy played with her "private parts" when she was four years old. No additional information about the episode could be obtained.

When the case came to the attention of the behavioral therapist, the target behavior was Valerie's low rate of school attendance, and the goal was to increase and then maintain the rate. To do so, three factors were explored: (1) Valerie's reinforcements for staying away from school; (2) the consequences of her staying away from school for her and her family; (3) how the consequences of her staying away from school could be redesigned so as to reduce the probability of staying away from school, and increase the probability of her attending school.

A study was initiated of Valerie's activities when she did not go to school. On the basis of these observations, it was determined that whatever the "causes" of her initial resistance to school attendance, Valerie's school phobia was clearly maintained by the very pleasant and undemanding characteristics of her daily experiences with a neighbor who took care of Valerie while her parents were at work.

Further assessment procedures led to the conclusion that Valerie was not intimidated by the academic demands of school—she *could* do the work, and would probably respond to efforts to shape school attendance (e.g., she was willing to get into a car and drive towards the school with an assistant to the therapist).

Intervention required the following four basic procedures over a two-month period to achieve the behavioral goal of voluntary and consistent school attendance.

1. PROMPTING AND SHAPING OF SCHOOL ATTENDANCE

Valerie was initially reintroduced to the school at a time when school was nearly over for the day. She was dismissed along with the other children in an attempt to replicate some of the natural experiences of going to the school. Valerie seemed concerned when the plan was presented to her, but did not resist, especially when she learned that the therapist's assistant would remain with her. When Valerie arrived at school, her teacher, by prearrangement, welcomed her and gave her some classroom work to do. As Valerie and the assistant were leaving the school, they found Valerie's siblings. To encourage Valerie's getting approval for school attendance from her siblings, the assistant gave her some candy to share with them, and left her and her siblings to walk home together.

On subsequent days, Valerie was taken to school earlier each day by the assistant, who gradually decreased her own time in the classroom with Valerie. Each day, the assistant left a paper bag containing some prize for the teacher to give to Valerie when school was over. On the eighth day of this procedure, Valerie left for school, on time with her siblings, without the assistant. Both Valerie's teacher and the assistant later praised Valerie for going to school on her own. On the next day Valerie failed to go to school on her own, and the assistant picked her up and returned her to school. On six subsequent days Valerie stayed home while the procedure was being re-evaluated.

On the basis of the re-evaluation, it was decided that although the first procedure helped Valerie stay at school all day without running away, disturbing the other children, or demonstrating any panic reaction, there seemed to be insufficient motivation to get her there in the first place. Thus, the decision was made to focus next on the reinforcements Valerie received for her refusal to go to school.

2. WITHDRAWAL OF SOCIAL CONSEQUENCES UPON FAILURE TO ATTEND SCHOOL

The re-evaluation indicated that when Valerie refused to go to school, she would stay alone with her mother after her siblings had gone off to school until her mother went to work about an hour later. It was believed that the mother's additional, individual attention was reinforcing Valerie's school avoidance, and the mother was therefore instructed to inform her children that she would henceforth be leaving for work at the same time they left for school. However, when the mother left for work at the earlier hour, Valerie still refused to go to school, and she was taken to the neighbor's apartment as before. Despite the mother's efforts, Valerie refused to leave either her mother or the neighbor. Another 10 days of intervention seemed lost. Valerie still refused to go to school.

3. PROMPTING SCHOOL ATTENDANCE COMBINED WITH A HOME-BASED MOTIVATIONAL SYSTEM

Although Valerie was still not going to school, it had been shown that she could return to school through a prompting/shaping procedure, but it was futile if her attendance could not be maintained voluntarily. It was decided to try next to find some reinforcements, available at home, to be awarded contingent on school attendance. The mother observed that some of the things Valerie liked most were overnight visits with her cousin, and various sweets. In addition to the re-institution of a prompting/shaping program (this time carried out by the mother), a motivational system was implemented in which a large chart was put up at home, with stars for each day of voluntary school attendance by Valerie and each of her siblings. Five stars for the week (perfect attendance) would mean a special treat or trip on the weekend. Also, each day that a child went to school voluntarily, he would receive three pieces of a favorite candy. If the child had to be taken to school, only one piece of candy would be given. The placing of earned stars on the chart when the mother returned from work was to be made a special event. Also, if Valerie did not go to school voluntarily, her mother was to take her, accepting no excuses other than a genuine illness. (The mother was taught how to differentiate genuine from feigned illnesses.) This procedure resulted in Valerie's attending school, but only if accompanied by her mother. It failed to initiate Valerie's going on her own. On assessment, it appeared that the mother's taking Valerie to school might have reinforced Valerie's refusal to go on her own.

Now, it appeared that the natural consequences of school attendance and the motivational system employed in Procedure 3 reinforced Valerie's attending school, but she still would not go unescorted. Thus Procedure 4 was designed to provide an aversive consequence for the mother if Valerie did not go to school on her own. The motivational system of Procedure 3 was maintained as Valerie was moved into Procedure 4.

4. The Effects of Aversive Consequences on the Mother

The mother was instructed to leave the house ten minutes before the children were to leave for school. She would, however, meet them at school each day to see if they had arrived on time, and greet them with a reward. The procedure was designed to prompt Valerie's voluntary departure for school with her siblings, and to provide reinforcement for Valerie from her mother on arrival at school. If Valerie did not arrive at school the mother would have to return home and escort Valerie to school, necessitating a three-mile walk for the mother. On the first day of the procedure, Valerie did not join her siblings on the trip to school, and the mother had to retrieve her. At night, Valerie received only one piece of candy, and no stars on the chart. The mother emphasized that Valerie would have to earn five stars in order to have her cousin stay overnight with her.

The next day, Valerie again stayed home. The mother waited fifteen minutes, then walked home in a heavy rain. The extra walk in the rain was a major inconvenience for the mother, and when she reached Valerie, she scolded her, pushed her out of the house, and escorted her to school. When Valerie tried to explain her absence to her mother, she lost her temper and hit Valerie with a switch. When they reached school they were both soaked. That night Valerie received her one piece of candy, but no star.

That was the last day Valerie stayed away from school. Subsequently, she went to school along with her siblings, with her mother meeting them all at the school door with candy and praise.

Five days later Valerie had accumulated enough stars to have her cousin stay overnight. Valerie continued her regular attendance even after her mother no longer met her at the school, and, one month later, the chart was terminated.

Figure 22.1 shows the long-term effects of these procedures. Follow-up was made 6 and 9 months after Valerie's voluntary return to school. Her attendance continued to be regular, her grades, which formerly averaged "C," were now "A"s and "B"s. Her social skills had also improved, and she had been chosen to be a school guide for new students. She also joined the Brownies, and became friends with several other members. At home, she no longer suffered from insomnia nor felt sick or tired. Neither Valerie's mother nor her teachers noted any new dysfunctional behavior or "symptom substitution" since school attendance was resumed.

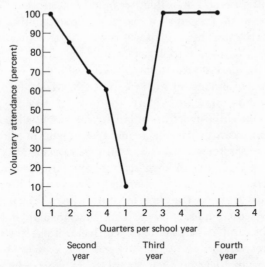

FIGURE 22.1. Valerie's voluntary school attendance. Each dot represents the percentage of voluntary attendance per school quarter (45 days). Intervention began in the second quarter of the third year.
Source: T. Ayllon, D. Smith, and N. Rogers, "Behavioral Management of School Phobia," *Journal of Behavior Therapy and Experimental Psychiatry*, vol. 1, 1970, p. 135.

CHAPTER 23:   Self-Care Behavior Problems

A problem frequently brought to the attention of social workers in various settings is the lack of self-care skills, a problem category that includes people who do not adequately feed, dress, or groom themselves, or who have inappropriate toilet habits. Such problems are most often—but not always—encountered in retarded or severely disturbed adults and children in institutions as well as in private homes.

Common as these problems are, they have traditionally been considered difficult, if not impossible, to modify. Countless manhours, including the time and energy of parents, nurses, and attendants, are expended on caring for individuals who are considered incapable of caring for themselves. The negative effect of requiring such care from others is broader than the necessary manpower, and includes the expenditures of substantial sums of money for such items as extra laundering, food, soap, deodorizers, and so on. Furthermore, the tasks of cleaning the products of an incontinent child or adult, or sitting for extended periods of time feeding someone, can evoke anger and resentment in those who must perform these tasks for others. This can generate negative feelings not only toward the recipient of such services, but also toward the role of "helper," whether vocational or familial. Conversely, the development of self-care skills frees up the time of those who would usually care for others, increases their morale, gives them time to help individuals with other problems, and enhances their positive feelings toward those for whom they are responsible.

More important, learning self-care skills can provide an individual with a basic first step toward functional independence and respect for the rights of others. Possessing basic self-care skills can enhance feelings of self-worth that can generalize by making the individual more responsive to potential reinforcers in his environment. Thus, teaching these skills can be a step toward the rehabilitation of an individual whose own behavior may have been minimally responsive to environmental reinforcers.

Self-care behaviors lend themselves readily to change through behavior modification. Often those who lack self-care skills are in settings (i.e., institutions and hospitals) in which the provision of reinforcers is under the influence of the social worker or other professionals. If need be, potential reinforcers can be withheld so as to build up a greater response to their presentation. There is often a ready supply of mediators who are motivated to try almost any procedure that would ultimately lead to a reduction of undesirable tasks. Furthermore, self-care behaviors tend to be quite specific; their occurrence can be clearly defined, their frequency easily noted, and their improvement accurately assessed. Generally, too, an increase in self-care behaviors is highly reinforcing to mediators, and thus likely to reinforce their participation in intervention plans. Finally, since many individuals who lack self-care behaviors have obtained relatively little reinforcement from their environment, simple reinforcers (e.g., candy and praise) can have considerable potency.

Types of Behavior Included

Included under the general heading of "self-care" are all those specific behaviors associated with taking care of one's physical needs (such as feeding oneself, dressing oneself, avoiding elimination except in the appropriate receptacle) as well as appropriate self-grooming behaviors (such as brushing one's teeth, combing one's hair, washing, and bathing). Although many individuals may lack self-care behaviors in only one of these areas, quite often the deficit occurs in more than one.

The absence of such behaviors may be a product of physical limitations; muscles may be incompletely developed, or there may be a nerve or brain impairment that interfered with the coordination or dexterity required to perform these tasks. Such limitations can usually be ascertained by medical evaluation; they may or may not be reversible.

Often, however, physically irreversible limitations are assumed when they do not exist. For example, it is often inaccurately assumed that the profoundly mentally retarded are incapable of any self-care. Expectations of self-care for such individuals may be minimal, and little or no efforts may be expended on teaching them to feed themselves or control their elimination. Since self-care (like most behavior) is learned, one cannot expect its emergence without some focused influence from the environment. Thus, lack of self-care skills is often merely a behavioral or learning deficit, and one that is amenable to training through a new learning experience.

Finally, while its occurrence may be exaggerated, it sometimes does happen that those who care for other individuals find such service reinforcing. Some people, for example, are more reinforced by feeding or dressing their children (or spouses or patients) than having them feed or dress themselves. In such cases, the focus of intervention might well shift from the non-self-carers to the "caretakers."

Interventive Strategies

There are numerous reports of successful applications of behavior modification with a wide spectrum of self-care behaviors ranging from toilet training to buttoning shirt buttons (Karen & Maxwell, 1967). This chapter will review intervention with two of the more common and basic problems in self-care: toilet training (including the treatment of enuresis and encopresis) of both institutionalized and noninstitutionalized adults and children, and eating (including influencing noneaters to eat and developing appropriate eating behaviors). A final section will review some environmental programs aimed at improving total self-care of retarded and severely disturbed individuals in institutions.

TOILET TRAINING

Although both enuresis and encopresis involve complex neurological and muscular as well as learned processes, behavior modification procedures have led to the development of fairly simple and effective interventions. These methods are of particular importance to social workers who frequently receive requests from parents and other mediators for help in toilet training children.

Indeed, enuresis was one of the first human problem behaviors to which behavior modification procedures were applied. In 1938, for example, Mowrer and Mowrer (1938) reported 100 percent success in treating 30 enuretic children by: (1) using an electrical device that, when moistened by the urine of a child, set off an alarm that woke the child or someone attending to him; (2) reversing a popular approach (which had the enuretic child cut down on liquid intake to avoid a full bladder and thus, hypothetically, reducing the probability of bed-wetting) by having the child *increase* his consumption of liquids so that he would have a greater opportunity to learn bladder control by responding to a full bladder, rather than simply waking up at night in response to anxiety.

In the more than 30 years since Mowrer and Mowrer's report, studies have been reported on modifications and improvements of their procedures. Further refinements of the conditioning apparatus and procedures have led to greater success rates with fewer relapses. Lovibond (1963a), for example, developed a "Twin Signal Apparatus" that, when activated, sets off a loud, aversive "Hooter" that causes the child to tighten his sphincter muscle. Since the noise is set to end after one second, sphincter tightening becomes negatively reinforced by the escape from the aversive sound of the "Hooter."

A second signal (a quieter buzzer) is then set off which wakes a mediator (e.g., parent) who must switch off the buzzer and then take the child to the bathroom—thus reinforcing functional behavior (i.e., going to the bathroom) rather than only punishing undesirable behavior (i.e., wetting the bed).

There seems to be considerable evidence that treatment of enuresis by use of an apparatus such as that described above has a high success rate (Davidson & Douglass, 1950; Freyman, 1963; Geppert, 1953; Gillison & Skinner, 1958; Lovibond, 1963, 1964). Since enuresis is often perceived as a "symptom" of underlying "pathology," the use of such effective conditioning procedures also provides a test of "symptom substitution." Many of the published reports on the conditioning treatment of enuresis have attempted to evaluate any evidence of symptom substitution once enuresis was extinguished. No such evidence has been found. Indeed a number of reports (Mowrer, 1938; Davidson & Douglass, 1950; Geppert, 1953; Gillison & Skinner, 1958; Freyman, 1963) suggest that not only was there no symptom substitution, but that there was often marked positive improvements in other areas of the child's behavior, plus positive "personality" changes, suggesting that " . . . maladjustments may often be the effect rather than the cause of enuresis" (Geppert, 1953, p. 383). Baller and Schalock (1956) conducted before and after personality tests of children who underwent conditioning for enuresis. The results of these tests confirmed that there was no deleterious personality effects of the elimination of enuresis. Based on these observations as well as a study of over 800 children (Tapia, 1960) that showed no correlation between the incidence of enuresis and either general adjustment or the presence of other "behavioral symptoms." it would seem safe to conclude that " . . . there is no evidence whatsoever that enuresis is a symptom of some underlying conflict or disturbance; that successful treatment of the enuresis does not produce adverse personality changes; and that it does not produce symptom substitution" (Yates, 1970, p. 97).

In view of the effectiveness of conditioning procedures in reducing or eliminating enuresis, it would be helpful for social workers practicing in settings where enuresis tends to be one of the problems presented to them by clients to be familiar with enuresis control systems and, indeed, suggest their use in appropriate cases. Either the social worker or the parents themselves can order the apparatus. An example of one such device is the "Enurstat" (available from Medical Devices, Inc., 833

Third St., S.W., St. Paul, Minnesota 55112). The Enurstat is a battery-operated device that incorporates small gauze pads that are easily attached to the inside of underpants and worn over the vagina or penis of the enuretic child during the night. The pad is extremely sensitive to moisture, and even a drop of urine will instantly set off a loud buzzer. (A previous popular device utilizing a bed pad required a substantial amount of urine to set off the alarm. The delay between the onset of urination and the sounding of the alarm tended to reduce the effectiveness of the conditioning procedure.) The procedures recommended to be used (Sloggett, personal communication) together with the Enurstat include the following:

1. Mediators (such as parents) should make sure that the child is fully awakened by the alarm so that he is aware of the associated physical cues and his subsequent behavior.
2. The child should turn off the alarm, go to the bathroom, void completely (often enuretic children do not do this) return to his bed, and make a note on a chart or note pad of the time he got up and the degree of bed-wetting that had occurred (e.g., just a drop, a small amount, a substantial amount). Such recording insures that the child is fully awake and taking a part in eliminating his enuresis. He then resets the alarm and goes to sleep.
3. In the morning, the parents give the child 10¢ for each night time recording or 50¢ for a dry night (it is unlikely that the child will engage in activities that would get him more money from the recording, as contrasted with the greater satisfaction plus the 50¢ for a dry night). Of course, any other reward that will be reinforcing for the child (prizes, candy, etc.) can be substituted for the money.

In addition to the use of the training device, it may be desirable to help train the enuretic child to retain his urine for longer periods of time during the day. Liquid intake may even be increased (rather than decreased) and the child trained to stretch his bladder and go for longer and longer periods between urination, thus learning to better perceive and control the cues for voiding. Such training procedures follow the preferred behavior change strategy of putting an emphasis on the child's learning appropriate behavior (i.e., how to control the time and place of urination), rather than emphasizing the elimination of undesired behavior (i.e., bed-wetting).

Successful behavioral approaches to the treatment of encopresis (i.e., soiling or defecating in one's clothes) follow a similar formula. The emphasis is placed on reinforcing the child for defecating in the toilet rather than punishing the child for defecating in his clothes. If the child is conditioned to hold back from defecating as a result of punishment for soiling, he may tend to hold back too long. "A child who holds back overly long will lose the internal feedback of cues of the necessity to move his bowels. At a certain point, without any feedback whatsoever, the muscular processes of digestion will lead to soiling" (Ullmann & Krasner, 1969, p. 540). The emphasis, then, in treating encopresis is on reinforcing the child for sitting on the toilet and defecating. For example, Peterson and London (1965) reported on a severely encopretic child whose retention of bowel movements made it very painful when defecation did occur, thus reinforcing bowel retention and subsequent soiling. Intervention involved helping the child to relax, suggesting that bowel movements need not be painful, and reinforcing appropriate defecation with candy and praise. Similarly, Neale (1963) reported success with three out of four severe cases of encopresis by placing the children on a toilet four times a day and giving them substantial reinforcement such as praise and candy for defecating in the toilet. There was no punishment or aversive response if soiling did occur.

Toilet training is, of course, a major concern of those working with the severely mentally retarded. Caring for retarded individuals who lack (or do not use) bladder or bowel control is one of the most time-consuming and unpleasant tasks of parents or custodians who are responsible for their care. Such tasks may tend to make the retarded aversive to those who care for them, thus interfering with their developing positive social relationships. Furthermore, soiling is a health hazard, and interferes with the retarded child's ability to carry out constructive learning experiences in the classroom. Giles and Wolf (1966) report a successful effort to toilet train a group of five severely retarded children living in an institution. Again, the focus was on positively reinforcing self-initiated defecation on the toilet. While individualized programs were initiated for each of the five children, the basic procedure initially involved rewarding all appropriate defecation in the toilet by giving sweet foods such as candy and ice cream. In addition, individualized reinforcers had to be found. Two children, for example, refused candy, and baby food was substituted. Others were reinforced by rides in a wheelchair, or a shower. In addition, such social reinforcers as hugs and enthusiastic comments of "Good boy!" were given immediately after defecation. In addition, mild aversive stimuli (such as ignoring the child, allowing them to remain in their soiled clothing, and confining them) were used to suppress soiling, but only after positive reinforcement alone had not developed appropriate toilet behavior. These aversive stimuli were omitted as soon as the child began to use the toilet consistently. Subsequently, in every case, the positive reinforcers maintained appropriate toilet behavior. By the end of the eight weeks of the program, all five children were defecating consistently in the toilet. Similar successful uses of behavior modification in toilet training severe retardates have been reported by Dayan (1964), and Hundziak, Maurer, and Watson (1964).

Toilet training, of course, is not confined to retardates, or to children who are old enough to have developed adequate muscular coordination but still soil or wet their beds and clothing. Toilet training is carried on almost universally by parents of young children who function adaptively in the natural environment. As noted by many of those concerned with child development, toilet training can be a significant learning experience since it is one of the first major experiences a child has with complying with the expectations of his parents and society. Learning experiences associated with toilet training, both negative and positive, may well generalize to other subsequent learning situations. Behavior modification provides some procedures that can facilitate effective training with less emotional turmoil for both parents and children.

For example, fairly rapid toilet training of a young child using operant procedures was reported by Madsen (1965), who was approached by parents who were planning an extended automobile trip in a month. They wanted their healthy, nineteen-month-old daughter to be toilet trained before the trip. Again, the intervention plan was to positively reinforce the child for appropriate toilet behavior. The reinforcements included: (1) a candy bar after successful elimination; (2) praise from one or both parents; (3) advance information that the child would receive the candy bar, and that her parents would consider it very nice indeed if she gave her parents advance warning of her need "to go."

The training progressed rapidly. On the fourth day, she asked about the "potty," on the fifth day she asked to use the potty and she did so twice. By the twelfth day, her parents considered her fully trained. After the fifteenth day, candy was given as a reinforcer only if the child requested it. A follow-up after six months indicated that there had been only one brief relapse during an illness, at which time the reinforcer was successfully reinstituted.

Using an elaboration of the previous strategy, one of the present authors used behavioral principles to toilet train both of his children. Out of eagerness to have the first child trained, a behavioral program was begun at age 18 months. The main ingredient of the program was positive reinforcement, both social and primary (candy), for going on the potty. After three weeks, the child was still having a substantial number of "accidents," and it was decided that the toilet training was premature.

At the age of two and a half years, a second, more systematic attempt was made. First, there was an attempt at antecedent control. The child was told that she would receive rewards for going on the potty. Then she was placed on her trainer potty several times a day at times when it appeared likely that she might have to urinate or have a bowel movement (e.g., after meals and first thing in the morning). When on the potty, she was encouraged to use it. A wider range of reinforcers than previously used were made available, including social reinforcement (praise, hugs, handclapping by parents), candy, and a bucket full of inexpensive little trinkets, each of which was wrapped up in an attractive manner (these proved especially reinforcing). The rewards were offered immediately upon completion of elimination. The result with the older child was that she was completely potty trained within only three days, with only one subsequent "accident." With a younger child, potty training was also begun at two and a half years and essentially completed in three and a half weeks, with five subsequent accidents. In both situations, the schedule for use of material and primary reinforcers was reduced to an intermittent schedule and gradually phased out.

In summary, then, an effective strategy for toilet training children consists of the following procedures:

1. Making sure the child is physiologically ready. Children vary tremendously in their rates of physical growth. Any questions about readiness should be referred to the child's pediatrician.
2. Informing the child about the program.
3. Modeling the appropriate behavior. Parents can bring children into the bathroom with them and show them appropriate toilet behavior. Often, the younger children in a family request to begin going on the potty on their own because they see their older brothers or sisters doing it.
4. Engaging the child's cooperation.
5. Prompting the child. The child can be encouraged to tell his parents when he has to go. He can be asked periodically to tell when he has to go.
6. Placing the child on the potty at regular intervals.
7. Making sure the child is not afraid of sitting on a high toilet seat. If so, a portable potty can be used and placed on the floor. Also, the parent should be sure that the child is not in danger of falling through the toilet seat, and is not afraid of the flushing sound.
8. Ignoring mistakes. They will cease soon enough. Parents should not make a big fuss over accidents. At most, a parent might say, "Now, Johnny, next time don't forget to tell me when you have to go."
9. Using a good deal of affection. Enthusiastic social reinforcement should be given every time the child goes.
10. Selecting additional reinforcers carefully. For example, some children are not sufficiently reinforced by candy, while others are. Reinforcers appropriate for the individual child should be used.
11. Reinforcing each elimination *immediately,* but waiting until the child is finished eliminating before reinforcing.

12. Changing to an intermittent schedule once the behavior is fairly well established.
13. Making the whole experience as pleasant as possible for the child.

The procedures outlined above can provide a reasonably rapid, pleasant and nontraumatic experience for both parents and children in toilet training, an important first step toward eventual self-care.

EATING

Poor eating habits can create a range of problems, ranging from inconvenience and waste of time for the caretakers of those who will not feed themselves or do so messily, to a matter of life or death for those whose consumption of food falls below minimal nutritional needs.

Situations in which individuals virtually starve themselves through inadequate intake of food are particularly distressful for those around them. Such diverse approaches as bribing, coaxing, threatening, spoon-feeding, tubefeeding, intravenous feeding, and even electroshock are often futile in such cases. Paradoxically, food itself has been found to be an effective reinforcer in getting some such individuals to eat. Ayllon and Houghton (1962) for example, worked with twenty elderly, "chronic schizophrenic" women in a mental hospital who generally refused to eat, almost to the point of starvation. It was the researchers' conclusion that, to a great extent, the women's eating problems were shaped and reinforced by those who attended to them during meals by their coaxing and attempts to feed the women. When this social reinforcement was withdrawn, food alone reinforced adaptive eating behavior. Once the social reinforcement for non-eating was removed, and food was established as a reinforcer, the women's behavior was shaped so that they were reinforced (by food) for engaging in specific efforts that earned them admission to the dining room. Thus they still achieved social reinforcements, but now for the positive desirable behavior of eating, not for the undesirable behavior of noneating.

A similar approach involving the reinforcement of eating behavior was reported by Milby et al. (1967) in the case of a 44-year-old institutionalized man who was confined to a wheel chair as a result of brain damage from a self-inflicted gunshot head wound. Punishment had not been effective in getting him to eat. Indeed, his non-eating might have been reinforced by the attention and coaxing that attended his *not* eating. Subsequently, at meal times, all social reinforcements were withheld and he was ignored unless he was propelling his wheel chair to the dining room. If he did go to the dining room to eat, he was reinforced with smiles, conversation, and other social reinforcers. (The authors noted that social reinforcement from attractive female staff members was significantly more effective.) The man was wheeling himself to 80 percent of his meals after 13 weeks of intervention, despite some intervening surgery.

Sometimes, the withholding of food from those who will not feed themselves is impractical or undesirable. In such cases creative use of other reinforcers is called for. A classic example of the use of negative reinforcement of self-feeding is provided by Ayllon and Michael (1959).

> Mary was a resident of a psychiatric hospital who adamantly refused to eat unless her nurses spoonfed her. She was relatively indifferent to social reinforcement from nurses, other staff, and fellow ward residents. Her only interest was in grooming herself and keeping her clothes neat and clean. The case consultant noted Mary's concern for her appearance and thus assumed that Mary would find any food spilled by the attendant during her feeding quite aversive. The attendant was therefore instructed to spill some food while feeding Mary. To escape or avoid the aversive consequences of the food spills (i.e., messy clothes), Mary would either have to feed herself or go hungry. In addition to this negative reinforcement, Mary received social reinforcement from staff contingent on feeding herself. The program rapidly proved effective. In a span of eight weeks Mary went from a pretreatment level of five meals a week at which she fed herself and a weight of 99 pounds, to feeding herself at all meals and a weight of 120. Success at this program led directly to her discharge from the hospital. (See Figure 23.1.)

Improving eating behavior is also an ongoing concern in institutions for the mentally retarded. Often, individuals in such institutions find few reinforcements in their daily lives to match those provided by food. However, they may not have learned, or perhaps do not understand, the requirements of considerate, orderly social eating in the presence of others. Indeed, it may be quite difficult to teach the retarded to give up some of their eating behaviors that are so intensely and immediately self-reinforcing, for example, eating rapidly, stealing food from a neighbor's plate, or eating handfuls of food.

In working with a group of four profoundly retarded boys in a state training school, Henriksen and Doughty (1967) attempted to teach "proper" eating behavior, such as eating relatively slowly, using utensils rather than hands, not stealing food from other children's plates or hitting other children at the table, and avoiding spilling or throwing food. Henriksen and Doughty operated on the assumption that their first step in modifying these behaviors was to immediately and consistently interrupt them to prevent their successful completion and consequent reinforcement. Thus the four boys selected for modification (who were considered the worst behavior problems on the ward) were placed, at

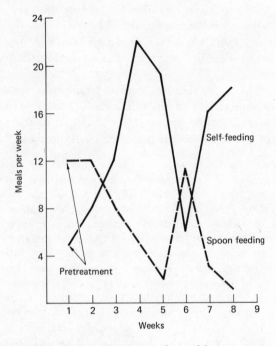

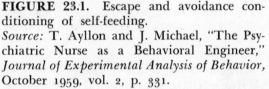

FIGURE 23.1. Escape and avoidance conditioning of self-feeding.
Source: T. Ayllon and J. Michael, "The Psychiatric Nurse as a Behavioral Engineer," *Journal of Experimental Analysis of Behavior,* October 1959, vol. 2, p. 331.

meal times, around a square table away from the other boys on the ward. Two mediators sat at opposite corners of the table, and each mediated the behaviors of the two children adjacent to his corner. The mediators responded to the children's undesirable behavior (e.g., eating food with their hands when a utensil was called for, or throwing or stealing food) by quickly interrupting the behavior by holding down the boy's arm thus preventing reinforcement for their unacceptable behavior, while indicating disapproval by facial expression and verbal comments. The mediators taught the boys appropriate sitting behavior by replacing their feet on the floor whenever they put them on their chairs. Appropriate table behavior (e.g., using a spoon, eating neatly) was reinforced with extra food and such comments as "That's a good boy," smiles, and pats on the back.

Considerable improvement was noted for all the boys in the first four weeks of the program. The boys were able to determine which foods were appropriate to eat by hand and which required a spoon, and they were able to sit quietly until the others were finished eating. The improved behavior continued as the mediators began to "fade out" their direct influence over the boys' eating behavior and as the boys returned to eating along with the others on the ward. Occasional verbal instructions seemed adequate to maintain the boys' desired eating behaviors.

Edwards and Lilly (1966) describe a somewhat similar approach on a not atypical, closed ward for 26 profoundly retarded (IQ 5 to 25), assaultive female adolescents and adults who, before the initiation of an operant training program, required a staff of four or five to feed them and maintain order on the ward at meal time. In fact, because of the typical chaos—which included rushing for the food, pushing, throwing, smearing, and stealing food, and eating with hands—only a small group of women could be served at any one time.

Again, food itself was used as a positive reinforcer to bring about order and more appropriate eating behavior. The women were provided with additional portions of food contingent on their eating in an orderly way. However, any woman who threw, smashed, or stole food was immediately removed from the room. Within ten weeks of the intervention, mealtime had become the most orderly activity of the day. As time went on, fewer attendants were required at mealtime, and women who "misbehaved" would remove themselves from the room. While the program was successful in modifying eating behavior, it was noted that there did not seem to be any carryover into improved behavior in other ward activities. Furthermore, there were subsequent relapses in the women's dining room behavior as new staff personnel came into the ward.

Although procedures such as those described above may require ongoing intermittent reinforcement as well as initial focused intensive activities by the staff, they do lead to more order, and in the long run, more satisfaction and pleasure around a basic and recurrent human activity.

DIVERSE SELF-CARE PROBLEMS

The social workers and others employed in institutions for the retarded or severely disturbed encounter a large proportion of residents who lack a variety of self-care skills. A number of such institutions have successfully used token systems to reinforce self-care and other skills that increasingly approximate the behaviors of people functioning in the community. For example, Ayllon and Agrin (1965), working with a group of hospitalized "psychotic" women, used a token system with tokens redeemable for a choice of activities that the individuals involved would usually perform if they had the opportunity and free time (see Table 23.1). The program was designed to increase such behaviors as self-grooming, washing dishes, mopping floors, helping to serve meals, typing,

T A B L E 2 3. 1. List of Reinforcers Available for Tokens on a Psychiatric Ward

	TOKENS
I. Privacy (cost per day)	
Selection of room 1	0
Selection of room 2	4
Selection of room 3	8
Selection of room 4	15
Selection of room 5	30
Personal chair	1
Choice of eating group	1
Screen (room divider)	1
Choice of bedspreads	1
Coat rack	1
Personal cabinet	2
II. Leave from the Ward	
20-min. walk on hospital grounds (with escort)	2
30-min. grounds pass (3 tokens for each additional 30 min.)	10
Trip to town (with escort)	100
III. Social Interaction with Staff	
Private audience with chaplain, nurse	5 min. free
Private audience with ward staff, ward physician (for additional time—1 token per min.)	5 min. free
Private audience with ward psychologist	20
Private audience with social worker	100
IV. Devotional Opportunities	
Extra religious services on ward	1
Extra religious services off ward	10
V. Recreational Opportunities	
Movie on ward	1
Opportunity to listen to a live band	1
Exclusive use of radio	1
Television (choice of program)	3
VI. Commissary Items	
Consumable items such as candy, milk, cigarettes, coffee, and sandwich	1–5
Toilet articles such as Kleenex, toothpaste, comb, lipstick, and talcum powder	1–10
Clothing and accessories such as gloves, headscarf, house slippers, handbag, and skirt	12–400
Reading and writing materials such as stationery, pen, greeting card, newspaper, and magazine	2–5
Miscellaneous items such as ashtray, throw rug, potted plant, picture holder, and stuffed animal	1–50

Source: T. Ayllon and N. H. Azrin (1965). "The Measurement and Reinforcement of Behavior of Psychotics," *Journal of the Experimental Analysis of Behavior,* Vol. 8, p. 360.

answering the phone, doing the laundry, selling at the commissary, guiding tours, and assisting the staff in caring for other residents.

Atthowe and Krasner (1968) used a token economy, accompanied by social reinforcement, to improve the self-care behaviors of older men on a closed ward in the custodial section of a V. A. hospital, as well as attendance at scheduled activities and such complex behaviors as responsible decision-making and "learning to delay immediate reinforcement in order to plan for the future" (p. 37). The token economy led to significant increases in general self-care and responsibility, while apathy was dramatically decreased.

Token economies have also proven effective in improving the general self-care of the institutionalized retarded. Girardeau and Spradlin (1964), for example, introduced a token economy in a cottage of 28 severely retarded adolescent girls. The program was mediated by two 21-year-old women (with high school diplomas) during the residents' waking hours. There were different target behaviors for each of the girls, depending on their capacity to engage in such behaviors, including making beds, dressing for meals, brushing teeth, setting hair, cleaning the cottage, shining shoes, and feeding the goldfish. In addition to the influence of the mediators of the token systems, all personnel who came in contact with the girls in the cottage were informed about the program and encouraged to reduce their use of punishment to influence the girls' behaviors and increase their social reinforcement of the girls' desirable behaviors.

Many institutionalized retarded are not able to respond to a token system. In such cases such primary reinforcers as food, used in conjunction with social reinforcers, are, once again, effective in modifying a variety of self-care behaviors. Kimbrell *et al.* (1967) used these reinforcers with 40 severely and profoundly retarded young girls to increase and improve general self-help skills, communication, dressing, bathing, and eating. Bensbeng *et al.* (1965) used similar reinforcers to shape such self-help behaviors as use of the toilet, self-cleaning, and table manners as well as "socialization" and response to verbal instructions. The clients were a group of seven young boys who had the lowest tested mental and social age of those in their cottage.

Even the behavior of the profoundly retarded, who are often thought to be too retarded to gain from teaching efforts, may be influenced by such procedures. Minge and Ball (1967) had some success in increasing basic skills (e.g., standing up upon request) in a group of profoundly retarded girls, age 8 to 15. In addition to learning partial self-care skills, the shaping program (which took only a half-hour a day for approximately two months) led to the girls' becoming generally more attentive and responsive to basic verbal cues.

Such institutional programs as these often require careful planning and the involvement of many individuals—not only the clients whose behavior is to be modified, and their mediators, but also other institutional personnel who work with the clients, the clients' families, institutional administration members, and others. In order to mount a successful systematic environmental program based on behavior modification, considerable time, skill, and thought is necessary. The case illustration that follows reflects such a comprehensive program.

Case Illustration

Most of the case illustrations in Part 3 of this book have described behavior modification strategies applied to a particular client experiencing a particular problem. In this chapter, the illustration shows how various aspects of an institutional program may be involved in the development of a systematic environmental program for increasing various self-care behaviors of retardates.

Hamilton (1971) describes a behavior modification program developed at a "typical" overcrowded, understaffed state institution for the retarded. Generally, the 2000 residents' activities (especially for the more severely retarded) revolved around their cottages; therefore, the behavioral programs were organized at the cottage level.

A unit of five cottages housing 300 retarded females was selected as the site of the initial program. It was felt that the residents of those cottages were representative of the residents of the total institution, so that any programs developed in the unit, if successful, could be applied to other units at the institution.

The first problem confronted in developing new behavioral self-care procedures was the general inertia in the institution with respect to the development of new programs. Personnel directly involved with the care of the residents generally thought that the residents were already operating at their optimal level. Furthermore, the personnel in the cottages were quite isolated from the institutional staff who could bring about change. Therefore, as an initial, relatively acceptable step, the administration agreed to make some changes in the physical environment of the residents in the five cottages. The residents (who were originally assigned to cottages on a random basis) were regrouped in such a way that two of the four cottages that had been locked became open and more homogeneous. The greater homogeneity in the cottages permitted the development of programs specific to the needs and capacities of each cottage. Changes in the furnishings in the cottage were also made (financed, as was the rest of the program, by an NIH Hospital Improvement Project grant), which allowed for more space (by replacing beds with double bunks), more privacy (by installing toilet, shower, and bedroom dividers) and a more pleasant environment (by replacing institutional furnishings with more homelike tables, chairs, and couches).

As important as these physical changes may have been, Hamilton considered changes in management and treatment philosophies and practice even more significant for the residents. The organizational structure of the unit was shifted (although it is not clear how) from an authoritarian, centralized form of administration in which employees were expected to carry out the goals and procedures established by the central administration, to an ". . . employee-centered approach which emphasizes individual and group participation in organizational goals and methods of implementation." As the shift took place, morale at all levels seemed to improve, there was less staff tension, and, under a new staffing structure, those staff members who had the most influence over the care and day-to-day life of the residents were better able to express themselves and fully participate in cottage programming. They were also given more direct responsibility for their own job assignments and scheduling. As a result of these changes, direct care staff were willing and able to make a more active and creative contribution to the treatment of the residents than they had under the previous authoritarian structure.

Under the reorganized program, the majority of residents who were exhibiting the most disruptive behaviors were placed in one cottage. Such behaviors as fighting, destroying property, and tearing clothes had become effective "attention getters" that required most of the attendants' time. These behaviors were substantially reduced by placing the residents in a particular "time out area" for 30 minutes immediately after the undesired behavior was noticed. The offending resident was confined to a chair that was bolted to the floor. Each chair had a bell-ringing timer that ensured the resident that his time out would be for the prescribed period. No one was permitted to interact with the resident during time out. This process substantially reduced the rate of disruptive behaviors in the cottage.

In addition to the program for reducing disruptive behaviors, several programs aimed at enhancing patients' self-care behavior were initiated. One of these was a system to toilet train some of the profoundly retarded residents. A unified attempt at toilet training a group of ten such girls succeeded in eliminating most accidents within two months. The residents continued to use the toilets with very few accidents even after the training program was discontinued. However, as soon as there was staff turnover, the accidents recurred in significant numbers, and the residents stopped using the toilets unless they were told to by the staff. Upon exploration, it was discovered that the staff had inadvertently received cues from the residents when any of them needed to go to the bathroom and had, in response, been prompting them to use the bathroom, often with no more than a nod of the head. Thus, the most essential component of effective toilet training had not been provided, that is, teaching the residents to go to the toilet on the basis of their own cues from their internal organs (bladder and bowel) rather than relying on cues from the mediators.

The next attempt, with another group of twelve profoundly retarded girls (IQ less than 20) who could not talk, feed, dress, or bathe themselves, was directed toward teaching them to respond appropriately to their own cues for going to the toilet. They were first given a week of "command training," which, through food and social reinforcement (praise), prepared them to respond appropriately to 18 simple statements such as "Come here," "Sit down," "Stand up," and "Go to the toilet." Within a week the girls responded appropriately to an average of 16 of the 18 statements. Based on this response, the girls were moved on to a 6-phase toilet training program:

Phase 1 (11 days): The girls were checked for soiling and wetting every two hours on an around-the-clock basis.

Phase 2 (19 days): Based on a schedule determined by the base rate for each girl derived from Phase 1, each girl was placed on a toilet chair in her room nine times each day according to the following procedure: (1) called to the toilet; (2) told to pull down her pants; (3) told to sit on the toilet; (4) allowed to sit on the toilet for five minutes or until after voiding; (5) told to pull up her pants. A potato chip was given for each step the girl completed appropriately, and a candy was given immediately if the girl voided. (Voiding and soiling were treated similarly.)

Phase 3 (28 days): The toilet chairs were moved into the open cottage, and some of the girls began to use them without specific commands from the mediators. However, this made it difficult to maintain records of the girls' toilet behaviors and to give them appropriate reinforcements. Therefore, the toilets were enclosed in a locked area with a buzzer on the gate. The girls were now called individually to the toilet by a mediator at specified times. By rewarding successive approximations, the mediators taught the girls to press the buzzer. Once the girl pressed the buzzer, she was let through the gate to the toilet and reinforced. The girls could also use the toilet any time they chose to by pressing the buzzer, after which they were allowed through the gate and given a reinforcer if they voided. This phase was significant in helping the girls move from responding to cues to go to toilet from the mediators to cues from within themselves.

Phase 4 (19 days): During this period, the mediators discontinued giving cues to the girls at the scheduled times, and the responsibility was shifted entirely onto the girls for responding to their own bladder and bowel stimuli. The girls continued to be reinforced with a potato chip for pressing the buzzer and a candy for eliminating. As might be expected, accident rates increased from the daily average of 11 for the group to 18.

Phase 5 (13 days): The purpose of this phase was to determine the effect of the training thus far. Therefore, while the girls were still checked for accidents, all prompting, scheduling, and reinforcements were terminated. The girls were given free access to the toilet chairs. The daily average of accidents remained at 18, compared with 103 during the pretraining period. Furthermore, four of the girls had become completely toilet trained; another four were free of accidents during their waking hours but still wet their beds. The other four girls sometimes still had accidents day and night. (See Figure 23.2 for a comparison of accident rates for phases 2 and 5.)

Phase 6 (29 days): The twelve girls continued to have free, unscheduled access to the toilet area. However, food reinforcements for successes were given by the mediators, who were alerted by a buzzer activated when a girl went into the toilet area. This succeeded in reducing the accident rate of the girls still further and strengthening the toilet-going behavior of those girls who were already toilet trained. Collectively, the girls averaged only 5 accidents a day by the end of this period, mainly

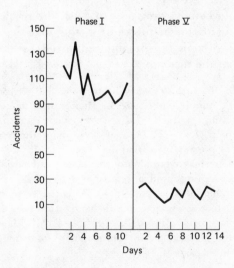

FIGURE 23.2. Total number of accidents per day for 12 girls before and after toilet training.

Source: J. Hamilton, "Environmental Control and Retardate Behavior," in H. Rickard (ed.), *Behavioral Intervention in Human Problems,* New York: Pergamon, 1971, p. 395.

as a result of residual bed wetting by a few of the girls. The girls were essentially toilet trained to the extent of even using toilet tissue without any assistance.

Upon subsequent transfer to a different section of the cottage that had different mediators, the girls continued to be toilet trained without any formal scheduling or reinforcement program. Other groups were then trained with equal or greater success, especially as training groups were smaller, enabling the staff to develop more flexible programs.

The unit also initiated a reinforcement procedure to shape self-dressing. Initially, the girls were reinforced for performing only the last task in dressing themselves, and then successively more difficult tasks in the dressing procedure were added (and reinforced) until the residents were completely dressing themselves:

> For example, in teaching a resident to put on socks, the first response to be reinforced may be pulling on the sock after it has been placed over the foot. When this has been learned the next increment may be pulling the sock over the heel and up. The trainer continues in this backward manner until the total response has been mastered" [Hamilton, 1971, p. 399].

Individual applications of this procedure were geared to the level of skill and competence of the residents.

Similarly, in developing programs to teach the residents self-feeding, they were first taught, and reinforced for, the final step in eating, with successive backward steps taught and reinforced by the food itself as well as praise from the mediator:

> For example, the first step may be to hold a filled spoon a few inches from the child's mouth and guide his hand until it touches the spoon before feeding him, gradually fading the guidance until he touches the spoon without help. The next step may be to shape the response of grasping the spoon before the reward of eating. Next, the distance he has to reach for the filled spoon may be gradually increased until he is lifting the spoon from the plate. The rate of advancement is determined by each individual's progress, but should be sufficiently gradual so that errors and failures are minimal. Eating too fast, grabbing with hands, throwing utensils, and other such inappropriate behaviors can be controlled by withdrawing and withholding food for a brief period immediately following the undesirable behavior [Hamilton, 1971, p. 403].

Profoundly retarded residents were successfully taught self-feeding in this way within a few weeks, providing they were given unhurried, individualized training. This was sometimes found to be difficult in crowded, somewhat chaotic rooms. However the problem was partially overcome by using the more capable residents as volunteer mediators, using "incentive payments" or special privileges to reinforce their help. Each volunteer was assigned to a particular resident; each carried out the self-feeding training procedure under a supervisor who would indicate the points at which the volunteer should should proceed to the next step in the self-feeding sequence.

Disruptive and noisy behaviors in the dining room were reduced by instituting a program in which residents who broke into the food line, threw or stole food, fought with other residents, or engaged in other disturbing behaviors were immediately removed from the dining room and not allowed to finish that meal. The initiation of this program rapidly created a more pleasant and relaxed atmosphere at meal times, and gave the staff time to work on more training programs.

In addition to the basic self help programs described above, the unit developed a sheltered workshop program. The workshop had a significant effect on many of its residents, who, for many years, had been lethargic, compliant, and dependent. Those residents who were able to participate in the workshop became far more alert and active, not only in the workshop, but in their other cottage and institutional activities as well. Moreover, they showed greater motivation to do a variety of things for themselves. They also became more responsive to the other residents, were generally more helpful in the cottage, and took on regular job assignments around the institution.

The development of the new programs in the unit also included stimulating greater involvement of the parents of the residents. Although parents had been encouraged to talk with staff members, in the past they had not felt welcome in the cottages, and saw little of their children's natural environment. To bridge this gap between parents and their children, the unit initiated an experimental open house for one of the cottages. Over 100 relatives attended the program, which gave the families a chance to eat with their children, get to know the personnel who cared for their children, meet their children's cottage mates and their families, and learn, in detail, about the goals and procedures of the new programs initiated in the cottage.

The program proved successful in giving the parents an opportunity to become familiar with—and give support to—the new cottage programs. The aura of mystery that had previously obscured their children's lives gave way to clear information. "Another outcome was that the staff became more relaxed with the parents, and a group feeling appeared to emerge in which all were interested in attaining the same goal—improved care for the children" (Hamilton, 1971, p. 405).

CHAPTER 24. Severely Disturbed Behavior Problems

Although the patterns of dysfunctional behavior described in the other chapters in Part III of this book *can* create major disruptions in the lives of those who emit them as well as for those in their environment, the behaviors described in this chapter tend to preclude effective social functioning almost totally. These behaviors are often perceived as so bizarre or potentially destructive that custodial care is considered necessary.

Those who engage in severely disturbed behaviors appear to most observers to be violating basic laws of human behavior. Their behaviors seem unrelated and even inappropriate to the environmental circumstances under which they occur. At best, these behaviors appear unlikely to bring about reinforcement for the individuals concerned, and, at worst, they seem self-destructive. The individuals who emit these behaviors seem unable to comprehend or deal with the environmental contingencies of their behavior. Indeed, they seem to lack the capacity to catch on to the conventional norms of successful social interaction, and they may even have withdrawn from such interactions.

People who exhibit such apparently illogical, inappropriate behavior are often given such labels as "psychotic," "schizophrenic," or "autistic" by the mental health professions; "insane" by the law; and "crazy" by the general public. Parsons (1951) has suggested that such labels confer a deviant status on those to whom they are given, which provides them with certain rights, such as giving up social and vocational obligations, not being held responsible for their behavior, deferring to others to make decisions, getting help from others for essential care, and being excused from the basic rules of social relations. These "rights" can reinforce the behaviors that earn the labels. Such reinforcements come at great cost to those so labeled—through the loss of freedom and the reinforcements generally available from functional interpersonal behavior—as well as to their relatives (although some may be reinforced by the dependency or other attributes of their relationship with a severely disturbed relative). Ultimately there are also losses for the community, which must support the expensive institutions that house the severely disturbed as well as the programs that deal with them. For social workers and other professional or "care-giving" personnel, these behaviors have traditionally been among the most difficult and frustrating to deal with, to the extent that people with severely disturbed behaviors are often permanently labelled as "hopeless," and simply deposited in the back wards of state hospitals.

Types of Behavior Included

Severely disturbed behavior includes a diffuse group of behaviors such as social withdrawal, delusional-obsessive or disorganized thinking, hallucinations, self-destructiveness and incoherence, and other behaviors inappropriate to general societal behavioral expectations. A general characteristic of those exhibiting such behaviors is their apparent unresponsiveness or inappropriate response to environmental stimuli. A behavioral perspective on such disorders would suggest that such patterns may be a response to deficient or distorted perceptions of the reinforcement systems that generally serve to guide functional behavior (Ullmann & Krasner, 1969).

There may well be organic dysfunctions in many individuals who exhibit severely disturbed behavior. Neurological damage or biochemical imbalances can interfere with the cognitive processes essential to independent decision-making and functional behavior. But even when such impairment exists, it does not necessarily preclude the possibility that those individuals can still *learn*. Except, perhaps, in profoundly damaged individuals, those with organic impairments can still be influenced in varying degrees by contingencies in their environment.

Optimally, however, for individuals to engage in appropriate, reinforceable behavior, they must, to some extent, be able to attend to and perceive those significant social stimuli in their environment that provide cues for appropriate responses. Moreover, they must possess adequate discrimination, memory, and reasoning to use these perceptions to make choices among various behavioral options. When individuals lack any of these cognitive components (attention, perception, discrimination, memory, or reasoning) they are likely to experience disorganized thinking, and may be unable to engage in those everyday behaviors that elicit reinforcements. In essence, such individuals possess an ". . . extremely limited and undifferentiated behavioral repertoire with respect to environmental stimuli" (Schaffer & Martin, 1966, p. 1147). The resulting absence of environmental reinforcement may lead to withdrawal from attempts to bring about such reinforcement. Withdrawal also serves to reduce the pain or discomfort that may have frequently been associated with failure in having behaviors reinforced.

When repeated attempts at seeking reinforcement fail, or are perceived to fail, the individual may also retreat from those basic behaviors that normally elicit reinforcements. Grooming, speech, and civility may deteriorate. The individual may stop making decisions and even stop attempting to perceive environmental cues. When this happens, he may well simply follow the path of least resistance, and develop automatic responses to environmental pressures, such as routine obedience, or routine resistance. "Taking a strategy and sticking to it has two advantages: first, if the person is making minimal discriminations about his environment, one way of playing it cool is to do what he is told. The other aspect is that he has a ready-made response, and the bothersome process of attending and decoding, which has not had great success, can be short-circuited" (Ullmann & Krasner, 1969, p. 385).

As severely disturbed individuals withdraw from attempts to derive reinforcement from their social environment, they may well turn to their inner world of ideation for stimulation and reinforcement. When the ideational becomes perceived as real, delusions and hallucinations occur. Delusional and hallucinatory behavior may be reinforced because it provides shelter from a nonreinforcing, confusing environment. These and other apparently inappropriate or bizarre behaviors may bring about some intermittent reinforcement or a reduction of aversive elements in the environment. For example, it has been reported (Ayllon & Michael, 1959; Ayllon & Haughton, 1962) that such bizarre behavior as the delusional talk emitted by mental hospital residents seem to be reinforced by the responses those behaviors elicit from institutional staff. Furthermore, when reinforcement is made contingent on an individual's making sense when he talks, his bizarre talk tends to extinguish. Lovaas (1965) showed that even the severe self-inflicted injuries of autistic children tend to increase in response to the physical care and concern showed by staff members in response to these behaviors—and Ullmann et al. (1965) have demonstrated that it is possible through differential reinforcement to extinguish delusional "crazy" talk and increase the number of rational verbal responses in interview sessions.

Furthermore, Haughton and Ayllon (1965) found that apparently useless and irrelevant behaviors may be shaped by simple reinforcement procedures. To demonstrate this, a 54-year-old woman labeled "schizophrenic" who had been hospitalized for 23 years and who was an active cigarette smoker was deprived of cigarettes. The cigarettes were then provided to her contingent on her holding a broom in an upright position. Subsequently she would walk around the ward holding on firmly to the broom, aggressively resisting any attempts to remove the broom from her hands.

Two psychiatrists observed the woman's behavior through a one-way mirror. Both interpreted the broom holding as "symbolic" behavior. The evaluation by one of the psychiatrists follows:

> Her constant and compulsive pacing holding a broom in the manner she does could be seen as a ritualistic procedure, a magical action. When regression conquers the associative process, primitive and archaic forms of thinking control the behavior. Symbolism is a predominant mode of expression of deep-seated, unfulfilled desires and instinctual impulses. By magic, she controls others, cosmic powers are at her disposal and inanimate objects become living creatures.
>
> Her broom could be then:
>
> 1. a child that gives her love and she gives him in return her devotion;
> 2. a phallic symbol;
> 3. the sceptre of an omnipotent queen.
>
> Her rhythmic and prearranged pacing in a certain space are not similar to the compulsions of a neurotic, but because this is a far more irrational, far more controlled behavior from a primitive thinking, this is a magical procedure in which the patient carries out her wishes, expressed in a way that is far beyond our solid, rational and conventional way of thinking and acting [Haughton and Ayllon, 1965, pp. 97–98].

Those individuals who continue to exist more or less exclusively in their inner world over extended periods of time and who become unresponsive to environmental demands may be unable to function without continuous care. Many such individuals are ultimately placed in institutions. This institutionalization often only serves to reinforce their already dysfunctional behavior patterns. Since their ability to operate effectively on their environment is already limited, they are even more vulnerable to the powerful influences that institutions generate. Attendants, nurses, and other staff members in custodial mental hospitals have very influential reinforcers at their command, and will often use them to make their own formidable tasks more manageable. In many hospitals, the staff members use their reinforcers to maintain compliance and submissiveness. Complaints, assertiveness, and demands for care, treatment, and other individual needs—even discharge—are therefore rarely reinforced (Ullmann & Krasner, 1969). Given the regimentation, anomie, and lack of stimulation in many hospital wards, residents have little choice but to withdraw even further into their inner worlds; their behavior becomes even less active, creative, and spontaneous than it was prior to hospitalization. Indeed, a study by Mahrer and Mason (1965) suggests that individuals who have been in a mental hospital even a short time had more "symptoms of mental illness" than those tested just before admission. This may well result from what Ullmann and Krasner

(1969) call the "degradation ceremonies" of mental hospitalization, and at least in part from the modeling of those behaviors of long-term residents that seem to be successful in getting attention from the staff.

It would seem, then, that part of the problem behaviors of the severely disturbed may be a product of the very "treatment" that our society provides (see Hollingshead & Redlick, 1958). The illustrations of institution-based approaches to severely disturbed behaviors described in this chapter, therefore, emphasize those programs that attempt both to reinforce the functional behaviors of these individuals and to modify the environmental contingencies that seem to sustain their dysfunctional behaviors.

Interventive Strategies

As was noted earlier, the common denominator of severely disturbed behavior is inappropriate response to the minimal requirements of functional interpersonal behavior. This chapter will provide examples of interventions with two groups of individuals who engage in severely disturbed behaviors: long-term psychiatric hospital residents and "autistic" children.

THE LONG-TERM PSYCHIATRIC HOSPITAL RESIDENT

While institutionalization can reinforce the withdrawal from attempts at successful interaction with the environment, it can also provide significant reinforcers to shape more responsive, functional behaviors. Token economies attempt to use the staff and other reinforcers available in the hospital in a deliberate and focused way to achieve such changes in the residents' behavior as are appropriate to their development of greater independence and to their ultimate rehabilitation. Illustrations of the use of token economies to shape self-care behavior—an important component of responding more appropriately to environmental expectations—were presented in the previous chapter.

Beyond self-care, there are various behaviors, particularly those associated with enhanced socialization and work performance, that are incompatible with social withdrawal and likely to increase the probability that functional behavior will be reinforced by the environment.

Extensive work on the use of token economies in mental hospitals has been reported by Ayllon and Azrin (1968). They have chosen to reinforce such diverse behaviors of long-term psychiatric hospital residents as serving meals, cleaning floors, sorting laundry, and washing dishes.

They found that giving individuals the opportunity to engage in these activities was often, in itself, reinforcing. In developing other reinforcements for desirable behaviors incompatible with social withdrawal, they observed what residents actually did when they were given free choice (the Premack Principle). Based on these observations, they established a system in which tokens were used to bridge the gap between observed functional behavior and the ultimate use as reinforcers of those items that residents were observed to seek out, such as particular bedrooms, a choice of dining companions, visits with particular staff members, the chance to watch television, passes out of the hospital, and candy and cigarettes. Using their token system, Ayllon and Azrin (1968) carried out a series of experiments in which various resident behaviors necessary for rehabilitation increased significantly.

Another extensively reported, successful token program was initiated in a closed psychiatric ward of a Veterans Administration Hospital in California (Krasner, 1965b, 1969; Atthowe & Krasner, 1968). The ward housed 86 patients with a median age of 57. (More than a third were over 65 years old). The median length of residence in the hospital was 22 years. The majority of the residents had been labelled "schizophrenic," and the others "organic." Over half of the residents required constant supervision.

The staff developed a token economy for the 60 oldest residents who presented the most dysfunctional behaviors. They tried to incorporate significant aspects of these residents' ward lives into the token system. Their acquisition of all the important activities, materials, and privileges they might want were made contingent on their behavior. Residents were reinforced for basic behaviors that were considered incompatible with withdrawal from the social environment, including attending a variety of scheduled activities, helping on the ward, and interacting with other ward residents. Tokens used to reinforce these behaviors were exchangeable for ward privileges and access to television, money, and cigarettes. However, the researchers found that individualized reinforcers such as giving a resident the assignment of feeding kittens were most effective. The presentation of tokens to the residents was always accompanied by praise from the staff as well as a statement of the reason the token was being given.

Twelve of the residents on the ward were able to achieve the ultimate reinforcement of the token economy—a *carte blanche* by accumulating a substantial number of tokens as a result of their willingness and ability to accumulate tokens and thus delay gratification. This card essentially took them out of the token system by entitling them to all the privileges of the system, as well as several other special privileges. The *carte blanche* also carried with it considerable prestige. Once residents were given this status, however, they were required to work at least 25 hours a week in special vocational assignments around the hospital, and to maintain some special ward operation responsibilities.

After a year of operation, the program showed considerable success in increasing resident responsiveness in such areas as social interaction, visiting the ward canteen, requesting passes, and attending ward activities. Apathy decreased markedly. More than twice as many residents were discharged or moved to more discharge-oriented wards than in previous periods. However, of the 24 residents discharged during this period, 11 returned within nine months, thus suggesting the need for greater emphasis on including the shaping of community functioning into the token system as well as for creating reinforcement contingencies in the discharged residents' home environment.

Figure 24.1 shows the overall group improvement in attendance at group activities before and after the introduction of the token system. As noted in the figure, group attendance seemed associated with both the introduction of the token system and the increase in the value of the tokens.

A token program in a ward of a large state hospital in California, described by Schaefer and Martin (1966, 1969), directly addressed itself to mental hospital residents' "apathy" as the specific target of intervention. Schaefer and Martin point out that individuals who present an apathetic or nonresponsive behavioral pattern offer little reinforcement to the responses made by therapists and other staff members charged with their rehabilitation, and therefore extinguish conventional therapeutic efforts directed at changing the residents' behavior. Therefore, a token system would seem a desirable alternative.

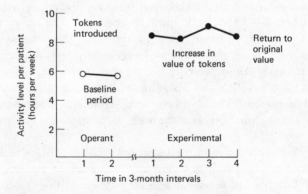

FIGURE 24.1. Attendance at group activities. *Source:* J. M. Atthowe and L. Krasner, "Preliminary Report on the Application of Contingent Reinforcement Procedures (Token Economy) on a 'Chronic Psychiatric Ward,'" *Journal of Abnormal Psychology,* 1968, vol. 73, p. 39.

In many psychiatric wards' behavioral programs, the authors contend, intervention aimed at decreasing the residents' undesirable behaviors do not necessarily decrease their apathy, and, thus, do not adequately prepare them for functioning in their home communities:

> Our own experience has been that apathy sometimes disappears as soon as the various behavioral problems of a patient have been solved. But this is by no means true of all patients. . . . Many of them were still limited, having repertoires lacking behaviors normally expected by the community outside the hospital. This was often true even though the problems which had caused that community to reject them had been eliminated" [Schaefer & Martin, 1966, p. 1148].

In order to test their approach, the authors developed an "apathy score" that was based on carefully detailed observation made by ward nurses of each patient's natural range of behaviors. Apathy was measured by the frequency with which a patient was observed to engage in any one behavior to the exclusion of all others during the regular observation period (for example, just sitting, pacing, rocking, etc.). Higher scores meant that the particular resident was engaging in a variety of activities involving his environment, while lower scores meant fewer activities and, thus, greater apathy. Based on these data a program was initiated for a group of residents who had no organic brain damage but were labelled "chronic schizophrenics," seemed habituated to hospital life, and had poor prognoses for therapeutic success.

After extensive discussions with ward staff, a general list of behaviors incompatible with apathy was developed for which reinforcers would be offered. The list was intended to give general guidelines to the staff for evaluating individual residents' behavior. The basic list is reproduced below along with the authors' explanation of how these behaviors were related to apathy.

> (1) *Personal hygiene:* reinforce thoroughness of showering, manicuring, toothbrushing, hair-combing, use of cosmetics, use of costume jewelry, inquiries about fashions, use of sewing machine, and, as appropriate, evidence of any of these behaviors such as clean feet, absence of body odor, and attractive appearance. The rationale for reinforcing this complex of behaviors is that evidence of sloppy appearance is often, and quite correctly, taken as absence of these behaviors. This absence, in turn, serves as the basis for the inference that the patient does not care about anything—not even herself—and thus is apathetic.

> (2) *Social interaction:* reinforce the patient for asking questions, saying "Good morning," etc., speaking up in group therapy sessions, playing card games with other patients. The rationale here is that the non-emission of these behaviors serves as the basis for the inference that the patient has "no interest" and thus is apathetic.

> (3) *Adequate work performance:* reinforce assignments the patient was given, such as emptying wastepaper baskets, wiping tables, vacuuming sewing room, and similar household chores that patients on this ward are

given; reinforce, also, verbal statements about the quality of accomplished work and requests for work assignments. Here, again, the rationale is that the patient who emits these behaviors "cares" and thus cannot be said to be apathetic [Schaefer & Martin, 1966, p. 1150].

Individualized behavioral approaches to each ward resident included not only lists of those specific behaviors to be increased but the manner in which they would be reinforced. Generally, the tokens used could operate such automated devices as T.V. sets, cafeteria turnstiles, and food and goods automats; they could also be exchanged for almost anything else a resident might want on the ward. Occasionally, however, a primary reinforcer as well as praise was presented at the same time as the token in the early phases of the program. A heavy smoker, for example, might be given a cigarette (contingent on specified behaviors) at the same time a token was dispensed in order to condition responses to the tokens. Individual reinforcement programs were chosen by the entire ward staff based on the general list (above) as well as the staff's evaluation of the characteristics of a particular resident's apathetic behavior. For example, one resident might be reinforced for appropriate smiling, another for appropriate answers to brief questions, and still another for not overwhelming ward visitors with overly enthusiastic talking. (The last example was considered "apathetic" since these verbalizations seemed inappropriate to the responses made by the visitors.) In essence, the criterion the staff used for the selection of the particular behaviors to be modified was the extent to which they would be considered as evidence of "apathy" or unresponsiveness by the community outside the hospital. The program also included a process of "weaning" the residents from the artificial token reinforcements to the normal reinforcements that would be available in the residents' natural home environments.

The authors compared 20 residents who had been in the token program with 20 similar residents who had not been in the program. There was a marked increase in the non-apathetic behavior of the experimental group (that is, the frequency with which residents were observed to be engaged in a variety of behaviors rather than a single behavior to the exclusion of others), while the apathetic behavior of the control group remained the same. The psychiatric and nursing staff also evaluated the behaviors of the experimental group as being greatly improved. Furthermore, the recidivism rate of the experimental group was about half of the hospital's overall rate. The authors attributed the positive results of the program both to the introduction of "success" to the residents as a result of their non-apathetic, responsive behavior and to the program's emphasis on "weaning" the residents from artificial token reinforcers to natural social reinforcers.

Token systems have also been used to restore specific functional behaviors in place of bizarre dysfunctional behaviors. Azerrad and Stafford

(1969) describe the use of a token system to increase food consumption by a girl hospitalized as a result of anorexia nervosa. Various treatment approaches prior to hospitalization had been unsuccessful—indeed, she had continued to lose weight. After she was hospitalized, a supportive counseling relationship that made no attempt to explore the "dynamics" of her eating behavior was initiated, and continued concurrently with the token system, which began in her second week.

The token system was presented through four sequential reward systems:

System 1 (12 days): The girl was weighed each morning. She was allowed—but not forced—to eat at meals, but not allowed to take food out of the dining room. Nurses and other staff were not to discuss her eating problems with her. She was allowed a one-hour visit with her parents each week, but no phone calls. A token system using handwritten index cards was initiated. The cards were redeemable for items often used by the girl such as hair curlers and stationery, and for such special events as movies and trips. Later, the points could be used toward the purchase of items at local department stores or through a Sears and Roebuck catalogue. In the first reward system, a point was earned for maintaining the weight from the day before, with additional points awarded for each 0.1 kg gained. If she had lost weight, no points were given until the lost weight was regained. This system failed to bring about weight gain since it focused on weight rather than the girl's purposeful consumption of food.

System 2 (23 days): During this period, points were rewarded each day on the basis of the amount of food consumed during her three meals. This system had limited success because the reinforcements were still somewhat remote from the specific behaviors to be rewarded.

System 3 (23 days): Each type of food was now assigned a specific point value according to a list given to the girl. Token cards were given to her by a nurse immediately after each meal. Again, the points were exchangeable for items available at a store or through the catalogue.

System 4 (50 days): In addition to being able to exchange points for material items, the girl could (and did) exchange points for home visits of varying duration depending on the points she had accumulated.

Concurrent with the token system, the girl's parents were being seen to help them understand the rationale of the treatment plan and to teach them a behavioral approach that would facilitate continuance of the treatment program when the girl returned to the community. Follow-up for five months after discharge revealed a continued slow rate of weight gain. Figure 24.2 (over) shows the history of weight gain by the girl during her hospitalization.

Many of the reports on token economies used with individuals on psychiatric wards (Ayllon & Azrin, 1965; Atthowe & Krasner, 1968; Winkler, 1970) note that there are long-term "apathetic" psychiatric hospital

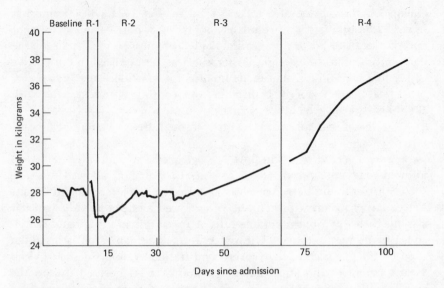

FIGURE 24.2.   Effect of reinforcement on weight in a case of anorexia nervosa.

Source: J. Azerrad and R. L. Stafford, "Restoration of Eating Behavior in Anorexia Nervosa through Operant Conditioning and Environmental Manipulation," *Behaviour Research and Therapy*, 1969, vol. 7, pp. 165–171.

residents who refuse to accept tangible rewards and, thus, do not respond to token systems. In trying to help such resistant individuals, Mitchell and Stoffelmayr (1973) have done exploratory work in applying the Premack Principle to increase functional behavior. Two residents who did not respond to tangible reinforcers were observed by the staff to determine which high-probability behavior they engaged in when they were left alone by the staff. The observations showed that the response that occurred with very high frequency was "just" sitting. Subsequently, "sitting" was made contingent on the completion of certain work projects. As a result, work performance of these residents significantly increased.

Another approach that avoided the complexities of a token system was described by Liberman *et al.* (1973), who were able to increase rational talk 200 to 600 percent in a group of four individuals labeled "schizophrenic" who frequently exhibited paranoid and grandiose delusions and had been hospitalized for an average of 17 years. The procedure used was: (1) to terminate scheduled 10-minute daytime interviews as soon as the individual talked delusionally; (2) to reinforce the daytime interviews in which the individual talked rationally with an informal 30-minute evening chat with a nurse-therapist during which coffee, snacks, and cigarettes were provided. However, as in a somewhat similar study by Wincze *et al.* (1972), the decrease in delusional speech was incomplete and did not generalize to other ward situations.

"AUTISTIC" CHILDREN

"Autistic" is a label applied to the behavior of children who do not seem to respond appropriately, if at all, to external stimuli, particularly to other human beings. Rather their responses seem limited to those made in response to stimuli within their own bodies. Affectionate and other affective responses seem lacking from their behavioral repertoire. They appear able to concentrate on only one stimulus at a time. Many engage in self-mutilating behaviors such as banging their heads against a wall and tearing at their flesh with their fingernails. Many children who emit such behaviors do not seem to lack intelligence or sensory acuity, yet their behaviors have proven particularly resistant to therapeutic interventions.

Extensive applications of behavioral approaches to autism have been developed by Lovaas and others at U.C.L.A. (Lovaas *et al.*, 1973). Lovaas believes that while autistic behaviors may well have some organic components the essence of an effective interventive approach is to make continual demands on the children for appropriate behaviors. His approach is a very physical one; he and his associates frequently use hugging, touching, kissing, and even spanking contingent on specific behaviors.

In his approach to developing functional interpersonal relations and essential social skills, Lovaas works closely with parents as mediators. He teaches the use of arduous shaping procedures, for example, first reinforcing eye contact and then reinforcing successive approximations of appropriate verbal communication (i.e., first imitating sounds, then syllables, then words, then identifying objects and concepts, then sentences and requests and finally, conversation) with bits of food coupled increasingly with hugs and praise.

Lovaas includes in his program teaching the children to express affection. Based on the belief that the physical expression of affection is learned and not innate, and that the autistic child has for some reason not successfully learned such behavior, Lovaas engages the child in a process of "building a hug." To do this, the child is deprived of breakfast, and given bits of food as he comes closer and closer to his mother. Later, he must raise his arms toward his mother in order to be given food, and still later, he must put his arms around her. The process may be painful for the mother as she perceives her child's only apparent motivation for touching her as the desire for bits of food, but ultimately the child learns to express affection spontaneously without any immediate primary reinforcement.

A controversial aspect of Lovaas' program is the use of punishment, including slapping and, occasionally, electric shock. For example, in traditional approaches to self-mutilation by autistic children, the child is restrained and comforted. Lovaas perceived self-destructive behavior, however, as a dangerous, painful behavior used by the child to communicate with the outside world. He noted that such behavior tends to extinguish if not reinforced by those around the child. However, he also noted that before such behavior is extinguished, the child may do considerable physical damage to himself, and could conceivably kill himself. He further noted that if a self-mutilating behavior were immediately followed by an aversive stimulus such as a slap, the behavior would stop. In fact, when electric shock is administered to a child at the point he initiates self-mutilation, the behavior stops immediately, with rare repetitions. Like most behavior then, self-mutilating behavior will continue if reinforced, and cease if punished.

Lovaas also used punishment to decrease inward directed, ongoing self-stimulation such as long-lasting twirling or rocking, which seems to block out perception of environmental stimuli for long periods of time. Lovaas found that if shock or, preferably, other aversive stimuli such as slaps or loud verbal rebukes are administered to a child while he is engaging in such behaviors, and if other appropriate behaviors are reinforced, the useful behavior will eventually predominate.

Lovaas also used aversive stimuli to negatively reinforce approach behavior to the child's parents. Mediators would shout at a child, or even spank him, in the presence of his parents until the child approached his parents. Eventually, the child learned to associate his parents with safety, security, and the reduction of anxiety.

An alternate approach to using punishment to eliminate the physical self-attacking behavior of autistic children was reported by Wolf et al. (1967). A 5-year-old child who had previously been successfully treated for a variety of autistic behaviors (including severe tantrums) was released from a hospital setting. Treatment was then continued in a nursery school where attention was directed at self-attacking behavior, particularly self-slapping and pinching. The interventive strategy was based on the assumption that the self-slapping and pinching were being negatively reinforced by their consequences in class, such as being able to avoid class activities, demands from the teacher, and social interaction. Therefore, after attempts at extinction had failed, the child was required to leave the classroom and go to another room immediately after he slapped or pinched himself. In addition to this time out from any reinforcements the classroom *did* provide, the child was concurrently taught to gently pat himself as a temporary substitute for the more destructive behavior. The self-attacking behaviors were soon eliminated.

The question may be asked: is punishment a necessary or desirable treatment for autistic behavior? Corte et al. (1971) have compared various interventive strategies in eliminating the self-injurious behavior of profoundly retarded adolescents. They found (as had Lovaas & Simmons, 1969) that the elimination of all apparent social reinforcers for the self-destructive behavior was ineffective, and also likely to result in physical damage to the child while waiting for extinction to occur. Reinforcing periods of non-self-injurious behavior had minimal success. Punishment of the self-injurious behavior had clear and immediate success. However, in addition to the general problems associated with the use of punishment, described earlier in this book, Corte *et al.* pointed out that the effects of the punishment on self-injurious behavior seemed to be quite specific to the circumstances in which it occurred (see also Risley, 1968, and Lovaas & Simmons, 1969), and thus the punishment would have to be carried out by various individuals in many of the settings in which it usually occurs. However, the problem in generalization of responses to punishment would seem much greater with retarded than with autistic children (Lovaas *et al.*, 1965).

Therefore, while the occasional use of punishment to eliminate dysfunctional behaviors may seem cruel and inappropriate, the approach of Lovaas must be measured in large part in terms of how successfully it enables previously unresponsive children to relate appropriately to their social environments.

In evaluating the effects on those children treated in almost 10 years of operation of Lovaas' clinic (Lovaas *et al.*, 1973), it was observed that although the treated children were quite heterogeneous (despite their shared label of "autistic") there was much they had in common as a result of the program. First: Undesired behavior such as ritualistic self-stimulation and echolalia decreased, and desired behavior such as functional speech, appropriate play, and functional social behavior increased. Second: Measured IQs and social quotients showed improvement. Third: While the amount of improvement varied considerably, the behavior of all children who went through the program showed some measurable improvement. Fourth: Follow-up studies of the children one to four years after leaving Lovaas' clinic showed that those children who were able to return to homes in which the parents were trained and motivated to carry on a behavioral program in which expectations for functional behavior were maintained and reinforcement provided continued to progress. They developed at least marginally effective social functioning in adulthood. On the other hand, the behavior of those children who were placed in institutions and who were not expected to improve deteriorated (although not to pre-intervention level) and lost many of the functional behaviors acquired at the clinic. However, it was possible to re-establish some of the behavioral gains of those who were institutionalized if a behavior modification program was reintroduced. Fifth: The younger the children are at the beginning of treatment, the more likely that there will be a significant improvement in their overall behavior.

Reports on the treatment of autistic behavior have generally been based primarily on institutional or clinic programs, such as in Lovaas' clinic, that often require complex apparatus and procedures carried out by expensive, highly trained professionals or paraprofessionals. One difficulty reported in such programs is that behavior learned in institutional settings may not generalize to the child's home (Risley, 1968). Efforts have been made to circumvent the problems associated with the institutional treatment of autistic behavior by a greater focus on training and supervising parents to mediate the behavior of their children in their own home. Nordquist and Wahler (1973), for example, reported their work with the parents of an autistic child over a two-year period. The specific targets of intervention were to decrease ritualistic behavior (flapping hands, twirling objects) crying, and whining and to increase compliance with parental requests, and non-verbal and verbal imitation. The parents were able to accomplish these behavioral goals successfully once adequate contingencies (time-out, and reinforcement using high-frequency behaviors) were discovered and rigorously applied.

Case Illustration

As noted earlier in this chapter, the major characteristics of those who emit severely disturbed behavior is their apathy and lack of interpersonal skills. Their dysfunctional behaviors—or lack of functional behaviors—may be a direct result of the lack of reinforcement or even the presence of pain in earlier interpersonal relationships, and, ultimately, of the learning of social withdrawal to avoid the aversive elements of such social contacts. It would therefore seem logical that a major goal of hospital programs for these individuals would be the reversal of such patterns through the reinforcement of successful interpersonal relationships.

An application of a token system to systematically reinforce effective interactive behavior is described by Bennett and Maley (1973). Their program was aimed at reinforcing appropriate social responses (talking, attending, questioning, and answering) of withdrawn, noncommunicative long-term residents of a psychiatric hospital. The program also had the goal of evaluating the extent to which any increase in appropriate inter-active behavior generalized from the treatment setting to other situations.

Four women residents of the Behavior Therapy Unit at Weston State Hospital in West Virginia were selected for the program. They had a mean of 6.3 years of psychiatric hospitalization and had all been labeled as "chronic schizophrenics." They were selected from a ward of twenty women because they had received the lowest scores on a measure of social interaction. They were then randomly assigned either to an experimental or to a control dyad.

The treatment of the experimental dyad occurred in ten 30-minute treatment sessions held on the weekdays of two consecutive weeks. The sessions were held in a room equipped with a set of four lights used to indicate the occurrence of desired responses. The lights were visible only to the woman sitting directly in front of them. Each of the four lights under the control of the mediator were to signal particular desired responses, and were labeled "talking," "paying attention," "asking questions," and "answering questions." A timer measured the length of time each light was turned on.

Before each treatment session, the mediator would inform the women about the desired responses during that particular session, as well as the contingencies of reinforcement. Although the desired responses changed from session to session, the amount of reinforcement (tokens earned) remained contingent on the length of time any of the woman's lights were on in that session. One token was earned for every 50 seconds of appropriate verbal behavior. (Tokens could be exchanged—along with others earned through the ward's token system—for various items available through the ward's store).

In addition to giving instructions and operating the lights, the mediator also offered suggestions for discussion topics at the beginning of each session, offered praise for good responses during the sessions, maintained a cumulative record of the length of time each woman's lights were on, and dispensed the earned tokens at the end of each session. The mediator's judgments of the women's responses were evaluated by two psychologists during two sessions. There was 100 percent agreement with the mediator's decisions on whether the women's responses met the reinforcement criteria. The intervention process occurred in four phases:

Phase 1 (sessions 1 and 2): During this phase, the "talking light" was turned on as long as anything was said by one of the women, regardless of the content of what was said or to whom it was directed. (The woman was considered to have stopped talking when three seconds elapsed following the last word.)

Phase 2 (sessions 3 and 4): During this phase, reinforcement was made contingent on not only talking, but attending to what was being said. "Attending" was defined as facing the other woman while she was talking. Reinforcement was based on how long either their "talking" or "paying attention" lights were on.

Phase 3 (sessions 5, 6, and 7): During this phase, the women were reinforced contingent on their asking questions and offering appropriate answers. Reinforcement was no longer given for "paying attention" nor for "talking," only for questions and answers exchanged between the two women. Thus, only the "asking questions" and "answering questions" lights were used during this phase. However, the lights were only lit when the women were facing each other. Answers had to be relevant to the preceding question to warrant reinforcement.

Phase 4 (sessions 8, 9, and 10): This final phase required considerable cooperation between the two women. The new criteria for reinforcement in this phase were that there be a sequence of one woman asking a question and the other answering it before either was reinforced; furthermore, the answer had to be longer than two words. Each completed sequence produced ten seconds of token-earning time for each woman.

The two women in the control group also went through ten 30-minute treatment sessions in the same room with the same mediator. They also received reinforcers (tokens) in similar numbers to the other two women, but it was not contingent on specific kinds of verbalizations. The function of the control group was to control for any effects of attention from the mediator, the project as a whole, and the passage of a similar amount of time on the treatment ward.

The results on a variety of tests showed that the treatment procedure had a powerful effect on the women in the experimental dyad compared to the women in the control dyad during the treatment sessions. Furthermore, clear generalization of the treatment experience was observed in the women's behavior on the ward. While the number of interactions of all four women was essentially similar during the baseline period, during the treatment period the number for the two women in the experimental group rose to 36 and 43 occasions respectively, while the number for the women in the control group remained near the baseline rate of 7 and 12 occasions. After treatment, the number of interactions for the experimental dyad was 75 and 44 while the control dyad's remained at 7 and 9.

Other tests revealed substantially higher ratings for the experimental dyad on assessments of withdrawal, social contact, mood, and communication skills. The social functioning scales for the control group remained essentially the same (except for improvement in one of the woman's cooperation-mood ratings) as during the baseline period. The perception that the experimental group benefited greatly from the treatment procedure was further supported by informal staff observations that the women in the experimental dyad sought out interpersonal relationships more often after treatment, and appeared much more "relaxed" and "spontaneous" in their interactions.

It would appear that these social activities of the experimental group, artificially reinforced during the treatment sessions, became reinforcing in and of themselves after treatment. The treatment process, then, served the function of a pump-primer in initiating (or re-initiating) social interaction activities. It is possible that the treatment of the women in dyads was also successful as a result of the modeling that occurred when each woman observed the other being reinforced for appropriate interpersonal activities.

Whatever the factors were that led to improvement, this project suggests that a fairly replicable, short-term treatment process may increase social responsiveness—a core component of effective social functioning—through the application of systematic reinforcement of basic social behavior in the context of an interpersonal relationship. It is unfortunate that this study involved such a small sample size. A replication of the project using larger experimental groups would be useful.

CHAPTER 25.   Sexual Behavior Problems

Social workers in virtually all practice settings encounter a wide variety of sex-related problems. However, they and their clients often resist dealing directly with these problems partly because of their attitudes toward sexual problems (Gochros, 1971) and partly because of the difficulties inherent in the nature of many of the problems themselves. Sexual problems often are a product of many factors—social, legal, psychological, genetic, and physiological—that combine to produce complex behaviors. Some of these problems can appear insurmountable, especially since there are few categories of behavior that are either so powerfully reinforced or powerfully punished (and sometimes both) as sexual behavior. However, procedures have been developed that have proven effective with a number of specific sex-related problems, some of which will be discussed in this chapter.

There are several characteristics of sexual behavior that make it susceptible to behavior modification approaches: First, most sexual behaviors are learned responses that have been powerfully reinforced by fairly predictable physiological stimuli—including tactile enjoyment and the tension release of orgasm—and, often, by social reinforcement. The behavior modifier, therefore, has potentially available these significant reinforcements to motivate client cooperation, and to bring about the desired behavior.

Second, many desired sexual behaviors such as orgasm, erection, ejaculation, and even pleasurable affective experiences are fairly easily pinpointed and counted. Third, society has already built in—for better or worse—powerful aversive stimuli for unacceptable sexual behavior. These negatively reinforce participation in programs aimed at decreasing undesired sexual responses.

Societies generally have considerable influence over sexual expression. The sexual response is a powerful one, and one of its products—reproduction—is of prime concern to the survival of any group. Indeed, there are few areas of behavior that are more carefully regulated (Marshall & Suggs, 1971). Until very recently, the strength of any group very much covaried with its ability to more than reproduce itself. This reproductive imperative, along with other factors, led to strong reinforcements—or, at least, freedom for the reinforcement intrinsic to sexual behavior—to be enjoyed by those engaging in certain prescribed sexual behaviors. These generally were related to semi-permanent, monogamous, heterosexual relationships in which children would be conceived, born, cared for, and socialized. Thus, through a complex system of learning experiences provided by parents, peers, teachers, the media, and others, certain behaviors are shaped, varying somewhat with the culture, the place, and the time.

For example, those sexual behaviors that are consistent with, and bring about, socially approved pregnancies are reinforced: These behaviors have included focusing sexual activities on a man's seeking a responsive woman, his achieving and maintaining a firm erection, and her accepting his penis into her vagina, where, in due time, he ejaculates. Such behaviors are certainly conducive to pregnancy, and are considered by most reinforcing agents as ideal, natural, normal, and mentally healthy activities associated with sexuality. Other sexual behaviors that can potentially provide physical or psychological pleasure (or both) but cannot lead to pregnancy—self-stimulation or manual, oral, or anal stimulation of a partner's genitals, or sexual activities with a partner of the same sex—have often been met with aversive social consequences ranging from feelings of guilt to peer ridicule and even legal sanctions.

The societal reinforcement for reproduction has somewhat abated among the 15 percent of Americans who are college educated and who, because they include most of the educators, writers, journalists, lawyers, politicians, and doctors, greatly influence sexual attitudes. Thus recent studies (Hunt, 1973) show that these non-reproductive behaviors are gaining greater acceptance. However, the old powerful patterns of social reinforcement and punishment change slowly. To compound all these problems, our society has also generally punished open, honest, and direct communication about sexual behavior.

Professionals (including social workers) are no less immune to the present confusions about sex-related behavior (including talking about sex) than others. Their own ideas and the directions they take as professional helpers are both affected by and affect their changing social environment. One hopes that once their own values are clear, they can help others work through the welter of conflicting stimuli and reinforcements to give and receive joy from this basic aspect of humanness.

Types of Behavior Included

Sexuality is a broad field that includes diverse interrelated behaviors and ideas associated with sensuality (including pleasurable tactile and other sensations derived from the body, especially, but not limited to, the "erogenous zones" and the tension release of orgasm), intimacy, gender identity, object choice, and reproduction.

The broad areas of sex-related problems most often encountered by social workers include the following:

PROBLEMS OF THE SEXUALLY OPPRESSED

As a result of social learning, members of various groups who are unable to produce socially desirable pregnancies have traditionally had their rights to sexual satisfaction (as well as other rights) curtailed or totally blocked. Some members in these groups have learned to perceive themselves as ineligible for sexual satisfaction. The extent of sexual pro-scriptions for members of these groups vary with the place and the time. These groups have included the mentally retarded, the aged, the homo-sexually oriented, prisoners, the young, and the handicapped (Gochros and Gochros, 1976). Sex education programs in general, and advocacy on behalf of these groups, will, one hopes, reduce the sanctions against their sexual expression.

PROBLEMS OF SEXUAL RESPONSES

Even some of those who generally have society's sanction for sexual expression may experience problems in their physical sexual relationship. They are often the victim of their high expectations of themselves and their partners for quality sexual "performance". They may consider their adequacy as a human being or as a woman or man "tested" by how well they "perform" sexually. For a man, this involves, at the very least, being sexually aggressive, achieving an erection, inserting it in his partner's vagina, sustaining it, and avoiding ejaculation until the partner has had her orgasm. The pressure to perform and the anxiety of having—or repeating—a sexual failure is, of course, incompatible with sexual enjoy-ment, and is a major factor in such common male "plumbing" prob-lems as "impotence" and premature ejaculation along with the less tangible problems of sexual dissatisfaction.

For the woman, the problem can be even more complex. Whereas the man has learned to be strong, sexually oriented, and aggressive, the woman may have received reinforcements for conflicting behaviors. Until the recent revolution in the role of women, they were taught to be attractive, perhaps a bit seductive, oriented eventually to motherhood, but only passively interested in sexual behavior. Indeed, too much inter-est and enjoyment in sex was often considered unacceptable, and was subtly punished. Conflicting messages and reinforcements are offered today; women are encouraged by their peers and the media to enjoy sex, obtain a maximum number of orgasms, and be as sexually aggressive as men. This latter orientation has increased the number of women who are seeking help to undo the damage of their and their partners' earlier learning experiences, which have contributed to the inability to let loose, enjoy sex, and experience the satisfaction of orgasms.

The preoccupation with performing learned sexual roles well in bed can create a pairing of anxiety with sexual activity, which can contribute to the lack of enjoyment, the plumbing problems (that is, the malfunction of the sexual physiology), and the terror that some of the sexually elite experience in their sexual behavior.

UNDESIRED SEXUAL BEHAVIORS

A third group of people tend to achieve sexual enjoyment or psychological stimulation and satisfaction from activities that they themselves consider undesired, or significant other people in their environment consider unacceptable. These include people who have been labeled by themselves or others as rapists, fetishists, pedophiles, homosexuals, and transvestites. Frequently, these behaviors violate state or local laws. They often create difficult dilemmas both for the individual who engages in them as well as for the social worker who works with them. They may, to a large extent, be satisfying and even functional to the individuals involved; yet they are subject to punitive laws or condemned by influential segments of those who control powerful contingencies for their behavior—ministers, law enforcement officers, employers, and landlords, to name a few. The individual engaging in these activities may either be satisfied with them or find them simultaneously reinforcing and aversive. They may, indeed, feel a great deal of conflict about whether their behaviors are "normal" and whether they should try to extinguish them. However, sexual responses (particularly orgasm) highly reinforce such behaviors and the stimuli that are associated with them, making these behaviors highly refractory to change efforts.

PROBLEMS OF THE VICTIMS OF SEXUAL OFFENSES

Many of those who are victims of sexual offenses (e.g., rape, child molestation, exhibitionism) experience emotional and behavioral problems long after the offense has occurred. Often these problems arise more from the reaction and sometimes over-reaction of others—including insensitive professionals—to the event rather than to the offense itself. Although social work efforts with these problems is best focused on preventing such offenses and minimizing the environmental contingencies on the victim after the event, sometimes behavioral techniques such as thought stopping and systematic desensitization to the stimuli associated with the offense may be helpful to the victim.

Interventive Strategies

The two areas in which behavior modification strategies have frequently proved useful can be categorized as: (1) increasing desired sexual responses such as achieving and maintaining an erection at the appropriate times, achieving orgasm with reasonable frequency and at a desirable point in sexual activity, and obtaining and giving enjoyment in sexual activities; (2) decreasing undesired sexual responses, such as eliminating sexual responses to stimuli if they are considered inappropriate or undesirable to the individual experiencing them, or are clearly harmful to others, including such behaviors as those labeled fetishism, rape, transvestitism, pedophilia, and homosexuality. Strategies which have been reported in accomplishing these goals will be described in this chapter.

1. INCREASING DESIRED SEXUAL RESPONSES

The specific patterns in which an individual behaves sexually are, to a great extent, the product of the history of reinforcements and punishments that have followed particular sexual thoughts and overt behaviors. An individual may have learned that sexual behavior with a partner can be reinforced both by the physical pleasure experienced and by the pleasure communicated by the partner.

On the other hand, unsatisfying sexual experiences can be highly aversive not only because of the unpleasant physical sensations, such as tension, congestion, and irritation experienced by one or both partners, but also because of the considerable emphasis and premium placed on "normalcy" and competent sexual performance or, at least, adequacy by many contemporary Western societies. Thus, a woman who has rarely experienced orgasm, or whose vagina has tightened in anticipation of penile penetration, or the man who has had occasional difficulty in maintaining erection or delaying ejaculation, may well begin to associate sexual behavior with failure, embarrassment, and pain. It is possible that they will subsequently avoid any sexual contact that could have such aversive consequences.

But sexual abstinence may involve too much of a cost. More likely, such individuals will, as a result of respondent learning, begin to approach sexual activities with anxiety, yet continue to seek or engage in sexual activities in the constant hope that next time it will be better. However, the conditioned anxiety is likely to preclude satisfaction in such attempts and thus compound the problem. Although many sexual problems manifest themselves in obvious physiological malfunctions, the behaviors are often conditioned responses such as anxiety and counter-productive attitudes that prevent natural responses (such as receptive, lubricated vaginas, erect penises, and satisfactory orgasms) from occuring.

A number of procedures have been found useful in reducing anxiety and performance expectations that can inhibit desirable, intrinsically reinforceable sexual behavior (Masters & Johnson, 1970; Lo Piccolo & Lobitz, 1973; Gochros, 1972; Annon, 1974; Shusterman, 1973). They include the following:

ASSESSMENT

Because of the complexity of some sex-related problems, the social worker should carefully assess the presenting problems. Simple self-labeling by the individual can be quite misleading and possibly destructive. If individuals label themselves as "impotent," "frigid," or "homosexual," the labels themselves can affect subsequent sexual behavior. Overlooking other aspects of a couple's relationship apart from the specific labeled sexual plumbing problem can lead to serious problems (Kaplan & Kohl, 1972).

Since direct observation of the sexual behavior by the social worker is not practical, the social worker should obtain a clear behavioral description of, and, ideally, data on, the individual problem behavior. Questions that may be useful in obtaining such information include:

Has the problem always existed? If not, what were the circumstances of its onset?

Does the problem always occur, or does it occur only at certain times and under certain circumstances, such as when the individual is drunk, tired, or angry?

What are the individual's (and the partner's) expectations for sexual behavior? What are their behavioral goals? Are they realistic? For example, ejaculation after a half hour of intravaginal thrusting may not be productively labeled "premature" even if the partner considers it so.

How has the individual's sexual behavior changed, over time, in frequency and in pleasure? For example, if the problem occurs in the context of a pair relationship, have other aspects of the relationship covaried over time?

What does the individual consider to be the environmental contingencies that affect the sexual relationship (e.g., the individual's health, the setting in which the sexual behavior occurs, the proximity of children and others)?

What, specifically, have the individuals attempted to resolve the problem (e.g., medications, psychotherapy, variations in the sexual behavior)?

If there is a suspicion of a physical source for the sexual problem (such as diabetes in the case of impotence), medical consultation may be advisable. However, the social worker might do well to select a medical consultant carefully. Until recently, medical schools did little to prepare their students for working with sex-related problems (Vincent, 1968). Destructive attitudes and, possibly, misinformation communicated by a biased physician could set back a behavioral program rather than facilitate it.

PROVISION OF INFORMATION

Many sex-related problems have their origin in misinformation or lack of accurate information. For example, a man may approach sexual relationships with considerable anxiety (or not approach them at all) out of concern that his penis is not large enough. Realistic reassurance can be provided by pointing out that the outside inch or two of the vagina along with the clitoris provide the most physiological stimulation to the woman. Thus, even a reasonably "small" penis can stimulate a woman to orgasm. Accurate direct information about basic sexual anatomy, physiology, and common behavior patterns, as summarized in such books as McCary (1973), Katchadourian and Lunde (1972), or Gochros and Schultz (1972), when clearly and comfortably presented, can eliminate dysfunctional sexual myths.

MODIFICATION OF DYSFUNCTIONAL SELF-REGULATION

Closely related to the provision of information is the debunking of the dysfunctional "shoulds" and "musts" that often rigidly regulate many individuals' sexual behavior, and prevent satisfying sexual experience. Typical "shoulds" are: the woman should experience orgasm through her vagina, not her clitoris, and only while a penis is in it; all sexual contact should culminate in genital intercourse, and the man should be above the woman in intercourse; married people should never masturbate. The informed, empathic social worker can help the client get reinforcement from a wide range of satisfying sexual behaviors that may have been proscribed prior to intervention.

STIMULUS CHANGE

The pain, embarrassment, and anxiety related to sexual problems can become paired with stimuli associated with the time and place of the sexual activities. For example, the couple's bed, and even the bedroom, late at night may provide cues to sexual anxiety and failure. To reduce the impact of such stimuli, Masters and Johnson (1970) bring their couples to St. Louis. While in residence in their program, the couple stays in a new environment, free from home distractions (children, phone calls, etc.) and reminders of their sexual disappointments. A less extensive stimuli change is Gochros' (1972) "motel therapy," in which couples spend a weekend early in the intervention process at a motel or hotel where they carry out several homework assignments such as learning about what each partner enjoys in sexual activities and trying out new modes of sexual activities, while avoiding demands for sexual performance. A still more economical plan is to simply rearrange the furniture in the couple's bedroom.

SHAPING DESIRED SEXUAL BEHAVIOR

Much of the anxiety experienced by those with sexual problems is a product of anticipating each planned sexual contact as a major test of their sexual competence, a case of "do or die." Such expectations of performance mitigate against successful sexual behavior: the participants can become spectators of their own sexual test in which the bed becomes the arena for their contest with their bodies. Since anxiety coupled with performance expectations is a breeding ground for sexual disaster, such an orientation is inevitably self-defeating. The social worker can help the couple approach the desired sexual activity by shaping the end goal rather than meeting it head on. The social worker can suggest to the couple, for example, that they explore each other's body and stimulate each other, but not make any premature demands for genital satisfactions. As they feel comfortable at each step along the way they can both discover and more closely approximate the desired sexual behaviors.

Along with these general procedures for achieving desired sexual responses, various researchers have reported on specific procedures that have proved useful with particular sexual problems. Two of the most common, orgasmic dysfunction in women and erection difficulties in men, will be discussed here.

2. ORGASMIC DYSFUNCTION

The most common of the sexual problems presented to social workers and other professionals by women is the lack either of orgasms or of enjoyment of sexual activities in general. In a recent survey of sex-related problems in the caseloads of social workers in family agencies and mental health clinics in Honolulu, "Female loss of interest in sex" and "Orgasmic dysfunction" accounted for 41 percent of the encountered cases (Gochros *et al.,* 1974). Lo Piccolo and Lobitz (1973) report that 80 percent of the cases seen in their program for sexually dysfunctional couples involve women who never (or only irregularly) reach orgasm or who find all sexual behavior aversive. The high incidence of women seeking help with these problems may reflect either a growing social acceptance of the expression by women of unhappiness with their sexual life or, more likely, the existence of a large number of women ". . . who have internalized our society's implicit and explicit norms that 'good' women do not have a sex drive, and that sexual needs are something to be ashamed of . . ." (Lo Piccolo & Lobitz, 1973, p. 343). Such learned proscriptions often lead to sexual ignorance. Many women are strangers to their own bodies, and have not allowed themselves to learn about their own sexual responses. Often women who experience orgasmic dysfunctions have paired such responses with fear and shame.

Since orgasmic dysfunctioning is often a result of anxiety or hostility that prevents the occurrence of physical and emotional responses that would, if uninterrupted, probably culminate in orgasm, systematic desensitization has been utilized successfully in its treatment. Lazarus (1963) reported on the use of systematic desensitization with sixteen women who differed significantly in personality, background, and lifestyle, but who all experienced chronic difficulty in reaching orgasm. All had previously undergone some form of treatment such as advice on sex techniques, hormonal injections, and ointments from physicians as well as conjoint marital counseling, psychoanalysis, and other forms of psychotherapy. Lazarus approached all the cases by first teaching the women to relax. Then, using data obtained in interviews with the women, hierarchies of anxiety-provoking situations were developed, ranging from descriptions of mildly anxiety-provoking situations to those which provoked a great deal of anxiety. For example, Lazarus cites one case in which a twenty-four-year-old woman had permitted intercourse less than twenty-four times during her 2½-year-old marriage. She experienced both dyspareunia and "disgust for the whole messy business." She could tolerate some kissing and caressing without anxiety, and even enjoyed these activities on occasion. She had a puritanical upbringing in which she was taught the "sinful qualities of carnal desire." The woman was afraid of losing her husband because of her sexual inhibitions, and sought treatment.

Following a series of diagnostic interviews and psychometric tests, the following hierarchy was developed (Lazarus, 1963, pp. 275–276):

1. dancing with and embracing husband while both fully clothed
2. being kissed on the cheeks and forehead

3. being kissed on the lips
4. sitting in husband's lap, both fully dressed
5. husband kissing neck and ears
6. husband caressing hair and face
7. shoulders and back being caressed
8. having buttocks and thighs caressed
9. contact of tongues while kissing
10. embracing while semiclothed and being aware of husband's erection and his desire for sex
11. breasts being caressed while fully clothed
12. naked breasts being caressed
13. oral stimulation of the breasts
14. caressing husband's genitals
15. husband's fingers being inserted into the vagina during precoital loveplay
16. manual stimulation of the clitoris
17. having intercourse in the nude under the bed covers
18. having intercourse in the nude on top of the bed (uncovered)
19. having coitus in the nude in the dining room or living room
20. changing positions during intercourse
21. having intercourse in the nude while sitting in husband's lap

Systematic desensitization based on the hierarchy was then administered. Modifications were made as the process proceeded. For example, the woman was able to visualize, without anxiety, certain caresses (item no. 8) in the dark several sessions before she could accept them in the light. Throughout the period in which desensitization was going on, the husband was asked not to request intercourse with his wife so as not to reactivate anxiety around their sexual relationship.

Using such procedures for an average of six months and twenty-nine sessions, Lazarus reported that nine of the sixteen women subsequently enjoyed sexual intercourse, almost always had orgasms, and would even occasionally initiate sexual activities with their partners.

In situations in which a woman experiencing anxiety regarding sex is married, Madsen and Ullmann (1967) suggest that the husband participate in the systematic desensitization process by helping construct the hierarchy and by presenting the items on the hierarchy to his wife. Madsen and Ullmann found that involving the husband in this way enhanced his cooperation and communication with his wife. Furthermore, his participation tended to diminish his own anxiety and enabled both partners to explore their total relationship as it bore on their sexual interactions. In contrast to Lazarus and others, Madsen and Ullmann encouraged their couples to have intercourse during the desensitization process, believing that this would reinforce any progress the couples were making as long as they engaged only in those sexual activities that were mutually desired.

A number of therapists working with orgasmic dysfunction have reported on the successful use of self-regulated masturbation as a vehicle of behavior change (Annon, 1973; Lo Piccolo & Lobitz, 1973; Marquis, 1970; Dengrove, 1971; Hastings, 1963). These procedures are based on the findings that masturbation is the most probable way for a woman to reach orgasm (Kinsey, 1953) and that it generally produces the most intense orgasms (Masters & Johnson, 1966). Because of the intensity of the orgasm resulting from masturbation, it becomes a very powerful reinforcer of the fantasies that accompany or precede it. Annon (1971, 1973) describes a procedure in which masturbation is used. The goal for women who report difficulty in sexual responsiveness is to increase their awareness of their sexual reactions until they are able to experience orgasm. The woman is helped to learn about her own sexual responses through "self-exploration" so that she can transfer this knowledge to her relations with her partner. (The label "masturbation" is avoided to prevent any conditioned aversive responses to the term.) If the woman encounters limited progress, the therapist may suggest the use of a battery-operated vibrator and appropriate reading materials. The woman is also encouraged to be cognizant of her bodily sensations, particularly in her breasts and genitals, even when not specifically engaging in masturbation, such as when showering or bathing.

Once orgasm can be reached with some regularity through masturbation, the practitioner then helps the woman successively approximate heterosexual intercourse by changing the position of her arms, legs, and torso while she is "self-exploring." She is also instructed to move from direct clitoral stimulation to labial and vaginal stimulation. Finally these procedures may be faded into sexual intercourse with a partner.

Another program that uses self-stimulation as well as the training of husbands in sexual techniques has been reported by Lo Piccolo and Lobitz (1973). The program is described as extremely effective in producing orgasms for women who have never before experienced them from any source. The procedures are carried out as supervised homework, and the couple must fill out daily record forms. A refundable penalty deposit is used to insure the completion of the sometimes difficult assignments. There are nine steps in the procedure:

Step 1: Since the woman is usually found to be both unfamiliar with, and unappreciative of, her own body, particularly her genital organs, she is instructed to study her own nude body (particularly the genitals) carefully, using a hand mirror, and is given diagrams to facilitate her self-study. She is also started on a program of exercises for her pubococcygens muscles (Kegel, 1952) in order to increase the responsiveness of her pelvic muscles and increase her orgasmic potential.

Step 2: The woman is now asked to use her hands—as well as her eyes —to become familiar with her body. She is *not* led to expect that this will or should sexually arouse her, but only desensitize her to the sight and feel of her genitals.

Step 3: The woman is now asked to explore thoroughly her clitoral shaft and hood, major and minor labia, vaginal opening and all surrounding areas and try to locate any sensitive areas in her genitals that may produce pleasurable feelings.

Step 4: Once such areas are discovered, she is asked to learn how to stimulate these areas manually. The female co-therapist gives such pointers as how variations in stroking and pressure and the use of lubricants can aid in the enhancement of pleasure.

Step 5: If orgasm does not result from the activities in Step 4, the woman is asked to increase the intensity and duration of self-stimulation (to the point of diminishing returns) and to use fantasy as well as pornographic material to increase arousal.

Step 6: If orgasm has still not been reached the woman is instructed to use a mechanical vibrator, along with lubricants, pornographic materials, and erotic fantasies. The authors report that most women are orgasmic by this point.

Step 7: Once the woman has acquired the capacity to experience orgasm through self-stimulation, the focus shifts to having her experience orgasm brought about by her sexual partner. Initially this invoves her stimulating herself while her partner watches. While such a procedure may well be quite embarrassing, it serves to desensitize the woman—and perhaps her sexual partner—to the display of sexual arousal and orgasm in his presence. The partner can also observe what physical stimulation turns the woman on.

Step 8: The man now does for the woman exactly what she has learned to do for herself, whether it involves manual stimulation or mechanical stimulation with a vibrator.

Step 9: Once the man has been successful in bringing the woman to orgasm through the procedures of Step 8, intercourse is initiated in one of several positions in which the man has easy manual access to his partner's genitals. He continues manual procedures to bring her to orgasm concurrent with intromission. The man and woman may then choose to go on to learn how to bring about orgasm without manual stimulation.

In addition to these steps, Lo Piccolo and Lobitz have found other procedures that often facilitate orgasm. For example, the woman may facilitate real orgasms if, with her partner's knowledge, she role-plays gross exaggerations of orgasm, including violent convulsions, wild thrusting, and even screaming. This is particularly helpful with women who fear or are embarrassed by loss of control with orgasm, and thus lose arousal as orgasm approaches. "Knowing that the orgasm is not real, the couple is free to make a game, even a parody, of the response. We instruct them to repeat this until they pass from their initial anxiety and embarrassment to amusement and finally boredom with the procedure."

Laughter is an effective means of decreasing anxiety, and can be a useful tool in enhancing sexual pleasure in an "uptight" couple.

3. ERECTION DIFFICULTIES

Erection of the penis is usually a spontaneous response to sexual stimulation. However, the response may be inhibited when the cues associated with sexual activity are paired with anxiety about the likelihood of the response.

"Due to our society's great emphasis on successful sexual behavior, and due to the perceived unpleasant bodily sensations of unsuccessful behavior, inadequate sexual performance is quite unpleasant to the suffering male. In many cases because the impotent male has experienced unpleasant consequences for his sexual behavior, he anxiously tries to perform adequately on subsequent occasions. Since the anxiety he feels may actually prevent further adequate sexual performance, the impotent man may not learn successful behavior" (Shusterman, 1973, p. 226).

Behavior modification procedures may be useful in removing the learned obstacles to functional sexual responses.

One of the earliest reports on the use of learning principles to overcome impotence was presented by Wolpe (1958). He attempted to increase the probability of erection in sexual activities by reducing the incompatible response of anxiety through the use of systematic desensitization. The process involves the following steps:

1. A general behavioral history related to the individual's sexual problem is collected.
2. An explanation of the learning principles that may relate to impotence is presented.
3. Relaxation procedures are taught.
4. A hierarchy of stimuli that create anxiety is developed.
5. In a series of sessions, the man is asked to imagine each of these stimuli while, at the same time, relaxing.

In some cases reported by Wolpe (1958), systematic desensitization to imagined scenes was not necessary. Instead, the man was taught assertive sexual responses as well as relaxation. In one case, for example, a man was instructed to lie nude in bed with his wife and engage in sensual caresses, but not to attempt genital intercourse unless he experienced an "unequivocal" physical impulse to do so. Within a week, the man was having "successful" intercourse.

Lazarus also reported on the use of systematic desensitization both in individual treatment (1965) and in groups (1961). In his group procedure, he used a ten-item hierarchy of progressively intimate sexual situations entailing increasing amounts of initiative on the part of the man. The members of the group were first taught muscle relaxation procedures that they were to practice at home for fifteen minutes, twice each day. At the group's second meeting, the group leader began to present the hierarchy. If any group member felt anxious while imagining the scene, the item was withdrawn. Subsequent items were presented only if all group members indicated no anxiety for ten seconds. There was an ongoing attempt to make sure that all group members were able to visualize the scenes. By the last group meeting, all the men could visualize all the hierarchy scenes, and all reported that they no longer considered themselves impotent.

The most widely read and discussed behavioral approaches to impotence are those developed and reported by Masters and Johnson (1970). Since they recognize that the preoccupation about "performance" is in itself a major obstacle to satisfying sexual functioning, they de-emphasized erection *per se* as the focus of their procedures.. Although their approach involves a complex of counseling, testing, and other activities that includes both sexual partners as well as a dual sex treatment team, most of their procedures are based on behavioral principles, particularly a structuring of a hierarchy of sexual activities by the couple while in a state of relative relaxation. Their approach to impotence is to encourage the couple to concentrate on achieving pleasurable sexual stimulation from and for each other with the male experiencing as little pressure as possible to get an erection or engage in genital intercourse. Reducing this pressure, they found, increases the couple's enjoyment as well as the probability that nature will take its course, and erection spontaneously occur.

In early "homework" sessions, the couple is encouraged to learn about what "pleasures" each other and to give each other sensual pleasure, bypassing the genitals and suppressing feelings that intercourse "should" accompany such activities. Once the man has erections with some frequency and duration, the female partner is taught to "tease" the man to erection, then allow the erection to subside, and then bring him to erection again. Once erection is fairly predictable, the couple is instructed to attempt intercourse, with the woman above the man.

4. DECREASING UNDESIRED SEXUAL RESPONSES

Certain sexual behaviors are considered "problems" because they deviate from norms of acceptable sexual behavior. Various aversive social consequences (ridicule, legal penalties) as well as emotional respondents (guilt, anxiety) often accompany any reinforcements that maintain these behaviors, thus producing considerable conflict.

The social worker confronted with individuals whose sexual responses are considered undesired by themselves or others (or both) is confronted with several value issues. Does society—through the social worker—have the right to proscribe sexual behaviors that are not intrinsically harmful to the individual or society? How should the social worker respond when a person asks to change his sexual patterns primarily in order to avoid both the subtle and the overt oppression he experiences (such as harassment, ridicule, discrimination, etc.)? What should the social worker do when a client is ambivalent about his sexual behavior—decrease his anxiety and guilt about the socially undesirable behavior, or initiate behavior change procedures to reinforce socially approved sexual patterns?

Certainly such cases call for the social worker's ability to evaluate the behavior objectively in the light both of the individual's total life situation and of changing community standards. The social worker, understanding the factors that maintain the behavior as well as its consequences, will probably accept the individual's own choices. If the individual's tension or anxiety is high, the focus may not be on the alteration of the sexual behavior itself but on the modification of those contingencies that bring about the anxiety. Furthermore, the anxiety and guilt that often accompany an atypical sexual behavior can be reduced if the factors that reinforce these respondents are weakened. Discussions with empathic social workers who approach such behavior without criticism or disapproval can significantly reduce anxiety and the resulting pressure for major changes in the individual's sexual choices (Dittes, 1957).

However, if an individual clearly chooses to decrease a sexual response he finds undesirable, or if his behavior is believed dangerous to himself or others, there are several procedures that have proven useful in bringing these changes about. One such approach is to train the individual to avoid those situations that are likely to lead to the undesirable behavior. Bergin (1969) reports on a procedure that focuses on determining those specific stimulus and response links that form a behavioral chain leading to the unwanted behavior. For example, a twenty-four-year-old man requested help in terminating his homosexual behavior. Bergin treated his fear of heterosexual behavior through counterconditioning, but the homosexual pattern remained. A careful assessment of the man's typical homosexual encounters indicated a consistent stimulus–response ($S \to R$) sequence that led to the reported unwanted homosexual acts. A typical chain was described by Bergin as follows (1969, p. 144):

S (male person in a public place)———▸R (glance toward person) —
S (return of glance)———▸R (mild emotion and fantasy plus
additional glance) —
S (establishment of visual contact)———▸R (intensified
emotion and fantasy plus movement toward person) —
S (physical proximity)———▸R (heightened desire) —
S (heightened desire)———▸R (verbal exchange) —
S (verbal exchange)———▸R (interpersonal engagement) —
S (interpersonal engagement)———▸R (intense feelings, memories,
and fantasies) —
S (feelings, memories, and fantasies)———▸R (physical involvement) —
S (body contact)———▸R (consummatory behavior)

Once these sequences were identified, the man was taught to watch for the onset of such a chain and to interrupt the sequence quickly by deliberately attending to other stimuli or engaging in unrelated activities before the intensity of the situation got out of hand. After several attempts, the man was increasingly successful in avoiding involvement in the undesired sexual activities, and continued to be successful in regulating his behavior through a two-year follow-up. It should be noted, however, that Bergin used other procedures in his approach to the problem, and it is therefore difficult to determine which specific procedure brought about the change.

A procedure which more directly attacks unwanted sexual responses is based on covert sensitization, developed by Cautela (1967) and applied to unwanted sexual responses by Davison (1968), Anant (1968), and Barlow, Leitenberg, and Agras (1969). In this procedure, the individual is trained to relax and then is instructed to imagine vividly a series of scenes leading up to the unwanted sexual behavior. As each scene begins to arouse the individual, it is turned into a powerful aversive one. The individual is then instructed to visualize turning away from the sexual object and, as a result, escaping from the aversive stimuli, thus finding himself feeling much better. To be most effective, the scenes used in the procedure should incorporate situations that *could* exist in the individual's natural environment, as well as both arousing and aversive stimuli known to have a strong effect on the individual. Cautela provides the following example of such a scene (1967, p. 164):

> I want you to imagine that you are in a room with X. He is completely naked. As you approach him you notice he has sores and scabs all over his body with some kind of fluid oozing from them. A terrible foul stench comes from his body. The odor is so strong it makes you sick. You can feel food particles coming up your throat. You can't help yourself and you vomit all over the place, all over the floor, on your hands and clothes. And now that makes you even sicker and you vomit again and again all over everything. You turn away and then you start to feel better. You try to get out of the room but the door seems to be locked. The smell is still strong but you try desperately to get out. You kick at the door frantically until it finally opens and you run out into the nice clean air. It smells wonderful. You go home and shower and you feel so clean.

After several sessions in which the individual is helped to turn on these visualized scenes at will, he is instructed to practice visualizing them on his own, with the relief scenes comprising the escape and avoidance training in the procedures. Subsequently, whenever the individual begins to be stimulated by the unacceptable object, he is to turn on the noxious scene automatically and then switch to the escape scene once the impulse has subsided.

Sometimes it is difficult to invent a scene sufficiently noxious to overcome the strong reinforcement present in the unwanted sexual behavior.

Anant (1968) reported on a case of an intellectually limited twenty-year-old girl who kept losing her job because she continually seduced her co-workers. She was trained to visualize aversive scenes that made use of the young woman's fear of venereal disease, the embarrassment of an unplanned pregnancy, and the danger of being hurt or killed by a sexual partner. The covert sensitization program was successful within ten sessions. The woman took another job in which she avoided seducing co-workers during an eight-month follow-up.

Covert sensitization was also one of the procedures used with a young unmarried man greatly upset by the sadistic fantasies he had been experiencing for ten years. Anant (1968, p. 86) introduced the covert sensitization procedure as follows:

> With his eyes closed (the patient) was instructed to imagine a typical sadistic scene, a pretty girl tied to stakes on the ground and struggling tearfully to extricate herself. While looking at the girl, he was told to imagine someone bringing a branding iron towards his eyes, ultimately searing his eyebrows. A second image was attempted when this proved abortive, namely, being kicked in the groin by a ferocious-looking karate expert. When he reported himself indifferent to this image as well, the therapist depicted to him a large bowl of "soup," composed of steaming urine with reeking fecal boli bobbing around on top. His grimaces, contortions, and groans indicated that an effective image had been found, and the following five minutes were spent portraying his drinking from the bowl with accompanying nausea, at all times while peering over the floating debris at the struggling girl. After opening his eyes at the end of the imaginal ordeal, he reported spontaneously that he felt quite nauseated, and some time was spent in casual conversation in order to dispel the mood.

After eight sensitization sessions, the man's sadistic fantasies no longer occurred.

One of the procedures Davison used with the man was directed masturbation fantasies. The man was instructed to replace the sadistic fantasies that usually accompanied his masturbation with fantasies of nonsadistic relations. Only if the man lost his erection was he to revert to his former fantasies, but just long enough to restore his erection. Such replacement of lost fantasies—or any other unwanted sexual stimuli—are essential to any program that aims at removing unwanted sexual responses. Clients will more likely decrease behaviors that have been strongly reinforced if they learn to respond to acceptable alternate behaviors. Reinforcement for such new behaviors can be covertly self-administered, as in a case reported by Cautela (1970) in which heterosexual approach behaviors were shaped in a man whose behaviors had previously been exclusively homosexual. The man was taught to reinforce himself covertly for each step toward heterosexual relations by vividly visualizing a scene that was very reinforcing to him—"swimming on a hot day, feeling the refreshing water and feeling wonderful." A similar procedure was found useful by Rehm and Marston (1968) in working with a group of college students who were experiencing difficulties in relating to women.

Another strategy commonly used to decrease undesired behaviors is one or another form of aversion therapy. Although these procedures have been used only rarely, if at all, by social workers, they have provided some degree of success in work with some of those sexual behaviors that have proved most refractory to other interventive methods such as undesired homosexual behavior, fetishes, and so on.

"Aversion therapy" is a term that actually includes at least three different operations (for comprehensive reviews of aversion therapy techniques, see Rachman & Teasdale, 1969a; Rachman & Teasdale, 1969b; Feldman & MacCullough, 1971; Bandura, 1969). The first of these is operant punishment, application of an aversive stimulus following the performance of a behavior in order to decrease that behavior. The second, closely related to punishment, is what is called avoidance conditioning or aversion relief (also called "anticipatory avoidance" by Feldman & MacCullough, 1971), in which, in order to avoid an aversive stimulus, the client must perform some desired behavior (hence, the goal of decreasing an undesired behavior, say, unwanted homosexual behavior, by increasing desired behavior, say, heterosexual behavior). The third is the use of classical conditioning (aversive counterconditioning), the conditioning of an aversive stimulus and resulting anxiety to a previously attractive, but undesired, stimulus. Actually, there is not clear evidence of a substantial difference in the relative effectiveness of these three procedures (McConaghy and Barr, 1973) so, pending further research, selection of one or another appears to be based largely on the preferences of the practitioner and his familiarity with the procedures.

Although it is possible to use chemicals as the aversive stimuli, there has been an increasing use of electrical stimuli on grounds they are more controllable, less unpleasant, more efficient, and more effective. Actually, probably because of the very difficulty of the problems with which such procedures have been used, none has achieved 100 percent success. On the other hand, the use of aversion therapy procedures with such behaviors as undesired homosexuality and fetishes has achieved far higher success rates than any other procedures—behavioral or nonbehavioral— and it is on these grounds, and when the proper cautions are taken (e.g., client willingness, no other more positive procedures available, safety, etc.), that these procedures may loom as increasingly more important in the clinical interventive armamentarium.

A quote from the work of Feldman and MacCullough (1965, pp. 170–171) might illustrate their use of anticipatory avoidance conditioning, which is combined with reinforcement and other procedures to increase responsiveness to heterosexual stimuli (such as introducing slides of females contiguous with the relief of anxiety), in work with undesired homosexual behavior:

> The patient is told that he will see a male picture and that several seconds later he might receive a shock. He is also told that he can turn off the slide by pressing a switch, with which he is provided, whenever he wishes to do so, and that the moment the slide leaves the screen the shock will also be turned off. Finally he is told that he will never be shocked when the screen is blank. It is made clear to him that he should leave the slide on the screen for as long as he finds it sexually attractive. The first slide is then presented. The patient has the choice of switching it off or leaving it on the screen. Should he switch it off within eight seconds he is not shocked and this is termed an avoidance response. Should he fail to turn it off within 8 seconds, he receives a shock. If the shock strength is not sufficiently high to cause him to switch it off immediately, it is increased until he does so. In practice this has hardly ever been necessary. The moment a patient performs the switching off response the slide is removed and the shock is terminated. This is termed an escape trial. In addition to switching off, the patient is told to say "No" as soon as he wishes the slide to be removed. It is hoped that a further increment of habit strength will accrue to the avoidance habit by means of this further avoidance response. The usual course of events is: (i) several trials in all of which escape responses are made; (ii) a sequence of trials in some of which the patient escapes, and some which he avoids; (iii) a sequence of trials in which the patient avoids every time.

Because of the intensity of reinforcement and the complex learning that may be involved in the development of patterns of sexual behavior, it may be difficult to extinguish one set of unwanted responses while developing a new set. The case illustration that follows involved the sequential use of several previously described procedures to extinguish unacceptable (to the client and the community) sexual responses and develop socially acceptable and personally rewarding behaviors.

Case Illustration

In the case of Mr. Jones, Annon (1971, 1973) describes in detail the use of several procedures to eliminate unwanted pedophilic desires and behavior. In an interview with Miss Kato, a social worker, Mr. Jones, a 32-year-old unmarried man, hesitantly revealed that since his early teens he had always been attracted to eight- and nine-year-old girls. He had frequently engaged in mutual sexual explorations with girls ranging in age from two to twelve, and although he had never attempted intromission, he became highly aroused by these encounters. He would usually follow these episodes with masturbation to fantasies of sexual relations with the girls. He was at that time involved in a relationship with an older woman who had two young daughters. He reported being sexually repulsed by the woman but very much attracted to her daughters.

Mr. Jones was disgusted by his behavior, and was afraid of being caught and either sent to prison or committed to a psychiatric hospital. He desperately wanted to rid himself of his interest in young girls and to develop the capacity to relate sexually to mature women.

Miss Kato proceeded to assess Mr. Jones's behavioral patterns, including his sexual responses to both young girls and women as well as the content of his masturbatory fantasies. She also gave him articles on learning theory approaches to sexual problems to prepare him for subsequent procedures.

A sexual history revealed sex exploration with neighborhood children when he was between the ages of six and thirteen, and then no further sexual experiences until a visit to a prostitute at the age of nineteen. Subsequently, he had affairs with several women, none of which he considered as satisfying. He considered sexual intercourse "dirty" and adult female vaginas repulsive to look at. The bulk of his contacts with children were through his work as a medical assistant and as a volunteer in the pediatric section of a hospital, where he had frequent opportunities to handle children's genitals during routine tests. Records kept by Mr. Jones during the assessment period showed him to be sexually aroused by young girls an average of once or twice a day, with no arousal by adult women.

The use of conditioned masturbation was considered as a way to reinforce attraction to women, but was rejected for the following reasons: Since he considered fantasies about adult women aversive, and not just neutral, he would probably be unable to arouse himself with these fantasies, and thus revert to fantasies of young girls. Even worse, masturbation could cease to provide him with the reinforcement it was then providing, and he might be inclined to initiate even more physical contact with children. Furthermore, he did not currently have a solid relationship with an adult woman, and he lacked the skills to develop such a relationship. Therefore, as a preliminary procedure, systematic desensitization was used to decrease his negative attitudes toward sexual stimuli involving adult females.

The first hierarchy used consisted of stimuli associated with adult female genitals. Since Mr. Jones expressed a general rejection of adult female genitals, he had a difficult time discriminating degrees of response to particular aspects of the genitals. To facilitate the development of a hierarchy, he was given a book of photographs of female genitalia. He was able to identify "definite negative responses" to some of the pictures as well as minor sexual arousal to others. He was asked to take the book home and attempt to select those pictures that provoked the most negative response and write a "one-line, objectively descriptive sentence" about each of these pictures. He was then to rank each of these sentences according to the intensity of discomfort they provoked.

The five descriptions Mr. Jones gave Miss Kato were hardly "objective," but they *did* clearly reveal Mr. Jones's attitudes. In order of increasing degrees of unpleasantness, the descriptions were as follows (1971, pp. 395–396):

1. The lack of smoothness and symmetry destroys the concept of beauty.
2. The black thick pelt of hair reminds me more of a beard than of a female.
3. With three fingers in place, I would doubt my ability to please her (the picture was illustrating the distensibility of the vagina by showing the insertion of three fingers).
4. The grossness of the labia minora reminds me of sickness.
5. The worst looking flabby caricature of a female sex organ to be seen— active revulsion.

Several changes were then made in the five items Mr. Jones had presented for the hierarchy in order to make the items more neutral. It was found that medical terms such as "labia minora" failed to elicit vivid images, and his own words such as "cunt" and "bush" were too embarrassing for him. Finally, after trying out several modifications in the wording over several sessions, Miss Kato used the following workable items (1971, pp. 396–397):

1. See a vagina asymmetrically developed with a darkening and wrinkling of the inner lips.
2. See a vagina with a heavy growth of black pubic hair that obscures the outline of the genitals.
3. See an exposed vagina large enough for three fingers to be inserted.
4. See a vagina with particularly large inner lips that are apparently rough and darkened.
5. See a vagina with enlarged and drooping inner lips.

A byproduct of the wording of the hierarchy was Mr. Jones's apparent desensitization to the use of sexual words. He reported that their use during the systematic desensitization procedure enabled him to use them casually and with less anxiety. Moreover, Miss Kato noted a similar change in her own responses to the words. Positive changes in Mr. Jones's attitudes toward adult female genitalia—including some arousal—were noted within a month after the initiation of the systematic desensitization.

In addition to the systematic desensitization procedure, Miss Kato proceeded to provide him with sexual information and guidance for social contacts with women. For example, she debunked some of the myths he held about penis size, and showed him research reports and life-size models to support her points. She also discussed adult masturbation, and gave him articles to read about it. As a result of these discussions, Mr. Jones reported that he was no longer concerned about the size of his penis and that he felt great relief from learning how common adult masturbation was. This paved the way to the second major phase of intervention, masturbatory conditioning.

Mr. Jones was asked to focus on fantasies of sexual contacts with adult females while he masturbated at home. After several attempts, he reported to Miss Kato that he was unable to do so. He would consistently resort to fantasies that he found more stimulating. To aid him in focusing on adult women, Miss Kato provided him with several magazines with illustrations of nude women engaging in various activities. He was asked to select those pictures that elicited any "interest" at all. While pictures of preteenagers were eliminated from his choice, he selected several pictures, generally of teenagers with small breasts and light growth of pubic hair. It was hoped that fantasies generated by these pictures would serve as an initial step in reinforcing successive approximations to arousal with adult women.

In addition to using fantasies generated by these photographs while masturbating, Mr. Jones was asked to imagine himself fondling the women and engaging in mutual petting behavior with them in ways he had fantasized with children in the past. As he approached the point of ejaculatory inevitability, he was to vividly imagine intromission with the female, with all the specific accompanying sensations.

Within a short time, Mr. Jones reported that he could use the pictures exclusively during masturbation, but did not find the experience particularly arousing. He was assured that this was to be expected, but that continuing with the procedure would ultimately increase the arousal level of the fantasies. Subsequently, at each session, Mr. Jones exchanged his fantasy-stimulating pictures for those of progressively older women with greater breast development and more pubic hair. By the fifth session, he was selecting pictures of women about 20 years of age, with fairly large breasts and mature genitalia. Later, he reported a single "breakdown" of the masturbatory conditioning when he reverted to "old fantasies." He was surprised and disappointed, however, to discover that the old fantasies were no longer as arousing or satisfying as his "new" fantasies. He also reported he was now turning on to older teenagers (16-18) in his natural environment. Next, he was provided with pictures of adult couples petting and engaging in oral-genital activities and sexual intercourse, and he found these quite arousing.

At this time social behavior training was also initiated, including such formal procedures as reinforcement of successive approximations of social relations with women, behavior rehearsal and role playing with the use of video tape feedback, and such informal procedures as "bull sessions" on social skills with Dr. Annon.

Since Mr. Jones was now responding to socially acceptable sexual stimuli, aversive conditioning to unacceptable stimuli was introduced as a final interventive procedure. In particular, covert sensitization to sexual activities with young girls who might conceivably arouse Mr. Jones was used. In order to individualize the procedure, situations were developed which incorporated stimuli that were likely both to occur and to arouse Mr. Jones. For example, his likely unacceptable behaviors included being aroused by looking at a young girl's legs, hips, and crotch. The girls who had been most attractive to him were described as "cute, tan, with long black hair and graceful smooth legs," and the most attracting attire was "tight pants or Levis or sheer dresses." The activities he most frequently watched included "running, stooping over, squatting and sitting with legs spread open exposing tight underpants," and the most stimulating situations included "wrestling, having a child sit on his lap, patting her fanny, touching her buttocks and vagina, and the friction of rubbing his penis against her body."

It was also necessary to know which situations related to sexual approaches to children might be most aversive to Mr. Jones. These included being caught while involved with a young girl, "being yelled at, laughed at, insulted and arrested." He also considered bleeding as very aversive.

Based on such information, covert sensitization was begun by having Mr. Jones imagine the following scene while completely relaxed:

> It is a nice day and you are walking along the sidewalk (pause for signal of clear image). Off in the distance you see a mother and her young daughter walking toward you (pause for signal of clear image). As they come closer you notice the sunlight is behind them and shining through the little girl's sheer dress. You *think* about dropping your eyes and looking closer. You are *about* to drop your eyes. You *do*—you look at her hips and zero in on her crotch. Immediately the little girl screams and points at you. The mother grabs her daughter in terror and screams for help. People come running from all directions yelling and screaming at you. You're trapped. You can't escape. In anger they grab and tear at your clothes and beat your head and naked body. You feel hurt and trapped and desperately try to get away but you can't. You are bleeding from your wounds and people continue to hit you and call you "skinny bastard" and "child molester." Several big policemen arrive and start beating on you and they put handcuffs on you. You feel alone and defenseless and hurt and bleeding [Annon, 1971, p. 425].

He was asked to practice the covert sensitization procedure on his own along with such escape scenes as the following:

> You think about dropping your eyes and looking closer. You are about to drop your eyes—but you DON'T. You look away and notice the beautiful clouds and trees around you. You begin thinking of an attractive woman you saw in class that day. You barely notice as the mother and daughter

pass you and you think of what a beautiful day it is and how good you feel as you continue walking peacefully down the sidewalk [Annon, 1971, p. 426].

Finally, he was given practice in the use of covert reinforcement in place of escape scenes, as follows:

You think about dropping your eyes and looking closer. You are about to drop your eyes—but you don't. Immediately you are out in the country camping on a splendid day. You are thoroughly enjoying yourself as you admire the beautiful country around you [Annon, 1971, p. 426].

Mr. Jones responded well to these procedures, and was told to use them whenever he encountered unwanted stimulation in his natural environment.

Some additional sessions with Miss Kato focusing on behavior rehearsal and role playing in social relationships completed the intervention procedures.

By the end of their rehearsals Mr. Jones had advanced to the point where he not only appeared comfortable in initiating various dating behaviors but he began asking Miss Kato about her personal sexual experiences. . . . It

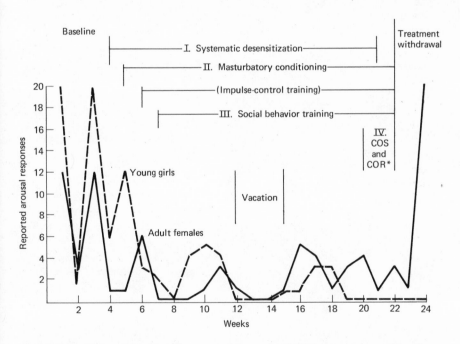

FIGURE 25.1.   Mr. Jones's arousal record. COS is covert sensitization; COR is covert reinforcement.
Source: J. Annon, "The Extension of Learning Principles to the Analysis and Treatment of Sexual Problems," Doctoral dissertation, University of Hawaii, Ann Arbor, Mich.: University Microfilms, No. 72-290.

was at this time that he was told of the plan to withdraw treatment procedures [Annon, 1971, p. 435].

Figure 25.1 shows Mr. Jones's record of arousal to girls and women before, during, and after interventive procedures. It is noted that he experienced no arousal to girls during the last six weeks of the intervention program, and that his responses to adult women at the end of the program equaled his previous rate of response to young girls.

When Mr. Jones was seen five months after the discontinuance of all interventive procedures, he reported strong sexual responses, and sexual activities with adult women. He experienced no sexual response to, or sex-related contacts with, young girls. Another follow-up contact with Mr. Jones nearly two years later (Annon, personal communication, 1974) indicated that the new sexual behavior patterns had been maintained and that he was enjoying mutually satisfying relations with women. Mr. Jones looked back on his prior sexual feelings and behavior as having belonged to "another man."

PART 4

PROBLEMS AND ISSUES

CHAPTER 26. Issues in the Use of Behavior
Modification In Social Work

The value base of social work existed long before there was a systematic attempt to introduce borrowed knowledge from the social sciences to implement these values. Social work is primarily a value-oriented field that uses technology—i.e., applied knowledge—to further its goals. It is only appropriate, then, that any technology be carefully scrutinized before it is accepted in practice as to whether it furthers the mission of the field and, at the same time, does no violence to its value base.

Behavior modification, perhaps more than any other technology, has been examined meticulously in the last few years by social work educators and practitioners (Carter & Stuart, 1970; Bruck, 1968; Thomas, 1968; Morrow & Gochros, 1970; Jehu, 1967, 1972; Hollis, 1968). The very potency of this technology, its relative newness, its origins in the "non-real-world" laboratory, and its departure from many traditional approaches have made it suspect for many social workers.

It is not surprising that social work, with its dual perspective on both the individual and society, is concerned with the long-range implications of this technology. The history of the last thirty years has taught us that technological advancements can have serious unanticipated consequences: consider, for example, the effects of atomic energy and television. As with any other tool, whether behavior modification is used for good or for evil is not inherent in the technology itself. Rather, the value system that governs the application of behavior modification (or any other technology) must come from the individuals who utilize it. It cannot be denied, however, that the more powerful a technology is, the greater its potential for both good and evil. With the development of behavior modification techniques, individual practitioners, the professions, and even governments have a growing capacity to influence—effectively, swiftly, and often subtly—the behavior of individuals, groups, and communities. The development of such new technologies is, perhaps, inevitable, and it carries with it certain hazards. And, while social workers may utilize this body of knowledge for the welfare of the individuals about whom they are concerned, they should, at the same time, consider the potential long-range effects of its use.

This concern is made greater because behavior modification is, in essence, a direct, action-oriented system; that is, behaviors of individuals are modified directly through the application of behavior modification procedures. Changes are usually brought about by the social worker, the mediator, and, perhaps, the client through the alteration of those variables in the client's environment that directly influence his behavior.

In traditional psychotherapeutic approaches, the usual method of bringing about change is for the social worker and the client to make changes in the client's cognitive system, which may or may not be supported by the attitudes or behaviors of those in the client's environment. These changes, then, are generally mediated by the client. In essence, clients hypothetically have, at any point, the option of making any use they choose of the "insights" or other cognitions that the social worker helps them achieve.

However, it is difficult to say how much real free choice a client has in making such decisions when treated through traditional methods. Clients, like everybody else, are already under the influence of many people in their environment, even though these controls may be subtle indeed.

In behavior modification, on the other hand, once a contract is set and the environment modified, behavioral change can become almost automatic. Thus, the use of behavior modification places even greater responsibility on social workers, since they take more significant roles in influencing their client's behavior than they would if the client's own cognitions serve as the principal mediator of behavior change. The very effectiveness of behavior modification, however, demands that the social worker—and the profession—carefully evaluate the rights of the individuals involved in such interventions.

In addition to the general concern about the values underlying behavior modification, there are some very specific concerns often expressed in the literature (Bruck, 1968; Morrow & Gochros, 1970; Hollis, 1968) about the application of this technology in social work practice. Some of the basic issues are posed below in the form of the more common questions asked about behavior modification. These questions reflect legitimate concerns about the ethics of the approach along with some misconceptions about it. While many of these issues have been discussed throughout this book, the purpose of this chapter is not only to summarize previous discussion but to highlight these issues, and focus attention on their importance.

For the sake of clarity, the questions are divided into three general categories:

1. questions about the value issues inherent in the use of behavior modification;
2. questions about the nature of human behavior that are raised by the behavioral model;
3. questions about the application of behavior modification procedures in social work practice.

1. Questions about the Value Issues Inherent in the Use of Behavior Modification

Does behavior modification have its own value base?

The determination of whether behavior modification is used for good or evil, of course, in large part is dependent on who is practicing it, and to what end. Implicit in this is the need to place heavy emphasis in the education of social workers on the value issues associated with the use of these approaches. The potential power of behavior modification makes it necessary to consider such questions as: who should evaluate the goals of those who are trying to influence others; under what circumstances can we deliberately try to influence the behavior of those who may not want to change their behavior; do we have any models of a functional life style for our clients to guide our interventions, or do we go along with any model they choose? There is always a danger of using any therapeutic approach to force an individual (or class of individuals) to engage in behaviors that conform with our standards rather than to help him behave in a way that is consistent with his own goals.

Whichever approach to practice a social worker uses, his value base is, to a great extent, influenced by that of the profession. Over the years the National Association of Social Workers, as well as individual social work practitioners and educators, have enunciated and continually re-evaluated the complex of values that provides the foundation for all social work practice (see, e.g., Bartlett, 1970).

But beyond the questions of the individual practitioner's and the profession's values there is the question of values implicit in the behavior modification approach itself. Although based to a large extent on objective studies of behavior, behavior modification does have certain values that are intrinsic to its use. Although there is some overlap between values (beliefs) and knowledge (empirically testable propositions) in the following list, it covers some of the basic precepts involved in the use of behavior modification.

1. Human suffering should be reduced by the most effective, efficient, and harmless methods that can be found.

2. The scientific method is the best available method of ordering knowledge; it can, and should be, applied to studying human behavior.

3. Scientific, objective knowledge about human behavior is available, and should be utilized by practitioners to bring about greater satisfaction for those who lack appropriate behaviors or exhibit dysfunctional behaviors.

4. Labels of "mental illness" or concepts of intrinsically bad behavior are not helpful. All behaviors must be evaluated in their environmental contexts. Thus, the practitioner must evaluate a behavior in terms of its effects both on the persons who emit it and on their social environment. Similarly, any change in behavior must be considered in terms of both its positive and its negative effects on the individual and his environment. Psychiatric labels related to the disease model (such as "anxiety hysteria") are both conceptually unsound and potentially harmful, since they can create a chain of responses that reinforce expected patterns of dysfunctional behavior.

5. Much of human behavior is modifiable; hence, a sense of optimism pervades the use of behavior modification. Since a great deal of behavior is a product of individuals' interaction with their environment, maladaptive behavior can be altered by modifying such interactions. This has led behaviorists to work with a range of behaviors traditional approaches have considered "hopeless," or, at least, in need of indefinite therapeutic intervention (e.g., "autistic" behavior, behavior of people institutionalized for years in the back wards of psychiatric hospitals, and so on).

6. A focus on inferred inner states (such as "autonomous ego," or "unfulfilled dependency needs") or assumptions about interpersonal relations (such as "transference," or "unresolved Oedipals") obfuscate problems, since their existence can neither be proved nor disproved. Therefore there are advantages in basing interventions on observable behavior. While much goes on in human beings that is, indeed, unobservable, there is also much that *is* observable in human behavior that can be modified to bring about greater positive reinforcement and pain reduction for people.

7. The goals of interventions are those of the client as long as they do not conflict with the appropriate goals of others. Exploration of the client's perceptions of his problem is essential for its resolution.

8. The relationship between practitioner and client must be open and honest. Goals, strategies, and techniques should be clearly explicated. No hidden agendas or secret labels should be used.

9. The value of any intervention plan is determined by whether it

works (i.e., whether it changes behavior in a desirable direction), not whether it somehow "sounds good" or "feels good."

10. Interventions should be focused on the client's behavior in his everyday life. The intervention process should focus on the client's reactions to, and activities in, his natural environment. The social worker should attempt to bring about changes through his client's regular relationships, rather than depend on the special relationship between him and his client.

11. Interventions should focus on environmental events as they relate to specific behaviors rather than on extensive talk and conceptualization between the person experiencing stress and a professional talker.

12. Social work interventions should be applicable with individuals from all social classes, rather than limited largely to upper- and middle-class clients. Behavior modification is widely applicable to people from all social class backgrounds. Furthermore, the behavior modification approach is such that clients need not be very intelligent, sophisticated, or verbal to be "treatable."

13. The client should be as full and active a participant in the intervention process as possible. However, the social worker should take responsibility for the successful application of his knowledge to each case.

14. It is desirable to emphasize positive change through positive reinforcement. "The good society is one in which all people are social reinforcers" (Franks, 1969, p. 544). While a society can and often does unnecessarily impinge on the rights of its citizens, the individual must still derive his satisfaction from that society. We can best help individuals receive their share of reinforcements by helping them derive their own positive reinforcements from their environment. Behavior modification runs contrary to totalitarian approaches that influence behavior through punitive control. Although behaviorists recognize the need for those within a society to influence each other's behavior, the goal clearly is to do this through mutual positive influence.

15. The social worker should be honest, open, direct, and human in his relations with clients, mediators, and significant others. There should not be a focus on mystical elements in these relationships. The treatment relationship consists of one person with a problem working with another person who has both special skills and an interest in helping people. Although the relationship should be mutually reinforcing, it should not be a replacement for the relationships in the client's—or social worker's—natural environment.

16. The social worker is accountable, in each case, for developing a system for ascertaining the success or failure of an intervention

on the basis of objective criteria and data. These data should be shared with the client, who has a right to participate both in goal selection and in the evaluation of the outcomes of intervention.

Isn't behavior modification essentially the manipulation of those without power by those who have power, and thus unethical?

Social workers may be concerned that behavior modification can be used coercively and to violate client self-determination. Hollis (1968), for instance, warned that if "the current operant conditioning approach is given a central theoretical position . . . it means the abandonment of our presently highly valued principle of giving priority to enhancing the client's control over his own treatment" (p. 195).

While the loss of a client's—or anyone else's—rights is a serious threat, it is not necessarily any more a threat in thoughtfully practiced behavior modification than in any other interventive strategy. Human behavior, after all, *is* profoundly and continuously influenced and directed by the behavior of other humans. Some condemn behavior modification because of its emphasis on planned behavioral influence. The criticism is made that such influence interferes with freedom. However " . . . control is not the opposite of freedom. The opposite of human control by humans might be many things. It is certainly, for example, a defining characteristic of schizophrenia. It may be hermithood . . . Freedom can better be viewed as the achievement of a most singular and exquisite pattern of control— one in which joy, creativity, surgency and dignity are fostered" (Tharp & Wetzel, 1969, p. 205).

The issue is not whether to engage in influencing behavior, but, rather, to what end. If the client perceives the goals as being clearly in his self-interest, and if he is, furthermore, willing to participate in change efforts, and the goals and change efforts are not harmful to others, ethical problems are minimized. Ethical problems arise when social workers find themselves influencing the behavior of others because of the rules and demands either of the institutions they are affiliated with or of an oppressive environment. In such situations, social workers cannot avoid the issues of fairness and justice. They must ask: are the target behaviors reasonable, really helpful, and compatible both with what the social worker knows about human behavior and what he holds to be basic human rights?

The social worker, finally, must also consider carefully the environmental contingencies that influence his own behavior and the case decisions he makes as a social worker, such as the sources of his own reinforcements and punishments on the job. Behavior modification, no less than any other interventive method, requires that practitioners look into their own reinforcement network to understand their own behavior in relation to their practice.

As was noted earlier, behavior modification leads to direct changes in behavior through changes deliberately made in the environmental contingencies of such behavior. Many forms of psychotherapy involve the use of therapeutic conversations with clients in the attempt to change their perception of themselves, their situation, and their options. However, it would be naive to believe that the social worker who uses an insight-oriented approach attempts to modify *only* his clients' perceptions, and not their overt behavior as well. Much of this influence is, of course subtle—so subtle, in fact, that sometimes neither the social worker nor the client is aware of what is going on. Hollis (1968), for example, noted that social reinforcement in interviews is a potentially useful technique to be used " . . . selectively within the total casework approach under certain limited conditions" (p. 195). She underestimates, however, the prevalence of such activity on the part of social workers. Research has increasingly demonstrated that interpersonal helpers of diverse orientations shape their client's statements, thinking, and other behaviors through differential reinforcement during interviews (Krasner, 1965). Such reinforcement takes the form of differential levels of attention, praise, encouragement, and approval of those behaviors the social worker is attempting to increase and inattention to, or disapproval of, behaviors he is trying to decrease. In fact, detailed evaluations of interviews of even so "nondirective" a therapist as Carl Rogers reveal that he systematically, if not necessarily deliberately, selectively reinforces certain client verbal behaviors with a resulting increase in the rate of these behaviors (Truax, 1966). Rogers concedes that: "In client-centered therapy, we are deeply engaged in the prediction and influencing of behavior, or even the control of behavior. As therapists we institute certain attitudinal conditions, and the client has relatively little voice in the establishment of these conditions. We predict that if these conditions are instituted, certain behavioral consequences will ensue in the client" (Rogers, cited in Goldstein, 1966, p. 58). If the goal of all approaches is *not* to have some influence on clients and their problems, what *is* it?

Behavior modification, however, offers considerably more effective and varied procedures than the mere reinforcement of verbal behaviors in interviews (although such reinforcement is, indeed, a legitimate technique). Social workers can provide their clients with many different vehicles for changing behavior within the context of their natural environment, without the added burden, expense, and loss of privacy and independence that an extensive therapeutic relationship involving a series of "therapeutic" interviews might demand.

Furthermore, although social workers bear the primary responsibility for the care and management of each case, they can be, in a real sense, partners of their clients. Indeed, in many cases the social worker *must* draw on the client's observations and knowledge to develop case goals and interventive strategies cooperatively. Since the approach is behaviorally specific, there is no place or need for secret labeling, which only tends to isolate the client from the social worker, and brands clients as "sick" and incompetent.

Whenever possible, both the social worker and the client should work together in the problem-solving process, defining and then influencing target behavior according to a clear, concise, behaviorally specific intervention contract concerned with the specific problem that the client brings to the social worker. This contract may, of course, change as a product of further negotiations. The social worker should not view the client's perception of his problem merely as an indicator of some deeper (and inferred) conflict (as a psychiatrist once said to one of the authors, "a patient's presenting problem is merely the ticket of admission to a person's *real* problems").

The ethical problems associated with attempts to influence institutionalized clients, children, and involuntary clients who are under the potentially coercive control of social agencies, correctional programs, child welfare organizations and so on are more serious. Complex issues of professional ethics and civil rights are often raised by the use of any interventive approach with people who are not specifically asking for behavioral change.

The social worker should obviously avoid using his influence to alter his client's behavior if such intervention clearly violates the rights of his client. But the balance of individual rights and social expectations is sometimes difficult to establish. The process of making the difficult ethical decision of who, indeed, the social worker represents in such situations, and who should control those who modify others' behaviors is, of course, a problem, and one very difficult to resolve. It is perhaps significant, however, that the potential strength of behavior modification technology as well as the clarity and explicitness of its procedures bring the ethical issues involved in its utilization into sharp focus, whereas the use of less explicit technologies may permit the illusion of self-determination for involuntary clients when, in fact, such self-determination does not exist (Morrow & Gochros, 1970).

Special concern is often expressed about the use of aversive procedures to eliminate behaviors that are perceived by the client or significant others as self-destructive, such as problem drinking, "autistic" behavior, and undesired, dysfunctional sexual behaviors. The ethical dilemmas in such situations include determining who defines these problems as dysfunctional. Is the client forced into behavioral change because the behavior is truly dysfunctional, or because others in his environment have made him believe so? Can aversive techniques be avoided by positively reinforcing competing desirable behavior? If the client participates voluntarily—and is not in any way coerced into the process—if there is no known non-aversive procedure that would bring about the same desired terminal goal, and if he fully understands and accepts the procedures that are to be followed, including their rationale and the probabilities that the intervention will be successful, then the temporary discomfort of aversive procedures *may* be as legitimate in terminating the client's suffering as surgery is for relieving a physical disorder.

Many professionals who use behavior modification are concerned about the use—or overuse—of aversive procedures. As Tharp and Wetzel (1969, p. 207) noted: "aversive control is rarely the most effective choice as a permanent socialization technique, and frequently so objectionable in its experiential concomitants for the [client] and in its brutalizing effects on the mediator as to be distasteful and unethical." However, in the following sentence they add: "This is not to say that we would never endorse punishment as a control technique . . . ; for grossly intolerable behaviors, such as autistic-self-destruction, pain—infrequently and judiciously administered—can create conditions which allow for instituting positive control." The point is that, sometimes, aversive procedures may be the only effective strategy for initial intervention into grossly damaging behaviors or self-destructive behaviors, or in situations where the potential positive effects of such intervention outweigh the potential negative effects. But such situations are rare, particularly considering the total range of problems with which social workers deal. The overwhelming emphasis in behavior modification—from both an ethical and functional viewpoint— is on the use of positive reinforcement to increase desired behaviors.

In sum, there are a multitude of variables that constantly influence our behavior. Such influences are obviously necessary. The influences brought about through behavior modification can be evaluated according to the extent to which they free individuals to engage in chosen behaviors that bring them satisfaction from their natural environment and that allow them to exert a maximum degree of control over their own destinies.

Doesn't behavior modification dehumanize people and relegate them to the roles of robots or animals, ignoring the particularly human aspects of thoughts and feelings?

It is not uncommon to hear practitioners using behavioral procedures described as people devoid of feelings, perceiving those whom they treat as being devoid of feelings as well—robots fixing robots, in other words. For example:

Now obviously this kind of conditioning approach to psychotherapy means that the patient is conditioned to the goals of the therapist, as the therapist controls the patient, but the therapist also takes no real responsibility for this, because the therapist, himself, is a programmed IBM machine, and one does not need to go into detail to indicate that the full meaning of human freedom—freedom and responsibility in any meaningful sense —is thereby undermined, but to the extent that this would be our approach to therapy, freedom would be destroyed [May, 1962].

Another example:

"Behaviorism is a psychology of despair and self-contempt. If man is simply a complex machine, then ethics and decency are nonsense and our philosophers, both ancient and modern, were fools" (LeShan & LeShan, 1968, p. 100) .

There may be some individuals who have been attracted to the practice of behavior modification because they *perceived* it as an approach that requires neither the helper nor the recipient of help to express feelings, thus obviating the need to "get involved." There are others who may have been attracted by a curiosity about human behavior and a desire to figuratively poke their fingers around in human behavior just to see what would happen. There are still others who may have been attracted to this area of practice because of the control they think they might gain over other people's behavior, or possibly even because they desire the sanctioned use of aversive control. One hopes that normal professional controls will be effective in preventing any malpractice by individuals such as these, whether they use behavior modification or any other interventive approach in work with their clients.

There are, no doubt, numerous, complex motivations—many self-serving—that determine which approach to practice a particular social worker will use. One major factor in this decision is simply the approaches the social worker has been exposed to in his education and practice. Another is which approach seems to be "most comfortable," and therefore easiest to use. Both of these factors may reflect how actively a particular practitioner seeks effective treatment approaches and how willing he is to push or extend himself on behalf of those he serves.

The motivations that determine a social worker's choice of interventive strategies can usually only be inferred. But it would be hoped that a more common factor than those cited above would be a deep concern on the part of each social worker that he is using the most effective and efficient interventive procedures available to alleviate human suffering. It is likely that if a social worker does not want to use a particular approach, or uses it but is unhappy with it—whatever the reason—he may not be successful in using it. However, from an ethical viewpoint, the selection of intervention strategies should be based not on the personal comfort or desires of the social worker, nor only on what he learned years ago, but on what approaches have the most evidence of effectiveness.

The practitioner is wrong if he believes that behavior always and uniformly can be effectively changed without taking into consideration the thoughts and feelings of the individuals whose behavior is to be changed. Cognition and emotion play a major role in determining behavior. Behavior modification without a recognition of the "humanness" of people probably could not succeed, since all intervention should take into account the uniqueness of the life experience of each client. Assessment should generally include an exploration of what the individual really wants, what feelings impede his accomplishing his goals, and how he perceives his environment. Many of the techniques of behavior modification—such as systematic desensitization, covert sensitization, and assertive training— work directly with emotions and feelings. Behavioral procedures to aid clients with decision-making and self-control all require exploration of a client's thoughts and wishes.

Even in working with operant behaviors, the reinforcements used are only effective to the extent that they touch on the needs, desires, hopes, and goals of the individual. Social reinforcers are effective only to the extent that they are perceived and felt as reinforcing. And, as has been noted frequently in this book, the core conditions of nonpossessive warmth, accurate empathy, and genuineness are major factors in the success of any helping situation.

The criticism that a behavioristic orientation "depersonalizes" individuals may, in part, be based on the point of view in behavior modification that the probability of a behavior occurring is largely a function of its environmental contingencies. That orientation does not deny, however, the amazing complexity of the factors that influence behavior. Human behavior is partly a product of genetic, biological, chemical and other non-environmental processes. Science does not yet (and may never) understand all the variables within individuals and their environment that determine behavior. What can be shown, however, is that certain behaviors occur with a certain frequency, rate, intensity, and duration. That behaviorally-oriented practitioners focus on observable or reportable behavior does not negate that they also should be aware of the complex processes that influence behavior going on *within* individuals. However, the orientation of those who use behavior modification is to work primarily with what is known, especially when it results in observable success, rather than with what we only can infer.

Doesn't behavior modification emphasize control of behaviors, and thus present a threat to individual freedom, both in clinical practice and in behaviorist schemes for social planning?

Social workers—along with other interested citizens—have long been concerned about the dangers involved when any individual or group exercises "control" over another. On the other hand, many practitioners who use behavioral procedures have been concerned about how they might apply emerging knowledge about human behavior in actually intervening with the increasingly complex problems involved in the interaction of individuals with each other and with larger social systems. The concern of most behaviorists does not reflect the belief that they have ready-made solutions to all social problems. However, many behaviorists think that some of the understanding and approaches that have derived from studies of human interaction might be successfully used in understanding and resolving broad social problems (see, e.g., Burgess & Bushell, 1969).

These approaches inevitably bring up issues about the use of control. Two contradictory positions often emerge from discussions about these issues (Kanfer & Phillips, 1970). There is a concern about individuals in power (including those in the helping professions) who ignore humanistic values in exerting impersonal dictatorial control over those without power in order to accomplish selfish or materialistic ends. At the same time there is increasing public support for the use of power by those possessing it to control some individuals and groups (e.g., burglars, big business, politicians) to prevent their potentially dangerous behavior and create a better environment for society in general. The inconsistency in these two perspectives can be summarized as: "People should not control each other, unless it does *me* some good." A position taken by some would be that "good people" (such as poor people, social workers, consumers, Democrats, minority group members, "us") should not be controlled, but "bad people" (such as rich people, manufacturers, Republicans, our spouses, children and parents, and "them") should. (The casts differ according to who is writing the script.) Obviously such labels rarely stand up under careful analysis. As one graduate social work student wrote: "There is so much bad in the best of us and so much good in the worst of us, that it makes it tough for some of us to diagnose the rest of us!" (Omori, 1972).

A common misconception, attacked by such authors as Skinner (1973), Kanfer and Phillips (1970), and Schiller (1968), is that freedom is a product of unlimited individual choice. They argue instead that the individuals within a society will suffer an erosion of their freedom unless there is sound, centralized governmental action to control the influence of technological "progress." Indeed, if society does not regulate, to some extent, the behavior of individuals, then the fulfillment made possible by any technological and social progress may well be prevented. In other words, many efforts by society to control behavior—such as limiting the harmful emissions of autos and factories—may require limiting the choices of some people to allow the freedom of others. In fact, the strategies and procedures for influencing group behavior on a large scale (e.g., Burgess & Bushell, 1969) may not be substantially different from the procedures (described in this book) for influencing the behavior of individuals and small groups.

However, there are many more problems in inducing change in the sociocultural environment and predicting the outcomes of such intervention than there are in changing the behavior of individuals. Social theorists such as Bauer (1966) have suggested several procedures to minimize these problems and to increase the probability of success of efforts to influence the general social environment, including using scientific systems of decision-making, national data banks, and regular assessment of both the social performance and the status of the country.

There are, of course, numerous hazards in these approaches—the problems of checks and balances in controlling the abuse of power, the danger of the emergence of bureaucratic totalitarianism, the difficulty in resolving conflicting social goals, the development of public apathy in a controlled society. There is already considerable concern over the mechanization of government at all levels, which has resulted both in people becoming social security numbers and in ten-digit telephone numbers. Although such procedures can be efficient, they may overlook individual differences. In such cases, however, it may not be due to the approach, but to the values of those who use it and to the inappropriate ways in which it is used.

Criticisms of the application of the scientific method to human problems—whether in government planning or in clinical practice—should not confuse the potential *usefulness* of the interventive procedures with the *appropriateness* of their use. Obviously, technology alone cannot solve man's social problems; events over the last decades confirm that observation. Nor can behavioral technology alone solve clinical problems. It is the artful, creative application of the knowledge about human behavior applied by individuals who are guided by their values and their concern for those they are helping that can bring about worthwhile change.

The question of the potential violation of individual freedom and clients' rights to self-determination through the use of behavior modification techniques is an important one. While it should be of concern to anyone in clinical practice, it becomes even more significant when these techniques are used, because of their potency. Not only must the social worker ask, "To what extent does my use of these techniques violate this person's freedom," but also, "Would my refusal to use behavior change techniques violate this person's freedom or that of others in his environment, or society as a whole?"

It is necessary in evaluating the use of behavior modification to be quite sure, however, that the choice of behavioral goals is not limited to social expectations (that is, what does society expect my client—or me—to do), but considers the client's rights and emotional needs as well. This is true whether the social worker is developing a behavioral change program for a particular individual, or for the entire population of an institution. Such programs should not violate the right of the clients to think, to express their views, to satisfy their basic human rights, to question or protest about elements of the program, or to maintain their uniqueness. The rationalization used by some professional helpers that what they are doing is "in the client's best interest" should be used cautiously, and not be an excuse to carry out control methods that have as their goals behavioral changes *not* in the client's interest, but that involve the maintenance of a self-serving bureaucracy. Also, the social worker must guard against having his clients behave according to his own personal value system rather than that of the clients or of society.

Of course, the issue of control is not unique to behavior modification. The expectations and goals of practitioners of all persuasions influence their clients behavior (Frank, 1961; Goldstein, 1962). It would seem that at least some of the difference in concerns between traditional therapies and behavior modification stems, in part, from the inherent clarity of the specific behavioral goals and procedures and the effectiveness of behavior modification on the one hand, and the absence of specificity, less focused assessment and intervention, and less obvious effectiveness of the more traditional approaches on the other. These differences may lead some to perceive traditional approaches as less controlling than behavior modification.

2. Questions about the Nature of Human Behavior Related to the Use of Behavior Modification

Don't the advocates of behavior modification think that people are simply helpless pawns, completely at the mercy of their environment?

If people were perceived as nothing but reactors to their environment, there would be little that the social worker could offer to clients other than urging passive acceptance of their fate. Few conscientious observers of human behavior subscribe to this pervasive image of human behavior. Philosophical debates over free will versus determinism often obscure the complexities of human behavior. Much of human behavior is certainly a product of the interactions individuals have with their environment. But the very activities individuals engage in—both what they say and what they do—constantly affect their environment and, in turn, the impact of their environment on them. Indeed, Urban and Ford (1961) have suggested that people can be conceived of as "pilots," not robots, in the sense that they have considerable power to influence their own direction: "This view sees man himself as exercising control over his responses and the situations which he encounters. He influences situations as much as they influence him" (p. 3).

Practice frameworks based on Freudian models are more likely to view the behavior of individuals as a result of repressed, unconscious, or hidden factors that have a profound effect on the functioning of the personality. People are seen as very much weighted down by their history in their interactions with their contemporary environment.

In contrast, the behavioral perspective views people as continually acting on and being acted upon by their environment (indeed, as noted early in this book, the very term "operant" refers to the way an individual's behavior *operates on,* or has an effect on, his environment). To ask which takes precedence, or which is more important (the individual's self-direction, or the influence of the environment) parallels the futility of asking which came first, the chicken or the egg. The social worker need not choose one emphasis or the other. In fact, the most effective course of intervention involves both working on the environmental contingencies of an individual's behavior, and helping individuals experiencing stress be more accurate in their perception of their environment, and make wise choices on how to operate on it.

Isn't positive reinforcement just another term for bribery? Shouldn't people behave appropriately because it is the "right" thing to do?

One of the features of behavior modification that may tend to alienate some is its emphasis on positive reinforcement. Strangely enough, many critics of behavior modification would more readily accept punishment as the principal method of influencing behavior. Most people find the *act* of rewarding more acceptable than the *act* of punishment, and may be less likely to notice when their behavior is being influenced by positive reinforcement than when it is being controlled by punishment. But they perceive positive reinforcement as more dangerous and of less moral virtue than changing behavior by punishment (Kanfer & Phillips, 1970). People recall their own experiences with punishment, and, judging by its prevalence in our society, prefer to use it—or the threat of it—when they see a need to influence the behavior of others. There is a prevailing attitude, certainly in most of middle-class American society (from which most of our social workers are drawn), that there must be something wrong if something feels too good—and positive reinforcement generally feels good. Many philosophers, theologians, and personality theorists have considered man to be in a constant struggle between his conscience or superego and his negative libidinal nature and thus dependent on his own or others' aversive devices to keep his evil nature under control (Kanfer & Phillips, 1970).

Perhaps it should not, therefore, be too surprising that most deliberate controls on behavior tend to be punitive. Our prison system and much of our parental discipline, as well as the controls in most schools, are based on aversive control—that is, undesirable behavior is punished, and positive behavior is developed as a way of avoiding punishment (negative reinforcement). It sometimes seems that this form of behavioral control—using aversive or punitive methods—is more acceptable to many people than focusing on helping people work toward the rewarding aspects of life through the provision of positive reinforcement for desirable behavior. Perhaps this is a reflection of our work ethic, which dictates that doing good is only to be expected of man and that rewarding positive behavior is unnecessary; only negative behavior should be attended to. In this way, the child who acts in a well-behaved way all day in school is ignored. But a deviation from this pattern, say, talking out of turn for only one minute, is immediately punished. Unfortunately, many people do not develop, for one reason or another, certain desirable behaviors; these functional behaviors are sometimes prevented by circumstances often beyond their control. Use of behavior modification can help rectify these situations so that a person can draw his gratification and satisfaction from his natural environment and, in return, provide reinforcements to others. The point is that, as noted above, practitioners using behavior modification openly recognize that there are many types of control—both overt and covert—operating in everyday life. The behavioral perspective suggests first, that these controls should be as overt as possible, and second, and even more important, these controls should be positive rather than aversive. Thus, people would learn to operate on their environment for what is rewarding and desirable, rather than for avoiding punishment.

A related objection to using positive reinforcement that has been raised is that it somehow seems wrong to reinforce others for behavior that they should be emitting anyway. In other words, people should behave appropriately because it is the "right" thing to do, not because they will be reinforced for it. Some parents, for instance, ask why they should reinforce their children for doing something they *should* be doing. Or a wife might question why she has to give special reinforcement to her spouse for being a "good husband" when that is expected of him.

This argument implies that "good" behavior, or, for that matter, any behavior, is self-generating, that people, almost innately, know what is right and what is wrong. This position ignores almost everything that is known about human behavior and the laws of learning. People are not born with the ability to distinguish between what is right and what is wrong. This knowledge is a product of learning, sometimes subtle and often covert, but learning nevertheless. A whole variety of learning principles apply here, including the modeling of behavior displayed by significant others, as well as the positive reinforcement of selected behaviors as individuals gradually assume certain roles. Few of us would go to work, write books, or kiss our mates unless we derived some satisfaction out of it. Of course, such reinforcement is often found in the behavior itself. But when the behavior is not intrinsically reinforcing, then the deciding factor in whether or not the behavior occurs may lie in the availability of external reinforcement.

Generally, intrinsic reinforcement, or internal, self-reinforcement ("I am a good person") is developed only after extensive experience with external (extrinsic) reinforcement. It is unrealistic to expect a child or an adult to operate on internal reinforcement before he has been taught by repeated positive experiences with his environment that there is a high probability he will be reinforced for desirable behavior. Indeed, it is unlikely that much good would be done at all if it were not for at least occasional external reinforcements. The point is that, whether subtle or obvious, laws of learning do apply in the development of most behavior, and their systematic (rather than haphazard or arbitrary) application can have rewarding and predictable consequences for the people involved. As Krumboltz and Krumboltz (1972, p. 250) noted: "A harmonious society is one in which all members feel reinforced in their contact with one another."

One result of the distrust of the emphasis of behavior modification on positive reinforcement is the often-heard objection, expressed particularly by many teachers and parents, that to advocate the use of positive reinforcement to influence behavior is, in effect, bribery and, therefore, morally objectionable and of questionable long-term effectiveness.

The question of bribery can be approached as at least partly a semantic one. Webster's Seventh New Collegiate Dictionary (1971) defines bribery as, "money or favor bestowed or provided to a person . . . to pervert his judgment or corrupt his conduct." Reinforcement, then, can certainly be bribery if the goal is to pervert judgment or corrupt conduct. There are many ways to view transactions in which one item of worth is exchanged for another: wages, rewards, bribery, reinforcements, blackmail, reparations, and so on (Krumboltz & Krumboltz, 1972). Many of our daily interactions with others are the product of such exchanges, which can be used to bring about functional or dysfunctional, desirable or undesirable behaviors. Reinforcement can obviously be used for good or evil. Only if reinforcement is used for negative purposes can it be truly called a bribe. Just as we can have "wages for sin" and "wages for a hard day's work," we can also have reinforcement for truancy and reinforcement for toothbrushing. Clinical applications of positive reinforcement are not (and should not be) used to strengthen antisocial acts.

However, the power of behavior modification still frightens some, in the same way that the power of automobiles does. Both can be used wisely or foolishly. In a heterogeneous society, it is often unclear what is good behavior and what is bad (is hard work always a virtue?). There may, therefore, be disagreements over what exactly should be reinforced. But the reinforcement process itself can be neither praised nor condemned —it is a fact of social life that can be used either to do harm or to enhance social functioning. It is the value system, art, and wisdom of the social worker (or other change agent) that makes the difference.

The concept of bribery sometimes has other meanings besides its antisocial one (Patterson, 1971). Bribery can also refer to the offering of something of worth to cover up prior inadequate training. Thus, a parent may offer a child a dollar if he "promises" not to insult a visiting relative. In that case, the parent is making up for his or her own difficulties in being a parent by offering money to the child. It usually does not work. Even if it does, it offers little carry-over to similar situations in the future unless another, perhaps larger, "bribe" is offered. Effective reinforcement of a complex behavior demands a history of reinforcement of the steps that lead up to it. Stop-gap measures such as bribes rarely can make up for past deficiencies.

Similarly, coaxing, which is an attempt to persuade someone to do something he really does not want to do *before* he does it, is rarely effective. Repeated episodes of coaxing may actually strengthen an individual's refusal; indeed, coaxers may establish a behavior opposite to what they wanted to by reinforcing through their attention the refusal to engage in the target behavior, rather than reinforcing the target behavior itself (Krumboltz & Krumboltz, 1972).

What may be most abhorrent about bribery (and, perhaps, coaxing) is not the use of an exchange (reinforcement) to bring about desired goals or outcomes, but rather the balance in benefits (the outcome of reinforcement) for those who reinforce and those who are reinforced. An undesired—and perhaps immoral—balance exists when the individual who is doing the reinforcing has as his major (or only) goal and motivation his own well-being rather than that of the individual being reinforced, of the mutual relationship, or of society as a whole. In such a situation, the reinforcements may well be perceived as bribes, since they are really intended only to benefit the dispenser.

Also underlying some of the concerns about the appropriateness of reinforcement may be the feeling that there is danger in a behavioral system that may be reinforcing for some, but aversive to those who do not have the skills or ability to behave in such a way as to obtain reinforcement. There is no question that in an ideal world, everyone should have successes as often—and failures as infrequently—as possible. The reality, however, is that we optimize our reinforcements by behaving in ways that are perceived by others as reinforceable. This certainly has its unfortunate consequences. For instance, "children from disadvantaged backgrounds start [school] slowly, seldom catch up, and are humiliated by low grades and teacher disapproval. They are seldom rewarded for the progress they do make. It is no wonder that they often become dropouts, truants or vandals. The present system is aversive to those who do not perform correctly" (Krumboltz & Krumboltz, 1972, pp. 246–247). There are numerous other situations that social workers are all too aware of in which it seems that people just cannot win—in prisons, mental hospitals, or through the bureaucratic obstacles that block access to some needed service. It is, therefore, incumbent on the social worker —as it always has been—to help his clients maximize the probability of obtaining reinforcement in their environment for functional behavior. Such help involves not only the development of skills (through appropriate reinforcement) that would generate natural rewards in the client's natural environment, but also the modification of the environment itself so that it is more responsive to the client's appropriate behaviors.

Don't reinforcers spoil people?

"Spoiling" people is a problem only when reinforcement is used inappropriately, in which case "spoiling" means the doing of harm to their patterns of interaction with other people. There are three misuses of reinforcement that could have deleterious effects:

First: The mediator (parent, teacher, etc.) may routinely provide reinforcement well in excess of what is needed to bring about desired behavior, and then maintain excessive levels of reinforcement on a continuous schedule even after the behavior is established. Such patterns of reinforcement could lead to satiation of the client, or to the client's need for higher and higher levels of reinforcement to bring about desired behavior. For example, the parents of a retarded child may underestimate his mental capacity and consistently overpraise each of his accomplishments. This could result in the child's being reinforced only by his parents' overwhelming social reinforcements (as well as by primary reinforcers, of course), rather than the intrinsic reinforcement of the satisfaction of a job well done.

Second: A mediator may provide reinforcement under inappropriate conditions, thus teaching the client inappropriate behaviors. For example, a technician on a psychiatric ward might pay attention to a particular individual committed to the ward only when he engaged in "crazy talk" or vigorous head movements, but ignore relatively more functional behaviors. Parents who make a fuss over their children every time they cry, regardless of their reason for crying, may be "spoiling" their children in that the children would be learning that crying for whatever reason is always rewarded with parental attention.

Third: A mediator may provide reinforcement inconsistently to a client. This is a pattern that many parents recognize as "giving in." For example, a parent may limit a child's intake of sweets at home, but be unwilling to say no to the child's loud demands for candy in a crowded department store. As a result, the parent might buy the candy "just to keep the child quiet." The irony in such a situation is that the parent may indeed be "spoiling" the child (i.e., reinforcing the child for undesirable behavior) in order to present to others the image of their child as "unspoiled".

The continual misuse of reinforcement through excessive, inappropriate, and inconsistent use can indeed have a negative effect on the client's overall patterns of behavior. However, it is not reinforcement itself that "spoils" the individual, but rather the *ways* it is used and the *goals* for which it is used. Much of our learning—whether it is learning to talk, ride a bicycle, play poker, or even something as complex as keeping a job or making friends—is, at least in large part, a product of reinforcement. Such reinforcement is often so subtle that we may not even notice it. We may therefore become uneasy about the deliberate use of reinforcement. Furthermore, as noted earlier, the work ethic that permeates much of our society teaches us to be good and to work hard because it is *right* to work hard and be good—not because there are worldly rewards. Nevertheless, much of what we do is influenced by the history of approval, praise, and tangible rewards we garner for our behavior—whether it be the salary received for a job, or the congratulations of a congregation for a religious conversion. If the laws that determine much of our daily life are applied in a systematic, appropriate manner, there is far less risk of "character destruction" than there is from the more haphazard reinforcement of behavior that usually goes on.

Isn't cognitive and affective self-awareness necessary, however, before real, lasting change can take place in people's overt behavior?

Most changes in the daily life of individuals occur without their being aware of the "reasons" for them. Behaviors generally change subtly because of a complex of equally subtle internal and external events. Although individuals in such fields as psychotherapy try to explain how these events bring about such changes, these "explanations" are often just guesses. Even in situations where people are fairly well acquainted with the environmental factors that bring about specific changes in behavior, or "cause" certain behaviors, they often find that they are unable to change their behavior simply on the basis of their knowledge.

People who smoke, overeat, or feel anxious or depressed may well know what events precipitated or followed such behaviors or affects, but can still do little about them. Indeed, it is not unusual for individuals, in their own thoughts or in discussions with others, to use elaborate descriptions of these causes as a justification of their behavior and a rationale for continuing such behavior.

The idea, however, that insight is necessary to change behavior has been well reinforced in social work and in the other helping professions. Although self-awareness can be useful in avoiding and sometimes coping with dysfunctional behaviors, there is little reason to assume either that it is necessary to have insight to change behavior, or that insight, alone, will change behavior. Indeed, as was discussed more extensively in Chapter 8, what is frequently perceived as insight often follows rather than precedes changes in behavior. It is not unusual for clinicians to note that "self-awareness" and attitude change often occur only after a client engages in new behaviors (Ullmann & Krasner, 1969).

Freud himself questioned whether insight was enough to change certain behaviors, and whether new behaviors can precede any new self-understanding. In discussing a case of agoraphobia, Freud suggested that direct behavioral change was as important as insight in altering the problem: "One can hardly ever master a phobia if one waits till the patient lets the analysis influence him to give it up. . . . One succeeds only when one can induce them . . . to go along and to struggle with their anxiety while they make the attempt" (Freud, 1957, p. 400).

The evidence is overwhelming that many different behaviors can be changed through the modification of antecedent and consequent environmental events without any concomitant cognitive or emotional changes (Ayllon, 1964; Bijou, 1967; Eysenck, 1960, 1964; Hart, 1968; Hawkins, 1966; Krasner, 1965; Staats, 1963, 1964, 1968; Ullmann, 1965; Ulrich *et al.,* 1966; Atthowe & Krasner, 1968; Ayllon & Azrin, 1968; Franks, 1964; Bandura, 1969; Schaefer & Martin, 1969). The notion that attitude change must precede behavioral change has also been contradicted by research in other areas such as the modification of racial prejudice (Clark, 1953; Raab, 1959), which showed that changes in approved policies and practices created rapid change in discriminatory behavior despite previous prejudices.

The intent here is not to deny that cognition has an important role in behavioral change. In fact, as was suggested in Chapter 8, the facilitation of client understanding of the behavioral program can play an important part in enhancing its effectiveness. Flexibility in attitudes can help individuals to expose themselves to situations that could lead to new behavior. By definition, attitudes are cognitive guides to behavior. However, attitudes themselves are influenced by environmental factors. The point is, of course, that the social worker who uses behavior modification should do everything in his power to help the client make positive changes in behavior. When the research indicates that such changes can be facilitated through the addition of procedures that enhance self-awareness, such procedures should be incorporated into practice.

If one deals only with explicit, specific behaviors, isn't there a risk of symptom substitution occurring?

This often-expressed concern is based on the assumption that dysfunctional behavior is analogous to physical disease—that is, that "surface symptoms," whether they be specific problem behaviors or fever are merely the external reflection of some underlying disease. If one merely "masks" the symptom, one has really ignored the core problem—the disease—and, this argument goes, other symptoms and problems will emerge after the superficial symptoms are removed. Such a view pictures the psyche as a steam boiler. If it gets overheated, the steam pressure will get too high, and perhaps blow a hole in the boiler's surface. If someone merely plugs the hole, little is accomplished, since another hole will soon appear. The corollary of this psychodynamic perspective on dysfunctional behavior is that, unless the person understands his problem and goes through some "internal" changes first, no significant or lasting behavioral change will occur; the steam's pressure will remain dangerously high.

Since early psychiatric thinking was an outgrowth of medical experience, such a view of dysfunctional behavior seemed logical enough. Moreover, many clinicians see a recurrence of problem behavior in their clients, which they feel can only be explained by the notion of symptom substitution. However, in extensive research that carefully evaluated the use of behavior modification techniques, there have been very few incidents of new dysfunctional behaviors emerging following the modification of old ones (Franks, 1969; Ullmann & Krasner, 1969). In those rare cases in which new dysfunctional behaviors did appear, one can account for such appearances either through new learning experiences, or through the relearning of old behaviors as a function of the return to similar environments. When a client, for example, finds that a particular antisocial behavior is no longer reinforced (or is punished), he may try other antisocial behaviors. However, if his circumstances are altered so that functional behaviors bring about reinforcement, his antisocial behavior likely will extinguish.

Typically, individuals who show an increase in functional behavior or a decrease in dysfunctional behavior (or both) obtain far more positive responses from their natural environment. Those in their families, their friends, employers, and co-workers may all respond more positively to the individual, both in relation to the individual's new behavior and, perhaps, to the individual's general mood ("Laugh and the world laughs with you; cry and you cry alone"). The new desirable behaviors, therefore, receive more positive reinforcement, and the more infrequent dysfunctional behaviors extinguish. The newly acquired desirable behaviors are, therefore, sustained by the natural environment as the individual experiences less trauma as a result of the reaction of others to his overall behavior.

3. Questions about the Application of Behavior Modification Procedures in Social Work Practice

Isn't behavior modification just a fancy term for the old idea of giving rewards and punishments?

In many respects, the reinforcements and punishments used in behavior modification seem similar to traditional rewards and punishments. There are, however, some significant differences. Contingencies (including reinforcement and punishment) are developed and tested for their specific effect at a particular point in time on particular behaviors of particular individuals. Traditionally defined rewards and punishments tend to be generalized—that is, the same reward may be used for a class of people, or a class of problems. Furthermore, in behavior modification, contingencies are used in a planned program of intervention according to a specific schedule, and their effects carefully checked out. Traditional rewards and punishments are more usually provided without any particular plan or schedule, and are more often related to the mood of the rewarder (or punisher) than to the behavior of the individual who is the object of the change procedure. Also, as was discussed in Part I, reinforcement and positive and negative punishment, as used in the behavioral sense, are defined by the effects they have on behavior. The conventional notion of reward and punishment refers mainly to a subjective sense of pleasure or pain, or to the intent of the rewarder or punisher, whether or not behavior changes at all. In essence, the use of reinforcement and punishment in behavior modification is planned, systematic, related to the problems of the client and his environment, and applied in a manner consistent with the ethics of all the parties involved. For better or for worse, rewards and punishments as traditionally defined are not subject to any of these restrictions.

Isn't behavior modification simply a new explanation for what social workers have always known and done anyway?

The laws of human behavior are not new—they have existed since man emerged as a social being. The laws have been observed in operation—and the principles derived from the laws utilized—as long as people have looked around themselves and noted what other people (and they, themselves) were doing. Playwrights, authors, poets, philosophers, religious leaders, and behavioral scientists have made keen, accurate descriptions of what people tend to do in their interaction with their environment. Psychiatrists, politicians, social workers, propagandists, parents, and spouses have long used their own and others' observations about behavior to try to influence other people's behavior, sometimes with considerable effectiveness.

What is new in behavior modification is the systematic, planned application of laws about behavior derived from careful, scientific studies and observations. These applications are then carried out with as much scientific rigor as the observations upon which they are based, including a careful evaluation of their efficacy. This, quite simply, is different from what traditionally has been the case in the practice of social work, where the connection (if any) between the scientific principles of human behavior and the application of these principles in practice has been tenuous. Furthermore, where some knowledge of the laws of learning was applied, e.g., using reinforcement in interviewing, the application was limited to only a small aspect of practice, and clearly lacked the breadth and scope of the interventive procedures derived from the behavior modification model. Finally, the major emphasis in behavior modification on the application of specific techniques to specific problems has been missing in traditional social work practice. This specificity is one of the major advantages of the behavioral approach.

Does behavior modification recognize individual differences?

The behavior modification approach, like most systems that try to understand and deal with human behavior, recognizes that in some ways all people are alike, and in other ways all people are different. Certainly, some behavior modification procedures seem to work effectively with general classes of behavior (such as stuttering and bed wetting). However, the main thrust of behavior modification is individualization: precisely pinpointing the problem behaviors experienced by particular individuals, tailoring reinforcements to particular individuals at particular times, making use of the specific characteristics of a client's particular natural environment, and developing specific programs for shaping desired behavior in successive steps based on the individual's circumstances and his behavioral repertoire.

Behavior modification requires that the individuality of each person be recognized, and specifies the ways in which individual differences should be used. Individual applications of behavior modification are based on the understanding of certain basic laws of learning, genetic and biological factors, and prior patterns of reinforcement. Research has demonstrated that these principles apply to individuals from a variety of social class, ethnic and cultural groups. However, the social worker who uses behavior modification also must understand the individual client's behavior. The social worker would study the relation between the behavior and the client's social and cultural situation, the goals of the client and those around him, and the circumstances in the client's environment that can be modified to affect those behaviors that have been determined to be significant. Thus, behavior modification recognizes and deals both with commonalities, and with individual differences. But always, the focus is placed on specific behaviors of each individual at a particular time.

Doesn't behavior modification limit itself to oversimplified details of behavior rather than the whole person in the context of his total environment?

Frequently, this question is raised because behavior modification is based on laboratory research on simpler animals engaging in simple activity ("People are not rats or pigeons!"). Such criticisms often reflect erroneous ideas of how knowledge is transferred from the laboratory to the "real world" (Morrow & Gochros, 1970). Laboratory research is often limited to a few variables that are manipulated experimentally. Intervening variables are deliberately kept to a minimum so that concise, reliable interpretations of the results of the experiment may be made. Obviously, then, experimental work may involve research on animals in a simple environment before the knowledge involved is applied to humans in a more complex environment. Indeed, such an approach has made much of the impressive progress in the field of medicine possible.

It is a reasonable observation that often these laboratory settings are quite different from those in which human beings live. However, as Goldiamond (1962) has observed, such research has proved to have broad applicability to complex human problems. Procedures such as systematic desensitization and many of the findings about positive reinforcement originated in laboratory studies. On the other hand, conceptual frameworks for verbal therapy (e.g., psychoanalysis), which are described and developed in rather general terms—which may *sound* impressive—may turn out to have very little applicability in developing purposeful change in diverse problem behaviors.

Critics of behavior modification may feel that the focus on behavioral change is limited to very small, relatively unimportant units of behavior rather than complex human behaviors. We hope this book has dispelled that notion by illustrating the use of behavior modification with a variety of complex problem behaviors typically found in everyday practice. In addition, numerous published reports have presented data on the successful application of behavioral procedures to a variety of broad and complex problems (such as were summarized in the chapters dealing with the tools and procedures of behavior modification). As was noted in earlier chapters, however, the approach to such complex problems requires their partialization into manageable, specific (but psychologically and socially significant) behaviors in order for them to be modified sequentially.

Finally, while behavior modification does focus on specific behaviors, one of the goals inherent in the behavioral approach is to insure that this behavior is carried over into other situations. There is much to suggest that such carry-over from one situation in which improved behavior is exhibited and reinforced to other situations is more of a rule than an exception (Vernon, 1972).

Even if we accept manipulation, on whose behalf do we manipulate—the individual's or the society's?

For many years, one of the most frequently debated issues in social work has been whether it is right to participate in efforts to have individuals adjust to a patently unjust environment. For instance, do we help prisoners of an unjust prison system be "good prisoners"; can we allow welfare recipients on unrealistic budgets to get away with cheating? In situations in which the needs and rights of individuals seem to be constantly violated by the organizations that possess considerable power to punish reasonable behaviors, the social worker in direct services would seem to have little choice but to try to teach the consumers of these "services" how to optimize their reinforcements and how to avoid punishment for reasonable behaviors, while attempting to modify the behavior of those who establish the rules as to what is to be reinforced and punished. Social work ethics require such a dual orientation and commitment. The first position statement of the NASA Code of Ethics is: "I regard as my primary obligation the welfare of the individual or group served, which includes action for improving social conditions." Both activities can and should go on simultaneously.

There are occasions, however, when the social worker encounters problems in which there is a disparity between clients' values and those accepted by most members of their culture. Societies generally prescribe such diverse behaviors as preferred marriage forms, ways parents should discipline their children, sexual behaviors, work orientation, and patterns of behaving in social gatherings. Sometimes, individual choices do not conform to these expectations. For instance, some people prefer being alone, or having sexual relations with partners of their own sex, or not being gregarious at the office.

Fortunately, while some cultures may openly condone or advocate only one set of behaviors, they often informally permit—and even allow reinforcement for—a much wider spectrum of behavior patterns (Kanfer & Phillips, 1970). One of the major functions of the major functions of the social worker, then, becomes to explore and expand the alternative behaviors open to individuals, and seek ways their behaviors can be reinforced: "If you don't like to mess with people, how about changing your job"; or, "If you don't want to work, you could move back with your family"; or, "If you don't want to get married, but want a choice of partners, how about moving to a bigger city?"

Those who use behavior modification are well aware of the significance of cultural values for the reinforcement of individuals. This awareness should lead to two simultaneous activities: (1) helping individuals make behavioral choices in the context of the potential reinforcers for these behaviors; (2) trying to change broad social systems so that they allow and reinforce more individual freedom in determining functional behavioral patterns.

Doesn't behavior modification pose piecemeal solutions when larger social changes are necessary?

No single approach, regardless of its effectiveness, can alter all those social forces that bring about human suffering. All social institutions are flawed: the contemporary family faces a multitude of problems, including the confusion of roles for family members, and the dwindling away of external supports for family unity; our health delivery systems are not delivering quality medical care to citizens of all economic levels; our legal and correctional systems do not provide "equality before the law," and often do little to reduce the probability of subsequent offenses. These and other social injustices require constant pressures for change from social workers as well as other citizens. We cannot, however, leave the wounded on the field because we are busy trying to win a war.

Social work historically has divided its resources between trying to improve the general human condition and helping those individuals whose social functioning is impaired. Those who use behavior modification procedures need not abdicate this dual responsibility. Indeed, the more efficient and effective the interventive strategies that social workers use, the more social work manpower is freed to work on the more complex and demanding challenges of social change. In fact, behavior modification emphasizes and provides effective procedures for the prevention of behavior problems. This preventive potential can help alleviate the pressures on the many who experience a heavy weight of behavior problems yet have the least resources to cope with them, such as the poor, the overcrowded, the undereducated.

The limited resources to work with these groups can be allocated more effectively by using behavior modification in the following four ways:

First: The social worker can offer clear and systematic ways of instructing care givers (e.g., nurses, attendants, parents, teachers) to deal both with problems in everyday development and with crises. Indeed, these principles are clear enough so that they could be made part of the regular high school curriculum in courses on such topics as "Being an Effective Parent." The teaching of such courses is only one of the ways in which behavior modification can be used to help prepare young people to take responsible, creative, and effective roles in society.

Second: Social workers who use behavior modification appropriately should not be completely satisfied with their interventions unless the individuals involved are equipped with the behavioral knowledge to deal with future problems. This is one of the most important aspects of behavior modification: a preventive emphasis—providing people with the tools to deal with new problems as they emerge, as well as the knowledge to avoid the occurrence of such problems by establishing positive, desirable conditions for the growth and development of those close to them.

Third: Behavior modification practitioners should clearly specify their interventive goals, and accumulate data to determine whether these goals have been reached.

Fourth: The techniques developed in behavior modification, can, to some extent, be utilized by social engineers in attempting to achieve broader goals of social change through an understanding of some of the factors that shape the behaviors of those involved in the development of public policy. Not only could this apply to understanding and changing the behavior of individuals or groups involved in decision making, but also to helping plan social systems that insure that positive reinforcement is maximized and distributed in an equitable way, and the use of punishment or aversive conditions minimized in order to foster the goal of a society composed of mutually reinforcing individuals and groups.

Can behavior be controlled by artificial reinforcers forever?

No thoughtful practitioner of behavior modification would support a program for intervention that relies on indefinite artificial reinforcement from a mediator. The goal of the social worker is to naturalize the reinforcement of goal behavior as soon as possible, so that the behavior is maintained by intermittent reinforcement from those in the client's natural environment (who, themselves, are being reinforced by the client's new behavior) and by the client's own self-reinforcement from the direct and indirect benefits of the new behavior. Even in situations in which new behavior is taught outside of the environment where the new behavior usually occurs, an attempt is usually made to replicate the client's natural environment (Franks, 1969). Such an arrangement provides a safe and structured setting in which to evaluate the client's problem behaviors and experiment with new behaviors without the hazard of aversive consequences.

Again, part of the behavior modification approach is a planned replication of aspects of the learning experiences that people encounter in their daily lives. Whenever a new skill is learned (e.g., walking, talking, playing a game), there is often need, initially, for immediate and continual reinforcement from the environment, e.g., in the form of praise from others. As skills develop and new behaviors are learned, the reinforcements need not be presented as often or at the same intensity. Furthermore, the results of the new behavior tend increasingly to reinforce the occurrence of the behavior, and the individual gains more and more self-confidence about the behavior.

If, indeed, the behaviors are well chosen in that they are appropriate to the reasonable demands of the client's environment, they will increasingly come to be supported by the "natural" reinforcers available in the environment, and will not need planned, structured, artificial reinforcement.

Isn't the practice of behavior modification devoid of human warmth and compassion?

The goal of behavior modification is to alter events so that: (1) functional, self-fulfilling, and socially beneficial behavior is reinforced and not punished; (2) self-destructive behavior, or behavior detrimental to the well-being of others, is not maintained. This dual goal reflects the concern of social workers who are behaviorally oriented to ease pain and optimize joy and satisfaction. Since this approach avoids secret labeling of inferred inner states and diseases, the focus, with few exceptions, is on what the client wants. There is respect and concern for the client's wishes and perceptions.

The client and those in his environment are partners in the interventive activities. Indeed, there is little mysticism in this approach, and, thus, no need for maintaining aloofness or social distance between the social workers and those with whom they work. The absence of concern about "over-identifying" with clients or about such phenomena as transference and its manipulation allows the social worker and the client to enjoy the closeness and honesty of peers. The social workers are seen—and present themselves—as open, concerned individuals who have competence and interest in teaching the client and mediator how to change behaviors in a desired direction. This absence of "pseudo-professionalism" facilitates the social worker's warmth and genuineness. Moreover, behavior modification often requires that behaviors of the client and the mediator be reinforced by the social worker's concern and praise. In the absence of warmth and compassion, these reinforcements will probably have little effect.

It would seem that, given the concern and commitment of social workers to alleviate suffering, enhance human joy, and remove artificial conceptual obstacles to relating to clients as living, real, total human beings (as opposed to labels or pathologies), the genuine humanity and concern of the social worker can emerge. Certainly, within the context of behavior modification, there are no arbitrary limits on the involvement of the social worker and his client in a relationship that is both facilitative for the client and mutually rewarding and growth-producing for all parties to the interaction.

Isn't the use of behavior modification in social work just a fad?

Any practitioners who work with problems as complex and seemingly insoluble as those encountered by social workers would, understandably, search for help from any source that seems to offer it. It is not surprising, then, that in an era when there seems to be a new therapeutic approach born every day, social workers try out many practice frameworks only to discard them in despair until the next approach comes along. After a while, practitioners can become skeptical about the value of *any* organized approach.

How, then, does the social worker judge whether an approach actually has something to offer? The merits of any intervention model, obviously, should not be equated with the charisma of its advocates, or the intricacy of, or fascination with, its concepts. A range of predetermined, rationally based, systematically applied criteria seem appropriate in evaluating an intervention approach (Fischer, 1973b). Some of the questions the social worker might ask in such an evaluation include:

1. Does the approach sound rational? Does it make sense, and are its principles internally consistent? Does it rely on inferences about things that are not testable or on factors that are unobservable? Is the approach understandable and communicable?

2. Are its principles based on research involving many people, experiencing diverse problems, with clearly reported findings showing relevant data relating the approach to successful practice? In other words, is it effective?

3. Is the approach applicable in various settings to a wide spectrum of problems experienced by people having various levels of intelligence and verbal ability?

4. Does the approach provide objective criteria for its evaluation?

5. Does the approach provide specific procedures—techniques—for changing behavior, in the context of a system for assessing their appropriate use? Are its procedures clearly connected to its principles about human behavior?

6. Is the approach practical? Can it be utilized by present manpower, or does it require intensive training for a very select group? Can its principles and procedures be taught to people with limited professional education, who can thus spread the impact of the interventive approach? Does it allow or even encourage individuals to work on their own problems so that the need for professional help is kept at a minimum?

7. Is the approach compatible with such social work values as respect for the dignity of the client, and starting where the client is?

If the approach does not meet these criteria, it is possible that it may offer very little to the client. On these bases, it would seem that behavior modification could not be considered "just a fad" in view of its broad applicability, clarity of concepts, specific interventive procedures, foundation in research, emphasis on accountability, practicality, compatibility with social work goals, settings, and values, and, most importantly, demonstrable effectiveness.

Conclusion

The growing use of behavior modification in social work has generated concern among many practitioners and educators about whether it is really useful in working with the problems typically encountered by social workers, and, even if it does work, whether its use is compatible with social work values and professional ethics. These concerns, to a large extent, reflect the newness of the approach, its power, and its departure in significant ways from many traditional concepts of social work practice.

Some of the questions critics raise concerning the use of behavior modification in social work relate to important issues discussed in this chapter about the determinants of human behavior, the relationship of professional activities dealing with individual adjustment to those dealing with social change, the hazards of social control of behavior, and the relationship of overt behavior to the "real" person. It is difficult to find clear answers to such issues. But they are legitimate issues that each social worker must consider. Many of the concerns about behavior modification, however, reflect misconceptions about it. These misconceptions include the notions that behavior modification ignores thoughts and feelings, that it deals only with isolated behaviors and thus has little significance for the total person, that it is cold and mechanistic and ignores individual differences, and that it is applicable only to a limited number of problems in limited types of settings. While some of these errors in practice do occur, they are neither intrinsic to, nor desirable in, behavior modification.

Finally, the most common objections to the use of behavior modification often result from a lack of understanding about human behavior and how it can be changed. These objections often derive from non-supportable hypotheses such as the notion that self-awareness and attitude change must occur before behavior can change, or that if dysfunctional behavior is removed, another dysfunctional behavior will take its place ("symptom substitution"). This chapter has presented explanations—as well as references to research data—that neither of these hypotheses is accurate.

There are, of course, less obvious resistances to incorporating behavior modification into social work practice. Some social workers, for instance, express discomfort in utilizing a technology that has been largely developed by another profession. While social workers are responsible for adapting this technology to the range of problems and settings—and the values—of our own profession, it would seem irrelevant whether the technology itself is borrowed, or developed in our own agencies. Our professional self-esteem is in more jeopardy from not using available, effective knowledge for carrying out our work than it is for borrowing from another discipline. Medicine borrows without hesitation from biology, anatomy, physiology, biochemistry, and other fields without suffering the loss of professional identity that some social workers fear.

In fact, through its long history, social work has borrowed from practitioners in other fields. There are, of course, hazards as well as benefits associated with the process of adapting material from one profession to the use of another. Differences exist in the orientation and practice of psychology (which has provided the bulk of research and development of behavior modification) and that of social work. As noted in the Introduction of this book, Kadushin (1959) thoughtfully explored the problems inherent in borrowing knowledge from another field. Although problems exist in the adaptation of behavior modification concepts to social work practice, they are not insoluble. Some of these problems include the following:

1. Because of the time lag in incorporating knowledge from other fields, we may tend to borrow outdated knowledge. The field of behavior modification is new and rapidly growing. The social worker who uses this approach should be prepared to keep up with the advances in the field.
2. We may well endow the borrowed knowledge with a greater degree of certainty than the donor discipline itself. For this reason, we must evaluate the relevance and utility of any borrowed methodology with respect to the specific social work problems for which it is to be used.
3. We are likely to be misled by oversimplified versions of the borrowed material. There is a temptation to seek quick, simple answers to some of the overwhelming problems social workers deal with. Behavior modification concepts have often been oversimplified to the point that they are useless. The effective application of behavior modification technology requires more than a superficial review of basic learning principles as they apply to complex human behavior.
4. The danger of confusion of professional identities resulting from borrowing knowledge has been discussed above.
5. There is a danger that the borrowed knowledge will become "an undigested lump" in social work practice. The limitations on the utility of behavior modification concepts, suggested by Hollis (1968) and Bruck (1968), suggest this sort of indigestion. Behavior modification provides nothing more nor less than a way of understanding and changing dysfunctional human behavior. Its utility is limited only by the social worker's perception of the role of behavior as a factor in the problems he deals with.

As has been mentioned repeatedly throughout this book, many of the underlying principles and procedures of behavior modification depart considerably from those practice concepts taught for many years in most practice and methods courses in schools of social work. These courses, largely based on psychodynamic theories, have espoused extensive historical diagnoses and secret psychiatric labeling. The product of such assessment procedures has often been intervention that sometimes included some vaguely defined "environmental manipulation," but primarily focused on "talk" in which change was supposed to result somehow from the social worker–client relationship and enhanced self-awareness. Behavior modification in large part rejects—on the basis of research, not commitment—an exclusive or excessive reliance on such approaches. Traditional social work interventions, although well-intentioned, are expensive, time consuming and can have negative byproducts (such as overdependence on the social worker, and the selection of clients who are intelligent and verbal). A more serious problem, however, is the finding in outcome research that these interventions seem to be of limited effectiveness (Fischer, 1975b).

Despite the authors' convictions about the utility of behavior modification in social work practice, we recognize that this methodology is not enough to solve all of the problems about which social workers are concerned. Social work need have no binding *or* blinding attachment to any single view of the human condition or to any set of interventive strategies. The core of social work is its values, responsibilities, and commitments, *not* its technology.

Yet commitment without effective methodology is powerless. But what methodologies do we use? Much of what many consider to be "the" social work approach is a product of tradition and not of rational choice of a process through which social work goals can effectively be carried out. The choice of procedures to be employed by social workers to achieve their goals should be made on the basis of empirical evidence (i.e., what works) rather than on the basis of emotion (i.e., it's what I know; what I've always done; what our leaders say is right; or what I feel comfortable with). Neither tradition nor uncontrolled clinical impressions would seem the best criteria for the selection of an interventive system. What matters is, does it really help?

Glossary of Basic Terms Commonly
Used in Behavior Modification

Antecedent. A stimulus (or stimuli) that precedes the occurrence of any behavior. *Operant Antecedents* set the occasion for the occurrence of behavior
(time and place). *Respondent Antecedents* actually elicit the behavior.

Anxiety. An intense emotional response usually accompanied by changes in
physiological responses mediated by the autonomic nervous system. Anxiety
generally involves subjective feelings of uneasiness or apprehension in anticipation of some unpleasant threat. (Contrast with *fear,* which is generally a reaction to more objectively defined threats, and is typically more realistic.)

Aversive Stimulus. See *Reinforcer, Negative.*

Avoidance. Behavior that increases in frequency in order to postpone or avoid
an aversive stimulus.

Back-up Reinforcers. The items or privileges used in token economies to be
exchanged for the tokens.

Baseline. The rate or frequency of occurrence of behavior as measured and
charted prior to the beginning of intervention.

Behavior. Any activity or movement of an individual that is observable or
potentially observable (or measurable) by another individual.

Behavior Deficit. Failure to perform certain behaviors that would be considered adaptive in a particular situation.

Behavior Excess. Performance of behaviors at such a high rate that they are
maladaptive or dysfunctional for the individual or those in his environment.

Behavior Modification. The planned, systematic application of experimentally
established principles of learning to the modification of maladaptive behavior.

Behavior Therapy. Synonymous with *Behavior Modification* (although some
writers do refer to use of respondent procedures as behavior therapy and use of
operant procedures as behavior modification).

Behavioral Model. The body of knowledge and assumptions underlying behavior modification based on the view that learning and the environment are
important in the development of most forms of behavior.

Behavioral Repertoire. The total of all behaviors that might be performed by
any individual. Frequently used to refer predominantly to operant behaviors.

Chaining. The linking of several operant behaviors to the point where one behavior leads to the next. Involves all three major operant dimensions—discriminative stimulus, behavior, reinforcement—with the stimuli from one performance serving also to trigger the following performance.

Classical Conditioning. Synonymous with *Respondent Conditioning.*

Coaching. See *Prompting.*

Conditioned Reinforcer. Synonymous with *Secondary Reinforcer.*

Conditioned Response, Operant. A response that has been strengthened by consequent reinforcement.

Conditioned Response, Respondent (CR). A response that is elicited by a conditioned stimulus; a learned response.

Conditioned Stimulus, Respondent. An initially neutral stimulus that has been paired with an unconditioned stimulus and has acquired the property of eliciting a response on its own.

Conditioning. Synonymous with learning. Refers to a change in behavior as a result of interaction with the environment; respondent or operant.

Contact Desensitization. Combination of modeling and physical guidance (guided practice) used to decrease anxiety.

Contingency. A consequent event that is conditional (dependent) upon some response being performed.

Contingency Management. Arrangement of consequences so that desired behaviors will be reinforced and undesired behaviors not reinforced.

Continuous Schedule. Provision of reinforcement after every occurrence of the target behavior.

Counterconditioning, Respondent. Learning of a new response that is incompatible with a previous response but elicited by the same stimulus.

Control. The functional relationship between the performance of a behavior and the event or stimulus of which it is a function.

Coverant. Covert *operant;* thoughts and imagination, etc. Assumed to follow laws of all operant behaviors.

Deprivation. Withholding of a reinforcer to the point where its effectiveness will be increased.

Differential Reinforcement. Reinforcement of selected behaviors among many that are performed, and non-reinforcement of others (also called Selective Reinforcement).

Differentiation. Development of a specific response through differential reinforcement.

Discrimination Training. Training an individual to perform a behavior in one situation and not in another by reinforcing the behavior in the presence of one stimulus (the discriminative stimulus) and not in the presence of other stimuli. This places the target behavior under stimulus control.

Discriminative Stimulus (S^D). An antecedent stimulus that signals that a given behavior will be followed by a reinforcer.

Disease Model. The body of knowledge and assumptions underlying most traditional therapeutic approaches emphasizing the analogy between physical and biological illness and social and psychological problems (internal causation, symptoms, etc).

Elicited Behavior. An involuntary or reflexive (respondent) behavior performed in direct response to an antecedent stimulus (S^E).

Eliciting Stimulus (S^E). The stimulus that directly brings forth involuntary, reflex (respondent) behavior.

Escape Behavior. Behavior that increases in frequency in order to terminate (not postpone or avoid) an aversive stimulus.

Extinction, Operant. Non-contingent discontinuation of reinforcement resulting in a decrease or weakening in the occurrence of the behavior previously maintained by that reinforcement.

Extinction, Respondent. Continued presentation of the conditioned stimulus without the unconditioned stimulus resulting in a decrease in the rate of occurrence of a behavior.

Extrinsic Reinforcement. Reinforcement that originates outside the individual.

Fading. The procedure in which a stimulus controlling an individual's behavior is gradually changed to another stimulus that gains control of the behavior.

Fixed-Interval Schedule. Reinforcement delivered after regular (fixed) periods of time elapse.

Fixed-Ratio Schedule. Reinforcement delivered after a regular (fixed) number of target behaviors are performed.

Free Operant. An operant behavior not under stimulus control.

Functional Relationship. A relationship in which changes in one part of a relationship between an individual and his or her environment produce or lead to changes in other parts.

Generalized Reinforcer. A conditioned reinforcer that is reinforcing for several types of behaviors in several situations.

Generalization. Performance of behavior under conditions similar to but not identical to the conditions under which the behavior was learned; also called Stimulus Generalization.

Higher-Order Conditioning. Using a conditioned stimulus as though it were an unconditioned stimulus by pairing it with a new stmulus that will eventually come to elicit behaviors similar to those elicited by the original CS and UCS.

Incompatible Behavior. Behaviors that cannot be performed at the same time.

Intermittent Schedule. Any schedule of reinforcement where reinforcement is not provided after every occurrence of the behavior.

Intrinsic Reinforcement. Reinforcement experienced internally, such as feelings of success.

Learning. A change in the behavior of an individual as a result of some interaction with the environment.

Mediator. The person (s) in direct contact with the client who actually carries out the intervention program; the dispenser of reinforcers. Can be the social worker or someone in the client's natural environment.

Motor Behavior. Physical movements such as walking.

Modeling. The process of learning, or the procedure through which that process is conducted, in which behavior is performed as a result of watching it being performed (actually or symbolically) by others.

Negative Reinforcement. An increase (strengthening) in the probability that a behavior will occur as a result of withdrawing, or escaping or avoiding, some stimulus (aversive) following that behavior.

Negative Reinforcer. See *Reinforcer, Negative.*

Neutral Stimulus. A stimulus that does not evoke or elicit specific responses.

Operant Behavior. Voluntary, purposive behavior mediated by the gross muscle and central nervous system that generally has some effect on its environment and which includes most of the daily, ongoing behavior of human beings. This behavior is learned and modified by the principles of operant conditioning.

Operant Conditioning. The process through which operant behaviors are learned. Specifically, changes in the probability of occurrence of behaviors as a result of the arrangement of the consequences of those behaviors.

Pavlovian Conditioning. Synonymous with *Respondent Conditioning.*

Phobia. A strong, persistent, and irrational fear elicited by specific or specificable stimuli.

Positive Reinforcement. An increase (strengthening) in the probability that a behavior will occur as a result of the presentation of some stimulus (positive reinforcer) following that behavior.

Positive Reinforcer. See *Reinforcer, Positive.*

Premack Principle. The principle that a high-probability behavior can be used as a reinforcer for a low-probability behavior.

Primary Reinforcer. Unlearned or innate stimuli that increase behavior and satisfy basic human requirements (e.g., food) .

Prompting. An antecedent cue or clue to an individual (e.g., a verbal instruction) to perform a behavior (also called Coaching) .

Punishment, Negative. A decrease (weakening) in the probability that a behavior will occur as a result of the removal of a positive reinforcer following that behavior.

Punishment, Positive. A decrease (weakening) in the probability that a behavior will occur as a result of the presentation of an aversive stimulus following that behavior.

Reciprocal Inhibition. The principle that a response inhibiting anxiety, made to occur in the presence of stimuli eliciting anxiety, can be used to weaken the bond between the stimuli and the anxiety.

Reflex. An involuntarily occurring behavior elicited by a stimulus (e.g., startle elicited by a loud, unexpected noise).

Reinforcement, Negative. See *Negative Reinforcement.*

Reinforcement, Positive. See *Positive Reinforcement.*

Reinforcer, Negative. Any stimulus that either increases (strengthens) the probability that a behavior will occur by its termination, removal, or postponement (*Negative Reinforcement*), or decreases (weakens) the probability that a behavior will occur by its presentation following that behavior (*Positive Punishment*). Also called Aversive Stimulus.

Reinforcer, Positive. Any stimulus that either increases (strengthens) the probability that a behavior will occur when it is presented following that behavior (*Positive Reinforcement*) or decreases (weakens) the probability that the behavior will occur when it is removed following that behavior (*Negative Punishment*).

Respondent Behavior. Automatic, involuntary behavior elicited by a stimulus, and mediated by the autonomic nervous system.

Respondent Conditioning. The process through which respondent behaviors are learned. Specifically, the pairing of a neutral stimulus with an unconditioned stimulus over time, to the point where the neutral stimulus comes to elicit behavior similar to the behavior elicited by the UCS.

Response. Synonymous with *Behavior.* Sometimes used to refer to an individual element or component of behavior.

Satiation. Decrease in the effectiveness of a reinforcer as a result of overuse of that reinforcer.

Schedule of Reinforcement. The patterns and ways reinforcers are arranged for presentation to the individual (See *Continuous Schedule* and *Intermittent Schedule*).

S-Delta ($S\Delta$). A stimulus that sets the occasion for non-reinforcement, as opposed to other stimuli that let the individual know he or she will be reinforced (S^D).

Secondary Reinforcer. A stimulus that has acquired reinforcing properties after previously being neutral. A learned reinforcer; synonymous with Conditioned Reinforcer.

Self-Control. A response repertoire in which an individual can increase or decrease his own responses in relation to his own perceptions of what is desirable, e.g., by arranging his own contingencies.

Self-Reinforcement. Intrinsic reinforcement where thoughts or feelings are used to maintain or increase certain behaviors.

Selective Reinforcement. See *Differential Reinforcement.*

Shaping. The process of reinforcing increasingly complex units of behavior that successively approximate some goal or terminal behavior in order to achieve the terminal behavior that is desired.

Social Reinforcer. A reinforcing stimulus that consists of the behaviors of other people (e.g., attention).

Stimulus. Any situation, event, or item—internal or external—including an individual's own behavior. Generally defined in terms of its specific behavior-change properties, e.g., discriminative stimulus, eliciting stimulus, reinforcing stimulus.

Stimulus Control. The performance of behavior in the presence of one stimulus and not others. See *Control* and *Discriminative Stimulus.*

Stimulus Generalization. See *Generalization.*

Successive Approximation. The "steps" in the shaping process. Each step that approximates or comes closer to the terminal or desired behavior is reinforced.

Target Behavior. The behavior specifically identified as either desired or undesired and hence, as needing to be increased or decreased.

Terminal Behavior. The final or goal behavior, described in terms of how, where, and when it will be performed.

Time-Out. A punishment procedure in which an individual is removed from all sources of reinforcement in an effort to decrease undesired behaviors.

Token. An item, usually of no value in and of itself, that is given as a reward and that can be exchanged for desired items or privileges (*Back-up Reinforcers*).

Token Economy. A more or less comprehensive token exchange system in which most privileges must be earned and bought with tokens.

Unconditioned Response (UCR). In respondent conditioning, the unlearned behavior that is elicited by an unconditioned stimulus.

Unconditioned Stimulus (UCS). In respondent conditioning, the stimulus that elicits the UCR without prior training or experience.

Variable-Interval Schedule. Intermittent reinforcement supplied following a variable or irregular period of time, but set around some mean.

Variable-Ratio Schedule. Intermittent reinforcement supplied following a variable or irregular number of occurrences of behaviors, but set around some mean.

Vicarious Reinforcement. An increase in the occurrence of some aspect of an individual's behavior following his observation of another individual being reinforced for that behavior.

Bibliography

Included here are the references cited in the text, and, because of the proliferation of material on behavior modification in recent years, for the convenience of the reader, a listing of books published on the topic of behavior modification up to mid-1973.

ABRAMSON, E. E. (1973) "A Review of Behavioral Approaches to Weight Control." *Behaviour Research and Therapy*, 11, 547–556.

ACKERMAN, J. M. (1972) *Operant Conditioning Techniques for the Classroom Teacher*. Glenview, Ill.: Scott, Foresman.

ADDISON, R. M., AND HOMME, L. (1966) "The Reinforcing Event (RE) Menu." *National Society for Programmed Instruction Journal*, 5, 8–9.

AGRAS, W. S. (ed.) (1972) *Behavior Modification: Principles and Clinical Applications*. Boston: Little, Brown.

ANANT, S. S. (1968a) "Verbal Aversion Therapy with a Promiscuous Girl: Case Report." *Psychological Reports*, 22, 795–796.

ANANT, S. S. (1968b) "Treatment of Alcoholics and Drug Addicts by Verbal Aversion Technique." *International Journal of Addictions, 3*, 2.

ANANT, S. S. (ed.) (1969) *Readings in Behavior Therapies*. New York: MSS Educational Publishing Co.

ANNON, J. S. (1971) *The Extension of Learning Principles to the Analysis and Treatment of Sexual Problems*. Unpublished Doctoral Dissertation, University of Hawaii. Ann Arbor, Mich.: University Microfilms. No. 72–290.

ANNON, J. S. (1973) "The Therapeutic Use of Masturbation in the Treatment of Sexual Disorders." In R. D. Rubin, J. P. Brady, and J. D. Henderson (eds.), *Advances in Behavior Therapy*, vol. 4. New York: Academic Press.

ANNON, J. S. (1974) *The Behavioral Treatment of Sexual Problems. Vol. 1. Brief Therapy*. Honolulu: Kapiolani Health Services.

ARKOWITZ, H. J., AND BRINK, R. (1973) *The Training of Behavior Therapists*. New York: Pergamon.

ASHEM, A. B., AND POSER, E. G. (1973) *Adaptive Learning: Behavior Modification with Children*. New York: Pergamon.

ASTRUP, C. (1965) *Pavlovian Psychiatry: A New Synthesis*. Springfield, Ill. Charles C Thomas.

Atthowe, J. M., Jr., and Krasner, L. (1968) "Preliminary Report on the Application of Contingent Reinforcement Procedures (Token Economy) on a 'Chronic' Psychiatric Ward." *Journal of Abnormal Psychology, 73,* 37–43.

Ayllon, T. (1963) "Intensive Treatment of Psychotic Behavior by Stimulus Satiation and Food Reinforcement." *Behaviour Research and Therapy, 1,* 53–61.

Ayllon, T. (1965) "Some Behavioral Problems Associated with Eating in Chronic Schizophrenic Patients." In L. P. Ullmann and L. Krasner (eds.), *Case Studies in Behavior Modification.* New York: Holt, Rinehart and Winston.

Ayllon, T. and Azrin, N. H. (1964) "Reinforcement and Instructions with Mental Patients." *Journal of the Experimental Analysis of Behavior, 7,* 327–331.

Ayllon, T., and Azrin, N. H. (1965) "The Measurement and Reinforcement of Behavior of Psychotics." *Journal of the Experimental Analysis of Behavior, 8,* 357–383.

Ayllon, T. and Azrin, N. H. (1968) *The Token Economy.* New York: Appleton-Century-Crofts.

Ayllon, T., and Haughton, E. (1962) "Control of the Behavior of Schizophrenic Patients by Food." *Journal of the Experimental Analysis of Behavior, 5,* 343–352.

Ayllon, T., and Michael, J. (1959) "The Psychiatric Nurse as a Behavioral Engineer." *Journal of the Experimental Analysis of Behavior, 2,* 323–334.

Ayllon, T., and Skuban, W. (1973) "Accountability in Psychotherapy: A Test Case." *Journal of Behavior Therapy and Experimental Psychiatry, 4,* 19–30.

Ayllon, T.; Smith, D.; and Rogers, M. (1970) "Behavior Management of School Phobia." *Journal of Behavior Therapy and Experimental Psychiatry, 1,* 125–138.

Azerrad, J., and Stafford, R. L. (1969) "Restoration of Eating Behavior in Anorexia Nervosa through Operant Conditioning and Environmental Manipulation." *Behaviour Research and Therapy, 7,* 165–171.

Azrin, N. H., and Holz, W. C. (1966) "Punishment." In W. K. Honig (ed.), *Operant Behavior: Areas of Research and Application.* New York: Appleton-Century-Crofts.

Bachrach, A. J. (ed.) (1962) *Experimental Foundations of Clinical Psychology.* New York: Basic Books.

Baer, D. M.; Wolf, M. M.; and Risley, T. R. (1968) "Some Current Dimensions of Applied Behavior Analysis." *Journal of Applied Behavior Analysis, 1,* 91–97.

Baller, W. R., and Schalock, H. (1956) "Conditioned Response Treatment of Enuresis." *Exceptional Children, 22,* 233–236 and 247–248.

Ban, T. A. (1964) *Conditioning and Psychiatry.* Chicago: Aldine.

Bandura, A. (1967) "Behavior Psychotherapy." *Scientific American,* March 1967, pp. 78–86.

Bandura, A. (1965) "Vicarious Processes: A Case of No-Trial Learning." In L.

Berkowitz (ed.), *Advances in Experimental Psychology,* vol. 2. New York: Academic Press.

BANDURA, A. (1969) *Principles of Behavior Modification.* New York: Holt, Rinehart and Winston.

BANDURA, A. (1971) "Psychotherapy Based Upon Modeling Principles." In A. E. Bergin and S. Garfield (eds.), *Handbook of Psychotherapy and Behavior Change.* New York: John Wiley.

BANDURA, A., AND WALTERS, R. H. (1963) *Social Learning and Personality Development.* New York: Holt, Rinehart and Winston.

BANDURA, A., GRUSEC, J. E. AND MENLOVE, F. L. (1967). "Vicarious Extinction of Avoidance Behavior." *Journal of Personality and Social Psychology,* 5, 16–23.

BARLOW, D. H.; LEITENBERG, H.; AND AGRAS, W. S. (1968) "Experimental Control of Sexual Deviation Through Manipulation of the Noxious Scene in Covert Sensitization." *Journal of Abnormal Psychology, 74,* 596–601.

BARRETT-LENNARD, G. T. (1965) "Professional Psychology and the Control of the Human Behavior." *Australian Journal of Psychology, 17,* 24–34.

BARRISH, H.; SAUNDERS, M.; AND WOLF, M. M. (1969) "Good Behavior Game: Effects of Individual Contingencies for Group Consequences on Disruptive Behavior in a Classroom." *Journal of Applied Behavior Analysis, 2,* 79–84.

BARTLETT, H. (1970) *The Common Base of Social Work Practice.* New York: National Association of Social Workers.

BATTLE CREEK (MICHIGAN) VETERANS' ADMINISTRATION HOSPITAL. (1966) *Symposium on Behavior Modificaiton Techniques in the Treatment of Emotional Disorders.* Battle Creek, Michigan.

BAUER, R. A. (1966) *Social Indicators.* Cambridge, Mass.: MIT Press.

BECKER, W. C. (1971a) *Parents Are Teachers: A Child Management Program.* Champaign, Ill.: Research Press.

BECKER, W. C. (ed.) (1971b) *An Empirical Basis for Change in Education: Selections on Behavioral Psychology for Teachers.* Chicago: Science Research Associates.

BECKER, W. C.; ENGLEMANN, S.; AND THOMAS, D. R. (1971) *Teaching a Basic Course in Applied Psychology.* Chicago: Science Research Associates.

BEECH, H. R. (1969) *Changing Man's Behavior.* Harmondsworth, England: Penguin Books.

BEM, D. J. (1967) "Self-Perception: The Dependent Variable of Human Performance." *Organizational Behavior and Human Performance, 2,* 105–121.

BENNETT, P. S., AND MALEY, R. (1973) "Modification of Interactive Behaviors in Chronic Mental Patients." *Journal of Applied Behavior Analysis, 6,* 609–620.

BENSBERG, G. J. (ed.) (1965) *Teaching the Mentally Retarded: A Handbook for Ward Personnel.* Atlanta: Southern Regional Educational Board.

BENSBERG, G. J.; COLWELL, C. N.; AND CASSEL, R. H. (1965) "Teaching the Profoundly Retarded Self-Help Activities by Behavior Shaping Techniques." *American Journal of Mental Deficiency, 69,* 674–679.

BENSON, F. A. M. (ed.) (1969) *Modifying Deviant Social Behaviors in Various*

Classroom Settings. Eugene, Oregon: University of Oregon, Department of Special Education.

BERGIN, A. E. (1969a) "A Technique for Improving Desensitization via Warmth, Empathy and Emotional Reexperiencing of Hierarchy Events." In R. D. Rubin and C. M. Franks (eds.), *Advances in Behavior Therapy, 1968.* New York: Academic Press.

BERGIN, A. E. (1969b) "A Self-Regulation Technique for Impulse Control Disorders." *Psychotherapy: Theory, Research, and Practice, 6,* 113–118.

BERGIN, A. E. (1971) "The Evaluation of Therapeutic Outcomes." In A. E. Bergin and S. Garfield (eds.), *Handbook of Psychotherapy and Behavior Change.* New York: John Wiley.

BERKOWITZ, B. P., AND GRAZIANO, A. M. (1972) "Training Parents as Behavior Therapists: A Review." *Behaviour Research and Therapy, 10,* 297–317.

BERLIN, I. N. (1967) "Preventive Aspects of Mental Health Consultation to Schools." *Mental Hygiene, 51,* 34–40.

BERNAL, M.; DURGEE, J.; PRUETT, H.; AND BURNS, B. (1968) "Behavior Modification and the 'Brat Syndrome'." *Journal of Consulting Psychology, 32,* 447–455.

BERNSTEIN, D., AND BORKOVEC, T. (1972) *Relaxation Therapy.* Champaign, Ill.: Research Press.

BIJOU, S. W., AND BAER, D. B. (1967) *Child Development: Readings in Experimental Analysis.* New York: Appleton-Century-Crofts.

BIJOU, S. W.; PETERSON, R. F.; AND AULT, M. H. (1968) "A Method To Integrate Descriptive and Experimental Field Studies at the Level of Data and Empirical Concepts." *Journal of Applied Behavior Analysis, 7,* 175–191. *ment, 30,* 151–170.

BIJOU, S. W., AND RIBES-INESTA, E. (1972) *Behavior Modification: Issues and Extensions.* New York: Academic Press.

BIJOU, S. W., AND STURGES, P. S. (1959) "Positive Reinforcers for Experimental Studies with Children—Consumables and Manipulatables." *Child Development, 30,* 151–17.

BIRK, C. L. (1969) "Combined Aversive Conditioning and Group Psychotherapy for Homosexuals." Unpublished manuscript.

BLOOMFIELD, H. H. (1973) "Assertive Training in an Outpatient Group of Chronic Schizophrenics: A Preliminary Report," *Behavior Therapy, 4,* 277–281.

BRADFIELD, R. H. (ed.) (1970) *Behavior Modification: The Human Effort.* San Rafael, Calif.: Dimensions.

Bradfield, R. H. (ed.) (1971) *Behavioral Modification of Learning Disabilities* San Rafael, Calif.: Academic Therapy Publications.

BRIAR, S. (1967) "The Current Crisis in Social Casework." In *Social Work Practice, 1967.* New York: Columbia.

BRIAR, S. (1968) "The Casework Predicament." *Social Work, 13,* 5–11.

BROWN, D. B. (1972) *Behavior Modification in Child, School, and Family Mental Health: An Annotated Bibliography.* Champaign, Ill.: Research Press.

BROWNING, R. M., AND STOVER, D. O. (1971) *Behavior Modification in Child Treatment.* Chicago: Aldine.

BRUCK, M. (1968) "Behavior Modification Theory and Practice: A Critical Review." *Social Work, 13,* 43–55.

BRUTTEN, E. J., AND SHOEMAKER, D. J. (1967) *The Modification of Stuttering.* New York: Prentice-Hall.

BUCKLEY, N. K., AND HILL, M. W. (1970) *Modifying Classroom Behavior: A Manual of Procedure for Classroom Teachers.* Champaign, Ill.: Research Press.

BUDDENHAGEN, R. G. (1970) *Establishing Vocal Verbalizations in Mute Mongoloid Children.* Champaign, Ill.: Research Press.

BURCHARD, J. D. (1967) "Systematic Socialization: A Programmed Environment for the Habilitation of Anti-Social Retardates." *Psychological Record, 17,* 461–476.

BURGESS, E. P. (1969) "The Modification of Depressive Behaviors." In R. D. Rubin and C. M. Franks (eds.), *Advances in Behavior Therapy.* New York: Academic Press.

BURGESS, R. L., AND BUSHELL, D., JR. (eds.) (1969) *Behavioral Sociology—The Experimental Analysis of Social Process.* New York: Columbia University Press.

BURKE, W. W. (1970) "Training Organization Development Specialists." *Professional Psychology, 1,* 354–358.

BURNS, L. E., AND WORSLEY, J. L. (1971) *Behavior Therapy in the Seventies.* Baltimore: Williams & Wilkins.

BUSHELL, D., JR., AND BURGESS, R. L. (1969) "Characteristics of the Experimental Analysis." In R. L. Burgess and D. Bushell, Jr. (eds.), *Behavioral Sociology—The Experimental Analysis of Social Process.* New York: Columbia University Press.

BUTTERFIELD, W. H.; THOMAS E. J.; AND SOBER, R. J. (1970) "A Device for Simultaneous Feedback of Verbal and Signal Data." *Behavior Therapy, 1,* 395–401.

CAHOON, D. D. (1968) "Symptom Substitution and the Behavior Therapies: A Reappraisal." *Psychological Bulletin, 69,* 149–156.

CAPLAN, G. (1970) *The Theory and Practice of Mental Health Consultation.* New York: Basic Books.

CARKHUFF, R. R. (1969) *Helping and Human Relations* (2 vols.) New York: Holt, Rinehart and Winston.

CARKHUFF, R. R., AND BERENSON, B. G. (1967) *Beyond Counseling and Therapy.* New York: Holt, Rinehart and Winston.

CARTER, R. C., AND STUART, R. B. (1970) "Behavior Modification Theory and Practice: A Reply." *Social Work, 15,* 37–50.

CASE, H. W. (1960) "Therapeutic Methods in Stuttering and Speech Blocking." In H. J. Eysenck (ed.), *Behavior Therapy and the Neuroses.* Oxford: Pergamon.

CAUTELA, J. R. (1965) "Desensitization and Insight." *Behavior Research and Therapy, 3*, 59–64.

CAUTELA, J. R. (1966) "A Behavior Therapy Treatment of Pervasive Anxiety." *Behaviour Research and Therapy, 4*, 99–109

CAUTELA, J. R. (1967) "Covert Sensitization." *Psychological Record, 20*, 459–468.

CAUTELA, J. R. (1969) "Behavior Therapy and Self Control." In C. Franks (ed.), *Behavior Therapy: Appraisal and Status*. New York: McGraw-Hill.

CAUTELA, J. R. (1970) "Covert Reinforcement." *Behavior Therapy, 1*, 33–50.

CAUTELA, J. R. (1971) "Covert Conditioning." In A. Jacobs and L. B. Sachs (eds.), *The Psychology of Private Events: Perspectives On Covert Response Systems*. New York: Academic Press.

CAUTELA, J. R. (1972) "Rationale and Procedures for Covert Conditioning." In R. D. Rubin, H. Fensterheim, J. D. Henderson and L. P. Ullmann (eds.), *Advances in Behavior Therapy, 1972*. New York: Academic Press.

CAUTELA, J. R., AND KASTENBAUM, R. (1967) "A Reinforcement Survey Schedule for Use in Therapy, Training and Research." *Psychological Reports, 20*, 1115–1130.

CHAMPAGNE, D. W., AND GOLDMAN, R. M. (1972) *Teaching Parents Teaching*. New York: Appleton-Century-Crofts.

CHASSAN, J. B. (1967) *Research Design in Clinical Psychology and Psychiatry*. New York: Appleton-Century-Crofts.

CHITTICK, R. H.; ELDRED, D. M.; AND BROOKS, G. W. (1965) *The Use of Programmed Instruction with Disturbed Students*. Waterbury, Vermont: Vermont State Hospital.

CIBA FOUNDATION (London). (1969) *The Role of Learning in Psychotherapy: Proceedings of 1968 London Ciba Foundation Symposium*. Boston: Little, Brown.

CLARK, F. W.; EVANS, D. R.; AND HAMMERLYNCK, L. A. (eds.) (1972) *Implementing Behavioral Programs for Schools and Clinics*. Champaign, Ill.: Research Press.

CLECKLEY, H. (1964) *The Mask of Sanity*. St. Louis: Mosby.

CLEMENTS, C. B., AND McKEE, J. M. (1968) "Programmed Instruction for Institutionalized Offenders: Contingency Management and Performance Contracts." *Psychological Reports, 22*, 957–964.

COHEN, H. L.; FILIPCZAK, J.; AND BIS, J. S. (1967) *Case I, An Initial Study of Contingencies Applicable to Special Education*. Silver Spring, Maryland: Educational Facility Press—Institute for Behavioral Research.

COHEN, H. L., AND FILIPCZAK, J. (1971) *A New Learning Environment*. San Francisco: Jossey-Bass.

COHEN, J. (1969) *Operant Behavior and Conditioning*. Chicago: Rand McNally.

CORTE, H. E.; WOLF, M. M.; AND LOCKE, B. J. (1971) "A Comparison of Procedures for Eliminating Self-Injurious Behavior of Retarded Adolescents." *Journal of Applied Behavior Analysis, 4*, No. 3, 201–213.

DAVIDSON, J. R., AND DOUGLASS, E. (1950) "Nocturnal Enuresis: A Special Approach to Treatment." *British Medical Journal, 1*, 1345–1347.

DAVIS, D.; KAUSCH, D. F.; AND GOCHROS, H. L. (1968) "Psycho-Social Characteristics of Check Offenders." *Comprehensive Psychiatry, 9,* 474–481.

DAVISON, G. C. (1968) "Elimination of Sadistic Fantasy by a Client-Controlled Counterconditioning Technique." *Journal of Abnormal Psychology, 73,* 84–90.

DAVISON, G. R. (1969) "Appraisal of Behavior Modification Techniques with Adults." In C. Franks (ed.), *Behavior Therapy: Appraisal and Status.* New York: McGraw-Hill.

DAYAN, M. (1964) "Toilet Training Retarded Children in a State Residential Institution." *Mental Retardation, 2,* 116–117.

DEIBERT, A. N., AND HARMON, A. J. (1970) *New Tools for Changing Behavior.* Champaign, Ill.: Research Press.

DE LEON, G., AND MANDELL, W. (1966) "A Comparison of Conditioning and Psychotherapy in the Treatment of Functional Enuresis." *Journal of Clinical Psychology, 22,* 326–330.

DENGROVE, E. (1966) "Treatment of Non-Phobic Disorders by the Behavioral Therapies." Lecture to the Association for Advancement of the Behavioral Therapies, New York, December 17.

DENGROVE, E. (1971) "The Mechanotherapy of Sexual Disorders." *Journal of Sex Research, 7,* 1–12.

DILORETO, A. O. (1971) *Comparative Psychotherapy: An Experimental Analysis.* Chicago: Aldine-Atherton.

DITTES, J. E. (1957) "Extinction During Psychotherapy of G. S. R. Accompanying 'Embarrassing' Statements." *Journal of Abnormal and Social Psychology, 54,* 187–191.

DYER, W. G. (1972) *The Sensitive Manipulator.* Provo, Utah: University of Utah Press.

D'ZURILLA, T., AND GOLDFRIED, M. R. (1971) "Problem Solving and Behavior Modification." *Journal of Abnormal Psychology, 78,* 107–126.

EBNER, M. J. (1967) "An Investigation of the Role of the Social Environment in the Generalization and the Resistance of the Effect of a Behavior Modification Program." Unpublished doctoral dissertation, University of Oregon.

EDWARDS, M., AND LILLY, R. T. (1966) "Operant-Conditioning: An Application to Behavioral Problems in Groups." *Mental Retardation, 4,* 18–22.

ERICKSON, G. D., AND HOGAN, T. P. (eds.) (1972) *Family Therapy.* Monterey, Calif.: Brooks-Cole.

ERON, L. D.; WALDER, L. O.; AND LEFKOWITZ, M. M. (1971) *Learning of Aggression in Children.* Boston: Little, Brown.

EYSENCK, H. J. (ed.) (1960) *Behavior Therapy and the Neuroses.* New York: Pergamon.

EYSENCK, H. J. (ed.) (1964) *Experiments in Behavior Therapy.* New York: Pergamon.

EYSENCK, H. J., AND RACHMAN, S. (1965) *The Causes and Cures of Neurosis.* San Diego: Knapp.

EYSENCK, H. J. (1959) "Learning Theory and Behavior Therapy." *Journal of Mental Science, 105,* 61–75.

EYSENCK, H. J., AND BEECH, H. R. (1971) "Counter-Conditioning and Related Methods in Behavior Therapy." In A. Bergin and S. Garfield (eds.), *Handbook of Psychotherapy and Behavior Change*. New York: John Wiley.

FAIRWEATHER, G. W. (ed.) (1964) *Social Psychology in Treating Mental Illness: An Experimental Approach*. New York: John Wiley.

FAIRWEATHER, G. W.; SANDERS, D. H.; MAYNARD, H.; AND CRESSLER, D. L. (1969) *Community Life for the Mentally Ill: An Alternative to Institutional Care*. Chicago: Aldine.

FARGO, G. A.; BEHRNS, C.; AND NOLEN, P. (eds.) (1970) *Behavior Modification in the Classroom*. Belmont, Calif.: Wadsworth.

FAZIO, A. F. (1970) "Treatment Components in Implosive Therapy." *Journal of Abnormal Psychology, 76,* 211–219.

FELDMAN, M. P., AND MacCULLOUGH, M. J. (1971) *Homosexual Behavior: Therapy and Assessment*. New York: Pergamon.

FELDMAN, M. P., AND MacCULLOUGH, M. J. (1965) "The Application of Anticipatory Avoidance Learning to the Treatment of Homosexuality." *Behaviour Research and Therapy, 2,* 165–183.

FERNSTERSHEIN, H. (1971) *Help Without Psychoanalysis*. New York: Stein/Day.

FERSTER, C. B., AND PERROTT, M. C. (1968) *Behavior Principles*. New York: Appleton-Century-Crofts.

FESTINGER, L. A. (1962) *A Theory of Cognitive Dissonance*. Stanford: Stanford University Press.

FIELDING, H. T. (1969) *The Modification of Human Behavior*. Minneapolis, Minn.: Oakdale Medical Center.

FISCHER, J., AND HARRIS, R. E. (1966) *Reinforcement Theory in Psychological Treatment—A Symposium*. Sacramento: California Dept. of Mental Hygene, Bureau of Research.

FISCHER, J. (1972) "Theories of Social Casework: A Review." *Social Work, 17,* 105–108.

FISCHER, J. (1973a) "Is Casework Effective?: A Review." *Social Work, 18,* 5–20.

FISCHER, J. (1973b) *Interpersonal Helping: Emerging Approaches for Social Work Practice*. Springfield, Ill.: Charles C Thomas.

FISCHER, J. (1973c) "Systematic Desensitization: An Effective Technique for Clinical Practice." *Child Welfare, 52,* 493–502.

FISCHER, J., AND MILLER, H. (1973) "The Effect of Race and Social Class on Clinical Judgments." *Clinical Social Work Journal, 1* (2), 100–109.

FISCHER, J.; PAVEZA, G.; AND KICKERTZ, N. (1975) "The Relationship Between Theoretical Orientation and Therapists' Interpersonal Skills." *Journal of Counseling Psychology* (in press).

FISCHER, J. (1975a) *Effective Casework Practice: An Eclectic Approach*. Fair Lawn, N.J.: R. E. Burdick (in press).

FISCHER, J. (1975b) *The Effectiveness of Social Casework*. Springfield, Ill.: Charles C Thomas.

FO, W. AND ROBINSON, C. H. (1972) "Behavior Modification in Group Therapy." Unpublished Paper Presented at the Annual Convention, American Psychological Association, Honolulu.

FOXX, R. M., AND AZRIN, N. H. (1971) *Rapid Toilet Training of the Retarded.* Champaign, Ill.: Research Press.

FRANK, J. D. (1961) "The Role of Influence in Psychotherapy." In M. I. Stein (ed.), *Contemporary Psychotherapies.* New York: Free Press.

FRANKEL, A. J., AND GLASSER, P. H. (1974). "Behavioral Approaches to Group Work." *Social Work, 19,* 163–175.

FRANKS, C. M. (ed.) (1964) *Conditioning Techniques in Clinical Practice and Research.* New York: Springer.

FRANKS, C. M. (ed.) (1969) *Behavior Therapy: Appraisal and Status.* New York: McGraw-Hill.

FRANKS, C. M., AND WILSON, G. T. (eds.) (1973) *Behavior Therapy: Theory and Practice. Vol. 1.* New York: Brunner/Mazel

FRANKS, C. M., AND WILSON, G. T. (eds.) (1974) *Annual Review of Behavior Therapy.* New York: Brunner/Mazel.

FREEMAN, H. (ed.) (1968) *Progress in Behavior Therapy.* Bristol, England: John Wright.

FREUD, A. (1958) "Adolescence." In *The Psychoanalytic Study of the Child,* vol. 13. New York: International Universities Press.

FREUD, S. (1950) "Analysis Terminable and Interminable." In *Collected Papers,* vol. 5. Translated by Joan Riviere. London: Hogarth Press.

FREUD, S. (1957) "Turnings in the Waves of Psychoanalytic Therapy." In J. D. Sutherland (ed.), *Collected Papers,* vol. 2. London: Hogarth Press.

FREYMAN, R. (1963) "Follow-up Study of Enuresis Treated with a Bell Apparatus." *Journal of Child Psychology and Psychiatry, 4,* 199–206.

GAGNÉ, R. N. (1970). *The Conditions of Learning* (2d Ed.). New York: Holt, Rinehart and Winston.

GALLIMORE, R.; THARP, R.; AND KEMP, B. (1969) "Positive Reinforcing Function of Negative Attention." *Journal of Experimental Child Psychology, 8,* 140–146.

GARDNER, W. I. (1971) *Behavior Modification in Mental Retardation.* Chicago: Aldine.

GARVEY, W., AND HEGRENES, J. (1966) "Desensitization Techniques in the Treatment of School Phobia." *American Journal of Orthopsychiatry, 36,* 147–152.

GEISINGER, D. L. (1969) "Controlling Sexual and Interpersonal Difficulties." In J. Krumboltz and C. E. Thoresen (eds.), *Behavioral Counseling.* New York: Holt, Rinehart and Winston.

GELFAND, D. M. (ed.) (1969) *Social Learning in Childhood: Readings in Theory and Application.* Belmont, Calif.: Brooks-Cole.

GELFAND, D. M., AND HARTMANN, D. P. (1968) "Behavior Therapy with Children: A Review and Evaluation of Research Methodology." *Psychological Bulletin, 69,* 204–215.

GEPPERT, T. V. (1953) "Management of Nocturnal Enuresis by Conditioned Response." *Journal of the American Medical Association, 152,* 381–383.

GILES, D. K., AND WOLF, M. M. (1966) "Toilet Training Institutionalized Severe Retardates: An Application of Operant Behavior Modification Techniques." *American Journal of Mental Deficiency, 70,* 766–780.

GILLISON, T. H., AND SKINNER, J. L. (1958) "Treatment of Nocturnal Enuresis by the Electric Alarm." *British Medical Journal, 2,* 1268–1272.

GIRARDEAN, F., AND SPRADLIN, J. E. (1964) "Token Rewards in a Cottage Program." *Mental Retardation, 2,* 345–351.

GLUECK, S., AND GLUECK, E. (1950) *Unraveling Juvenile Delinquency.* Cambridge, Mass.: Harvard University Press.

GOCHROS, H. L. AND GOCHROS, J. (1976; in press) *The Sexually Oppressed.* New York: Association Press.

GOCHROS, H. L. (1971) "Sexual Problems in Social Work Practice." *Social Work, 16,* 3–5.

GOCHROS, H. L. (1972) "Treatment of Common Marital Sexual Problems." In H. L. Gochros and L. Schultz (eds.), *Human Sexuality and Social Work.* New York: Association Press.

GOCHROS, H. L., AND SCHULTZ, L. (eds.) (1972) *Human Sexuality and Social Work.* New York: Association Press.

GOCHROS, H. L.; WASHBURNE, B.; COLES, W.; GLUMP, S.; AND PETERS, M. (1974) "Characteristics of Sexual Problems Brought to Social-Workers and of the Social Workers who Respond to Them." Unpublished manuscript.

GOCHROS, H. L., AND FISCHER, J. (1975) "Introducing Behavior Modification into Social Agencies" Paper presented at N.A.S.W. Twentieth Anniversary Professional Symposium, Hollywood-by-the-Sea, Florida, Oct., 1975.

GOLDFRIED, M. R., AND MERBAUM, M. (eds.) (1973) *Behavior Change Through Self Control.* New York: Holt, Rinehart and Winston.

GOLDIAMOND, I. (1965a) "Stuttering and Fluency as Manipulatable Operant Response Classes." In L. Krasner and L. P. Ullmann (eds.) *Research in Behavior Modification.* New York: Holt, Rinehart and Winston.

GOLDIAMOND, I. (1965b) "Self Control Procedures in Personal Behavior Problems." *Psychological Reports, 17,* 851–868.

GOLDIAMOND, I. (1968) "Programs, Paradigms and Procedures." In A. L. Cohen (ed.), *Training Professionals in Procedures for the Establishment of Educational Environments.* Silver Spring, Md.: Educational Facility Press–Institute for Behavioral Research.

GOLDSTEIN, A. P. (1962) *Therapist–Patient Expectancies in Psychotherapy.* New York: Pergamon.

GOLDSTEIN, A. P.; HELLER, K.; AND SECHREST, L. B. (1969) *Psychotherapy and the Psychology of Behavior Change.* New York: John Wiley.

GOTESTAM, K. G.; MELIN, G.; AND DOCKENS, W. A. (1972) "Behavioral Program for Intravenous Amphetamine Addicts." Paper presented at International Symposium on Behavior Modification, Minneapolis.

GRAY, B. G., AND ENGLAND, G. (eds.) (1969) *Stuttering and the Conditioning Therapies.* Monterey, Calif.: Monterey Institute for Speech and Hearing.

GRAZIANO, A. M. (1973) *Child Without Tomorrow.* New York: Pergamon.

GRAZIANO, A. M. (ed.) (1971) *Behavior Therapy with Children.* Chicago: Aldine.

GREGORY, H. H. (ed.) (1968) *Learning Theory and Stuttering Therapy.* Evanston, Ill.: Northwestern University Press.

GREENSPOON, J. (1955) "The Reinforcing Effect of Two Spoken Sounds on the Frequency of Two Responses." *American Journal of Psychology, 68*, 409–416.

GRIPP, R. F., AND MAGARO, P. A. (1971) "A Token Economy Program Evaluation with Untreated Control Ward Comparisons." *Behaviour Research and Therapy, 9,* 137–149.

GRONLUND, N. E. (1970) *Stating Behavioral Objectives for Classroom Instruction.* New York: Macmillan.

GROSSER, C. F. (1965) "Community Development Programs Serving the Urban Poor." *Social Work, 10,* 15–21.

GROUP FOR THE ADVANCEMENT OF PSYCHIATRY (1964) *Pavlovian Conditioning and American Psychiatry.* Symposium No. 9. New York.

HALL, J. F. (1966) *The Psychology of Learning.* New York: Lippincott.

HALL, R. V. (1970) *Managing Behavior* (3 parts) . Lawrence, Kansas: H and H Enterprises.

HALL, R. V.; LUND, D.; AND JACKSON, D. (1968) "Effects of Teacher Attention on Study Behavior." *Journal of Applied Behavior Analysis, 1,* 1–12.

HALL, R. V.; PANYAN, M.; RABON, D.; AND BRODEN, M. (1968) "Instructing Beginning Teachers in Reinforcement Procedures Which Improve Classroom Control." *Journal of Applied Behavior Analysis, 1,* 315–322.

HAMERLYNCK, L. A.; DAVIDSON, P. O.; AND ACKER, L. E. (eds) (1969) *Behavior Modification and Ideal Mental Health Services.* Calgary, Alberta, Canada: University of Calgary.

HAMERLYNCK, L. A.; HANDY, L. C.; AND MASH, E. J. (eds) (1972) *Behavior Change: Methodology, Concepts, and Practice.* Champaign, Ill.: Research Press.

HAMILTON, J. (1971) "Environmental Control and Retardate Behavior." In H. Rickard (ed.) , *Behavioral Intervention in Human Problems.* New York: Pergamon.

HARING, N., AND WHELAN, R. (eds.) (1966) *The Learning Environment: Relationship to Behavior Modification and Implications for Special Education.* Lawrence, Kansas: University of Kansas Press.

HARRIS, M. B. (1972) *Classroom Uses of Behavior Modification.* Columbus, Ohio: Charles E. Merrill.

HART, B. M., AND RISLEY, T. R. (1968) "Establishing Use of Descriptive Adjectives in the Spontaneous Speech of Disadvantaged Preschool Children." *Journal of Applied Behavior Analysis, 1,* 109–120.

HARTUP, W. W., AND SMOTHERGILL, N. L. (eds) (1967) *The Young Child: Reviews of Research.* Washington, D.C.: National Association for the Education of Young Children.

HASTINGS, D. W. (1963) *Impotence and Frigidity.* Boston: Little, Brown.

HAUGHTON, E., AND AYLLON, T. (1965) "Production and Elimination of Symptomatic Behavior." In L. P. Ullmann and L. Krasner (eds.) , *Case Studies in Behavior Modification.* New York: Holt, Rinehart and Winston.

HAWKINS, R. P.; PETERSON, R. F.; SCHWEID, E.; AND BIJOU, S. W. (1966) "Behavior Therapy in the Home: Amelioration of Problem Parent-Child Relations with the Parent in a Therapeutic Role." *Journal of Experimental Child Psychology, 4,* 99–107.

HECKEL, R. V.; WIGGINS, S. L.; AND SALZBERG, H. C. (1962) "Conditioning Against Silence in Group Therapy." *Journal of Clinical Psychology, 18,* 216–217.

HEDQUIST, F. J. AND WEINHOLD, B. K. (1970) "Behavioral Group Counseling with Socially Anxious and Unassertive College Students." *Journal of Counseling Psychology, 17,* 237–242.

HENRIKSEN, K., AND DOUGHTY, R. (1967) "Decelerating Undesired Mealtime Behavior in a Group of Profoundly Retarded Boys." *American Journal of Mental Deficiency, 72,* 40–44.

HESS, R. D., AND BAER, R. M. (eds.) (1968) *Early Education: Current Theory, Research, and Practice.* Chicago: Aldine.

HEWETT, F. H. (1968) *The Emotionally Disturbed Child in the Classroom.* Boston: Allyn and Bacon.

HILGARD, E. R., AND BONER, G. H. (1966) *Theories of Learning.* New York: Appleton-Century-Crofts.

HILL, J. P. (ed.) (1967) *Minnesota Symposium on Child Psychology.* Minneapolis: University of Minnesota Press.

HODGSON, R. J., AND RACHMAN, S. J. (1970) "An Experimental Investigation of the Implosion Technique." *Behaviour Research and Therapy, 8,* 21–27.

HOFFMAN, M. L., AND HOFFMAN, L. W. (1964, 1966) *Review of Child Development Research,* 2 vols. New York: Russell Sage Foundation.

HOGAN, R. A. (1968) "The Implosive Technique." *Behavior Research and Therapy, 6,* 423–431.

HOGAN, R. A., AND KIRCHNER, J. H. (1967) "A Preliminary Report of the Extinction of Learned Fears via a Short-Term Implosive Therapy." *Journal of Abnormal Psychology, 72,* 106–109.

HOLLAND, C. J. (1970) "An Interview Guide for Behavioral Counseling with Parents." *Behavior Therapy, 1,* 70–79.

HOLLAND, J. G., AND SKINNER, B. F. (1961) *The Analysis of Behavior.* New York: McGraw-Hill.

HOLLINGSHEAD, A., AND REDLICH, F. (1958) *Social Class and Mental Illness.* New York: John Wiley.

HOLLIS, F. (1968) " . . . And What Shall We Teach? The Social Work Educator and Knowledge." *Social Service Review, 42,* 184–196.

HOLLIS, F. (1970) "The Psychosocial Approach to the Practice of Casework." In R. Roberts and R. Nee (eds.), *Theories of Social Casework.* Chicago: University of Chicago Press.

HOMME, L. E. (1965) "Control of Coverants: The Operants of the Mind." *Psychological Record, 15,* 501–511.

HOMME, L. E. (1966) "Contiguity Theory and Contingency Management." *Psychological Record, 16,* 233–241.

HOMME, L.; CSANYI, A. P.; GONZALES, N. A.; AND RECHS, J. R. (1969) *How to Use Contingency Contracting in the Classroom.* Champaign, Ill. Research Press.

HOMME, L. E.; DE BACA, P. C.; DEVINE, J. V.; STEINHORST, R.; AND RICKERT, E. J. (1963) "Use of the Premack Principle in Controlling the Behavior of

Nursery School Children," *Journal of the Experimental Analysis of Behavior, 6*, 544.

HONIG, W. (ed.) (1966) *Operant Behavior: Areas of Research and Application.* New York: Appleton-Century-Crofts.

HOTCHKISS, J. (1966) "The Modification of Maladaptive Behavior of a Class of Educationally Handicapped Children by Operant Conditioning Techniques." Unpublished doctoral dissertation, University of Southern California.

HOWE, M. W. (1974) "Casework Self-Evaluation: A Single-Subject Approach." *Social Service Review, 48*, 1–23.

HULL, C. L. (1943) *Principles of Behavior.* New York: Appleton-Century-Crofts.

HUNDZIAK, M.; MAURER, R. N.; AND WATSON, L. S. (1964) "Toilet Training Severely Handicapped Children by Operant Conditioning Techniques." Unpublished doctoral dissertation, University of Southern California.

HUNT, G. M., AND AZRIN, N. H. (1973) "A Community-Reinforcement Approach to Alcoholism." *Behaviour Research and Therapy, 11*, 91–104.

JACOBS, D. (ed.) (1969) *Behavior Therapy: New Directions.* Cleveland: Western Reserve Press.

JACOBSEN, E. (1938) *Progressive Relaxation.* Chicago: University of Chicago Press.

JEHU, D. (1966) *Learning Theory and Social Work.* New York: Humanities Press.

JEHU, D.; HARDIKER, P.; YELLOLY, M.; AND SHAW, M. (1972) *Behavior Modification in Social Work.* New York: John Wiley.

JOHNS, J. H., AND QUAY, H. (1962) "The Effect of Social Reward on Verbal Conditioning in Psychopathic and Neurotic Military Offenders." *Journal of Consulting Psychology, 26*, 217–220.

JOHNSON, W. G. (1971) "Some Applications of Homme's Coverant Control Therapy: Two Case Reports." *Behavior Therapy, 2*, 240–248.

JONES, M. R. (ed.) (1969) *Miami Symposium on the Prediction of Behavior, 1967: Aversive Stimulation.* Coral Gables, Florida: University of Miami Press.

KADUSHIN, A. (1959) "The Knowledge Base of Social Work." In A. Kahn (ed.), *Issues in American Social Work.* New York: Columbia University Press.

KANFER, F. H. (1968) "Verbal Conditioning: A Review of its Current Status." In T. R. Dixon and D. L. Harton (eds.), *Verbal Behavior and General Behavior Theory.* Englewood Cliffs, New Jersey: Prentice-Hall.

KANFER, F. H., AND PHILLIPS, J. S. (1970) *Learning Foundations of Behavior Therapy.* New York: John Wiley.

KANFER, F. H., AND SASLOW, G. (1969) "Behavioral Diagnosis." In C. M. Franks (ed.), *Behavior Therapy: Appraisal and Status.* New York: McGraw-Hill.

KANFER, F. H., AND SASLOW, G. (1965) "Behavioral Diagnosis." *Archives of General Psychiatry, 12*, 529–538.

KAPLAN, H., AND KOHL, R. (1972) "Adverse Reactions to the Rapid Treatment of Sexual Problems." *Psychosomatics, 13*, 185–190.

KAREN, R. L., AND MAXWELL, S. J. (1967) "Strengthening Self-Help Behavior in the Retardate." *American Journal of Mental Deficiency, 71,* 546–550.

KARLINS, M. (ed.) (1972) *Man Controlled: Readings in the Psychology of Behavior Control.* New York: Free Press.

KASWAN, J. W.; LOVE, L.; AND RODNICK, E. (1968) *The Effectiveness of Information and Consultation.* Unpublished manuscript, Ohio State University.

KATCHADOUVIAN, H. A., AND LUNDE, D. T. (1972) *Fundamentals of Human Sexuality.* New York: Holt, Rinehart and Winston.

KAU, M. L., AND FISCHER, J. (1975) "Self Modification of Exercise Behavior." *Behavior Therapy and Experimental Psychiatry, 5,* 213–214.

KEGEL, A. H. (1952) "Sexual Functions of the Pubococcygens Muscle." *Western Journal of Obstetrics and Gynecology 60,* 521.

KEIRSEY, D. W. (1965) "Transactional Casework: A Technology for Inducing Behavioral Change." Paper presented to the convention of California Association of School Psychologists and Psychometrists, San Francisco.

KEIRSEY, D. W. (1969) "Systematic Exclusion: Eliminating Chronic Classroom Disruptions." In J. D. Krumboltz and C. E. Thoresen (eds.) *Behavioral Counseling: Case Studies and Techniques.* New York: Holt, Rinehart and Winston.

KELLER, F. (1969) *Learning: Reinforcement Theory.* 2d ed. New York: Random House.

KENNEDY, T. (1964) "Treatment of Chronic Schizophrenia by Behavior Therapy: Case Reports." *Behaviour Research and Therapy, 2,* 1–6.

KIMBLE, G. A. (1964) *Conditioning and Learning.* London: Methuen.

KIMBRELL, D. L.; LUCKEY, R. E.; AND PAUL, F. P. (1967) "Operation Dry Pants: An Intensive Habit-Training Program for Severely and Profoundly Retarded." *Mental Retardation, 5,* 32–36.

KINSEY, A.; POMEROY, W.; AND MARTIN, C. (1948) *Sexual Behavior in the Human Male.* Philadelphia: W. B. Saunders.

KINSEY, A. C.; POMEROY, W. B.; MARTIN, C. E.; AND GEBHARD, P. H. (1953) *Sexual Behavior in the Human Female.* Philadelphia: W. B. Saunders.

KLEIN, F. C.; HAPKIEWICZ, W. G.; AND RODEN, A. H. (eds.) (1973) *Behavior Modification in Educational Settings.* Springfield, Ill.: Charles C Thomas.

KNOX, D. (1971) *Marriage Happiness: A Behavioral Approach to Counseling.* Champaign, Ill.: Research Press.

KRAFT, T., AND AL-ISSA, I. (1967) "Behavior Therapy of Frigidity." *American Journal of Psychiatry, 21,* 116-120.

KRAFT, T. (1969b) "Treatment of Drinamyl Addiction." *International Journal of Addictions, 4,* 59–64.

KRAFT, T. (1970) "Treatment of Drinamyl Addiction." *Journal of Nervous and Mental Disorders, 150,* 138–144.

KRAFT, T., AND AL-ISSA, I. (1967) "Behavior Therapy of Frigidity." *American Journal of Psychotherapy, 21,* 116–120.

KRASNER, L. (1962) "The Therapist as a Social Reinforcement Machine." In

H. H. Strupp and L. Lubrosky (eds.) *Research in Psychotherapy,* vol. 2. Washington, D.C.: American Psychological Association.

KRASNER, L. (1965) "Verbal Conditioning and Psychotherapy." In L. Krasner and L. P. Ullmann (eds.), *Research in Behavior Modification.* New York: Holt, Rinehart and Winston.

KRASNER, L. (1969a) "Behavior Modification—Values and Training." In C. Franks (ed.), *Behavior Therapy: Appraisal and Status.* New York: McGraw-Hill.

KRASNER, L. (1969b) "Discussion." In I. P. R. Guyett (chmn.), *Tribulations of Token Programs in Hospital and School Settings.* Symposium presented at the American Psychological Association, Washington, D.C.: August 1969.

KRASNER, L. (1970) "Token Economy." In D. J. Levis (ed.), *Learning Approaches to Therapeutic Behavior Change.* Chicago: Aldine.

KRASNER, L. (1971) "The Operant Approach in Behavior Therapy." In A. Bergin and S. Garfield (eds.), *Handbook of Psychotherapy and Behavior Change.* New York: John Wiley.

KRASNER, L., AND ULLMANN, L. P. (eds) (1965) *Research in Behavior Modification.* New York: Holt, Rinehart and Winston.

KRASNER, L., AND ULLMANN, L. P. (1973) *Behavior Influence and Personality.* New York: Holt, Rinehart and Winston.

KRUMBOLTZ, J. D. (ed.) (1966) *Revolution in Counseling: Implications of Behavioral Science.* Boston: Houghton-Mifflin.

KRUMBOLTZ, J. D., AND KRUMBOLTZ, H. B. (1973) *Changing Children's Behavior.* Englewood Cliffs, N.J.: Prentice-Hall.

KRUMBOLTZ, J. D. AND THORESEN, C. E. (eds.) (1969) *Behavioral Counseling: Cases and Techniques.* New York: Holt, Rinehart and Winston.

KUBANY, E. S., AND SLOGGETT, B. S. (1973) "Child Management Therapy." Paper presented at Hawaii Psychological Association Annual Convention.

KUBANY, E. S.; WEISS, L. E.; AND SLOGGETT, B. S. (1971) "The Good Behavior Clock: A Reinforcement/Time Out Procedure for Reducing Disruptive Classroom Behavior." *Journal of Behavior Therapy and Experimental Psychiatry, 2,* 173–179.

KUNZELMANN, H. P. (ed.) (1970) *Precision Teaching: An Initial Training Sequence.* Seattle, Wash.: Special Child Publications.

LANG, P. J. (1969) "The Mechanics of Desensitization and the Laboratory Study of Human Fear." In C. M. Franks (ed.), *Behavior Therapy: Appraisal and Status.* New York: McGraw-Hill.

LANSEN, L. A. AND BRICKER, W. A. (1968) *A Manual for Parents and Teachers of Severely and Moderately Retarded Children.* Nashville, Tenn.: John F. Kennedy Center for Research on Education and Human Development.

LAWRENCE, H., AND SUNDEL, M. (1972) "Behavior Modification in Adult Groups." *Social Work, 17,* 34–43.

LAZARUS, A. A. (1961) "Group Therapy in Phobic Disorders by Systematic Desensitization." *Journal of Abnormal and Social Psychology, 136,* 504–570.

LAZARUS, A. A. (1963) "The Treatment of Chronic Frigidity by Systematic Desensitization." *Journal of Nervous and Mental Disease, 136,* 272–278.

LAZARUS, A. A. (1965) "The Treatment of a Sexually Inadequate Man." In L. P. Ullmann and L. Krasner (eds.), *Case Studies in Behavior Modification.* New York: Holt, Rinehart and Winston.

LAZARUS, A. A. (1966) "Behavior Rehearsal vs. Non-Directive Therapy vs. Advice in Effecting Behavior Change." *Behaviour Research and Therapy, 4,* 209–212.

LAZARUS, A. A. (1968) "Learning Theory and the Treatment of Depression." *Behaviour Research and Therapy, 6,* 83–89.

LeBow, M. D. (1973) *Behavior Modification: A Significant Method in Nursing Practice.* Englewood Cliffs, N.J.: Prentice-Hall.

LEITENBERG, H. (1973) "The Use of Single Case Methodology in Psychotherapy Research." *Journal of Abnormal Psychology, 82,* 87–101.

LESER, E. (1967) "Behavior Therapy with a Narcotic User: A Case Report." *Behaviour Research and Therapy, 5,* 251–252.

LeSHAN, E., AND LeSHAN, L. (1968) "A Home Is Not a Lab." *New York Times Magazine,* April 7, 97–107.

LESLIE, G. R. (ed.) (1968) *Behavior Modification in Rehabilitation Facilities.* Hot Springs, Arkansas: Arkansas Rehabilitation Research and Training Center.

LEVIS, D. J. (ed.) (1970) *Learning Approaches to Therapeutic Behavior Change.* Chicago: Aldine.

LEVIS, D. J. AND CARRERA, R. (1967) "Effects of Ten Hours of Implosive Therapy in the Treatment of Outpatients: A Preliminary Report." *Journal of Abnormal Psychology, 72,* 504–508.

LEWINSOHN, P. M.; WEINSTEIN, M. S.; AND SHAW, D. A. (1969) "Depression: A Clinical-Research Approach." In R. D. Rubin and C. M. Franks (eds.) *Advances in Behavior Therapy, 1968.* New York: Academic Press.

LIBERMAN, R. P. (1968) "Aversive Conditioning of a Drug Addict: A Pilot Study." *Behaviour Research and Therapy, 6,* 229–231.

LIBERMAN, R. P. (1969) "Reinforcement of Cohesiveness of Group Therapy." Paper presented to the annual convention of the American Psychiatric Association, Miami Beach, Florida.

LIBERMAN, R. P. (1970a) "A Behavioral Approach to Group Dynamics: I. Reinforcement and Prompting of Cohesiveness in Group Therapy." *Behavior Therapy, 1,* 141–175.

LIBERMAN, R. P. (1970b) "A Behavioral Approach to Group Dynamics: II. Reinforcing and Prompting Hostility-to-the-therapist in Group Therapy." *Behavior Therapy, 1,* 312–327.

LIBERMAN, R. P. (1970c) "Behavioral Approaches to Family and Couple Therapy." *American Journal of Orthopsychiatry, 40,* 106–118.

LIBERMAN, R. P. (1972) *A Guide to Behavioral Analysis and Therapy.* New York: Pergamon.

LIBERMAN, R. P.; TEIGEN, J.; PATTERSON, R.; AND BAKER, V. (1973) "Reducing

Delusional Speech in Chronic Paranoid Schizophrenics." *Journal of Applied Behavior Analysis, 6,* 57–64.

LINDSLEY, O. R. (1966) "An Experiment with Parents Handling Behavior at Home." *Johnstone Bulletin, 9,* 27–36.

LINDSLEY, O. (1968) Personal Communication.

LLOYD, K. E., AND GARLINGTON, W. K. (1968) "Weekly Variations on a Token Economy Psychiatric Ward." *Behaviour Research and Therapy, 6,* 407–410.

LOCKE, E. A.; CARTLEDGE, N.; AND KOEPPEL, J. (1968) "Motivational Effects of Knowledge of Results: A Goal-Setting Phenomenon?" *Psychological Bulletin, 70,* 474–485.

LONDON, P. (1964) *The Modes and Morals of Psychotherapy.* New York: Holt, Rinehart and Winston.

LONDON, P. (1969) *Behavior Control.* New York: Harper & Row.

LOVAAS, O. I. (1966) "A Program for the Establishment of Speech in Psychotic Children." In J. K. Wing (ed.) , *Early Childhood Autism.* Oxford: Pergamon.

LOVAAS, O. I.; FREITAG, G.; GOLD, V. J.; AND KASSORIA, I. C. (1965) "Experimental Studies in Childhood Schizophrenia: Analysis of Self-Destructive Behavior." *Journal of Experimental Child Psychology, 2,* 67–84.

LOVAAS, O. I.; FRIETAG, G.; GOLD, V. J.; AND KASSORIA, I. C. (1965) "Experilishment of Imitation and Its Use for the Development of Complex Behavior in Schizophrenic Children." *Behaviour Research and Therapy, 5,* 171–181.

LOVAAS, O. I.; LITROWNICK, A.; AND MANN, R. (1971) "Response Latencies to Auditory Stimuli in Autistic Children." *Behaviour Research and Therapy, 9,* 39–49.

LOVAAS, O. I.; KOEGAL, R.; SIMMONS, J. Q.; AND LONG, J. S. (1973) "Some Generalization and Follow-Up Measures on Autistic Children in Behavior Therapy." *Journal of Applied Behavior Analysis, 6,* 131–166.

LOVAAS, O. I., AND SIMMONS, J. Q. (1969) "Manipulation of Self-Destruction in Three Retarded Children." *Journal of Applied Behavioral Analysis, 2,* 143–157.

LO PICCOLO, J., AND LOBITZ, W. C. (1973) "Behavior Therapy of Sexual Dysfunction." In L. A. Hamerlynck, L. C. Handy, and E. J. Mash (eds.) , *Behavior Change: Methodology, Concepts, and Practice.* Champaign, Ill.: Research Press.

LOVIBOND, S. H. (1963a) "Intermittent Reinforcement in Behaviour Therapy." *Behaviour Research and Therapy, 1,* 127–132.

LOVIBOND, S. H. (1963b) "The Mechanism of Conditioning Treatment of Enuresis." *Behaviour Research and Therapy, 1,* 17–21

LOVIBOND, S. H. (1964) *Conditioning and Enuresis.* London: Pergamon.

LOVITT, T. C.; GUPPY, T. E.; AND BLATTNER, J. E. (1969) "The Use of a Free-Time Contingency with Fourth Graders to Increase Spelling and Accuracy." *Behaviour Research and Therapy, 1,* 151–156.

LUNDIN, R. (1969) *Personality: A Behavioral Analysis.* New York: Macmillan.

LIPPETT, R.; WATSON, J.; AND WESTLEY, B. (1965) *The Dynamics of Planned Change.* New York: Harcourt, Brace and World.

McBREARTY, J. F.; DICHTER, M.; GARFIELD, Z.; AND HEATH, G. (1968) "A Behaviorally Oriented Treatment Program for Alcoholism." *Psychological Reports, 22,* 287–298.

McCARY, J. L. (1973) *Human Sexuality.* New York: Van Nostrand.

McCONAGHY, N., AND BARR, R. F. (1973) "Classical, Avoidance and Backward Conditioning Treatments of Homosexuality." *British Journal of Psychiatry, 122,* 151–162.

McCORD, W.; McCORD, J.; AND ZOLA, I. K. (1959) *Origins of Crime: A New Evaluation of the Cambridge-Somerville Youth Study.* New York: Columbia University Press.

MacDONALD, W., AND TANABE, G. (eds.) (1973) *Focus on Classroom Behavior.* Springfield, Ill.: Charles C Thomas.

McGINNES, E., AND FERSTER, C. B. (eds.) (1971) *The Reinforcement of Social Behavior.* Boston: Houghton-Mifflin.

McINTIRE, R. W. (1970) *For Love of Children: Behavioral Psychology for Parents.* Del Mar, Calif.: C. R. M. Books.

McLEAN, P. D.; OGSTON, K.; AND GRAUER, L. (1973) "A Behavioral Approach to the Treatment of Depression." *Journal of Behavior Therapy and Experimental Psychiatry, 4,* 323–330.

McNEMAR, Q. (1940) "Sampling in Psychological Research." *Psychological Bulletin, 37.*

MADSEN, C. H. (1965) "Positive Reinforcement in the Toilet Training of a Normal Child." In L. P. Ullmann, and L. Krasner (eds.), *Case Studies in Behavior Modification.* New York: Holt, Rinehart and Winston.

MADSEN, C. H., JR.; BECKER, W. C.; AND THOMAS, D. R. (1968) "Rules, Praise and Ignoring: Elements of Elementary Classroom Control." *Journal of Applied Behavior Analysis, 1,* 139–150.

MADSEN, C. H., AND ULLMANN, L. (1967) "Innovations in the Desensitization of Frigidity." *Behaviour Research and Therapy, 5,* 67–68.

MADSEN, C. K., AND MADSEN, C. H. (1970) *Teaching/Discipline.* Boston: Allyn and Bacon.

MADSEN, C. K. (1971) *Parents/Children/Discipline.* Boston: Allyn and Bacon.

MAHONEY, M. J.; KAZDIN, A. E.; AND LESSWING, N.J. (1974) "Behavior Modification: Delusion or Deliverance?" In C. M. Franks and G. T. Wilson (eds.), *Annual Review of Behavior Therapy.* New York: Brunner/Mazel.

MAHONEY, M. J., AND THORESEN, C. E. (eds.) (1974) *Self-Control: Power to the Person.* Monterey: Brooks Cole.

MAHRER, A. R., AND MASON, D. J. (1965) "Changes in Number of Self-Reported Symptoms During Psychiatric Hospitalization." *Journal of Consulting Psychology, 29,* 285.

MAIER, S. E.; SELIFMAN, M. E. P.; AND SOLOMON, R. L. (1970) "Pavlovian Fear Conditioning and Learned Helplessness." In B. A. Campbell and R. M. Church (eds.), *Punishment.* New York: Appleton-Century-Crofts.

MALOTT, R. W.; WHALEY, D. L.; AND ULRICH, R. E. (eds.) (1967) *Analysis of*

Behavior: Principles and Applications. Dubuque, Iowa: William C. Brown Company.

MANGAN, G. L.; AND BAINBRIDGE, L. D. (eds.) (1969) *Behavior Therapy.* St. Lucia, Queensland, Australia: University of Queensland Press.

MARKS, I. M. *Fears and Phobias* (1969) New York: Academic Press.

MARKS, I. M.; AND GELDER, M. G. (1966) "Common Ground Between Behavior Therapy and Psychodynamic Methods." *British Journal of Medical Psychology, 39,* 11–23.

MARQUIS, J. N. (1970) "Orgasmic Reconditioning: Changing Sexual Object Choice Through Controlling Masturbation Fantasies." *Journal of Behavior Therapy and Experimental Psychiatry, 1,* 263–271.

MARQUIS, J. N.; MORGAN, W.; AND PIAGET, G. (1971) *A Guidebook for Systematic Desensitization.* Palo Alto, Calif.; Veterans Administration Workshop.

MARSHALL, D. S., AND SUGGS, R. C. (1971) *Human Sexual Behavior.* New York: Basic Books.

MARTIN, B. (1967) "Family Interaction Associated with Child Disturbance: Assessment and Modification." *Psychotherapy: Theory, Research and Practice, 4,* 30–35.

MARTIN, D. G. (1972) *Learning-Based Client-Centered Therapy.* Monterey, Calif.: Brooks-Cole.

MASLOW, A. (1954) *Motivation and Personality.* New York: Harper & Bros.

MASTERS, W. H.; AND JOHNSON, V. E. (1966) *Human Sexual Response.* Boston: Little, Brown.

MASTERS, W. H.; AND JOHNSON, V. E. (1970) *Human Sexual Inadequacy.* Boston: Little, Brown.

MAYER, J., AND TIMMS, N. (1969) "Clash in Perspective Between Worker and Client." *Social Casework, 50,* 32–40.

MAZUR, A. (1972) *Biology and Social Behavior,* New York: Free Press.

MEACHAM, M. L.; AND WIESEN, A. E. (1969) *Changing Behavior in the Classroom: A Manual for Precision Teaching.* Scranton, Pa.: International Textbook Company.

MEAD, M. (1949) *Male and Female.* New York: William Morrow.

MEALIEA, W. L. (1967) "The Comparative Effectiveness of Systematic Desensitization and Implosive Therapy in the Elimination of Snake Phobia." Unpublished doctoral dissertation, University of Missouri.

MEHRABIAN, A. (1970) *Tactics of Social Influence.* Englewood Cliffs, N.J.: Prentice-Hall.

MERTENS, G.; LUKER, A.; AND BOLTUCK, C. (eds.) (1968) *Behavioral Science Behaviorally Taught.* Minneapolis: Burgess.

MEYER, V., AND CHESSER, E. S. (1970) *Behavior Therapy in Clinical Psychiatry.* Baltimore: Penguin.

MICHAEL, J. (1970) "Principles of Effective Usage." In Ulrich, R.; Stachnik, T.; and Mabry, J. (eds.), *Control of Human Behavior,* vol. 2. Glenview, Ill.: Scott, Foresman.

MICKELSON, D. J., AND STEVIC, R. R. (1971) "Differential Effects of Facilitative and Non-Facilitative Behavioral Counselors." *Journal of Counseling Psychology, 18,* 314–319.

MIKULAS, W. L. (1972) *Behavior Modification: An Overview.* New York: Harper & Row.

MILBY, J. B.; STENMARK, D. E.; AND HORNER, R. F. (1967) "Modification of Locomotive Behavior in a Severely Disturbed Psychotic." *Perceptual and Motor Skills,* 25 no. 25, 359–360.

MILLENSON, J. R. (1967) *Principles of Behavioral Analysis.* New York: Macmillan.

MILLER, L. K., AND MILLER, O. L. (1970) "Reinforcing Self-Help Group Activities of Welfare Recipients." *Journal of Applied Behavior Analysis, 6,* 57–64.

MILLER, P. M. (1973) "Behavioral Treatment of Drug Addiction: A Review." *The International Journal of the Addictions, 8* (3) , 511–519.

MILLS, A. B. (ed.) (1968) *Behavior Theory and Therapy: Research Symposium No. 2.* Sacramento: California Department of Mental Hygiene, Bureau of Research.

MINGE, M. R., AND BALL, T. S. (1967) "Teaching of Self-Help Skills to Profoundly Retarded Children." *American Journal of Mental Deficiency, 71,* 864–868.

MISCHEL, W. (1968) *Personality and Assessment.* New York: John Wiley.

MITCHELL, W. S., AND STOFFELMAYR, H. (1973) "Application of the Premack Principle to the Behavioral Control of Extremely Inactive Schizophrenics." *Journal of Applied Behavior Analysis, 6,* 419–423.

MOORE, C. H., AND CRUM, B. C. (1969) "Weight Reduction in a Chronic Schizophrenic by Means of Operant Conditioning Procedures." *Behaviour Research and Therapy, 7,* 129–131.

MORREAU, L. E., AND DALEY, M. F. (1972) *Behavioral Management in the Classroom.* New York: Appleton-Century-Crofts.

MORROW, W. R., AND GOCHROS, H. L. (1970) "Misconceptions Regarding Behavior Modification." *Social Service Review, 44,* 293–307.

MORROW, W. (1971) *Behavior Therapy Bibliography.* Columbia, Mo.: University of Missouri Press.

MOWRER, O. H., AND MOWRER, W. M. (1938) "Enuresis: A Method for Its Study and Treatment." *American Journal of Orthopsychiatry, 8,* 436–459.

MOWRER, O. H. (1960) *Learning Theory and the Symbolic Processes.* New York: Wiley.

MURRAY, E. J. (1963) "Learning Theory and Psychotherapy: Biotropic Versus Sociotropic Approaches." *Journal of Counseling Psychology, 10,* 250–255.

NAGOSHI, J. (ed.) (1969) *Progress in Behavior Modification.* Honolulu: Social Welfare Research and Development Center.

NAWAS, M. M. (1971) "Existential Anxiety Treated by Systematic Desensitization: A Case Study." *Journal of Behavior Therapy and Experimental Psychiatry, 2,* 291–295.

NEALE, D. H. (1936) "Behavior Therapy and Ecopresis in Children." *Behaviour Research and Therapy. 1,* 139–149.

NEISWORTH, J. T.; DENO, S. L.; AND JENKINS, J. F. (1969) *Student Motivation and Classroom Management: A Behavioristic Approach.* Newark, Del.: Behavior Technics, Inc.

NEURINGER, C., AND MICHEL, J. (eds.) (1969) *Behavior Modification in Clinical Psychology.* New York: Appleton-Century-Crofts.

NEWMAN, D. R. (1969) "Using Assertive Training." In J. Krumboltz and C. E. Thoresen (eds.), *Behavioral Counseling.* New York: Holt, Rinehart and Winston.

NORDQUIST, V. M., AND WAHLER, R. G. (1973) "Naturalistic Treatment of an Autistic Child." *Journal of Applied Behavior Analysis,* 6, 79–87.

O'BRIEN, J.; RAYNES, A.; AND PATCH, V. (1972) "Treatment of Heroin Addiction with Aversion Therapy, Relaxation Training and Systematic Desensitization." *Behaviour Research and Therapy, 10,* 77–80.

O'CONNOR, R. D. (1969) "Modification of Social Withdrawal Through Symbolic Modeling." *Journal of Applied Behavior Analysis, 2,* 15–22.

OFFER, D.; AND SAHSHIN, M. (1966) *Normality: Theoretical and Clinical Concepts of Mental Health.* New York: Basic Books.

O'LEARY, K. D.; O'LEARY, S.; AND BECKER, W. (1967) "Modification of a Deviant Sibling Interaction in the Home." *Behaviour Research and Therapy, 5* 113–130.

O'LEARY, K. D., AND O'LEARY, S. G. (1972) *Classroom Management: The Successful Use of Behavior Modification.* New York: Pergamon.

OMORI, S. (1972) "Diagnosis in Social Work Practice." Unpublished manuscript, School of Social Work, University of Hawaii.

OSIPOW, S. H. (1970) *Strategies in Counseling for Behavior Change.* New York: Appleton-Century-Crofts.

OSIPOW, S. H., AND WALSH, B. (1970) *Behavior Change in Counseling.* New York: Appleton-Century-Crofts.

PACKARD, R. G. (1970) "The Control of Classroom Attention: A Group Contingency for Complex Behavior." *Journal of Applied Psychology, 3,* 13–28.

PARKER, R. D. (ed.) (1969) *Readings in Educational Psychology.* Boston: Allyn and Bacon.

PARSONS, T. (1951) "Illness and the Role of the Physician: A Sociological Perspective." *American Journal of Orthopsychiatry, 21,* 452–460.

PATTERSON, G. R. (1965) "An Application of Conditioning Techniques to the Control of a Hyperactive Child." In L. P. Ullmann and L. Krasner (eds.), *Case Studies in Behavior Modification.* New York: Holt, Rinehart and Winston.

PATTERSON, G. R. (1971a) *Families.* Champaign, Ill.: Research Press.

PATTERSON, G. R. (1971b) "Behavioral Intervention Procedures in the Classroom and in the Home." In A. Bergin and S. Garfield (eds.), *Handbook of Psychotherapy and Behavior Change.* New York: John Wiley.

PATTERSON, G. R., AND GULLION, M. E. (1971) *Living with Children: New Methods for Parents and Teachers.* Champaign, Ill.: Research Press.

PATTERSON, G. R., AND HARRIS, A. (1968) "Some Methodological Considerations for Observation Procedures." Paper presented at the meeting of the American Psychological Association, San Francisco.

PATTERSON, G. R.; JONES, R.; WHITTIER, J.; AND WRIGHT, M. A. (1965) "A Behavior Modification Technique for the Hyperactive Child." *Behaviour Research and Therapy, 2,* 217–226.

PATTERSON, G. R.; LITTMAN, R.; AND BRICKER, W. (1967) "Assertive Behavior in Children: A Preliminary Outline of a Theory of Aggressive Behavior." *Monograph of Society for Research in Child Development,* vol. 1, pp. 1–43.

PATTERSON, G. R.; MCNEAL, S.; HAWKINS, N.; AND PHELPS, R. (1967) "Reprogramming the Social Environment." *Journal of Child Psychology and Psychiatry, 8,* 181–195.

PATTERSON, G. R.; RAY, R. S.; AND SHAW, D. A. (1968) "Direct Intervention in Families of Deviant Children." *Oregon Research Institute Research Bulletin, 8* (9).

PATTERSON, G. R.; AND REID, J. (1969) "Reciprocity and Coercion: Two Facets of Social Systems." In C. Neuringer and J. Michael (eds.), *Behavior Modification in Clinical Psychology.* New York: Appleton-Century-Crofts.

PATTERSON, G. R.; SHAW, D. A.; AND EBNER, M. J. (1969) "Teachers, Peers, and Parents as Agents of Change in the Classroom." In Benson, F. A. M. (ed.), *Modifying Deviant Social Behaviors in Various Classroom Settings.* Eugene, Oregon: University of Oregon.

PAUL, G. L. (1966) *Insight vs. Desensitization in Psychotherapy: An Experiment in Anxiety Reduction.* Stanford: Stanford University Press.

PAUL, G. (1969) "Outcome of Systematic Desensitization in Groups." In C. M. Franks (ed.), *Behavior Therapy: Appraisal and Status.* New York: McGraw-Hill.

PAUL, G., AND SHANNON, D. T. (1968). "Treatment of Anxiety through Systematic Desensitization in Groups." *Journal of Abnormal Psychology, 17,* 124–135.

PAVLOV, I. P. (1927) *Conditioned Reflexes.* Translated by G. V. Anrep. London: Oxford University Press.

PEINE, H. (1969) "Programming the Home." Paper presented at the meetings of the Rocky Mountain Psychological Association. Albuquerque, New Mexico.

PERLMAN, H. H. (1970) "The Problem Solving Model in Casework." In R. Roberts and R. Nee (eds.), *Theories of Social Casework.* Chicago: University of Chicago Press.

PETERSON, D. R., AND LONDON, P. A. (1965) "A Role for Cognition in the Behavioral Treatment of a Child's Eliminative Disturbance." In L. P. Ullmann and L. Krasner (eds.), *Case Studies in Behavior Modification.* New York: Holt, Rinehart and Winston.

PHILLIPS, E. L. (1968) "Achievement Place: Token Reinforcement Procedures in a Home-Style Rehabilitation Setting for Pre-Delinquent Boys." *Journal of Applied Behavioral Analysis, 1,* 213–223.

PINCUS, H., AND MINAHAN, A. (1970) "Toward a Model for Teaching a Basic First-year Course in Methods of Social Work Practice." In L. Ripple (ed.),

Innovations in Teaching Social Work Practice. New York: Council on Social Work Education.

PITTS, C. E. (1971) *Operant Conditioning in the Classroom.* New York: Crowell.

PIZZAT, F. (1973). *Behavior Modification in Residential Treatment for Children.* New York: Behavioral Publications.

PLOWMAN, P. D. (1971) *Behavioral Objectives: Teacher Success through Student Performance.* Chicago: Science Research Associates.

PORTER, R. (ed.) (1968) *The Role of Learning in Psychotherapy.* London: Churchill.

PREMACK, D. (1959) "Toward Empirical Behavior Laws. I. Positive Reinforcement." *Psychological Review, 66,* 219–233.

PUMROY, D. K., AND PUMROY, S. S. (1973) *Modern Child Rearing: Behavioral Principles Applied to the Raising of Children.* Chicago: Aldine-Atherton.

PUMROY, D. K., AND PUMROY, S. S. (1965) "Systematic Observation and Reinforcement Technique in Toilet Training." *Psychological Reports, 16,* 467–471.

QUAY, H. C., AND HUNT, W. A. (1965) "Psychopathy, Neuroticism, and Verbal Conditioning: A Replication and Extension." *Journal of Consulting Psychology, 29,* 283.

RACHMAN, S. J. (1969) *Phobias: Their Nature and Control.* Springfield, Ill.: Charles C Thomas.

RACHMAN, S. J. (1972) "Clinical Applications of Observational Learning, Imitation and Modeling." *Behavior Therapy, 3,* 379–397.

RACHMAN, S. J., AND TEASDALE, J. D. (1969a) "Aversion Therapy: An Appraisal." In C. M. Franks (ed.), *Behavior Therapy: Appraisal and Status.* New York: McGraw-Hill.

RACHMAN, S. J., AND TEASDALE, J. D. (1969b) *Aversion Therapy and Behavior Disorders.* Coral Gables, Fla.: University of Miami Press.

RAMP, E. A., AND HOPKINS, B. I. (eds.) (1971) *A New Direction for Education: Behavior Analysis, 1971.* Lawrence, Kansas: Dept. of Human Development, University of Kansas.

RASHKIS, H. A. (1966) "How Behavior Therapy Affects Schizophrenics." *Diseases of the Nervous System, 27,* 505–510.

RAY, R. S. (1965) "The Training of Mothers of Atypical Children in the Use of Behavior Modification Techniques." Unpublished master's thesis, University of Oregon.

RAYMOND, M. (1964) "The Treatment of Addiction by Aversion Conditioning with Apomorphine." *Behaviour Research and Therapy, 1,* 287–291.

REESE, E. P. (1966) *Analysis of Human Operant Behavior.* Dubuque, Iowa: William C. Brown.

REHM, L. P., AND MARSTON, A. R. (1968) "Reduction in Social Anxiety Through Modification of Self-Reinforcement: An Instigation Technique." *Journal of Consulting and Clinical Psychology, 32,* 565–574.

REID, W., AND B. SHAPIRO (1969) "Client Reactions to Advice." *Social Service Review, 43,* 165–173.

RESNICK, J. H. (1968) "The Control of Smoking Behavior by Stimulus Satiation." *Behaviour Research and Therapy, 6,* 113–114.

REYNOLDS, G. S. (1968) *A Primer of Operant Conditioning.* Glenview, Ill.: Scott, Foresman.

REYNOLDS, N. J., AND RISLEY, T. R. (1968) "The Role of Social and Material Reinforcers in Increasing Talking of a Disadvantaged Preschool Child." *Journal of Applied Behavior Analysis, 1,* 253–262.

RICKARD, H. (ed.) (1971) *Behavioral Intervention in Human Problems.* New York: Pergamon.

RIESSMAN, F. (1963) "The Culturally Deprived Child: A New View." *The Education Digest, 29,* 12–15.

RISLEY, T. (1968) "The Effects and Side-Effects of Punishing the Austistic Behaviors of a Deviant Child." *Journal of Applied Behavior Analysis, 1,* 21–34.

RITTER, B. (1968) "The Group Desensitization of Children's Snake Phobias Using Vicarious and Contact Desensitization Procedures." *Behaviour Research and Therapy, 6,* 1–6.

RITTER, B. (1969a) "Treatment of Acrophobia with Contact Desensitization." *Behaviour Research and Therapy, 7,* 41–45.

RITTER, B. (1969b) "Eliminating Excessive Fears of the Environment Through Contact Desensitization." In J. D. Krumboltz and C. E. Thoresen (eds.), *Behavioral Counseling.* New York: Holt, Rinehart and Winston.

ROBERTS, R., AND NEE, R. (eds.) (1970) *Theories of Social Casework.* Chicago: University of Chicago Press.

ROSE, S. D. (1969) "A Behavioral Approach to the Group Treatment of Parents," *Social Work, 14,* 21–30.

ROSE, S. D. (1972) *Treating Children in Groups.* San Francisco: Jossey-Bass.

ROSEHAN, D. L. (1973) "On Being Sane in Insane Places." *Science, 179,* 250–258.

ROTTER, J. B.; CHANCE, J. E.; AND PHARES, E. J. (eds.) (1972) *Applications of a Social Learning Theory of Personality.* New York: Holt, Rinehart and Winston.

RUBIN, R., AND FRANKS, C. M. (eds.) (1969) *Advances in Behavior Therapy, 1968.* New York: Academic Press.

RUBIN, R. D.; FENSTERSHEIM, H.; HENDERSON, J. D.; AND ULLMANN, L. P. (eds.) (1970) *Advances in Behavior Therapy, 1969.* New York: Academic Press.

RUBIN, R. D.; FENSTERSHEIM, H.; HENDERSON, J. D.; AND ULLMANN, L. P. (eds.) (1972) *Advances in Behavior Therapy.* New York: Academic Press.

RUBIN, R. D. (ed.) (1973) *Advances in Behavior Therapy.* New York: Academic Press.

RUTNER, I. T., AND BUGLE, C. (1969) "An Experimental Procedure for the Modification of Psychotic Behavior." *Journal of Consulting and Clinical Psychology, 33,* 651–653.

SAGE, W. (1974) "Autism's Child." *Human Behavior, 3,* 16–26.

SARASON, I. G., AND GANZER, V. J. (1969) "Developing Appropriate Social Behaviors of Juvenile Delinquents." In J. D. Krumboltz and C. E. Thoresen (eds.), *Behavioral Counseling.* New York: Holt, Rinehart and Winston.

SARASON, I. G.; GLASSER, E. M.; AND FARGO, G. A. (1972) *Reinforcing Productive Classroom Behavior: A Teacher's Guide to Behavior Modification*. New York: Behavioral Publications.

SCHAEFER, H. H., AND MARTIN, P. L. (1966) "Behavioral Therapy for 'Apathy' of Hospitalized Schizophrenics." *Psychological Reports, 19,* 1147–1158.

SCHAEFER, H. H., AND MARTIN, P. L. (1969) *Behavioral Therapy*. New York: McGraw-Hill.

SCHILLER, H. I. (1968) "Social Control and Individual Freedom." *Bulletin of Atomic Scientists,* May 1968, pp. 16–21.

SCHOFIELD, W. (1964) *Psychotherapy: The Purchase of Friendship*. Englewood Cliffs, N.J.: Prentice-Hall.

SCHWITZGEBEL, R. (1964) *Street-Corner Research*. Cambridge, Mass.: Harvard University Press.

SHAFTEL, F. R., AND SHAFTEL, G. (1967) *Role-Playing for Social Values: Decision-Making in the Social Studies*. Englewood Cliffs, N.J.: Prentice-Hall.

SHAPIRO, D., AND BIRK, L. (1967) "Group Therapy in Experimental Perspective." *International Journal of Group Psychotherapy, 17,* 211–224.

SHAW, F. J. (ed.) (1961) *Behavioristic Approaches to Counseling and Psychotherapy: A Southeastern Psychological Association Symposium*. University, Alabama: University of Alabama Press.

SHEPPARD, W. C.; SHANK, S. B.; AND WILSON, D. (1972) *How to Be a Good Teacher*. Champaign, Ill.: Research Press.

SHERMAN, J. A., AND BAER, D. M. (1969) "Appraisal of Operant Therapy Techniques with Children and Adults." In C. M. Franks (ed.), *Behavior Therapy: Appraisal and Status*. New York: McGraw-Hill.

SHLIEN, J. J., *et al.* (eds.) (1968) *Research in Psychotherapy*. Washington, D.C.: American Psychological Association.

SHOSTROM, E. L. (1968) *Manual for the Personal Orientation Inventory*. San Diego: Educational and Industrial Testing Service.

SHUSTERMAN, L. S. (1973) "The Treatment of Impotence by Behavior Modification Techniques." *Journal of Sex Research, 9,* 226–240.

SIMON, B. (1970) "Social Casework Theory: An Overview." In R. Roberts and R. Nee (eds.), *Theories of Social Casework*. Chicago: University of Chicago Press.

SKINNER, B. F. (1953) *Science and Human Behavior*. New York: Macmillan.

SKINNER, B. F. (1948) *Walden Two*. New York: Macmillan.

SKINNER, B. F. (1966) "What Is the Experimental Analysis of Behavior?" *Journal of the Experimental Analysis of Behavior, 9,* 213–218.

SKINNER, B. F. (1957) *Verbal Behavior*. New York: Appleton-Century-Crofts.

SKINNER, B. F. (1968) *The Technology of Teaching*. New York: Appleton-Century-Crofts.

SKINNER, B. F. (1969) *Contingencies of Reinforcement*. New York: Appleton-Century-Crofts.

SKINNER, B. F. (1971) *Beyond Freedom and Dignity*. New York: Knopf.

SKINNER, B. F. (1972) *Cumulative Record* (3rd ed.) New York: Appleton-Century-Crofts.

SLOANE, H. N., AND McCAULEY, B. D. (eds.) (1968) *Operant Procedures in Remedial Speech and Language Training*. Boston: Houghton-Mifflin.

SLOGGETT, B. A. (1971) "Use of Group Activities and Team Rewards to Increase Individual Classroom Productivity." *Teaching Exceptional Children,* Winter 1971.

SMITH, J. M., AND SMITH, D. E. (1966) *Child Management: A Program for Parents and Teachers*. Ann Arbor, Michigan: Ann Arbor Publishers.

SMITH, R. E., AND SHARPE, T. M. (1970) "Treatment of a School Phobia with Implosive Therapy." *Journal of Consulting and Clinical Psychology, 35,* 239–243.

SMITH, W. S. (1966) *Conditioning and Instrumental Learning: A Program for Self-Instruction*. New York: McGraw-Hill.

SPREGEL, H., AND LINN, L. (1969) "The 'Ripple Effect' Following Adjunct Hypnosis in Analytic Psychotherapy." *American Journal of Psychiatry, 126,* 53–58.

STAATS, A. W. (1968) *Learning, Language, and Cognition*. New York: Holt, Rinehart and Winston.

STAATS, A. W., AND STAATS, C. K. (1963) *Complex Human Behavior: A Systematic Extension of Learning Principles*. New York: Holt, Rinehart and Winston.

STAMPFL, T. G. (1970) "Implosive Therapy: An Emphasis on Covert Stimulation." In D. J. Levis (ed.), *Learning Approaches to Therapeutic Behavior Change*. Chicago: Aldine.

STAMPFL, T. G., AND LEVIS, D. J. (1967) "Essentials of Implosive Therapy: A Learning-Theory-Based Psychodynamic Behavior Therapy." *Journal of Abnormal Psychology, 72,* 496–503.

STEINFIELD, G. (1970) "The Use of Covert Sensitization With Institutionalized Narcotic Addicts." *International Journal of Addiction, 5,* 225–232.

STRAUGHAN, J. H. (1964) "Treatment with Child and Mother in the Playroom." *Behaviour Research and Therapy, 2,* 37–41.

STUART, R. B. (1967a) "Applications of Behavior Theory to Social Casework." In E. J. Thomas (ed.), *The Socio-Behavioral Approach and Applications to Social Work*. New York: Council on Social Work Education.

STUART, R. B. (1967b) "Analysis and Illustration of the Process of Assertive Conditioning." Paper read at the National Conference on Social Welfare, 94th Annual Forum, Dallas.

STUART, R. B. (1969) "Operant-Interpersonal Treatment of Marital Discord." *Journal of Consulting and Clinical Psychology, 33,* 675–682.

STUART, R. B. (1970a) *Trick or Treatment*. Champaign, Ill.: Research Press.

STUART, R. B. (1970b) "Behavioral Control of Overeating." In R. Ulrich, T. Stachnik, and J. Mabry (eds.), *Control of Human Behavior, vol. 2*. Glenview, Ill.: Scott, Foresman.

STUART, R. (1971) "Research in Social Work: Casework and Group Work." In R. Morris (ed.), *Encyclopedia of Social Work*, vol. 2, 16th Issue. New York: National Association of Social Work.

STUART, R. B., AND DAVIS, B. (1971) *Slim Chance in a Fat World.* Champaign, Ill.: Research Press.

SULZBACKER, S. I., AND HOUSER, J. E. (1968) "A Tactic to Eliminate Disruptive Behaviors in the Classroom: Group Contingent Consequences" *American Journal of Mental Deficiency, 73,* 88–90.

SULZER, B.; MAYER, G. R.; AND CODY, J. J. (1968) "Assisting Teachers with Managing Classroom Behavioral Problems." *Elementary School Guidance and Counseling, 3,* 40–48.

SULZER, B., AND MAYER, G. R. (1972) *Behavior Modification Procedures for School Personnel.* Elk Grove, Ill.: Dryden Press.

SULZER, E. S. (1965) "Behavior Modification in Adult Psychiatric Patients." In L. P. Ullmann and L. Krasner (eds.), *Case Studies in Behavior Modification.* New York: Holt, Rinehart and Winston.

STURM, I. E. (1965) "The Behavioristic Aspect of Psychodrama." *Group Psychotherapy, 18,* 50–64.

SZASZ, T. (1961) *The Myth of Mental Illness: Foundation of a Theory of Personal Contact.* New York: Hoeber-Harper.

TAPIA, F.; JEKEL, J.; AND DOMKE, H. R. (1960) "Enuresis: An Emotional Symptom?" *Journal of Nervous and Mental Diseases, 130,* 61–66.

THARP, R. C., AND WETZEL, R. J. (1969) *Behavior Modification in the Natural Environment.* New York: Academic Press.

THOMAS, D. R.; BECKER, W. C.; AND ARMSTRONG, M. (1968) "Production and Elimination of Disruptive Classroom Behavior by Systematically Varying Teachers' Behavior." *Journal of Applied Behavior Analysis, 1,* 35–45.

THOMAS, E. J. (1968) "Selected Socio-Behavioral Techniques and Principles: An Approach to Interpersonal Helping." *Social Work, 13,* 12–26.

THOMAS, E. J. (ed.) (1967) *The Socio-Behavioral Approach and Applications to Social Work.* New York: Council on Social Work Education.

THOMAS, E. J. (ed.) (1974) *Behavior Modification Procedure: A Sourcebook.* Chicago: Aldine.

THOMAS, E. J.; CARTER, R. D.; AND GAMBRILL, E. D. (1969) "Some Possibilities of Behavior Modification with Marital Problems using 'SAM' (Signal System for the Assessment and Modification of Behavior)." In R. D. Rubin, H. Fensterheim, A. A. Lazarus, and C. M. Franks (eds.), *Advances in Behavior Therapy—1969.* New York: Academic Press.

THOMAS, E. J.; CARTER, R. D.; GAMBRILL, E. D.; AND BUTTERFIELD, W. H. (1970) "A Signal System for the Assessment and Modification of Behavior (SAM)." *Behavior Therapy 1,* 252–259.

THOMAS, E. J., AND GOODMAN, E. (1965) *Socio-Behavioral Theory and Interpersonal Helping in Social Work.* Ann Arbor, Mich.: Campus Publishers.

THOMAS, E. J. (1970) "Behavioral Modification and Casework." In R. Roberts and R. Nee (eds.), *Theories of Social Casework.* Chicago: University of Chicago Press.

THOMPSON, T. S. (1972) *Behavior Modification of the Mentally Retarded.* New York: Oxford University Press.

THORNE, G. L.; THARP, R. G.; AND WETZEL, R. J. (1966) "The Behavioral Research Project: An Interim Report on the First 14 Months of Operation." HEW Grant 65023 and 66020, Office of Juvenile Delinquency and Youth Development. Washington, D.C.: Government Printing Office.

THORNE, G. L.; THARP, R. G.; AND WETZEL, R. J. (1967) "Behavior Modification Techniques: New Tools for Probation Officers." *Federal Probation, 31,* 21–26.

TIFFERBLATT, S. M. (1970) *Improving Study and Homework Behavior.* Champaign, Ill.: Research Press.

TRUAX, C., AND CARKHUFF, R. R. (1967) *Toward Effective Counseling and Psychotherapy.* Chicago: Aldine.

TRUAX, C., AND MITCHELL, K. M. (1971) "Research on Certain Therapist Interpersonal Skills in Relation to Process and Outcome." In A. Bergin and S. Garfield (eds.), *Handbook of Psychotherapy and Behavior Change.* New York: John Wiley.

TRIPODI, T.; FELLIN, P.; AND MEYER, H. J. (1969) *The Assessment of Social Research.* Itasca, Ill.: F. E. Peacock.

ULLMANN, L. P.; FORSMAN, R. G.; KENNY, J. W.; McINNIS, T. L., JR.; UNIKEL, I. P.; AND ZEISSET, R. M. (1965) "Selective Reinforcement of Schizophrenics' Interview Responses." *Behaviour Research and Therapy, 2,* 205–212.

ULLMANN, L. P., AND KRASNER, L. (eds.) (1965) *Case Studies in Behavior Modification.* New York: Holt, Rinehart and Winston.

ULLMANN, L. P., AND KRASNER, L. (1969) *A Psychological Approach to Abnormal Behavior.* Englewood Cliffs, N.J.: Prentice-Hall.

ULRICH, R.; STACHNIK, T.; AND MABRY, J. (eds.) (1966) *Control of Human Behavior,* vol. *1.* Glenview, Ill.: Scott, Foresman.

ULRICH, R.; STACHNIK, T.; AND MABRY, J. (eds.) (1970) *Control of Human Behavior,* vol. *2.* Glenview, Ill.: Scott, Foresman.

URBAN, H., AND FORD, D. (1961) "Man: A Robot or Pilot?" Paper presented at the Annual Meeting of the American Psychological Association. New York, September 1961.

VALETT, R. E. (1969) *Modifying Children's Behavior: A Guide for Parents and Professionals.* Palo Alto, Calif.: Fearon.

VALETT, R. E. (1970) *Effective Teaching.* Palo Alto, Calif.: Fearon.

VERNON, W. M. (1972) *Motivating Children.* New York: Holt, Rinehart and Winston.

VERPLANCK, W. S. (1955) "The Control of the Content of Conversation: Reinforcement of Statements of Opinion." *Journal of Abnormal and Social Psychology, 51,* 668–676.

VINCENT, C. E. (1968) *Human Sexuality in Medical Education and Practice.* Springfield, Ill.: Charles C Thomas.

VITALO, R. (1970) "Effects of Facilitative Interpersonal Functioning in a Conditioning Paradigm." *Journal of Counseling Psychology, 17,* 141–144.

VOGLER, R. E. (1970) "Electrical Aversion Conditioning with Chronic Alcoholics." *Journal of Consulting and Clinical Psychology, 34,* 302–307.

WAGNER, M. K. (1968) "Parent Therapists: An Operant Conditioning Method." *Mental Hygiene,* July 1968.

WAHLER, R. G. (1967) "Behavior Therapy with Oppositional Children: Attempts to Increase Their Parents' Reinforcement Value." Paper presented at the Meeting of the Southeastern Psychological Association, Atlanta, Ga.

WAHLER, R. G.; WINKEL, G. H.; PETERSON, R. F.; AND MORRISON, D. C. (1965) "Mothers as Behavior Therapists for their Own Children." *Behaviour Research Therapy, 3,* 113–124.

WALDER, L. O.; BREITER, D. E.; COHEN, S. I.; DASTON, P. G.; FORBES, J. A.; AND McINTYRE, R. W. (1966) "Teaching Parents To Modify the Behaviors of their Autistic Children." Paper presented at the 74th Annual Convention of the American Psychological Association, New York.

WALDER, L. O.; COHEN, S. I.; BREITER, D. E.; DASTON, P. G.; HIRSCH, I. S.; AND LEIBOWITZ, J. M. (1967) "Teaching Behavioral Principles to Parents of Disturbed Children," Paper presented at the meeting of the Eastern Psychological Association, Boston.

WALDER, L. O.; COHEN, S. I.; BREITER, D. E.; WARMAN, F. C.; ORNE-JOHNSON, D.; AND PAVEY, S. (1971) "Parents as Agents of Behavior Change." In S. Golann and S. Eisdorfer (eds.), *Handbook of Community Mental Health.* New York: Appleton-Century-Crofts.

WALDER, L. O.; COHEN, S. I.; AND DASTON, P. G. (1967) "Teaching Parents and Other Principles of Behavior Control for Modifying the Behavior of Children." Progress Report, U.S. Office of Education, 32-31-7515-5024. Washington, D.C.: Government Printing Office.

WALDER, L. O.; COHEN, S. I.; DASTON, P. G.; BREITER, D. E.; AND HIRSCH, I. S. (1967) "Behavior Therapy of Children Through Their Parents." Revision of a paper presented at the meetings of the American Psychological Association. Washington, D.C.

WALKER, E. L. (1972) *Conditioning and Instrumental Learning.* Monterey, Calif.: Brooks-Cole.

WARD, H., AND BAKER, B. L. (1968) "Reinforcement Therapy in the Classroom." *Journal of Applied Behavior Analysis, 1,* 323–328.

WARREN, S. A., AND MONDY, L. W. (1968) "Which Behaviors are Reinforced by Attending Adults?" Paper read at Midwestern Psychological Association. Chicago, May 1968.

WATSON, D. L., AND THARP, R. G. (1972) *Self-Directed Behavior.* Monterey, Calif.: Brooks-Cole.

WATSON, J. B. (1930) *Behaviorism.* New York: W. W. Norton.

WATSON, J. B., AND RAYNER, R. (1920) "Conditioned Emotional Reactions." *Journal of Experimental Psychology, 3,* 1–14.

WATSON, L. S. (1973) *Child Behavior Modification.* New York: Pergamon.

WEINER, H. (1962) "Some Effects of Response Cost upon Operant Behavior." *Journal of the Experimental Analysis of Behavior, 5,* 201–208.

WEINROTT, M. R. (1974) "A Training Program in Behavior Modification for the Siblings of the Retarded." *American Journal of Orthopsychiatry, 44,* 362–375.

WELSH, R. S. (1968) "The Use of Stimulus Satiation in the Elimination of Juvenile Fire-Setting Behavior." Paper presented at the Eastern Psychological Association. Washington, D.C., April 1968.

WENRICH, W. W. (1970) *A Primer of Behavior Modification*. Monterey, Calif.: Brooks-Cole.

WERRY, J. S. (1966) "The Conditioning Treatment of Enuresis." *American Journal of Psychiatry, 123,* 226–229.

WERRY, J. S., AND QUAY, H. (1969) "Observing the Classroom Behavior of Elementary School Children." *Exceptional Children, 35,* 461–470.

WHALEY, D. L., AND MALOTT, R. W. (1971) *Elementary Principles of Behavior.* New York: Appleton-Century-Crofts.

WILLIAMS, C. D. (1959) "The Elimination of Tantrum Behaviors by Extinction Procedures." *Journal of Abnormal and Social Psychology, 59,* 269.

WINCZE, J. P.; LEITENBERG, H.; AND AGRAS, H. S. (1972) "The Effects of Token Reinforcement and Feedback on the Delusional Verbal Behavior of Chronic Paranoid Schizophrenics." *Journal of Applied Behavior Analysis, 5,* 247–262.

WINKLER, R. C. (1970) "Management of Chronic Psychiatric Patients by a Token Economy Reinforcement System." *Journal of Applied Behavior Analysis, 3,* 47–55.

WISOCKI, P. A. (1973) "The Successful Treatment of a Heroin Addict by Covert Conditioning Techniques." *Journal of Behavior Therapy and Experimental Psychiatry, 4,* 55–62.

WITTES, G., AND RADIN, N. (1969) *The Reinforcement Approach: Helping Your Child to Learn.* San Rafael, Calif.: Dimensions.

WOLF, M. M.; GILES, D. K.; AND HALL, V. A. (1968) "Experiments with Token Reinforcements in a Remedial Classroom." *Behaviour Research and Therapy, 6,* 51–64.

WOLF, M. M.; RISLEY, T.; JOHNSTON, J.; HARRIS, F.; AND ALLEN, E. (1967) "Application of Operant Conditioning Procedures to the Behavior Problems of an Autistic Child: A Follow-Up and Extension." *Behaviour Research and Therapy, 5,* 103–111.

WOLPE, J. (1958) *Psychotherapy by Reciprocal Inhibition.* Stanford, Calif.: Stanford University Press.

WOLPE, J. (1964) "Conditioned Inhibition of Craving in Drug Addiction." *Behaviour Research and Therapy, 2,* 285–287.

WOLPE, J. (1969) *The Practice of Behavior Therapy.* New York: Pergamon.

WOLPE, J., AND LAZARUS, A. A. (1966) *Behavior Therapy Techniques: A Guide to the Treatment of Neuroses.* New York: Pergamon.

WOLPE, J.; SALTER, A.; AND REYNA, L. T. (eds.) (1964) *The Conditioning Therapies: The Challenge in Psychotherapy.* New York: Holt, Rinehart and Winston.

YATES, A. (1970) *Behavior Therapy.* New York: John Wiley.

ZEILBERGER, J.; SAMPEN, S.; AND SLOANE, H. N. (1968) "Modification of a Child's Problem Behavior in the Home with the Mother as Therapist." *Journal of Applied Behavior Analysis, 1,* 47–53.

ZIMMERMAN, E. H., AND ZIMMERMAN, J. (1962) "The Alteration of Behavior in a Special Classroom Situation." *Journal of the Experimental Analysis of Behavior, 5,* 59–60.

Name Index

Subject Index